Charles Matthew Clode

The Early History of the Guild of Merchant Taylors of the Fraternity of Saint John the Baptist

Vol. 1

Charles Matthew Clode

The Early History of the Guild of Merchant Taylors of the Fraternity of Saint John the Baptist
Vol. 1

ISBN/EAN: 9783337400521

Printed in Europe, USA, Canada, Australia, Japan

Cover: Foto ©ninafisch / pixelio.de

More available books at **www.hansebooks.com**

THE EARLY HISTORY

OF THE

Guild of Merchant Taylors

OF THE

FRATERNITY OF ST. JOHN THE BAPTIST,

LONDON.

WITH

NOTICES OF THE LIVES

OF

Some of its Eminent Members.

(IN TWO PARTS.)

Part I.—THE HISTORY.

BY CHARLES M. CLODE.

[Master for 1873-4.]

LONDON:
HARRISON AND SONS, ST. MARTIN'S LANE,
Printers in Ordinary to Her Majesty.
1888.

[PRINTED FOR PRIVATE CIRCULATION.]

14, Ashley Place, S.W.

St. John Baptist Day, 1888.

My dear Master,

I may perhaps in a few lines addressed to you explain to others who may be interested in the subject how it is that this work has been written for the Company.

Some months since the issue of the "Memorials," which were printed for the Company in 1875, came to an end, the copies that were taken off having been distributed. It then became a question whether that publication should be reprinted with such additional information as was available, or whether the materials which it contained should be made the basis of the "Early History of the Company." The latter appeared to me to be the better course for two, not to mention other, reasons—one, not the least important, that it would be far less expensive, and the other that a connected history would present to the reader a more intelligible outline of the Company than the "Memorials." Therefore I have written the history which is to be found in Part I of this volume.

But Part II has been written from other inducements. It had long been felt by some of us to be a subject of regret—if not of reproach—that so little was known by the guildsmen of the present day of those guildsmen of earlier days, who were great benefactors, founders of schools, and liberal providers for the poor much of whose time must have been passed in the hall premises, and whose munificence can be best illustrated from our archives. When, therefore, the information that was available for the life of *Richard Hilles* came under my notice not long since, I prepared a sketch of his life and letters. In doing so, I came upon other materials which had reference to *Sir Thomas White*, and these I proceeded to incorporate with it as one memoir of these two guildsmen.

But there appeared to me to be no sufficient reason why an outline of the lives of other guildsmen should not be attempted as for instance of *Sir John Percyvale*, then of Sir Stephen Jenyns and after that of Sir W. Harper, all founders of schools that are flourishing in the present day. Other notable men of the Guild were afterwards added because their lives were full of usefulness, both to the guild and to the city, and illustrate the condition of London at the several periods when they lived. Everyone whose life is given is a corporate ancestor of whom every guildsman must feel proud. The result is before you in Part II.

In undertaking this Work I imperfectly estimated the time that it would require to produce it. Unfortunately, none of our records have any index, and besides the difficulty of deciphering the various handwritings in which the several entries are made, there is little by way of marginal note to indicate the contents of each entry. However, others, as the Memorials prove, have laboured before me, and the investigations which I have had to make have been always lightened and ever made agreeable from the cheerful way in which each member of the Company's staff has aided me by his intelligence and labour.

But, after all, the Work would never have been undertaken had it not been for the hearty sympathy which you have always expressed, and the wish of many of your colleagues on the Court that it should proceed.

It has therefore been completed in the hope that the perusal of it may prove to be interesting to yourself and other members of the Company.

Yours faithfully,
CHARLES M. CLODE.

JOHN BLACKETT GILL, Esq.
    Master of the Merchant Taylors Company.

PART I.

TABLE OF CONTENTS.

INTRODUCTION.

Object of the work, p. 1.—Government of London, p. 2.—Of the Guild, p. 2.—Ward or Guild the unit of London government, p. 2.—Characteristics of the Livery Companies' (1) Charity, p. 3 ; (2) Religion, pp. 4 and 5 ; (3) Hospitality, pp. 6, 7, and 8.—Eminent members, p. 8.—Richard Hilles, p. 9.—Commerce and colonisation, p. 10.—New enterprises by the Guilds, p. 10.

CHAPTER I.

THE GOVERNMENT OF LONDON.

London governed by the same continuous rule from the earliest to the present day, p. 11.—The area and population, p. 12.—Percyvale, first Taylor who became Mayor, p. 12.—Freedom gained by Indentures, p. 12.—Chamberlain's advice to Apprentices, p. 13.—Freemen, their duties and oath, p. 13.—As traders liable to Guild authority, p. 14.—Wards and the Mote, p. 14.—Duties of the Bedel, p. 14.—Of Wardsmen, p. 15. —Common Council, p. 16.—Duties of members thereof, p. 16.—Control of Council over Expenditure, p. 17.—Sheriffs' election, p. 18.—Sheriffs' Riding, p. 18.—Duties, p. 19.—Aldermen, p. 19.—Election, p. 20.— Duties, p. 20.—Mayor, p. 21.—Election, p. 21.—Duties : (1) to the King ; (2) his fellow Citizens, p. 23.—His riding to Westminster, p. 23. —His Feast, p. 23.—Visit to William's Tomb and Beckett's Grave at St. Paul's, p. 24.—Service in scot and lot, p. 24.—Importance of the office, p. 25.—As at the Meeting of the York and Lancaster supporters in London, 1458, p. 25.—Ceremonials of the office, p. 26.—Precedence of the Mayor in the City determined in Henry V's reign, p. 28.—Insisted on at Serjeants' Feast, 1464, p. 28.—Sheriff subordinate, p. 29.—Precedence out of the City, p. 30.—Recorder's duties, p. 30.—Access of Corporation to the Throne, p. 31.—Butlership at the Coronation, p. 32.

CHAPTER II.

THE GOVERNMENT OF A LONDON GUILD.

Every trader governed by a Guild, p. 33.—Taylors and Linen Armourers, p. 33.—Petition of 1327 for Charter and grant of it, p. 34.—Names of 24 Taylors to certify Freemen, p. 34.—Order of 1371, p. 35.—Charter of Richard II (1390), p. 35.—Henry IV (1408), p. 36.—Henry VI (1439), p.

36.—Edward IV (1456), p. 36.—Henry VII (1502), p. 37.—Agreement for Perpetual Obit, p. 37.—Method of becoming a guildsman, p. 38.—Government of a Guild explained, p. 39.—Ordinances made by the whole Fraternity, p. 39.—Mayour's Preface, p. 40.—Freeman's oath to the Guild, p. 41.—Women members of the Guild, p. 42.—Ordinances of 1507, p. 42.—As to dress, p. 43.—Liverymen, p. 44.—Wardens, p. 45.—Court of Assistants, p. 46.—Master, p. 47.—Election dinner, p. 47.—Jenyns's orders as to payment, p. 47.—Attendance at St. Martin's, p. 48.—Post-Reformation ceremonial, p. 49.—Master's oath, p. 50.—Meetings of (1) Quarterly Court and Annual Court of the whole Fraternity, p. 51 ; (2) Court of Assistants, p. 51 ; (3) Master and Wardens, p. 51.—Audit of Master's Expenditure, p. 52.—Gratuitous Office by Jenyns's orders, p. 52. —The Clerk, p. 52.—The Bedel, p. 53.—The Guilds as subordinate to the Mayor, p. 54.—Place in London Government, p. 55.—Precepts for Mayor (1) Personal service, Standing Watch, p. 56 ; (2) For money, p. 57.—Bridewell Hospital, p. 58.—Gunpowder, p. 59.—Service of the Crown, p. 59.

CHAPTER III.

THE BACHELOR OR YEOMAN COMPANY OF TAYLORS.

The Yeoman Taylors, p. 60.—Disputes of 1411, p. 61.—Of 1415, p. 61.—Of 1417, p. 63.—Came under control of the Merchant Company, p. 64. —Traces of the Company in 1446-56, p. 64.—When Companies separated, p. 64.—Bachelors Company seldom mentioned on Merchant Company's records, p. 64.—Number of the Bachelors, p. 65.—Ordinances of 1507, p. 65.—Ordinances of 1613, p. 65.—Organisation of Bachelors Company, p. 65.—Offices not readily filled up, p. 66.—Workman and Employer, p. 67.—Seeds of Disunion, p. 68.—Disadvantages of separate organisation, p. 68.—Division of funds and separate distribution of alms, p. 68.—Merchant Company held the trust estates, p. 68.—Members of the wealthy class, p. 68.—Poor Taylors in the Bachelor Company, p. 68. —Which became the Almoner of the Merchant Company, p. 68.—Sources of income to Bachelor Company, p. 68 : (1) Benefactions ; (2) Quarterages ; (3) Fines ; (4) Donations from Merchant Company, p. 68.—Distribution to the poor, p. 69.—Method of it, and changes made, p. 70.—Donations in 1655-9, p. 70.—Merchant Company take the distribution in 1663, p. 70.—Merchant Company's control over Bachelors Treasury, p. 71.—Disputes in 1601, p. 71.—Army Contracts declined by Merchant Company, p. 72.—Disputes of 1608, p. 72.—Sumptuary expenses excessive, p. 72.—Agreement for future government of the Company, p. 73.—Ceased to be appointed by the Merchant Company in 1661, p. 74.—Merchant Company take charge of business of the Bachelors Company, p. 74.—Corporation refuse to interfere, p. 74.—So also the Privy Council, p. 74.—Note as to assessment of 1602-5.

CHAPTER IV.

THE STAR CHAMBER AS TO THE LONDON CORPORATION AND GUILDS.

Star Chamber Jurisdiction relating to London, p. 75.—Eden's case, p. 76.—As to Corporation, p. 76.—As to Guild, p. 76.—Foreign Workmen p. 77.

—Statutes of Henry VIII, p. 77.—Report as to foreigners, p. 78.—Samuel Pepys' father admitted to the Merchant Taylors Company, p. 79.—Dutch and French Taylors, p. 79.—Agreement with them, p. 80.—Meeting of the Company to hear Star Chamber decrees, p. 80.—NOTE. List of Clerks and Beadles, 1397 to 1624.

CHAPTER V.

THE HALL AND ITS CONTENTS.

The Hall, antiquity, p. 82—Purchase in 1331, p. 83.—Sir O. Ingham tenant thereof, p. 84.—Ingham's Hall rebuilt, p. 84.—Hall in 1575, p. 84.—Ambassadors lodged in (1518 and 1619), p. 85.—Fire of London, p. 85.—Dates of different parts of the Building, p. 85.—Description of the Hall, p. 86.—Saltpetre diggers, p. 87.—Floor covered with rushes, p. 87.—Erasmus's description, p. 87.—Flooring of Hall, p. 87.—Glazed in 1419, p. 87.—Inventories of 1512 and 1609 as illustrating two distinct periods, p. 88.—St. John Baptist's Statue, p. 88.—Tapestry, p. 89.—Furniture, p. 90.—Table trestles, p. 90.—Laying the Cloth, p. 90.—Plate of 1491, p. 91.—"The Jowell House," p. 91.—Basyns and Ewres, p. 92.—Saltes, p. 93.—Spones, pp. 93, 94.—Stondyng Cuppes, p. 95.—Pottes, p. 96.—Bolles, p. 97.—Plate for kepyng of Obyttes, and Masers, p. 98.—One knife, p. 99.—"The Parloure," p. 99.—St. John's Statue, p. 99.—Tapestry, p. 99.—Sir John Skevington's will (note), p. 99.—Furniture, p. 100.—For Funerals, p. 101.—For Triumphs, p. 102.—The Yard, p. 102.—Almery, p. 102.—The King's Chamber, p. 103.—The Kitchen and the Larder, p. 104.—The Pastry, p. 104.—The Buttery, p. 104.—The Storehouse, p. 105.—No napery, p. 105.— No Glass, p. 105.—Pewter, p. 106.—Butler, p. 106.—Additions in 1609, p. 106.—The Brasse, p. 107.—The Lynnen, p. 107.—Clock in the yard, p. 108.—Armour, p. 109.—Note as to the dimensions of the Halls, p. 109.

CHAPTER VI.

RELIGION AND ALMSGIVING.

Care of the Fraternity as to the two objects of Religion and Almsgiving, as evidenced by the early records, p. 110.—Acquisition of Religious Privileges by Merchant Taylors Company from (1) St. John's Jerusalem, p. 111 ; (2) Chapel in St. Paul's, p. 112 ; (3) Papal and Episcopal Pardons, p. 113.—Our Lady of Rounceval, p. 114.—And other grants, p. 115.—Contracts for performance of Obits, p. 116.—Chapel at the Hall, p. 117.—Payments for Religious Service, p. 119.—Charities of the Company, p. 120.—Endowments for both objects, p. 121.—Illustration of expenditure in 1399-1400 enumerated, p. 123.—Coronation of Henry IV and Banquet, p. 124.—Expenditure of 1466-7, p. 125.—Grant of Arms, 1480, p. 126.

CHAPTER VII.

SECULAR AFFAIRS AND POSITION OF THE COMPANY AT THE CLOSE OF THE FIFTEENTH CENTURY.

Continued action of the Guild, p. 127.—As to trade, p. 127.—Search, p. 128.—Yard measure, p. 128.—Authority of the Master and Wardens, p. 129.—

Fines, how enforced, p. 129.—The Mace, p. 130.—Company used for secular purposes, p. 130.—Piers' contract, p. 130.—Class and status of ordinary members, p. 131.—Honorary members as (1) Kings, pp. 132, 133 ; (2) Nobles, p. 134.—Company in relation to (1) Corporation, p. 134.— Dispute with Clopton in 1441, p. 135.—R. Holland rejected as Sheriff, p. 136.—Charter of 1439 disputed, p. 136.—(2) The Skynners' dispute, p. 137.—Billesden's award, p. 137.

CHAPTER VIII.

THE EARLIER HALF OF THE SIXTEENTH CENTURY AND THE DISENDOWMENT OF RELIGION.

Two great changes in the sixteenth century : Disendowment of religion and destruction of Guild monopoly, p. 138.—Religious and eleemosynary gifts from 1507 to 1531 to the Company, p. 138.—Example of an Obit from Sir John Percyvale's will, p. 139.—Act for Chauntries Collegiate, p. 140. —Effect of it, p. 140.—37 Henry VIII, c. 4, p. 141.—Commissioners' return under it, p. 142.—Extracts from cash books, p. 142.—Payment to the Crown, p. 143.—Edward VI's Act and preamble, p. 143.—Royal Commissioners to ascertain sums due from Guilds, p. 144.—Court of Merchant Taylors Company in 1548-9, p. 145.—Execution of Commission and Extracts from cash books, p. 145.—Obit omitted, p. 145.—Annual payment to the Crown, p. 146.—Purchase of obit charges from the Crown, p. 146.— Extracts from Commissioners' Report of 1884, p. 146.—Extortion against the Guilds, p. 147.—Conveyance of Property to Guilds, p. 148.—Petition to Parliament for Act 5 and 6 Edward VI to confirm same, p. 149.— Religious services extinguished, p. 149.—Eminent members of the Guild, p. 149.

CHAPTER IX.

AFTER DISENDOWMENT—LATER BENEFACTIONS.

Days of racked consciences, Obit moneys applied to secular uses, p. 152.— Hall chapel used for secular purposes and fitments removed, p. 152.— Religion the vital principle of the Guilds, p. 152.—Constitutional changes in the Guild, p. 153.—Effects of on benefactions and expenditure, p. 154.— As to benefactions, p. 155.—Character of Post-Reformation gifts, p. 155. —Robert Donkyn, p. 155.—His charity of 1570, p. 156.—Progress of it and scheme of 1872, p. 157.—Bognor House, p. 157.—Robert Dowe, p. 157.—His charities, p. 158.—(1) For prisoners in Newgate, condemned in death, p. 159.—In City prisons for debt, p. 161.—(2) Pensions for Guildsmen, p. 162, *et. seq.*—For parishioners, p. 165.—For Improvement in Church singing, p. 167. — School probation, p. 168. — Commendatory sentences in favour of poor Tailors and St. John's Oxford, p. 168.—Almshouses, p. 169.—Schools founded, p. 171.—No contract with non-members to charity endowment, p. 171.—William Roper's offer declined, p. 171.— Guildsmen made such, p. 172.—What religious observances were kept up, p. 172.—Grant of arms with secular emblems, and payment for same, p. 173.—NOTE. Cooke, the Herald, and payment for same, p. 173.

CHAPTER X.

AFTER DISENDOWMENT—LATER EXPENDITURE.

Object of the Chapter, p. 174.—As to expenditure in hospitality in Edward VI's reign, p. 175.—Sir F. Palgrave on civic hospitality, p. 175.—Feasting traditional in London, p. 175.—As to feasting, sanctioned by Charter of Richard II, p. 175.—Guild funds have borne such charges, p. 176.—Early records of this, p. 176.—As to method of accounting, p. 176.—Renter Wardens, p. 176.—Master's accounts, p. 176.—Auditors, p. 177.—Master's fees of office, p. 177.—As to income, p. 177.—Subsidy Return, 1556, p. 178.—Other sources of income, p. 180.—Total of receipts and payments for decennial periods, p. 180.—Two great feasts, St. John the Baptist's and Decollation days, p. 180.—Contributions thereto, p. 181.—Changed to quarter days, p. 181.—The charges in Edward's and Mary's reigns, p. 181.—Sumptuary expenses of Elizabeth's reign, p. 181.—Livery increased, p. 181.—Guildsmen acted as Waiters, p. 181.—Election Dinner, 1593, p. 182.—Increase of Allowance, p. 183.—Gore declines it, p. 183.—Accepted by Elwes in 1605, p. 183.—School dinner, p. 184.—Sir Thomas White's, p. 184.—View and search dinners, p. 184.—Increase in Elizabeth's reign, p. 184.—Court Dinners in James I's reign, p. 185.—Dowe's convivium dinner, p. 185.—Cook's employment (note), p. 185.—Funeral dinners, p. 187.—Dowe's grace, p. 187.—Extraordinary cost of a mayoralty, p. 187.—Feast postponed for scarcity, p. 188.—As to expenditure for alms, p. 189.—Charities administered without costs, p. 189.—School at St. Lawrence, p. 189.—University Exhibitions, p. 190.—Almsmen, p. 191.—Qualifications and duties in 1507, p. 191.—Altered, p. 192.—Widows, p. 192.—Almshouses not full, p. 192.—Provision for Livery, p. 192.—Grants to Freemen made under circumstances, p. 193.—John Stowe's pension, p. 194.—Wakefield's for leprosy, p. 194.—Refused to general applicants, p. 194.—Analysis of receipts and payments, p. 194.—Explanatory notes thereon, p. 195.

CHAPTER XI.

THE TRADE MONOPOLY OF THE GUILD DESTROYED.

Persons of various occupations admitted to the Merchant Taylors Company in 1399, p. 197.—The Merchant Taylors became Clothworkers, p. 198.—Charter of Henry VII, p. 198.—Hereditary principle of the London franchise, p. 199.—Impossible for all trades to become hereditary, p. 199.—Complaint of Clothworkers against the Taylors, p. 200.—Controversy of 1550, p. 200.—Claim right of search, p. 200.—Refuse to grind Taylors' shears, p. 200.—Their claims overruled by the Lord Mayor, p. 200.—Order as to apprentices, p. 201.—Claims renewed in 1566, p. 201.—White, Hilles, and other Taylors engaged in clothworking, p. 201.—Vital importance of the question, p. 202.—Lease of the Mora estate by Taylors, p. 202.—Various tenants thereof, p. 202.—Return of the number of Taylors, &c., occupied in clothworking, p. 202.—Appeal to Parliament, p. 202.—Parliamentary Bills prepared by Clothworkers, p. 202.—Rejected by Parliamentary Committee, p. 203.—Other two Bills proposed by the

Committee, p. 203.—No Bill passed, and the controversy ended, p. 203.
—Complaint of the Haberdashers, p. 204.—Order of 1571 to employ
guildsmen in clothworking, p. 204.—The principle of Guild monopoly
raised in 1571 by fourteen other Guilds, p. 204.—Their case as stated to
the Lord Mayor and Council, p. 205.—Remedy sought, p. 205.—Richard
Hilles and others as a Committee answer the case, p. 205.—Decision in
the Clothworkers' case adhered to, p. 206.—No order made by the Lord
Mayor and Council, p. 206.—Attempt at Legislation in 1575, p. 206.—
Haberdashers asked by Taylors to join in search, p. 206.—Taylors in the
Company, p. 207.—Though Guild monopoly destroyed, guildsman could
not quit his Company without licence, p. 208.—Wilkes' case with the
Widow Hodgson, p. 208.—Nor sue a brother guildsman without licence,
p. 208.—Arbitrament, p. 208.—I. Jurisdiction of Master and Wardens :
(a) In partnership quarrels, p. 209.—(b) Apprentices, p. 209.—(c) Dress,
p. 209.—(d) Bad work, p. 210.—(e) Recovery of debts, &c., p. 210.—(f)
Slander, p. 110.—II. Manners and Amenities of the guildsmen: Assault,
p. 211.—Hitting in the face, p. 211.—Provoking words, p. 212.—Insult to
a Warden, p. 212.—Evil words in anger, p. 213.—Bastardy, p. 213.—
Insult to the Master and Wardens, p. 214.—Eminent guildsmen during
the controversy, p. 215.

CHAPTER XII.

The Guild without Monopoly in Trade—Disintegration.

Primary use of Guild destroyed, p. 215.—Opening up of foreign trade, p. 215.—
Increase of London, p. 215.—Apprenticeship needful for London citizenship, p. 216.—Franchises of Guild and Corporation not sought after, p.
216.—Burthens to be avoided, p. 216.—Apprentices the cheapest
labourers, p. 216.—Scot and lot, p. 216.—Return of apprentices and
freemen, p. 217.—Freedom not taken up, p. 217.—No presentment, p.
217.—Fleetwood fined, p. 217.—Membership of Company not sought for,
p. 217.—Guild offices neglected, p. 217.—Master absent on election, 1565,
p. 217.—Refusal of Shottesham, 1572, p. 217.—Assistants absent, p. 218.
—Master and four Wardens absent on election, 1589, p. 218.—Auditors
absent, p. 218.—Great neglect in 1595, p. 219.—Committee appointed, p.
219.—Report, p. 219.—Ordinances to be amended, p. 220.—Increasing
punishment, p. 220.—Neglect in 1602-3, p. 220.—Wardens to be removed
from office, p. 220.—Warden a defaulter in account, p. 220.—Dowe's
opinion of the evil, p. 221.—Court renewed by thirteen members, p. 221.
—Master and Wardens are absent on election in 1611, p. 221.—Result of
changes in the Guild, p. 222.—New basis of Guild, without religion or
monopoly, p. 222.—Table of Apprentices and Freemen, p. 224.

CHAPTER XIII.

Matters Miscellaneous in the Later Half of the 16th Century.

Matters found on records of the Merchant Taylors Company, p. 225.—School
and St. John's College, p. 225.—Claim of the Crown on School site, 1565,
p. 226.—Grant from James I, 1620, p. 226.—The Royal Exchange, p.
227.—Corporation desire Percyvale's House, p. 227.—Lombard Street
oldest Burse in Europe, p. 227.—Deputation from Guildhall, p. 228.—

PART I.] *Table of Contents.* xi

Company object to sell, p. 228.—Conference with the Recorder, p. 228.—
Offer to exchange land declined, p. 228.—Subscriptions raised, p. 228.—
First lottery established (1568), p. 229.—The second, 1585, p. 230.—
Lotteries in the city sanctioned by Lord Mayor, p. 231.—Abolished in
1826, p. 231.—Norfolk's treason, 1572, p. 231.—Guard at the city gates,
p. 231.—Conduct of citizens towards foreigners, p. 232.—Lord Mayor's
precept in 1573, p. 232.—The two terrors of London, p. 233.—Plague in
1563, p. 233.—In 1575, p. 233.—Fire and precautions against, p. 233.—
Plays and playhouses, p. 234.—Plays not favoured by citizens, p. 234.—
Plays by scholars of the Company's school, p. 234.—Prohibited in the
Hall, 1573, p. 235.—Act of Common Council, 1574, p. 235.—Measures of
the Crown, p. 235.—Players licensed, p. 235.—Master of the Revels, p.
236.—Lord Mayor's proposal, 1591, declined by the Company, p. 236.
—The Bible set up in the Hall, 1578, p. 237.—The Exchequer suit
against the Company in 1578, p. 238.—Fish's and FitzWilliam's scholarship at St. John's, pp. 238–240.—Alleged concealment by the Guilds, 1582,
p. 240.—Patent of concealed lands to Adams and others, p. 240.—Negotiations with Sir C. Hatton, p. 241.—And the patentees, p. 241.—Company's
tenants proceeded against, p. 242.—Suit dismissed, p. 242.—Offer to pay
200*l.*, p. 242.—Statement laid before Elizabeth, 1587, p. 243.—Sir Philip
Sydney's funeral, p. 243.—Thanksgiving at St. Paul's for taking of Cadiz,
p. 244.

CHAPTER XIV.

The Company at the Close of the Reign of Elizabeth.

Object of the Chapter, p. 245.—Guild consisted of Taylors, Clothworkers, and
Merchants, p. 245.—Wealth of the Company, p. 246.—Assessments on
Precepts, p. 246.—The Principle of, p. 246.—Assent of Common Council
essential, p. 247.—Freemen represented on Assessment authority, p. 247.
—Assessment of Common Council, 1562, p. 247.—Corn assessments of two
kinds, pp. 247, 248.—Of 1564, p. 249.—Of 1565, p. 249.—Of 1596, p. 249.—
Merchant Taylors assessed in highest amount, p. 249.—Precepts for
military service, p. 250.—In 1572, p. 250.—In 1577 and 1579, p. 250.—
In 1585, p. 251.—Wealth of the guildsmen, p. 251.—In 1565, p. 251.—
Precept to meet the Lord Mayor in gold chains in 1578, p. 251.—
Demands for Crown loan of 5,000*l.* on Privy Seal in 1588, p. 252.—Loan
notes issued, p. 253.—Imprisonment of defaulters, p. 254.—Offley and
others command trained bands, p. 254.—As to the Merchants, p. 254.—
Wealth of citizens in 1557 and 1590, p. 254.—Russia Company, p. 255.
—Establishment of East India Company, 1599, p. 255.—Part taken by
guildsmen, p. 256.—Mayors and Sheriffs, p. 256.—Common Councilmen,
p. 257.—Political influence, p. 257.—M.P. for London, p. 257.—List of
the wisest and best Merchants, p. 257.—High position of the Guild, p.
257.—What were their household expenses, p. 258.—Their house rent, p.
258.—Cost of living, p. 258.—Rise of prices, p. 258.—Wild Darrell's
expenses in 1589, p. 259.—Attendant servants, p. 259.—Locomotion, p.
259.—Educational attainments of guildsmen, p. 260.—The admirable
discharge of duty in the 16th century, p. 260.

CHAPTER XV.

THE COMPANY IN THE EARLIER YEARS OF JAMES I.

James I's reign opens a new era in Guild history, p. 261.—Fortunes of Merchant Taylors at his accession in the ascendant, p. 261.—Lord Mayor, Sir Robert Lee, p. 262.—Sir John Swynnerton, Sheriff, p. 262.—Richard Gore, M.P., Master, p. 263.—Nowel Sotherton, p. 263.—Assessments by precepts, p. 264.—Number of members in the Company, p. 264.—Merchant Taylors premier Company for Lee's year, p. 264.—Payments to John Stowe and for school boys' pageant, p. 264.—Order for Speech by school boy to the King, p. 265.—Plague, p. 265.—Lee knighted, p. 265.—Coronation, p. 266.—Three other members knighted, p. 266.—Fine for renewal of charter, p. 266.—Reduction thereof by the Lord Chancellor's man, p. 266.—Claim for concealed lands, p. 267.—Reference to Mr. Baron Saville, p. 267.—Letter of January, 1604, from Crown officers, p. 268.—Master and Wardens of that period, p. 269.—Court of 9th February, p. 269.—Recorder retained, p. 270.—Mayoralty of Sir L. Halliday, p. 270.—Session of 1606, p. 270.—Recorder's advice as to claim of Crown, p. 271.—Clothworkers agree to support Bill, p. 271.—Merchant Taylors contribute 100*l*., p. 272.—Act of 4 James I (local and personal), p. 272.—The case against the Guilds under the Chauntries Collegiate Act, p. 273.

CHAPTER XVI.

THE BANQUET TO JAMES I AND HIS SON HENRY PRINCE OF WALES, 1607.

Royal guests in earlier years, p. 275.—The feast of St. John, p. 276.—Celebrated in song, p. 276.—Clothworkers' dinner, p. 276.—James I expresses his intention to dine with the Taylors, p. 277.—Merchant Taylors' record of the feast, p. 277.—Number of guests, p. 277.—Preparations made on 27th June, p. 278.—Money from the Treasury, p. 278.—Standing Committee, p. 278.—Stewards, p. 278.—Two Caterers, p. 279.—Butler and wine, p. 279.—Ben Jonson's engagement, p. 280.—Hangings, &c., for the Hall, p. 280.—Plate hired, p. 281.—Waiters appointed, p. 281.—Watch on the Hall premises, p. 282.—Committee to meet daily, p. 282.—Court of 7th July, p. 283.—King, Prince, and Queen invited, p. 283.—Lord Mayor and Aldermen not to be invited, p. 284.—Recorder attends to remonstrate, p. 284.—Purses of gold to be provided, p. 285.—Provision laid in for the feast, and the cost of it, p. 286.—Butlers, Cooks, and Waiters, p. 286.—Utensils for the table, p. 287.—Messes for the King and others, p. 287.—Preparation of the Hall for guests, p. 287.—Reception of the King, p. 288.—Plague, p. 288.—Lord Mayor and Aldermen at the Hall, p. 288.—Retinue of the King, p. 289.—The Physician, p. 289.—Cooks, p. 289.—Lords, p. 290.—Enters the Hall, p. 291.—Performances, p. 291.—Pageant of performers, p. 291.—King's dinner, p. 291.—Dr. Bull's and Mr. Gyles' performance, p. 291.—The Prince's dinner, p. 291.—The Recorder's address, p. 292.—Master presents the purse of gold, p. 292.—The Clerk the roll of Honorary Members, p. 292.—List of these from 1351 to 1562, p. 293.—Notes of these Members, p. 293.—Purse presented to the Prince, p. 304.—Made an Honorary Member, p. 305.—Lords also, p. 305.—Master and Wardens installed into office with garlands, p. 305.—Farewell, p. 305.—Settlement of accounts, p. 305.—Dr. Bull and Mr. Gyles made Liverymen, p. 305.—Ambassadors apply for certificate of freedom, p. 306.—Master's contribution to the feast, p. 306.—Final items, accounts, and total costs, p. 306.—NOTE. Items of expenditure for feast, pp. 307-17.

CHAPTER XVII.

THE COMPANY TO THE DATE OF THE NEW ORDINANCES (1613).

New enterprises in Elizabeth's reign, p. 319.—Contract with Rochelle merchants, p. 320.—In James's reign London population excessive, p. 321.—American (Virginia) Plantation, p. 322, *et seq.*—Lottery, p. 325.—Disastrous result, p. 326.—Ulster plantation, p. 326.—Precept for voluntary offers, p. 327.—Result, p. 327.—Compulsory assessment of the Guilds, p. 328.—Merchant Taylors' payments of first and second instalments, p. 328.—New Assessment, p. 329.—(Note on same, p. 329).—Payment of third and fourth instalments, p. 329.—Irish Society, p. 330.—Allotment of lands to the Guilds, p. 330.—Manor of St. John Baptist, p. 330.—Plantation of Church and people, p. 330.—Taylors' Irish estates sold, p. 330.—Ill behaviour of members, p. 331.—Difficulty in filling Guild offices, p. 331.—Power of fine and imprisonment, p. 333.—Guilds upheld by the Crown, p. 333.—Lady Elizabeth's marriage portion, p. 333.—Favours solicited from them, p. 333.—Prince Henry's request, p. 333.—Lady Elizabeth's for Cook's place, p. 334.—Sir John Swynnerton's mayoralty, p. 334.—Dekker's pageant, p. 335.—Opening of New River, p. 339.—Masque at Merchant Taylors' Hall, p. 340.—Ordinances of 1613 confirmed, p. 341.—Eminent members of the Company, p. 342.—Conclusion, p. 342.—Expenditure for 1612-13, p. 343.

APPENDICES.

		PAGE
1.	Indenture of Apprenticeship of 20th December, 1451 (30 Henry VI)	344
2.	Petition of the Tailors and Armourers of London to Edward III for a Charter granted 10th March, 1327	344
3.	Nota Bene, &c., of the great costs, Tempore Lokok, Master, 1439-40	345
4.	22 Henry VI (1443), William Auntrus, Master. "Thise been the Paiementz and Costz made by the Meistre and Wardeins upon dyvers Men for the Serche of Barthilmew Faire"....	346
5.	Agreement with Henry VII, that in consideration of the New Charter certain religious ceremonies shall be observed and masses said for him	347
3.	"Th'ordynnaunce for the kepyng of the Queene's Obite and of the Kynges when it shall happen	350
7.	Epitome of the Ordinances of the Merchant Taylors Company relating to the persons undermentioned: (A) Freemen; (B)	

	PAGE
Apprentices ; (C) Wardens ; (D) Assistants ; (E) Master ; (F) Master ; (G) Beadle and Wardens, as approved in 1507, under 19 Henry VII, Chap. 7	351
8. The Ordinance (1507) for the Election of the Master and Four Wardens	357
9. The Prayer of the Guild.—The First Entry in the Merchant Taylors' Ordinance Book of Henry VII's Reign	359
10. Muster and Shew of the Standing Watch	360
11. Assessments made upon the Company to Provide for the Purchase of Corn	360
12. Account of the Repayment of Corn Money which the Corporation had made to the Master and his Distribution of it.—List of the Merchant Company	362
13. A Threat of Imprisoning the Master and Wardens for not making a Provision of Gunpowder	363
14. Eden's Case in the Star Chamber	363
15. "The Othe of ev'y foreyn broder admitted into their said fraternitee"	366
16. 1467, February 22nd.—Agreement transferring a Taylor's business from father to son on terms	367
17. The Payments Made in the Years Preceding and Succeeding the Act as shown in the Company's Cash Books	371
18. The Financial Effect of the Sales (1549–50) upon the Yearly Revenue of the Company at that and at the Present Time	371
19. In Chancery (1514). Merchant Taylors Company *v.* Thomas Howden's Executors	372
20. Memorandum of the Merchant Taylors Company	374
21. Robert Dowe's Midnight Exhortation to the Condemned Prisoners in Newgate	388
22. Robert Dowe's Morning Exhortation to the People to Pray for the same Prisoners	389
23. Sir Richard Lee's Mayoralty	389
24. Expenses Concerning the Law for our Defence in the Suit made by the Company of the Clothworkers	390
25. An Ordinance for Nourishing and Relieving the Poor Members of the Merchant Taylors Company	393
26. Mr. Wilkes's Petition to Marry and to be Translated from this to the Vintners Company	394
27. Confirmation by James I (1620) of Title to School Site	396
28. 1564.—Interviews between the Corporation of London and the Court of Merchant Taylors Company as to the Acquisition of Perevvale's House for the Burse	396
29. "A Precept to Watch at ev'ry Gate and Posterne in the City"	400

	PAGE
30. Sir W. FitzWilliam's Obit and Fish's Exhibitions ...	402
31. List of Freemen in the Lansdowne MS.	404
32. Table showing Assessments of the Livery Companies by the Corporation of London in 1548, 1562, 1599, and 1603–4....	405
33. Ancient Acquisitions of the Merchant Taylors Company, 1331 to 1531	407

INTRODUCTION

Object of the work, p. 1.—Government of London, p. 2.—Of the Guild, p. 2. —Ward or Guild the unit of London government, p. 2.—Characteristics of the Livery Companies' (1) *Charity, p. 3;* (2) *Religion, pp. 4 and 5;* (3) *Hospitality, pp. 6, 7, and 8.—Eminent members, p. 8.—Richard Hilles, p. 9.—Commerce and colonization, p. 10.—New enterprises by the Guilds, p. 10.*

THE present work is an attempt to trace from the antient records, the history of the Merchant Taylors Company from initiation, when trade in its infancy was nurtured by religion, to the full development of corporate life, when trade passed into other organizations.

To show also the position which the Company occupied, and the work that it did as a factor in the government of London, while it was the monopolist of the trade it protected, the patron of the craftsmen it enrolled, and the almoner of the poor it relieved. For the three centuries which come under our notice each citizen was governed by his Guild, and to estimate aright the value of that organisation we must bring under notice the lives of those members, interwoven with the growth of the Company, who living guided it by their counsel and afterwards endowed it by their wealth. But eminent as guildsmen they were something more, living as they did not only for their Guild but for their city, the offices of the one leading not unfrequently to the dignities of the other. It would, therefore, be impossible to write effectively either the early history of a London Livery Company or the lives of its eminent members, without describing, at least in outline, those corporate offices in the civic Government which on election they were bound to fill.

London, though so worthy of it, has unfortunately no constitutional history, and each writer must, as best he can, frame one for his readers from the materials which lie scattered in various works.[1] To treat of the rights of the citizens as contained in their charters, and to show how they first secured for themselves those liberties which afterwards they got extended to their fellow countrymen, would be too long a digression. London has, for upwards of 500 years, been governed by officers each freely elected by his fellow citizens, and then sworn faithfully to discharge his office. The duties of these office bearers are, therefore, to be found in their oaths, for to quote the words of Lord Somers, "there is no better

---

[1] Chapter I, page 11.

measure to be taken of what is the natural and proper business of antient officers than what is compendiously and significantly expressed in the oaths, which have with great care and wisdom been formed and instituted for them to take."[1] At the present day the government of London is carried on under the sanction of oaths formulated 500 years past, which still continue to be administered.[2]

The rights and duties of the guildsman[3] lie in a narrower compass, for each Company has its own charters, ordinances, Court books and accounts, dating from various eras of greater or less antiquity, and the Merchant Taylors Company, from whose records our extracts will be taken, are fortunate in having preserved some of these, but had the antient civic, like the antient State papers, been deposited in safe custody, viz., at the Guildhall, under a competent Record Keeper, with regulated access to them; what an advantage would have been secured not only to the Guilds whose records are lost, but to those seeking information on the constitutional history of London?[4]

London has been more or less governed, though both have been co-existent, by wards and by Guilds; for the Guild was once, as the ward is now, an unit of London government. "The whole population of London," writes the Venetian ambassador, in May, 1551, "is divided into Companies or Fraternities of artificers; as for instance, all the workmen purchase from the King the privilege of forming Companies amongst themselves, holding their meetings, forming their statutes, regulating the price of cloth, preventing others from exercising the trade, nor can anyone enter these Companies until he has served those in the trade six or seven years."[5] The government in ward by the Alderman is here wholly ignored.

The history of all the London Livery Companies on constitutional subjects is the same, because their relationship—and

---

[1] The Banker's Case, 14 State Trials, page 63.

[2] Compare oaths set out in Vol. 1, Statute Realm, page 349, with oaths in Report on Oaths (1867).

[3] Chapter II, page 33.

[4] The most important of the early records of the Merchant Taylors Company are Charters, old ordinance book 1507, and ordinance book 1613, Master and Wardens' receipts and payments A.D. 1397 to 1445; 1453 to 1484, 1545 to 1557, 1569 to 1648; Treasury accounts 1489 to 1503; rough Court Minutes 1486 to 1492; freeman's book 1530 to 1888; apprentices book 1583 to 1888; Court Minutes 1562 to 1663.[a] *We have recently lost a most valuable book containing the list of all the Masters and Wardens from the foundation of the Company, and an epitome of its affairs.*

[5] Cal. Ven. St. Papers, page 703.

[a] 1654 to 1663 missing.

usually their contact—has been the same with the Legislature (civic or imperial), with the Crown, and with the Lord Mayor (as the civic King), but in a popular view of their position, and omitting for the present any reference to trade (which has little to do with the Livery Companies of to-day) we find in the antient Guild three leading characteristics which we will describe in the relative order of importance which we think our progenitors attached to them, taking our illustrations from the Merchant Taylors' records.

First, as to benevolence :[1]

1. The earliest mention made by Stowe of the Taylors is that on St. John Baptist's Day, in 1300, they chose Henry de Ryall, as Master, "to be their pilgrim," and the Wardens were then called "purveyors of alms" of the said Fraternity. It was in the next century that their benevolence assumed a substantial shape; for in 1406 the Company built almshouses near their hall, adjacent to St. Martin's Church, "for the brethren of the livery or clothing falling into poverty." But their charity was not to be a blind benevolence, poor the brother might be, but if he had "fallen into poverty through ryot! or wanton or lavish expenditure—his own negligence, or other misdemeanour," he was no fit candidate for their alms. Having elected him as a meritorious man, he was not deemed to be degraded by his poverty, for he had a place at their great feasts. Thus runs an entry (after a quarterly court had ended) in 1607: "And then preparation was made for dinner whereunto were invited the whole Assistants, and the ladies, and old Masters' wives and the Warden's wives of the present year, and the preacher and the schoolmaster, Wardens Substitute, and almsmen of the livery as in antient time hath been accustomed." The provision was for life provided no misconduct forfeited it, "for if found to be either drunkard or of unchast life or conversation, he was to be displaced by the Master and Wardens," and upon his death "he was to be honestly buried at the costs and charges of the said Fraternity, the Master and Wardens, and divers of the clothing in their whole livery to be present at his burial." But though this was the original it was not the only mode of relief, for the account books show that alms were given to poor brethren, though not inmates of the almshouse; and in course of time benefactions came to the Company (there being then no poor rate) for the poor of the

---

[1] Chapter VI, page 110.

Fraternity,—which are still distributed according to the testators wishes by the Court of Assistants.

Next as to religion :[1]

2. The society was founded in honour of some saint, that of the Taylors Company being St. John the Baptist, and the election of officers was made on the feast connected with that saint. The Taylors attended service on St. John Baptist's Day at their chapel upon the north side of St. Paul's; the yeomanry[2] on the day of his Decollation at the Chapel of St. John's Clerkenwell, the crypt in which they worshipped being still to be seen by the visitor. In 1455, if we may believe the Company's petition to Pope Calixtus, recited in his Bull (a copy of which is still extant) the Chapel of St. Paul's was *too small*, therefore, with his sanction, another was erected in St. Martin's Outwich parish. In 1465 the Company associated itself with the Hospital of St. John in Jerusalem in Clerkenwell, and with other religious societies enumerated in the *Book of Ordinances*, some particulars of which are printed elsewhere. The young Taylor upon entering into his apprenticeship was thus instructed by the Corporation of London, under its order of June, 1527 : " Ye shall constantly and devoutly on your knees every day serve God, morning and evening, 'to make conscience in due learning of the Lord, and endeavour the right practice thereof in your life and conversation,' and according to your course to expect your reward, for good or ill, from God and your friends." When the Bible had been rendered into English by Miles Coverdale (who, be it mentioned, was the Company's tenant for a house in Finch-lane, and preached before them in 1548-9 for a fee of 6s. 8d.), he Company ordered a Bible to "be bought and set up in their common hall for such as resort unto the said hall"—"to occupy themselves while they attend the hearing of their causes." The quarterly courts (if not other meetings) of the Company, were kept with religious observances, in the earlier years possibly in their chapel, but at a later date in their hall as this entry shows : "After which said quarterly meeting, so concluded and agreed upon, the whole assistants resorted into the Common Hall, where the whole Livery were called, and the default marked and prayers reverently said, every man kneeling upon his knees; but forasmuch as the

---

[1] Chapter VI, page 110.
[2] The entry of 1417 has reference to such attendance without the Master and Wardens.—Chapter III, page 63, *post*.

forenoon was spent, there was no time left either to read the
ordinances or the names of the benefactors, therefore the same were
deferred until the next quarters day." The prayers used are set
out in the Court books and printed in the *Memorials*,[1] that of
Henry VII's reign is here printed.[2] As a final act of brotherhood, when a member died, he was not shuffled under the
earth by strangers but the beadle's duty was to summon every
member of the fraternity to the funeral, and each was liable at the
call of the Master and Wardens " to bear the said brother or sister
to burying," and fined if no appearance were made. Descriptions
of such funerals by Machyn are frequent, and in September, 1558,
he thus writes of Dalbeney's[3] : "Many morners in blake, and many
clarkes and preste's and all the Compene of the Marchand Tayllers,
and after home to drynke as the compane with spycyse bred, and
the morrow masse and after to dener." The dinner was always
given by legacy of the deceased, and here again a devout grace or
prayer (still extant) was pronounced by the chaplain.[4] The costly
furniture of a funeral was kept by the Company for the use of its
members. Thus in the Inventory of 1512, there are found " a
coffyn of Estriche borde, with the burying clothe and half a shete
to lay within it." " The coffyn and shete " no longer exist, but two
rare and beautiful " herse cloths," which illustrate the decollation
of the Baptist, are to be seen hung upon frames in the west gallery
of the hall. It is well known that around the hall itself the
history of the event was given in tapestry of very ancient date,
some of which continued until the reign of George II, when it was
sold by one Mr. Alderman Salter to Deputy Tatem for the sum of
20*l*. A statue or, as the records call it, " an image of St. John "
stood in the hall from the years 1401–2 until the Reformation, but
recently (1873–4) as a memorial of that mastership, a copy of
Benedetto de Majano's 1442 statue from the Ufizzi Gallery at
Florence was placed in the hall entrance. A later and more
practical development of this religious feeling was the foundation
of the school, in 1561, "in honour of Christ Jesu," for the education
of good manners and literature, wherein "such a catechisme as

---

[1] In the mastership of 1873-4 the charters, ordinances, extracts from records, and all the parliamentary reports relating to the Merchant Taylors Company were printed for " private circulation " in royal octavo, and are quoted throughout this volume as " Memorials." The prayers will be found at pages 128 and 130.

[2] Appendix 9, page 359.

[3] It was probably Dawbeney, a well-known family in the Company.

[4] It was composed for the funeral dinner of John Swynnerton, at the instance of Robert Dowe, page 187, *post*.

shall be approved by the Queen's Majesty (Elizabeth) that novices" shall be taught—stamping the school as one established by the promoters of the "new learning."

As to hospitality :[1]

3. Under the Taylors' second charter (1390) permission was given "to hold and keep in an honest manner their feast of meat and drink on the feast-day of St. John the Baptist," and the oath of the liveryman obliged him " to attend the feast kept yearly about Midsummer, and holden in the Common Hall of the said Fraternity," a strange necessity, as we should now think, to swear a man to a strict attendance for a good dinner, but at that time necessary, because the expenses of these feasts were borne, not as now, wholly by the Company, but partly at the personal cost of the members. For this reason only a scant record of them is preserved, save when a King or Lord Mayor was entertained, and then we have amusing entries. However, who were the guests, what was their "menu," and what their amusement, are questions not admitting of a definite answer. In pre-Reformation times the feast of St. John was the event of the year, religious as well as social. Thus, in 1453, the Company paid for " preparing the hall and chambers for the feast of St. John, including hire of altar clothes, 40s.; flourishing with green bolles, three torches before the image of St. John in the hall, 16d.; and other expenses for the public worship at the two chapels of St. John (in St. Paul's and at the hall). All the Company, with the women, were entertained, and "the garlands" were provided "for the Masters and their wives." Guests of a higher class were invited; thus, in 1454-5, the Master and Wardens go by boat to Lambeth to invite the Chancellor, and in 1455-6 to invite the Archbishop of Canterbury; and in 1464-5 to Greenwich to invite the King and Queen, and to Westminster and Lambeth to invite lords " to the feast," but with what success these invitations were given is not recorded. A "menu"[2] for 1438 has been accidentally preserved on the fly-leaf of one of the Company's account books. The reader will find fairly good cheer, such as brawn, chines of pork, beef, swan, pheasant, chickens, venison, partridge, plovers, rabbits, snipe and quail, fruit and quinces. All the articles provided for King James's banquet in 1607 are recorded

---

[1] Chapter X, page 174.

[2] See the courses " for dyner and soper" provided for the noblemen and gentlemen of the Emperor Charles V, on his visit to London in 1522.—Rutland Papers (Camden Society, 1842), page 96.

in the Company's books, and will repay perusal.[1] The poultry will probably be thought to offer the greatest variety, for, besides the ordinary birds, and those before enumerated, you find "hernes, bitters, shovelers, godwitts, owles, cookoes, ringdoves, martins, mallards, and browsses." Whatever else might be lacking in entertainment, music was never wanting; but there—in the gallery over the screen in the Hall—sat the minstrels, or City waits, to amuse the guests. In 1434-5 they appear to have passed the whole day with the Company. Thus, "To the waytes of London attending upon the Company at the feast of St. John, and going before them to the Hospital of St. John, 10s.; to Henry Luter 3s. 4d.; to Thomas Reyner, with the trumpe, 12d." At King James's banquet they were, we fear, displaced by more distinguished performers, for "Ben Jonson, the poet," was engaged to frame a speech, and Dr. Bull to compose a song, but that he composed the "National Anthem" for the occasion is an absolute fiction. The existing "daïs" indicates where the principal guests sat, but where the "salt" was placed, or who sat above or who below it, no record explains. What the guests drank admitted of some variety —wine, beer, and ipocras;[2] while the large number of standing cups—the usual gifts of esteemed members of the Company—show the estimation in which the "loving cup" was held at City feasts. "I give" (were the words of FitzWilliam's will in 1534) "to the Master and Wardens of the Fellowship of the Merchant Taylors, in the City of London, my best standing gilt cup, with covers, for a perpetual remembrance of me, to be kept in their hall, and they to pray for my soul;" but these and others were destroyed at the fire of 1666. Those entertainments did not in later years include "the yeomen," who, in each third year, kept their feast at the decollation of St. John, after service, in the church at Clerkenwell. In course of time their contributions by way of quarterages were not received, and in 1696 their connection with the Company ceased.

Another feast—annual since A.D. 1484—must be noticed, though the history of it is to be found on the stained glass windows in our corridors. It is briefly this: The Skynners and

---

[1] Chapter XVI, page 275.

[2] Arnold, writing in the year 1502, gives the following "Ressaite to make Ypocras": "For a galon and a pint of red wy take synamon iij vncis, gynger tryed an vnce, greynes and longe peper di: vnce, cloves and masys a q'rt' of an vnce, Spignard a quartir of an vnce, sugar ij lb."—The Customs of London; or, Arnold's Chronicle. (London), 1811, f. 187.

Taylors were at that time in controversy as to precedence in the City processions, and, according to the wise customs of those times, they referred the subject to the Lord Mayor. Samuel Pepys, a shrewd observer in later days, wrote: "It is strange to see how a great dinner and feasting reconciles everybody," but the Lord Mayor (Sir Robert Billesden) had arrived at that conclusion 200 years before Pepys wrote, as he decreed, "for norishing of peas and love between the fellowships aforesaid they should dine with each other yearly, and take precedence in each alternate year," a decree which is still in full force and observance.

It only remains to add that the feasts of the citizens were then always made subordinate to the higher law of charity. Thus, in 1593, the Privy Council (through the Lord Mayor) required the guilds to give the cost of their annual election dinners to the relief of the poor visited by plague; and again, in 1603, the Company itself decided that all entertainments should be wholly given up during the time of the plague, "and that one-third part of the charge and expence intended to be spent on the said entertainments shall be bestowed upon the poor, miserable, and needy persons whose houses it shall please Almighty God so to visit"—an example not unworthy of imitation in any days of present distress.[1]

Turning now from the Guild to the citizens, who were its founders and benefactors; in the desire to rescue their good deeds from oblivion, and to show how London has been advanced to commercial greatness by the quiet integrity and public virtue of these guildsmen, we have gathered up from civic records such incidents as we can find of their lives (including one, who, though not a guildsman, was connected with the Company as the tenant of the Taylors' Hall in 1331, Oliver, Lord Ingham). These are Sir John Hawkwood, 1310–94; Sir John and Lady Percyvale, 1450–1509; Sir Stephen Jenyns,[2] 1524; Sir W. Fitzwilliam, 1450–1534; Richard Hunn, 1460–1514; Sir Thomas White, 1492–1566; Richard Hilles, 1510–87; and Sir Thomas Offley,[3] 1512–1582; Sir W. Harper, 1496–1573; Recorder Fleetwood, 1536–1596; John Stowe, 1515–

---

[1] During the Plague of 1603 all public feasting and common dinners in the several halls of the Corporation were wholly given up, and one-third of the expense of such dinners "bestowed upon the poor, miserable, and needy persons whose houses it shall please Almighty God so to visit."—(11th July, 1603).

[2] Part II.   [3] Page 172.

1605; Sir William Craven, 1548–1622; John Speed, 1568–1629; Sir Leonard Halliday,[1] 1564–1620.

This list contains two families ennobled, but from one Taylor now to be mentioned, four noble families can be traced. In the account books for A.D. 1399–1400 is to be seen this entry of "confrers" admitted to the Fraternity, "Johan Gore, Taillour," 20s. In 1603 there are seven Gores contributing as Taylors to the City assessment for James I's coronation, and in 1615 the Sheriffs were two Gores, members of the Company. One of these, Sir John, became Lord Mayor in 1624, and his mayoralty was celebrated by the Company, when Webster wrote for it his piece of the "Monuments of Honour." From Johan Gore four peerages are to be traced—the Earl of Ross and Lord Annalley (both extinct), the Earl of Arran and Lord Harlech (existing). Some years since the late Earl, as claiming, through Sir John Gore, came for any further information as to his family. The account books enabled him to trace his family to its source—to Mr. John Gore of 1399—a fact not yet stated in any edition of the Peerage.

But we can not close this sketch without noticing for special approval one benefactor to learning, whose life hitherto has been unrecorded, we mean Richard Hilles, who, in the reign of Elizabeth, and in furtherance of the Reformation, established for the children, not only of London, but indeed "of all nations and countreyes," the famous school at St. Lawrence Poultney, with Richard Mulcaster as the Chief Master, who in his early years had the glory of training amongst his pupils "Edmund Spenser," "the greatest ornament of the allegorical and imaginative school of poetry"—a London school which for upwards of three hundred years has sent out men who have gained renown in various ranks of life.

Such were the men who were honoured in their day, "but some there be," as wrote the son of Sirach, "who have no memorial—merciful men whose righteousness hath not been forgotten." If this experience needs confirmation, it would be found in the study of Guild records, for of the righteousness of these citizens no other memorial is extant; and, therefore, for the period embraced in this sketch, we propose to bring these records under the notice of the reader, to illustrate both the corporate life of a London Livery Company and the individual lives and actions of some of its eminent members.

---

[1] Page 235.

The religious aspect of the Guild in its initiation and development, with the great changes made in its endowment as a consequence of the Reformation, will come under our notice.[1] It will be seen how earnest supporters of the old and of the new "learning" were to be found amongst the guildsmen, and in looking back at the past, it is interesting to see how the efforts of each to support his own views have been brought into harmony and made subservient to the interests of Church and State from the Tudor to the present time.

Under the Tudors the commerce of London came into existence. If it be true, as the Bishop of Chester writes,[2] "that their period was that of the birth of modern commerce and colonisation," it is no less so that the London Guilds were the parents of each, and their halls the places of incubation and nurture until both trade and colonisation were firmly established, spreading far beyond the walls of London—even to the area of the civilised world.

With James I's reign a new era opens belonging more to the history of commerce and colonisation than to the London Livery Companies. In Elizabeth's reign[3] guildsmen had, rather as merchants than as guildsmen, initiated new enterprises to India and America, but in James's reign[4] they became—at the instance of the Crown—involved in schemes lying beyond the purposes of their charters of incorporation, and therefore not within the scope of the present work.

---

[1] Chapter VIII, page 138.
[2] Oxford Lectures (Clarendon Press), 1886, page 335.
[3] Page 255.
[4] Chapter XVII, page 319.

CHAPTER I.

THE GOVERNMENT OF LONDON.

London governed by the same continuous rule from the earliest to the present day, p. 11.—The area and population, p. 12.—Percyvale, first Taylor who became Mayor, p. 12.—Freedom gained by Indentures, p. 12.—Chamberlain's advice to Apprentices, p. 13.—Freemen, their duties and oath, p. 13.—As traders liable to Guild authority, p. 14.—Wards and the Mote, p. 14.—Duties of the Bedel, p. 14.—Of Wardsmen, p. 15.—Common Council, p. 16.—Duties of Members thereof, p. 16.—Control of Council over Expenditure, p. 17.—Sheriffs' election, p. 18.—Sheriffs' Riding, p. 18. —Duties, p. 19.—Aldermen, p. 19.—Election, p. 20.—Duties, p. 20.— Mayor, p. 21.—Election, p. 21.—Duties: (1) to the King; (2) his Fellow Citizens, p. 23.—His riding to Westminster, p. 23.—His Feast, p, 23.—Visit to William's Tomb and Beckett's Grave at St. Paul's, p. 24.—Service in scot and lot, p. 24.—Importance of the office, p. 25.—As at the Meeting of the York and Lancaster supporters in London, 1458, p. 25.—Ceremonials of the office, p. 26.—Precedence of the Mayor in the City determined in Henry V's reign, p. 28.—Insisted on at Serjeants' Feast, 1464, p. 28.— Sheriff subordinate, p. 29.—Precedence out of the City, p. 30.—Recorder's duties, p. 30.—Access of Corporation to the Throne, p. 31.—Butlership at the Coronation, p. 32.

THE Guilds formed part of the civic government, and as some of those whose lives are to be noticed attained to the supreme authority, it will be useful if we endeavour to give an outline of the government of London during the Tudor period; a task not altogether useless for the practical purposes of the *present* day, for here there has been a continuity of rule for many hundred years which is possibly without parallel elsewhere.

London at that period was divided into the city and its liberties, both subject to the authority of the Mayor. The *City*, an area of 380 acres of land, was enclosed within a boundary wall of two miles extent, having seven principal gates, such as Ludgate and Newgate. The *Liberties* consisted of a belt of land of 300 acres lying outside the walls and having, as its other boundary, bars such as the Temple and Holborn, with chains to separate this area from the surrounding counties. Both areas together were one square mile of land.[1]

---

[1] See Vol. I, Londiana, page 15; French Chron. (Camden Society), page v.

Within the smaller area of the *City*[1] there was in 1560 a constant resident population of not less than 130,000[2] souls, living in streets in which religious houses, mansions, and gardens were to be found interspersed with hovels. In the larger area—after the religious houses had been suppressed[3] and gardens had been covered with modern houses of greater size—the population was returned (in 1851) at 131,129 souls, so that we may reasonably presume that the *City* was overcrowded in 1560 and that one could "scarcely[4] pass along the streets on account of the throng."

The residents were governed by the Mayor as the supreme head of the municipal institutions, under several charters, either as wardsmen under an Alderman, or as guildsmen under a Master, or indeed as both. Taking Percyvale (he being the first Taylor who became Mayor) as an illustration, we will follow him through the different civic offices devolving upon a wardsman until he reached the supreme authority of the Mayor of London, and thus show how the city was governed in *wards*.

First to show how the right of citizenship was to be gained. His initiation would commence with obtaining the assent of some guildsman of London to take him for seven years as an apprentice. To become such he must have been more or less of gentle breeding[5]

---

[1] Of the city in the earlier Tudor reigns we have several descriptions by the Venetian ambassadors in their periodical reports to the Doge. In August, 1531, a Venetian visitor thus writes : " In various parts of the city there are many palaces of divers citizens and merchants, but the larger ones are on the river, the owners being the chief personages of the kingdom. The population is immense, and comprises many artificers. The houses are in very great number, but ugly, and half the materials of wood, nor are the streets wide. It is a very rich populous and mercantile city, but not beautiful."[a] In the same year an ambassador writes that London is divided into 26 wards and 86 parishes,[b] with a population of 70,000.[c] Another in August, 1554, described London as having a dense population, said to number 80,000 souls, and as beyond measure commercial, the merchants of the entire kingdom flocking thither, " so they soon became very wealthy.[d] Again in 1557.[e] London is most opulent, not only from the trade and great commerce but from the privileges of her citizens, containing, with Westminster, 185,000 souls, having handsome streets and buildings. However, " their building materials are very coarse, as not having good clay for making bricks, they use wood mixed with mortar, earth, or straw, so that the walls are ugly, which is why they use tapestries or canvas on which they paint foliage.

[2] Norton's London, page 141. Report on City P.C. (1880), page 5. See Vol. 6, Brayley, page 70, which gives the population in wards as 130,178 in August, 1631.

[3] The religious houses and their enclosures are said to have occupied two-thirds of the city area.—Vol. 10, part 2, page 39, Beaut. of E. and W. (1814).

[4] Fred, Duke of Wirtemberg, 1592, Rye's England, page 7.

[5] The 7 Henry IV put a property qualification on apprentices.

[a] Cal. State Papers (Venetian), page 682.   [b] *Ibid.*, page 694.

[c] See Preface to Anderson's History of Commerce, 1801, page v.

[d] Cal. State Papers (Venetian), page 934.   [e] *Ibid.*, 884.

and a natural born subject of the King. The master and apprentice entered into articles which for 500 years past have been the same in substance, and all but identical in words. The master was to find the apprentice in all necessaries (as food, clothing, shoes, and bed), the apprentice not to injure or waste his master's goods ; not to frequent taverns ; nor, in or out of his master's house, to commit sins of inchastity, nor contract marriage; not to play at dice, &c., but to conduct himself justly and piously as a good servant according to the use and custom of London.[1]

When placed under articles of apprenticeship these had to be registered in the Chamber of London, and the apprentice, when brought into contact with the great Corporation, received from the Chamberlain these devout instructions :—

"Ye shall constantly and devoutly on your knees, every day, serve God, morning and evening, and make conscience in the due learning of the word preached, and endeavour the right practice thereof in your life and conversation. You shall do diligent and faithful service to your master for the time of your apprenticeship, and deal truly in what you shall be entrusted. You shall often read over the covenants of your indenture, and see and endeavour yourself to perform the same to the utmost of your power. You shall avoid all evil company, and all occasions which may tend to draw you to the same ; and make speedy return, when you shall be sent on your master's or mistress's business. You shall be of fair, gentle, and lowly speech and behaviour towards all men; especially to all your governors. And according to your carriage expect your reward, for good or ill, from God and your friends."[2]

And let it be noted that this custom is not yet altogether extinguished, as an apprentice still receives from the Master of the Merchant Taylors Company a book of good sound religious advice such as he would do well to follow.

Having faithfully discharged his duty to his master under his articles the apprentice would claim his freedom to the city, for until he had been enrolled as a Freeman and sworn to discharge his duty as such he would be unable to practice his art or craft in the city of London. This enrolment could only be made upon "the security of six respectable men of the mystery or craft through which he was to obtain his freedom."

This certificate being obtained he was then admitted and sworn:
(1.) To obey the Mayor and ministers of the city.

---

[1] See Appendix, page 344.
[2] C. C. Act, 1st June, 18 Henry VIII, 1 Mait., pages 229-30.

(2.) To maintain the franchises and customs.
(3.) To contribute to and bear all manner of charges (*inter alia*), scot and lot, as a freeman ought to do.
(4.) Not to conceal foreign goods or foreigners.
(5.) Not to implead or sue any fellow citizen out of the city "whilst ye may have right and law within the city."[1]
(6.) To take no bondsman's or alien's son as an apprentice.
(7.) To make his apprentice free of the city, if his service has been good and true to him.
(8.) To keep the peace and warn the Mayor of all conventicles or conspiracies against the city.[2]

By enrolment he came under a double allegiance to the Mayor as the supreme authority over him; (*a.*) as a resident freeman, in regard to the city bye-laws; and (*b.*) as a trader of a Guild or Company, in regard to its laws and ordinances; in each of which relationships he would have to discharge duties, both personal and pecuniary, as he had solemnly pledged himself to do. Here we take under review those claimed from him as a wardsman through the Alderman, and leave those claimed from him as a guildsman until a later chapter.

London was a quasi republic, governed by its own citizens annually elected by their fellow citizens in common hall, under rules and regulations which they framed for their own observance. All that the Crown was required to do was to approve the supreme ruler after his election, but the two sheriffs needed no such approval. So long, therefore, as the executive and administrative officers of the city acted within the powers conferred upon them by charter their authority within the city was supreme.

It is scarcely necessary to say that London was, and still is, divided into wards, each presided over by an Alderman, with an executive officer, the "Bedel," and that Percyvale, as a resident, would have to take his part as a wardsman. The Bedel was elected by the Wardmote, and had the charge of the ward under oath. By that he pledged himself to suffer no man accused of robbery or of evil courses, or hucksters of ale, or woman keeping a brothel, or other women commonly reputed of bad or evil life, to dwell there, but to report the same to the Alderman, so that he might turn them out in fifteen days. Any affray he was forthwith to report to the Chamberlain and Sheriffs. He was not to be an officer in any Christian court, nor to trade in certain

---

[1] This oath is modified by 11 George II, cap. 18, sec. 19, as to 4, 5, and 6.
[2] Enlick, page 214, *note*.

specified things while holding the office of Bedel.[1] Twice a year all the residents in a ward were brought together by the precept of the Lord Mayor, directed to the Aldermen, and when the Alderman received his biennial precept to hold a Wardmote, he summoned thereto all the freemen and hired servants, who were bound to attend under a penalty of 4d. for absence.[2]

The Alderman having taken his seat "with the more opulent men of the ward, each in his proper place," attention was called. The Clerk then read the warrant for the meeting, and the "bedel" the name roll of residents, and of those who, being absent after proclamation aloud, had to be fined. The ward constables then came forward with the jury panel "of the respectable men of the ward," and articles of enquiry were given to the jury touching the ward (*inter alia*)—

(1.) As to the peace of God and Holy Church and of the King being strictly kept between clerks and laymen, rich and poor in common.

(2.) As to residents not under frankpledge, and that no one receive a stranger beyond one day and night.

(3.) As to lewd women, to be driven out or else placed in the Compter.

(4.) As to furnaces and chimneys.

(5.) As to lepers or usurers.

(6.) As to night walkers.

(7.) As to extortion in any city officers;[3] or

(8.) As to no wages being paid at a higher rate than the assize.[4]

The jury had to give in their verdict in detail in duplicate by a stated day, so that the Alderman might bring any matters needing correction before the Court of Common Council. The manner in which they executed their office may be seen by an extract from a return in 1523 printed at the foot.[5]

---

[1] Liber Albus (London, 1861), pages 34 and 272.

[2] Liber Albus, page 33. See the form of it, 2 Mait., London, page 121.

[3] The city at a very early stage in its history made an order forbidding their officers to ask for *Christmas Boxes*:—" It is not agreeable or proper that those who are in service with the advantage of befitting clothes and raiment as also received and remunerated in a competent degree, should after a known custom be begging aught of people like paupers" (A.D. 1419), Riley's Memorials, page 670.

[4] Liber Albus, page 288.

[5] In December, 1523, the Broad Street Wardmote presented (*a*) *St. Benet's Fynk*, that the cage is very noisome and adible and a well dampned thereby; a noisome and dangerous draught in Thomas Howell's house, defective pavement before St. Anthony's, &c.; and showing the Inquest Jury met then (as sanitary authorities

The wardmote then proceeded to more general business, such as the election of officers, " the scavagers, all commoners, and other officials" to carry on the local government of the ward, to seal the weights and measures, to bring all freemen on to its roll, and to put others upon the oath of " frankpledge," viz. :—(1) To keep the peace ; (2) To be obedient to the city officers, and assist them at all times in arresting misdoers, as well denizens as strangers ; (3) To make the watches, and to bear other charges for the safeguard of the peace ; (4) To keep the rules of the Wardmote ; and lastly, to withstand evil courses within the Ward and to make known the same to the Alderman.[1]

Such was the Wardmote, and one other duty had to be performed by it—viz., the election of Alderman, which will be explained when we deal with that office.

The greater affairs of the whole city were dealt with by the citizens, as a Council, originally formed by the Mayor and Aldermen summoning, through the Serjeants of the Chamber, a varying number of the Ward (as sixteen, twelve, eight, or even four,) according to its size, " of the wisest and most wealthy persons, while no one was to appear unless duly summoned, or presume to be present under penalty of imprisonment."

All those summoned and appearing were to be thus sworn :

(1.) To be true to the King.

(2.) To come quickly to the Common Council when summoned.

(3.) To give good and true counsel after his wit and cunning.

(4.) To maintain no singular profit against the public, or against the common profit of the city.

(5.) Not to depart from the Council without licence ; and

Lastly, Not to disclose what was there spoken.

In later times—the oath remaining the same—changes were made, which did not continue. During John Warde's mayoralty in 1375 the Council was elected " by the respective mysteries " (or Livery Companies) as six, four or two, according to the importance

---

do now) with a little abuse when interposing to secure good sanitary arrangements, William Delke for threatening certain persons of the Inquest. The parish of St. Martin Outwich was then visited, and their presentment was :—The rerydosts in Charterhouse rents and a hayloft under them are dangerous for fire ; defective pavement before the Taylors' almhouses, and a noisome gutter through it. Then follows this general presentment :—Spencer's wife, Harrison's wife, and Badcock's wife for scolding (who we may hope were not the wives of the Merchant Taylors who bore those names).—Vol. 3, Part 2, Henry VIII, Cal. S.P.

[1] Liber Albus, page 273.

CHAP. I.]   *Control of Council over Expenditure.*   17

of the Company, and not by Wards. This was thought to work to the disturbance of "peace and quiet amongst the people," and therefore in Sir Nicholas Brembers' fourth mayoralty of 1384 (his opponent, John Northampton, the late Mayor, being in prison and his goods confiscated[1]) "the Mayor, with his Aldermen and the good Commoners did choose certain persons with deliberation to advise thereupon how tumult and peril might be best avoided and remedied." The result was that the Common Council should be annually elected by Wards, and that to each Ward according to its size a number of members was assigned (then constituting a total of 96 members) as Common Councillors for the government of the city.[2]

Those who duly appeared were to form a "congregation," and if they could not agree they were to be examined by the Common Serjeant "upon their oath," as no delay or obstruction to the practical work of the city was permitted.

This Council made all the assessments and bye-laws in the city, which were levied and enforced by the Mayor's precept. It was the supreme court of appeal for any (municipal) grievance. All controversies arising between the Guilds were referred by petition to its arbitrament, and the Acts of the Common Council, like those of Parliament, had to be obeyed by the citizens.[3]

All other "matters affecting the common weal" were there dealt with. No alien was admitted to the Freedom[4] or corporate letters sealed unless with the consent of the commonalty, for the common seal, which is "the hand and mouth" of every Corporation, was placed in a certain chest, which had six locks, three keys of which were to be held by the Alderman, and the other three "by certain reputable men of the commonalty."[5] Thus it was that the Common Council became in August, 1312, what the Commons of England afterwards attained to be, viz., the Comptrollers of expenditure.

Whether a member of Common Council or not we have n record, but the first office in which we *know* Percyvale served his fellow citizens was as one of the Sheriffs of London and Middlesex. These two officers were then quaintly described "as the eyes of

---

[1] Liber Albus, page 397.
[2] Regulated by 11 Geo. II, c. 8, freemen householders paying scot and bearing lot in their wards being the electors.
[3] See Norton's London, page 314.
[4] As to this see Collection of Letters, &c., by Reg. Sharpe, D.C.L., London 1585.
[5] Liber Albus, page 317.

VOL. I.   C

the Mayor," ever on the watch, and taking their share in his anxieties. They and all their officers were to be subservient to the Mayor for the time being ("as the limbs are subservient to the head") performing all mandates issued by him.

In their own courts they were judges as to personal pleas, and in the Hustings Court not only judges but also executors of the Mayor's precepts. Their appointment was not like that of other Sheriffs upon the nomination of the Crown, but by free election of all their fellow citizens until the Act of the Common Council of 15 Edward IV conferred the franchise on the Livery—as the honest men of the mysterie—*coming in their last livery to the elections*.[1]

The Mayor, Recorder, Aldermen, and Electors being assembled, one Sheriff was nominated by the Mayor, either by way of duty or privilege, for it is not clear which, "as the King's Sheriff," and the Mayor, if he so nominated, was responsible to the Crown[2] for the money due from the Sheriff during his year of office.[3]

The other Sheriff (or both, if the Mayor did not nominate) was elected by the commonalty, and for such election the city was in like manner responsible to the Crown. The Sheriffs were apparently upon an equality when serving, save that the Mayor gave the "cocket," or seal of Newgate, to the Sheriff whom he may have nominated for election at Midsummer.[4]

But the Sheriffs, though elected, could not act as such until they had been admitted to the office under sanction of an oath which was administered in the city, but in later years at Westminster. For this purpose they went in procession (much as did the Mayor) to be sworn before the Barons of the Exchequer, but two such ridings in the year caused a feeling of rivalry, "as the usage was for citizens to array themselves in new suits, to hire horses, and to incur many other expenses, when shortly after, on the Morrow of St. Simon and St. Jude, they again incurred the like expenses," it was thought, therefore, that the Sheriff's riding ought not to be continued. So "on the Feast of the translation of St. Edward the King and Confessor (13th March, 1389) the Mayor, Aldermen, and an immense number of the Commonalty agreed

---

[1] At the present day the Beadle's summons to the Livery is to appear in their gowns, though it is not observed, nor possibly the reason known. These elections by the Livery are now regulated by the Act of Common Council, 7th April, 1748. [2] Riley's Memorials, page 515.

[3] The Lord Mayor may still, between 14th April and 14th June, nominate freemen, not exceeding nine, as candidates, and the method of nomination is prescribed by order of 7th April, 1748.

[4] As to the Sheriff's office and customs, see Harper's Life, Part II, page 258.

that no Sheriff should in the day of his presentation "give any vestments save to the servants of the city, and his own officers and serjeants, or should have any riding," but should go by water or proceed by land without there being any men of the trades in like suits for that purpose, but that men of the trades wishing to accompany them should walk in the livery of their respective trades as they might have.[1]

The duties of the Sheriffs as laid down in their oath were:—

(1.) To be true to the King.
(2.) To maintain the city franchises.
(3.) To keep the limits of London and Middlesex.
(4.) To do right as well to poor as to rich.
(5.) To break no good custom, nor evil one maintain.
(6.) To keep the assize of bread, &c.
(7.) Not to delay judgments or executions, nor any right disturb.
(8.) Not to return any writs touching the state or practice of the city without the advice of the Mayor and Common Council.
(9.) On warning from the Mayor to keep and maintain the peace and state of the city.
(10.) Not to farm out the county of Middlesex or the government of Newgate.[2]

Percyvale's next advance would be to the office of Alderman, for which the laws and ordinances of the city had laid down some definite qualifications:

"No person was accepted by the Mayor and Aldermen as Alderman unless he was free from infirmity in body, wise and discreet in mind, rich, honest, trustworthy, free, and on no account of low or servile condition, that perchance the disgrace or opprobrium that might be reflected on him by reason of his birth might have the additional effect of casting a slur upon the other Aldermen and the whole City as well."

That an Alderman should then have been an able-bodied man was an absolute necessity, for police, as we understand them, did not exist. All watch in his ward was under his personal control, and his functions as a Guardian of the Peace had often to be discharged on horseback.

---

[1] Liber Albus, page 266.
[2] Ibid., page 39.

The election as Alderman[1] was made by his fellow wardsmen acting under the presidency of the Mayor, who, whenever the office became vacant, issued his summons according to the regulations of 1397, which ran in these words[2]:—

"To avoid the damages, dissensions, and perils, by reasons of the headstrong, partial, and imprudent elections of Aldermen," it was ordered that "at every such election at least two reputable and discreet men, either of whom in manners and worldly goods is fit to be a Judge and an Alderman of the city, shall by the men of the Ward which is so destitute of an Alderman be peacefully and quietly chosen and presented to the Mayor and Aldermen to the end that one of those men of whom the Mayor and Aldermen shall deign to make choice may be admitted and sworn to office."

The candidate selected by the Mayor and Aldermen was presented by his fellow citizens to be sworn. By his oath he was to inform the people of his ward of such things as pertained for them to do for keeping the city, maintaining its peace, and its laws, usages, and franchises. He was to maintain the rights of orphans according to the laws and usages of the city; to come on the Lord Mayor's summons to speed the assizes, pleas, and judgments of the hustings, and other needs of the city; and to give good and lawful counsel touching the common profit of the city, and lastly he was *not* to be a common victualler during his office.

By election he became a member of the "Court of Aldermen in the Inner Chamber," who, when summoned by the Lord Mayor, acts (1) Judicially, as for instance, in investigating controversies arising between the Guilds, and imprisoning those officers who may refuse to obey their order or decree; or (2) In an executive capacity. The office, originally one of annual election, was in Percyvale's time held for life, but the Alderman was not a Justice of the Peace till he had passed the office of Mayor.[3] In the Common Council he voted as an ordinary member thereof.

As a guildsman who had passed through the offices of Alderman and Sheriff, Percyvale became qualified for election as Mayor of London. The electors were his fellow citizens, originally em-

---

[1] These elections are regulated by 11 Geo. II, c. 18, and 19 Geo. II, c. 8, and made by the Freemen paying scot (rates to church, poor, scavengers, orphans, and for watch and ward), and bearing lot.

[2] Liber Albus.

[3] By later charters, some, and in 1741 all, Aldermen became Justices of the Peace on election.

bracing all the apprentices and serving-men of the city; but by order of 1404, in which it was written "that so loud and clamorous was their shouting that the Mayor and Aldermen were unable to understand the reason of their noise," it was decreed "that at the election of Mayor, Sheriff, or Officers, no person shall presume to enter the Guildhall unless summoned to make such election," and no one was to be summoned unless he were one of the more substantial men of the city or one of the Common Council thereof.[1] This, however, was thought to leave too much power in the hands of the Mayor, and therefore the Common Council Act of 15 Edward IV (before referred to), limiting the franchise to the Livery, was passed.[2]

These electors appear to have fallen into the mistake of supposing that they were the sole electors, and sent up to the higher Court *one* name only; but on being reminded by the Mayor and Aldermen that as citizens they had also a voice in the election the Commoners assented thereto. Hence it became the custom by common consent of both Aldermen and Commoners for the Commoners to retire to the other end of the Hall (the eastern or Sheriff's Court end), and there to nominate two Aldermen, which done, they returned, and by their own Common Pleader presented to the Mayor and Aldermen two names asking which of them they would be pleased to admit. Upon this the Mayor and Aldermen ascending to the upper chamber elected one of these by plurality of votes, then returning below, they made known to the people in the Guildhall, by the mouth of the Recorder, which of the two had been elected Mayor for the ensuing year.[3]

The procedure observed at the election of a Lord Mayor in later times is carefully explained by Recorder Fleetwood,[4] in one of his letters containing a diary of a week's work in 1573, written to Lord Burghley. After reading it we shall probably think that if the citizens failed to make a wise choice it was from no lack of previous counsel. He writes:

"Upon Thursday we all in our gounes and cloks in scarlett furred, were in the Yelde Hall Chappel, where a very learned and godly sermon was preached, and at the end of the sermon my Lord

---

[1] Liber Albus, page 17; Riley's Memorials, page 560. The Livery now elect under 11 Geo. II, c. 18.
[2] 11 Geo. II, c. 18, sec. 1.
[3] Liber Albus, page 19.
[4] See also Day's Pamphlet of the Customs of 1532, in Vol. 2, Allen's London, page 249.

and all his brethren received the Communion. And that done, we went into the Counsell Chamber, and there pawsing a while until all the comons of the citie were placed in the greate Halle, every man in his degree. Then, in a decent order we came forth, sat downe in the est ende of the Halle in the Hustings Court, and then myself did stand forth upon the chekker borde there, and used a simple speake unto the Comons, partlie noting unto them brefelie the chiefest points of the sermon that tended to the order of the election. And then I put them in remembrance of their dutie in the forme of their chosing, and what qualities the man ought to have whom they were of dutie bound to chose.

"That done, my Lord and his brethren returned to the Great Counsell Chamber, viz., the Maior's Courte, leaving behind us the two Sheriffs with the Comon Sargaunt. The which Comon Sargaunt doth then stand up, and either doth or should recite unto the Comons what the preacher and I had spoken, and add somewhat more to the same. And that done, the Comons name three or four of the most antient. And after question is asked which two of them they meane to present unto my Lord and his brethren; and then as menie as meane to have ———— to be Maior do hold up their hands and saie never a word.

"And so the names of the two that have most hands are sent up to my Lord and his Brethren, and then myself go down to a windowe, and beginning with the youngest Alderman, and in order to take their votes; and that done, we all returne to our place in the Halle againe, where I do declare and pronounce to the people the man upon whom the lott of the election is fallen, and then ask them 'Whether they like thereoff?' And they said a'l 'Yea, yea.' That done, my Lord elect standeth forthe in my place, and there doth desable myself, and in the end is well contented, and so giveth their thanks in like manner, and then dothe he take his leave."[1]

The election having been thus made the Mayor had to attend the Feast of St. Simon and St. Jude at the Guildhall "about the 10th hour by the clock" with the Aldermen and Commoners to receive the insignia and take the oath of office which was administered by the Common Serjeant-at-Arms "holding before him the book with the Kalendar with the effigy of Him crucified on the outside thereof, and he in the meanwhile placing his hand upon the Book," which he duly kissed.

Then the record continues, "The old Mayor delivered to him

---

[1] Part II, page 278

the seal of the Statute Merchant together with the seal of the mayoralty enclosed in two purses.

The Mayor's[1] oath embraces (a.) his duties to the King; (b.) to his fellow citizens.

(a). To the King:

(1.) He is to give true and lawful service in his office as Mayor.

(2.) Surely and safely to keep the city for him and his successors, Kings of England.

(3.) To do profitably for the King all things belonging to him to do.

(4.) To keep the rights of the King within the city; not to assent to their decrease or concealment, but where concealed or withdrawn to repel it, or, if that be not possible, to disclose the same to the King or his Council.

(b.) To his fellow citizens:

(1.) He is "lawfully and rightfully to treat the people and right to do unto everyone thereof as well unto strangers as unto denizens, to poor as to rich in that which belongeth to you to do, and that neither for highness nor for riches, nor for promise nor for favour, nor for hate or wrong you shall do unto any one, nor the right of any one disturb."

On the Morrow of the same Feast, this oath had to be repeated before the Barons of the Exchequer at Westminster. The riding and pageantry will be described in the lives of later Lord Mayors. At this date the new and past Mayors, the Aldermen and Sheriffs, and the several mysteries, all arrayed in their respective suits, met on horseback at 9 A.M., and rode "along Chepe through the gate of Newgate and then turning into Fletestreet passed on to Westminster."

On their return (by water after 1434) a dinner was given at the Guildhall (possibly at about noon), and "after dinner it was the custom of the new Mayor to proceed from his house to the church of St. Thomas de Acon (now the site of the Mercer's Chapel) those of his livery preceding him, and after the Aldermen had there assembled they proceeded together to St. Paul's," a custom which the Corporation continued to observe until the destruction of St. Paul's in 1666.

---

[1] This and the other oaths which have been set and are still administered, were enacted by a Statute of early and unknown date. See Vol. I, St. Re., page 249, and Liber Albus, page 266.

The purpose of their visit aptly illustrates the religious feeling of those times. In the nave of the Cathedral stood a tomb with this inscription:—

> Hæc tibi, sancte Pater, posuerunt Marmora cives,
> Præmia non meritis æquiparanda tuis
> Namque sibi populus te Londoniensis amicum
> Sensit, et hinc urbi non leve præsidium
> Reddita Libertas, duce te, donataque multis,
> Te duce, res fuerat publica muneribus.
> Divitias, genus, et famam brevis opprimit hora;
> Hæc tua sed pietas, et benefacta manent.

The man so revered was William, first Chaplain to the Confessor and then Bishop of London under the Conqueror. "Through his intercession (writes Dean Milman) the Conqueror restored and confirmed all the antient privileges of the citizens of London," and in grateful memory of this service, the first official act of every Mayor was to visit his shrine and there, in pre-Reformation days, to pray for the soul of Bishop William.

Nor was this the only duty which the Mayor and Corporation then discharged, as from thence they "moved to the churchyard where lie the bodies of the parents of Thomas, late Archbishop of Canterbury, and there they also repeated the 'De profundis' on behalf of all the faithful of God departed."[1]

Such then were the different offices through which Percyvale had to pass to become "the principal and immediate representative of the sovereign power in London," as conferred by the various Charters that had been granted to the citizens. Let it be remembered that in regard to the personal discharge of duty a citizen has no choice, for when admitted to the freedom his oath, by the charter of Edward II,[2] pledges him to serve "in scot and lot," and the fine (in lieu of personal service) is accepted at the option of the Corporation.

Thus, in the year 1415, in the mayoralty of Thomas Falconer, (the Mercer), one John Gedeney, a Draper (who was afterwards Sheriff in 1417 and Lord Mayor in 1427), the duly elected Alderman, refused to take his oath before the Lord Mayor, and set forth his inability and his insufficiency for the office. But the Court held him to be a fit person, and he was told that he could not refuse

---

[1] Liber Albus, page 21.
[2] Norton's London (1869), page 231.

the office without break of his oath of freedom which bound him "to be a partaker in *Lot* (which is liability to hold office) and in *Scot*, which means contribution to taxes and other charges."

John Gedeney still refused "to accept the office like a person who was utterly obdurate." "If" (runs the decree for his punishment) "any one so elected could at his own will and pleasure refuse the post and pass it by, not improbably the City before long would be left destitute of all rule and governance." Therefore, he was imprisoned, his shop and houses shut up and his goods sequestered.[1]

These duties have been, as we shall see, enforced by imprisonment, as in Sir Thomas White's case,[2] or by disfranchisement in FitzWilliam's.[3]

It was, at the period of time we are considering, an office greatly affecting in its due discharge not only the safety of the city, but of the realm. The holder needed to be a man possessing high personal qualities, such as some did possess in an eminent degree, as these records are intended to show. Take an incident of history happening in 1458, when possibly Percyvale was in apprenticeship: the meeting in London of the two great hostile parties of York and Lancaster, after the battle of St. Alban's, for conference with the King. Look at the retinues with which these leaders approached the city and consider how they were to be disposed of or controlled, that the peace of the city or of the kingdom should not be imperilled. Holinshed[4] gives the facts:

Richard, Duke of York, came with 400 men and was lodged at his own house, Barnard's Castle. The Earl of Salisbury with 500 men, at his own house, the Herbour. The Dukes of Exeter and Somerset with 800 men and were lodged without Temple Bar. The Earl of Northumberland, Lords Egremont and Clifford with 1,500, and lodged without the citie. The Earl of Warwick with 600 men and lodged at the Grey Friars. Thus the Yorkists and Lancastrians were lodged, the one within and the other without. Then the King and Queen came to London and were lodged in the Bishop's Palace.

London with the suburbs became an armed camp, and to preserve the citizens from the danger of it the Mayor and Aldermen "kept great watch, (as indeed well they might do)—as well by daye as by night—riding about the citie by Holbourne and Flete Street with 5,880 well armed and arrayed."

---

[1] Riley's Memorials, page 603.
[2] Part II, page 102.
[3] *Ibid.*, page 46.
[4] Vol. III, page 227.

The Mayor was not only the Chief Magistrate, the Speaker or Chairman of the civic parliament—which he alone can summon or prorogue—the head of the city administration, and the great dispenser of hospitality, but an officer of high ceremonial. Distinctive robes of various colours and trimmings had to be worn upon certain stated days on which the Corporation gave attendance at various festivals or celebrations. These, in the year 1562,[1] were subjected to regulation which would be too long to set out *in extenso*, but one or two illustrations may be taken from them.

First, then, a secular duty of special interest to the Taylors— the opening of the Annual Cloth Fair:[2]

"*On St. Bartholomew even, for the fair in Smithfield.* The aldermen meet my lord and the sheriffs, at the Guildhall Chapel, at two of the clock after dinner, in their violet gowns lined, and their horses, without cloaks, and there hear evening prayer; which being done, they take their horses and ride to Newgate, and so forth of the gate, entering into the Cloth Fair, and there make a proclamation. The proclamation being made, they ride through the Cloth Fair, and so return back again through the churchyard of Great St. Bartholomew to Aldersgate, and so ride home again to the lord mayor's house."

The others are two religious ceremonials:

"*For Good Friday.* My lord and the aldermen meet at St. Paul's-cross, at one of the clock, to hear the sermon, in their pewk gowns, and without their chains and tippets.

"*For Monday and Tuesday in Easter-week.* All the Aldermen and sheriffs come unto my lord's place before eight of the clock, to breakfast, in their scarlet gowns, furred, and their cloaks and horses, and to Spital, and there put on their cloaks, and so sit down in order to hear the sermon; which done, they ride homeward, in order, till they come to the pump within Bishopsgate, and there so many of the aldermen as do dine with the sheriffs, take their leave of my lord, and the rest go home with him.

"*For Wednesday in Easter-week.* Like as before, in the other two days, save that my lord and the aldermen must be in their violet gowns, and suitable cloaks; but the ladies in black."

The yearly rota included these days:—

---

[1] The ceremonials at present in use were collected in 1845 and published by authority of the Corporation. The two codes should be compared.

[2] Vol. 1, Allen's London, page 251, and page 128, *post*.

a. St. Bartholomew's Day. For wrestling; dinner with the Lord Mayor.

b. The next day for shooting.

c. Our Lady in Southwark to St. Magnus's Church.

d. Michaelmas Even. For swearing in the Sheriffs.

e. Michaelmas Day. Election of Lord Mayor, Guildhall Chapel.

f. Presenting the Lord Mayor to the Lord Chancellor.

g. Presenting the Sheriffs at the Exchequer to be sworn.

h. St. Simon and St. Jude. The Lord Mayor invested with the insignia of office.

i. "The morrow after." To swear the Lord Mayor at Westminster; dinner; and after that "to Paul's with all the Company."

j. All Saints' Day.
Christmas Day.
Twelfth Day.
Candlemas Day.
} Prayer at Guildhall and sermon at St. Paul's.

k. St. Thomas's Day. The Wardmotes.

l. Innocents' Day. Dinner with the Lord Mayor.

m. Good Friday. Paul's Cross at one P.M. for sermon.

n. Easter Monday, Tuesday, and Wednesday, Spital sermons.

o. Low Sunday. Sermon at Paul's School.

p. Whit Sunday.

q. Monday and Tuesday at Paul's to hear sermon.

r. First Sunday in each term to St. Paul's.

Frequently on these days a dinner would follow, and each day had a particular dress assigned to it. Thus, scarlet gown, lined, on *a, c, d, e, p,* and *r* ; scarlet gown, furred, on *i, j, n, o,* and *q* ; violet gown, furred, *d, f, g, h, k,* and *n,* and if any one failed to appear in his robes or dress, the fine appears to have been a dinner at his expense to the Lord Mayor and Aldermen, and to produce thereat his robes or dress.[1]

To the Mayor's office from the earliest times the highest respect has been shown. In later years courtesy titles have been added as of "Lord," derived, as one writer states, from the first charter of Edward III, 1349,[2] and of the "Right Honourable" because summoned,[3] though not as a member, to the Privy Council,

---

[1] Riley's Memorials, page 66. It is the duty of the Lord Mayor's sword-bearer to notify the costume to be worn.

[2] Vol. I, Enlick's London, page 254.   [3] Page 261, *post.*

to hear the proclamation read at the commencement of every reign.

It has been held for 400 years that he is supreme over every subject within the city. When, as an early record shows, the King (Henry V) sent the Archbishop of Canterbury, many Bishops, and his own brothers to consult the Mayor at Guildhall, " diligent counsel was held as to the order in which they ought to sit, and there being called before them, as is usually required, certain of the more substantial Commoners of the same city, the Lords agreed together to the effect that the Mayor, in consideration of the reverence due to our most excellent Lord the King, of whom he is the representative in the city, should have his place in the middle, and that the Lords of Canterbury and Winchester on the right hand, and the King's brothers on the left there to make declaration on behalf of our said Lord the King."[1]

This precedency thus resting on authority was asserted on future occasions, of which an illustration is preserved both in Holinshed's[2] and Gregory's[3] chronicles. It was usual for the Serjeants-at-Law before their own Hall was built to have an annual dinner which was not unfrequently held at the Bishop of Ely's place in Holborne. To such a gathering the Mayor and Corporation were usually invited, and in 1464 they were present when, according to Holinshed, Lord Grey de Ruthin, who was then Lord Treasurer, appears, unknown to the Serjeants and against their will, to have placed himself in the seat of State in the Hall.

Gregory names the Earl of Worcester (Tiptoft not Somerset) as the offender, and his narrative we will follow.

"And at denyr tyme the Mayre of London come to the feste with his offecers, a-greyng and a-cordyng unto hys degre. For with yn London he ys next unto the King in alle maner thynge. And in tyme of waschynge the Erle of Worseter was take be-fore the mayre and sette downe in the myddys of the hys tayblle. And the mayre seynge that hys place was occupyd hylde him contente, and went home a gagne with owt mete or drynke or any thonke, but rewarde hym he dyd as hys dygnyte requyryd of the citte. And toke with hym the substance of hys bretheryn the aldyrmen to his place, and were sette and servyd also sone as any man couthe devyse, bothe of the sygnet and of othyr delycatys i-nowe, that alle the howse mervelyd howe welle alle tynge was

---

[1] Riley's Memorials, page 665. [2] Vol. III, page 283.
[3] Page 222.

done in soo schorte a tyme, and prayde alle men to be mery and gladde, hit shulde be a mendyd a nothyr time.

"Thenn the offesers of the feste, fulle evylle a schamyd, informyd the maysters of the feste of thys mysse happe that ys be-falle. And they consyderynge the grete dygnyte and costys and charge that longgyd vnto the citte, and a-non sende unto the mayre a present of mete, brede, wyne, and many dyvers sotelteys. But whenn they that come with the presentys say alle the gyftys, and the sarvyse that was at the borde, he was fulle sore a schamyd that shulde doo ye massage, for the present was not better thenn the servyse of metys was by fore the mayre, and thoroughe owte the hyghe tabylle. But hys demenynge was soo that he hadde love end thonke for hys massage, and a grette rewarde with alle. And thys the worschippe of the citte was kepte, and not loste for hyn. And I truste that nevyr hyt shalle, by the grace of God."

But between a Mayor and a Sheriff there would seem to have been an appreciable distance in rank[1] as may be illustrated from another incident: In 1478 and for many earlier years the pride and glory of St. Paul's and the richest fountain of wealth was the shrine of St. Erkenwald,[2] before which the greatest made their devotions and paid their oblations. This saint was the Bishop of London, A.D. 675, who founded the Abbeys of Chertsey and Barking, and died in 693. After his death at Barking his place of interment was a subject of bitter strife, but the population of London poured forth, seized his bier, and he was buried in St. Paul's. At his shrine the Mayor, Richard Gardener, the Mercer, went to worship, possibly on the 30th April or 14th November, when the Sheriff (Robert Byfield) also came: but let the old Chronicler tell his own story: "The Maior being in Paules kneeling in his devotions at St. Erkenwald's shrine, Robert Bifield, one of the Sheriffs, inadvisedly kneeled down nigh unto the Maior, whereof afterwards the Maior charged him to have done more than becomed him, but the Sheriff answering rudely and stubbornly would not acknowledge to have committed any offence, for the which he was afterwards fined by the Court of Aldermen, 50*l.* to be paid towards the reparation of

---

[1] Note as to arrest of the Sheriff for disobedience to the Mayor's orders.—Riley's Memorials, page 417.
[2] Milman, St. Paul's, page 151. Simpson, St. Paul's, page 19.

the conduits of London, which fine" (adds the Chronicler, to prove that it was not a nominal sentence only) was trulie paid."[1]

But beyond the walls of the city or in a Royal procession he had of course no such precedence. In those days[2] when the Pope having "no peer" was before King or Emperor, the Mayor was placed after the Chief Justice and before the Chief Baron of the Exchequer. At the funeral of Edward IV[3] (1483), it was noted "that after the Lords that were within the herse and Bishops had offered, the Mayor of London offered, next after him the Chief Judges and other Judges;" and in the procession of March, 1494, when Prince Henry was created Duke of York[4] "the best ordered and most prysed of all the processions that I have heard of in England" (so writes the author of it) the King walking as the centre figure and the Mayor in those preceding him came after the Archbishop of York, and nearer therefore to the King.[5]

The officers and attendants upon the Lord Mayor and Corporation, and their various duties, is too large a subject for us to enter upon, but one officer "accustomed" (as the *Liber Albus* states) "to set forth all matters touching the city in the presence of his Lordship the King, and his Council, as also in all the Royal Courts by his mouth, as being more especially embued with knowledge and conspicuous by the brilliancy of his eloquence"—viz., the Recorder—must be referred to. The office was too important to be altogether omitted, and its duties (as fulfilled by our guildsman "the honest Recorder" Fleetwood) will come under our notice in the later pages of this work.[6]

"The Recorder should be, and of usage hath been, one of the most skilful and most virtuous apprentices at law in the whole kingdom, and the duties of his office are thus laid down in his oath:—

1. To be true to the King and his successors.
2. To maintain the city franchises, and not to discover the city counsels.
3. To keep and rule the King's Courts in the chamber and hustings, according to the city customs.
4. Not for gift or favour, promise, or hate, to omit to do equal law and right to all manner of people, as well poor as to rich, to denizens as to strangers, who before you shall plead,

---

[1] Holinshed, Vol. III, page 318. [2] Babus Book, 1658, pages 186, 284, 381.
[3] Letters of Richard III, &c., Vol. 24, Roll's Series, page 4.
[4] *Ibid.*, page 363, and see Part II, page 33, Jenyn's mayoralty.
[5] Part II, Chapter XIX.

and in all pleas lawfully to record the same, and the same enrol, and no right to disturb.

5. To delay no judgment without reasonable cause.
6. To show to the Mayor and Aldermen any rights or profits of the King or of the city concealed, for the saving of the same.
7. To come at the warning of the Mayor and Sheriffs, or of their officers, for good and wholesome counsel unto them to give, and at all times when needed shall he to go and ride with them, to keep and maintain the state of the city.
8. To take nothing from any person, denizen or stranger, who has before you any cause to plead, and no fees or robes to take except one only from the chamber of London.
9. To be attentive to save the rights of orphans according to city usages.

When delivering judgments his seat is at the right hand of the Mayor, and he has a seat with the Mayor at his dinner table. Further, he receives robes and vestments (lined or edged with fur) as often as the Mayor and Aldermen receive the same, and he is the highest officer of the Corporation.

The rights and privileges of the Corporation would be too large a subject to enter upon, but one at least should claim our attention, viz., the antient right which the Lord Mayor and Corporation possess of presenting an address to the Sovereign, from themselves or their fellow citizens, at the foot of the throne. This is one of the occasions when the Recorder, "in the presence of his Lordship the King," reads the address ultimately delivered into the hands of the Sovereign by the Lord Mayor. But it is not without precedent that the Lord Mayor, with the permission of the Sovereign, has spoken, and in words of remonstrance not to be found in the address presented by the Recorder.[1]

If an extraordinary occasion arises, by which the Lord Mayor requires an audience of the Sovereign, the request is made through the Lord Chamberlain, and up to the present reign has been granted.[2] To this he goes in state, but unaccompanied by the Recorder. Another privilege (long may its exercise be deferred) arises on the coronation of the Sovereign. "The Mayor of London

---

[1] Beckford as Lord Mayor in 1770, Ann. Reg., Vol. XIII, pages 103 and 111, Vol. XIV, page 15.

[2] In the mayoralty of Alderman Wilson, 1839.

claymeth to serve the Queen [Mary] after meate with a cuppe of wyne, and he to have the cuppe of golde for his labor," a claim which has arisen (it is said) from his connection with the wine entries in the Port of London; to be butler with 360 men in scarlet, and to have a cup of gold with a cover, and an enamelled ewer of the value of 90*l*. However, the right stands recorded in the reign of Richard III, and is to be traced back to the second coronation of Richard I[1] (1191).

Such are the institutions for local government which the citizens of earlier centuries raised for themselves and for their successors, under which they sought out their liberties, and we must preserve our own. Parliament has hitherto respected the government of London as the model upon which our national institutions have been framed, but how long this protection may last, or the time come before the Corporation be swept away, depends in these evil days more on the exigences of party strife than on any higher considerations.

---

[1] Rutland Papers, page 120; Hales' History of the Customs, page 12; and Ceremonials of the City (1845), Norton's London, page 129.

CHAPTER II.

THE GOVERNMENT OF A LONDON GUILD.

Every trader governed by a Guild p. 33.—Taylors and Linen Armourers, p. 33.—Petition of 1327 for Charter and grant of it, p. 34.—Names of twenty-four Taylors to certify Freemen, p. 34.—Order of 1371, p. 35.—Charter of Richard II (1390), p. 35.—Henry IV (1408), p. 36.—Henry VI (1439), p. 36.—Edward IV (1456), p. 36.—Henry VII (1502), p. 37.—Agreement for Perpetual Obit, p. 37.—Method of becoming a guildsman, p. 38.—Government of a Guild explained, p. 39.—Ordinances made by the whole Fraternity, p. 39.—Mayour's Preface, p. 40.—Freeman's oath to the Guild, p. 41. — Women members of the Guild, p. 42.—Ordinances of 1507, p. 42.—As to dress, p. 43.—Liverymen, p. 44.— Wardens, p. 45.—Court of Assistants, p. 46.—Master, p. 47.—Election dinner, p. 47.—Jenyns' order as to payment, p. 47.—Attendance at St. Martin's, p. 48.—Post-Reformation ceremonial. p. 49.—Master's oath, p. 50.—Meetings of (1) Quarterly Court and Annual Court of the whole Fraternity, p. 51 ; (2) Court of Assistants, p. 51 ; (3) Master and Wardens, p. 51.—Audit of Master's Expenditure, p. 52.— Gratuitous Office by Jenyns' order, p. 52.—The Clerk, p. 52.—The Bedel, p. 53.—The Guilds as subordinate to the Mayor, p. 54.—Place in London Government, p. 55.—Precepts for Mayor (1) Personal service, Standing Watch, p. 56.—(2) For money, p. 57.—Bridewell Hospital, p. 58.—Gunpowder, p. 59.—Service of the Crown, p. 59.

As shown in the last chapter every resident was governed by the Mayor and Corporation, and every trader in the city by the Master and Wardens of a Guild. Of this latter government under Royal Charters and the ordinances made by the Fraternity in 1507, an outline will be given in the present chapter.

The earliest trace that we have of the "Tailors" as a craft is when, in their quarrel with the Goldsmiths in March, 1267, they disturbed the peace of the city; and of the "Armourers" when on their feast of the Conversion of St. Paul in 1322, they enrolled in the presence of the Mayor an ordinance relating to their covering of hacquetons and gambesons by their workmen.[1]

The Taylors and Linen Armourers appear as one craft in the petition to Edward III, for their first Charter[2] of 1327, wherein they claimed to be a guild or corporation (by prescription) to govern their workmen for the common profit of the city, and prayed the King's

---

[1] Riley's Mayors, page 104, and London, page 145.
[2] Appendix 2, page 344.

authority for so doing, and for holding their guild once a year to redress all wrongs by the Mayor of London. Further they prayed for a monopoly, *i.e.*, that no one but a freeman of the guild should hold a shop, and that none should be made free as Taylors unless vouched for by the Fraternity. The official answer to this petition was "let right be done with the advice of the Mayor,"[1] and in pursuance of this authority on the 10th March, 1327, the earliest Charter was granted by Edward III, "to the Taylors and Linen Armourers," whereby he accepted and ratified the existing guild, and enabled them (1) to hold their guild once a year; (2) to govern their mysteries and servants by view of the Mayor; (3) and to correct them by the more honest men of the mystery. It also provided that no one should hold a shop or counter of their mystery in London unless free thereof, or be admitted to the freedom unless his "honesty, faithfulness, and fitness, were testified by the honest and lawful men of the mystery," who, according to the City Charter of Edward II, were to be six in number.[2]

This Charter is entered in the earliest Ordinance Book of the Company, and following it (as of the mayoralty of Andrew Aubery in 1339) is an entry of 24 names of guildsmen, from some of whom a certificate was needed to obtain the freedom of London through the fraternity of Taylors. These were as under :—

Henri de Cauntebrigge.	Willms de lyndefrith.
Egidius de Westmelle.	Williams Spark.
Robertus de Gildford.	Henry ab Shawe.
Thomas de Cornewayll.	Joh⁹ Kyng.
Robertus de Uttokeshater.	Alanus de ffyshbourn.
Joh⁹ de Martynscrost.	Adam de Essex.
Joh⁹ de Walssh.	Joh⁹ de Drayton.
Ric⁹ de Carlell.	Joh⁹ pynchebek.
Joh⁹ ab Brok.	Walter⁹ de Bedeford.
Al⁹ˣ de Waldeby.	Joh⁹ de ffarle.
Steph⁹ de Royston.	Robt⁹ de Grandon.
Joh⁹ de Dobenhm̃.	Hugo de Portesmouth.

Under the powers of this Charter the "good men of the trade" submitted an ordinance for the approval of the Mayor and Aldermen on 19th February, 1371 (in the 45th year of Edward's reign) to enable them to order and regulate their trade. The object was

---

[1] See page 55, *post*. [2] Norton's London (1869), page 334.

to make every workman responsible for his work by having to make amends "for his misdeeds to the complainants;" thus if he miscut or otherwise spoilt the cloth entrusted to him he should pay as a fine "to the chamber at the Guildhall 6s. 8d., and to the alms of St. John the Baptist, that is to say, to the priests and poor men, 3s. 4d." for the first and for after offences higher fines. Then followed this additional penalty "that if any of the said trade pray for anyone after he is attainted for his misdeeds or favour the said offender in his misdeed he shall pay to the chamber half a mark,[1] thus placing the offender under a religious interdict.

Such then was the legal origin of the Fraternity, but to trace it down to its present existence we must give an outline of their other charters, which may be thus briefly summarised:—

The Company's second Charter from Richard II (1390) recognised St. John Baptist as their patron saint, and enabled—

(a.) The Fraternity to elect a Master and four Wardens (who had a prior existence, as Thomas Carleton,[2] in December, 1382, devised land to them), as often as they pleased, or as was needful; and

(b.) The Master and Wardens—

(1.) To give one livery garment in each year to the brothers and sisters of the Fraternity;[3]

(2.) To cause meetings and assemblies of the Fraternity in places of the City belonging to them;

(3.) To hold and keep in an honest manner their feast of meat and drink on St. John Baptist's Day;

(4.) There to make ordinances amongst themselves[4] for the

---

[1] Memorials, page 513; and see an order of 1573 giving similar fines to a poor blind brother of the mysterie living on London Bridge, ib., page 533, and see 123, post.

[2] See Appendix 33, page 407.

[3] This is referred to in the Order of 5th May, 1490 (post). The use or giving of livery was the subject of much legislation in earlier days (16 Richard II, cap. 4; 2 Henry IV, cap. 21; 7 Henry IV, cap. 14; 8 Henry VI, cap. 4; and 8 Edward IV, 1468). The Star Chamber had authority to punish persons giving or receiving liveries, a jurisdiction not unfrequently exercised. See 3 Henry VII, cap. 1, and Mr. Bruce's paper, Vol. 25, Arch., page 364. The 19 Henry VII, cap. 14, reciting that there were divers statutes for the punishment of such persons that give or receive liveries, imposed a penalty upon any one giving any livery or sign to any person "other than such as he giveth household wages unto," but a proviso was inserted (sec. 11) that the Act should not extend to any livery to be given (inter alia) by any Serjeant-at-Law or by any executor at the interment of any person for any mourning array, or by Guild, Fraternity, or Craft corporate (Stat. Realm, Vol. ii, page 660). Scarlet and puke were adopted as colours for the livery and clothing of the Company, 25th September, 1568, and blue (for gowns) appears to have been asked from the Lord Mayor in October, 1624.

[4] Page 39, post.

better government of the Fraternity as they had theretofore for a long time been accustomed to do.

The third Charter of Henry IV (1408) marks a considerable change in the constituency of Freemen, as the two earlier Charters only sanctioned existing usages and bestowed various powers for the future management of the trade or mystery, but this Charter incorporated the Fraternity as "The Fraternity of Taylors and Linen Armourers of St. John the Baptist in the City of London," and gave them a corporate seal and perpetual succession, with powers of self government and to sue and be sued in their corporate name. These and similar charters of incorporation were therefore looked upon with great jealousy by the Corporation as tending to make the guilds independent of the Mayor and of his government.[1]

Between the dates of the second and third Charters, other estates had been acquired and conveyed to the Fraternity by various names or designations, and this latter Charter confirmed these estates to the Taylors, notwithstanding the Statute of Mortmain.

The fourth Charter of Henry VI (1439) which was obtained "at the grete coste"[2] of 71*l.* 5*s.* 3*d.*, and was afterwards (as we shall show) a subject of controversy, enabled the Company—

(1.) To make full search in, and concerning the mysteries within the City and the suburbs, and concerning all those persons that may be privileged with the Taylors, and concerning such mysteries which they or any of them use.

(2.) To correct and reform all defects found among them according to their discretions by the survey of the Mayor, and that no other persons should make any search, but only the aforesaid Mayor or his deputies privileged of the aforesaid Taylors, and to be elected (in default) by the Master and Wardens of the Taylors.

The fifth Charter of 5 Edward IV (1465) only confirmed and approved the previous Charters, but it is recited in the ordinances of 1507, as justifying the powers of search.

The sixth Charter of 18 Henry VII (1502), the last that need

---

[1] Sec. 17, page 25, Report (second) on Municipal Corporations (April, 1837).
[2] See Chapter VI, page 135, and Appendix 3, page 345.

be mentioned, was considered by the Guildsmen of that period to be the grant of a "new corporation," and the King under special contract was to be prayed for in perpetuity "as the first Founder of the said Fraternity of St. John Baptist of Merchant Taylors of London." Whether it was the change of name by adding that of "Merchant" to "Taylors" or the grant of greater powers which was the special advantage for which the Guild was so grateful, is not apparent. However it recites and confirms the earlier Charters, and then gives these greater privileges to the Fraternity:—

(1.) To be styled "The Guild of the Merchant Taylors of the Fraternity of St. John the Baptist in the City of London."

(2.) To increase the Fraternity by whatever persons (natives) they may be willing to receive without any hindrance from any other guild.

(3.) To hold all the lands, goods, and privileges which they then held.

(4.) To purchase, sell, plead, and defend in their new name.

(5.) To make statutes and ordinances for good government, and search without impeachment from the King or his officers, so that the same be not contrary to the laws of the realm, nor in prejudice to the Mayor of London.

(6.) To make search and survey of all men of the Fraternity in the city liberties and suburbs as well in the making, cutting, and working of men's apparel or otherwise using the same mysteries.

(7.) To correct all natives, strangers, and foreigners in all matters pertaining to the mystery for the benefit of other liege subjects, but according to the laws of the realm and of the city of London.

(8.) None to work in the working, cutting, and making of men's apparel unless first admitted thereto by the Master and Wardens.

(9.) None to search any liege members or their goods or wares, woollen cloths, ells or measures, save only the Master and Wardens, so that nothing be done or suffered to the prejudice of the authority of the Mayor of London.

The new Charter was granted to Richard Smith, as Master, Hugh Acton,[1] and James Moncastre, being two Wardens, all of them benefactors to the Company, and that it was highly appreciated by the Company at large is conclusively shown by the agreement of the whole Company in the year following, when Edmund Flower was Master, and Thomas Speight, another benefactor, one of the Wardens, to keep a perpetual obit with all due solemnity in com-

---

[1] Freeman in 1486. MS. Court Records, page 25, and Part II, page 99, as to the Actons.

memoration "of their most excellent prince," the grantor, in the parish church of St. Martin's, which agreement was sealed "unanimously, knowingly, and deliberately, in the common hall" on the 3rd December, 1563.[1]

To carry on the trade or business covered by these Charters it was necessary to become a member of the Fraternity, which might be done in one of three methods :—1st. By apprenticeship, which was the usual method, and has already been described. 2nd. By patrimony, *i.e.*, by being born as the child of one free of the Company ; or Lastly, By redemption, *i.e.*, by grant made by the Company either with or without a pecuniary consideration to a particular person named, a procedure which in Tudor times was usually adopted at the instance of the King[2] or Mayor of London, and was hotly resented by the craftsmen upon whose privileges these redemptioners infringed.

But the Charters were silent on many matters of detail which were carried out by the rules and ordinances made by the Fraternity. They are silent for instance with regard to the government by the Court of Assistants, and make no reference to the distinctions in class of a freeman or a liveryman ; these we propose to explain, and, as in the "Government of London," we followed Sir John Percyvale through the various offices of the Corporation, we shall here follow Sir Stephen Jenyns through the various offices of the Merchant Taylors Company, and endeavour to show *by the oaths and ordinances, substantially the same now as in the Tudor period,* what were, and indeed what are, the duties which by the oaths and ordinances the various members of the Company have to discharge towards their fellow citizens.

These ordinances were originally made or assented to by the *whole* Fraternity at the annual or quarterly meetings, at which

---

[1] Appendix 5, page 347.

[2] "11th September, 1575, Court Minutes, page 21.—Itm, Richard Loynt was this daye made free by the Queen's Maties lre gratis and hathe promysed the Master a Buck to be delivered him at his pleasure.

"16th March, 1579, folio 91.—Itm, John Davisone made free per redempcon per warrant from my Lorde Mayor and Court of Aldermen at the sute of my Lord Chamberlain lres, the saide Davison dwelleth at Baynards Castell."

Note by the late Mr. Nathaniel Stephens.—There are many entries of freedom by redemption, generally "at the sute" of some influential person, and promise by the freemun to give the Master a buck, or a sugar loaf, and sometimes both ; and see entry of Court Minutes, 16th July, 1606, for King James I's request, Part II, page 203.

every liveryman was bound to attend. For instance, the two oldest ordinances[1] that are extant in the Merchant Taylors' records run in these terms:—

"Also at a Quarter-day held the 16th day of April in the 6th year of Edward IV (1466), in the presence of John Stodard, then Master, *and the whole body together* assembled, it was concerned and remembered by the same Master and whole body, &c." [Then follows a decree against taking Irish apprentices.]

Again, on the 18th August, 1490 (at a meeting which will be noticed hereafter), the entry is that the ordinance was "made and established by the authority of the Master and Wardens, and by the authority *and with the whole body of the said Craft in this Hall assembled.*"

The language of the Statute law in 19 Henry VII, c. 7, leads to the same conclusion, for the complaint recited in the preamble is not against the ordinances of the Master and Wardens only, but of these *and the people of the guilds, fraternities,* and other Companies corporate, and the restraint imposed is upon ordinances so made. These, then, were the act and agreement of the whole Fraternity, and therefore it was not so much a protection against themselves as against others not of the Fraternity whom they might by their legislation injure, which led Parliament to enact under a penalty that no ordinance should be put in force unless previously sanctioned by the Ministers and Judges mentioned in the Act.

Considered in this aspect the ordinances have an additional interest as illustrating what was the accepted duty which the members of a guild voluntarily imposed upon themselves, having regard to their continuously existing obligations as citizens to the Corporation of London.

The grant of a "new corporation," by Henry VII in 1502, was followed up by a codification of all the bye-laws or ordinances of the Guild, which, to give them quasi validity and to protect the Guild from penalties, needed approval under the 19th Henry VII, cap. 7. This Act obliging the Guilds to submit their ordinances for the approval of the Lord Treasurer and others, according to the original entry of Henry Mayour, was obtained by Sir Robert Sheffield, the Recorder, whose motive, Mayour represents, as a sinister one. His entry is rather prolix, but it is worth transcribing.

As a preface to the ordinances he writes—

"Forasmuch as many sundry acts and divers ordinances and provisions that were made in times past amongst fellowships

---

[1] See also the agreement with Henry VII, on the last page.

corporate within this City for the good refinement, sad direction, common profit, public weal, encrease, and also in conservation of very good order and due obedience in every fellowship, amongst which one was that no man of what company that he were of should sue, vex, trouble, or implead any brother of his in Court spiritual or temporal, but if the matter were first shewed afore the Governors of the Company that the party complaint was of, and if they could not pacify the matter and cause of complaint and do him remedy therein, then the complainant and defendant were put at their free liberty to take and sue for their remedy in the law where they listed; and as long as this Rule and Ordinance was so used and kept within this said City, so long good obedience was used in crafts, and perfect love and charity was had between brother and brother of every mystery without any suit in the law, by reason whereof the citizens of the said City did richly encrease and grew into wealth and prosperity, Sir Robert Sheffield, Knight, then Recorder of this City, and one of the Knights of the Parliament for the same City, knowing the Secrecies and Ordinances made as well within this City as of many sundry fellowships of the same, perceiving that sad directions, good policy, and discreet justice was indifferently taken and ministred among fellowships of and in pacifying matters that were debateful, grew to the prejudice of the learned men of the said City, and also of other out of the same. Therefore he, by his great labour, subtle wit, and crafty means, caused an Act of Parliament to be made that no Masters nor Governors of Guild or Fraterities within this Realm from henceforth should use or exercise any Acts or Ordinances, but such only as should be ratified, approved, and confirmed by the Lords Chancellor, Treasurer, and two Chief Justices of England, upon the pain of 40*l*., as in the same Act thereof made more plainly is contained; and inasmuch as the Fellowship of Merchant Tailors of London had very perfect knowledge of the said Act, and how that the Master and Wardens of the same had a great number of householders, with their servants, to rule and govern, which could not be ordered and well justified without good acts, reasonable Ordinance, and laudable provisions were had for the politic governance, regiment, and wise ordering of the same. Therefore, and in avoiding of the penalty comprised in the said Act of Parliament, the Right Worshipful Richard Conhyll, late Master, and the four Wardens with him afore in this book named, with the advice, counsel, and consent of the more part of the most worshipful persons, councillors, and assistants of the said Company, commanded me Henry Mayour, Notary Public and their Common Clerk, to compile and make a book or two in paper of all such Ordinances and Oaths as should concern and appertain to and for the good refinement and common weal of their said Company, and conservation of the same, whose commandment, I the said Henry, diligently according to mine oath and duty obeyed and fulfilled, which book of ordinances and oaths the four Lords named in the said Act of Parliament have approved, ratified, and confirmed and sithen the approbation, ratification, and confirmation of the same book. I the aforesaid Henry at desire and request of my right singular good master William Grene, now Master, John Tresawell, John Wright, Richard Hall, and John Sexsy, Wardens with the said Master Grene, have written, compiled, engrossed, and ordered the same book after the manner and form as it appeareth to every man's sight, that listeth to see or read. And it was clearly written finished, engrossed, and ended by me the same Henry within my dwelling house, pertaining to the whole body of this said fellowship, the 20th day of June, in the year of Our Lord God 1508, and in the 23rd year of the reign of Our Most dread Sovereign Lord, King Henry the 7th."

We thus have a code of oaths and ordinances of which the details are given elsewhere.[1] The authorities approving the ordinances were the Lord Chancellor (Warham), Thomas, Earl of Surrey, High Treasurer, and Sir John Fineaux, Chief Justice of the King's Bench, and Sir John Read, Chief Justice of the Common Bench, and the date of the approval 1507.

Sir Stephen Jenyns' initial step in membership was that of an apprentice, leading up, as we have seen in Percyvale's life, to the freedom of the Company. When this freedom was obtained Jenyns became one of the Guild or Fraternity, and immediately eligible to hold office as Master or Warden.

So long as he was in the Company he remained under his oath responsible for specific acts of duty, and general obedience to the summons of the Master and Wardens, and the rules and ordinances of the Company.

The Freeman's oath is in these terms :—

(1.) To be true to the Company; (2.) not to disobey the summons of the Master and Wardens, but to be obedient to them; (3.) to be secret in Council; (4.) to conceal no foreign craftsman, but to warn the Chamberlain of such; (5.) to take only workmen who had duly served the Company as apprentices; (6) to register

---

[1] Appendix 7, pages 351-7.

apprentices at the Hall; (7.) not to withdraw another man's apprentice or servant; and (8.) to obey all the ordinances.

What part (if any) the women or "sisters of the Fraternity" took in the proceedings, or what rights (if any) they had to take apprentices and admit to the freedom of the Company are questions not easily answered, but it is clear that women were originally admitted as members and took apprentices.

That it was customary in later years for women to dine or be present at the quarterly meetings is evidenced by a notice of their absence in an entry of the Quarterly Court on 5th July, 1603. Ambassadors and Scottish knights were guests, and the record goes on thus:—"and the upper table near to the garden, commonly called the '*Mistris* Table,' was furnished with sword-bearer and gentlemen strangers, there being no gentlewomen at *this* Quarter Day."

In many of the wills of early benefactors, sisters as well as brethren are named as "devisees." Thus in Sibsay's (1404) the devise is "to the Master and Wardens and brethren and sisters"; so in Churchman's (1403), in Sutton's (1432), in Candish's (1460), in Richard Smith's (1515), in John Harris's (1520), and in others the same.[1]

When an almsman of the Livery married with the Company's consent, his widow remained during her life as an almswoman, and was buried by the Company. In that sense she was treated as a sister of the fraternity, but she probably exercised no rights as a member of it.

The ordinances[2] of the Merchant Taylors Company, as confirmed in 1507, may be dealt with as divided into three heads:—

(*a.*) The duty of personal service.
(*b.*) The duty of contribution in money; and
(*c.*) The duty of loyalty to their brother craftsmen in their trade or business.

(*a.*) As to this, the freeman upon summons was to attend upon the Master and Wardens, and with them to be present "at all noble triumphs for the honour" of the King; at all civic pageants and religious ceremonies (including obits and burials of deceased members), and upon the Mayor and Sheriffs when chosen from the Company, appearing on these occasions in costume, when entitled to wear such. Further the freeman was to be present in the Common Hall at the great annual feast on St. John Baptist's day

---

[1] Appendix 33, page 407.   [2] See Appendix 7 for an epitome of these, pages 351-7.

and at all Quarterly Courts. Lastly, to take charge in watch and ward for the protection of the city.

(b.) The payments, indefinite in amount, were (*inter alia*) for the feast of St. John (whether present or absent); the assessments made from time to time by the Master and Wardens under a Mayor's precept, for civic purposes, or on their own authority for guild purposes.

(c.) This will be best understood by a study of the ordinances relating to this subject epitomised elsewhere.

Stipulations are also to be found relating to general good behaviour. Thus the ordinances required that the apprentices should wear no weapon within the City, that the guildsman should wear only such array as was suitable to his calling as a citizen, that he should not attend any unlawful assembly, nor be rude in manner or behaviour, and further should aid the Master against rebellious members, and not associate with such, that he should keep the Queen's obit, and the King's (Henry VII) whenever his death should happen.

The dress or apparel to be worn by each class of the community was a subject of legislation in the early years of our constitutional history. These statutes originating in the 37th Edward III, cc. 8 and 14, were amended and enforced until the reign of James I, when the 25th chapter of the first of his reign closed the legislation upon this subject.

Strype in his Annals of Elizabeth's reign sets forth proclamations and Council regulations in the years 1559, 1565, 1577, and 1579, but in May, 1582, the City took up the subject and the Common Council passed an Act to regulate the apparel of apprentices. No apprentice[1] was to wear any apparel but at his master's cost or appointment; the fashion and quality of which was set forth with great exactness. Then he was to wear neither jewel of gold or silver, nor any silk in or about his apparel; nor was he to carry any sword or dagger, but only a "meate knife."

Should the apprentice break any of these regulations he was to be punished: 1. For the first time, by his master at his discretion with some convenient punishment; 2. For the second by open whipping at the Hall of his Company; 3. For the third, by six months' longer service than the term of his apprenticeship.

It is certain that some earlier law or ordinance was in force, dating as far back as 1463-4, from the entries in our records of fines received for the breach of it.

---

[1] By the Indenture the Master covenants to provide him "with meat, drink, apparel, lodging, and all other necessaries according to the custom of London."—Appendix 1, page 344.

In ordinary course the next grade to that of a Freeman was being chosen to the Livery or Clothing of the Fraternity, which from the entry of 5th May, 1490,[1] would appear should be conferred only upon men of substance, able to bear the sacrifice of time and money which the choice entailed, as of attending civic ceremonies, paying higher assessments, acting as stewards or providers for public entertainments. The manner of this calling is set forth in the entry of 10th July, 1602, which also shows the precedence given to Aldermen or Sheriffs, as upon this occasion Mr. John Swinnerton was elected one of the Livery, but before being sworn he became an Alderman and Sheriff. "So by reason of such worshipful calling he did overleap the said other inferior place and was never of the Livery, nor paid any fine for the same."

To meet the expenses of Sir Robert Lee's mayoralty money had to be raised, and therefore many freemen were called to take up their livery. "The Master, Wardens, and Assistants having received sufficient testimony of their habylities, wysdom, and civill conversations," they were told that the fee payable was 25l. a-piece, to prepare their livery gowns and hoods all of one cloth (and not to provide any old hoods), and to bestow on the clerk and beadle a new hood besides a gratuity. Further they were advertised that it "hath been an ancient and usual custom and courtesy to present and help our Master with venison against his 'feaste.' These terms being complied with, a special day was appointed for them to take the oath, when, "in the presence of the Master and his Wardens, and Mr. Dowe, Mr. Offley, Mr. Prockter, and Mr. Plomer, foure of the old masters, and all the said psons with their hoods upon their shoulders, and kneeling upon their knees, they did receive and take the usuall othe upon admittance into lyvery, and then were taken by the hand, saluted, and hartely bidd welcome by the said Master and the ould Masters and Wardens."

Whether service as a liveryman was that of "Scot and Lot," under the ruling of John Gedency's case, was raised but not decided in Charles II's time; but at any rate the Court then held that the Taylors had by custom the right to commit to prison one of the Guild, who, being duly chosen, refused without reasonable cause, to serve as a liveryman.[2]

The oath of "the whole brother admitted to the Livery" contained these additional clauses to his former oath, as a freeman :—

---

[1] Part II, Chapter III. Each person when chosen had his place or seniority assigned to him, 1 Mait., page 287.
[2] King v. Merchant Taylors Company, 2 Lev., page 200.

(1.) To come to quarter day or other assemblies for the worship and profit of the Fraternity or pay the penalty for default.

(2.) Not to withdraw from the feast yearly kept in the Common Hall about Midsummer so as to escape the office and charge of Master or Warden.

(3.) Not to give his livery to another.

(4.) Not to use customably any unlawful or ungodly usages whereby the Fraternity might be brought into great infamy.

(5.) If a member should so offend to warn the Master and Wardens thereof.

(6.) To keep the lawful ordinances and the wills of Churchman and Beatrice Lady de Ros, Carleton, Percyvale, and others, that shall be read quarterly by the Clerk of the Fraternity.

Upon him the Company had to rely for the discharge of its higher offices, and he was not to withdraw himself from election to such services. He was to be more careful of his own conduct, and to be observant of that of other members of the clothing.

Jenyns would next be elected one of the four Wardens of the Company, the manner of this election being laid down by the ordinance relating to the Master's election. The office has by custom been held twice before the mastership. First as "Renter," and then (after a longer or shorter interval of time) as "Upper" Warden. The day and time of election were the same as those of the Master's, and in later years the election was made by the twenty-four Assistants, on the nomination of the Master and Wardens, who presented eight names from the Livery or Clothing as of men capable of holding office, and out of these were to be chosen four by the common voice of the Fellowship. This being done, was to be kept secret until the Master's election was disclosed; but if a Warden failed to serve he was liable to fine and imprisonment.[1]

The nature of the Warden's office is to be learned from the ordinances and oath, which oath is—

(1.) To rule and govern with the Master all the brethren.

(2.) On complaint from any one with the advice of the Master to examine and determine the same without favour, &c.

(3.) To see the ordinances carried out and to levy the amercements and fines for the common profit of the mystery, of all that come not to quarter-days, ridings for the Kings, dirges, offerings, or obits for brethren and sisters deceased, processions and other

---

[1] The King v. Merchant Taylors Company, 2 Lev., page 201.

assemblies concerning the worship and common profit of the mystery.

(4.) Twice a year to make search for apprentices and foreigners.

(5.) To see that the Master renders a good and true account of the land revenue of the mysterie and of the payments made, written by the Clerk on the day of his account.

(6.) To see that quarter-days be kept.

(7.) To see paid at the Common Hall the priests, officers, and almsmen, and the almsmen within their house.

(8.) To be present with the Master in livery at all manner of obits kept at the costs and charges of the mystery.

(9.) To give personal attendance on the Master in the Common Hall, as in every other place within the city, for matters pertaining to the common profit of the Company.

The Wardens are joint Governors with the Master, having from 1489 precedence over the other members of the Company, but of the few matters in which they have a special duty or authority, notice has been taken elsewhere.

In the Charters no mention is made of "the Court of Assistants," nor is the origin of this "Court" shown on the records. It may be assumed that *after* a freeman had served the Fraternity as Master or Warden faithfully, the wish of his colleagues would be to retain him as an Assistant in the future government of the Company. This was, probably, the origin of the office, and a suggestion has been made that since the date of Aubery's mayoralty in 1339, there had been twenty-four, because that number is given in the old Ordinance Book after the entry of Edward III's Charter.

However this may be it is certain a Court of twenty-four persons were in existence in Jenyns' time if not in his mastership; for in the Treasury accounts (1490 to 1502) "the Council of the craft" are referred to "as Assistants," and as the "hole twenty-four"; and in the records of 1507 both in the election ordinance and the Assistants' oath, twenty-four Assistants are mentioned.

The records are silent as to the qualifications or the manner of the election of an Assistant. By his oath he was:—

(1.) To attend on summons of the Master and Wardens without a let or hindrance, to be proved by oath, and to give the best advice.

(2.) To inform the Master and Wardens and Court of Assistants of anything which shall hurt the Fraternity.

(3.) In all matters and causes before the Master and Wardens between parties to give sentence according to truth and good conscience, without affection or malice, and according to equity and good conscience.

(4.) To keep these and other matters secret.

He had therefore to be attendant on the Master and Wardens when summoned, and when his services were needed in cases of arbitration (which are frequently mentioned in the Merchant Taylors' records), for the settlement of trade disputes.

Under the first Charter any freemen is eligible to serve in any office, and the election is left to the whole Fraternity, but the ordinances of 1507 constitute the Court of Assistants as the electors, who are to be assembled on the *vigil* of St. John Baptist's Nativity, in the Common Hall, at a certain hour limited, and after the Wardens for the ensuing year have been elected, the Master is to be chosen and put into room by the then Governor, the four Wardens then being, and the Assistants who have been Master.[1]

The great festival of the Company[2]—now apparently forgotten —was the day of the Nativity of St. John Baptist (afterwards superseded by "the Master's election dinner") day, held with the express sanction of the Fraternity in 1490, and to which they contributed from the corporate funds. The early ordinances, however, provided that each man should make his payment or contribution towards the expenses of this feast, and the only charges which the earlier account books show as paid out of the corporate funds were for inviting public guests and wages of the city waytes or minstrels, and for the charges of public worship after the feast.

The brethren of the Fraternity would appear in Jenyns' mastership to have made their payments "for meat and alms with some words sounding rather to dishonour them in worship," "others savouring of irreverence," and as the place for making these payments was then "the cloisters," adjacent to the chapel, Sir Stephen ordered that the brethren should from henceforth pay their duties not in the cloisters but in the Hall.

---

[1] Appendix 8, page 357. King *v.* Attwood, 4 B and Adel, 406.
[2] According to the old ballad, there were only four feasts in England, all other *banquets* being only *dinners*. On St. George's Day (by the King), the Lord Mayor's Day, the Serjeants' Day, and St. John's Day (by the Merchant Taylors Company.—Songs and Ballads (Percy Society), 1841, page 143.

The ceremonial of declaring the election to the whole Fraternity was laid down by the ordinance : "nigh about the end of the same feast, the Master and four Wardens with garlands upon their heads and two others that have been Master that shall be for the same appointed, and their officers attending upon them, shall come forth openly into the Hall afore such noble estates, men of honour, and worshipful guests as shall be then and there present and do admit and choose the new Master that was afore named in the said vigil, and none other; and after that done then the four Wardens and every of them in his order shall elect and admit openly the same four persons that were afore appointed to be Wardens in the said vigil, and none others."

All were present and at the close of this feast the Master's first official act (like that of the Mayor of London) was to go with every brother of the said Fraternity to Divine Service, to the church, not of St. Paul's, but St. Martin's, "where for ever shall be kept a solemn dirge by note for all the brethren and sisters of the said Fraternity deceased"; which service was to be followed up the next morning by every member of the Fraternity attending mass and offering the mass, 1d.[1]

The post-Reformation ceremonial is fully set out in a Court entry of 1573. The election having been made, "it was then solemnly and openly in the Common Hall put in execution" by the old Master and his Wardens in the presence of the Lord Mayor, and many other worshipful persons towards the latter end of the dinner, "and before waifers served in accordinge to the rigte laudable and ancyent custom of this mystery yearly used and accustomed."

The election was thus declared to the Livery: "After the hall is served wth the seconde course, the Mr and his Wardens, accompanyed with officers do at evry table chere their gests, wch beinge done the Mr preparinge to make solempn publicacon of the said secrete elecon, havinge before him, firste, the wayts of the Cytie playinge, then the beadill and clarke followinge together, the beadill having a verger of sylver in his hande and the clerke a scrole of paper which importeth the names of Brethern, after whome followeth the yongest Warden goinge alone, havinge one of the elecon cupps in his hande and his garlande on his head, and in like manur appoynted, all the other Wardens followinge accordinge to their places, so that the flirste or Mr

---

[1] The conventional name for the offering made by the chief mourner at a funeral.

Warden goinge hindermost next the Mr carrieth the Mr's cuppe wth ipocras,[1] whom the Mr ffolowith, havinge onlly his garlande on his hedd, being accompaned wth two old Mr's, the elder of whome goeth on his righte hande, and the yonger on the Mr's left hande. The Officers, Wardens, &c., in order of aforesaide p'cede righte over the herthe[2] (wch is then fynely set wth flowers) to the chief geste sittinge at the highe table, to whome, after the officers have rendered dutie and he with the Wardens declyned to the syde of the north or liv'ry table, the Mr pffereth hym his garlande, who chearefully accepteth it and putteth it on his hedd, and after giveth yt agayne to the Mr, who, from one of his gests to another, setteth yt upon so many of their hedds as he lyketh at that table. Afterwards the waits, officers, and Wardens descende alonge by the liv'ry table, leavinge comodious place for the Mr to sett his garlande on the olde Mrs' hedds, with certen of the assistants syttinge abowte the newe Mr (or where he should sytt, yf he be absente), one whose hedds he setteth the garlande twyse yf the Mr electe be presente, and when he setteth his garland the second tyme on the hedd of the Mr electe, he letteth yt stande, and taketh his cuppe of the Mr Warden, and drynketh to him whom he publisheth to be Mr of the Company for the year ensuinge.

Wch being done, the waits, officers, and Wardens descende, and come aboute the scryne at the nether ende of the hall, where the fower Wardens substitute[3] attende to receive theire cuppes, wch they do beare afore them, viz.: the Warden substitute for M'chaunttaillo's Hall quarter before the youngest Warden Renter, and the Warden substitute for Fleate Streate quarter before the thirde Warden, the Warden substitute for Candilwicke quarter beareth the seconde Warden's cuppe, and the Warden substitute for Watling Streate quarter beareth the Maister Warden's cuppe, who then pcede, and go righte over the hearthe towards the chief gest, where, dutye being rendered, they goe unto the livry table, where evry of them pseth lyke ceremonyes wyth their garlands among suche as have not bene maisters, as the Mr dyd before among the maisters, and soe publishe the elecon of the newe

---

[1] Arnold, writing in the year 1502, gives the following " Ressnite to make Ypocras ": "For a galon and a pint of red wy take synamon iij vncis, gynger tryed an vnce, greynes and longe peper di. vnce, cloves and masys a q'rt' of an vnce, Spignard a quartir of an vnce, sugar ij lb."—*The Customs of London; or, Arnold's Chronicle.* (London.) 1811, f. 178.

[2] Standing in the centre of the Hall, page 86, *post.*

[3] On 13th July, 1601, this duty of the Wardens Substitute was reasserted, and the ipocras was "thereafter not to be sent by any such meane persons as of late, and the Masters and Wardens were to have a pottle of ipocras sent to them."

Wardens one after another by mutuall courses, viz., the Mr Warden and the most ancient Warden ovr ffirste after the like forme, as is described the manner aforesaide when a Maister elect pseute or absente, is published untill all be done, and then the hall is served with wafers."

Jenyns having been installed into office as the Master of the Merchant Taylors Company, served it as we shall see as an example of absolute disinterestedness.

The Master of the Merchant Taylors Company ought at this period at least to have been a man of scrupulous integrity, for he was a layman elected as the head of a quasi-religious Fraternity whose corporate life was essentially religious, symbolised by the highest type of humanity, emblems of whom surrounded the walls of the Common Hall, and whose figure was then present at all their assemblies.

The Master's duties of government are laid down in his oath :—

(1.) To rule and govern all the Brethren.

(2.) On complaint from anyone to call the offenders before him and examine the complaint with the advice of the Wardens and such of the Assistants as the Master sees fit to summon, that the matter (with the consent of the parties) may be truly determined.

(3.) Not to show favour or partiality to either party save as right, equity, and good conscience asketh.

(4.) To keep and maintain the ordinances, and levy the fines with the advice of the Wardens and Assistants.

(5.) To keep the Quarter-days.

(6.) To pay the priests, officers, and almsmen.

(7.) To keep the obits of Henry VII, Churchman, Carleton, Percyvale, Holland, &c., and of all others maintained at the cost of the mysterie.

(8.) To punish those of the mysterie keeping foreigners, &c.

Thus it will be seen that he was to hear and redress with strict impartiality all complaints arising within the craft, to hold the quarterly assemblies, to pay the chaplains, officers, and almsmen, to fulfil the benevolent trusts of deceased members, and to maintain the rights of the Company to monopoly.

The most important assemblies over which he had to preside were the Quarterly Courts in the Hall,[1] at which the whole body

---

[1] In 1489-90 these was held on September 16, January 25, May 5, and June 18.

was present, and where "every man kneeling upon his knees," the prayer which is found in the Ordinance book was used.[1] The first petition was for "the King," and then in obedience to the Psalmist's injunction to every good, true citizen[2] "for their noble city" of London. Then for the Fraternity for their due discharge of trusts, for an increase of well wishers, benefactors, and sound members; for grace honestly to discharge the trusts reposed in those assembled, as to be a good example and incitement to others to become benefactors.

All the names were then called and noted, the wills and endowments of deceased benefactors read, the business relating to landed property and their charities attended to, and if assessments were called for by the Mayor or the Masters and Wardens, they were made and adjusted according to the rank of the contributors as Mayor, Sheriff, or Alderman (if any such) of the Corporation, and as Master, Warden, Assistant, Livery or Free man of the guild.

The meetings of less importance, held in the Parlour, were those of the Master and Wardens and Assistants,[3] in whom the administration of affairs rested whenever the Master and Wardens *alone* had not the power to act. Such a meeting, constituted as a Court, elected to the Livery and exercised the power of fine and imprisonment over the members of the Fraternity, and was in this respect (under Lord Holt's judgment)[4] a Court of Record.

The meetings of the Master and Wardens in Jenyns' year were sixty in number distributed as at the foot,[5] but in later years often bi-weekly.[6] All the ordinary work relating to the trade, to apprentices and servants, had to be settled, and not unfrequently by personal reference and award.

The hour of assembly was according to the custom of that

---

[1] Appendix 9, page 359.   [2] Psalm 122, v. 6.

[3] In 1489-90 these were held on October 12, November 9, February 3, March 19 and 24, May 10, and June 4, and see Appendix 12.

[4] College of Physicians' case, 12 Med. Rep., page 386.

[5] In July   7   August   3   September 2
    October   9   November 5   December 5
    January   4   February 6   March   8
    April   4   May   4   June   3
    ──   ──   ──
    24   18   18

[6] In 1486 they were held on Monday and Friday, but on the 1st March, 1573, it was decreed that the Court days shall be kept on Mondays and Saturdays during this term of Lent, that the members may hear the Friday sermon before the Queen as hath been used aforetime.

period eight o'clock A.M., or early in the forenoon, and the meeting continued until the work was discharged.

All the cash received and paid for the current year was originally under the authority of the Master, who, at his own risk of disallowance, had to make disbursements, and, after the Master had left the chair, the last duty to be discharged was to come before the whole assembly and render up his accounts to them. The balance (if any) was paid into the "Treasury," the keys of which were held by others, and from which nothing could be withdrawn without the order of the "Council of the crafte to gyders assembled," and the presence of the authorities of the Company.

At a time anterior to Jenyns' mastership some allowances to the Master and Wardens, and, indeed, also to their wives, had crept into their corporate accounts, which he thought to be a great charge and hindrance to the craft, and, therefore, acting like an honest man, he put it from him, paid it to the treasury, and on the 18th August, 1490, obtained an ordinance "from the whole body of the craft in this Hall assembled" abolishing such allowances and decreeing that whosoever should hereafter attempt to break the ordinance should forfeit 20*l*. to the alms and 20*l*. to the Chamber of London, and that the Master, on his admission, should take his oath to observe it.[1]

Holding office involved, it is clear, a great sacrifice of time, and to the Masters after Jenyns some sacrifice of money. The Taylors, like the modern Freemasons, gave their time gratuitously to the benefit of their fellow-craftsmen, and Jenyns laid down a perpetual ordinance that this rule should continue.

It remains to be shown what were the duties of the subordinate or paid officers of the Fraternity, viz., the Clerk and Bedel,[2] who were to be true brothers of the mysterie, and sworn to discharge duties laid down in their oaths.

The Clerk is (1) To disclose no counsels nor give copy of any writing under pain of fine. (2) To be obedient to the Master and Wardens, and to be ready to attend the Wardens in their searches. (3) To inform the Master and Wardens of all ordinances, that they should not run into errors *or damage to the peril of their souls* through *his* negligence. (4) To "enter the names of all the Brethren that come not to the Quarter dais [Obites, diriges,

---

[1] No record of such an oath is now extant.
[2] A list of these officers is given at page 81.

offerings, ridings, processions] and other assemblies when they be summoned, and to help to gather and levy the amerciaments of the same according to the Ordynaunce thereof made. (5) To enter into the Books all the Receipts received by the Maister to the use of the said fraternity. And all manner payments made by the said Maister for the time being to the [Priests] Officers, Almsmen, & of all quitt Rents, [Obites] Reparacōns & all other casual payments & expences to & for the necessary causes of the said fraternitie. And all of the said Receipts & Payments to engrosse & make a true reckoning and accompt in writing & the same shewe & declare to the whole company or the more parte of them assembled for that purpose, openly in the Comōn Hall in the day of the yeelding up of the Maisters Accompt. (6) To declare once or twice every year the wills and compositions of all the Benefactors of the said Fraternitie at quarter dais holden in the presence of the Maister and Wardens & the whole body then assembled." The last clause is one of vast importance and shows clearly that the office was designed for an officer of great knowledge, intelligence, and integrity. "And yf the Maister and Wardens for the tyme being would desire you to compile or make any new Acts or Ordynaunces which *should grow to the disworshipp* of the said fraternitie, ye shall lett it as far forth as ye may. And yf you may not then, ye shall *warn* the most *substantiall & wysest* persons of the Assistants which have experience and wisdome to lett & adnull the same. Thus shall ye behave you well & truly to the said Companie as nigh as God shall send you Grace. Soe help you God."

The Master and Wardens as annual officers were the Judges, the Clerk was the Recorder of their Court, and was in duty bound to see that they did not, through ignorance, exceed their powers under the ordinances. He was to be the legal adviser of the Court, and it was needful that he should be versed not only in all the learning or traditions of the Company, but familiar with all the benefactions and the trusts which either the wills of the several founders, or the contracts of the Master and Wardens, might have imposed on the Fraternity. By the intelligence of some former Clerks the interests of the Fraternity have been secured.

As of the "Ward" so of the "Company" the Bedel was the executive officer. He was bound (1) To see the ordinances duly observed, or to report the breach thereof, and that no foreigner should occupy contrary thereto; (2) That no " Ryotor, Robber, night walker nor slaundered person of the said fraternity abyding within this Citty and liberties of the same, but that ye shall shewe the names of them as soone as yee have knowledge thereof to the M^r and Wardens for the tyme being, to the intent that the party so using himself theire wholesome counsell and good advertisement, may the sooner be reformed and reconciled to grace. (3) To goe with the Wardens or with the Clarck at all manner searches and all other needefull errands pertayning to the common proffitt of the said fraternitie as you shalbe thereto called or assigned. (4) Doe all manner sumons and warnings within the said fraternity or mistery, without any Penny receaving for your labour, whether it be betweene party and party of the same mystery or else betweene Maister and apprentice or servant, except of every stranger complayning of any person of this mistery, for your sumons doing fower pence. (5) To search all manner distresses, fynes, debts, amerciaments and all other duties belonging to the said fraternitie, and the same so gathered in and make thereof a true accompt unto the M^r and Wardens or else to the Clarck."

His authority is of course limited to the members of the Fraternity, but he would, we presume, have legal power to carry out the lawful orders of the Master and Wardens as affecting their corporate rights and duties. In the early history of the Company, in 1399–1400, before the higher functions of the Master and Wardens arose, the annual pay of the Bedel (David Kelly) was 3*l*., and of the Clerk (Johan Brenchal) 2*l*. 13*s*. 4*d*., with 2*l*. 12*s*. pur sa table; but in the year 1491, the wages of each were augmented, for there were taken out of the treasury and "delivered to William Duryvale, the Clerk, and Thomas Gresyll, Bedyll of this craft, in augmentation of their wages 23*s*. 4*d*., that is to say, to the Clerk an old noble and a half in gold and 4*d*. in white money, sum 13*s*. 4*d*., and to the Bedyll, 10*s*. in gold."

In the inventories it will be noticed that amongst the donations to the Company, the Clerk, Henry Mayour, is entered for a double Almery, and William Erle, late Bedel, for a standing Notte.

It now only remains for us to see in what relationship the Guild stood towards the Mayor as the head of the City Councils, and what place it occupied in the government of London in matters other than those of trade. It will be noticed that in the Charters granted to the Master and Wardens of the Guild the powers there given, recognised, and were to be exercised in due subordination to, the supreme authority of the Mayor. Therefore the Mayor and his Councils held supreme control over the Guilds, and were arbiters in case of differences between them.[1] Of this we shall read hereafter, but we may now refer to the Skynners' case as decided by Billesden in 1484, and the fourteen Companies' case as decided by the Mayor and Aldermen in 1571, when the Merchant Taylors, by their answers submitted themselves "to the Mayor and Aldermen in all things, both high and low."[2]

Every citizen, as already pointed out, was under a double allegiance; sworn as a freeman to obey the Mayor and to bear scot and lot; and as a guildsman to obey the Master's summons for personal service and to bear all cessings and charges. It was indifferent through which channel the assessment came, for if made by the Common Council the freeman was present by representative, or if made by the Guild at quarter-day or general assembly he was present in person. The Guild under the Master and Wardens became a better unit for civic administration[3] than the Ward under the Alderman, and for this reason, the Mayor's precepts were frequently addressed to them. Indeed in the assessment for the military muster of 1585, the yield of the Wards (with foreigners and others included) was only 289l. 3s. 2d., while that of the Guilds amounted to 4,735l. 1s. 1d.[4] What, therefore, the Court of Common Council, or of Assistants, determined should be done, and the Mayor by his precept, or the Master and Wardens by order, called on the liegemen to do, was in obedience to their oaths done.

It is not proposed here to deal with the subject at any length, as at a later period it will arise for much fuller consideration, but one or two of the Mayor's precepts will be given, having reference to personal service, and money assessments will be referred to.

I. As to Personal Service.[5]—Watch and ward were the incidents of citizenship. The city was in the charge of the Mayor and of his fellow citizens, not of the Crown and its executive officers. The setting of the standing watch was celebrated by two festivals, the Vigil of St. John Baptist's Day being one, and of St. Paul the other. The summer watch setting usually lasted from 11 P.M. to 2 A.M. "I do not believe" (writes the Venetian ambassador, who witnessed the watch of June, 1521) "that any where else in the

---

[1] See pages 137 and 201, *post*.

[2] On 25th January, 1562, the Merchant Company gave the Bachelors leave to promote a Bill in Parliament, but subject to the Lord Mayor's licence being given to them.

[3] The Halls of the several Guilds facilitated the assembly of the citizens for civic purposes.

[4] Vol. I, Antiquarian Repository, page 253.

[5] Appendix 10, page 360.

world a similar mark of rejoicing is usual." Our guildsman, Sir John Skevington,[1] was one of the Sheriffs in that year, and formed part of the procession. The Mayor[2] was in armour on horseback, clad in crimson damask, with his sword-bearer in armour (for he is never wont to go abroad unless preceded by his sword), and with two sheriffs[3] on horseback in armour, but with crimson surcoats, two pages likewise on horseback carrying their helmets."[4]

The worthy Taylor, John Stowe, gives this pleasing picture of city life at the Tudor period:—"In the months of June and July, on the vigils of festival days, and on the same festival days in the evenings after the sun setting, there were usually made bonfires in the streets, every man bestowing wood or labour towards them; the wealthier sort also, before their doors near to the said bonfires, would set out tables on the vigils, furnished with sweet bread and good drink, and on the festival days with meats and drinks plentifully, whereunto they would invite their neighbours and passengers also to sit and be merry with them in great familiarity, praising God for his benefits bestowed on them. These were called bonfires as well of good amity amongst neighbours that being before at controversy, were there, by the labour of others, reconciled, and made of bitter enemies loving friends; and also for the virtue that a great fire hath to purge the infection of the air. On the vigil of St. John the Baptist, and on St. Peter and Paul the apostles, every man's door being shadowed with green birch, long fennel, St. John's wort, orpin, white lilies, and such like, garnished upon with garlands of beautiful flowers, had also lamps of glass, with oil burning in them all the night; some hung out branches of iron curiously wrought, containing hundreds of lamps alight at once, which made a goodly show, namely in New Fish Street, Thames Street, &c. Then had ye besides the standing watches all in bright harness, in every ward and street of this city and suburbs, a marching watch, that passed through the principal streets thereof. The whole way for this marching watch extended (and here the memory of Stowe's old craft came upon him) to three thousand two hundred *tailor's* yards of assize; for the furniture whereof with lights, there were appointed seven hundred cressets, five hundred of them being found by the companies, the other two hundred by the chamber of London. Besides the which lights every constable in London, in

---

[1] See his will, page 99, note.
[2] Sir John Bruge, the Draper.
[3] Sir John Skevington and John Kyme.
[4] Cal. State Papers (Venetian correspondence) at date July 14th (244).

number more than two hundred and forty, had his cresset: the charge of every cresset was in light two shillings and four pence, and every cresset had two men, one to bear or hold it, another to bear a bag with light, and to serve it, so that the poor men pertaining to the cressets, taking wages, besides that every one had a straw hat, with a badge painted, and his breakfast in the morning, amounted in number to almost two thousand. The marching watch contained in number about two thousand men, part of them being old soldiers of skill, to be captains, lieutenants, sergeants corporals, &c., wiflers, drummers, and fifes, standard and ensign bearers, sword players, trumpeters on horseback, demilances on great horses, gunners with hand guns, or half hakes, archers in coats of white fustian, signed on the breast and back with the arms of the city, their bows bent in their hands, with sheaves of arrows by their sides, pikemen in bright corslets, burganets, &c., halberds, the like billmen in almaine rivets, and apernes of mail in great number; there were also divers pageants, morris dancers, constables, the one half, which was one hundred and twenty, on St. John's eve, the other half on St. Peter's eve, in bright harness, some overgilt, and every one a jornet of scarlet thereupon, and a chain of gold, his henchman following him, his minstrels before him, and his cresset light passing by him, the waits of the city, the Mayor's officers for his guard before him, all in a livery of worsteds or say jackets party-coloured, the Mayor himself well mounted on horseback, the sword-bearer before him in fair armour well mounted also, the Mayor's footmen, and the like torch bearers about him, henchmen twain upon great stirring horses, following him. The Sheriffs' watches came one after the other in like order, but not so large in number as the Mayor's; for where the Mayor had besides his giant three pageants, each of the Sheriffs had besides their giants but two pageants, each their morris dance, and one henchman, their officers in jackets of worsted or say, party-coloured, differing from the Mayor's, and each from other, but having harnessed men a great many, &c."

For this assembly the Guild was ordered to provide "12 Fayre Cressetts with two bearers for each light," and they did so under precept of June, 1567.[1]

---

[1] The cresset, so named from a French word, was a portable fireplace used chiefly in processions at night, or by watchmen or guides. It was usually placed at the top of a pole and carried for safety by two bearers. (See an illustration in Wright's Domestic Manners, page 454).' In 1547-8, when a Merchant Taylor was Lord Mayor, the expenses were these: "Charges concerning the watch at Midsummer. Cleaning 13 pair of Almain rivets and other pieces of harness, 12s. 2 yew bows, 4s.

II. As to Assessments for Money.—The money would appear to have been levied for two distinct objects: one, as a loan to the city for corn, &c.; the other for use by the city, as for Bridewell, &c. Assessments were also made for the service of the Crown. The corn assessments to provide against dearth originated in the year 1521, by an order of the Common Council. Money was to be levied from the several Guilds by way of "Prest and lone;" and it was enacted that the Lord Mayor and Aldermen should, at their discretion, "appoint what sum should be levied of each Company," and each person in the Company "be assessed by the Wardens thereof."[1] The Merchant Taylors Company have no books to show what sum this assessment amounted to, but in 1546-7 we have an account showing the repayment by the city of 51*l*. 3*s*. 4*d*. which had been previously levied on the members of the Court and Livery, with the amount repaid and the persons who were the recipients.[2] Of such an assessment that of 2nd October, 1562, given in the Appendix,[3] will do as an illustration.

Bridewell Hospital in 1548-9.—The history of the Hospital assessment may be thus given:—Bridewell in West Smithfield was founded by Henry VIII for the relief of the poor within the house and the suburbs of the said city. The Corporation of London had by indenture under its corporate seal agreed with the King to pay 500 marks annually towards the institution. This sum the Corporation thought would be best raised from the Guilds; thereupon "an Act of Common Council" was passed in 2nd Edward VI (1548), enacting that the said sum should thenceforth be borne and paid of and amongst the said Companies or fellowships thereunder written in such manner and after such allotment as thereafter appeareth and is expressed, the payments being made quarterly. The act then gives power of distress to the collectors appointed by the Master and Wardens upon every person contributory and chargeable to the said payments, as he or they should thereafter be reasonably assessed or taxed, until he paid such assessment to the Warden. It made no provision for the assessment or distribution of the total sum amongst the various members of the Guild which therefore was made by the Master and Wardens under the charter and ordinances of the Company. In the schedule then added

---

3 sheaves of arrows, 6*s*. 1,600 cressett lights, 53*s*. 4*d*. Washing and trimming the fustian coats for the 8 bowmen, and sewing red crosses on their coats. 3 doz. straw hats with scutcheons sewn on them, 4*s*. 2*d*. To 24 cresset bearers and 10 bagbearers, at 6*d*. a night, etc. Total 7*l*. 10*s*. 11*d*."

[1] Vol. 1, Her. O. C., page 133. Appendix 11, page 360.
[2] Appendix 12, page 362.
[3] Appendix 32, page 405.

Companies were named and the 500 marks distributed amongst them by a separate sum placed opposite the name of each Company. In this schedule the Mercers Company stands first and bears 24*l*., as the highest assessment; then the Grocers and Drapers, each 20*l*.; then the Fishmongers and Goldsmiths, each 16*l*.; the Skynners, 13*l*. 6*s*. 8*d*.; and the Merchant Taylors Company, 20*l*., the sum which we find entered in their cashbooks as paid in 1548–9. For how many years this assessment lasted does not appear, but probably in the course of later years the smaller Companies were withdrawn from future assessments. In March, 1600, the Merchant Taylors Company was assessed in 16*l*. 16*s*. 0*d*. as its proportion of 500*l*.

The Gunpowder Assessment not only involved the payment for but the storage of gunpowder upon the hall premises, and the Company appear to have delayed, if not demurred, to obey the precept.[1] However, the Mayor, by a second precept of October, 1586, reminded the Master and Wardens[2] of the neglect, and of his power to commit them to ward or prison should they continue disobedient. Thereupon two members of the Court, Mr. Robert Dowe and Mr. Richard Maye, were directed to make a purchase of part of the amount demanded.

The assessments for the service of the Crown for soldiers or ships, were usually made upon the Companies by the Lord Mayor; that is, the Crown put him in motion, and if the Common Council saw fit to call on their fellow citizens for contributions, his precept issued.[3]

Other precepts might be given to any number, but the present will suffice for the purpose for which they are cited, as the subject is entered upon at greater length in a later chapter (14).

---

[1] Appendix 13, page 363.
[2] These were William Widnell, Reginald Barker, William Saulte, Nowell Sotherton, and William Webbe.
[3] Appendix 13, page 247, *post*.

CHAPTER III.

THE BACHELOR OR YEOMAN COMPANY OF TAYLORS.

The Yeoman Taylors, p. 60.—Disputes of 1411, p. 61.—Of 1415, p. 61.—Of 1417, p. 63.—Came under control of the Merchant Company, p. 64.— Traces of the Company in 1446-56, p. 64.— When Companies separated, p. 64.—Bachelors Company seldom mentioned on Merchant Company's records, p. 64.—Number of the Bachelors, p. 65.—Ordinances of 1507, p. 65.— Ordinances of 1613, p. 65.—Organisation of Bachelors Company, p. 65.— Offices not readily filled up, p. 66.— Workman and employer, p. 67.—Seeds of Disunion, p. 68.—Disadvantages of separate organisation, p. 68.—Division of funds and separate distribution of alms, p. 68.—Merchant Company held the trust estates, p. 68.—Members of the wealthy class, p. 68.—Poor Taylors in the Bachelor Company, p. 68.—Which became the Almoner of the Merchant Company, p. 68.—Sources of income to Bachelor Company, p. 68; (1) Benefactions; (2) Quarterages; (3) Fines; (4) Donations from Merchant Company, p. 68.—Distribution to the poor, p. 69.—Method of it and changes made, p. 70.—Donations in 1655-9, p. 70.—Merchant Company take the distribution in 1663, p. 70.—Merchant Company's control over Bachelor's Treasury, p. 71.—Disputes in 1601, p. 71.—Army Contracts declined by Merchant Company, p. 72.—Disputes of 1608, p. 72.—Sumptuary expenses excessive, p. 72.—Agreement for future government of the Company, p. 73.—Ceased to be appointed by the Merchant Company in 1661, p. 74.—Merchant Company take charge of business of the Bachelors Company, p. 74.—Corporation refuse to interfere, p. 74.— So also the Privy Council, p. 74.—Note as to Assessment of 1602-5.

IN the last chapter we have deemed it best to describe the Fraternity as consisting of one Company, which may be conveniently called the Merchant Company, but for many years anterior to 1661 there existed an organisation attached and subordinate to the Merchant Company, of which the records have been lost. This was the Bachelor or Yeoman Company, composed originally of the craft of Taylors, either masters or workmen, or in later years of any members of the Guild. We propose therefore in this chapter to give an outline of the Bachelors so far as it can be traced from the records of the Merchant Company or elsewhere.

It was a principle of civic government in the early times that no working man could be permitted to be masterless or unattached—living as or where he pleased, without or beyond the control of some lawful authority. This principle would seem to have been disputed in Henry V's reign by the working Taylors, and to have led them into controversy with the Master of the Taylors and Linen Armourers, then (as those records show) one Thomas Tropewell. The men lived in a place of evil repute (quoting from a legal document), and the existence in the city of Yeoman Taylors claiming to be a separate craft, was brought to the notice of the Mayor (Thomas Faucover) when, on the 19th April, 1415, they were informed against as living by themselves alone against the licence of their superiors, and as having beaten Thomas Tropewell, one of the Masters [in 1411] of the aforesaid trade.[1]

The evil is stated thus: "by incessant reports, that certain servants and apprentices of the tailors of the said City, called 'yeomen taillours,' live by themselves alone in companies, and take and inhabit divers dwelling-places in the said city against the licence or will of their superiors of the said city or the masters of the same art. The inhabitants of which houses in former times, like irregular and lawless men without a head or government, have often assembled together in great numbers, and made divers assemblies and conventicles in divers places within the said city and without, and have beaten, wounded, and ill-treated many lieges of our lord the king, and especially now lately one Thomas Tropewell, one of the masters of the foresaid trade, severely, from malice and design aforethought; and have made many rescues against the servants and officers of the said city while arresting malefactors and disturbers of the peace of our lord the king; and have committed, and daily endeavour to commit, very many other evils and enormities to the injury of the peace of our lord the king and the manifest disturbance of his people. Whence divers evils and dangers to our lord the king and his people, as well as scandals and injuries to the masters of the foresaid art, who know nothing of the said evil deeds, have often happened, and will probably continue to happen for the future, unless a remedy is soon and speedily applied by the governors of the said city."

Now the authorities who were primarily responsible for this state of affairs were the Master and Wardens of the Taylors Company, and therefore they were first to be summoned to give their explanation. The record therefore continues: " Concerning which the said Mayor and Aldermen, after careful deliberation on the premises being inclined to repress this malice and these enormities, and wishing to oppose to their power, as they are bound to do, the

---

[1] Memorials, page 514.

evils, scandals, and injuries of this kind, which are likely easily to happen (which God forbid) unless they are speedily resisted, caused to appear before them in the Chamber of the Guildhall of the said city on the 25th of April then next following, Thomas Whityngham, now master, and the wardens of the trade aforesaid, to discuss the premises why, although they have the special government of the foresaid trade, under the Mayor and Aldermen and other governors of the foresaid city, they allow their servants and apprentices to inhabit houses of this kind alone by themselves, in companies, without a superior to rule them, and to commit and perpetrate these evils and crimes so lawlessly."

The Master and Wardens appeared accordingly, and "having first obtained leave to address the Mayor and Aldermen, by their grievous complaint signified that they were deeply grieved at these misdeeds and crimes, because scandals and many injuries daily happen to the master and good men of the foresaid art by the lawlessness of these men, and are likely to happen in the future, which God forbid, unless they are repressed. They are much concerned at the companies of these men living alone by themselves in houses, because, although they have been often warned by the same masters of the said trade to evacuate their houses, on account of their crimes committed by reason of their fellowship together in the foresaid houses, they disregard the warnings of the said masters and will not leave the foresaid houses, but have expressly refused so to do and still refuse; requiring the said Mayor and Aldermen with due instance, to deign to send for the said causes for David Brekenhok and John Stanbury, and others living in a certain house at Garlykhyth,[1] alone by themselves, in company together."

These offenders were therefore summoned and appeared on the 29th April, who admitting their residence to the Mayor had their case further adjourned until the 2nd May, when the decision of the Court was given in these words:

"At which day there came thither the said David Brekenhok and John Stanbury and others for themselves and the rest of the foresaid company living together. And the foresaid Mayor and Aldermen, after careful consultation together upon the premises, being of opinion that the livery or dress in which the said servants

---

[1] In Vintric Ward, running from Bow Lane to Thames Street. "Three Shear Court" (small and ordinary) "was over against the Church."—Stowe, Book III, page 14.

and apprentices, like young and unstable people, congregate and assemble together yearly by themselves without the government or supervision of their superiors of the said trade, or of any others, within the said city, and further that the houses in which they live together continuously by themselves alone without any fixed government, expressly tend and redound to the breach of the peace of our lord the king, the disturbance and probably the commotion of his people, which God forbid; consider and adjudge that the servants of the foresaid trade shall be hereafter under government and rule of the Masters and Wardens of the foresaid trade, as other servants of other trades in the said city are, and are bound by law to be, and that they shall not use henceforth livery or dress, meetings or conventicles, or other unlawful things of this kind.

"And further the said Mayor and Aldermen then and there enjoined the said David Brekenhok, John Stanbury and others then and there present, that they and all their fellows inhabiting the said house at Garlykhyth, and other houses of the same kind in the said city, should depart from and leave them before Sunday, the 6th day of May next, and should not take them again or others to live in them together by themselves alone together, in any wise for the future, on pain of imprisonment and fine, to be levied at the discretion of the Mayor and Aldermen for the time being."

This decree was not acceptable to the Yeoman Taylors, for they came before the Mayor in August, 1417,[1] for permission to assemble yearly on St. John's Decollation Day in the church of St. John

---

[1] See further as to their attendance at St. John's, Clerkenwell, in order of August, 1417, as under:—

"On the 5th day of August in the 5th year of the reign of King Henry the Fifth after the Conquest [1417], there came hither William Davenish, John Elis, John Spencer, and John Cobbe, and others of the said trade, commonly called 'Yomantaillours,' and by their petition presented to Henry Barton, then Mayor, and the Aldermen, prayed that they would deign to grant to them and others their fellows being of the brotherhood of 'Yomantaillours' that they might assemble on the feast of the Decollation of St. John the Baptist next following and so henceforth yearly, in the Church of St. John of Jerusalem near Smythfeld, there to offer for the deceased brothers and sisters of the said brotherhood, and to do other things which they have been accustomed to do there, etc.

"The Mayor and Aldermen after the inspection of a certain record concerning the government of the said trade, and of the servants and yeomen of the same, in the time of Thomas Fauconer, then Mayor, entered in Folio 151, of this book, and after consultation concerning the premises, considering that an assembly of this kind, although it is sought and prayed for under a pious pretext of goodness, if it were permitted, would nevertheless manifestly tend to the infringement of the foresaid ordinance and the disturbance of the peace, as other similar assemblies in the said trade have done, order and consider that in future times no servant or apprentice of the said trade shall presume by themselves to make or enter assemblies or con-

Jerusalem, and there to offer for the deceased brothers and sisters of the brotherhood. The Mayor and Aldermen turned to Faucover's decree and after consideration concerning the provisions, considered that such an assembly though sought and prayed " under a pious pretext of goodness " would manifestly lead to an infringement of that decree and to a disturbance of the peace, therefore their order was that no servant or apprentice should presume by themselves to make or enter assemblies or conventicles at the aforesaid church or elsewhere, unless with and in the presence of the Masters of the said trade on pain of imprisonment or fine to be levied by the Mayor and Aldermen.

Thus it was that the Yeoman Taylors came under the government of the Guild. We have traces of the Bachelors' Company as governed by Substitutes in 1446 and 1456, for when differences arose in January, 1639, as to the election of Substitutes, the Sixteen Men claiming to influence their election, a reference was then made "to an antient entrance of a book of this Society made 25 Henry VI (1446), and which showed that the oath concurred with the antient usuage," whereupon the Merchant Company decided that such custom should be observed.[1] And again that the office of " Warden of the Yeoman " existed in 1458–9, is shown from the accounts of William Boylet (Master) having this entry: "Paid to the Warden of the Yeomen Feleship" for the search of "foreigns at the Mayor's order, 20d."

In the absence of the records of the Bachelors' Company we are left very much to conjecture as to the exact dividing line between the two Companies, and the year in which it was originally laid down. In treating of the Merchant Company, we shall find that considerable constitutional changes were made in the Guild in the sixteenth and principally in the early half of the century. When the Court records of the Merchant Company commence (in 1561-2) they have reference to the affairs of that Company, and those of the Bachelors' are mentioned only so far as the Merchant or dominant Company had to give directions concerning the meetings or elections, or contributions by the Bachelors. Although the

---

venticles, at the foresaid Church of St. John or elsewhere, unless with and in the presence of the Masters of the said trade, etc., on pain of imprisonment and fine to be levied according to the discretion of the Mayor and Aldermen for the time being, etc. But that the foresaid ordinance and all the other ordinances ordained for preserving the good of peace and quietness in the said trade shall remain unbroken and entire."

[1] Memorials, page 565.

CHAP. III.] *Number of the Bachelors.* 65

latter Company originated with Taylors, yet when Taylors exercised the trade of clothworkers these became, we presume, members of the Yeomen or Bachelors'. At any rate the latter Company far exceeded in number that of the other. If it were true that "great multitudes" of the brethren attending "mass" in 1455 made the chapel of St. John's in "Powles" too small "to hold so many persons of the Company," rendering it necessary to found another chapel at the hall "for the more commodious performance" of their devotions, those brethren must have been largely supplemented in numbers from the Yeomen. So again in the attendance and assessments for pageants, as in Lee's mayoralty (1603) and Halliday's in 1605 their numbers were very considerable.[1]

It is, therefore, remarkable that the rules and orders for the government of the Bachelors, which were in force in 1507 should not have been incorporated in those ordinances which then were submitted for statutory confirmation. Why it should have been so is not apparent, but it is the fact that only a slight reference is made to the Bachelor Company in the code of 1507, possibly no additional authority being thought needful.

However, whatever may have been the occasion of the change in policy in this respect, we find in the ordinances of 1613 some additional ones relating to the Bachelor Company inserted which must now be considered.

The Company is there shown to consist of two classes, first, the Bachelors "in Foyne" (paying a higher assessment), and those "in Budge"; their rights and duties in other respects are not defined;[2] and, secondly, freemen or brethren electing to be recorded on the Company's books as such.[3]

The ordinance for the election of the Master and Wardens had an addition providing for the election of Wardens Substitute of the Bachelors Company and their Sixteen Men as Assistants, upon the Eve of the St. John's Decollation "according as heretofore hath been accustomed. But the more important additions were the two oaths relating to the "Substitutes" and Sixteen Men. It will be seen from the context that these oaths were

---

[1] Note at the end of the chapter.   [2] Appendix 7, page 351.

[3] I think many (as now) having taken up their freedom in the Company had no further fellowship with it as subscribing or participating members. If so these men did not pay the quarterage of 2s. 2d. prescribed by the ordinances for the poor, nor would they be recognised as eligible for alms. In August, 1578, the Master and Wardens ordered that every servant or journeyman free of the city and a brother of this mistery should pay to the Wardens Substitute quarterage after 8d. a year or 2d. a quarter. This may have been the origin of quarterages for the Yeomen.

post-reformation and different from the oaths of other guildsmen. The deponents were not sworn to attend upon the King in ridings, &c., or at obits. The Warden Substitute was to exercise his office as the Court of Assistants of the Merchant Company willed him to do. No meetings, either the four quarterly or otherwise, were to be held, save only at the hall, and such as were sanctioned by the Master and Wardens upon the day and time when they could attend them. The Wardens Substitute were named by the Court, and the Sixteen Men were to appoint none other. The dinner for the Bachelors Company was to be in the hall on St. John's Decollation Day, with the like assent, and the four Wardens named by the Court of Assistants were to be elected thereat. They were to levy the assessments and fines on those not attending quarter-days and burials of brothers or sisters deceased; to obey all the ordinances approved under the Statute, and then these words:—
"And also such resonable and lawful ordinaunces of old time made by the antient faders and Go^{r}rs of the said Fraternity for our comon weal and profit wch were devised and ordained for ye to have and wch old ordinaunces by the late Master, four Wardens, and Assistants be of new ratified, approved, and confirmed to your said increse and profit;" ordinances of which no copy is held by the Merchant Taylors Company.

The freeman was elected as a Bachelor, and then as a Warden Substitute. Serving this office led to election on the Livery at lower fees as a reward, but the office was not popular, for it was laborious and chargeable, while the younger men of the better class held it to be disparagement to serve in it. Thus, in March, 1596, we find the Merchant Company going to extremities against Philip Cotton, an elected Substitute, who would not serve.[1] The Court entry of the Merchant Taylors runs thus:—"And therefore at divers Courts of Assistants it was resolved that he should be committed to prison by the authority of this house. But forasmuch as the said Cotton opposing himself wilfully against the Company did keep his house so close and walk so secretly that the officer could not come where he might lawfully carry him away. Therefore this Company were dryven to make their complaynt to the right honourable the Lord Mayor of the city, and by the greate care and paynes at the right woor^{ll} Mr. Edward Kympton now M^r of this society, who spent many dayes for the bridling of so contemptuous a brother in thend procurred a warrant from the Lord

---

[1] The same proceedings had to be taken in 1613 against the Master elect and two Wardens of the Merchant Company.

Mayor for his apprehension, who by virtue hereof, was at last apprehended and committed to the compter in the Powltrey where he remaynde for the space of twenty daies, and then was released upon his recognizance to submit himself to the judgement of the Mayor and Aldermen, the Company doing the same, when Cotton was fined 20*l*. & to be discharged from all offices in the Company."[1]

The Sixteen Men were to attend when summoned, and to give their advice, both to the Master and Wardens or Wardens Substitute; whilst in all causes and matters between party and party they were to act without partially.

The supervision of the workmen was placed in the hands of the Bachelor Company. Each man's residence was registered, and he was placed under contribution of 2*s*. 2*d*. a quarter, which these ordinances provide should be paid "for the poor of the Fraternity," and which the Wardens Substitute distributed amongst them. Lastly, they were to see that the accounts of the common goods of the Fraternity should be yearly made and placed before the whole body of the Fraternity for registry and enrolment.[2]

How much of the 1613 code may have been a new organisation in the interval between the two codes we cannot determine, but under the ordinances of 1613 the Yeomen or Bachelors Company was governed, having a (quasi) Court of Assistants of four Wardens Substitute and Sixteen Men, with a separate (1) Treasury, (2) Clerk, (3) Bedel, and (4) Benefactors. Of this Company all the working Tailors were members, their names were entered upon the roll, London being apportioned into four quarters or districts, over each of which a Warden took the charge. Each of these quarters comprised a given area which from time to time was adjusted as the population and wealth of the residents varied.

"In the old time," writes Palgrave,[3] "the workman was the brother, the Compagnon, the Gesell of his employer, perhaps poorer in purse, inferior in station, younger in age, but all united by the most kind and sociable bonds, they repeated the same creed, met in the same church, lighted their lamp before the same altar, feasted at the same board. Thus, they constituted the elements of the burgher aristocracy which, as far as institutions can answer that end, reconciled poor and rich, equally protecting the rights and claims of capital and labour."

---

[1] In April, 1602, it was proposed that the Livery fine (without substitute service) should be raised to 25*l*., of which 23*l*. 6*s*. 8*d*. was to go to the Bachelor Company (for the poor), and the residue to the common box and officers.

[2] See an instance, 1st March, 1595.

[3] Page 112 of the Merchant and the Friar.

Such was the Merchant Taylors Guild in its inception: the union of capital and labour, but the code of 1613, whether original or not, led to its disintegration, until, as we shall see, the labour element ceased to exist, save as the poorer members who ultimately became the recipients of eleemosynary funds of the *Merchant* Company.

The seeds of disunion are not difficult to discover. The feasts of the Merchants and of the Yeomen were held on different Church festivals, and there was no social equality or relationship between them. The Yeomen met only once in three years or not so often, to entertain the "generalte" and almsmen;[1] whereas the Merchants met once in every year or oftener to entertain the Honorable and Worshipful guests under the Charter.

The division of funds and a separate distribution of alms were the results. Each Company had its own sumptuary expenses for separate guests and the care of its own poor. The Merchant Company held the trust estates and distributed the rents as directed by the several wills. Their own members being of the wealthier class, little was needed by way of alms for them. Far different was the case of the Bachelor Company, for if the poor Taylors were to be found it was in one or other of the quarters into which London was divided, and over each of which a Warden Substitute had charge. The Bachelor Company became, therefore, the channel through which the working men were provided with alms, in fact the almoners of the Merchant Company for such pensions as they had to fill up or sums as they were pleased to entrust them with.

The sources of income to the Bachelor Company were:—

(1.) Benefactions made expressly to them.
(2.) The quarterages from their own members.
(3.) Fines received from the same, including Livery fines.
(4.) Annual donations from the Merchant Company.

The first source of income was not large; thus Dowe gave for the "almsmen's dinner at the Bachelors' feast" 1*l*., and for the shooting dinner 13*s*. 4*d*.; Vernon gave 13*s*. 4*d*. to the shooting dinner, and 16*s*. to the Sixteen Men, and 12*d*. every third year on St. John's Decollation day, when kept; while these benefactors besides Craven and William Parker gave small sums to the officers of the Bachelor Company.

---

[1] Dowe's almsmen had their gowns given them and attended church on this day, but it was not always certain "that a general feast shall be kept every third year," but when kept they were "to be sit at the table in the Hall where the said almsmen have been before placed."—Deed of August, 1605.

The quarterages in 1663, when they came to the Merchant Taylors, realised 108*l*. 4*s*. 10*d*. net.

The fines must have varied considerably in total amount, and those from the calling to the Livery were dependent on the pleasure of the other Company, as to their grant of the Livery. As a rule, of the latter fine, any sum which was received in excess of 1*l*. 13*s*. 4*d*. (which was distributed as 1*l*. to the Merchant Company, 5*s*. to the Master, 6*s*. 8*d*. to the Clerk, and 1*s*. 8*d*. to the Beadle) went to the Bachelors, towards the relief of their poor.[1] In exceptional cases another division would be made by the Merchant Company, thus in 1609-10,[2] when twenty-eight new Liverymen were called on a fine of 30*l*. each, but only 838*l*. 6*s*. 8*d*. was realised to the Merchants, of which 500*l*. was paid to the Bachelor's Company, and the residue retained in their own Treasury.[3] Again in March, 1618, 106*l*. was paid to the Bachelors out of 206*l*. raised by the Merchant Company.

By order of December, 1619, the whole brotherhood money or first year's quarterage money raised from the Livery, viz., for 244 received into the brotherhood at the rate of 3*s*. 4*d*. a man = 40*l*. 13*s*. 4*d*., was paid to the Wardens Substitute, and for many years a similar payment was made. Then an annual donation from the Merchant Company was paid and increased by order of the Court. In October, 1630, the sum paid was fixed at 60*l*.,[4] to be distributed quarterly by the Wardens Substitute and Sixteen Men amongst the "poor brethren and sisters of the Fraternity and *none others*," and "for divers years prior to July, 1645," the annual allowance had been increased to 150*l*.

The distribution of this sum to the poor was left wholly to the discretion of the Wardens Substitute for the time being, who, in sums varying from 2*s*. 6*d*. to 1*s*., gave it every three months to some of the poor living in the quarter over which each had the oversight. The only certainty was the amount to be distributed in each quarter, which was fixed, as in Watling Street, 6*l*. 5*s*. 0*d*.; in Candlewick 6*l*. 15*s*. 0*d*.; in Fleet Street 10*l*., and in Merchant Taylors' Hall 14*l*. 10*s*. 0*d*., but who were to be the recipients

---

[1] See entries in Court Minutes of the 7th June, 1595; 24th April, 1610.
[2] Order of Court, 23rd May, 1610.
[3] Order, 20th June, 1610.
[4] In 1640 two separate payments of 60*l*. were made to two of the Wardens Substitute on different occasions, to be employed "in the affairs of the Company," not probably for the poor."

depended on the selection of an officer who was changed every year, and this chance or uncertainty lessened the good of the gift to those who ultimately received it, and created numberless beggars all hoping to receive it. What was the number of these casual applicants is not recorded, but the Court sensibly adopted this better course, which is laid down in the Minute of 15th July, 1645: The Wardens Substitute and Sixteen Men do "reduce the n° of such poor wh receive that Charity to 300 of the fittest persons wh may receive 2s. 6d. for the next quarter only, and discharge the Books of all the rest, and if upon exam^n of those persons p^{r}sented and paid by the Ward. Sub. and 16 Men wh are the fittest persons to be continued to receive that Charity during theire life by 2s. 6d. quarterly payments then they are to be continued, & as any of them die another to be chosen in the room of the dec̄ed once every year, as the free *noble pensioners*[1] are, and the choice to be in the beginning of Decr yearly, and we think fit that a Com̄ee of the Court join the Ward. Sub. and 16 Men to choose the poor people in the places void."

Either the inability of the Merchant Company to pay more, or the lessened needs of the poor may have led to the reduction of this annual grant; from the minutes of a Court of the 3rd May, 1654, we fear the former, as the Report of a Committee appointed for mitigation of the Company's charge suggested "that, whereas heretofore there hath been allowed to the M^r of this Society the sum of 20l. per ann. to be by him distributed to the poor, that for the time to come there be allowed the sum of 10l. only . . . . . . that no more pensioners that receive 2s. 6d. per quarter be admitted until the Company be better able and think it convenient . . . . . ."

Possibly, as consequent on this recommendation (for the Court records are missing from 1654 to 1663), we find in the Master's accounts these smaller sums entered:—"1655-6.[2] Paid to the Wardens Substitute, which was distributed by them to — poor people of this Company at 2s. 6d. a piece quarterly 131l. 10s. 0d." In 1656-7 125l. 5s. 0d. In 1659-60, 105l. 5s. 0d. And in 1663, after the Wardens Substitute had ceased to act, the Merchant Company made these payments to the poor. "Paid to 77 poor persons of this Company at Michaelmas and Christmas, and to 74 at Lady day and Midsummer by 6s. 8d. a piece, as by book appeareth,

---

[1] No explanation suggests itself as to the persons here referred to, unless they be the "Almsmen of the Livery" or Dowe's.

[2] In several years 6l. 13s. 4d. is charged in the Master's accounts as fines for not enrolling apprentices, paid to poor people.

100*l.* 13*s.* 4*d.*" (which is 7*l.* 11*s.* 6*d.* less than the net quarterages received); and "Paid 133 people of the said Company at Michaelmas, and 131 at Christmas, to 129 at Lady day, and 126 at Midsummer by 2*s.* 6*d.* a piece, 64*l.* 17*s.* 6*d.*"

Over the Bachelors' treasury the Merchant Company exercised a supreme control. Thus, Mr. Albany and Mr. Dowe having in December examined their treasury to see what store of money was therein, the Court on the 24th February, 1585, "ordered and agreed that 400*l.* shalbe borrowed of the Wardens Substitute to be taken out of ther Treasurie, *never* to be paid them againe, but to be imployed and bestowed uppon and towards the buildinge of the hall."

Again, when the Lord Mayor's precept was sent to the Merchant Company, they decided what proportion of the sum assessed should be raised from the Bachelor Company, and required the Wardens Substitute or special members named by the Master and Wardens to collect the sum and pay it to the Merchant Company to be sent in to the Lord Mayor by them.

In the interests of the Yeoman Taylors the organisation was not successful, as it led to disputes between the four Substitutes and the Sixteen Men in regard to their conduct towards each other. At the opening of the 17th century the trade appears to have been overrun with foreigners, and the Yeomen came to the Merchant Company for its assistance. Legislation was proposed and the subject referred to a Special Committee, who reported in December, 1601, against any application being made to Parliament, but suggested that the powers which the Company held were sufficient if they were put in exercise, and recommended that application should be made to the Lord Mayor for authority to commit offenders.

Soon after the report had been presented to the Company the Army contracts for clothing were obtainable, in February, 1601, and the Wardens Substitute, with others of the Bachelor Company solicited the Merchant Company to procure from Her Majesty the providing of the Brabant work or soldiers' apparell which Mr. Bromeley[1] and Mr. Babington, who were members of the Company, have for many years done, and which would be the means for setting a number of poor freemen to work and expelling of foreigners. The Merchant Company doubted if the contracts would not bring much trouble to them, but they entreated certain

---

[1] We had three Bromleys who were Freemen—Robert, 16th January, 1561; John, 16th September, 1575; and George, 29th January, 1592; and five Babingtons—Anthony, 22nd May, 1559; William, 2nd May, 1567; Richard, 2nd March, 1581; Ury, 4th September, 1615; Thomas (per Anna Turner), 25th October 1637.

of their members to meet and consider what they should think fit to be done therein, and on the 24th April, 1602, such a meeting was held, which resolved "that it would prove a 'matter likely to bring great trouble and loss to this house,' and advised the Company by no means to meddle therewith." The contract became one notorious for fraud, and brought trouble upon Babington and Bromeley, for in Trinity term, 1608, one Beecher sued them for his share of the profits made under the contract, and in the action it appeared that the contractors had defrauded the Crown to the extent of 180,000*l.*, whereupon the Attorney-General (Bacon[1]) filed an information in Trinity term, 1615, against them.

In 1608 disputes and mutual recriminations arose between the Substitutes and Sixteen Men. The latter, when accused by the former of wasting the money of the House in public-house meetings, and of usurpation of authority, answered that their usual allowance of 10*s.* for the quarterly meetings had been withheld from them, and that if extravagant, their administration had been successful, for since they held office the foreigners[2] had been diminished by 1,000 in number, and their yearly collections raised from 88*l.* 12*s.* 10*d.* to 122*l.* 8*s.* 10*d.*, and the poor of the Fraternity, to whom these fines were distributed, thereby proportionately benefitted. However, the presence of a common enemy in some strength in London (the Dutch and French Tailors) led to an agreement, first with the foreigners (which will be hereafter referred to[3]), and then with each other, both sanctioned by the Merchant Company.

The difficulty then, as in times since, seems to have arisen from sumptuary expenses, and the unwillingness of the poorer members to control themselves or be controlled by others. There was "great want and necessity of the poor," and the Bachelors were to be "admonished and entreated to be frugal and sparing in their expenses and to keep as few dinners at the charges of the house as conveniently they might," an injunction which leads to the conclusion that the Bachelors had a greater power to incur such an expenditure than the Merchant Company. The agreement, therefore, had more reference to these sumptuary expenses than to other matters.

---

[1] Hall's Elizabethan Age, page 124.

[2] Orders from the Lord Mayor and Privy Council to the citizens to behave courteously to foreigners were not unfrequent. See 8th March, 1573, and 14th March, 1580. In this year the residents were 6,462, being an increase of 3,762 in 13 years.—3 Nichol's Elizabeth, page 56. But what are here meant are non-freeman.

[3] Chapter IV.

Firstly. The Treasury was to be put into the hands of the Substitutes as representing the Master and Wardens.

Secondly. The Treasury chest was to be kept with four locks to the chest and four locks to the two doors of the Treasury, and eight keys to be kept by these persons, viz., the four door keys by two Substitutes and two of the Sixteen Men (having Candlemas and Watling Street quarters), and the other four keys by other two and two (having the Fleet Street and Merchant Taylors quarters).

Thirdly. The Substitutes to keep proper accounts for audit by the two upper Livery Wardens and two of the Sixteen Men.

Fourthly. Certain matters of precedence were then settled, and that two of the Sixteen with their Clerk and Bedel with two others employed against foreigners should meet every other Monday for business, and a dinner at 10s. at the cost of the house.

Fifthly. The quarters were then readjusted, the "Stranger's" dinner[1] was abolished, but an annual Star Chamber decree dinner was established for the Substitutes and Sixteen Men at the cost of 3l. 6s. 8d.

Sixthly. The "Shooting" dinner "as of ancient contynuance was sanctioned at a cost of 8l. to the house, besides 13s. 4d. called "Mr. Dowe, his mite."

And lastly. "As all victualls are growne to a very high rate," it was ordered that the four Substitutes should keep only four Quarter dinners on St. Luke's, All Saints, Christmas, and St. Mathias ("with moderate chere without excuse or drawing any great company to the hall"), and an audit dinner on Trinity Tuesday.

In August following, a special agreement was made that the "great dinner for the generality" (usually held every third year and now in arrear to the sixth year) should be held on the next "Decollation Day," and so these amicable agreements were consummated.

A few sentences will complete the history of the Bachelors Company, as other controversies arose. In 1623, freemen ceased to be summoned to the quarterly courts, and as the tailor element felt that no encouragement was given to their craft, they asked in 1642 (not unreasonably) that two of the Substitutes should be of their trade, and that orders against foreigners should be put in force at the cost of the Fraternity. But the monopoly could not be maintained, and the machinery of the Bachelors Company was too expensive a remedy for what was irremediable, therefore in 1661

---

[1] This dated as far back as 1390.—Memorials, page 67.

the Merchant Company refused to swear in the Substitutes, and took the business into their own hands. For a time their organisation remained in abeyance, but on the 13th August, 1663, the Court took their several officers into employment and settled the remuneration to be paid to them for the collection of quarterages. They awarded to John Milner, Clerk, 10*l*. per annum for his pains and care; to John Sutton and Henry Halliman, the two collectors of quarterages, an allowance of 3*s*. per 1*l*. for all such monies as they shall receive, and that Sutton (in lieu of all allowances that were heretofore paid him by the Wardens Substitute) shall have a salary of 8*l*. per annum from the Merchant Company.

The Court of Common Council (to whom an appeal was made) upheld the action of the Merchant Company, after the parties to the controversy represented by Counsel[1] had been fully heard. From this decision of the Common Council, the Bachelors Company appealed by petition to the Privy Council, but beyond making a reference in January, 1696, of their petition to the Law Officers of the Crown for report no order was made by the Council, and thus the separate organisation of the Bachelors Company ceased to exist, and all their records have been lost or destroyed.

NOTE referred to at page 65, and see page 314, note.
The sums received on each occasion are given in the Merchant Taylors' accounts as follows:—

	"Sir R. Lee. 1602.			Sir L. Halliday. 1605.		
	£	s.	d.	£	s.	d.
Received of Bachelors in Foynes..	133	6	8	120	0	0
„ Budge..	130	0	0	96	0	0
By assessment in Watling Street Quarter	176	4	0			
Candlewick Street	112	18	9	329	19	8
Fleet Street	67	9	4			
Merchant Taylors	100	2	10			
	720	1	7	545	19	8
Received of the Lord Mayor and Sheriffs	13	0	0	[2]30	0	0
Stuff over	1	7	0	—		
	734	8	7			
Excess payments over receipts paid out of Master's Account..	12	14	3			
Received from sundry brothers of the Company	—			33	0	0
From the Treasury of the Bachelors..	—			100	0	0
An extra assessment upon the Bachelors	—			25	0	0
	747	2	10	733	19	8"

[1] Memorials, page 229.
[2] This was made up of 20*l*. from the Lord Mayor and 20*l*. from the Master (Juxon) for a dinner to the Bachelors, and see page 334, note 2.

CHAPTER IV.

THE STAR CHAMBER AS TO THE LONDON CORPORATION AND GUILDS.

*Star Chamber Jurisdiction relating to London, p. 75.—Eden's case, p. 76.— As to Corporation, p. 76.—As to Guild, p. 76.—Foreign Workmen, p. 77.— Statutes of Henry VIII, p. 77.—Report as to foreigners, p. 78.—Samuel Pepys' father admitted to the Merchant Taylors Company, p. 79.—Dutch and French Taylors, p. 79.—Agreement with them, p. 80.—Meeting of the Company to hear Star Chamber decrees, p. 80.—*Note. *List of Clerks and Beadles, 1397 to 1624.*

THE Records of the Merchant Taylors Company furnish abundant evidence of the interference of the Star Chamber in the affairs of the Corporation of London and its Guilds in two aspects:

First, as a Court of Appeal from the decisions of the Corporation and Guilds.

Second, as directing the course to be taken by the Guilds towards foreign workmen of their craft.

I. It may be premised of the Star Chamber's jurisdiction that the King, as the fountain " of justice, exercised his jurisdiction originally in the *concilium ordinarium*, out of which proceeded the Chancery and Common Law Courts, acting under a delegated authority from the King." In regard to matters not coming under the direct cognizance of these Courts, the King's prerogative was held to be in force, and over these matters he exercised judicial authority through the Court ultimately termed (from the ceiling of the room in which its sittings were held) the Star Chamber.

The proceedings were taken at the instance of the King's officers or of private subjects, and were either *ore tenus*—that is, by summons for personal appearance before the Court (of which Sir Thomas White's case is an instance), when the defendant was often dealt with summarily—or by bill, subpoena, and answer as analogous to Chancery, of which Eden's case (*infra*) is an instance.

Any person from whom the payment of costs could be enforced was allowed to appear as plaintiff, and therefore discontented members of a corporation, or the governors of such, could invoke its assistance. "If a corporation (writes Hudson) be rent asunder by faction, and by wilful and heady practice displacing their officers, the Court would restore and punish, as in the Dyers' case (17 Henry VIII), and so if a troublesome man disquiet the rest (as Dunning, the pewterer, in 3 James I) the Court would punish him."

The matters dealt with by the Court were so undefined, and its decisions so unjust and so irrevocable, that the Court as an intolerable grievance, was suppressed.

The Star Chamber claimed to be a Court of Revision and Appeal from the judgment of inferior tribunals, and of this Eden's case, preserved in the records of the Merchant Taylors Company, is an illustration. Eden was admitted a Freeman of the Company on April 24th, 1556, by apprenticeship to Henry Suckley, and entered into partnership with a worthy Freeman, one George Toppe (Warden in 1580-4, Master in 1587), against whom he appears to have instituted a suit in the Lord Mayor's Court in or about 1573, which was ultimately settled by the award of Walter Fish (the Master) acting with the Wardens, on November 23rd, 1573. Like an ill-conditioned fellow, as he probably was, Eden went to the Star Chamber on bill, alleging against Walter Fish and his colleagues perjury and divers other misdemeanours, of which the Court held that there was no proof at all, but on the contrary that the Master and Wardens had acted simply and plainly with the parties' full consent, and without any manner of corruption or suspicion, and the case was dismissed with costs.

But surely not only should the case have been dismissed from the Court, but the man from the Company, if Dunning the pewterer was justly treated. However, instead of the Star Chamber suggesting this course, the Lord Chancellor advised the Company to confer a pension upon him, and as a craving suppliant he obtained it.[1]

II. The relationship which the City Guilds held towards the foreign craftsmen in former days is a matter of interest. The common halls are large ones almost of necessity, as they had to receive all the workmen of their trade, whether home or foreign, to hear from time to time the decrees of the Star Chamber, which regulated their mutual relationship.

---

[1] Appendix 14, pages 363-6.

Two statutes, passed A.D. 1523 and 1529, have a direct bearing on the subject. The first Act, viz., the 14 and 15 Henry VIII, c. 2, prohibited aliens from taking alien apprentices or from keeping more than two alien journeymen. It placed aliens using any handicraft and living in London under the search of the Wardens of the Craft, and one substantial householder of the same Craft chosen by the Wardens, and it authorised the Wardens to give the aliens a mark, which the aliens were bound to use upon their goods to distinguish them.

Should the Wardens abuse their authority the alien was to obtain relief by bill to the Lord Chancellor and Lord Treasurer, or to the Justices of Assize—words sufficient to give the Star Chamber jurisdiction.

After a few years' experience the Act was found not to work well, as the substantial householder either would not attend the search, or, if he did, gave the alien such early notice that he could, if so disposed, square all things before the search was made. The Act was, in fact, evaded, and the London artificers appealed to the Star Chamber for redress. The subject was under consideration of the Court on February 20th, 1528-9, and the result was further legislation on the lines laid down and recommended by its decree.

The second Act, 26 Henry VIII, c. 16 (1529), setting forth and exemplifying the Star Chamber decree, enabled aliens to employ natives as servants or apprentices without limitation of numbers, but subjected aliens to all the impositions and charges (imperial and local) which others of the same craft were liable to. It provided that all householders, strangers, or artificers resident in the city, or within two miles, should, on summons from the Wardens of the Craft, join in making search, under the first Act, and on refusal made them liable to be summoned for fine before the Lord Chancellor or Lord Mayor. Further, on summons from the Wardens, they were to present themselves at the "Common Hall of the Craft," and to be sworn before the Master and Wardens to be faithful and true to the King, to be obedient to all acts and decrees made by the King or Council. They were also to make search under the Act, and not to give prior notice or warning to the strangers of the intended search.

It was under the authority of this statute that foreign taylors were taken into the Fraternity and sworn in allegiance to the King, and to be a "loving brother" of the Merchant Taylors; the fruit of

---

[1] Appendix 15, page 366.

which was to be a donation (in life or at death) to the Fraternity or their priests and poor almsmen.

Denizens only were to be permitted to take shops in the city for the exercise of their craft, and alien artificers were prohibited from assembling in any company, fellowship, congregation, or conventicle, but only in the "Common Hall" with native subjects which be of the Company of the craft, and at such time as they should be commanded and warned by the Master and Wardens, and at none other place or time, or in any other manner.

Therefore it was that the "Common Hall" became the centre of all craftsmen, whether native or strangers, connected with the trade of the Merchant Taylors Company, and the place from which all rules and regulations concerning the craft were promulgated.

From early times the foreign workmen pressed very heavily upon the native craftsmen, taking work from them and keeping down the price of wages, so that proclamations were frequently issued and addressed to the citizens from the Sovereign and Lord Mayor requiring them to keep the peace towards them.

At the close of the Tudor period their presence became so intolerable that some remedial measures had to be adopted, and a Committee of the Court was appointed in December, 1601, the summary of whose report, dated the 6th, may be thus given :—

"Report of Committee against foreigners and strangers.—Application made to Parliament rejected.—The charters searched for authority, considered to be ample—no direct punishment appointed —considered to be at the discretion of the M^r and Wardens and the Lord Mayor—application to the Lord Mayor recommended for authority to commit offenders.—Master and Wardens to meet weekly, or to revive an ancient custom, some of the Bachelors' Company to meet every Monday fortnight.—This Committee to consist of four Wardens Substitute and two of the Sixteen Men.— To make search throughout the City (according to authority of their ancient charter) for foreigners and strangers making garments, to seize and carry such garments to the Chamberlain.—To summon all offenders before them, and freemen in default of appearance at the hall on quarter days and at burials, and that pay not their quarterage in due time, and all other lawfull demands.—To report all offenders to the Master and Wardens, to be dealt with at their discretion according to their offence.—Those that are ancient dwellers and married, and have children born within this City, or otherwise thought fit, shall, upon consideration had, be admitted into this Company (but not made free of the City), and so suffered to work. Foreign Bachelors now come into the City, or otherwise thought fit to be removed, after warning given, by four at a time be committed to the counter, upon the Lord Mayor's commandment, no further fine to be taken of them than the Chamberlain takes for garments found in their hands on Serch days. The care and zeal of this Committee commended, and their suggestions approved, with request that they may be done with gravity, judgment, and consideration, and the Master and Wardens to be informed from time to time of their proceedings."

And before passing from this entry we may mention another in connection with it, viz., the admission of "John Pepys," the father of Samuel Pepys, F.R.S. (the Diarist of Charles II's reign) to be a member of the Merchant Taylors Company, under the authority which this decree gives for admitting foreign taylors as members. It is in these words :—

"16th November, 1653.   Admission of Forren Tailors.

"This day R. Cumberland, and *John Pepys*, William Gyles, J. Waine, Robert Trevethen, Thomas Christmas, Edward Martin, and William Foster, forreiners, cutting tailors, inhabiting in Salisbury Court, Whitefriars and Blackfriars, were admitted free Brothers of this Company according to an ancient order of this Court of 6th December, 1601. And they presented the Company with their several pieces of plate following, viz.: R. Cumberland gave one silver tankard; J. Pepys gave one silver tankard and a trencher salt; W. Gyles, two silver cups; J. Waine, one silver tankard; R. Trevethen, one great salt and a trencher salt; T. Christmas, one silver bowl with the Company's arms; Edward Martin, one dozen spoons; and William Foster, three silver porringers, of all which this Court accepted.[1]

But the peace resulting from these measures suggested by the Company was of short duration, the Merchant Taylors endeavoured to expel the Dutch and French tailors who had come over for freedom and liberty of conscience, and had not the elders of the Dutch and French churches made application to the Privy Council for protection, might have succeeded, but after a conference with the Merchant Taylors Company a concordat was agreed upon.

The question affected the Yeomen or working rather than the Merchant Taylors, and therefore it was left a good deal to the Wardens Substitute and the Sixteen Men to manage. After a full

---

[1] I am indebted to Mr. Harcourt A. F. Chambers, of the Merchant Taylors Company, for bringing this and many other entries used in this work to my notice.

discussion a definite agreement under seal was come to with the foreigners on the 13th January, 1608.

"To this assembly resorted Sir Noel de Caron,[1] Ambassador to the State of the Lowe Countries, and fower Elders, viz'., two of the Dutch church, and two of the French church, and in the presence of two of the Warden Substitutes and fower of the Sixteen men. After a long discourse and many objections, *pro et contra*, it was in thend concluded and agreed as in and by certen articles of agreement Indented under the hands of the said parties, whereof one parte remayneth with the said Ambassador and thother wth this Company, and the copy thereof being entered in a faier vellum book remayning with the Warden Substitutes."

About the same time a disagreement arose between (the somewhat discordant elements of) the Merchant and the Taylor Companies, and terms of agreement had to be arranged between them.

The dinners of the Taylors had come to be allowed for out of the Treasury, and the expense had to be curtailed, but, as bearing upon our subject, which was dealt with in the last chapter, we need only refer to the "Strangers" dinner, given when the foreigners were summoned to hear the "Star Chamber" decrees, that they might, as policy required, be kept in good humour.

"Forasmuch as the Dynner yerely kept for the entertaining of strangers groweth to a great charge, and no reason that the strangers should be better entertained then the King's naturall subject. It is therefore ordered that the same Dynner shall be no longer kept. Nevertheless it is agreed that the House shal allow 3*l*. 6*s*. 8*d*. for a Dynner for the Wardens Substitute and Sixteene men upon the day that the strangers be yerely somond to appear before them to hear the Decree in the Star Chamber, and the orders lately agreed upon to be read before them."[2]

It may be noticed that the members of the Star Chamber, like those of the Merchant Taylors Court, dined together after each sitting, and the expense of the Star Chamber dinners are set out in the authorities quoted.

---

[1] This gentleman was ambassador for thirty-four years for the Netherlands in Elizabeth's and James I's reigns. He had a handsome house at South Lambeth (site of Beaufort's Distillery), with a deer park, where in July, 1599, he entertained Elizabeth. He was a donor to Lambeth parish, and in 1615 founded almshouses at Vauxhall, for seven poor women, with an annual pension of 4*l*. each. His house is shown in maps of the present century. He died in December, 1624.—Rye's England, page 251.

[2] The Star Chamber papers are to be published by the Record Commissioners, but till then see Hudson's Treatise (1635) printed Hargrave's Coll. Jur., vol. 2, and Mr. Bruce's paper in vol. 25 Archæologia, and cases printed in 32 (N.S.) Camden Coll., 1886.

List of Clerks and Beadles of the Livery.[1]

Date of Appointment.	Clerk.	Beadle.
Before 1397 1403 1420 1427	John Brenchele. — Nicholas Hoper. —	David Kelby. John Wenge (or Wynge)[1] Thomas Swaby (or Swatheby).
Before 1452 1453 1456 1462 1464	Nicholas Mille. William Bouchier. Thomas ffililode. — Thomas Kirton.	Reginald Burgate. Peter Ferrys.
Before 1492 1493	William Duryvale. Henry Mayour.	Thomas Gresyle.
Before 1512	—	William Erle.
Before 1545 1546 1569 1571 1575 1579 1586 1587 1590 1594 1598 1610 1621 1624	Roger Wylson. John Huchenson. — Nicholas Fuljambe. Thomas Hazelfote. — Barnabas Hilles. Richard Wright. — Richard Langley. — Richard Baldock. — Clement Mosse.	Thomas Carne (or Can). Richard Corryndon (or Carryngton). Francis Yoman. Robert Dowle. Edward Thruxton. Nicholas Hurdys. Robert Churchman.

[1] Mr. Chambers has furnished this list.

CHAPTER V.

THE HALL AND ITS CONTENTS.

*The Hall, antiquity, p. 82.—Purchase in 1331, p. 83.—Sir O. Ingham tenant thereof, p. 84.—Ingham's Hall rebuilt, p. 84.—Hall in 1575, p. 84.—Ambassadors lodged in (1518 and 1619), p. 85.—Fire of London, p. 85—Dates of different parts of the Building, p. 85.—Description of the Hall, p. 86.—Saltpetre diggers, p. 87.—Floor covered with rushes, p. 87.—Erasmus's description, p. 87.—Flooring of Hall, p. 87.—Glazed in 1419, p. 87.—Inventories of 1512 and 1609 as illustrating two distinct periods, p. 88.—St. John Baptist's Statue, p. 88.—Tapestry, p. 89.—Furniture, p. 90.—Table trestles, p. 90.—Laying the Cloth, p. 90.—Plate of 1491, p. 91.—" The Jowell House," p. 91.—Basyns and Ewres, p. 92.—Saltes, p. 93.—Spones, pp. 93 and 94.—Stondyng Cuppes, p. 95.—Pottes, p. 96.—Bolles, p. 97.—Plate for kepyng of Obyttes, and Masers, p. 98.—One knife, p. 99.—" The Parloure," p. 99.—St. John's Statue, p. 99.—Tapestry, p. 99.—Sir John Skevington's will (note), p. 99.—Furniture, p. 100.—For Funerals, p. 101.—For Triumphs, p. 102.—The Yard, p. 102.—Almery, p. 102.—The King's Chamber, p. 103.—The Kitchen and the Larder, p. 104.—The Pastry, p. 104.—The Buttery, p. 104.—The Storehouse, p. 105.—No Napery, p. 105.—No Glass, p. 105.—Pewter, p. 106.—Butler, p. 106.—Additions in 1609, p. 106.—The Brasse, p. 107.—The Lynnen, p. 107.—Clock in the yard, p. 108.—Armour, p. 109.—*NOTE *as to the dimensions of the Hall, p. 109.*

FOLLOWING upon the incorporation of the Guild in 1327 was the acquisition of the Hall premises in 1331, in which during succeeding centuries the corporate life of the guildsmen has been passed. Therefore it may be well before entering upon the record of the doings of these citizens to gather up some particulars of the Hall premises in which they passed much of their time and with which their labours for the craft are closely associated. The incidents in which they bore part will be better realized if we can make ourselves familiar with the Hall (in which they assembled the Fraternity) and its contents.

The Hall from the necessity for accommodation must have been large, as the place not only for the annual festival of St. John, at which many guests and all the Fraternity attended, but also for the assembling of all craftsmen, native or foreign, that were affiliated to the Company.

It would be interesting if we could determine with accuracy whether any and what parts of the present Hall premises are the same as those in which Sir John Percyvale, Sir Stephen Jenyns and other worthies conducted the Company's affairs during their masterships; but though we believe them to be so, yet the Company's records afford no positive proof of the fact.

The property was purchased by the Company of Crepin in the year 1331.[1] "It is needless to remind you that at that time no Bank of England, no Royal Exchange, no Mansion House, no Guildhall existed, but we had three grand religious foundations around us—St. Austin's, St. Helen's, and St. Antholin's—the pigs of which latter house often, we have no doubt, were found in our stable and on our dunghill. You must think of London as of a small city surrounded (as York and Lancaster now are) with walls and well-guarded gates. What the Merchant Taylors Company acquired in 1331 is carefully set out in the conveyance deed enrolled at Guildhall. Threadneedle-street sprang from our subsequent occupation as we abutted on Broad Street (then what its name signified), with a garden, stable, &c., in the rear, having a gate opening upon Cornhill. What adjacent residences then existed are facts not easily traceable, but their usual surroundings were open gardens, for when in later years Sir W. Pawlett and Lord Cromwell built their houses in the ward, they had large gardens.[2] In Cheapside a tournament was held in the year following our acquisition, at which Edward III and Queen Phillippa were pre-

---

[1] From a paper read in Merchant Taylors' Hall on the 8th day of December, 1886.

[2] The injustice which Cromwell, then "Sir Thomas," inflicted on Stowe's father, his son thus describes :—" On the south side, and at the west end of this church, many fair houses are built ; namely, in Throgmorton Street, one very large and spacious, built in the place of old and small tenements by Thomas Cromwell, master of the king's jewel-house, after that, master of the rolls, then Lord Cromwell, knight, lord privy seal, vicar-general, Earl of Essex, high chamberlain of England, &c. This house being finished, and having some reasonable plot of ground left for a garden, he caused the pales of the gardens adjoining to the north part thereof on a sudden to be taken down; twenty-two feet to be measured forth right into the north of every man's ground; a line there to be drawn, a trench to be cast, a foundation laid, and a high brick wall to be built. My father had a garden there and a house standing close to his south pale; this house they loosed from the ground, and bare upon rollers into my father's garden twenty-two feet, ere my father heard thereof; no warning was given him, nor other answer, when he spake to the surveyors of that work, but that their master, Sir Thomas, commanded them so to do ; no man durst go to argue the matter, but each man lost his land, and my father paid his whole rent, which was 6s. 6d. the year, for that half which was left. Thus much of mine own knowledge have I thought good to note, that the sudden rising of some men causeth them to forget themselves."

sent. Walbrook ran as a clear stream. The Maypole stood in Leadenhall, and the Ton for incontinent priests in the centre of Cornhill."

"What kind of premises we acquired may be judged of by the social position in London of the occupying tenant whom we succeeded. His name was Oliver de Ingham, first a knight and then a peer of Parliament. Born of a Norfolk family, and coming to his inheritance at 23, he became a great soldier and was the Seneschal of Gascony, then one of the guardians of the realm, and in 1328 (when resident here) a Royal Commissioner with the Lord Mayor to enquire into the City riots. The notable exploit of his life was the defence of Bordeaux against the French king (Philip) in 1340, when, by inviting the enemy within the gates, he captured them with a slender garrison. His occupation of our hall was from 1327 to 1331, in which latter year he was again sent on foreign service, and there died in 1344. In the village church at Ingham is to be seen his effigy, with his gilt spurs and the order of the Garter.[1]"

"Ingham's Hall, it is thought, was replaced in the fourteenth century by the present Hall, and no traces of his original hall are to be found, unless they are the kitchen or chapel and a crypt leading thereto from the street. The fire of 1666 burnt down the houses standing in front of the Hall in Threadneedle-street, but stopped at St. Martin's Church, which was slightly injured. It did not reach to the houses in Bishopsgate-street, but the hall was so injured as to need a new roof and general restoration, the area and general arrangement stand, it is thought as they existed when James I was entertained in 1607."[2]

We are not aware of any particular description of the Hall by any writer contemporary with the Tudor period, save in a MS. History of London,[3] by W. Smith, Citizen and Haberdasher, who, writing in 1575, describes the Hall "as of stone and of such byggnes that it passeth all the Halles in London for beauty and comlyness."[4] This description could scarcely apply to Crepin's

---

[1] Other incidents in his life are given in Part 2, Chapter I.

[2] I have examined all the extant leases granted before and after the fire that are held by the Company, and the text is the result. Other particulars as to the entertainment are given *in extenso*.—Chapter XVI, page 275, *post*.

[3] Possessed by Simpson Rostron, Esq., of the Inner Temple, London.

[4] In the Rutland Papers (Camden Society, 1842) there is a list of "lodgings" appointed for the Emperor Charles V and his retinue, when he visited London in 1522. Four of the Companies' Halls are described, but not the Merchant Taylors'. The accommodation which each house would afford, in rooms and feather beds, is given. A good proportion of the houses had "Halls" and "Chapels."—Page 86.

CHAP. V.] *Ambassadors lodged in* 1518 *and* 1619. 85

dwelling-house of 1331, and therefore at some time prior to 1575 the Hall which W. Smith refers to must have been built by the Merchant Taylors' Company.

Of the size of the Hall we have other incidental evidence.[1] It was used until 1502, alternately with the Grocers' Hall for the Mayor's Feast, and, like other Halls of the period, for the lodgement of ambassadors and other great men visiting London. The French ambassador who negotiated with Wolsey the four treaties of October, 1518, for the marriage of the Princess Mary with the Dauphin, the restitution of Tournay, the meeting of Henry and Francis in the Valley of Andern, and other matters, was quartered in the Hall. Upon the occasion of the Emperor Charles V's visit to London in 1522, the Emperor and his suite were lodged in the Blackfriars and Bridewell, and in the clergy-houses round St. Paul's, but in 1526 the ambassador from Scotland and in 1619 the Dutch ambassador[2] were lodged in it.

Leaving the date of the building for the present undecided, we will refer, by quotation, to the Company's records for the dates at which the Hall and the several rooms in and adjacent are mentioned thus :—

1. The gateway and solar over it in Cornhill (1331).
2. The chapel (1406–7).
3. The lord's chamber (great parlour), (1419).
4. The grand chamber (1422).
5. The hall (1406–7).
6. The pantry (1408).
7. The buttery (1433–4).
8. The larder (1408–9).
9. The scullery (1433–4).
10. The kitchen (1406–7).
11. The pastry—on Sital House (1408).
12. The chamber over the hall.
13. The laundry.
14. The bakehouse (oven), (1406).

---

[1] Note, page 109.

[2] Payments in Henry VIII's reign. To Sir John Daunce for provision made by him of wines, &c., at Tailor Hall, London, for the French ambassador, 134*l*. 19*s*. 10*d*. January, 1519.—For. and Dom. Letters, Henry VIII, vol. 3, page 1534. Richard Blakgrove (the Mercer), was the keeper of the Hall for that occasion.

1526, 12th July. 14 Henry VIII.—Hire of staff for Tailor Hall for the ambassador of Scotland.—2751, vol. 4, For. and Dom. Letters, Henry VIII, page 1228.

1619.—Dutch ambassadors.—Col. S. P., pages 8 and 486.

15. The brewhouse.
16. The gardener's house.
17. The stables (1422–3).
18. The clerk's chamber (1426–7).
19. Chequer (1421–2).
20. The spring (or well), (1421–2).
21. The storehouse (1426–7).
22. The ewery (treasury), (1422–3).
23. The wardrobe (cloth chamber), (1421–2).

This list is not exhaustive of the accommodation of the premises, while it must be noticed that the Hall stood in a garden (with a fountain and bowling green, grass plots, and allies), well cared for by the Company, and sufficiently private in 1625 as to induce the East India Company to solicit for the Lord Ambassador[1] from Persia "the liberty of walking therein for his recreation."

The present Hall is an accurate representation of one of the 14th century. In the arrangement of such we begin, writes Parker,[2] "with the dais or raised platform at one end, on which the high table was placed lengthways; in the centre was the seat of the lord, sometimes raised again in a separate chair. . . At one end of the dais in the recess stood the buffet, on which the plate was displayed, and opposite were two doorways, one to the cellars, and the other to the staircase leading to the saloon or principal chambers."

So far his description is exactly that of Merchant Taylors' Hall, and he proceeds with a closer analogy:—

"At the end of the Hall opposite to the dais was the screen, with the Minstrel's Gallery over it; and under the gallery was a passage through, with a door at each end. In the wall behind the screen there were three doors—to the kitchen (down a short flight of steps), to the buttery, and to the pantry or servants' apartments." Those who know the premises will be struck with the accuracy and applicability of this description to the present Hall and to that in which James I was entertained.

No chimney or fireplace exists, and the usual custom was to make the fire in the middle of the Hall,[3] and huge logs were piled

---

[1] He lived in Sir L. Halliday's house in Bishopsgate, and on 10th August, 1626, attended the funeral of his secretary, whose tomb was till lately to be seen in St. Botolph's Churchyard.—Vol. 10, p. 3, B. of E. and W. (1815), page 160, Bishopsgate Register, page 437. He was also entertained by the Company 20th March, 1625.

[2] Domestic Arch., Vol. II, page 39. [3] This was so here, page 49, *ante*.

upon the "andirons," and thrown upon the rere-dos or hearth, the smoke escaping from the louvre in the roof.[1]

In the year 1415-6 the Company made two chimney in their premises, and one of these in the Parloure, " for a pece of waynescote was framed " to cover it up.[2]

It will be noticed that the "fote pace" at the " high dais " was boarded, but that the dais was both matted and boarded, and so were the sides of the Hall, leaving the centre, or "Marsh" (to be covered with clean straw or rushes on the feast day of St. John's), for the convenience of the domestics or the display of pageants.

In the accounts of 1545-6 we find this entry: "Given in reward to my Lord Chancellor's officers (the Company's tenant, Lord Wriothesley, being Chancellor) to stay the saltpetre makers from turning up the floor of our Hall, 10s." Of English houses in Henry VIII's reign, Erasmus wrote thus: "The floors are in general laid with white clay and are covered with rushes,[3] occasionally removed, but so imperfectly that the bottom layer is left undisturbed, sometimes for twenty years, harbouring expectorations, vomitings, the leakage of dogs and men, ale droppings, scraps of fish, and other abominations not fit to be mentioned."[4] Before the floor was tiled the Court Minutes (July, 1646) describe it "as inconvenient and often times noisome"; which this entry in the Master's accounts for 1545-6 would seem to confirm : " Paid 10s. 2d. to 2 women for 12 days, taking 60 loads of rushes out of the Hall."

Rushes were used as early as 1399, and for the banquet to James I in 1607, Guy Robinson (who was reprimanded in July, 1595, for unseemly behaviour) supplied for the Hall upon that occasion twenty-four dozen of rushes at 3s. a dozen.

Late in the sixteenth century (November, 1587[5]) the Hall was ordered to be glazed, and the arms of benefactors to be set up at the cost of the Company, but from an entry in the account books for 1403-4 (Pour l'amendment de fenestre de glas, 3s.), and in 1419-20 (glazing the great window, 3l. 15s.) it would appear that glass[6] was used at an early period.

---

[1] Domestic Arch., Vol. II, page 39. [2] See Life of Percyvale, *post*.

[3] If clean ones were not provided for each new guest, the expression arose "that you did not care a rush for him," which has survived to the present day.

[4] Erasmus to Francis the Physician and Cardinal Wolsey, vol. 1, Brewer's Henry VIII, page 239, note.

[5] By a singular coincidence the Merchant Taylors Company adopted this course in November, 1887, as to their Library and Court Rooms.

[6] The cost of glass in the 15th century was 5d. per foot. When the Duke of Northumberland left his London house the windows were taken out and laid up ;

What were the furniture and garnishment of the Hall premises and how these were distributed in the different parts or rooms are shown in two Inventories of effects, the first taken originally in the year 1512 (but to which articles were subsequently added as they were acquired), and the other in 1609, taken under an express order of the Court of the 28th August in that year. These inventories represent two distinct periods of religion and manners; the first, say fifty years before, and the other fifty years after, the Reformation. The text is founded upon the first inventory, and the other is only used when distinct reference is made to it. In some particulars the differences in the inventories are noticeable. In 1609 all the religious emblems have been removed from the plate, and the statues of St. John, besides the splendid embroidered tapestry are not to be found on the premises. Some progress had been made in furniture, but still for the rooms and the banquets it is very sparse compared with our modern conveniences.

In the Hall, the place of assembly for the whole Fraternity at their Quarterly Courts, stood a statue of their patron saint John Baptist ("gilt standing in a Tabernacle also gilt") which was probably the gift of Henry, Earl of Northumberland, as we find 10s. paid to his servant in 1436 for bringing a statue of St. John to the Hall. This Earl was admitted to the honorary freedom of the Company in 1420, and was slain at the battle of St. Albans in 1455, as a follower of Henry VI.[1] "3 costrynges," *i.e.*, side pieces or hangings, "of red saye," probably of silk, "with borders stayned of the lyf of St. John hangyng there the more parte of the yere." Then "3 torches garnysshed hangyng afore St. John." The Hall at that time would seem to have been lit with wax, although candles date from the 13th century.

The distinguishing garnishment on the surrounding walls of the Hall was the embroidered tapestry, giving the incidents of the life and death of St. John Baptist, which Edmund Spenser may have often looked upon (Book 2, Canto ix). It is thus entered :

"Itm, 9 pieces of Arays richly made of the lyf of Saint John, wherof 2 of the first are made atte costes of the crafte, price 80*l*.

---

they appear to have been deemed more essential in Henry VIII's reign, when they became fixtures.—See Dom. Arch. (*passim*) and Northumberland's expenses (1512). Pickering, London (1827).

[1] See his life in Vol. 1, page 241, of The Annals of the House of Percy (1887).

"The 3de cloth of the same syde of the gyfte of Maistres Kateryn Pemberton,[1] whose soule God pardon, the price, 40*l.*"

After this follows the entry of Sir Stephen and Lady Jenyns and William Buk's gifts to the Company, which are thus described:

"The 3 clothes of the high doysse of the gyfte of the Right honourable Sir Stephen Jenyns, Knight, late Mayre of London, the price 100*l.* and aboue. And the last 3 clothes of the gyfte of the Right Worshipfull William Buk, late Maister of this fraternitee, decessed, on whom Jhu have mercy, price 123*l.*

"Whiche 9 Clothes of Arays are well lined with canvas, lyred lowped and corded, and ben putte in 9 seuerall bagges of canvas w strynges to them pertynent.

"Also the Right revered Dame Margaret, Wyfe of the forsaid Sr Sephen Jenyns, of hyr good mynde and zele that she bereth to this Company, hat gyffen a cloth of Saint John, richely browdered, sette vpon blewe velvet with a white Rose over the hed of Saint John, the sydes of grene velvet, browdered with floure de luces of venyce gold, and with thise Wordes browdered in golde *Entere tenere*, Which said clothe and all the forsaid 9 clothes of arays are remaynyng in a gret joyned chest w^t 2 lokkes, standyng in the Chapell."

Arras was introduced in the 14th century, and was often richly embroidered and used to furnish or ornament the back of th daïs. Frequently it was so costly that noblemen had it removed with them from one castle or mansion to another. Some appears to have been introduced into the Hall as early as 1421-2, when brackets were purchased for hanging it, and another part was bought in 1502. Looking at the vast cost of the gifts of Jenyns and W. Buk these were probably very fine specimens of the embroiderer's art.[2]

In the inventory of the great Hall in 1609 the images of St. John and the beautiful embroidered tapestry are not to be found, only "the nine pieces of arras" as "the hangings for the hall," with "nine bags wherein the same arras were kept." These pieces would appear from an earlier entry[3] of March, 1587, to have been 408

---

[1] This lady, the wife of Hugh Pemberton, was a donor of land still held by the Company in the Vintry, but lost sight of as a donor till 1885.

[2] The Hall was wainscotted in 1729, and what was left of the tapestry sold in 1736-2 to Mr. Deputy Tatem for 20*l.*—Memorials, page 37.

[3] Memorials, page 536.

Flemish olnes in length, and they were probably the same which survived the fire and were sold in Alderman Salter's mastership to Deputy Tatem for 20*l.*

The paucity of ordinary furniture contrasts strangely with our modern experience, but in the Inventory of the Earl of Northumberland for his two mansions of Wressel and Leckingfield, taken in the same year (1512), the furniture of the apartments consisted of nothing but long tables, benches, cupboards, and bedsteads. Thus the "great chamber" had one long table upon a frame, and a cupboard with a door; and the "Hall" sixteen great standing tables with six forms, three cupboards with two doors, but neither keys nor locks.

The boards and trestles were brought in by the domestics and made up into tables before each dinner, and the table was set out with great solemnity. Paul Hentzner in 1598 describes what he saw at Elizabeth's palace at Greenwich: "A gentleman entered the room bearing a rod and along with him another who had a table cloth, and after they had both knelt three times with the utmost veneration, he spread the cloth upon the table, and after kneeling again they both retired. Then came two others, one with the rod again and the other with a salt cellar, a plate, and bread, when they had knelt (as the others had done), and placed what was brought upon the table they too retired with the same ceremonies performed by the first."[1]

After dinner the tables were removed in the presence of the guests.[2] The Constable of Castile in his description of James I's banquet at Whitehall in 1604 writes: "The cloth having been removed, every one immediately rose up, the table was placed on the ground, and their Majesties standing upon it, proceeded to wash their hands, which is stated to be an ancient ceremony."[3]

The furniture of the Merchant Taylors' Hall was:—

"First an image of Saint John Baptist, gilt, standyng in a Tabernacle, gilt.

"Itm, 3 Costrynges of red Saye with borders steyned of the lyf of Saint John, haugyng there the more parte of the yere.

"Itm, the high table dormaunt[4] with a particion slydyng in the myddell.

---

[1] Rye's England, page 106, and see further Our English Home, page 36.
[2] Order, 1st July, 1588 (*post*).
[3] Rye, page 122.
[4] In Chaucer's description of the sumptuous Franklin he writes;
 "His table Dormaunt in his Halle alway
  Stood redy covered all the longe day."

" Itm, 9 double stoles Joyned with fote paces for the same table.

" Itm, a Joyned stole with a fote pace for thende of the same table.

" Itm, 4 syde tables dormaunt.

" Itm, 4 formes dormaunt.

" Itm, 4 formes remevable.

" Itm, 8 tables remevable.

" Itm, 3 torches garnysshed hangyng affore Saint John,[1]

" Itm, the high doysse matted and borded.

" Itm, both sydes of the said hall matted and borded.

" Itm, the fote pace atte high doysse borded thurgh oute.

" Itm, thall crested rownd aboute.

" Itm, a Cupborde with 4 fete in the South Wyndowe.

" Itm, in the Cupborde Room on the North syde 3 hawle paces for plate and a shelve bylowe.

" Itm, dyvers trestelles and stoles staked liying atte theste ende of the Hall."

The cupboard was the equivalent for our present buffet or sideboard, placed in a conspicuous position for the flagons and cups to be shown upon it. To serve at the sideboard was a post of honour. The absence of all chairs will be noticed, only " stoles " and forms being used. In 1609 only twelve great stoles belonging to the upper table are entered.

The earliest list of plate is A.D. 1491.[2] The contents are valued thus: White plate of 1,081 ozs. at 3s. 4d. the oz., 180l. 3s. 4d. The Nottes and Mazers had 52 ozs. and 2s. 8d. an oz., 6l. 18s. 8d. The gilt plate was 504 ozs. in weight and 3s. 8d. an oz., was in argent 147l. 8s., making a total of 334l. 10s., according to the entry.

But the plate of 1491 is included in the Inventory of 1512, many of the articles being set out in detail. It will be seen that the emblems were all more or less religious and frequently have a special reference to St. John Baptist.

The place of custody is thus described:—

" *The Jowell House.*

"First, a new Almery of waynescote, with 3 flores, 4 lokkes, and 6 keys of the prouysion and ordynance of the forsaid Maister Tresawell and his Wardeyns, for the conseruacion and sauf kepyng

---

[1] See an illustration of a torch before an Image. Wright's Domestic Manners, page 378.

[2] Purchases were made in 1428, amounting to 73l. 2s. 11d.—Memorials, page 62.

of the plate, jowelles, chartres, evydences, and munymentes concernyng and bilongyng to this fraternitee."

First in the enumeration are "Basyns and Ewres" which were essential articles of domestic use before James I's reign, when forks were introduced from Italy. The banquet being served both before and after its completion the attendants came with these articles and a napkin, offering them to each guest.

"Basyns and Ewres.[1]

"First, 2 gilt basyns of estate, with lambes and sonnes, pois togiders by the weight of troye (gift of W. Chapman, Master, 1428), 149 vnc.

"²Itm, 4 basyns of siluer parcell gilte, with lambes and sonnes in the botoms, pois togiders by the said weight, 191 vnc.

"²Itm, 4 ewres of siluer, with lyke tokens on the lyddes, pois togiders, 93 vnc.

"Itm, 3 basyns, with sterres and lambes in the botoms, pois togiders, 193 vnc. and di.

"Itm, 3 ewres, parcell gilt of the same makyng, with lambes on the liddes, pois, 87 vnc. and di.

"M^d that the Basyn and Ewer w^t tharmes of Mr. Hugh Pemberton,[3] late Aldreman (Master 1481), weyen togyders by the weight of Troye, 78 vnces lakkyng di qrt.

"Itm, of the gift of Master Henr. Dacres (Warden 1510), A Basyn and An Ewar of Siluer parsell gyft w^t his Armes in the Botom of the saied basyn, weyeng poiz."

It will be noticed that the Company possessed eleven basins, but in 1609 there were only seven in number of which one only bore the name of an old benefactor (Dacres), and other four were given by *new* benefactors (as Richard Maye, Master 1583; William Wilkes, 1592; Henry Lee, and Arthur Medlicote, Warden, 1604). Of ewers they possessed nine, of which seven only existed in 1609, and are accounted for as the basins have been. The old basins and ewers must, therefore, have been sold, or transferred to the Bachelors Company.

"The Saltes gilt." The Company had one large square salt and four others. The place in which the "salt" was fixed in the Hall

---

[1] John Stone, Warden in 1439, and Sheriff in 1464, was a donor of two Basons and Ewres. His widow, Margaret, gave a salt in 1465-6.

[2] Rose Swan (1498) gave two basons and two Ewres, weighing 174 ozs.

[3] Buried in St. Martin's, but now in St. Helen's, whose wife, Katherine, was a benefactress to the Company.

determined the seats of the guests. The principal guests were seated on the daïs, but the others at long tables in the body of the Hall; in the middle of each table stood the "great salt" and the guests were classed as they were placed either above or below the "salt." The better servants attended upon the first and the inferior on the other guests.

"*Saltes, gilt.*

"First, a large square salt, with a couer with torettes, and a lambe w^t a sonne on the pomell, pois, 70 vnc. and di.

"Itm, a square salt couered, with a pellycane on the knop, of the gyfte of Maistres Bate[1] (1418), pois, 42 vnc. and di.

"Itm, a round salt, gilt, couered, with a lambe and sonne on the pomell, pois, 44 vnc."

"Itm, 2 salters with a couer parcell gylt, chaced with sonnes and small roses of the biquest of Thomas Howden[2] (Warden 1494) late Master, weyen togyders 39 vnces and di.

In 1609 the same number but none of the old salts remained, one of the new being given in 1603 by Mr. Anthony Sprott, admitted to the Livery 21st August, 1602. The old salts weighed 195 oz. and the new 148 oz. only.

Then are entered:

"*Spones, gilt and white.*

"First, 6 spones of the gyfte of Mr. Barther Reed and Thomas Wyndowte, Shreffs (1497) (for the use of the hall for their dinner), w^t Saint John Baptist on the spones endes, pois togiders, 9 vnc. 3 quarters.

"Itm, 6 gilt spones, with wrethen knoppes, late Mr. Swannes ..

"Itm, 6 gilt spones, with strawbery knoppes, pois togiders ..
} 15 vnc.

"Itm, 6 gilt spones, with acornes, of the gyfte of John Herst (Warden 1490 and given in 1499), pois togiders, 10 vnc. quarter di.

"Itm, 2 gilt spones, with round knoppes and sonnes, pois, 3 vnc.

"Itm, a gilt spone, of the gyfte of Grey (a whole brother in 1495), with Saint John on the knoppe, and the stele graven w^t his name, 2 vnces di quarter lesse.

"Itm, spones, whyte, with Saint John vpon the knoppes, 12

---

[1] Ralph Bate was Master in this year, and Richard admitted to the freedom in 1485-6.

[2] See Bill in Chancery to recover this, Appendix 19, page 372.

dossen and one spone, pois togiders by the weight of troye, 181 vnc.

"Itm, 3 spones gylt, which Richard Barton gafe to thuse of this place for to haue his lees sealed w[t] the comen scale of the tent that he holdeth in Lumberd Strete, pois, 3 vnces.

"Itm, a gilt spone wt seint John of the gyft of Agnies Benet poys, 2 oz.

"Itm, 12 spones w[t] seint John of the gyfte of Alane Hubert, late deceased, weyen to gyders 20 vnces, quarter.

"Item, 1 dozen gilt spoons of the gift of Mr. John Wilkinson, Alderman (buried in St. Andrew's Undershaft), given in the time of John Goune, Master 1620, 26 oz. and 3 quarters."

One donor, the late Mr. Swannes, was a member of a family connected with the Company from 1399-40, as in the books of that year one "Johan Swayn, Taillour," is found entered as a confrère, paying 20s. for admission. John of the same name became Master in 1470 and Sheriff in 1485, and afterwards an Alderman; he died sometime before 1493, as in that year his widow, Rose, paid the Company (in the presence of Buk, Jenyns, and other worthies) 149l. 6s. 8d. (in gold and grotes) for establishing an obit under indenture with the Master and Wardens,[1] money which appears soon to have been spent in rebuilding the property of the Company in the Vintry. Another donor, Richard Barton, was probably the first lessee of part of the estate which Sir John Percyvale had devised to the Company in Lombard Street.

In the inventory of 1609 the spoons given by Hubert and Wilkinson are to be found. All the other spoons in the inventory of 1512 have disappeared, but these are entered as special gifts:—

"1 dozen spoons by John Pount, and 24 gilt spoons by our benefactor Robert Dowe, Master 1578."[2]

"Stondyng Cuppes," are then entered, which, with "Pottes and Bolles," were articles of necessity when glass and earthenware were not used. Many of these cups were gifts of guildsmen in commemoration of holding office: the earliest donation being that of John Fulthorp, who was Master in 1412; and one (Fener's) was given for an obit.

"*Stondyng Cuppes.*"

"*First, a gret gilt stonding cup*, couered, for the chosyng of the Maister, pois, 66 vnces.

---

[1] Memorials, page 72.
[2] Dowe's spoons were given 19th June, 1605.

" *Itm, an other gilt cup*, couered, with a lambe and the sonne graven in the fote, with gaudete in dño, pois, 51 vnc. 3 quarters.

" *Itm, a stondyng gilt cup*, couered, with 3 angelles on the fote, and ecce agnus dei on the couer, pois, 55 vnces.

" *Itm, a stondyng gilt cup*, couered, with a lambe and the sonne on the couer, of the gyffe of John Fulthorp (Master 1412), pois 45 vnc.

" *Itm, a standing cup*, couered, of the gyffe of Maistres Champernon (wife of Hugh, given in 1489), pois, 51 vnc. and di.

" Itm, a stondyng cup, couered, chaced wrethen, of the gyfte of Maister Stodard (Master in 1465, but the gift was made in 1490), pois, 40 vnc.

" Itm, a stondyng cup, couered, with a pomell castell wyse, of the gyfte of Maistres Rose Swan (1493), pois, 42 vnc.

" Itm, 2 stondyng gilt cuppis, couered, chaced with son beames, of Mr. Materdale's (Master in 1480 but given in 1499) yefte, pois togiders, 80 vnc.

" Itm, a stondyng gilt cup, couered, and chaced with the Resurrexion on the pomell, of the gyfte of my Lady Bergevenny (wife of Richard Naylor, Master in 1475, but given in 1499), pois 40 vnc. 3 quarters.

" Itm, 2 standyng cuppes, couered, a more and a lesse, of the gyfte of M$^{r\cdot}$ Petyt (Master in 1498), pois togiders, 63 vnces.

" Itm, a standyng cup, couered, of the gyfte of Mr. Boughton (Master in 1495), pois, 34 vnces and di.

" *Itm, a standyng cup*, couered, chaced di. gilt, of the gyfte of Mr. Prince, pois, 41 vnces.

" *Itm, a standyng cup*, couered, chaced di. gilt with a floure in the botom, pois, 22 vnces.

" Itm, a standyng cup, couered, with Saint Mighell on the knop, with a spere and a perle on thende, of the gyfte of Margery Materdale, pois, 32 vnces and di.

" *Itm, a grete notte*, garnysshed with siluer and ouergilt with Saint John on the knop, of the gyfte of Mr. Breux (Master 1463), pois, 39 vnc.

" Itm, a standyng cup, gilt w^t a couer, and a columbyn on the pomell, of the gyfte of Dame Thomasyn Percyvale, pois by the troye weight, 47 vnces.

" Itm, of hyr gyfte a layer of siluer parcell gilt, weiyng by the same weight, 39 vnces."

" Itm, a white standing cup, with a couer, of the gyfte of Thomas Gardyner (Warden 1501), poys by troy weight, 24 vnces.

" Itm, a standing gylt cup, couered chaced vpright of his said (Howdan's) biqueste, weicth by the weight afforsaid, 39 vnces and di.

" Itm, a gilt cup of the gifte of John Smith, w^t a couer weiyng of Troye weight 26 vnces and 3 quarters.

" Itm, a gilt cup of the gifte of Maister Richard Hill (Warden 1493), weiying of troye weight, 16 oz. and di. quarter.

" Itm, of the gift of Maister Flower (Master 1504), 1 gilt cup w^t 1 couer, w^t a columbyne weiying 28 oz.

" Itm, of the gift of Hugh Fener, towardes the fynding of an obite, 3 goblettes w^t a couer, w^t 10l. of redy mony, the goblettes weiyng 64 oz. 1 qrt.

" It, of the gyft of Sir Willm. Fitz Willm., Knyght, A standyng cupp w^t a cover all gilt, weying of Troye weight, — vnces.

" Itm, of the gyfte of the worshipfull Mr. Rychard Wadyngton (Master in 1548), A standynge Cuppe of Siluer w^t a couer, all gylte, poiz 80 ounces." (Presented 26th October, 1565.)

It will be noticed that the Company possessed twenty-four standing and gilt cups and " one greate notte." But in 1609 these cups had been reduced to fifteen, of which one only had the old arms of the Company, and ten were new cups given by these benefactors:—John Olyff, Master 1564; John God, Master 1565; William Albany, Master 1568; John Hutchinson, Clerk 1574; Robert Hawes, 1580; George Sotherton, Master 1589; John Mansbridge, Warden 1592; William Linfold, Warden 1596; William Price, Warden 1596–1602, Whitcoote, so that nineteen of the old cups had disappeared.

" *Pottes.*

" *First,* 2 *gilt pottes,* playne, with lambes on the lyddes, pois 123 vnc.

" Itm, 2 gilt pottes, with bayles, of the gyfte of Sir John Percyvale, Knight, late Mayre of London, pois, 251 vnces.

" *Itm, a layer of syluer* and ouergilt, of the gyfte of Roger Gerveys, pois, 14 vnc. and di.

" Itm, a potell potte, parcell gilt, whiche Mr. Richard Smyth, late Shreffe (1508, Master 1503) had to pledge for 10l., whiche 10l. he gafe freely vnto the crafte, and deliuered the same potte ayen wthout any peny therfore payng, weiyng of troye weight, 47 oz. and di."

" It, A little Ale pott, pownced parsell gylt w^t a cover, of the gyft of Master Ric. Gibson (in 1530), weying of troye weight — vnces.

" Itm, of the gifte of Robert Wilford,[1] one Ale pott, w' A couer of syluer, all gilte, poiz, — vnces."

In the inventory of 1609 the two gilt pottes of Sir John Percyvale's are entered as Flagons, and Mr. Gibson's ale pot survived. The only pot therein entered was given by Edward Davenant, the plaintiff against Hurdys the Beadle, in 1600.

" *Bolles.*

" *First,* 4 *bolles, with a couer,* parcell of 6 bolles, parcell gilt with lambes and sonnes, bought in Mr. Duplage (Master 1480) tyme, pois togiders the 4 w' the couer, 106 vnc.

" Itm, 6 bolles, playne gylt, with a couer, whiche late were Maistres Swannes, pois, 170 vnces.

" Itm, 6 gret bolles, with a couer, chaced, that late were Mr. John Kyrkebye's (Master 1502, and Sheriff 1507) pois togiders, 397 vnc.

" For the whiche 6 bolles and couer the Company is bounde by indenture vnder their comon seale to kepe an obyte for the said Mr. Kyrkeby, the 6th daye of Juyn, duryng the terme of 80 yeres, expendyng atte same obyte at the blak freres yerely, 20s. As in the said indenture thereof made more playnely is conteyned.

" Itm, 5 playne bolles parcell gylt wt the couer weyen to gyders by the same weight (Pinkerton's gift), 94 vnces 3 quarters."

The inventory of 1609 contains these bowles, viz. :—

" One nest of Bowles with a cover, all gilt, of the gift of Mr. Hulson (Master 1569) and Mrs. Hulson, weighing 99 oz.

" Five greate Beere Bowles, weighing 124 ounces and a half.

" Six other Beere Bowles, weighing 66 ounces and one quarter.

" Six middle Wine Bowles, weighing 72 ounces and a half.

" Six lesser Wine Bowles, weighing 58 ounces and a half."

The small statue of St. John, presented to the Company in liquidation of an assessment, is not in this inventory, nor are the Bolles of 1512, unless they can be identified with any of those before enumerated as in 1609.

The words used in making some of these gifts would suggest a doubt whether they were given for secular use, and this may be the reason why they disappeared before the inventory of 1609 was taken. Thus Mrs. Rose Swan in the time of the mastership of Thomas Randell, 1493, made her offering in these terms : "Of

---

[1] He was one of five of the same name who were Members of the Company in 1537.   [2] Moore's Reports, 576.

very grete zele and harty love that she oweth and beareth to God and St. John Baptist, patron of the Fraternitie" and "for a token and perpetual remembrance." And William Gray made his gift in 1496 in the same form of words. The inscriptions on things offered would lead to the same suggestion. Thus John Stodard in 1490 gave "of grete zele and love that he oweth to the Fraternitie" a standing cup of silver and gilt with a "lambe and sonne in the botom graven upon the fote with one 'Agnus dei qui tollis precatæ mundi miserere nobis.'" They must have had plate for religious services although the heading in the Inventory "Plate for kepyng of obyttes" is not a description of the articles enumerated, thus:—

"*Plate for kepyng of Obyttes.*

"First a blak Notte couered garnysshed with siluer and ouergilt pois, 15 vnc.

Itm, a maser couered with an Image of Saint Kenelme on the Couer of the gyfte of John Cober, pois, 9 vnc.

"Itm, a standyng maser without a couer, pois, 11 vnc.

"Itm, a standyng maser with a couer and a lowe fote of the gyfte (1491) of Roger Doget,[1] preste. As it appereth on the fote of the same maser, pois, 14 vnc. 1 quarter.

"*Itm, a gret lowe maser* with a couer and a floure on the couer, pois, 17 vnc."

Various articles not of silver follow, as a plate chest, weights and beames, with balances, and their "nottes and masers."

"Itm, a standing Notte, couered, garnysshed w^t siluer and ouergilt of the biquest of Willm. Erle, late bedell, decessed, weieth, 35 ovnces.

"It, a nott wt a handyll, and A couer fast to hyt of syluer and geltt, of the geft of John Gavncell, of Axtall (Master 1437), weyyng 21 ownces A quarter.

"Itm, of the gift of maistres Boughton widow (of Master 1495) a nut w^t a couer weiyng of troye weyght 24 oz. and 3 quarters, tree and al.

"Itm, of the gift of maister Button, a standyng maser garnysshed w^t siluer and gilt, poiz."

It was the custom of the Tudor period[2] for each guest to bring his own knife, a whetstone hanging in the passage behind the

---

[1] John was Master in 1501, and Roger Chantry Priest to the Company.
[2] See Percyvale's Life.

screen so that he might sharpen it before sitting down to table; and the only knife in the inventory is thus entered:

"Itm, of the gift of S Laurence Wareyn, chauntrie preest, of Sr John Percyval Knight, A pair of Knyves and a bodkyn harnesid w^t siluer, and the shethe also hernesid w^t siluer." The said Wareyn lying buried beside Sir John in St. Mary Woolnoth. There are no knives or forks in the inventory of 1609.

When feasts were given in the Hall or a member became Lord Mayor or Sheriff, then the plate was brought out for use, but otherwise it was kept like the money of the Company in the Treasury in the garden under several keys.

"The Parloure"

Is the other room to which the Inventory principally applies. As the place of meeting for the Master and Wardens with or without the Court of Assistants on the general business of the Fraternity, there was found—"First, a gret Image of Saint John Baptist in a clothe with browdery worke of tholde makyng." This probably stood originally in the hall for in 1415-6 "100 pins for the image of St. John" were purchased at a cost of 3d., and in 1457-8 John Halle "painted the Image of St. John" then standing "in the Hall."

The ordinary furniture were cushions and bankers, the latter being usually placed on the form which was to be the seat of the chief guest. This seat was often (as in this instance) embroidered with tapestry worked with scriptural or emblematical subjects.

"Itm, 18 newe quysshens of the gyfte of John Skevyngton[1] (Warden 1503), then beyng Maister, George Sall, Henry Dacre, Gefferey Vaughan, and John Harryes, Wardeyns that tyme, with Angelles holdyng tharmes of the said Mr Skevyngton and with the markes of the said 4 Wardeins and tholy lambe, which quysshyns coste .. .." } 7l. 14s. 10d.

---

[1] The will of Sir John Skevington, 31st December, 1524, Alderman, Member of the Staple at Calais, is to be found in Cal. State Papers, 16 Henry VIII, vol. iv, page 411. He was Sheriff in 1520, resident in St. Mary Woolnoth, and his executors were Robert Strether and Guy Rawlinson; his apprentice, Christopher Vavassour, was to be free of the Merchant Adventurers in Flanders at the testator's expense. He gave to the Company his "White Basyns and Ewres." To the six persons of the Fellowship who bear his body to burial 6s. 8d. each. To James Wilford and the Master of the Merchant Taylors Company a black gown each. His best gown of pecoke with fur of foynes, and a gold ring of five wounds to Sir Walter

"Itm, 6 quysshens with tholy lambe browdered of the gyfte and bequest of John Powke late a brother of this fraternitee decessed whose soul God assoyle .. ..

"Itm, the tapet liying upon the table there of the gyfte of Thomas Speight (Warden 1499), late Maister, whiche coste .. . .

"Itm, the hangyng aboute the parlour of the gyfte of Henry Dacre, Richa Hall, George Harward, and John Benet than Wardeins with the said late M^r, which coste .. ..

"Itm, a banker, with tholy lambe in a sonne and Ecce agnus dei, lyned thurghout .. ..

} 3*l*. 8*s*. 8*d*."

The other articles of furniture were few.

"Itm, a table of grene, paynted of Kyffyns (Warden in 1467) gyfte.

"Itm, an old verdour for the same table.

"Itm, 3 trestelles and 3 formes joyned."

Then are entered "two course olde Aundyrorons and a pair of tonges," meaning, we presume, andirons or dogirons which were originally used for the reredos or brazier in the middle of the Hall and then in the common fireplaces. As coal came into use they became gradually to be discarded.

The contents of the parlour in 1609 are thus given :—

"Itm, One old long table.
    One old greene carpet fringed with greene silk.
    One drawing table.
    Ten Waynescott ioyned stooles.
    2 Pictures of Sir Thomas White.
    1 Picture of Mr. Dow, with a Silk Curtain to it.
    3 Great Mapps in 3 great frames.
    Three large Silk Curtains to them.
    1 Green cloth chair.
    1 Pair brass andirons.
    1 Fire Shovel, 1 Pair Tongs.
    1 Large Iron rack in the chimney.
    1 Hand bell of brass."

Griffith. The witnesses are James Wilford (late Alderman) and Paul Withipotts, with John Devereux, the Notary. He was never Lord Mayor, but Master of the Merchant Taylors Company probably in 1510, see p. 55, *ante*.

This last item marks an advance in domestic manners. Until January, 1607, the Master had to use his hammer for two purposes: (*a*) to keep the Court in order; and (*b*) to summon the Beadles, who (as they now do) stand outside the door, to his service. How was the confusion incident to this arrangement to be avoided? The Court Minute of 9th January, 1607, decided that question :—It is agreed that there shall be provided a handsome little bell to stand upon the table for the Maister to ringe when he hath occasion to call for the beadle who attendeth without the dore, soe as he and others may take notice that the knock with the hammer is onely for silence, and that the beadle is not to come in but when the bell is rung."

" Itm, 1 Large Testament.
1 Hammer of Ivory."[1]

In 1609 two other rooms and their contents are given :—

"*In the Council Chamber.*
" Itm, 1 long table.
1 long form to this one table."

"*In the Chamber next to the Council Chamber.*
" Itm, One great old press of wainscot.
One great new press of wainscot.
One great old wainscot chest.
The State Cloth of Black Velvett ymbrothered with gould.
One Buryall Cloth of Black Velvett being in two parts and ymbrothered with gould.
One large Persia Carpett for the King's Chamber.
One large Cloth ymbrothered with the Company's Arms being in three sev'ral pieces."

The furniture used for the burial of a deceased brother is entered thus :—

" Itm, a Coffyn of Estriche borde with the buriyng clothe and half a shete to lay within it.
" Itm, 3 peces of led to lye vpon the bankers.
" Itm, an olde Curteyn w^t a wyre affore the dore.

---

[1] Not the one at present in use, which was given by Thomas Roberts in 1679 (Memorials, page 95).

"Itm, in a gret Coffyn 3 baners of silke, whereof one is beten with an Image of our Lady, the 2de with Saint John, and the 3de with tholy Crosse and a dyademe in paper gilt.

"Itm, 2 stremers and a banner of Saint John all closed in a cofyn of Estryche borde, whiche coffyn William Erle (the Beadle) hath gyffen to the crafte."

At the date of this Inventory each funeral had to be specially provided for and therefore the cost of it might be great, unless the deceased were a member of such a society as this. The almsmen were buried by the Company at a cost in 1545-6 of 2s. only, and in 1663-4 (Dowe pensioner) at 9s. 8d. The trade of an "Undertaker" did not come into existence until a much later period. The coffin was not buried but was brought into store and used as a chest with lock and key. The herse was a temporary structure in the church covered with black cloth on which the body was placed covered with the herse cloth, of which the Merchant Taylors' Company have two beautiful specimens still hanging on their walls.

The articles used in city triumphs were preserved and entered.

"Itm, 4 scochcons in bokeram, wth tharmes of Quene Elizabeth (of Henry 7th), late decessed (11th February, 1503).

"Itm, 8 trumpet banners whiche were made whan Sir John Percyvale was mayre.

"Itm, 8 large trumpet banners made in Mr. Duplage (Master 1481) dayes."

In 1609 all the old banners of 1512 have disappeared.

These items following are worthy of special notice:

"Item, a yerd of sylver and another of iron" with which the Company tested the measure used for the sale of cloth in the city and at St. Bartholomew fair.

"Item, a table of the suffragies bilongyng to this fraternitee," in substance, we should presume, the same as that referred to elsewhere, as placed in the chapel of St. Paul's.

The last entries relate to the "Almery" which took its name from being originally a receptacle for broken meat left after a feast and to be given away in alms, a custom not altogether extinct in the Merchant Taylors Company. Of these Almeries two larger ones existed in the "Larder House" and "Botery." These articles at a later period had another use—that of a cupboard or safe for the deposit of plate or muniments, and such was the use which those in the parlour[1] appear to have been applied to.

"Itm, a double Almery of the coste and gyfte of Henry Mayour (Common Clerk), wherein be dyuers boxes and bookes of Maisters Accomptes and other.

"Itm, vpon the same Almery an hawte pace of Estryche borde to set ouer plate.

"Itm, an almery with 3 dores, of the cost of Mr. Doget (Master 1501-2), behynde the parlour dore."

"*The Kinge's Chambre*"

was thus furnished:

"First, an olde longe table of vyrre.

"Itm, 4 trestelles with 4 fete.

"Itm, an horse trapper with tharmes of the crafte.

"Itm, a staf for the Resurrexion, the Crosse thereof gilt.

"Itm, a bedsted with strawe."

For whose use this *one* bedstead was provided is not apparent, though it might have been appropiated to more than one official. When the hall premises were assigned for the lodgment of ambassadors, their retainers (of either sex) must have slept (as was then usual) on the floor of the hall, then covered with rushes. Feather beds were introduced into English homes in the early part of the fourteenth century, but this bed was of *straw* only. Many of the houses were reported to the civic authorities as having feather beds when Charles V visited London in 1522, and the sparseness of these articles in the Merchant Taylors' Hall is the more remarkable.

In 1609, after James I had been a guest in this room, the furniture was thus entered:—

"One pair of faire brass andirons.

"One fair wainscot dining table.

"Two foot parts belonging to that table.

"One faire wainscot cupboard.

"Two square tables of wainscot.

"21 wainscot joyned tables.

"One greene velvet chair.

"6 chairs covered with red leather.

"12 low stools covered with red leather.

---

[1] Parker's Domestic Arch., Vol. III, page 133.

"*In the Drawing Chamber, next to the King's Chamber.*

"One playne wainscot cupboard.

"One wainscot settle in the closet.

"One wainscot lather which is used to set herbes and flowers about the King's chamber."

The other premises to which the inventory applies may be mentioned without enumerating the articles in each room or building. They were on the ground floor in the garden lying to the south-east corner of Crepin's site.

"*The Kitchen*"[1]

Formerly here, as elsewhere, as a security against fire, was a detached building connected with the Hall by an alley or passage. The Merchant Taylors Company's kitchen appears as having been repaired in 1408, and a large expenditure was made in enlarging or rebuilding it in 1425-6.[2] It was not then complete without "im portraiture del patron del cusine." In the kitchen butchers (as well as cooks) were useful, for carcases were flayed and dressed there.[3] The furniture was very scanty. The mess of meat with various ingredients was beaten with a pestle and mortar. No spits are to be found, but they were probably used as the meat was sent to table upon them.

"*The Larder*"[1]

Was the place of deposit for provisions, and where many such had to be stored for use must have been of considerable size. The larder was placed adjacent to the kitchen and to the "weyhouse."

"*The Pastry or Pantry*"[1]

Was the office for bread, butter and cheese, and was superintended by the "Panter" or "Pannetier" whose duty it was to raise and arrange these things on the Hall table. In this pantry the articles were mostly standards or wooden chests for the preservation of the food.

"*The Buttery*"[1]

Was the place for distribution of the wine or other drinkables, which were not laid down or kept in stock by the Guild.[4] The cups, casks, and vessels which were used more or less during the meal

---

[1] No entries relating to these in the inventory of 1609.

[2] Memorials, page 569.

[3] Domestic Arch., Vol. II, page 124.

[4] "Few people keep wine in their own houses but buy it for the most part at a tavern, and when they mean to drink a great deal they go to the tavern."— Venetian Ambassador (A.D. 1497). Rye, page xlii.

were kept there. It would appear from the mention of a "window" that it was still a moveable article of furniture.

"*The Storehouse*"[1]

Was usually what its name indicates, for in the earlier times there was no social machinery for an immediate or early supply of the wants of a large household, and provisions had in many places to be kept in "store."

When napery was first brought into store at the Merchant Taylors' Hall is not traceable. None appears in the inventory of 1492, and the inventory of 1512 is not a safe guide as to dates. Stowe says that the wearers of napery were brought over by Edward III, who appointed St. Lawrence Poultney as the place of their meeting. When Anthony Radcliffe was Sheriff in 1585, he made application for the loan of it at Guildhall, but it was agreed that as "this house had never been charged with the loan of napery, therefore, the Court thought it not mete to provide anie." As Kympton was the Sheriff of 1576, and made no such application, it is possible that the acquisition had been recent.[2] However, according to the Inventory of 1512 the "napery, playne," was abundant. There were twenty-eight pieces with various marks, J & B being the most frequent, and varying in length from 21 to 4 yards. "The Diaper Table Clothes" were seven in number and varied from $14\frac{1}{4}$ in length and $2\frac{1}{4}$ yards in breadth. There were seven "Towelles," the longest being 31 yards (with a sonne in one part thereof) and the shortest 4 yards. The last entry was:

"*In thandes of the Bedell.*
"2 old bankers of red saye lyned, both cont. 9 yerdes.
"Itm, 5 old quysshons stuffed with flokkes."

The inventory of 1609, though wanting in some of the valuable contents of 1512, has in it other articles which require notice. There is no glass entered, but it was used in the mastership of Walter Plumer (1599), and this entry is found in the account of Thomas Aldworth, Master in 1601–2:—

"Item, paid for a dozen and a half of botle glasses and for the cases to the same, which bottles be used for service with wine

---

[1] No entries relating to this in the inventory of 1609.
[2] Our English Home, page 38. Rogers on Prices, Vol. iv, page 553.

on the election day and quarter dayes, and other dinners in the hall, 20s."

This charge, however, was not allowed against the Company by the auditors or the Court of Assistants (so that Mr. Aldworth was obliged to pay it himself), the ground of the disallowance[1] being that the former Masters had at their own charge paid for the glasses, out of the grant annually made to meet all sumptuary expenses.

For the quarterly feasts the Company had found it necessary to provide plates, dishes, pots, and trenchers, besides other conveniences, which are thus entered:—

"*Pewter.*

"Inprimis, nyne greate Chargers.
    One dozen of 5 lb. platters.
    ffowre dozen of 4 lb. platters.
    Two dozen and tenn of 3 lb. platters.
    Three dozen of 2 lb. platters.
    Three dozen and eleaven sallett dishes.
    ffowre dozen and eleaven plate trenchers.
    Two dozen and eight py plates.
    Eight dozen and fyve sawcers.
    Two dozen of pottle potts.

"*More Pewter bought this yere Anno Dm.* 1609.

"Inprimis, nyne greate 7 lb. Chargers.
    Twelve lesser 5 lb. Chargers.
    Two dozens of 4 lb. Platters.
    Three dozen and two of 3 lb. Platters.
    Two dozen of 2 lb. dishes.
    Two dozen and one Sallett dishes.
    ffowreteen long pasty plates.
    Three dozen and fowre round plates.
    Seaven dozen and eight Sawsers.
    Two plate trenchers.
    Six Dansk Potts, viz., fowre of quarts and two of pottles.
    Six chamber potts."

Then we find a butler mentioned as attending upon the guests at the quarter dinners:—

---

[1] 21st August, 1602.

"Brasse.

"One Brasse Cesterne, which is used by the Butler at quarter dynners and other dynners kept in the Hall."

The linen is entered with some particularity with an initial letter, added to show probably the place for which it was adapted as the school, parlour, hall, &c,

"Lynnen.

"Inprimis. 1 Damask Table Cloth for the High Table in the Hall, length 12 Ells. Marked H.

"Itm, 1 Damask Towell, length 11 Ells for do. Marked H.

1 Do. Table Cloth, 6 Ells and ½ length for the long Table in the King's Chamber. Marked K.

1 Do. Towell, 7 Do. ½ Do. Do. Marked K.

8 Do. Do. sq. board Cloth, 2 Ells, King's Chamber. Marked K.

1 Do. Table Cloth, 5 Ells, Table in the Parlour. Marked P.

1 Do. Towell, 4 Ells ¾, for the same Table. Marked P.

1 Do. Cupboard Cloth, 1 Ell ¾, for the Parlour. Marked P.

2 Doz. Do. Napkins, much worne.

6 Damask Coverpanes edged with Gould, wanting 2 buttons.

6 other Do. Do. with Silver, Do. 4 do.

18 Do. Do. and bottomed with thread, Do. 1 do.

A Diaper Table Cloth for the waiting Women's Table in the Hall, 12 yards in length. Marked M.

Do. Guest Table in the middle of the Hall, 10 Ells. Marked G.

A Diaper Cloth for the Skreene in the Hall, 5 yds. and ½. Marked S.

2 Coarse Diaper Cowchers, 9 Ells each.

9 Diaper Livery Towells, 2¾ Ells each.

5 Doz. and 4 Do. Napkins.

3 Diaper Table Cloths for the Schoole, 7 yds. each. Marked S.

2 Do. Square board Cloths for do., 2 yds. ½. Marked S.

1 Do. old Cowcher for the Parlor, 6 yds. Marked P.

1 Do. Do. Cowcher, playne, somewhat torne. 8 Ells.
1 Do. Do. Do., 11 yds. ½, Wayting Women's Table in the Hall.
2 long diaper Towells for the Schoole, 7 yds. each. Marked S.
1 Damask Table Cloth, Maister's Table, 12 yds. ¼. Marked M.
1 Do. Towell, Do. 11 yds. ¼. Marked M.
12 Dozen and 9 Napkins.
1 Diaper Table Cloth, Lyvery Table, divided into 2 pts., 24 yds. ¼. Marked L.
2 long Diaper Towells for Lyvery Table, 12 yds. each. Marked L.
6 Square Do. Clothes for the Carving boards, 2 yds. ½ each.
10 Dozen and 8 Diaper Napkins.
A Cowcher of playne Cloth for the high board in the Hall, 11 Ells ½. Marked H.
A Do. for the Table in the King's Chamber, 6¼ Ells. Marked K.
7 Dresser Cloths, 4½ Ells each.
A Cowcher of plain Clothe for the Guest board, 11 Ells Marked G.
1 Sq. Board Cloth of Damask, 2¼ Ells. Marked P."

In the yard they possessed a clock, with a case of wainscot for the same clock; and lastly came the armour, of which no mention is made in the inventory of 1512. At what date the armoury of the Company originated has not been noted, but in 1548–9,[1] and in Wyatt's rebellion, and in later periods, as in March, 1577, it is certain that a store of armour was held at the house. The contents are thus given in 1609 :—

"*Armor.*[2]

"Itm, Three and fyfty Corsletts.
Thirty Curetts.
Thirty musketts.

---

[1] Memorials, page 526.

[2] The gallery over the King's Chamber would appear to have been the place where the armour was kept (October 5th, 1595). At the Court of 23rd March, 1603, George Bell was appointed the Company's armourer at 40s. per annum, for scouring and making clean the whole of the Company's armour.

Two and twenty muskett rests.
ffortey Calyvers.
ffyfteene Bandaleeres.
Thirteene long bowes.
ffowre and twenty sheaf of old arrowes.
Twenty and eight pykes.
Thirteen Armynge for pykes of red cloth.
One hundred and ten fflaskes and tutchboxes.
Fowre score and eight hed peeces.
One hundred and one new Swords and daggers.
fforty old Swords.
Three and twenty old Daggers.
ffowre black bills.
Thirty one payer of leather hangers.
Twenty and three leather girdles.
Eleaven muskett mouldes.
One little bundle of match."

THE DIMENSIONS OF THE SEVERAL LONDON HALLS WERE COLLECTED BY THE LATE MR. NATHANIEL STEPHENS.

	Feet in		
	Length.	Width.	Height.
The Merchant Taylors' Hall	82	43	43
School Hall Charterhouse	93	50	44½[1]
Lincoln's Inn :—			
Old Hall	71	32	32
New Hall	120	45	62
Westminster Hall	288	66	110
Guildhall	153	48	55
Lambeth Palace	93	38	—
Middle Temple :—			
Hall	100	42	47
Library	96	42	70
Bartholomew's Hospital	190	35	30
Freemasons'	96	37	38
Goldsmiths'	80	40	35
Christ's Hospital	187	—	—

[1] To the collar of the roof principals.

CHAPTER VI.

RELIGION AND ALMSGIVING.

Care of the Fraternity as to the two objects of Religion and Almsgiving, as evidenced by the early records, p. 110.—*Acquisition of Religious Privileges by Merchant Taylors Company from* (1) *St. John's Jerusalem, p.* 111 ; (2) *Chapel in St. Paul's, p.* 112 ; (3) *Papal and Episcopal Pardons, p.* 113.— *Our Lady of Rounceval, p.* 114.—*And other grants, p.* 115.—*Contracts for performance of Obits, p.* 116.—*Chapel at the Hall, p.* 117.—*Payments for Religious Service, p.* 119.—*Charities of the Company, p.* 120.—*Endowments for both objects, p.* 121.—*Illustration of expenditure in* 1399–1400 *enumerated, p.* 123.—*Coronation of Henry IV and Banquet, p.* 124.—*Expenditure of* 1466–7, *p.* 125.—*Grant of arms,* 1480, *p.* 126.

WE are now about to enter upon the business of the Guild with regard to two of the important objects which the Guildsmen had at heart at the earlier period of their association. It will be remembered that the earliest ordinances of 1371 gave the penalties for the workman's misdeeds " to the priests and poor men" of the mysterie, and that the oath of the foreign brother was in these words : " Ye shall give in your life time or else bequeath in your testament to the use and behoof of the said Fraternity more or less after your estate, and demean that ye bear and leave to the same in supporting and maintaining of the priests and poor almsmen of the said Fraternity."[1] The prayer (the first entry in the ordinance book) which was used at the meetings of the Fraternity was partly in these words : " Multiply thy mercies towards us with *increase* of well wishers, *benefactors*, and sound members of the same, settle and confirm faithfull and harty love amongst us all. Bless and direct (by the Holy Spirit) all our actions and endeavours, and give us grace *faithfully and honestly* to discharge the *trusts reposed* in us as well by our *good friends and bretheren deceased*, as any other way belonging to us to the glory of thy holy name and peace and comforte of our owne soules and *good* example and *incitement* to others."[2]

---

[1] Page 77 and Appendix 15.
[2] The Clerk was sworn twice in each year at quarter days to read out "the wills and compositions of old benefactors to the whole body there assembled." As to the prayer, see Appendix 9.

CHAP. VI.] *Acquisition of Religious Privileges.* 111

Such then is the evidence which the old records present on this subject—and the same facts find an echo in the post-Reformation benefactors to be afterwards noticed.

Having, therefore, acquired the Hall as a place of assembly for secular business, the next purpose was to secure a chapel for the public worship of the Fraternity. This was done as early as 1361-71, when during Simon de Sudbury's episcopacy of London the Merchant Taylors Company received a grant or admission to a chapel on the north side of Paules[1] in honour of their patron, St. John Baptist.

But some thirty years before this grant was made to the Company they had obtained from John Pavely (the Prior of 1333) an admission "to be partners in the right holy Hospital House of St. John in Jerusalem," a fact which—with others of the like character—is thus recorded in the ordinance book:—

1. For asmoche as amonges all werks medefull, most meritory is in this oure lyfe, naufrage and perilous, the allectyfes of goostly helth deryvied from the moste mercyfull and plenteous founteyn of oure moder holy chirche to be publysshed, ministred and declared to all Cristen people as the perfite preparatyfes guydyng mannes soule to eternall salvacyon; Therfore it ys that we—John Prynce,[2] late Maister, Thomas Pye, Richard Sutton, John Martyn, and Thomas Burgeys, late Wardeins of the ffraternitee of Seint John Baptist of Taillours in the Citee of London beyng possessed of goostly tresoure and willyng all Cristen people to be partiners of synguler and all suche Indulgences, Pardons, and Remissions by oures of blessed memory precessours and predecessours of entier charitee purchased long tyme secrete: now of oure goostly mocyon to meve the reders and herers to devocyon of all & singuler such Indulgences, Pardons and remissions in oure moder tonge as is in this table ensuyng, have made a declaracyon. First, this reverent ffraternitee stablisshed in hymself to have that blessed prophete Seint John Baptist for their patrone, thurgh[3] theire deservyng were admitted to be partiners of the right holy hospitall house of Seint John in Jerusalem[4] after the tenoure here ensuying.

---

[1] Built by Sir John Poultney in 1349. Fuller's Worthies, Vol. I, page 573.

[2] Prynce was probably Master between 1445-51. Burgeys (the Junior Warden) was Master in 1467.

[3] Through.

[4] The Ordinance of 1417 shows the celebration of the Feast of the Decollation of St. John the Baptist, at the Church of St. John's of Jerusalem, near Smythfield, to have been then an annual custom. Chapter III, page 63, note.

"Frere John Pavely,[1] of the holy hospitall house of Seint John in Jerusalem prioure of th'ordoure in England, and all the brethern of the same hospitall, to oures welbeloved in Crist, all and singuler Taillours in the Citee of London which are of the ffraternitee of Seint John Baptist in the saide Citee of London and to all other of the said ffraternitee brethren & sisters, helth in our Lord Jesu.

"Advertisyng & brynging to mynde the grete zele and right many benefyttes by you don to oure religion and trustyng to be don, we, yelding love for love, have receyved & receyve you all and singuler into our ffraternitee and of th'ole religyon we admitte you withouten ende,[2] grauntyng you to be partyners of masses, mateins and other houres of prayers, fastynges, almesdedes, hospitalitees, abstynences, watches, pilgrimages, goostly laboures and of all other goode dedes by the brethern of oure religyon don or to be don worlde withouten ende."

This graunte is confermed by Robert Malory[3] late prioure of the saide religion in England.

The entry is then continued with reference to the chapel in St. Paul's, and shows the special days which were to be observed there by the Fraternity, and the grant of indulgences made by Popes and English Bishops to any benefactors for the chapel and God's services therein.

2. This devoute ffraternitee willyng th'encrease of Godde's honoure by lowly supplicacion,[4] were admitted of theire right reverent fader in God, Symon[5] the Bisshoppe of London, to have in theire moder chirche of Powles a Chapell which is halowed in th'onoure of Seint John Baptist atte North syde of Powles where they have ordeyned, by graunt of their saide right reverent fader, preestes to the grete laude of God, specyally to sey masses dailly and to praye for the sowles of brethern and systers of the said

---

[1] Prior in 1333 and in 1371. Admiral of the Fleet in 1375 and 1377 (Dugdale).

[2] These conventions were said to be common with religious guilds.—See Brentano Essay (1870), p. lxxxiv.

[3] Prior in 1432, and made an honorary member of the Merchant Taylors Company in same year.—Memorials, page 619.

[4] Edward III's letter to the Dean and Chapter of St. Paul's, complaining of the deficiency of Priests there (1345).—Riley's London.

[5] Simon de Sudbury, *alias* Tybold, appointed to London in 1361, translated to Canterbury in 1371, and beheaded by the Rebels in Wat Tyler's rebellion, on 14th June, 1381, whose skull is said to be preserved in a niche in the vestry wall of St. Gregory, Sudbury, Suffolk.

CHAP. VI.] *Pupal and Episcopal Pardons.* 113

ffraternitee deceased from oure mortalytee, and dayly contynued ys in goodenes for the preservacyon of theym that are or shalbe of the said ffraternitee.

3. Oure [¹most holy fader in God Bonyface pope the ninth² of that name] hath of his mere mocyon to cause people to devocion, to all Cristen people that wyll putte to theire helpyng handes to the makyng of the said chapell or to the mayntenaunce of Goddes service in the said place and to all theym truly penitent and shryven that visyt the said chapell in the ffeestes of Cristmas, Circumcisyon, Epiphanie, Easter, th'Ascencyon, Pentecost, Corpus Christi, th'adnunciacyon, Purificacyon & th'Assumpcyon of our blessed Lady Saint Mary, and in the ffeest of the Nativitee of Seint John Baptist the ffest of Peter & Paule and in the ffeest of the dedicacyon of the said chapell, hath mercifully for eche of these ffeestes graunted vij yeres and vij lentes of remissyon, and whoso, within th'utasses of Cristmasse, th'Epiphanie, Easter, th'Ascencyon, Corpus Christi, the Nativitee and th'Assumpcyon of the blessed Virgyn Mary, the Nativitee of Seint John Baptist, the ffeest of the blessed Apostels Petir & Poule and of the vj dayes immediatly ensuying the ffeeste of Pentecost, are willyng devoutely to visyte the said Chapell or to put to theire helpyng handes for every daye within th'utasses hath mercyfully graunted [c dayes of indulgence].³

4. Also⁴ the right reverent faders in God Symon th'arche-

---

¹ There is an erasure here in the Ordinance Book, and a blank left, which Mr. Martin, of the Record Office, has revived and restored the words here given in [ ].

² This should be Bonyface IX (1389-1404) who interfered in the affairs of the English Church and established the payment of Annates or First Fruits to the Pope. Bonyface VI was deposed in 896 after a reign of fifteen days only.

³ The rest of this part of the record is erased and has been also revived.

⁴ I understand this document to be an enumeration of antecedent grants made to the Company which are here summarised or formulated in (say) 1464-5. This is conjecture, and by comparing the dates of these Bishop's consecrations with other circumstances I am enabled to identify the Prelates who are referred to. The names of Robert, Rauf, Adam, Roger, and others are easily identified, and were all in office from (say) 1360 to 1385. In other cases where the same Christian name is repeated in the text I have taken that prelate holding office in or about the same period.

Symon of Canterbury was Islip from 1349 to 1366, and Lingham from 1366 to 1368. William of London was probably Courtney, who held office from 1375 to 1381, and was an honorary member of the Merchant Taylors Company in 1378. William of Wynchestre was Wykeham 1367 to 1404. John of Lincoln was de Bokingham, 1362 to 1398. Robert of Coventry, Stretton 1360 to 1385. John of Bathe and Welles, Barnet, 1364 to 1366, or Harewell, 1366 to 1386. Thomas of Exeter, de Brentingham, 1370 to 1394. Thomas of Ely, de Insula or de Lisle 1345 to 1361. Rauf of Salisbury, Ergham, 1375 to 1388. John of Hereford, Gilbert, 1375 to

VOL. I.   I

bisshoppe of Caunterbury, William of London, William of Wynchestre, John of Lincoln, Robert of Coventre & Lychefelde, John of Bathe & Welles, Thomas of Excestre, Thomas of Ely, Rauf of Salesbury, John of Herforde, Henry of Norwych, William of Chichestre, Adam of Seint Davyd, Thomas of Rowchestre, John of Bangor, Roger of Landaffe and William of Seint Asse, Bisshoppes, have graunted to all theim that put to theire helpyng handes to the laude of God in this Chapell to be mayntened to exorte Christian people to devocyon eche of them [xl days of remissyon].[1]

Endowments were soon after given to maintain the worship there. In 1382 Thomas Carleton gave by his will a yearly rent of ten markes to find a priest to sing for him "within the chapel at the north dore at Paules." Thomas Sibsay by will of 1404 directed his body to be buried "within the chapel of St. John the Baptist within the north entrance of the church," and gave 40s. for his obit. In 1408 Beatrice De Ros (widow), founded by contract with the Company a chauntry priest for service in the same chapel, to which preferment Henry Chassure was appointed on the 28th May, 1461.[2]

Probably the fifth grant follows in order of date, as the chapel of which Martyn (the Graver) was the Master was suppressed in the reign of Henry V (1412-22). The entry runs thus:—

5. Also right reverent faders in God, first Garsias Martyn of Savoy Channon and proctour generall of the Convent of th'ospitall of oure Lady of Roscydevale (Rounceval),[3] Maister & keper of the Chapell founded atte Charyngcrosse, hath receyved this worthy ffraternitee into theire ffraternitee, grauntyng theym to be parcyall

---

1389. Henry of Norwich, Despenser, 1370 to 1406. William of Chichester, either William de Lenne, *alias* Latimere, 1362 to 1368, or Reade, 1369 to 1385. Adam of St. Davyd was Houghton, 1361 to 1389. Thomas of Rowchestre, Trillick, 1365 to 1372. John of Bangor, either Gilbert, 1372 to 1375, or Swafham, 1376 to 1398. Roger of Llandaff was Cradock, 1361 to 1382. William of St. Asaph was de Spridlington, 1376 to 1382.—Bedford Blazonry of Episcopacy, 1858.

[1] Another erasure and revival here.

[2] Vol. I, page 443, Materials for History of Henry VII's reign. One of the abuses in Chaucer's time was the neglect of country cures for London chauntries.

"His good parson
———— sette not benefice to hire
And let his sheep encumbered in the mire,
And ran unto London unto St. Paules
To seeken him a chauntry for soules,
But dwelt at home."

[3] Founded by William Marshall, Earl of Pembroke in Henry III's reign, on the site of Northumberland Avenue, and suppressed as an alien priory. The "gentil Pardoner of Rounceval" was one of Chaucer's pilgrims.

CHAP. VI.]   *Other Grants.*   115

of the benefyttes in theire religion don or to be don of all indulgies graunted or to be graunted confermed or to be confermed by holy faders worlde withoute ende.

This graunte ys confermed by the priours in the generall chapitre by name " Examinacion De Aynore."

The six other grants which are entered were probably made during the fourteenth century.

6. Also William Wardon,[1] Abbot of the monastery of oure Lady nygh the Toure of London hath receyved this saide ffraternitee into the brotherhed of theire religyon ever to be partyners of theire suffragies perpetually.

7. Also William, the Prioure[2] of the Monastery of the Trinitee in London, hath admitted this notable ffraternitee in breder of theire religion and to be prayde fore perpetually.

8. Also William Hesperby[3] the prioure of th'ospitall of oure Lady Withoute Bisshoppesgate of London hath graunted to this said ffraternitee to be partyners of theire suffragies for ever.

9. Also Robert Draycote,[4] prioure of the hospitall of oure Lady of Elsyngspitell within Crepilgate of London, hath graunted this saide firaternitee to be partyners with theym in all theire goode werkes goostly for ever.

10. Also William Gedney,[5] prioure of the monastery of Seint Barthilmewe in Smythfelde of London, hath by th'assent and consent of his brethern admitted this right devoute ffraternitee into theire all & singuler suffragies don or to be don in their religion withoute ende.

11. Also all these places of religion have graunted that whan any brother or sister of this devoute ffraternitee shall deccase from this mortalitee, that than they of the name certefied shall do and make to be done in all thynges as is or shall be don for any brother of the saide religion.

12. Also all they that are or shalbe of this blessed ffraternitee by the privilege of Roscydevale to them graunted ben released of the vijth parte of theire penaunce by oure most holy faders in God Nicholas[6] the iiijth and Innocente [7]the vjth popes of blissed memory confermed.

---

[1] Owborne, honorary member of the Merchant Taylors Company in 1423–5.
[2] The latter office was usually held by an Alderman.—Strype's Stowe, Book 2, page 3.
[3] Prior in 1388.   [4] Prior in 1400.   [5] Prior in 1381.
[6] Pope 1288–9.   [7] Pope 1352.

13. Also Elizabeth, abbasse, and Thomas, generall confessoure and all the congregacion of sisters & brethren of the holy monastery of Seinte Brigitte of Syon, have graunted unto this saide ffraternitee to be partiners with theym, as wele in this lyf as after, of all masses, prayers, prechynges, fastynges, abstynencies, watches, disciplynes, almesdedes and all other good dedes don or to be don by theym and theire successours for ever.

The record is not dated, but we believe it to have been originally composed or formulated in 1464-5, as the account books for the same year contain an entry of this payment for a somewhat similar document: "For composing, writing, illuminating, and painting a table of the indulgences and remissions granted to the fraternity by divers Popes, Archbishops, and Bishops, and other prelates of the Church, hanging in St. Paul's, 10s. and 1d." At a later period, 16th December, 1595, there was "a table pendant in the parlour," which was openly read at the quarterly Courts.

It may have been the religious characteristics which were the inducements for persons unconnected with the Company to enter into contracts with the Master and Wardens to carry out for a pecuniary consideration their obit endowments. The earliest contract of this kind which we have traced is that with Beatrice De Ros, widow of Sir Thomas De Ros, of Hamlake, Knight. In 10 Henry IV (1408–9) she obtained licence from the Crown to found a charity "within this Cathedral (St. Paul's) for one priest to pray for the souls of persons named (not being Merchant Taylors) and to grant twelve marks per annum issuing out of certain messuages in London for the maintenance of the said priest (Dugdale, p. 42). A contract was then made with the Merchant Taylors Company to carry out this arrangement between the Merchant Taylors' Company and Beatrice De Ros, widow, dated 5th March, 1408, whereby Thomas Sutton, the master, and John Warlock, Thomas Wylby, Adam Teryby, and Ralph Shackelacke, the Wardens, charged their Hall and other property with an annuity of 8*l*. per annum for a chauntry priest at St. John's Chapel in St. Paul's, for a consideration which appears to have been 10*l*. only.

The second of such contracts was made with an equally notable person, Sir Gerard Braybroke, the brother of the Bishop who held the See of London till his death in 1404. It is dated 6th March, 1419, for an obit in St. Martin's Outwich church, which was redeemed by the Company in 1550-1. These contracts and other contracts for similar purposes are enrolled in the Hustings Court.

There had been a chapel in the Hall premises from early time, probably during Ingham's tenancy, and certainly from 1406. The grant following might lead the reader to think that a new chapel had then recently been built, but the account books of the Company afford no corroborative evidence of this fact. The chapel is frequently mentioned in earlier years, and in 1454, but only for repairs, and these principally to the windows.

However, in the Mastership of George Ashton, and may be upon his petition, "The Chapel at the Hall" was established under the papal sanction of Calixtus in the year 1455, and is an evidence of the religious zeal then animating the Taylors, for although the church of St. Martin's Outwich (of which the Company were the patrons) was adjacent to the Hall, this was not enough, but to their patron saint, St. John, they must have a chapel *in* their Hall premises.

The Bull is entered in the Company's ordinance book in these terms:[1]

"Calixtus, bishop [servant of the servants of God] to his beloved children the Masters, Keepers, Wardens, and all the brethren of the Brotherhood or Company of St. John the Baptist, generally or commonly called Tailors Armourers of the linen armoury of London, of both sexes, present and future, greeting and apostolic blessing."

It then sets out by way of recital the inducements which have led the Holy Father to make the grant:

"The feeling of sincere devotion which you bear towards us and the Church of Rome, deserves that we should favourably consent to your petitions, as far as God will allow us, especially in those cases which concern the health of souls and the increase of Divine worship. Whereas a petition lately exhibited to us on your behalf, declared that formerly a certain perpetual chapel in the Church of London was founded and endowed by some deceased faithful servants of Christ, belonging to your company or brotherhood (in

---

[1] This Bull is printed from the contemporary copy in the ordinance book of 1507, rendered into English by Mr. C. Trice Martin. In one or two places the copy is manifestly incorrect, but the general sense is clear. The passages within brackets have been carefully erased in obedience to the Proclamation for the abolishing of the usurped power of the Pope, issued on 9th June, 1535, which orders the Bishops "to cause all manner of prayers, orisons, rubrics, canons of mass books, and all other books in the churches, wherein the said Bishop of Rome is named, or his presumptuous and proud pomp and authority preferred, utterly to be abolished, eradicated and rased out, and his name and memory to be never more (except to his contumely and reproach) remembered, but perpetually suppressed and obscured."

which as you assert, very many ecclesiastical prelates, nobles and divers other persons of both sexes are united, to the honour of Almighty God, the Glorious Virgin Mary and St. John the Baptist), for the persons of your company or brotherhood, and priests meeting in great multitude, to say masses and other divine offices there for [the souls] of the brothers and sisters of your brotherhood; certain other faithful servants of Christ of the same brotherhood now living, considering that the members of your company or brotherhood of both sexes, have increased so much in numbers that the said chapel is too small to hold so many persons of this company or brotherhood, have founded and endowed another perpetual chapel in the hall or inn of your brotherhood, called "Taillours Halle," within the bounds or immunity of the parish church of St. Martin of Oteswyche, London, with an altar in the chapel, for the more commodious performance of the devotions of your said brotherhood. And you desire that masses and other divine services may be celebrated and sung there, as often as necessary, and that the anniversaries of the faithful servants of Christ of your brotherhood or company, now and for the future, may be performed according to custom at the respective seasons of the year, the licence [of the apostolic see] for this being [first obtained]. Wherefore humble supplication was made to us on your behalf that we would deign of our apostolic goodness to provide lawfully for you and your convenience in the premises."

And then concludes with the grant:

"We therefore consenting to your petitions on this behalf, with [apostolic] authority, by these presents grant you and each one of you free and lawful permission to have masses celebrated whenever it is necessary, on the altars in the said chapel of "Taillours Halle" with due reverence and honour, other divine services to be sung, with the ringing of bells, and anniversaries to be performed by your own or other priests also of your brotherhood, in whatever number, whom you may choose for this purpose; saving always the right of the parish church of Oteswyche aforesaid, and any other. The [apostolic] constitutions [and those] of Otto and Ottobonus, formerly [legates of the Apostolic See] in England, and others, general or special, published in provincial or synodal councils; the statutes also and municipal customs of the City of London, whether enforced by oath [apostolic confirmation], or any other security, and any other thing to the contrary notwithstanding.

"[Let, therefore, no man infringe this page of our grant, or with rash daring dispute it. If any one presume to attempt this, let him know that he will incur the indignation of Almighty God and his blessed Apostles Peter and Paul.

"Given at Rome, at St. Peter's]. In the year of the Incarnation of our Lord, 1455, 7 June, in the first year of our Pontificate."

It would appear from the account books that there were quarters for the chaplain (Sir John Doyley in 1409) in the Hall premises, and the same books show many entries regarding the chapels at St. Paul's and at the Hall :—

"1453–4 :
To tapers in the chapel of St. John at St. Paul's and two in the chapel at the Hall 4 lb. at 7d. a lb.
Bread and wine to the Bishop of London after performing mass at St. Paul's on St. John's Day .. 9d."
"1455–6 :
To such chaplain for bread and wine for celebrating mass .. .. 20d.
Three chaplains of the Company each.. .. .. 10 marks."
"1456–7 :
Mass on St. John's Day by the Bishop of Lincoln."
"1458–9 :
Mending the glass window at the chapel at St. Paul's 5s."
"1460–1 :
Mending two vestments in the chapel at St. Paul's .. 3s. 4d."
"1463–4 :
To a joiner for making "lx pewes" in St. John's Chapel, St. Paul's .. .. 4l. 1s."
(An early instance of such in the Cathedral Church.)

But the founders of the guild were benevolent[1] as well as religious, and the first great acquisition of a mixed character (partly by contract and partly by gift) invites a special notice, as connecting the Company with the Otewiches, and with their church of St. Martin's and their beautiful monument to be seen in St. Helen's.

The church of St. Martin, according to Stowe, was called "Oteswich," after "Martin" of that name, as Martin, Nicholas, William, and John De Oteswich were the founders thereof, and at the instance of William and John the advowson was given to the Taylors by John Churchman. The Merchant Taylors' records show that the Taylors paid 40l. to King Henry IV on 15th July, 1405,

---

[1] See Appendix 33, page 406.

for a license enabling John Churchman to grant the advowson and other rentals to them, and that on the 20th July he made such a grant. It was not, therefore, altogether a gift, and so long as Churchman lived he was to receive an annuity of 10*l*. per annum, and after his death the Company were to maintain an obit for him, and to pay five marks (3*l*. 6*s*. 8*d*.) to the priest of the chauntry then late "founded for the soul of Master William De Oteswyche," in St. Martin's. Besides these obligations the grant lays down certain ordinances (to the observance of which the Master and Wardens are to be sworn) for the appointment to the living of St. Martin's, and for other matters which the Master or Wardens were to fulfil " as before God and His Saints they will answer."

The rents at the time of the grant in 1406 appear to have amounted to 26*l*. 13*s*., and so soon as this wealth came to them from Churchman they turned a portion of his estate to the use of their almsmen of the Livery by erecting almshouses in close proximity to their hall, so that those in want might ever be within sight and hearing.

From this initial opening a large fountain of benevolence has been developed and poured in upon the Guild. There was not, as we know, any legal provision for the poor until Elizabeth's reign, and the original purpose of these Guilds was to provide work, so far as they could do so, for the competent craftsmen, and by their benevolence, alms, and succour for those whom age or infirmity rendered incompetent to labour. For these charitable purposes an assessment was made under the ordinances of 1613 upon some members in order to supply the need of others.

The first devise "in pure and perpetual alms for relieving the poor needy brethren of the brotherhood" was that of Peter Mason in 1412. The second devise in November, 1418, was for coals[1] to be given to the poor at Christmas, and coals were also given by later benefactors, as Candish in 1460, Langwith in 1467, Percyvale in 1507.

The money to be given away by the Master and Wardens

---

[1] This is an early bequest of coals which, in 1306 were prohibited from use in London as a nuisance, but in 1400 very generally used there. The Merchant Taylors' books show the cost in early days to have been as under:—

"1418.—Creek gave 13 qrs., cost in 1443 (first entry I find) at 8*d*., 8*s*. 8*d*.

"1460.—Candish. 36 quarters coals, cost, 1463, 15*s*. 10*d*.

"1507.—Sir J. Percival. 30*s*. at three festivals.

" Account, 1515 :—

" Item, for three loads of coals at 5*d*. the quarter—every load containing 24 qrs., to be delv. in Ward of Langbourne for Sir J. Percival and my lady his wife, 30*s*."

was to be done with careful discrimination, so as to injure as little as possible the self-respect of the recipients. One donor, Candish, adds these directions :—The recipients were to be " poor," but " such who may have been honourable and discreet persons of the mysterie, and afterwards by the visitation of God come to poverty." Then he desires that the alms should be "paid to them in their dwellings and not in the Common Hall," for so to receive their alms "in the view of others oftentimes happening to be there" would put these "poor and needy persons to no small shame" which this worthy man would spare them.

Often for like purposes landed estates were entrusted to the Master and Wardens by their members, who gave a residue over to the Company when the primary trusts for religion or charity were fulfilled. By these donations, and by purchases made out of corporate funds, the Company acquired houses and tenements in London, which are still, thanks to the integrity of our predecessors, more or less intact with a vast increment of rent.

The hall, as we have stated, was purchased in 1331. In 1382 Carleton gave the Company an estate in Wood Street of 4*l*. 4*s*. 10*d*. per annum (sold in 1550–1). In 1392 Simon Wynchcombe increased by donation the area of the hall premises. In 1400 the Company purchased the site of the "Saracen's Head," in Friday Street of 2*l*. 5*s*. 10*d*. per annum, and assessed their members in Percyvale's mastership to rebuild the premises for the *second* time. In 1404–5 Thomas Sibsay gave another "Saracen's Head," that in Bread Street, of 7*l*. 6*s*. 8*d*. per annum. In 1405 John Churchman, the Grocer, gave the advowson of St. Martin with an estate adjacent to the church in Bishopsgate Street, and to the hall premises in Threadneedle Street of 26*l*. 15*s*. per annum. In 1412 Peter Mason gave the corner shop in Cheapside and Bucklersbury of 11*l*. 6*s*. 8*d*. per annum. In 1422 John Buck, the "Scutle on the Hoppe" in Gracius Street of 2*l*. 4*s*. 2*d*. per annum (sold in 1550). In 1432 Thomas Sutton Anchor Alley and lands adjacent of 10*l*. 12*s*. per annum. In 1451 Idonea Hallegate lands in St. Margaret Patyns of 1*l*. 6*s*. 8*d*. per annum (sold in 1550). In 1452 Ralph Holland lands in the city, partly sold in 1550-1, and the residue still held by the Company of 47*l*. per annum. In 1460 Hugh Candish, probably the son of "John," the Master in 1413, gave lands in Walbrook and Fenchurch Street of 6*l*. 5*s*. per annum, the acquisition of which by the Company appears to have been disputed by his cousin and namesake. These entries in the account books following relate to the controversy.

"32 and 33 Henry VI, 1455.—Payment for ale given to men assembled in Fenchurch Street to witness the agreement between the Master and Wardens of this brotherhood and Laurence Percy Chaplain, feoffee of Hugh Caundish, deceased, concerning a certain rent of 11s. 8d. to be received yearly by the Master, Wardens, Clerk, and Beadle, and making other declarations there, according to the last will of the said Hugh, 2d.

"Wine given to Percy John Scotte and others, for advice in collecting evidence touching the lands and tenements late belonging to Hugh Caundish in Walbroke and Fenchurch Street, given and bequeathed by the said Hugh to the brotherhood for ever, 1s. 8d.

"Other payments for advice and for writing the composition of the last will of Caundish and evidences.[1] 34–35 Henry VI, 1457.—Breakfast to the Clerks of Guildhall for a matter concerning the tenement late belonging to Hugh Caundish in Walbroke, 10s. 4–5 Edward IV, 1465.—Advice of Geoffrey Coytmore, lawyer, concerning the evidences of the lands and tenements late belonging to Hugh Caundish in Fenchurch Street, which Augustine Caundish, cousin of the same Hugh, claims, 3s. 4d." The Company's title prevailed, and it is a noticeable feature that eating and drinking were freely resorted to at the cost of the Taylors.

In 1467 Ellen Langwith gave tenements in Sherburne Lane of 12l. 6s. 8d. per annum, still held by the Company. These several estates then gave to the Company an aggregate revenue of 138l. 15s. 6d. charged to some extent with payments, and which after the sale 47l. 3s. 8d., part thereof, leaves a present surplus rental of 8,606l. 15s. 10d. in favour of the Company.

We must turn now to the account books—taking two[2] years 1399–1400 and 1468–9 as illustrations—to see what was the expenditure made by the Company in relation to the subject headings of this chapter—adding for future use the sumptuary expenses then incurred out of Corporate funds.

The first year's account is headed thus :—

"Fait a remembrer que ceux sont lez acomptz de Clement Kyrton, Mestre de la Fraternite Seint Johan le Baptistre des Taillours en Londres de les biens du dit Fraternite, renduz le xxme jour de August[3] l'an du regne Roy Henry quarte puis le conquest primer."

---

[1] Account Book, No. 2.
[2] The Account Books commence in 23 Richard II. but are not very legible."
[3] Over this date is written, " Vendredi devaunt le feste de Seint Michell."

CHAP. VI.] *Expenditure in* 1399-1400. 123

The income or receipts of the Company are set out from rents, benefactions, fines (Almoigne De veill, 45*l*. and De Novell 11*l*. 14*s*. 4*d*.), and admission of " Confrers," amounting to 29*l*. 6*s*. 8*d*. Then follow the payments thus :[1]

"Ceux sount les espensis faitz el noun du dicte Fraternite. Chapelins et Pours."

The Company's Ordinances[2] of 19th February, 1371, gave, as we have already pointed out, all the fines leviable under it to the "Alms of St. John Baptist, that is to say to the priests and poor men," and this heading shews the expenditure.

	li.	*s.*	*d.*
En primes. A Sir Wauter Edenestowe, pur l'an	vj	xiij	iiij
[3]David Kelby, bedell, pur l'an		iij	
[3]Johan Brenchele, clerk, pour soun salary pur l'an		liij	iiij
Item, pur sa table, pur l'an		lij	
Umfrey Dunham, pur l'an		iij	
Richard Walwayn, pur l'an		iij	
Cristian Wytham, pur l'an		iij	
Nicholas Cornewaill, pur l'an		iij	
Johan Bateman, pur l'an		iij	
Sare Lunt, pur l'an		xl	
Robert atte Pye		lvj	viij
William Herford, pur iij quarters		lij	
Geffrey Kent, pur iij quarters		xlv	
Adam Ladies, pur demi an		xxx	
Johan Cornewaill		xxviij	iiij
Richard Jardevyle, serjant, pur l'an		vj	viij
Item, pur l'enterment de Roger Dalby		vij	viij
Item, pur l'obit de Maister Thos. Carleton		vj	xj
Item, pur ij novelles torches et le peinture pur le lumir a Poulis et pur chaundelle en la chapelle, par l'an		xx	iij

The sumptuary expenses relate to the great feast of the year— "the day of the Nativity of St. John the Baptist," in whose honour it was kept under their Charters, and to the antient custom of entertaining "strangers" by the dinner then given to them. The items were these

	li.	*s.*
Item, alowance a le Mestre pur straminer[4] et apparailer la sale et lez chambres encontre le feste de Seint Johan		xl
Item, pur payn et vin pur chaunter messe en le chapelle par l'an		ij
Item, pur jarlondis as mestres et maistresses		ij vj
Item, pur loture de la naperie		ij vj

[1] Memorials, page 657. [2] Chapter II, page 35.
[3] Establishment Charges. [4] Strewing rushes on the floor of the Hall.

124   *Religion and Almsgiving.*   [PART I.

	li.	*s.*	*d.*
Item, pur Minstrellis pur la feste et pur autres estrangers		xxviij	viij
Item, pur le wafrer pur le feste....		xiij	iiij
Item, pur lez chaperons des mynstrelles et wafrer, et faisure		xij	ix
Item, paie a le peintour en parti de paiement del peinture de lez baners		xxii	

Which with two concluding ones :—

	li.	*s.*	*d.*
Item, pur paper et parchemyn pur l'an....			xij
Item, pur quitrente al abbe et covent de Westm', pur l'an		xx	

amounted to the total sum of 51*l.* 16*s.* 11*d.*

The account then contains the customary expenditure on giving of "cloth" to various officials, from the king downwards, as follows :

Drap alowe par le Companie.[1]	*li.*	*s.*	*d.*
En primes, a le Roi, vj verges drap de ix*s.* un pece tartaryn, xxviij*s.* iiij*d.*	iiij	ij	iiij
A le prince, iiij verges demi drap de ix*s.* un pece tarteryn, xxvj*s.* viij*d.*	iij	vij	ij
A le meire, un goune et chaperon,[2] pris		xviij	
Item, a le tresorer, un chaperon, pris		iij	
Le Recordour et ij viscontz, iij chaperons		vij	vj
Richard Whitynton, le chamberleyn et son clerk, iij chaperons		vij	
William Cressewik, une robe		xviij	
William Morehay, une robe		xvj	
Sir Wauter Edenestowe, une robe		xix	iij
Sir Hugues Tesdale, une robe		xij	iij
Richard Jardevyle, Credy, Battisford, Est, Rose, Otis, vj chaperons		xij	
Johan Berfayr, un chaperon		ij	vj
Johan Godeston et sa femme, ij robis		xlj	ij
William Herford, une robe		xiij	ij
Johan Brynchele, clerk, un robe		xj	

Summa xvj*li.* x*s.* iiij*d.*

The last section of the account includes the expenses incurred for the "Coronation of Henry IV" on Edward the Confessor's Day (13th October, 1399).

A great occasion was that coronation, which was made with the full consent of Parliament, and after " all the people with one voyce sayed that their wylles was to have him Kynge, and how

---

[1] Chapter VII, page 132.   [2] Hood.

they wolde have none other but hym..... Then the people lyfted up their hands on hygh, promising hym their faythe and allegyance." To such ceremony the King rode from the Tower on a white courser, and the Garter on his left leg. "All the burgesses and lombard merchants in London, and every craft with their livry and devyse accompanying him." "After the Coronation (continues the Chronicler) the king went to his Palays, and there was a fountayne that runne by divers branches, white wyne and reed.... At the first table sate the king, at the second the Peers of the Realm, at the thyrde *the valyant men of London*, at the fourth the new made knights," and so on other tables mentioned. "Thus the day passed of King Henry's coronation with great joy and feast."[1]

These are the items:

	s.	d.
Item, pur mynstrelles al coronacion du Roy	xxiij	iiij
Item, pur lours chaperons, et le fesure, et pur boire a icelle temps	vj	ix
Item, pur mynstrelles al chivache du meire	xxiiij	
Item, pur lours chaperons, le fesure et boire a icelle temps	viij	vj

The other year taken for illustration comes down to the date of Langwith's gift. The account would not repay perusal in its entirety, and this analysis is given of receipts and payments:[2]

1466–7.—Receipts 283*l*. 7*s*. 2*d*.

Payments.	£	s.	d.
Trust payments	7	11	8
Chantries	37	14	2
Salaries	15	10	0
Almsmen[3]	22	8	4
Obits, &c.	4	10	0
Cloth	9	9	0
Sumptuary[4]	14	7	0
Repairs	42	16	0
Sundries	13	1	3
	167	7	5
Rents—outstanding	42	2	0
	£209	9	5

---

[1] 2 Frois. Chro., vol. 2, page 752 (ed. 1812).
[2] I am indebted to Mr. Chambers for this analysis.
[3] MS. (1468–9).
[4] The chief item of this is, 7 dozen garnish against the feast, 4*l*. 13*s*. 4*d*.

1468–9. Almsmen were as follows :

John Calham, one whole year, 6*l*. 14*s*. 4*d*; Clement Ashton, Robert Enderley, William Whyte, for one whole year, 3*l*. 17*s*. 4*d*. each, made up thus, per week, the Company, 1*s*. 2*d*., Sutton, 2*d*., and Holland 1*d*., 11*l*. 12*s*. 0*d*.; Henry Ketelwell, whole of year, 3*l*. 17*s*. 4*d*.; William West, whole year, 1*l*. 6*s*. 8*d*.; Thomas Percyval, 2*l*.; Thomas Sele, 1*l*. 13*s*. 4*d*.

It only remains to say that towards the close of the century (October, 1480) the Company obtained a grant of arms with these *religious* emblems[1]:

"Silver, a pavilion between two mantles imperial, purple, garnished with gold in a chief azure, an holy lamb set within a sun; the crest upon the helm a pavilion, purple, garnished with gold, being within the same our Blessed Lady St. Mary the Virgin in a vesture of gold sitting upon a cushion azure, Christ, her son standing naked before her, holding between his hands a vesture called tunica inconsutilis, his said mother working upon that, one end of the same vesture set within a wreath gold and azure, the mantle purple, furred with ermine."

This grant taken voluntarily preceded by a few years the order of the Earl Marshall, for all the crafts to take grants under a penalty of imprisonment or fine for using any sign or token without his authority, thus[2]:

"And also to all craftes and Companies of this noble city of London to have tokens of armes devised and given unto the said Companies, so that it doth appear by the same what crafte and occupation they be of, and also that no Masters and Wardens of what occupation they or any of them be of, do not enterprize or bear any signs or token of armes or devices in targets, banners, &c., without they be authorized by Clarenceux King of Arms, upon pain of imprisonment and to fyne at the King's pleasure." The charges for such a grant of arms being 10*l*.

---

[1] The Corporate seal of 1502 has never been changed or altered, and bears a beautiful impression of these arms.

[2] Charles Suffolk, Earl Marshal from 1509–1547. Dallaway's Heraldry, 1793, page 170.

CHAPTER VII.

SECULAR AFFAIRS AND POSITION OF THE COMPANY AT THE CLOSE OF THE FIFTEENTH CENTURY.

Continued action of the Guild, p. 127.—As to trade, p. 127.—Search, p. 128.— Yard measure, p. 128.—Authority of the Master and Wardens, p. 129.— Fines, how enforced, p. 129.—The Mace, p. 130.—Company used for secular purposes, p. 130.—Pier's contract, p. 130.—Class and status of ordinary members, p. 131.—Honorary members as (1) *Kings, pp.* 132, 133; (2) *Nobles, p.* 134.—*Company in relation to* (1) *Corporation, p.* 134.—*Dispute with Clopton in* 1441, *p.* 135.—*R. Holland rejected as Sheriff, p.* 136.—*Charter of* 1439 *disputed, p.* 136.—(2) *The Skynners' dispute, p.* 137.—*Billesden's award, p.* 139.

IN the last chapter we have endeavoured to show the early connection of the Guild with religion and almsgiving, we propose now to trace its action in things secular, and to show the position in matters social or civic which the Taylors held towards their fellow citizens of other guilds at the close of the fifteenth century.

By the first charter (1327) the Company had committed to them the government of their mistery or trade and the state of their servants, as well forcigners (*i.e.*, non-freemen) as others taking shops. No one could hold a tailor's shop or counter within the city, or be admitted to the freedom thereof, unless testified by the freemen of the Company that he was honest, faithful, and fit for the same. By the charter of 1390 the right to use a livery garment was conceded as a distinction "to the brothers and sisters of the Fraternity;" and by the charter of 1439 the exclusive right of search within the city and the suburbs thereof was granted to the Company, over and against all members of the trade, with power to cancel and reform all defects by the survey of the Lord Mayor. These privileges were largely extended by their final charter of 1502. Their right of search included all natives, strangers, and foreigners in the city, liberties, and suburbs, making, cutting, and working of men's apparel, and no person could exercise this craft unless first admitted thereto by the Master and Wardens. The search was "as to their goods or wares, woollen cloth, ells and measures," and to carry out the powers conferred by these charters "ordinances" were made, imposing fines and penalties, which were recoverable by the authority of the Master and Wardens primarily, or of the Lord Mayor in case an extreme measure of suppression was needed.

Taking the ordinance for search-making[1] as an illustration, it was in these words:—

Also it is ordayned that according to the ould usage and custome the ffower Wardens of the said Mysterie and such other of the same as have bene Wardens as the Master will appoint with and by the oversight of the Lord Maior of London for the tyme being shall as often and when as the said Maister shall think beneficiale to the said Mysterie make search throughout the whole cittie and the suburbs thereof and also at Bartholomew Faier during the tyme of that Faier amongst all the occupiers and ffreemen of their owne mysterie, as well for waights, measures yardes and ells as for non presenting of Apprentices, non enrolling of them, and of keeping of fforeyns contrary to the Lawes and use of the said City and of the good Rules and Ordynances of the said Mystery and of all other defaults which shall happen them to finde in theire search-making; And the transgressors and Breakers of theire said Acts and Ordinances to be punyshed and payned accordyng to theire deserving (viz.) Every offendor in using a false waight or yarde, six shillings and eightpence, and for not presenting and enrolling of every Apprentice the like penaltie of six shillings and eightpence. And it is ordayned that this same ordynance be openly redd by the Clerk of the said Mysterie, twice or thrice in a yeare, at Quarter dayes holden at theire Comon Hall, upon payne of fforfeiture of 40s. to be forfeyted by the same clerk to the use of the said ffellowshipp."

Now the "yard" here referred to is still in possession of the Merchant Taylors. It was the measure of London from say A.D. 1445, and has the Lombarde H, the Hall Mark in that year.[2] "The Iron yard of our Lord the King contained (as the Statute of Edward II still provides) three feet and no more, and a foot ought to contain twelve inches by the right measure of this yard measured (to wit) thirty-six parts of this yard rightly measured maketh one inch neither more or less." Such the standard yard has continued to this day. Bartholomew Fair, instituted by Henry II, by grant to the "Prior" for three days, was the great occasion for the "search." The Lord Mayor and Aldermen went in proces-

---

[1] Page 26, ante.

[2] This letter also identified the yard of Henry VII. See House of Commons Report of 1758, page 42, and seventh Report (1873) on Weights and Measures, page 34.

CHAP. VII.]   *Authority of Masters and Wardens.*   129

sion and proclaimed the fair on the Eve at the great gate of the Cloth Fair. The search having been made, sales forthwith commenced, all the clothiers of England and the drapers of London resorting to it. The account books show the "search" to have been made as early as 1428, and until the fair was abolished in 1854. In earlier days it was attended with some conviviality, as in 1445 we find this entry:—" In expenses for the wardens, the clerke, and bedill, with other drynkyngs in the search time, and about gadering yn of the money for prentises, and at other tymes with consell and suche other necessary and nedful for the craft 1*l.* 15*s.* 2*d.*" These Wardens thought more (we fear) of their own enjoyment than of the cost to which they put the Company, for in 31 and 32 Henry VI the cost was 12*d.*; and in 32 and 33 Henry VI the entry runs thus: "Expenses of the wardens making a search ' super hominibus hujus misteriæ' at Bart fair 10½*d.*" Latterly the beadle only attended on one day of the fair with the silver yard to test those used by the cloth vendors, of which he made a return to the " Pie Poudre Court."

The question naturally arises, How were these fines enforced ? What were the powers of the Master and Wardens as rulers of the Guild : and had they any and what judicial functions ?

From the books of the Company it is abundantly clear that the Master and Wardens exercised the power of fine and imprisonment over the guildsmen, and were, according to Lord Holt's definition, " a Court of Record." The oaths have been already set out. That of the Master clearly points to his judicial functions—he is " descretely to examine the matter of complaint and of variance, truly to determine it." "No favor or partialitie to either party" is to be shown, and all breakers of the ordinances are be to punished by fine and amercement, for the benefit of the Company. The Wardens were also sworn in these respects to be assistants to the Master. The ordinance against "partiality" is most emphatic, and a penalty of 5*l.* each is to be levied against the Master and Wardens, if found guilty, by the "sadest and most discreete of the Fraternity." Both the livery and freemen were sworn "not to withstand or disobey the summons of the Master and Wardens." The beadle, as the summoning and executive officer, was sworn to do all the summonings or warnings without one penny receiving, "within the Fraternity, whether between party and party of the same mysterie, or else between masters and apprentice or servant," and, except of stranger complaining, he was also to gather in all distresses, fines, and amercements awarded by the Master and Wardens.

The emblem of the Master's authority was the "mace." The "Chronicle of London" states: "In this year (1338) King Edward graunted that the seriaunts both of the meire and the schirreves of London schulde beren before the maire and the schirreves of London maces of silver and other gilte with the Kinges Armes," and the charter of the same date confirms this statement. Under what express authority the Company adopted a "mace" we have not discovered; but the mace held is the work of Mr. Duckett, a notable goldsmith in 1597 (who probably lent Queen Mary 2,000*l.* in 1569, as one "Leonel" of that name did so according to Stowe). A mace had been in use before this date, but the original one was stolen 1596–7, and the present one was made to replace it, at a cost of 6*l.* 4*s.* (with the "yard," which was also stolen). The tribunal of the Master and Wardens held its sittings in the hall, and from the "daïs" justice was for many years dispensed to the members of the Guild in all the minor matters of trade and good manners.

It has already appeared that the Guildsmen used the Company as the executor or administrator of their devises and bequests for matters other than civil or secular, but it will be seen that there was a disposition on the part of its members to use the Company in a somewhat similar way to carry out or see executed their trade or family arrangements. An instance of this as to trade, originating during the mastership of Thomas Burgeys in the year 1467, is preserved.[1]

Stephen Piers was anxious to retire and to transfer his business, which he carried on in Bucklersbury, to his son John, giving him his stock-in-trade and book debts, and handing over to him all his servants and apprentices. But he was to have a provision for himself and for his wife, and for "Anne Parys, a poore mayden that is dief and dome." The terms as agreed upon by father and son are set forth in a memorandum. The stock-in-trade was valued at 220*l.* sterling, and besides paying the rent of the house and allowing his parents the "White Chamber," and another annexed called "the Rede," the son was to provide, when either walked out,[2] "an honest man chyld to wayte upon the father," and

---

[1] Appendix 16, page 367.

[2] This provision of a child to "wayte" on the parents when they walked out was (I suppose) a necessity. One writing in 1598, a century and a half later than Piers' time, says, "If the mistris ride abroad she must have 6 or 7 serving men to attend her—one to carry her cloake and hood, another her fanne, another her boxe with ruffles and other necessaries, and some (which could not apply to London), to open gates and supply other services that may be occasioned."—Rye's England, page 197. See also page 259, *post.*

"an honest mayde to wayte upon the mother." For their maintenance he was to pay 10*l.* per annum at the usual quarter-days.

Following upon the last entry is another[1] of the 4th December in the mastership of William Parker (1469), which leads to the impression that the first agreement had not been found to be altogether satisfactory. The son had married, and his wife, Margaret, was to be a party to the new arrangement. Whether or not, the old people resented the introduction of Margaret into the home, at any rate they agreed "from hensforth beyng good fader and moder to their sone and his wyf," that the annual payment was to be thereafter "20 marks" for both, and 10 marks for the survivor of the father or mother. The agreements are printed in the Appendix.

As another instance, a century later, as to family arrangements, is seen when Sir Thomas White married Lady Joan Warren, and we find the "Mercers Company" parties to the marriage settlement of November, 1558, in the interest of the lady.

We must now endeavour to ascertain something of the *personelle* of whom the Guild was composed. Originally Taylors and Linen Armourers, they so continued until after the charter of Henry VII was granted, when the tailoring element began to die out, and that of the clothworker or merchant to be introduced. The changes which ultimately resulted from this charter will be dealt with hereafter, but here we deal with the Company as it existed towards the close of the 14th century.

Early records show traces of some members of the Company in their dealings as "Taylors." Thus Roger Tego, who was Master in 1463, appears in the household expenses of Sir John Howard (Duke of Norfolk), under date 1462:

"Delivered to my Lord's own Armourer, for his cost by the way, 20*s*.

"For a Bannett, 15*d*.

"For a horse to Roger Tego, 30*s*.

"For a dagger for my Lord, 20*d*."

In 1466, the name of Henry Galle, whose widow became Lady Percyvale, appears as a Taylor — his relative "William" being Master in 1471.

The next enquiry which suggests itself is whether all the

---

[1] Appendix 17, page 371.

members of the Guild in the Tudor period which became, as we shall see, so conspicuous were of this class or status? All those who attended the Guild meetings and directed its affairs were certainly (so far as we know) of this class, to whom all gratitude from their fellow citizens is due. But the Taylors had a number of honorary members, tradition saying that Edward III enrolled himself as such, but that other Kings, including Henry VII, were members admits of little doubt.[1]

A note of a late Clerk[2] to the Company runs in these words:—

"Richard II and his Queen were both of the Livery, being admitted like other members at that period by a payment of 20s. to the Company on their admission.

"The earliest entry (1398-9) in this Account Book is as follows:

"'Allowance of cloth by the Company.—First for the King 6 (yards or ells) of cloth of 8s. and 1 piece of Tartain 30s.—3l. 18s. To the Queen 6 y^{ds} of cloth of 8s. and 1 piece of Tartain 30s.—3l. 18s.' But whether these were supplied to this Sovereign and his Queen as being members of the Company, or as a matter of courtesy, is uncertain.

"The next entries relate to Henry IV and his son, who, in 1400, were both members of the Company. Similar entries are contained in the account to 1404, when the allowance of cloth to the Prince ceases, but the allowance as regards the King is entered throughout the reign, though the quantity and price of cloth vary occasionally.

"In the entry of the admission of members in 8 Henry IV, A.D. 1407, is the following one of the King's son,—'Monsr John, fitz au Roy Henri quarte, xxs.'; from which it is clear that the members of the royal family paid for their admission like any other member, as in the same list in which this entry is contained, are the admissions of noblemen and tradespeople at the same price of 20s. each.

"In 10 Henry IV, A.D. 1409, another son of this King was admitted, as appears by the following entry,—'Monsr Thomas, fitz au Roy, xxs.'

"It is believed that the Queen of Henry IV was free of the

---

[1] The circumstances under which Henry VII granted his Charter will be referred to in the life of Sir W. FitzWilliam, but there is Strype's authority for saying that this King took a personal part in the affairs of the Company, sitting openly in the Common Hall in a gown of crimson with a citizen's hood upon his shoulder at the elections of the Master and Wardens.

[2] Mr. de Mole in 1830-3.

Company, for in the year 1408 is the following entry :—' To our lord the King, 8 yards of coloured [cloth] of 5s. 8d., and 1 piece "tarteryn" of 23s. 4d.,—3l. 8s. 8d. The Queen, 8 yards of cloth of 5s. 8d., and 1 piece of tarteryn of 23s. 4d.—3l. 8s. 8d.,' being the only year in which the Queen had cloth.

"Henry V ascended the throne in 1413, and was admitted to the Freedom in 1414, but he had cloth the first year of his reign.

"The following entry in the second year of his reign shows his admission to the brotherhood or 'confrères' :—' Nostre tres excellent Sʳ le Roi Henri Quinte'; but in the last three years of this reign no cloth seems to have been given to him, though the Queen had 9 yards of green cloth at 6s. 8d. in the 9th year.

"Henry VI commenced his reign in 1422, and was admitted to the Company between the years 1436 and 1437; but in the statement of cloth allowed by the Company in the second year of Henry VI (1424) is the following entry :—' Our Lord the King, 3 yards of colored cloth of 6s. 8d. the yard, xxs. For Tartaryn Robe, 12s.'

"The entry of the allowance of cloth to the King is regularly made up to and including 1445; but in 1446 (23 Henry VI) there is no entry of cloth to the King, but an entry as follows :—' First for the Privy Seal 5 yards of colour of 4s. 6d., sum 22s. 6d.' "

"There is a lapse in the Company's account from 1445 to 1453 in 31 Henry VI.

"The allowance of cloth appears to have been discontinued after 1453, for there appears no entry upon the subject in the account after that year nor in subsequent reigns."

These entries show the attendance of the governing body of the craft on the Sovereign at various dates :—

"In 1453–4:
A barge to London for the anniversary of Henry V .. 6s. 10d."
Expenses of the Master and Wardens appearing before the Council at Westminster, by the King's order .. 1s. 1d."
A barge for a member of the Company to meet the Queen coming from Greenwich to Westminster .. 4s."

"In 1461–2:
To 10 Brethren riding to meet the King (Edward IV) 3l. 6s. 8d."

"In 1462–3:
Boat hire with the Mayor to Westminster at the King's command, and eight horsemen to serve the King, each .. .. 6s. 8d."

"In 1463-4 :
To 10 Brethren riding to meet the King, each .. 6s. 8d."
"In 1464-5 :
Barge hire to Greenwich for the Master and others going to meet the King and Queene to the feste of St. John .. .. 4s."

The list of other (honorary) members given elsewhere[1] commences in 1351 with Roger Mortimer (summoned to Parliament in September, 1355, as Earl of March), and of the first 60 names ending with William Ferrers De Groby (summoned to Parliament in 1396) and admitted in 1413, almost all (save prelates and religious men) were related to the Plantagenet family. What were the inducements for men of the highest rank to associate themselves with the Taylors and Linen Armourers are not easy to determine, for there was little hospitality save at the cost of the individual members, and few other advantages of which they could avail themselves.[2] Still many of these did join the Company, paying for their admission, as it is supposed, like ordinary freemen, and exercising their privilege of taking apprentices and admitting to the freedom. One of such instances, at least, is known, and others may be extant. Thomas Ratcliffe, third Earl of Sussex, who stands on the list of honorary members as of 1562, presented John Bull as his apprentice on the 28th January, 1577, for admission to the freedom, and asked for John Evans, though not a member of the Company, to be appointed to the Clerkship in December, 1571.[3]

Something must now be mentioned of the position or relationship which the Taylors' Company occupied towards the Corporation and the other guilds of London.[4] Unfortunately, in the 15th century, controversy had arisen towards each of these bodies, which, at the intervention of the King in the one case, and of the Mayor in the other, had been adjusted.

The controversy with the Corporation arose out of the "great Charter" granted to the Company in February, 1439 (18th Henry VI), and which made one of their members obnoxious to the Mayor and Aldermen.

Under this charter the Master and Wardens had power "to

---

[1] See Chapter XVI, and notes thereto.
[2] Up to 1453 Livery cloth was given to them, Memorials, page 597.
[3] See page 305, post.   [4] Part II, Chapter III, as to this.

make full search in and concerning the mysteries and all those who are or may be privileged with the Taylors within our city and the suburbs thereof, and that no other persons or person shall in any manner make any search in or concerning the persons or mystery thereof."

It would appear from the Company's records that the right of search after those who infringed the rights of the Company, as foreigners, was exercised from a very early period of its history, for entries of money spent for meat and drink, "sur le serche faitz par les gardeins," occur as early as 6 Henry VI, 1427-8. Thus, in 7 Henry VI,—[1]

"Paie as dyvers foitz sur lez serchez del Mistier et autres hommes pour warnyng de dyvers forcins overantz en musset, 6s. 8d."

And in 13 Henry VI,—

"Espendu divers foitz en viaunde et boire sur lez gardeins pour le serche et gaderyng dez revenuz, xxs."

Again, in 14 Henry VI,—

"Spent in mete and drynke whan the Meister went to serche, sur luy et lez gardeins et le serjaunt, et autres, iij daies, xxjs. Item, Paie a Holgrave Serjaunt, pour son labour delserche, xld."

It was in this state of feeling that our guildsman, Ralph Holland, presented himself to his fellow citizens for election as Mayor in 1441-2 (the other candidate for the mayoralty being Robert Clopton, the Draper), and was rejected, with something like a riot. Holland was a noble benefactor to his guild, giving his estate "in pure and perpetual alms" by will "sealed in the presence of Roger Legg and other guildsmen, on the 5th day of May, 1442, executed between the sixth and seventh hours after noon, the said Ralph then lying in his upper chamber in his bed." And we may reasonably presume that the irritation arising out of the "grete Charter" was the cause of his rejection by the Court of Aldermen, as thus described by Holinshed:

"When the Maior brought down Clopton upon his right hand towards the Hall, whereby the Taylors present saw that Holland was not chosen, they cried out, 'Nay, nay.' Wherewith the old Maior being astonished, stood still upon the staire, and where he sat downe and his brethren about him. In the meantime continued their crie and incensed of base trades of the citie (as simple persons) to take their part and to cry as fast as they, not proffering to cease their misrule for all that the Maior could saie, no nor yet

---

[1] Account Books, passim.

where the Maior's Serjeant-at-arms had cried, 'O Yes.' Whereupon the Maior to appease the rumor, sent downe the Sheriffs and commanded them to take the offenders and send them to gaole;" which precept was fulfilled, and about twelve or sixteen committed to Newgate, where some of them abode a long time imprisoned.[1]

Holland's rejection shows at least that the election of a Mayor was then by choice and not by seniority, or surely the law-abiding Aldermen would not have rejected him.

One of the earliest of Robert Clopton's official acts was to require this charter to be suspended. A Council Order appears to have been obtained "from the King's Parlour at Sheene," dated the 21st August, 1442, stating that "it is advised and commanded that letters of Privy Seal be directed to the Wardens of the Craft of Taylors of London and to all the Taylors thereof, and then setting forth the grant and ordering and charging for certain causes, moving the King and his Council that after the sight of these presents they should surcease of putting in execution the said pleas as touching the said search, and that every and each of them obey the Mayor of London after the old usages, customs, and laws of London, and that they bring before the King at the Council the said letters patent at St. Michael next even, for to see the contents of the said letters."[2] This order was sent to Clopton on the 20th March with instructions to put in force "all the articles of the great Charter of the city," notwithstanding the aforesaid charter of the Taylors.

The search under the Charter made at St. Bartholomew's fair appears to have brought the Company into trouble, for some men of the craft were committed to Newgate. It involved the payment[3] of more fees to lawyers and Crown officials for procuring a letter from the king to the Mayor to set the matter straight and to save the Charter from being revoked.

The search in its continuance appears to have been a convivial meeting, for the next entry is:—

"23 Henry VI.—In expensis for the Wardens, the clerks and bedill, with other drynkynges, in the serchyng tyme and aboute gaderyng yn of the money for prentises, and at other tymes with consell and suche other necessary and needful for the craft, xxxvs. ijd."

So much for the controversy with the Corporation. The dispute

---

[1] Holinshed, Vol. 3, page 204.
[2] Vol. 5, page 196, Sir H. Nicholas' Privy Council.
[3] See Chapter II, *ante*, and for bill of payments, Appendix 4, page 346.

with the Skynners Company arose on a question of precedency and the claim of the Taylors to go before them in the Royal and other processions which were then frequent in the city. There would appear to have been no fixed rules to determine such a question, other than this one, namely, that the guild from which the Mayor was chosen should take precedence of all others.

The guilds varied from time to time too much in numbers and in wealth to make either of these facts the test of precedency. Thus in 1464 the Skynners furnishing only 20 men were placed before the Taylors furnishing 30 men for the entry of Elizabeth, the Queen of Edward IV, for her coronation in May, 1465. So again, in the watch for St. Peter and St. Paul, though there were 20 Skynners and 50 Merchant Taylors, and in November, 1483, when 24 Skynners and 30 Taylors rode out to meet Richard III coming to the city. The disparity was even greater in the order of 28th July, 1485, for the "marching watch," as only 60 Skynners paraded against 200 Taylors. However, the rule of precedency laid down in Shea's mayoralty of 1483, gave the Taylors precedency with 84 men over the Skynners 54 men, and when Henry VII entered the city in August, 1485, after the battle of Bosworth, the Taylors having John Swan, their guildsman, as Sheriff, and furnishing 30, they took precedence of the Skynners furnishing 20 men only. But, from the date of their Charter, or incorporation, the Skynners were entitled to precedence, for theirs is dated on the 1st and the Taylors on the 10th of March, 1327.

In this state of uncertainty controversy arose in one or other of the processions between the two Companies and their differences, according to the wise temper of those times, were submitted for decision to the supreme civic ruler, the Mayor Mr. (afterwards Sir) Robert Byllesden. The reference appears to have been a formal one, very soon disposed of. "For nourishing of peas and love between the Masters, Wardens, and Fellowships aforesaid," so runs his decree of 10th April, 1484, let them dine together at their respective Halls, the Taylors with the Skynners on the vigil of Corpus Christus Day and the Skynners with the Taylors on the Feast of the Nativity of St. John Baptist. As to precedency, let each Company take that on each alternate year, save that a Mayor of either shall give that Company precedence in his year of office. So the decree has for 403 years been observed, while "peas and love" has reigned between the two fellowships.[1]

---

[1] See page 175 for Sir Francis Palgrave's opinions on City Festivals.

CHAPTER VIII.

THE EARLIER HALF OF THE SIXTEENTH CENTURY AND THE DISENDOWMENT OF RELIGION.

Two great changes in the sixteenth century: Disendowment of religion and destruction of Guild monopoly, p. 138.—Religious and eleemosynary gifts from 1507 to 1531 to the Company, p. 138.—Example of an Obit from Sir John Percyvale's will, p. 139.—Act for Chauntries Collegiate, p. 140.— Effect of it, p. 140.—37 Henry VIII, c. 4, p. 141.—Commissioners' return under it, p. 142.—Extracts from cash books, p. 142.—Payment to the Crown, p. 143.—Edward VI's Act and preamble, p. 143.—Royal Commissioners to ascertain sums due from Guilds, p. 144.—Court of Merchant Taylors Company in 1548-9, p. 145.—Execution of Commission and Extracts from cash books, p. 145.—Obit omitted, p. 145.—Annual payment to the Crown, p. 145.—Purchase of obit charges from the Crown, p. 146.—Extracts from Commissioners' Report of 1884, p. 146.—Extortion against the Guilds, p. 147.—Conveyance of Property to Guilds, p. 148.— Petition to Parliament for Act 5 and 6 Edward VI, to confirm same, p. 149.—Religious services extinguished, p. 149.—Eminent members of the Guild, p. 149.

THE sixteenth century was the most eventful one in the history of the London Guilds, for in the earlier half religion was disendowed and in the later half their trade monopoly was destroyed. Taking these subjects in the order in which they arose we shall deal with the first in this chapter.

We have already seen how to the close of the fourteenth century the Merchant Taylors Company had been selected by many persons to carry out their religious and charitable purposes, giving to the Company in most instances estates, and in others money for rent-charges (created over their Guild estates) to provide priests (and other attendants), with all things needful for the due solemnity of religious worship.

The lives of Percyvale, Jenyns, and others will show that this current of benefactions did not cease with that century. From 1507 until 1531 fourteen estates were devised to the Company, besides (at least) two contracts, those of John Howdan and Sir William FitzWilliam made for obits. All these devises were of valuable estates, ten of which are still possessed by the Company. Howdan's contract was made in 1514 by nuncupative will, which his family refused to recognise. The Company asserted their title in Chancery before the Lord Chancellor (Warham), and the full circumstances of the gift, as made in the Common Hall, in favour of specific objects are set out in the Bill, which, as the trusts are now being carried out by the Company,[1] we presume was successful.

As the direction for an obit on the anniversary of a benefactor's death occurs in many wills of this period, it may be well to give the exact words of Sir John Percyvale's will in creating his obit.

The testator directs that it shall be done "solempnely by note "with placebo and dirige on night and masse of requiem on the "morne by the persone of the Church or by his deputee and "by my said ij Chauntry Preests and by oder ij Chauntry Preests "and the ij Clerks of the same Church (that is to say) vii "persones in all at which obite I woll that the Clerke cause to "be rongen iij solempne peales in the tyme of synging placebo "and dirige on night and oder iij like peals to be rongen on "the morne in the tyme of synging of the masse of requiem "and that the persone or his deputee shall sing the High Masse of "Requiem there praying for my soule and other souls aforesaid and "that the said Maister and Wardeyns of the said Fraternytee "shall so ordeyn ij tapers of wax weiyng booth xii lbs. to brenne "there during the tyme of the said service, paiying for the wax and "makin of the said ij tapers xvi*d*. and I woll that the Maister and "Wardeyns of the said fraternytee with a competent number of "bretheren of the same Fraternytee and with the Beadle and "Clerk of the same Felowship shall come together in one clothing "to the said obite as well to dirige and nighte as to masse of requiem "in the morne to say there 'De Profundis' and other prayers as "like as in such cases they may be accustomed to do and after "dirige done I woll that the said Maister, Wardeyns and Bretheren "and also the Preest and Clerk and other neighbours beyng at the "said obite shall come if it please them together into my said "dwelling place, if the tenant thereof woll suffre it and else to "the Merchant Taylors Hall and there the Maister and Wardeyns "for the time beyng to provide as much bread and ale to be spent "among them as shall amount unto xs."

They were to make divers payments thereat, *i.e.*—

---

[1] Appendix 19, page 373.

		s.	d.
2 wax tapers		1	4
Bread, cheese and ale		10	0
In worship of 5 wounds		0	6
The Parson		1	0
4 Chauntry Priests		2	0
2 Clerks		1	0
Chamberleyn of London		6	8

Now at these services the governing body and officials of the craft, together with the brethren who cared to attend, were present, and hence religion—whether false or aught else you can call it—had a very conspicuous place in the routine of corporate life, which the Fraternity thought it to be their duty to fulfil. But by the Act under notice all these religious services were swept away, and the rent-charges by which they were supported confiscated and misapplied to purely secular uses by the Crown and its courtiers.

Some few years before the "Act for Chauntries Collegiate" of Edward's reign became law, the monasteries and religious houses,[1] by the aid of the Roman[2] Parliament, had fallen into the King's

---

[1] The 26th Henry VIII, cap. 3, secs. 2 and 9, granted the first fruits of all bishoprics, monasteries, &c., to the Crown, and directed a Commission to issue in each diocese to enquire into and certify the true yearly value and the deductions therefrom allowed by the Act. Dr. Tanner[a] gives the detail of each house in each county, and then this general summary:—

	£	s.	d.
555 Religious houses of the yearly value of..	136,710	14	5
Knights Hospitallers	5,396	6	6
Friars	809	11	8
Total	£142,916	12	17

Another authority gives these figures:—

	£	s.	d.
186 The "greater" monasteries	104,919	13	3
374 The "lesser" monasteries	2,385	12	8
48 The Knights Hospitallers (London)	3,026	9	5
28 Do. do. (country)	851	9	0
608 Friars	£140,785	6	3

[2] See Mr. Gasquet's remarks on the formation of the Parliament of 1529, which passed these measures, Vol. 1, page 300, Henry VIII and the English Monasteries.

[a] Notitia, page lvii.

hands. Reform, either by themselves or by the State, they had resisted, opposing every attempt to bring them back to their earlier and purer mode of life. "It is" (writes Archbishop Trench) "the misfortune of institutions, which are merely human inventions, that after a while they overlive themselves, having contributed all which they were capable of contributing to the Church's good or the world's, they thenceforward cumber a ground which they may have profited once; the reason of their existence having ceased, there is now one supreme favour which they would confer, that is not to seek to exist any more. It is seldom, however, that those who are bound up with institutions which have thus overpast their time see things in this light, while yet the falseness of their position, and the consciousness of this falseness which they cannot wholly escape—in many ways tell mysteriously upon them. The elevating sense of a true vocation is gone. The sphere in which a healthy activity is possible has grown much narrower, or has quite disappeared, and under these conditions it is almost inevitable that a rapid deterioration, moral and spiritual, should follow. The decay of discipline, the dissolution of manners, the dying out of all sense of corporate life (in the monasteries) were everywhere making themselves visible to the eyes of all."[1]

But although the monasteries had fallen without opposition from the mitred abbots in Parliament, there were left other endowments for colleges, chauntries, guilds, &c., which stood somewhat on the same platform, and the founders and owners in possession fearing the same fate as the monasteries, thought (as some persons in our own day have done) to anticipate the action of Parliament. They entered into possession of the endowments for their own use, dividing the spoils, and it was the primary object of the 37th Henry VIII, cap. 4, to defeat these alleged misappropriations, which "some donors or patrons had of their avarouse and covetouse myndes" effected, whereby the said colleges, chauntries, and guilds had been clearly dissolved. To meet the war expenses of the King, the Commons with their "hole voice, petition, and intercession besought the King" that all these colleges, chauntries, guilds, &c., with their estates, which between the 4th February, 27th Henry VIII (1535-6) and the 25th December 37th Henry VIII (1544-5), had by such means aforesaid been dissolved should

---

[1] Page 420 of Archbishop Trench's Lectures (the Eve of the Reformation) on Mediæval Church History. Macmillan, 1877.

be deemed to be in the very actual and real possession of the King and his successors for ever.

This part of the Act had no operation against establishments not dissolved, and as all founders had not entered on these Guilds to dissolve them, another theory was put forth with regard to those remaining established for charitable purposes, viz.:—That they "were *not* so employed, to the great displeasure of Almighty God, and the discontent of the King," and as the King "of his most godly and blessed disposition intended to have the premises used to more godly and virtuous purposes," Parliament authorised him during his life to issue Commissions to "persons in any county or place to enter into any such colleges, chauntries, guilds, &c., and hold the same in his name and for his use, and that of his successors for ever."

Although the statute was drawn in such wide terms as to have swept away into the Royal coffers all the endowments of Winchester and Eton, if put in operation against those colleges, such a construction was not asserted against the Guilds, but the Act appears to have been brought into operation against them forthwith.

Before the King's death the Royal Commissioners, either in person or by their deputies, had visited the Company's Hall to execute their Commission, and had ascertained by enquiry what property was held by the Guild, and returned to the Court of Augmentation their certificate as to that property which they deemed to have passed to the Crown under the Act. The return of chauntries and obits made by the Merchant Taylors Company is still extant, and these entries in the account books relate to the subject.

"1545-6. Item, pd. for meat and drink ordained for them that was appointed to make the boke for the certificate of the Chauntries according to a commission to them directed, 40s.

"Item, pd. to Mr. Recorder[1] for his accounceill in making the said certificate, 15s.

"Item, pd. for a quire of paper, 3d.

"Item, pd. to Robert Christopher for his pains in writing the book for the same, 40s."

"Paid for refection at the 'Mermaid Tavern' when we put in our book to the Commissioners, 8d."

"Item, paid more for refection made at the 'Mermaid Tavern,'

---

[1] Robert Brook, Chief Justice of the Common Pleas in 1554.

when we met their to take counsel to answer Mr. Mildmay and other the King's Commissioners, touching the last will of Sir S. Jenyns, 1s. 6d."

"Paid, and giving more to the witnesses at the Lord Chancellor[1] when as we went to speak to his Lordship in the said matter, by the advice of them that were appointed for the said matter, 2s."

The certificate was accepted by the Crown and immediately acted upon, for the same year's accounts contain this entry:

"Paid to the King's Majesty for certain money which was given to this mystery by Sir Stephen Jenyns, Master Percival, and Master Acton for to keep an obit, and otherwise to be distributed by this Company, all which is dissolved[2] and now found due to the King's Majesty in areages, 52l. 10s."

By Henry VIII's death the Act expired and further legislation was absolutely needful, as, in the absence of it, the founders or owners of the existing endowments would again have taken possession of them for their own use.

Fortunately or unfortunately, as the case may be viewed by each reader, the late King had not declared upon the statute the "godly and virtuous purposes" to which (had he lived) he would have applied these endowments, but that there might be no mistake as to the intentions of Parliament these were declared by the preamble to the Act of Edward VI. Possible confiscation would be made more acceptable to the people if the Act were prefaced with an enunciation of the doctrines of the Reformed faith and of the necessity for their preservation to the State.

The ostensible object of Parliament, as declared by the preamble, was to convert uses deemed to be superstitious into godly uses. "To correct superstition and error in the Christian religion," which had been brought into the minds and estimation of men by reason "of their ignorance of their very true and perfect salvation through the death of Jesus Christ," which vain opinions "of purgatory and masses satisfactory to be done for the departed," by nothing more was maintained than by trentals, chantries, and other provisions for the continuance of such ignorance, "therefore (the preamble went on to declare) these funds

---

[1] Lord Wriottesley, the Company's tenant in Bishopsgate Street.
[2] As the House of the Grey Friars was dissolved these obits became vested in the Crown.

must be applied to better objects," as the *erection of Grammar Schools* for the education of youth in virtue and godliness; the further augmenting the *Universities* and better provision of *the poor and needy*" Godly uses truly had they been carried out.

As Parliament could not discharge administrative duties the Crown, having for its aid and assistance the officers of the Court of Augmentation, was constituted a trustee for the Realm to put the Act (which was framed on a narrower basis than that of Henry) into execution. Of course when all the rents or lands were applied to what was deemed under the statute to be a superstitious use, then all the lands were transferred to the King; but where part only[1] of the rents were so applied, then from Easter next coming for ever the King had such sums of money as in any one year within five years before the first day of the then present Parliament had been so expended or bestowed, holding the same as a rent-charge, which was to be paid half-yearly at Michaelmas and Lady-day, by even portions to the Court of Augmentation. Hence it became necessary (as the Act provided) that Commissioners should be appointed by the Crown to ascertain[2] and report after examination of all evidences, compositions, books of account, and other writings, what moneys, or other things, had been applied to or bestowed on such superstitious uses.

At that time the Merchant Taylors Company held 29 hereditaments, standing at an annual rental of 440*l*. 13*s*. 10*d*., *all* of which (to some extent) were charged either by the Company's contract or by will, with payments to provide for masses or obits called "superstitious uses." To ascertain the total amount of these payments another Royal Commission was issued to the Lord Mayor[3] and other persons selected by the Crown for their knowledge and ability to determine what rents were held for, or what sums had been applied to, these superstitious uses.

The Act was not directed against the City Guilds, indeed in its passage through the House of Commons an assurance was given to its opponents (according to Collier and Burnet), by the Ministers of the Crown that such should not be its operation, but as that of the last reign had been so loosely drawn, it was necessary to be watchful, and this emphatic declaration should have made the Guilds secure. Except for religious sentiment the Guildsmen had no reason for concealment, as instead of making, as theretofore, several payments to several priests and in several parishes, one

---

[1] Section 5.   [2] Section 6.

[3] Sir H. Hubbathorne, a member of the Court of Assistants of the Merchant Taylors Company.

payment of an ascertained and definitive sum had thereafter to be made to the Crown.

This Commission was also executed at the Halls of the several Companies by production to the Commissioners or their agents of the contracts or wills founding the masses or obits, and the books showing the payments for these superstitious uses. The results were summed up in the form of a certificate or return to the Court of Augmentation, which appears to have been framed under the advice of the Recorder (Brooke), a man who afterwards became Speaker of the House of Commons, and Chief Justice of the Common Pleas. Further, it was handed in to the Commissioners at the Company's Hall, when a dinner was given at the cost of the Company, "the Lord Mayor being there." The facts are evidenced by these entries:

" 1547-1548. Thos. Offley, Master.

" To Mr. Brooke, recorder of London, for his advice given in making our book of certificate as touching what priests, obits, lamps, and lights was found and kept by the Company, and what lands and other thing was given for the maintenance thereof, and how long they should endure, 13s. 4d. To the Clerk, John Huchenson, for drawing and engrossing the same book and searching evidence, 40s. To the pursuivant attending on the kings commissioners at Haberdasshers' Hall, when we desired a longer day to bring in our book, 3s. 4d.

"Item to one of the Commissioner's clerks for entering the said day that was given us for bringing in of our book, 1s. 8d.

" Item, pd. for making of a dinner unto the said Commissioners my lord mayor being *here* at the same when they sat *here* in receiving of our said book of certificate as appeareth by a bill of particulars thereof ready to be showed, 7l. 18s."

We shall see hereafter that one obit, that of FitzWilliam's, was omitted by the Royal Commissioners; but as might have been expected the former recipient informed against the Company, in the Exchequer Court, and out of these circumstances arose the exhibitions long known as "Fish's Battelings," given to the poor divinity students of St. John's, still administered by the Company.[1] By the Commissioners' certificate the sum of 98l. 11s. 6d. was due to the Crown, and the Company's books show that this sum was

---

[1] Chapter XIII, page 238.

paid half-yearly to the Augmentation Office, until (as we shall see) the Company was required to purchase up or redeem these payments.[1]

The dealing of the Crown with the chauntry lands is a matter of history upon which many authorities are to be found, all concurrent in their testimony, but none agreeing with the statements which, under the authority of some of the Royal Commissioners, appointed to enquire into the City of London Livery Companies, were laid before Parliament in 1884. After saying that—"In the course of the suppression of the religious houses many lands held by the Companies to superstitious uses, such as the performance of masses for the dead and the maintenance of chauntries were confiscated," they continue, "the Companies were, however, *allowed* to redeem the lands on a *representation that they were required for* the purposes of the eleemosynary and educational charities to which they were trustees;"[2] and again, "The terms of the grants (from the Crown) have been held by the Court of Chancery to have vested in the Companies the same absolute property in these lands which the Act of Edward VI vested in the Crown, and they have thus been since, in the eye of the law, the corporate property of the Companies free from any trust. *There is no doubt, however, that the lands were only allowed to be brought back because* the Companies *represented to the Crown*, as was no doubt the fact, that *the rent was required* for the support of their *Almshouses, Schools, and Exhibitions* many of which depended for *their* existence on these superstitious uses."[3]

Collier and Tanner[4] represent the Act of Edward VI as being one of subsidy, and state that there was little intention in the King's advisers ever to use the chauntry lands for the *pious* purposes set forth in the preamble. However that may be, urgent necessity for money obliged the Crown to sell the lands and rent-charges. "The King," writes Strype, "hastened in 1548 to sell them to make up the defects of "his Treasury and to get ready money for necessary uses." Burnet is more explicit, Parliament having given the chauntry lands "that they might be delivered from all subsidies, the "Commons were dismissed and then the whole Council did on the "17th of April unanimously resolve that it was necessary to sell "5,000*l.* a year of chauntry lands for raising such a sum as the

---

[1] Appendix 17, page 371.   [2] 13th Report, page 15.
[3] 13th Report, page 40.
[4] Page xxv. Mr. Rogers in his History of Prices so treats it, vol. 4, page 183.

"King's occasion required, and Sir Henry Mildmay was appointed
"to treat about the sale of them."

Stowe[1] gives the 8th April as the date of the Council Order,
and this as the method in which the order was carried into effect:
"The citizens of London having certain chauntry lands for priests'
"wages, obits, and lights, suppressed into the King's hand by Act
"of Parliament, valued by the Commissioners to 1,000*l*. a year,
"purchased the said yearly quit-rents of the King for 20,000*l*.
"to be paid within eight days after by the Council's commandment,
"which caused them to sell much of their best land, far better,
"cheaper than they bought their quit-rents as after 16 or 14 years'
"purchase." Heylin's[2] words are "for the redeeming whereof the
"Companies were constrained to pay the sum of 20,000*l*. to the
"use of the King by an order at the Council Table." The sale of
obits or chauntry lands became part of the ways and means for
assuring the King's debts, and in 1552, Lord Burleigh[3] proposed
for that year to realise 12,000*l*. in this manner.

Shortly after these transactions the city of London placed these
facts upon record thus :—

"In the third year of Edward's reign, having occasion to levy
"a great mass of money, the King did require the Companys to
"purchase those rents, which they were loath to do, but being urged
"by their duty of love and service to the King;

"The Companies accordingly purchased those rents, for which
"they paid to the King almost 19,000*l*.

"For the raising of this sum they were enforced to sell divers
"of the said lands and tenements to pay for the rest."

The terms of redemption imposed were extortionate.[4] At that
time the Crown was paying 14*l*. per cent.[5] per annum for money
borrowed, but the Company was required to purchase these rent-
charges at the rate of 5*l*. per cent. (*i.e.*, 20 years' purchase), and
to pay this purchase-money in eight days.

As a consequence such estates as were most marketable, and
therefore most valuable, had to be disposed of at such prices as
could be obtained for prompt payment, and had not Sir Thomas
White, Sir Thomas Offley, and other members of the Company
come forward as purchasers, the result would have been more
disastrous than it was to the Company.[6] To redeem the rent-

---

[1] Annals, page 604.   [2] Vol. 1, page 279.
[3] Vol. I, Burleigh Papers, page 127.   [4] Wriothesley's Diary, page 35.
[5] In England the rate was limited to 10*l*. per cent. by 37 Henry VIII, cap. 9,
secs. 3 and 4, but this Act was repealed in Edward's reign. See part II, page 275.
[6] Note, page 151.

charge of 98*l.* 11*s.* 5*d.* estates with a rental of 122*l.* 14*s.* 2*d.* had to be disposed of, inflicting then a percentage loss of 5*l.* 9*s.* 6*d.* with a continuous annual increase ; which, measured by the *actual* rental of the estates left *unsold*, would now amount to upwards of 10,000*l.* per annum ; and is therefore the present loss inflicted on the Company by the enforced sales of 1549–50.[1]

In this manner the money was realized, and the entries in the cash book show these payments.

"3 ells of canvas for bags to put the money in for redeeming the rent-charge, 2*s.* 4*d.*

"To the Clerk of the Mercers, who was appointed by the Lord Mayor to come to all the Companies to confirm the great patent for redeeming the rent-charge, 6*s.* 8*d.*

"To the Treasurer of the Court of Augmentation for redeeming and purchasing money and quit-rents lately due to His Highness out of the lands belonging to this mystery, 2,006*l.* 2*s.* 6*d.*"

The conveyance obtained by the Company is printed at length in Herbert's work. The grant was by letters patent, made at Leighes, and bearing date 14th July, 1550, to three several nominees of the Corporation in trust for the several Companies.

Nothing can be more specific than its terms. Each rent-charge is described in regard to the amount and to the estate out of which it had accrued. The use to which it had been applied under the deed or will (which is recited) is also set out, and the rent-charge is conveyed to the nominees, their heirs and successors for ever from St. Michael's day then last past (1549).

Until sanctioned by Parliament the transaction was illegal, for the purchase moneys were used by the Crown for purposes *other* than those to which the preamble of the Statute had *appropriated* them, besides the objections presented to the title of the purchasers or grantees of the Crown arising from the rights of re-entry or gifts over contained in the founders' wills, should any default be made (as it had been) in keeping up the superstitious uses.

Therefore in the mayoralty of Sir Richard Dobbes (the Skynner), 1551, a petition was presented to the King by the Corporation of London, and underwritten with the signatures of "T. Cant, R. Rychelane, W. Wiltesh^r, J. Bedford, T. Wentworth, T. Ely, N. Wotton," setting forth that by the authority of Parliament the superstitious uses had become vested in the King as annual rent-charges, and that these had been sold for "notable

---

[1] Appendix 18, page 371.

sums of money" paid for "thexployte of your waytie affairs," and granted to the suppliants and the Fraternities. That the suppliants and Fraternities had sold *of necessity* and must sell the "greatyste part or porcion" of their other estates for the "furnyture of the said sommes of money" and therefore they prayed an Act of Parliament (which was passed as in the 5th and 6th Edward), confirming the title of Corporations and Fraternities, or other persons who since the 1st February (1549–50) had purchased, or should thereafter purchase of the King, or of the aforesaid Corporations, Fraternities, or persons, any such rents or hereditaments absolutely in fee simple, and free from such re-entries or gifts over a statutory title against the Crown, as plain and emphatic as Parliament has ever conferred upon any subjects of the Crown.[1]

An exemplification of the Petition and Act are held at the Guildhall, and copies of both in the archives of the Merchant Taylors Company.

Thus was the religion of the Fraternity *disendowed* by a Parliament of Roman Catholics, the chapels at " Poules " and at the Hall both ceased to be filled by the "great multitude" of the brethren, the Guild became secular, and though the Baptist's name continued to be used in the antient terms of incorporation, no longer was the day of his nativity to be kept by the notable feast in his honour, nor his statue to remain in the hall, where little was left to remind the Fraternity to hold his character in reverence.

During the period embraced in this chapter, several other members of the Guild had risen to eminence in London, as shown by the civic and parliamentary offices to which their fellow citizens had elected them. Thus, in civic offices we have these names of guildsmen:—

James Wilford,[2] Master 1494 (Alderman), Sheriff in 1499.
Nicholas Nynes, Master in 1496, Sheriff in 1502.
William FitzWilliam, Master in 1499, Sheriff in 1506.
John Doget, Master in 1501, Sheriff in 1510.
John Kyrkeby, Master in 1502, Sheriff in 1508.
Richard Smith, Master in 1503, Sheriff in 1509.
John Skevynton, Master in 1510, Sheriff in 1521.
Robert Pagett, Warden in 1527, Sheriff in 1536.
Henry Suckley, Warden in 1527, Sheriff in 1541.

---

[1] The sale of the chauntry lands were also confirmed by 1st and 2nd Philip and Mary, cap. 8, sec. 12.

[2] One of the Subsidy Commissioners under 12 Henry VIII, cap. 13 (1496–7). —Memorials, page 283.

Thomas White, Warden in 1530, Sheriff in 1547, Lord Mayor in 1553.

Henry Hubbathorne, Sheriff in 1542, Lord Mayor in 1546.

John Wilford, benefactor in 1550, Sheriff in 1544.

John Yorke,[1] Sheriff in 1549.

In 1529 Paul Withypoll[2] was returned for the Parliament of 14 Henry VIII. He had been Warden in 1522, and no doubt at some later date Master. He was appointed with Will Wilford to have the survey of the provisions supplied to the Emperor Charles V on his visit to London in the same year (1522), and in 1515 he was discharged from jury service as being in the Commission of the Peace. His daughter married Emanuel Lucar, a highly esteemed member of the Company. In the next Parliament of which we have a record of names, 1542, we find Nicholas Wylford (an established family in the Company) the member for London.

But the men who may be supposed to have had control and influence with the Company between 1545–51 were notably Sir Thomas White and Sir Thomas Offley, each taking an opposite view of the policy of the Reformation; the one a protector of the *old*, the other an advocate for the *new* learning, and not therefore sure to agree as to the morality of the course taken by the Crown under the Chauntries Collegiate Act.

Men of the accepted character of White and Offley might have been held to be above the imputation of any public act of dishonesty, such as either concealing (even had the Lord Mayor, as the Chief Commissioner, lent himself to the fraud) or misapplying property acquired from the Crown, but these imputations stand recorded, and therefore we have given in detail all the facts to show that their characters are entirely beyond impeachment.

Towards the close of the century it will be seen that some of those citizens who rose to eminence in the government of London had previously held office as Masters of the Taylors Company, the three most notable being Sir John Percyvale in 1484, Sir Stephen Jenyns in 1489, and Sir W. FitzWilliam in 1499. In gathering up the particulars of their lives as passed within the hall premises, we shall gain some further insight into the affairs of the Company at the period when they lived, and note (if so disposed) the zeal and integrity with which they discharged their duties as guildsmen.

---

[1] A freeman and liveryman in 1545-6, but I do not trace him as Warden or Master. In the assessment of February, 1565, he is assessed after "Alderman" Rowe, and for the same sum.

[2] See Vol. 1, Mait., page 236, as to special grant to him by the Common Council in October, 1539.

CHAP. VIII.]   *Hereditaments sold in 1849–50.*   151

[*Note referred to at page 147.*]

THE HEREDITAMENTS SOLD (IN 1549–50), THEIR RENTS AND SALE MONEY, ARE SHOWN IN THIS SCHEDULE.

Description.	Parish.	Rent.			Purchase Money.			Names of Tenants.	Name of Purchaser.
		£	s.	d.	£	s.	d.		
"The Helme"	Cornhill	10	6	4	170	0	0	Richard Payne	John Jacks, *Master,* 1552.
One messuage	Bread Street	7	13	4				W. Bower	
One ditto	Watling Street	5	13	0				Henry Suckley	Thomas White, *Lord Mayor* in 1553.
One ditto	Friday Street	5	0	0	410	6	8	Mrs. R. Allen	
One ditto	Fenchurch Street	2	0	0				John Noxe	
Five tenements	Tower Street	2	0	0				W. Dewell	
One stable	At 10s. each.								
	St. Mary Axe, At 16s.	4	1	0	80	0	0	Sundry tenants	Alderman Sir Thos. Offley, *Master,* 1547.
One tenement and garden	At 15s.								
One messuage and eight tenements	Wood Street and Ad Lane	9	8	8	159	16	0	Dr. Cromer	Thomas Howe.
One messuage "The Three Kings"	Without Aldgate	3	6	8	50	0	0	M. Heythwayte	Michael Heythwayte (*the tenant*).
One messuage	Thames Street	5	0	0	100	0	0	R. Barne	Alderman John Wilford. *M.T.C.*
"The Three Nuns"	Aldgate	7	0	0	122	2	0	John Austin	John Ashton
One tenement	Lime Street (up to Ledenhall)	13	6	8	213	6	8	Stephen Kerton	S. Kerton, *M.T.C.* (*the tenant*).
One messuage "The Julyan"	Tower Street	5	6	8	93	6	8	R Chaloner (Stowe, pl. 53)	Roger Chaloner (*the tenant*).
Four small tenements	Aldermanbury	2	13	4	46	13	4	Four tenants, at 13s. 4d. each	Richard Botyll, *Master,* 1551.
One tenement "The Talbot"	Walbrook	5	16	0	66	16	0	W. Morren	Edward Lee, *Warden,* 1559-50.
Six tenements, gardens, chambers, &c.	St. Bartholomew-the-Less	6	1	0				Fourteen tenants, at 4s. to 20s. each	
One tenement	Fenchurch Street	2	6	4	620	15	8	R. Jolson	Simon Low, *Warden,* 1549-50.
Five tenements	St Margaret Patyns	6	6	4				Six tenants, at 16s. 8d. to 28s. 4d. each	
Six tenements	St. Lawrence Pountney	18	13	4				Six tenants at 13s. 4d. to 6l. each	
		120	10	0	2,133	1	6	Four tenants, at 7s. 6d. to 13s. 4d. each.	William Johnson, *Freedom, M.T.C.* 18th *July,* 1544.
Add sold 1550-1: Four tenements	Gracious Street	2	4	2	50	0	0		
		122	14	2	2,183	1	6		

CHAPTER IX.

AFTER DISENDOWMENT.—LATER BENEFACTIONS.

Days of racked consciences.—Obit moneys applied to secular uses, p. 152.— Hall chapel used for secular purposes and fitments removed, p. 152. —Religion the vital principle of the Guilds, p. 152.—Constitutional changes in the Guild, p. 153.—Effects of on benefactions and expenditure, p. 154. —As to benefactions, p. 155.—Character of Post-Reformation gifts, p. 155. —Robert Donkyn, p. 155.—His charity of 1570, p. 156.—Progress of it, and Scheme of 1872, p. 157.—Bognor House, p. 157.—Robert Dowe, p. 157. —His charities, p. 158.—(1) For prisoners in Newgate, condemned to death, p. 159.—In City prisons for debt, p. 161.—(2) Pensions for Guildsmen, p. 162, et seq.—For parishioners, p. 165.—For improvement in Church singing, p. 167.—School probation, p. 168.—Commendatory sentences in favour of poor tailors and St. John's, Oxford, p. 168.—Almshouses, p. 169. —Schools founded, p. 171.—No contract with non-members to charity endowment, p. 171.—William Roper's offer declined, p. 171.—Guildsmen made such, p. 172.—What religious observances were kept up, p. 172.—Grant of arms with secular emblems, p. 173.—NOTE. Cooke the Herald, and Payment for same, p. 173.

THOSE must have been "days of racked consciences" (as a later Court minute describes them) when the "service[1] of placebo and dirige, with the mass on the morrow," which Henry abolished for others, he directed by his last will should be celebrated for himself,[2] and when the outcome of the Act was the sale of the obits and the application of the purchase money not to religious but to secular uses.

Following upon if not the effect of this confiscation was that the worship of the sanctuary was silenced within the hall premises, that the chapel of Calixtus was dismantled and then secularised; the beautiful tapestry (save the hearse cloths which still hang on our walls) was sold, and that all the plate with any religious emblems was melted down into modern shape or pattern. That disendowment was a blow to religion as a principle cannot be reasonably doubted, and how vital religion was to the Guilds let a writer of authority declare :

---

[1] Wilson, Vol. 1, page 45, and Part II, page 20. [2] Test. Vct., Vol. 1, page 38.

"Religion was the foundation of the Guild. Divine worship the solid bond of the association. The members were constantly reminded that it was not to the contrivance of wit or the strength of the labouring hand that man owes his daily bread. Industry, they were taught, might be the applied means, but God's providence was the only source of our subsistence, its increase the result of His blessing, not of our frugality, the alms the testimony of our gratitude to Him from whom the bounty emanated and undeserved is obtained." * * * *

But other very considerable alterations were introduced during the reigns of the later Tudors into the ordinances of 1507. Besides those which we have already noticed, relating to the government of the Yeomen or Bachelors, others had reference to the Merchant Company.

In the first place all the changes which the Reformation rendered necessary in the oaths and ordinances were made as of course. As the Guild had become secular, no attendance at public worship after elections was prescribed, although it was followed out as a custom. With these exceptions the oaths and duties remain as they did in 1507.

The new Master or Wardens absent from their election or the dinner (an offence increasing in later times), were to be fined. The "brotherhood money," for the Master's feast, hitherto indefinite, was fixed at 3s. 4d. for the Assistants and Livery, and 12d. for other members for the general feast. Each member had also to pay to the Wardens assigned to receive it a quasi poor rate, viz., a quarterage of 2s. 6d. yearly to the use of the Fraternity.

The government of the Guild was placed on a narrower basis. Although for legislation affecting all the members a full assembly may still be needed, we find no trace of any such meeting being summoned; and the Master instead of yielding up his receipts and payments after the expiration of his year of office, openly in the common hall before the whole of the Fraternity, has only to do so to the Court of Assistants, or to auditors appointed by the Court.

Some of the old ordinances are altogether omitted, such as the previous licence of the Master and Wardens to open a shop[2] (A. 4), as to keeping secret chambers (*ib.* 5), as to employing foreigners

---

[1] Sir Francis Palgrave.
[2] Appendix 7, page 351.

(*ib.* 6), as to unlawful assemblies (*ib.* 7), as to taking houses to disturb tenants (*ib.* 8), as to attendance at burials[1] (*ib.* 10 and 25), as to rebels against the Master (*ib.* 12), as to the observance of holidays (*ib.* 16), as to those associating with the breakers of ordinances (*ib.* 19), and lastly, as to the Wardens and the purchase of stuff at Kingston (*ib.* 4, 5, and 7).

Some ordinances were amended thus, the limit to the numbers and to the fees paid for apprentices were omitted (A. 3), and the freeman had only to present his apprentice at the hall for examination as to his birth; and in case the fine for leaving the Guild was excessive (under A. 20) the appeal was given not to the Chancellor and Treasurer of England, but to the Lord Mayor and Court of Aldermen of London.

Lastly two ordinances were added to ensure impartiality in the Court of Assistants, and to give it jurisdiction over cases of masters and apprentices.

When Parliament passed the Chauntries Collegiate Act the charitable needs of the kingdom were declared to be the want of funds for three definite objects:—Grammar Schools, University Exhibitions, and Poor Relief. It therefore remains for us to examine into the effect which this Act had upon the generation of guildsmen experiencing the consequences, whether, as evidenced by future endowments, it lessened their desire to give property to the Guild either for "the Common Box" or for any charitable purposes, and whether the future expenditure of *corporate* funds, became either diminished or altered in regard to benevolent objects. The first of these questions we will deal with in the present chapter.

The main source of wealth to the Guild has always been the benevolence of its members. In the pre-Reformation gifts we find these often made to the Master and Wardens, as in Tressawell's will "in pure and perpetual alms," or in other cases "to the brethren and sisters of the Fraternity." Again other gifts were made as in Percyvale's case " to the common box for the support of the common charge," or in Slater's and Moncaster's in 1521 for the Master and Wardens "to do and dispose of their own free will." But no such gifts were made to the Guild after the Chauntries Collegiate Act was passed, and the post-Reformation charities

---

[1] Though the Bedel was to summon the Fraternity, the penalty for non-attendance was withdrawn.

of which there were fourteen during Elizabeth's reign,[1] took a different form.

The first, Wilford's (1550), was for the repair of roads, and others were for similar uses. Sir Thomas Rowe (1559) gave annuities to poor freemen of various Companies." from age or impotence unable to practise their craft;" but he did not forget the men of his trade, clothworkers, and knowing how others could become nominally such by joining the Company, he laid down the qualification that his recipients should be "shearers with the broad shears or rowing at the perch," an example which was followed by Richard Hilles in 1586, by Robert Dowe (in 1605), for Taylors, and Craven (in 1615) for both. Another form of charity was the release of prisoners by payment of their fees due for discharge. Special gifts were also made for sermons, as by Vernon on the day of his decease: and by Wilford for Good Friday.

But two benefactions of this period claim special mention, the first from the good which it confers or ought to confer on the "poor inhabitants within the city of London," and the other as marking the distinctive characteristics of a Guildsman of the 16th century.

Robert Donkyn, the first founder, was one of several of that name who were members of the Company. He was a contemporary of Richard Hilles, and became a freeman prior to 1530, and was called to the Livery in 1556–7. He was a resident in St. Michael, Cornhill, renting from the parish a house at 6*l*. 12*s*. 8*d*.,[2] and then from the Company one of Giles Slater's houses at 2*l*. 13*s*. 4*d*. per annum. In 1549 he served with William Machyn[3] the office of Churchwarden; and as his trade had reference to church vestments his name appears in the parish accounts of St. Dionis Backchurch, when purchasing after the Reformation in 1549, "a badkyn or carecloth" (which was held over the bride and bridegroom's heads at a marriage till the benediction) for 40*s*., and two best suits of vestments (one a cloth of gold and red velvet, and the other "ryche whylvet," having four copes and three vestments), for 42*s*.; and in those of St. Michael's when purchasing in 1550 copes, vestments, altar clothes, and curtains for 31*l*. 17*s*. 10*d*., and in 1552 five copes with certain banner staves for 40*l*.

It may be supposed that he was successful in his business, for

---

[1] In this I reckon Dowe's charities as *one*.

[2] St. Michael's Registry, by Waterlow, page 61.

[3] One of the Company's tenants of Sir John Percyvale's estate.

he was a benefactor to the parish as well as to the Merchant Taylors Company. To the former he gave two houses now 143 and 144, and formerly known as Waterbearers' Hall, in Bishopsgate Street Without. Towards the close of his life he purchased another estate in Bishopsgate parish consisting of houses and gardens with a rental of 26l. per annum or thereabouts, apparently with the noble purpose of dedicating it to the poor of London, as on the 13th March, 1569, he came to the Court and offered it for acceptance on the terms and for the purposes mentioned in his proposed will. The record runs in these words :—" Whereas Robt Donkyn, a loving mebre of this mystery, for the greate good will and hartye zeale he beareth to the same, hath declared unto the aforesaid M^r and Wardens that he is mynded to give and assure by his last Will and Testament unto this Mysterie fo'ever, All these his lands, tenem^{ts}, and gardens lienge in the pisshe of St. Botoulphe wthoute Bishopsgate, in London, being at this pnte of the yerely value of 26l. p^r ann^m or theire about."

He made his will on the 1st December, 1570, devising the estate to the Master and Wardens, to take the rents and thereout to give 12 poor men inhabitating within the city of London, of honest fame and most in need, and to 12 poor women of honest conversation, fame and name, and most in need; to each man a gown of freese, containing 7 yards at 1s. 4d. per yard, a shirt[1] at 2s., and a pair of shoes at 12d. To each women a cassock of like freese and price containing 5$\frac{1}{2}$ yards, a smock at 20d. per yard, and a pair of shoes at 12d., on every Christmas Day; with legacies of 10s. each to the Chamberlain and Town Clerk, first, to put the Master and Wardens in mind on All Saints' day, and then to attend and see the bequest performed. The residue of yearly rents (then 9l. 13s.), was received and for many years was thought to be given to the use of the Company.

In June of the same year he had been appointed one of the Renter Wardens, William Kympton being Master, but while he was holding office, in February, he died, whereupon the Company having accepted the trusts entered into possession, and the first appointment of men and women to receive the benefit of his

---

[1] Although Falstaff, before the Battle of Shrewsbury, thought to clothe his ragged soldiers with shirts stolen from the hedges, on which they were placed to dry, yet they only came into general use at the beginning of the 16th century, and 2s. would seem to have been a liberal price for a shirt. The freese was in 1540 at 8d. per yard, but afterwards it rose to 1s. 1$\frac{1}{4}$$d$., the allowance of 1$s$. 4$d$. was therefore liberal. The same authority put shoes at 1s. 2d. as the highest, and 3d. as the lowest price.—Rogers on Prices, Vol. 4, *passim*.

charity was made on the 28th March, 1572, and their successors have had continuance to the present day.

But the rents which in 1570 were 26*l.*, or thereabouts, amounted in 1843 to 386*l.* 2*s.* 6*d.*; in 1852 to 798*l.* 18*s.* 1*d.*; and in 1862 to 1,125*l.* 7*s.* 6*d.*, and the residue increased from 9*l.* 13*s.* to 1,001*l.* 1*s.* 6*d.* and was transferred to the Taylors' corporate funds.[1]

As the result of a suit instituted by the Company against the Attorney-General to get an authoritative decision on the construction of Donkyn's will, a scheme was framed for establishing a convalescent home at Bognor for the reception of poor men discharged from the Metropolitan hospitals, and sanctioned by the Charity Commissioners on the 22nd March, 1872. Other funds (as the Prison Funds), have subsequently been added, so that in December, 1875, there was 2,019*l.* 18*s.* 5*d.* annually available for this charity. Up to December, 1887, the poor who have been inmates of Donkyn's home amounted to a total number of 10,900, possibly not a tithe of whom ever heard of his name as their benefactor.

Robert Dowe, the second of these founders, was more munificent, for in his lifetime he deposited with the Company, and they agreed in consideration of various sums of money (which, fortunately for their successors in the Guild they invested in London houses) to see to the fulfilment of various charitable foundations, which, partly in his own words and partly in the legal language of the times, he defined in various deeds which are still held in the archives of the Company. The total of his benefactions amounted to 3,448*l.* 10*s.* 8*d.*, a vast sum of money at that period.

Dowe, as a guildsman, had had a long experience of London life, he would know not only what were the wants of the poor, and how, according to opinions then prevailing, they could be best relieved, but to whom and with what safeguards the distribution could be best entrusted, while the nature of his benefactions and the terms used in their creation reflect his experience and worthy characteristics upon the guildsman of later times. All that we know of him is but little, and is as follows:—

Robert Dowe (or Dove, as was his crest, and as his name first appears) was the second son of Henry Dove of Stradbroke, Suffolk, by Alice, the daughter of —— Nowell. He came to

---

[1] See the case of the Merchant Taylors Company stated in a Memorandum, dated 10th August, 1882. Appendix 20, pages 374-88.

London, and had the good fortune to be the apprentice of Nicholas Wilford, living, as was then usual, in his family, and through this channel he became a freeman on the 9th August, 1550, when about 27 years old. His ultimate place of residence was Houndsditch, Aldgate, and his business that of a taylor. He married Letitia, the daughter of Nicholas Bull, by whom he had five sons, all of whom (with his wife) predeceased him.

He was called to the Livery of the Company some time before September, 1562, his name being found as such in an assessment of that date. He first served as Warden in 1571, and the second time in 1575, and as Master in 1578, having Thomas Wilford and Reginald Barker as two of his Wardens. In 1605 he was a donor of gilt spoons (40½ oz. in weight) to the Company, and founded the "convivium dinner." In September, 1611, when he was 88 years of age, he attended its celebration at the "Angel," in Islington, for he was a vigorous man. His handwriting to the nomination of scholars to St. John's, Oxford, on the 12th June, 1611, is clear, the letters well formed, the strokes thick, with no appearance of age discernible. He was present at the probation of the school on the 17th March, and he died on the 2nd May, 1612, at the age of 89. At the desire of Mr. Ralph Hamer and Mr. Zachery Dow (two of his nearest kin) his body was buried from the hall, and a funeral dinner provided by them for such as accompanied the corpse to the church of Aldgate; all "the hall linen and plate being freely lent to perform the last duty to so worthy a brother."[1]

Such is the bare outline of Robert Dowe's life, a detail of whose charities will presently be given. His memory was sought to be perpetuated by a monument still standing in Aldgate church, erected at the expense of the Company in 1622, when "five nobles were given to the parson for his suffering ye church wall to be broken to sete up Mr. Dowe's picture there," as thus described in the Court minutes :—

"It was at this Court[2] ordered that twentie marks shalbe given of ye Stock of this house for to bestowe upon a picture engraven in stone for Mr Robt Dowe an antient M^r of this Societie and a memorable Benefactor to the same to be sett up in the Church of St. Buttulph without Aldgate where the said Mr Dowe was buried as a Remembrance of him to succeeding ages Our M^r to pay the same and have it allowed in his account."

---

[1] Court, 8th May, 1612.
[2] 14th August, 1622, Vol. 8, page 114.

He first comes prominently into notice as a benefactor in the establishment of the Widows' Almshouses, in Hog Lane, after Richard Hilles death, when, in 1592, he was appointed the Treasurer and one of three Assistants to act as "Surveyors" of that foundation. After an interval of ten years (5th June, 1602), we have this entry in the Court minutes respecting him:—

"Certain Assistants with whom Mr. Robert Dowe had former speech and conference do state to the Court that it hath pleased God to move the heart of said Mr. Robert Dowe, to disburse a further good sum for the relief of the necessitous brethren of the Company, for whom the Company do make public declaration of their thankfulness to Mr. Dowe and to Almighty God. A deed to be drawn and sealed to charge and bind the Company to see the charitable alms for ever justly and truly performed."

The earliest operative deed held by the Merchant Taylors Company is dated the 8th July, 1605, and commences thus:—that "an antient citizen of London, named Mr. Robert Dowe, one of the Societie of the Worshipful Companie of Merchant Taylors in his lyfe tyme of his own charges and charitable disposition hath delivered " 50*l*. into the hands of the parish officers of St. Sepulchre without Newgate, for the fulfilment of a "charitable deed" which he afterwards sets forth.

At the date of the endowment, capital punishments were frequent, and poor criminals condemned to death were thought to deserve and, indeed, received little spiritual aid or comfort. Dowe's anxiety was to prevent such from passing out of this world unrepentant, and his "charitable deed" was directed, first, to their conversion, and then to engage the sympathy of the parishioners in their fate. These were his plans.

With the previous assent of the Lord Mayor and Bishop of London he obtained a contract with the Vicar, Churchwardens, and Vestry of the parish to have these services performed. First for arousing the attention of the prisoner:—"about the hour of tenn of the clock in the quiet of the night next before everie execution daie they were to appoint one to goe unto Newgate there to stand soe neere the window as he can where the condemned prisoners do lye in the Dungeon the night before they shall be executed and wth a hand bell (given to the parishioners by the said Mr. Dow) shall give there twelve solemn tolls with doble strokes and then after a good pawse to deliver with a lowd and audible voice (his face towards the prisoner's window) to the end the poore condemned sowles maie give good care and be the better stirred up to watchfulness and praier certain words of exhortation and prayer . . . and then he shall toule his bell again."¹

The night ended, the morning of the execution arose, and all criminals then and indeed until 1783 were taken for execution from the prison to Tyburn. A church custom also prevailed (the observance of which was no doubt stimulated by paying the sexton's fees for his trouble) of having the "passing or soul" bell tolled when a soul was passing out of this life, to call all within its sound to prayer for its pardon and acceptance with God. "When any shall be passing out of this life a bell shall be tolled and the minister shall not then be slack to do his last duty." It should be tolled three for a man, two for a woman, and at the conclusion a peal on all the bells.²

On the morning of execution, Dowe made another exhortation both to the prisoner passing to execution and to the assembled crowd, thus : when the prisoners goe to execution the carte shall staie a small while against the church wall to hear this short exhortation pronounced by one standing there bareheaded wth the hand bell having first given twelve solemne toules with double strokes for better stirring up as well the prisoners' mynde as other good peoples' harts to praie for God his mercie towards them in the words," which are set out.³

He then provided for the "passing bell," "that the greatest bell of Saint Sepulchres shall alwaies begyn to toule from the 25th of March unto the 29th of September at six A.M. and from the 29th of September unto the 25th of March before seaven A.M. in manner as the passing Bell is used and that this Bell shall alwaies continue towling until tenn of the clock or until such tyme as the Sheriffs' Officers shall return home from the execution to the end and purpose that all good people hearing this passing Bell may be moved to pray for these poor Synners going to execution after which the said Bell shall cease towling and be rung out the space of one half hower or thereabouts."

If any neglect or default should arise in these observances the correction was left to the Lord Mayor and Bishop of London, and by a later deed (April, 1610) to ensure detection of neglect, " he gave to the Beadle of his Livery 3s. 4d. yearly that three times in the year, yearly for ever, in the evening and morning

---

[1] Appendix 21, page 388.
[2] Hook's Ch. Dict. (1887), page 566. Brand's Pop. Ant., Vol. 2, page 122.
[3] Appendix 22, page 389. The Charity Commissioners have recently settled a scheme for applying this charity to the benefit of poor prisoners.

before the execution of the prisoners at Newgate, he shall repair thither to see and hear whether the persons appointed by the parish of St. Sepulchre to come in the evening under Newgate and in the morning in the church to perform the ringing of the hand bell and exhortation to the prisoners, also the ringing out of the passing bell for the prisoners in such devout and discreet manner as is appointed."[1]

But these were not the only prisoners who came within the scope of Robert Dowe's benevolence, for there were those confined enduring a life of misery for small debts unpaid, of which the debtors of the present day endure nothing.

The City prisons for such debtors were four in number, all utterly wanting in furniture and sanitation, held by keepers who had purchased their offices, and whose pay or revenue was derived from exactions inflicted upon the inmates. Ludgate was a freeman's prison, and had an endowment from Stephen Foster in 1454, for freeing the prisoners from paying for lodging and water, but Newgate had no such advantages.

The Sheriffs' prisons were the two compters—that in the Poultry held by one, and that in Wood Street by the other Sheriff, the prisoners getting the scraps from their tables.[2]

These prisons were, or should have been, regulated by (as the keepers did not obey) the Common Council; indeed, such an act of disobedience obliged the City to build Wood Street in place of Bread Street Compter, for as the keeper of the latter was also the freeholder of the prison, he could only be displaced from office by building another prison.[3] "He was" (writes Stowe) "hard with his prisoners, having also servants such as himself liked best for their bad usage, and would not for any complaint be reformed . . . . whereof myself am partly a witness, for being of a jury (1552), we found the prisoners hardly dealt with for their achates[4] and otherwise, also that thieves and strumpets were there lodged for 4d. the night, whereby they might be safe from searchers that were abroad: for which enormities and others, he was indicted."

It was to "relieve poor prisoners—redeeming them that are

---

[1] The Beadle presented his proposal to the Court.—Memorials, page 18.

[2] Strype's Stowe, Book 3, page 51.

[3] The same circumstances applied to the Fleet prison. See Commissioners' Report, 1729, in note, Vol. 17, State Trials, page 298.

[4] From the French word "achat," and in English use meant provisions not made in the house, but purchased, say, of the baker or brewer.—Chaucer's Prologue, line 570. Spenser's Faerie Queen, Book 2, chapter 9, line 34.

in pryson for small debts or for their fees, and for relieving such that are very syck in prison, and not otherwise," that Robert Dowe gave 20*l.* per annum to be so distributed between the 20th and 24th August in each year. His almoners for this charitable business were the Wardens of his Company, but to aid them in a careful distribution (which except under special circumstances should be 5*l.* for each prisoner) the Beadle of the Livery eight or ten days before the distribution should go round to the prisons to get information of the wants and necessities of the several inmates.

The trust which Dowe reposed in the Wardens is thus expressed:[1] he "dothe repose this speciall trust and confidence in the said Wardens and well assured of their charitable and conscionable care herein that he doth give them this power and authoritie that if in some one or more of the said fower prysons they shall fynde more want either for redeeming or relieving as aforesaid then in the other and that a greater porc̄on of charity were fitter to be bestowed there then in th'others that then they may in their wisdomes encrease the porc̄on to such one or more of the said fower places or prisons where most charity is fitt to be bestowed and defalke the same out of th'other that shall have lesse neede."

His next thought was for the poor workmen of his Guild, and on the 28th August, 1605, he declared his intentions regarding them. The deed opens with these words, the said "Robert Dowe looking into the great decay of his poor brethren the Merchant Taylors using the handicraft of tailory and being moved with a charitable love and care towards the relief of the deceased estate of the said handicraft, hath placed in the hands of the Master and Wardens various sums of money to be laid out in the purchase of tenements, by the revenue whereof, as well certain decayed brethren of the handicraft might be from time to time relieved by yearly pensions, when either by age or other accident they were not of ability of body to get their living by their handy labour, and also whereby other deeds of charity and good uses might be performed."

One of such pensions, to his honour be it recorded, he specially conferred on "the loving brother of mysterie, John Stowe," who had been a taylor, and the other recipients were to have distinct qualifications, thus: "To the thirteene poore aged and decaied Brethren of the said Societie of Marchaunt-tailers which have exercised and

---

[1] Deed of 4th April, 1610.

have ben brought up in the handycraft of Tailory and have contynued their trade so long as their sight and strength would permytt them to worke being of the full age of three score yeres and which have ben househoulders and mayntainers of famylies and of honest sober and good reputation and which have been obedient and dutifull to the Master and Wardens and so long as they were of capabilitie paid their quarteridge and have borne other charges and duties belonging to the said Brotherhood" . . . .
"But if there happen ympotency lamenesse or blindenes vpo^n any brother of the said Handycraft of Tailory under the said age of threescore yeres (and being quallified as before at large is recited) he may in the discretion of the Warden Substitute be appoynted one of the fowre in Election Soe as he be not under fiftie yeres of age well approved."

Their continued good conduct was to be assured by the powers of removal :—" If found negligent in the Service of God or in doing the Duties appointed or be unquiet or of any other lewd behaviour duly proved or be insolent and hygh mynded or disdaine or be negligent in wearing his livery or in performing the Orders appointed by these presents . . . . So that none remayne with the name to receave the charitie of Mr. Robert Dowe but them that be knowne and approved to be of very honest and quiet behaviour and of a religious and holy conversation."

To each of these he gave a liberal pension (according to the then value of money) of 6l. 13s. 4d. with a gown at the cost of 2l. 3s. 4d. every third year.

Foreseeing from his experience how great would be the importunity for these pensions, he took the precaution of instituting six ones of lesser value, to which the candidate should be first elected, thus : "The better to avoid such requeste and petitions that may be made to the Mr Wardens and Assistants for placing Men into the Penc̃ōn of the said thirteene almesmen which may grow to their trouble and breede much evill will and thereby the good meaning of the said Robert Dow abused," he appointed "six parsons of like age trade quallitie and condition as is before mentioned who shall be elected and chosen in forme hereafter ensuing to stand in reversion of the said almes, which said six persons shal be placed in the roome of the said almesmen when and as often as any of the thirteene doe decease."

To each of these he gave 1l. 6s. 8d., and with a cloak at the cost of 1l. 10s. every third year.

Each of these gowns and cloaks to have a badge with a

"Dove" thereon. They were to be of broad cloth and good cotton, to be cut up in the common hall "by a discrete man or twayne," all of one colour, shape, and fashion, and delivered to each of the poor almsmen to make up for himself. Which done they were to be brought back and retained at the hall until St. John's Decollation, when at seven A.M. they were to be redelivered to the almsmen, who were then to have the first wearing of them, with this admonition " that they shall weare them faire and cleanly upon Sundaies holy daies quarter daies and other appointed tymes in seemely manner untill the three yeres be expired when they shall receave new gownes and cloakes and yet nevertheless their old gownes and cloakes to be preserved and to be usually worne upon the weeke daies."

Liberal as these pensions were it is clear that they were not designed for members of the Livery, as were the earlier pensions, but for those of the Bachelors Company. The strict impartiality which the founder desired should mark the elections is apparent on the deed. On a vacancy a name should be brought up from each quarter by the Wardens Substitute and presented to the Master "incontinent." Then, the four candidates being present, choice of one shall be made by the balloting box (first reducing them to two by scrutiny), "which way is thought briefest and best to avoid suspition of partiallitie. And the reason that moveth the said Robert Dow to comyt and repose this trust in the Wardens Substitute and Sixteene Men is because they best know the quallitie behaviour and necessity of the poor handicrafte men and which of them have most neede and best deserve the said pention or almes. Nevertheless the said Robert Dow doth not so restraine the M^r and Wardens and Court of Assistants but that if it shall appeare that the Wardens Substitute and Sixteene Men shall use partiallitie or affection in their choice and p'sentment of Names (which is hoped they will not) that then the said Mr Wardens and Assistants may refuse and put back the parsons so presented and cause them to present others more needy and fitt to be preferred to the said pension or almes according to the true meanyng of the said Robert Dow untill the Mr Wardens and Assistants allowe of the same. But the said Robert Dow is well persuaded that as well the Master Wardens and Court of Assistants as also the Warden Substitute and Sixteene Men will deale uprightly iustly and with the like integretie of mind and conscience as everie one of them would have his owne will and charitable disposition truly performed which the said Robert Dow desireth them all for Christ Ihesus sake to remember and dulie to observe as they will annswer to Almighty God for the same."

These pensioners were to be present at the hall on Decollation Day, and then—dinner or no dinner celebrated—they were to go either to St. Helen's or to St. Martin's Church to serve God and hear His Holy word preached. Nor was this all, for Robert Dowe required "That when the pensioners came to receive their pensions they should be put in memory and warned to frequent the Church and House of Prayer and Service of God, and that they do humbly and heartily praise to God for the good estate of the said fellowship, and that it would please Almighty God to raise up more good benefactors and men able and willing to relieve the poor, aged, and decayed brethren of their Company, according to the effect of a printed prayer appointed to be delivered to him or them at their elections which they shall all learn by rote and without book perfectly to say the same wheresoever they shall be examined by the said Master and Wardens; and if any of them cannot say the same prayer without book within such a time as he or they shall be limited or appointed, then he or they were to be fined at the discretion of the Master and Wardens, and the fine distributed amongst those that can perfectly say the same prayer."

His next thought "on perceiving the multitude of poore increaseth" was for those of his own parish, and in the Aldgate records his benefaction ought to be found, set forth to this effect.

Having agreed with the Merchant Taylors that they should pay 10l. 6s. to the parish for ever, he gave his directions as to the distribution of this sum by the parish officers which commences thus:

"I Robert Dow Citizen and Marchant Tailer of Londō now dwelling in this parish of St. Buttolphes without Aldgate (mynding alwaies to help the poore and through the goodness of Almightie God from whom all holy desires all good councells and all just works doe proceed) I have contracted with the Worshipfull Companie of Marchantailers under their Common Seale upon due satisfaction to them made to performe for me certen deeds of charitie by God's Grace for ever."

The Renter Warden and Common Clerk "on the eve or vigil of St. Thomas the Apostle by nine A.M. were to pay this money to the Churchwardens within the Church," and 10l. of this sum was before twelve at noon to be distributed to sixty poor parishioners (by 3s. 4d. each), thirty being taken from the upper and thirty from the lower end of the parish being warned by the Clerk and Sexton to be at the church before nine A.M.

"The poore of the upper end shall alwaies be first called and as they answer to their names they shall goe up into the north Isle of the Quier and shutt the partition dore to them and soe that noe other be amongst them then shall they of the lower end be called and as they doe answer goe up into the south Isle and shut the like partition dore to them and remayne as aforesaid."

All others are then to be shut out of the church, the door thereof locked, and "Then the churchwardens being within the Quier shall distribute first to them of the upper end and as they be paid the parish clarck shall call their names in the Booke and they shall goe down into the Body of the church this donne then the parish clarke shall call them up neere the Quier Dore and the Minister (or the Clerk in his absence) in presence of the churchwardens shall exhort them[1] to come to church to serve God at the tyme of Common Prayers appointed yf they maie and especiallie upon the Sundaies and other Holidays not to faile and if anie be found negligent in the same or be of anie other misdemeanor the Churchwardens in their precinct shall exclude such person and bestowe this charitie upon some more worthy person.

"This exhortation being done the said poore shall all kneele downe and humblie with harte and hand lifted up to God say with the Minister openlie The Lord's praier and lastly they shall say God reward all good Benefactors and bless the Worshipful Companie of Marchauntailers. Then shall the South Church Doore and Gate be sett open that they may all go out quietly three and three together."

The distribution of the 6s. 8d. was to be made in payments of 8d. each to Company's Clerk, the Minister, and to each Churchwarden; of 12d. to the parish clerk for keeping the list of names, and 6d. to the clerk and sexton for summoning the recipients.

These pensioners—subject, of course, to good behaviour—were appointed for life by the Churchwardens, who by the first deed were directed to give a preference "to aged poor widows," without other detail. But by a later deed increasing the benefaction by 10l., Dowe,

---

[1] By the later deed of 1610 he increased the pensions by 6l., making them 6s. 8d. each, and he set forth the exhortation, which Strype credits him with having written; its conclusion is the same as the present clause. He also gives full instructions for the selection of the pensioners by the Churchwardens.—Strype's Stowe, Book 2, page 21.

having experienced " how the poor are given unto too much idleness, and little labour to get, and much seeking after alms, howlittle so ever it be, whereby the Churchwardens were cumbered with feeling," gave directions " partly to excuse the honest Churchwardens from affection to any others than those who have most need," that four ancient and discreet neighbours should be associated with the two Churchwardens, to select as they will answer to God for the same, and for request of any whosoever to make no grant before the day of their meeting, whereby the most needy may have the charity.[1]

Another endowment was to improve the celebration of Divine worship, and for this purpose he gave 250*l*. to the Governors of Christ's Hospital, who, by indenture of 8th February, 1609, agreed to provide for a perpetual sum of 12*l*. per annum " a sufficient man skilful in music to teach the poor children of that house the knowledge and skill of Pricksong "[2]—that is, written or recorded music, singing by note and not by ear.

Music and singing in Divine worship have always been more or less a subject of controversy; people there were and are " who would not have the Psalms to be made a part of our common prayer, nor to be said or sung by turns, nor music to be used with them;"[3] but Robert Dowe, we may reasonably suppose, was not of that party in our Church, and that he (like Richard Hilles in the vestment controversy) sided with the moderate party.

According to Strype, the music in the London churches stood in some need of improvement; but however that may have been, having established the plan it must be looked after, and therefore Dowe gave to the Common Clerk yearly the sum of 3*s*. 4*d*. that " three times of the year, yearly for ever, he should resort to Christ Church on three Sunday mornings at the time of Divine service there to see and hear how and in what manner the schoolmaster and singing children do perform their singing in Divine service in the choir, and at some other convenient times likewise to resort to the place allotted to the schoolmaster for teaching the singing children to see that he has fit and convenient rooms within the Hospital for their teaching and for his own lodging, and that all things be performed concerning the singing children according to

---

[1] Strype's Stowe, Book 2, page 20.
[2] See Grove's Dictionary of Music, Vol 3, page 30.
[3] Hooker, Book 5, sec. 35.

the agreement with the Corporation."[1] Accordingly we find, shortly after the establishment of this charity, reports presented to the Court of Assistants[2] from the Clerk of his visits to the church.

The disposition of his charity would have been imperfect had he omitted all mention of the Company's school, and the only endowment held for it is that given by Robert Dowe.

In March, 1608, he had proposed that the school probation should be examined twice a year by two learned men, between the hours of six and eleven A.M. which commenced on the 22nd March, and was formulated by order of the Court, providing "money to be given and distributed" for these purposes :—

"There shalbee payd unto the maister of the schoole for beere, ale, and new manchet bread with a dish of sweete butter, which hee shall have ready in the morning, with two fine glasses set upon the table, and covered with two faire napkins, and two faire trenchers, with a knife laid upon each trencher, to th'end that such as please may take part to stay their stomacks, untill the end of the examination, ijs." To cover these and other expenses he gave 8l. a year, which continues as a charge on the tenements purchased with Dowe's money.

The perpetuality of his gifts he never doubted, "the whole (referring to the charitable payments) by the assistance of Almighty God shall be paid and performed by the Master and Wardens and their successors so long as the sonne and moone endureth in perpetual memory and remembrance of the said Robert Dowe," and these commendatory sentences stand at the end of his deed:[3]

"And the said M^r· Robert Dow doth hartilie praie the worshippfull assistants of this Companie (whome God hath blessed with habillitie) that they would rememb^r as well the poore of the Companie as also the said Colledge wch some relief towards their better help maintenance and encouragement for preferment of our Schollers in the Companies schoole at Saint Lawrence Pountnies in London to their said Colledge according to the Devise of the said Sir Thomas White Knight their good founder which reason hath moved the said M^r· Robert Dow to extend such help to the said Colledge as is before mentioned and the rather because he

---

[1] Dated 8th February, 1609.
[2] Memorials, page 18, note.
[3] He gave to St. John's 100l. and a fair Bible in vellum.

wisheth that perpetuall love and true friendshipp and amyty may for ever continue betwene this Companie and the said Colledge."

Nor was Dowe's the only individual gift which was made by guildsmen during their lives. At the instance of Richard Hilles[1] though not carried into execution by his brethren of the Court until after his death, almshouses in Hog Lane were erected and endowed originally for the widows of poor brethren dying in the almshouses at the Hall, for inconvenience had been experienced by their continued residence there.

In February, 1588, the Court came therefore to this resolution :—

"Upon the consideracōn that our almshouses are charged with the widdowes[2] of some of oure almesmen, deceased, and by theire residence & continuance there other of our almesmen are disappoynted & keapte oute, suche course should be taken to make some other provision for the said widdowes, and suche other poore which shall hereafter be left destitute and wantinge of reliefe. Whereupon it is called to remembrance that Mr. Richard Hills did before his death make a mocōn to the Courte that those Tenements which he purposed to devyse to this Companie situate upon Tower Hill might be employed to receive the widdowes of such deceased almesmen. For the furtherance of which motion and the performance of soe good a worke the right Worshipful Mr. Alderman Ratcliffe beinge charitablie affected to bringe the same to effecte, did voluntarilie offer to the same ende and for further benefitt of this howse to give to the Companie a Hundred Loade of Tymber to be delyvered them uppon his owne charge at the waterside at Reading soe as they woulde new build the said small Tenements and reserve them rent free for suche widdowes and other poore makinge theire buildinge of the same, from the foundacōn to the seconde storie of brick, and for the acceptinge of his offer dothe give the Companie respite of time to be advised hereof betweene this and our Ladie dai, whose offer this assemblie taketh verie thankefullie, and the Maister and Wardens doe promise to goe and survey the Grounde, between this & y⁶ tyme appoynted."

The offer made by the Alderman was too good to reject, and

---

[1] Part II, page 230.

[2] It was usual to take sureties for the quiet departure of their wives, children, and servants within forty days after the almsman's death, and some small tenements in Church Lane, Vintric, were used as Almshouses.—See Court Minutes, 22nd September, 1584, page 117.

therefore on the 16th April " Our Maister & Wardens accompanyed by Mr. Recorder and others of this companie were entreated to goe to the right wor.^{ll.} Mr. Alderman Ratcliff and to give him to understande howe kindlie & thankfully the Companie doe accepte of his charitable & liberall offer of the Hundred loade of Tymber to be given towardes the buildinge of Howses for the Poore:" and the Alderman " upon the declaracōn of the thankfulle mind of the Companie and the acceptation of his guifte doth continue his good purpose towards them and perform his promise made unto them to the uttermost."

The prosecution of the scheme was postponed until August, 1592, when it was ordered by the Court that the houses should be built " on Tower Hill upon the Land lately devized to this Company by Mr. Richard Hilles, that the building should be performed with convenient speed, and be committed to the consideration, order, and appointment of three surveyors : Mr. Robert Dowe, Mr. George Sotherton, and Mr. Richard Spencer ; and that Mr. Robert Dowe be appointed Treasurer."

In the beginning of the year 1593, 14 almshouses were erected for the dwelling and relief of poor Widows of Merchantaylors or otherwise as the company upon further consideration should be induced to receive. And on the 23rd of June, Mr. Robert Dowe delivered to the Court a Book of the charges of the Building, by which account it appeared that the particular charges of the same, amounted to the sum of 400l. 16s. 1d.

So far, so good—the houses had been erected by aid of Mr. Alderman Ratcliff and the Guild—but the funds of the latter were wholly unequal to maintain the objects of the charity, whereupon the then Master of the Company, Richard Procter, immediately came forward and pledged himself " at his own cost to maintain in perpetuity one widow's place, and Mr. Robert Hawes bound himself in like manner to provide for another."

The good example was contagious, and by June, 1594, the fourteen widows were put into possession, as fourteen members[1] of the

---

[1] Richard Procter, Master.
Anthony Radcliffe, Alderman and Sheriff, 1585.
Robert Lee, Lord Mayor 1602.
John Robinson, Warden, 1585-90.
Henry Offley, Master, 1594.
Robert Dowe, Master, 1578.
Robert Hawes, Master, 1580.

Leonard Holliday, Lord Mayor, 1605.
Roger Abdy, Warden, 1590.
Richard Venables, Master, 1598.
Robert Hampson, Sheriff, 1599.
Gregory Smith, Warden, 1590-5.
Gerrard Gore, Warden, 1601-4.
William Craven, Lord Mayor, 1613.

Court (notable men in their day) had each come forward at their own cost to maintain a poor widow for ever.

But in these benefactions we have not reckoned the noblest that were made by members of the Company, viz.: the foundation of schools, all still continuing to confer great benefits upon the present age, and these foundations were frequently made, not as *post mortem* gifts, but by donation during the lives of the founders.

The earliest dates from the pre-Reformation period, that at Macclesfield by Sir John Percyvale[1] in 1502. His example was followed by his wife, Dame Thomasin Percyvale,[2] who established a school at Launceston. The present school at Wolverhampton was founded by Sir Stephen Jenyns[3] in 1508. Then after a long interval Sir Thomas White[4] founded St. John's, Oxford, partly before and after the Reformation. Following upon his example Sir William Harper[5] founded the present school at Bedford when the same influence was spread to others of the Court, and notably to Richard Hilles, who, with the aid of other individual members, established in 1561 the Company's Grammar School in Lawrence Pountney Lane, in honour of Christ Jesu, and to teach boys of all nations coming there duly qualified to receive education.

But there are no contracts which can be traced for the execution of charitable trusts with persons other than members of the Guild, a fact which may arise not from the want of confidence in the Guild, but from the unwillingness of the latter to accept such responsibility, as one such case comes under our notice in the following entry of 10 November, 11th Elizabeth, 1569.

"Whereas, Mr Willm Roper, Esq., hathe made an offer to gyve certen Tents of his lyinge in the pysse of St Olave in Southwerke, in the county of Surrey, unto this Misterie for ev^r upon condytion That this Mystere shall yerely for ev^r give & dystribute ffowre pounds to and amongst the poore pryson's at the flowre pryson howses of Newgate, Ludgate, the Kingsbenche, and the M^{r}shalsea, viz., to evry of the sayde 4 pryson houses 20s. in brede or coles, and to kepe the same in due repacon, wch sayde Tents were sometime in the tenure and holding of Mr John Jenkyns while he lived, citizen and Mchaunttaylor, of London, yt is agreed by the foresayde M^r and Wardens & Assistants that the said Tents shalbe firste

---

[1] See Part II, Chapter III, page 37. [2] See *ib.*, page 20.
[3] See Part II, Chapter IV, page 34. [4] See Part II, Chapter XIV, page 160.
[5] See Part II, Chapter XVII, page 252.

viewed, and if it shall happen upon the viewe thereof had that it will be profytable for this house to take the same Laudes according as they are offered Then this house to accepte the same offer to them made and yf yt shall appeare otherways, then this house to make refusal of the accepting the sayde offer, and yet nev'theless to render there hartye thanks to the sayde M[r] Roper for his good wyll to them. Whereupon after vyewe made of the foresayde Tents, they the said M[r] and Wardens & other the vyewers agreed to refuse the takinge of the sayde Lande according to the foresayde offer to this house, for that the same lande be nowe in greate ruyne and decay & lyke to fall downe."[1]

But the guildsmen as freely used the Company as administrators of their charitable foundations after as they did before the Reformation, as that event made no difference in the execution of the charitable trusts which the antient governors and fathers of the Guild had entrusted to the Master and Wardens. Of this we shall find an instance in the life of Sir W. Craven, when we deal with that hereafter.

Although a great change was wrought in the Guild by the Chauntries Act, and all payments for priests and obits disappear from the Guild accounts, it must not be understood that all religion or religious observances were in fact abolished. At the annual election of officers, the Guild assembled at the Church of St. Martin's, or in plague time at St. Helen's, for service and sermon, and at every Quarterly Court prayers were read "each man," as the entry states, "devoutly kneeling on his knees." The form of prayer varied somewhat from that used in pre-Reformation times, including and praying for, as amongst the enemies of the Gospel, the Pope,[2] the Turk, or their adherents. The brethren continued to be devoutly buried by the Fraternity,

---

[1] I am indebted for this extract to the late Mr. N. Stephens, who added this note:—

"The above extract may derive some interest from the fact that the proposed donor, William Roper, was the husband of Margaret, Sir Thomas More's favourite daughter, and the ancestor of the noble house of Teynham. The rejected gift may probably be traced down to our own time, as a certain property in Bermondsey Street was given by William Roper, shortly after the date of the above extract, to the Parish Clerk's Company, upon the same condition as above. The said property was sold for the formation of the Greenwich Railway for about 3,000*l*., part of which sum was afterwards applied for the purchase of a house in Wood Street, Cheapside.

[2] Memorials, page 120.

and when a commemorative dinner was given a "commendable grace," still extant, was used by the Chaplain, who was on the staff of the Company, observances which were probably continued until the fire of 1666.[1]

But the religious emblems placed in the coat of arms in 1480 were, after a century's usage, removed from the Company's shield in 1586, under the plea that to further the worthiness of the fraternity this grant should be made to them, "that is to say, the field silver, a pavilion with two mantles imperial purple garnished with gold on a chiffe azure, a lion passant gold, and to the crest upon the helm on a wreath silver and azure on a mount (*vert*), a lamb silver in the sumbeams gold, mantled gules doubled silver, and supported with two camels gold."

The cost of the grant was 5*l*., and in March, 1586, the Herald[2] had a further sum of 15*s*. paid for arranging the arms in the west window in the hall, after (we may presume) the new roof, which was undertaken about the same time, had been completed.

---

[1] It was composed for the funeral dinner of Mr. John Swynnerton, November, 1608.

[2] The new arms were granted by Robert Cooke, a Herald of some repute, who was said to have been the son of a Tanner, ignorant of languages, of dissolute life and haunting taverns, but a very diligent man in his science and had a vast collection of descents and pedigrees. At his death in 1573, Lord Burghley as Earl Marshall sent to the Lord Mayor to take an inventory of his books, some of which he had taken out of the Heralds' office violently.[a]

[a] Strype's Stowe, 1754, Book 1, Chap. 23, *passim*.

CHAPTER X.

AFTER DISENDOWMENT—LATER EXPENDITURE.

Object of the Chapter, p. 174.—As to expenditure in hospitality in Edward VI's reign, p. 175.—Sir F. Palgrave on civic hospitality, p. 175.—Feasting traditional in London, p. 175.—As to feasting, sanctioned by Charter of Richard II, p. 175.—Guild funds have borne such charges, p. 176. —Early records of this, p. 176.—As to method of accounting, p. 176.—Renter Wardens, p. 176.—Master's accounts, p. 176.—Auditors, p. 177.—Master's fees of office, p. 177.—As to income, p. 177.—Subsidy Return, 1566, p. 178.—Other sources of income, p. 180.—Total of receipts and payments for decennial periods, p. 180.—Two great feasts, St. John the Baptist's and Decollation days, p. 180.—Contributions thereto, p. 181.—Changed to quarter days, p. 181.—The charges in Edward's and Mary's reigns, p. 181.—Sumptuary expenses of Elizabeth's reign, p. 181.—Livery increased, p. 181.—Guildsmen acted as Waiters, p. 181.—Election Dinner, 1593, p. 182.—Increase of Allowance, p. 183.—Gore declines it, p. 183.—Accepted by Elwes in 1605, p. 183.—School dinner, p. 184.—Sir Thomas White's, p. 184.—View and search dinners, p. 184.—Increase in Elizabeth's reign, p. 184. —Court dinners in James I's reign, p. 185.—Dowe's convivium dinner, p. 185.—Cook's employment (note), p. 185.—Funeral dinners, p. 187.— Dowe's grace, p. 187.—Extraordinary cost of a mayoralty, p. 187.—Feast postponed for scarcity, p. 188.—As to Expenditure for alms, p. 189.— Charities administered without costs, p. 189.—School at St. Lawrence, p. 189.—University Exhibitions, p. 190.—Almsmen, p. 191.—Qualifications and duties in 1507, p. 191.—Altered, p. 192.— Widows, p. 192.—Almshouses not full, p. 192.—Provision for Livery, p. 192.—Grants to Freemen made under circumstances, p. 193.—John Stowe's pension, p. 194.— Wakefield's for leprosy, p. 194.—Refused to general applicants, p. 194.—Analysis of receipts and payments, p. 194.—Explanatory notes thereon, p. 195.

THE effect of the disendowment of religion on the expenditure of corporate funds, and whether it was either diminished or altered in regard to religious or benevolent objects, now remains for consideration.

We have observed in the last chapter that salaries for priests and obits disappear from the Guild accounts, and for the future no payments for religious services were made, save for sermons delivered under some benefactors' wills. The other expenditure of the Company may be examined under the two headings of

Feasting and Almsgiving—which in civic custom are not unfrequently associated together.

As early as Edward VI's reign the sumptuary expenses of the Guilds were challenged as excessive. "Many rich Guilds," it was represented, "were spending 800*l.* or 600*l.* yearly in making great feasts every month or six weeks in their halls, and thereby causing victuals to be dear,"[1] which so far as the Merchant Taylors' records afford information is entirely destitute of truth.

By some readers all such expenditure, even though a rule of moderation be observed, may be considered as waste, serving no good end, but a high authority writing after he had (under the authority of the Crown given him in 1833), inquired into the existing state, and collected information respecting the defects of the Corporation of London, came to an opposite conclusion; for thus Sir Francis Palgrave wrote in 1844:

"Amongst the causes of the well-being of London we must not omit the kindly influence of civic hospitality—long may it continue. Constantly in the habit of assembling at the festive board, as well in the greater assemblies of the city as in the smaller bodies of the Guilds, our citizens, however much they might be at discord or variance, were always in the way of being brought together by good fellowship, when the rival parties at Florence would have been employed in razing each others towns to the ground, our London factions were united in demolishing the ramparts of a venison pasty."[2]

It must, however, be remembered that when these entertainments originated the individual citizen had not (as he has now) the wealth or the house, or the appliances in the house, to feast his friends, and that the only other alternative was to take them to the "Mermaid" or the "Sun," or another tavern; as the traditional custom of London has always been that of feasting. Those of Chaucer's Pilgrims who were clothed in the livery "of a solempne and a great fraternite," had with them a cook "to boyle chyknes with the Mary bones," and that "feasting in an honest manner" or, as we may interpret these words, without extravagance or excess, was one of the purposes which the guildsmen in Richard's reign had in view is clear, as in express terms that charter authorised them and their successors to keep such a feast of meat

---

[1] Strype's Stowe (1721), Book 5, page 252.
[2] The Merchant and the Friar, by Sir Francis Palgrave, page 60. See his Reports on London Corporation and London Companies, ordered to be printed, 25th April, 1837, and see page 137, *ante.*

and drink on St. John Baptist's day, although it furnished no authority for the Master to hold such a feast in the common hall or at the cost of the body of the Fellowship without their licence, as the incident of 1485 in Sir John Percyvale's mastership proves. Nor can there be less doubt but that sumptuary expenses even for others not of the Guild have always been borne out of its funds whether as payments for all to the men who assembled in Fenchurch Street in 1455 as witnesses in Candish's affair, or for suppers and dinners to the King's officers or to the men of law when the Guild had to procure its charter, or an adjustment of it, or to the watch in the hall or at the city gates, or to the volunteers who repulsed Wyatt—on all these occasions and numberless others the Guild funds were so used.

But with regard to these payments for the enjoyment of the guildsmen records are found of an earlier date; thus it is clear from the Master's account for 1408-9, that "a kitchen, larderhouse, and sotil-house" had been sufficiently long in use at the hall as to need the repairs which he expended upon them;[1] while the inventory of 1512 gives the contents of a "kitchen" and various other outbuildings necessarily connected with the entertainment of many guests.

But before entering into the subject of expenditure we must explain the changes which had been introduced in the method of account and audit at some time anterior to 1561.[2] The whole rental of the Merchant Company had been taken out of the Master's hands and transferred to the charge of the two Renter or lower Wardens, who divided the same into two districts, each taking one and receiving the rents thereof. Further, out of the rents of one district all repairs were paid for and superintended by that Renter, and out of the rents of the other all trusts, or as it is entered "payments under the dead's will," and quit-rents were made by the other Warden. Each paid half of the view and search dinners, and the balance due on each Warden's rent account was at the close of the year paid over to the Master, and brought to the credit of the Company in his account; thus responsibility was distributed and the Master's authority weakened.

The Master's account was composed of the receipts of apprentices and freemen's fees and fines, the balance of rents received from the Wardens, and various other miscellaneous items. Originally his payments were for salaries to officials both at the hall

---

[1] Memorials, page 566.
[2] In this year our Court records commence.

and at the school (until these also were brought to the Warden's account), and for such sumptuary expenses as he incurred (by decree), and for law costs.

The audit of the accounts, though nominally with the Assistants, was entrusted to four members who were annually appointed by the Court, the Livery and Freemen not being represented on the audit, after the election of the Master and Wardens. While any expenditure of which the Court and auditors shared the benefit was probably not objected to by either body.

The balance was handed over to the succeeding Master or paid over to the Treasury, the keys of which were kept by the most respected members of the Court, Richard Hilles being one for many years. Only a few years' have been preserved of the Treasury accounts, and none of the Bachelors' accounts exist.

The Master and Wardens, under the wills of deceased benefactors, had been made the recipients of small annuities as for obits (which became obsolete), under the wills of Langwith, Percyvale, Jenyns, and Acton, and for "potation" under other wills still in force,[1] but as early as 1484–5 we find 10s. on apprenticing, and in 1546-7 on Ralph White's admission to the Livery, 5s. 4d. paid to the Master, which in the first entry is styled the "Master's parte," and in the next "that which he is accustomed to have for himself,"[2] though for many subsequent years 5s. was the only fee paid to him, and that was on taking up the "Livery."

With regard to the general income of the Guild we have already pointed out how their resources were exhausted (both presently and prospectively) by the redemption of obits under the Chauntries Collegiate Act. Of the capital and income available for taxation we have satisfactory evidence in the Company's certificate returned to the Subsidy Commissioners under 8 Elizabeth, cap. 18.

The Commons by that Statute presented a subsidy "in most lowly thanks" for three special matters, one of such being the most comfortable "assurance and promise by your Majesty made and declared unto us that for oure weale and suritye your Majesty would marry assone as God shold give opportunitie to accomplish the same, whereof we have receyved infinite comfort and shall pray to Almighty God to furder and prosper all yo⁹ Maj^ties actions tendyng thereunto."

---
[1] The total sum still payable to Master, Wardens, and officials for this is 61l. 17s. 2d.
[2] Percyvale's Court Records, MS. page 9 (3). Memorials, page 525.

Then follows the usual machinery for raising and paying this subsidy which was to be assessed (*inter alia*) "of every Fraternitie, Guild, or Mysterie (being worth 3*l*.) for every pound as well in coyne and the value of every pounde that every such Fraternitie, &c., hath of their own use, as also plate, stock of merchandise, almaner of corn, household stuffe, and of all goods moveable, and of all such sums of money as to them owing whereof they trust in their conscience surely to be paide, excepting therefrom debts which they owe, &c.," and for every pound it had in fee simple or for years of the yearly value of 20s.

In regard to *personalty* nothing could be claimed, for their debts were larger than their assets. Thus to the Lord Mayor's precept of 24th January, 1566, the Master and Wardens made this return :

"They do certyfie, that all the Plate, Juells, & Good's belonginge to their Corporacion extends not above the value of 66*l*. 13s. 4*d*.[1]

"And further, They do Certifie that the sayde Corporacion is indebted at this time, and doth owe to dyverse persons as well by their bonds obligatory under theire Common Seale as otherwyse ov̄ and above all such debtes as be owinge to the sayde Corporacion, the some of 237*l*. 6s. 0*d*."

And this return is consistent with the Court records of that period, for a loan had to be raised in December, 1567, for paying off a debt of 300*l*.

"Whereas at this pnte this house is and stands indebted to divers psons in sondry somes of money amountinge in the hole to the some of 300*l*., the most parte is pntely due and payable, and for there is not any money remayning in the comen Boxe at this pnte to paye the same, Therefore the aforesayde Mr Wardens and Assistants agree that there shalbe levied of the Members of this Mysterie, being of the clothing by waye of Prete or lone towards the supplie and payment of the aforesayde debt, vizt.:—every Alderman, or of every one who hath been M^r of this Mystere 40s.; of every one which hath not yet obtained to be M^r 30s.; and of evry one of the reste of the Clothinge that hath not bourne the room of one of the Wardens 20s. To be repayed unto them as soon as the coen Boxe of this house shalbe of habilitie to paye it."
—[December, 1567.]

---

[1] In December, 1524, the money, plate, and jewels were assessed at 110*l*. 13s. 4*d*. (Cal. State Papers, page 411.)

As to their *real estate* the Company's return enters more into detail.

"The Master & Wardens do Certifie that all theire Rents and Revenues Issuing, Coming & Growinge of all the Lands and Ten^ts belonging to their saide Corporacion¹ at this daye extends to the some per annum of .... — 280 15 4

"Notwithstanding of late the same did extende to the some per annum of 308*l.* 7*s.*

[As they proceed to explain thus :]

"But at this presente there is parcell of the same Londes² situate and leyinge in the Parish of St. Martyn, in the Vyntrye of St James, at Garlickhithe, which was lately rented in the hole at the some of xiij*l.* vj*s.* viij*d.* per annum, wch is nowe vacant by reason of the decaye thereof and lack of Newe buildinge. So that the yearly value of the Londes at this day is 280*l.* 15*s.* 4*d.*

[They then claim these deductions :]

    "Whereof to be admitted as followeth—

"Fyrste for Quyte Rentes and other Rente Charge, wherewithal the sayde Londes is charges per annum 109 15 0

"Item, to the Reliefe of theire Almsmen & others, and for Coles gyven to the Poore according to the Devyses of the Donors of certen of their sayde Londes per annum 59 17 11

"Item, to the Schoolmaster and iij Ushers of theire late erected Grammar Schole, founded in the Parishe of St. Lawrence Pounteney, in London, and for the Vysytacon of the sayde Schole per annum 56 13 4

[They then deduct their establishment charges for salaries—]

"Item, to theire Offycers for theire ffees, per annum 22 6 8

"Soma totalis of the deductions and payments goynge out of the foresayde Londes & Annuyties .... ————— 248 12 11

"And so remayneth clere to the sayde Company towardes the repayringe of the sayd Londes & of Newe Buildings, of what is decayed thereof as is aforesaid, the some of .... — 46 6 8"

It is clear therefore from this return that the Corporate income was all but exhausted, and that the Guild then had no available asset for taxation.

---

¹ In December, 1524, the Company returned their lands in St. Martin's Parish at 132*l.* 11*s.* 1½*d.*

² This was the gift of Mr. Thomas Sutton, Master 1408-12.

The other sources of income to the Merchant Company besides rents were fees on the enrolment of apprentices, and the admission of freemen, fines, and other miscellaneous items. The annual rental was diminished in its actual increase by the habit which prevailed at this period of taking fines, sometimes monied ones of large amount which went to the Treasury (and did not always appear in the Master's account), and sometimes smaller ones in kind, as good fat bucks for the Master's election feast; an instance of the former was in a lease granted to Arthur Ingram on a letter of request in May, 1612, from Prince Henry (set out in the records) of a house in Fenchurch Street (since sold); and of the latter the instances are too frequent to need mention.

For years taken incidentally at decennial periods the account books shew these total receipts and payments :—

	Receipts.			Payments.		
	£	s.	d.	£	s.	d.
1545–6	512	10	3	408	5	7
1555–6	428	14	10	323	11	3
1570–1	711	9	11	655	2	4
1580–1	822	19	6	786	13	6
1590–1	989	19	4	847	10	6
1600–1	1229	13	8	935	5	3

Of which an analysis and notes are given more in detail at the end of this chapter.

As to Feasting.—That this was inaugurated on a larger scale after the disendowment of religion would seem to be absolutely certain. The occasion of the Commissioners meeting under the Chauntries Collegiate Act at the Company's hall in 1547 was celebrated with a banquet, which in regard to the sum of 7*l.* 10*s.* 11*d.* which was allowed for it must have been one of great liberality. However, to deal with the facts as they present themselves.

In earlier times the two great feasts of the Company were in honour of their patron Saint John Baptist—that on the Nativity kept annually by the Merchants, that on the Decollation triennially by the Yeomen. To these feasts each of the brethren subscribed as we have already shown. The Company contributed some of the expenses towards inviting great guests, providing music, cleaning the hall and laying down clean rushes, hiring pewter vessels, and washing the napery, with other smaller items, but "the meat and drink" were provided by and at the cost of the Master out of the "brotherhood money" of the Livery, which he received direct from them, and not from the corporate funds. All the members of the Livery were present.

At a later period, but as early as 1545, we find three other "quarter days" kept, and the sum of 3*l*. each (9*l*. as a total) allowed out of the corporate funds to the Master for three dinners. To these and to other dinners (as on St. Simon and St. Jude, and at the school) two Stewards, taken in seniority from the Livery, were appointed, so that each liveryman had in turn to bear the extra charge (if any) of these dinners. But at the close of Edward's reign by a decree of 26th April, 1553, in the mastership of John Jakes (Ralph White being a Warden) the charge of the quarter day dinners was raised to 13*l*. per annum, which was allowed to Sir W. Harper, his successor. The income in 1545-6 was a total of 512*l*. 10*s*. 3*d*.; the sumptuary expenses 17*l*. 17*s*. 0*d*., but at the close of the decennial period ending with 1555-6 the corporate income had fallen, from the forced sales for the purchase of obits, to 428*l*. 14*s*. 10*d*., and the sumptuary expenses had risen to 54*l*. 2*s*. 7*d*., and they probably continued to rise during Mary's reign.[1]

The sumptuary expenses of Elizabeth's reign increased not so much by reason of there being more entertainments, but more guests (so far as the Livery were such) and these being feasted at a higher cost.[2] All the Livery were summoned to dine on these occasions besides the younger brethren who were chosen to wait on the elder members, thus on the 1st July, 1588 :—

"This Court was informed that divers of the younge men, brethren of this Companie, that were chosen for waighters and the carrying most of the meate served into the hall at dynner, did murmer and mislike that they were kept soe longe wthout their dynners and not appointed to sitt downe before the Dynner was fullie served in, and the tables taken upp in the Hall, and thereupon contemptuouslie departed away without their dynners, using some harde speech and apparent shewes of ther discontentment. Agreed, that such as departed awaie should be sent for at the next

---

[1] We have no account books from 1557 to 1569.

[2] Take one item as an illustration. The waits in 1555-56 were paid 6*s*. 8*d*., but in 1602 their fee (for six in number) was raised to 40*s*.—*Memorials*, page 540.

Court to answer their contempt, and to receive such orders therein as the Court shall awarde."[1]

This service continued to be performed till a later period, for when the late Master, Thomas Aldworth, claimed, on the 21st August, 1602, an allowance of 50s. for thirty officers, six of the Lord Mayor and twenty-four of the Sheriffs, that waited on the election day, which sum the auditors had disallowed, because they did not hold fit to allow it without the consent of the Court. The Court disallowed it, "for on consideration and due regard had to the said demand, as the said 50s. was paid by Mr. Plomer and Mr. Palmer, late Masters, out of their own purses and no allowance by them demanded for the same, and because it is a *new custom* to have officers to wait which heretofore hath been supplied by brothers of the Company, and as it is at the Master's pleasure whether of them he will have, therefore the Assistants do not allow of the s^d demand."

But the Master's "election" dinner would seem from a Court minute of the 9th July, 1593, to have been held at his option, for when the Company received a precept "from the Lord Maior, by order of Her Majesties most hon^{ble} Privie Counsell to this effecte, videlicet, that the Master and Wardens of this Societie should under their hands make certificate to the Lord Maior of the value of the yearly charge which is disbursed at the election dinner to th'end the same beinge certified to the councell that it maye be ordered and employed to the reliefe of the poore visited with the plague," the Court "considered that the same charge is p^{9}formed by the Master of the Company at whose choice it is either to have an election dinner or none at all, and that the usual and ancient allowance of the Company to the Master's cleration of his charges of the same dinner was eighte pounds (viij$l$.) and thereupon it is ordered that a certificate shall be made to the Lord Maior that the charge beinge the private charge of the Master of the Companie, there is no accompt kepte with us of the same, nor of any p^{9}ticular thereof more than of the eight pounds putt to the common accompte of this Societie which is ready to be disposed as other companies shall dispose of theirs."

At a later period, in 1605, the quarter day dinners, which

---

[1] It would appear in other respects they came under reproof :—

"16th July, 1622.

"Whereas divers of the Liverie at this Eleccon daie did rise from ye table before the Eleccon was finished. It is ordered that notice shall be given them at ye next Quarter daie that such disorder maie be amended."

began to be allowed for as three in 1545, were increased to four; the Master's election dinner in July being substituted for St. John's day. The occasion which suggested the increase was the calling of 27 freemen in 1602 to meet the cost of Sir Robert Lee's mayoralty. Richard Gore, the M.P. for London, was the Master of the Company, and in April, 1603, he was requested to postpone his quarter day dinner beyond the season of Lent, "in consideration thereof, and of the great recent increase of the Livery a resolution" was come to that an extra allowance of 20*l*. should be given to him. While the subject was under discussion the Master very properly left the Court, and during his absence the affirmative vote was carried. Another resolution was then put and carried that the allowance should to all succeeding Masters be 100*l*., but at the next Court of the 1st June this resolution was revoked.

If we may judge from the later action of the Master neither of these resolutions for increasing the allowance had his concurrence, for in accordance with the best traditions of the Company he refused to accept it, and desired that the resolution might be expunged, "so as to leave no precedent to posterity of any such increase while he was Master."

However, the question once raised was not allowed to rest, for when Jeffrey Elwes[1] (who was afterwards Sheriff in 1608) was Master, the Court by resolution of the 19th June 1605, resolved to raise the allowance, imposing these conditions[2]: "that the Master should keep three quarter days and his election day, and upon these occasions invite the wives of the Aldermen (being members) of the old Masters, and of the Wardens."

After the foundation of the school the examinations of scholars at St. Lawrence Poultney, brought together many of the Church dignitaries of London, besides the Oxford examiners which neces-

---

[1] Jeffery Elwes was possibly a man by whom money was needed. On 16th December, 1595, when three Assistants absent from former Courts were wanted by the Master to put down a self-imposed fine, Shepham gave 5*s*., Lydford 2*s*. 6*d*., and Elwes 6*d*. His descendants intermarried with the Gores—Herald's Visit. of Berks (1666).

[2] To make a bargain with the Master may appear strange, but it was necessary. The allowance for each dinner did not pay the cost of it, and therefore a Master would claim his allowance from the auditors for dinners which he never gave. Thus 1592-3, 60*l*. was paid for three dinners, and nothing for the election dinner—as for that the "Brotherhood Money" was taken. Again, the late Master, Richard Procter, claimed 80*l*. for four dinners, but was allowed 60*l*. for the *two* quarter day dinners which he had given.

sitated a dinner originally held at the hall, but in 1579 discontinued, for the reason thus explained in the Court minute of 23rd June:—" To avoid so great a charge as the dynner comonlye made here in oure hall upon St. Barnabas daye for theloction of scholers is growen unto. The said Master, Wardens, and Assistants have decreed that the said dynner shall no more be made & kepte here, but from hensforth at their schole in St. Lawrence Pountney accordinge to the wise discretion of the Masters and Wardens for the tyme beinge."

Such expenses as were allowed for this dinner appeared in the Master's account, but the funeral dinners directed to be given by deceased members at the expense of their estates were not unfrequently celebrated on these occasions to avoid cost to the Company. Take Sir Thomas White's gift as an illustration:—

"26th February, 1568:—The Master & Wardens appoynted their scole to be visited upon Monday the vijth of Marche by such learned men as they shall appoynt. A dinner to be made by Thos Ludwall & George Sanders in their Coēn Hall for the Lyverie of y^e Company & for such learned men as they shall appoint to be with them at theire said scole, and to have towards the making of the said dynner ix$li.$ which was bequeathed by S^{ir} Thomas White, Knight & Alderman, deceased, for & towards a refecc͠on or repaste to be made for the Lyverie of the said Companye accordinglie."

To these must be added the ordinary sumptuary expenses which appeared in the Wardens' accounts which were (1.) The view dinners, when they and others took their periodical surveys of the Company's houses; and (2.) The search dinner after St. Bartholomew's Fair, a custom possibly kept up by the dinner long after the search was of any practical utility.

The ordinary sumptuary expenses increased during Elizabeth's reign[1] from 77$l.$ 15$s.$ 5$d.$ in 1570-1 to 141$l.$ 6$s.$ 10$d.$ in 1600-1, and

---

[1] *Cook to the Company.*—The first entry which has come under our notice is of the 28th March, 1563, when Sylvester Clarke was admitted to the place. The value of it is not given, but in May, 1613, the Lady Elizabeth (James I's daughter) wrote to the Company a letter set out on their minutes of the 5th, asking the appointment on the next vacancy for one John Warde, but as the Princess had left England no answer was returned. From a Court entry of the 16th October, 1621, his suit was pressed on the Court by the Common Sergeant, but it was thought better that no permanent appointment should be made.—Chapter XVII, 331.

"16th October, 1621, folio 71.

"To this Court came Mr. Comon Seriant in the behalf of Jno. Ward, who is a

continued to increase during the reign of James I, when a new departure took place in having dinners for the Court, which is explained in the Memorials of May and August, 1606.

"Forasmuch as divers of ye Assistants, by reason of their age and remote dwelling from the Hall, cannot make their appearaunce untill a good part of the day be spent, and also by reason yt Courts of Assistants holdeth so long that they cannot return home to their dynners in any convenient time, doe therefore make default of appearance at many Courts: it is therefore ordered that at every Court there shalbe a convenient dynner provided by one of the Renter Wardens for the said Assistants at the coste of the Company, not exceeding 40s.," *i.e.*, 1s. a head, which was increased to 53s. and 4s. in March, 1611, when thirteen of the Livery were added to the Court; "if any more be expended the Renter Wardens shall beare the same, saving only that over and above the forty shillings, ye fynes of such Assistants as shalbe absent, shall be collected by one of the Renter Wardens and added to the charges of the said dynner."

"Be it remembered that this day ye Assistants dyned here at the charges of the Company, and, after dynner, sate and dispatched much business, so as there was more matters ended at this Court than hath ben accustomed at 2 or 3 other Courts."

It was in the same reign that another dinner for the Court only was established. We had occasion in the last chapter to enter at some length into a description of the charitable works of Robert Dowe, in accord with the best traditions of the Company —religion and almsgiving—and the benefaction now to be mentioned is in accord with the third characteristic of the Guild, viz., feasting or hospitality, towards which he granted a perpetual endowment. He was, therefore, a genial lover of good fellowship, and no cold ascetic.

By deed of August, 1605, Dowe established what was afterwards kept as the Convivium dinner, thus: "he gave to the Master and Wardens 40s. like other money given them by benefactors deceased for potation to be dispended by them either in Lent or some other convenient time during their year of

---

suitor to be the Company's Cook, whereupon the Co'te, considering how p'iudiciall it might be to make permanent choice of such officers, have ordered that every M^r of this Society for the time being or the Wardens, Stowards, or any other of this Society, who shall have the charge of any dinner or supp in this hall shall have power to make choice of their *own Cook and Butlers.* And any committee having the building or repaying any of the Companyes houses shall make choice of ye Carpenter, Bricklayer, and all other workmen, &c."

office, they and their wives to use that day or meeting for their comfort and recreation; to which repast he prayed them to invite some ten or twelve of the ancient Masters and chief of the Assistants, to perform the old saying 'The more the merrier,' and then and there to remember the charitable acts done by the good brethren of the Company with intent and purpose to increase the same to their powers, and also in perpetual remembrance of the said Mr. Robert Dowe to give the name of this meeting the 'Convivium or banquet of Mr. Robert Dowe and other good brethren deceased,' and if they shall leave to perform this friendly meeting (the which the said Robert Dowe hopeth they will not) or do not expend the said 40s. then the said yearly gift should be distributed and given to the almspeople."

The dinner was held at the Angel at Islington, in September, 1611, and this is the entry :—[1]

"Memorandum, the Convivium Dynner was kept at the Aungell at Islington, upon Monday, 9th September, 1611, where Dyned the Right Woor{ll} Mr. Richard Wright, Mr, Mr. Geo. Lyddiatt, Francis Evington, and John Gore, three of his Wardens, with other Right Woor{ll} p'sons, Assistants and Counsellors of this Mystery, whose names hereafter ensue, viz. :—

Sir Leonard Halliday, Knight, Ald{n}.
Mr. Jeoffrey Elves, Alderman.
Mr. Robert Dow.
Mr. Thomas Juxon.

Mr. Humphrey Streete.
Thomas Henshaw.
Randolph Woolley.
Raph Hamer, and
Thomas Johnson."

Further, on the death of an almsman Dowe left a sum to be

---

[1] It would appear to have been a dinner frequently paid for out of the potation money; but in 1620 the expenses came upon the Corporate funds, limited in 16l.

"Whereas divers several somes of money are given by good beenefactors to this Company towards a yearly Convivium dinner which hath been duly kept according to the will of the deceased, and some other somes given by the will of the dead only to the Maister and Wardens for their paynes,[a] have also hitherto by consent of the Maister and Wardens then being, beene spent with the former somes at the said convivium dinner, whereby the charge out of the stock of the house was soe much the less. But nowe the Master and Wardens, hereafter not willing to breake the will of the dead, but to receive their due, desire to be left at liberty whether they will doe as their predecessors have done or noe, which this Court doth not deny, but order and agree that a convivium dinner shalbe yearly kept according to the will of the dead, for to continue mutual love and society in this Company, but to be more frugal in expenses than heretofore, and therefore have ordered and agreed that the money spent at the said dinner shall not exceed the some of 16l. at the most."— [18th July, 1620.]

[a] Probably the potation money is here referred to.—Memorials I, page 8.

expended upon a recreation and drinking for the surviving almsmen who were attendant upon his funeral, but that this might not lead to excess he laid down these conditions regarding the expenditure "to be bestowed in cakes bread butter cheese ale or beer (but noe wyne) in some honest victualing and that the Clarke of the Bachilers Companie shall bring with him the hower glasse deliuered him by the said Robert Dowe for that purpose the same to be renewed by the M^r and Wardens as often as it shall decaie and presentlie upon their sitting downe at the table shal turne the said glasse, and take especiall care that they remayne not there above an howre, and the hower growing neer to an end some one of them by hart distinctlie and openlie to say the printed praier deliuered unto them at their elections (all being bareheaded reverentlie giving God thanks at the saying thereof) and then in civill sort everie man to rise and departe homeward."

Nor is this all that he did, funeral dinners given by the legacies of deceased guildsmen were in constant observance, and to prevent such an entertainment from degenerating into a funeral orgie or wake Robert Dowe gave the Common Clerk yearly the sum of 5s. "upon condition and in consideration that when any good brother or sister of the Company as shall departe this world shall bestowe upon the lyvery a funerall dynner at the Hall for the Company to meete there in remembrance of him or her that then the said common clarck shall openly reade and pronounce a comemorable Grace approved and allowed by the whole assistants and which by the moc̃on of the said Robert Dow was devised by learned men as a matter religious and comendable thereby to put the whole Company present as well in remembrance of their own mortality as the losse and want of that good brother or sister deceased."

But it must be remembered that there were other *extraordinary* sumptuary expenses which the members of the Bachelors Company took upon themselves when any of their guildsmen held one of the higher offices of the Corporation. Such an occasion arose in 1602 when two of their members, Merchants by profession (as it was emphasized), held the offices of Lord Mayor and Sheriff. This is the Court minute of 23rd September, 1602:—

"Itt is concluded and agreed that against Symon and Jude's Day for the triumph before the Lord Maior, there shalbe preparacion made of a Pageon, a Ship, a Lyon, and a Cammell. The Pageon being a thing ordinary, and th'other three doe properly belong unto our Companie, and are very fitt and answerable for this tyme, namely, the Ship in regard two Wor^ll Members of this Company are to bear great offyces in this Cittie for this nexte yeare ensuing, viz., Mr Robt Lee, Alderman, the hon^ble place of Lord Maior, and Mr John Swinnerton, Alderman, the place of one of the Sheriffes of this Cittie, and they both being merchants. And we, as well in regard of the Companies' Incorporacion and name of Merchantailors, as also in regard, the said two Wor^ll persons are merchants by profession, the shippe is proper and very apte for this occasion and tyme, and the Lyon being part of the Companie's Armes, and the Cammell the Companie's supporters. And our Master and Wardens are entreated to have a speciall care, that every thing maye be very sufficientlie p^rformed, to the worship and creditt of the Company, being long free from the same chardge not havinge had a Maior of our Company sithence Sir Thomas Rowe was Lord Mayor, being now thirty and three years since."

The money was raised by a calling of the Livery and by assessment.[1] The items of the expenditure are given in the appendix.

We have already shown how hospitality and feasting had to give place (according to the orders of the Common Council) to charity when provisions were scarce and the wants of the poor urgent; of this another instance may be given as happening in this reign.

At the Assembly on the 12th of August, a letter from Sir Stephen Slaney, the Lord Mayor, dated 28th July, 1596, " to my very loving friends " the Master, Wardens, and Assistants of the Company of Merchant Taylors was read, setting forth that " a very charitable and godly motion has been moved in the Common Council that considering the present dearth of all manner of victuals and especially of bread, and the exceeding number of poor and miserable people within the city which want relief it was very convenient to plead that the Master and Wardens of the several Companies whose feast and dinners are not passed would

---

[1] In 1605 a similar expense fell upon the Company, when Sir L. Halliday was elected Lord Mayor, with an additional cost for repeating the show. Page 75, *ante*.

" Memo.—This year, by reason of the great rain and fowle weather hap'ning and falling upon the morrow after Symon and Jude's day being the day my Lord Mayor went to Westminster, the great costs the Company bestowed upon their pageant and other shows were in manner cast away and defaced. And therefore upon a general request made by the Batchelors the same shows were new repaired and carried abroad upon All Saints Day, at a cost of 64*l.* 14*s.* 1*d.*"

forbear to give dinners for this time and that the Master and Wardens who do use or ought to bear that charge would be pleased liberally and charitably to impart some good portion of such charge as they should otherwise expend, to the intent that the same may be employed and bestowed in corn and bread for the present relief of the poor within the city, which motion and suit being gladly embraced and recommended by the Common Council." The Lord Mayor and his brethren the Aldermen had thought fit to communicate the same to the Company.

But the necessity of the times had induced the Company "long before the receipt of the said letter to forego feasting this year," and they had bestowed the charge so spared upon St. John's College, Oxford, for the expenses of building their library, a fact which was communicated to the Lord Mayor with a hope that he would rest satisfied with so reasonable an answer.[1]

As to Almsgiving, including the School and University Scholarships.

As a matter preliminary, it must be noticed that all the charities arising from trusts were duly executed by the Company, without any expenses to the trusts, that is neither establishment charges nor any percentage or expenses for collecting rents or for superintending repairs were ever deducted from the rents, a rule which has been uniformly observed in Guild administration.

Then under this head there has usually been included in the Company's books the cost of the school and university scholarships, so far as these were paid for out of the corporate funds, but it will be seen from the life of Richard Hilles, that the school at St. Lawrence Poultney Hill was originally established in 1562 rather at the cost of individual members than of the "common box" of the Company, and it would seem to be clear that the payment of the Masters' salaries out of the latter fund was contemplated rather as a tentative measure, "until such tyme as the same shall be *otherwise* discharged by the gifts and legacies of good and well-disposed men," than as a permanent endowment out of Guild funds.

However, no such gifts or legacies were made, save that of Robert Dowe which has been already referred to.

Shortly after the establishment of the school an appeal was

---

[1] "Master's Account, 1596–7.—Item, received of 73 of the Livery of the Company for brotherhood money after the rate of 3s. 4d. the man, being this year collected to the use of the house, because there was not any feaste kept this year, the sum of 12l. 3s. 4d., and the names of such as are unpaid was delivered over to our new Master, by him to be collected to the use of the Company ; I say received, 12l. 3s. 4d."

made to the Company from the Lord Mayor to establish scholarships at the Universities, one of the evil effects of Henry VIII's legislation of the Reformation period having been to withdraw young men from the Universities as an avenue to Church preferment.

To stop this evil and encourage the study of divinity there Queen Elizabeth[1] wrote in 1560 to the Lord Keeper (Nicholas Bacon) directing him to confer on "divinity students that have need of Exhibitions all prebends in his disposition for one year, or longer if required, till there was some repair of this lamentable lack," and to the Vice-Chancellors of the Universities[2] telling them that she had determined to prevent the decay of the study of divinity, and to bestow both the promotions in her gift, and the prebends in that of the Lord Keeper, on students recommended by them. In reply to this appeal, the Vice-Chancellor of Cambridge was not long in sending up to Sir W. Cecil his list of candidates. "There was never," wrote the Vice-Chancellor, "a larger number of learned youths, but poverty had often made their studies mercenary; they had gone to law or medicine for fear of want, and *deserted the study* which the Queen's measures would rectify."

It was Elizabeth herself who originated the movement, but following upon the Queen's letter came that from the Corporation of London soliciting the Guilds to promote the same object. The Lord Mayor[3] had taken counsel with the Bishop of London (Edmund Grindall), and as a consequence the Corporation made request to each of the twelve Companies in April, 1564, to establish "Exhibitions" out of their corporate incomes for one or more students at the Universities.[4]

The result, so far as the Merchant Taylors were concerned, is set out in the order of the Court of the 19th April. "Finding the

---

[1] Cal. State Papers (Dom.), on date.
[2] The number of students matriculating at Oxford at the periods below are thus given in the Register of the University, Vol. 2, page 416. For the names of London students in 1575 see Lansdowne MS., Vol. 20, page 82.

	1567 to 1573.	1574 to 1578.	1579 to 1583.	1584 to 1589.	1590 to 1594.
Bristol	3	10	7	3	4
London	24	77	92	92	80

[3] Sir John White, the Grocer.
[4] City Records Reports, Vol. 15, page 328; Vol. 18, pages 398 and 238, *post*.

Company not to be of ability to sustain or bear any further charge," it was "agreed that no such charge as requested by the Corporation shall be borne out of the common box of this mystery." There the matter might have ended but for the benevolence of individual Taylors, who taxed themselves (a fair criterion that the "common box" was empty) upon this scale, "every member, being a Sheriff of the city, should give what he pleased; Sir Thomas Rowe (an Alderman) should give 20s.; the Master, 6s. 8d.; and every Assistant 5s. a year, payable quarterly;" but the scholar, it must be noticed, was to be appointed by the Master and Wardens, and to make promise "to study and be student in divinity," and these contributions of 5l. for each scholar were continued in subsequent years,[1] but ultimately paid out of corporate funds.[2]

As to almsgiving.—To relieve the poor of the Guild, it is probable, if not certain, as we have already shown, that each Company, *i.e.*, the Merchant or Yeomen, looked after their own poor, and that none but *members* were recipients of Guild funds, and having already shown what contributions the Merchants made to the Yeomen for their poor, we shall here confine ourselves to the almsgiving of the Merchant Company to their own poor.

The almshouses at the hall, the enjoyment of which was, under the ordinances of 1507, defined as "the full alms of the Fraternity,"[3] were seven in number and reserved for the "brother being of the *clothing* fallen into poverty not through ryott, wanton and lavish expenditure, negligence, or other misdemeanour," who had kept obedience and had borne all manner of impositions, lot, scot, and other charges. The alms consisted of an almshouse to dwell in for life, and a weekly sum, originally of 17d., but afterwards increased, with a share of coals distributed under various benefactions.

On appointment the brother was to make promise to be "person-

---

[1] 1 Wilson, page 31, note, and page 196, note.

[2] Sir Thomas Rowe died in September, 1570, and in the Master's accounts for 1569-70, is this entry :—

"Item, this accountant asketh allowance of 10l., wherewith he charges himself in the title of his receipts, forasmuch as he hath paid the same as followeth, viz., to Sir Huchenson, Fellow of St. John Baptist College in Oxford for his whole Exhibition, due and ending at Midsummer anno 1570; 5l., and more paid to Mr. Wythers, late Fellow of Trinity College in Cambridge, for a half-year Exhibition to him, due before his departure from the said University, ending at Christmas last, and also for more paid to John Huchenson, Student in Pembroke Hall, who succeeded the said Mr. Withers for the enjoying of the exhibition to him granted by this house for one half year also to him due at Midsummer, anno 1570, total, 10l." Page 196, *post.*

[3] Ordinance 4.

ally present in St. Martin's Church, there serving God and all his Saints and praying every day for Henry VII, *the chief and first founder* of the said Fraternity of St. John Baptist, of London, for the good estate of the Master, Wardens, Brethren, and Sisters, and all the benefactors of the said Fraternity being alive, and for the souls of those deceased." The alms people were bound to leave all their bedding and household stuff for the use of their successors, but they were to be buried honestly at the cost[1] and charges of the Fraternity by the Master and Wardens, divers of the clothing in their whole livery being present at a " solemn dirige and at masse as they used to do laudably for other brethren and sisters when they depart out of this present life."

This, like other ordinances was altered after the Reformation. The service in St. Martin's was watered down to a weekly attendance, and the almsman's tenure was limited to good behaviour with a proviso that if he married without leave of the Master and Wardens he should at once forfeit his privileges, but if he married with leave the widow by survivorship enjoyed his privileges. It was this frequent survivorship of widows (possibly some years younger than their late husbands) which induced some benevolent members of the Court to provide almshouses in Hog Lane for widows of the Livery.[2]

Although the amount of the weekly payment was increased making the annual payment in 1545–6 3*l*. 13*s*. 5*d*., and in 1590–1 5*l*. 4*s*., with an addition of 1*l*. from Walter Fish's will, yet strange as it may seem, few members were recipients of these alms. Thus, in 1545–6 we have only four; in 1555–6 only two, and one for half a year; in 1570–1 the same; in 1580–1 only four; but in 1590–1 the full number of seven is reached.

In later years other relief, as of pension only,[3] was given to members of the Court or Livery who had fallen into decay. Thus, at a Court of 17th May, 1563, we find a grant of 20 marks per annum made to George Heton (Master in 1556–7) for the great losses he had sustained "both by land and sea," which he continued to hold until he came before the Court on the 9th June, 1572,[4] and surrendered it.

---

[1] The wife was buried by the Company, and in the account books of 1545–6 we find this entry :—" Item for burying Isham's wife, 2*s*."

[2] Page 169 and Part II, page 230.

[3] In 1600–1 I find 11 out-pensions of various sums amounting to a total of 37*l*. 6*s*. 8*d*.

[4] It was on his petition re-granted to him in April, 1576, and in June following

CHAP. X.] *Grants to Liverymen.* 193

"Mr. George Heton, now Chamberlain of this honorable Cytie of London, giving his most hearty thanks unto this Worshipfull Companye for their greate benevolence in relyving him by annull pension of 13*l.* 6*s.* 8*d.*, wch was to him lovingly and largely granted, of his free and good will hathe declared this psent daye in open courte that he is well pleased (God having otherwise well pvided for him) that the said annuity or anuual pension should henceforth cease and be no longer paid; nevertheless it is agreed, notwithstanding his free release, that the some of 3*l.* 6*s.* 8*d.* shall be paide to him for the quarter ending at the feaste of the Annunciation."

It was evidently not of course, but a strong case must be made for the Merchant Company to relieve those *not* of the Livery, and the relief when given did not come out of the common box but from such fines as might be leviable. A Court minute of the 24th September, 1564, illustrates this:—

"This daye a supplication was offered by dyvrs honeste men dwelling uppon London Bridge, in the behalf of William Ferman, their neighbo^r and a poor brother of this mystery, whom God hath lately stricken, together with his wiffe and mayde servant wth blyndness, that it would please this Company to extend their Charities for their relief, Whereupon y^t was accorded and dcreed that all such penalties wch hereafter shall be due by any Brother of this Company for non-appearance uppon lawfull summons shall be from tyme to tyme gathered by the Coen Clarke and disposed for the saide blind people until they may be otherwise pvided. And it is further decreed that 20*s.* wch Mr. Geo. Heton, Chamberlin of this honorable Cytie, hath received to the use of this Mystery for the half of 40*s.* fyne, receved of a Stranger dwelling in Cornhill, for the makynge of certen newe clothes and garments, which was seassed uppon by the Wardens of this Mystery, and now by the saide Mr. Chamberlin paide in courte, shalbe also given to the relief of the sayde blind people, &c. &c."

It is true that "John Stowe" who was not of the Livery was a pensioner out of the "common box" but the minute of 31st March, 1578, states that the grant was made "for divers good considerations them specially moving."

During the same mastership, that of "Robert Dowe," we find 20*s.* paid to Francis Wakefield "of the benevolence of the Com-

---

revoked, Mr. Richard Hilles being present at the Court, "as the said George Heton standeth not in so great need thereof as others." He was removed from his office in December, 1577.—Memorials, page 534.

pany" which is explained in the minute of 30th October, 1578, thus :—

"Decreed that Francis Wakefield, apprenticed some time to Francis Gore, of this mystery, and afflicted with leprosy, shall have 20s. delivered unto him by the Master of this mystery to bring him down to Bath, where he is persuaded to have hope of his disease," a persuasion which we fear was not realised, as he never became a freeman of the Company.[1]

The danger of using the Company's funds to satisfy the needs of persons other than guildsmen arose for consideration in 1586, and this was the decision:

On the 14th June, a letter from the Bishop of London, Dr. Aylmer, sent on by the Lord Mayor, in favour of our Mr. Stockard, a preacher, recommending his poor estate to the several companies of the city came before the Court, "but upon full consideration had thereunto and also what a precedent it would be hereafter in the like cases, and also how many poor brothers we have of this Company more than we are any way able to relief, this Company did not think it convenient neither do find their estate able to give or bestow any contributions in such or the like cases, and therefore the said Mr. Stockard is to be entreated to rest satisfied with this the Company's answer."

There was every reason why the Master and Wardens should not bestow benefits on other persons than those of their own Guild. The funds so far as they were subscribed came from their own guildsmen, and the benefactors who were such in early years, made the "bretheren and sisters of the Fraternity the donees."[2] Again, every citizen was of some Guild, and other residents not of any were, in the language of those times, foreigners, thought of with little favour by the citizens, and, therefore, never recipients of the Guild alms.

Donations for public purposes stood upon a different footing, and were made in answer to an appeal to them as citizens,[3] or to their patriotism or religious sympathies,[4] or indeed to both.

EXPLANATORY NOTE ON RECEIPTS AND PAYMENTS.

These are the receipts and payments (consolidated) made by the Master and Renter Wardens of the Merchant Taylors Company, and do not include those of the Bachelors nor of the "Treasury," but only the current account for each year.

[1] These were admitted freemen: Wakefield, William, per William Todd, October, 1539; Wakefield, Radus, per Thomas Wilson, 13th May, 1558; Wakefield, William, per William Maryatt, 4th November, 1577; but not Francis.

[2] Page 400.   [3] Page 228.   [4] Page 320.

194

CHAP. X.]   *Note on Receipts and Payments.*   195

Each of the two Wardens had a district assigned to him and collected the rents of such district. One Warden paid all the repairs of the whole property, and the other all the trust payments and quit-rents. At the close of the year each made up his account of receipts and payments and brought the balance to account with the Master and paid it over to him.

If in the course of the year the Master's account needed cash and the Warden had such in hand for his use, the same was handed over to the Master and then credited to the Warden.

Each Warden paid half of the view dinner and that at the search of St. Bartholomew's Fair, and for further illustration we will refer to each item of the receipts and payments for the year 1570-1.

Receipts.

1 and 2 are regulated by the 22 Henry VIII, c. 4, as 2s. 6d. for apprentices and 3s. 4d. for freemen.

3. These are for the non-enrolment of apprentices and non-presentment of freemen, and for each liveryman admitted. The lesser fines were taken by the Wardens Substitute, and are not therefore included in this account.

4. When leases were granted on fine, the fine was received by the Treasury and the ordinary rent by the Warden. The rent here given is only that received by the Warden.

5. Miscellaneous sums other than fines as last mentioned were received by the Master.

6. The corn supply of London was first made by the Corporation with money borrowed from the Guilds. It was afterwards made by the Guilds buying and selling corn at rates named by the Corporation. These transactions were not part of the ordinary income of the Guild.

7. The Treasury was equivalent to the banking account of the present day, and advanced to and received from the Master moneys to be accounted for. The Company's outstanding assets and obligations were retained there for safe custody, and the keys were held by appointed members of the Court of Assistants.

Payments.

8. These included (*inter alia*), the School, 40l.; the Clerk 16l. 13s. 4d.; the Beadle 7l. 3s. 4d.; two counsel at 1l. 6s. 8d. each.

Although Strype's statement as to the sumptuary expenses of the Guilds in Edward VI's reign[1] was an exaggeration so far as the Merchant Taylors are concerned, yet the fact is clear that such expenses were increased[2] at a date (1545) co-incident with the disendowment of religion.

9. These included in the Master's account: Audit, 4l. 9s. 8d.; View, 1l.; four quarter days at the hall, 20l.; by decree, St. Simon and St. Jude's for livery, 3l.; the like for school dinner, 10l.; Assistants who specially viewed Sir Thomas Rowe's estate, 2l. 17s. 7d. Then came special payments for St. John's feast, or rather the Master's election dinner: music, 1l. 10s. 0d.; clean straw, 18s.; hire of rich arras cloths for the parlour and gallery, 2l. 1s. 0d.; hire of vessels, 1l. 17s. 8d.; washing of napery, 1l. 2s. 0d.; purchase of napery, 11l. 15s. 10d.

In the Warden's account: Search at St. Bartholomew's Fair, 7l. 13s. 4d.; and view dinner at the hall (each charging a half), 5l. 17s. 7d.

---

[1] Page 173.   [2] Page 181.

The expenses of each year would be for similar occasions, but the quarter day dinners were increased to 60*l.* in 1581, to 80*l.* in 1591, and to 100*l.* in 1605.

10. These would necessarily vary and in time would be imposed on the tenants.

11. The annual fee to the standing counsel was included in the salaries, but the other items would vary as litigation arose. Thus, in 1578-9 35*l.* 7*s.* 6*d.*, and in 1579-80. 74*l.* 6*s.* 8*d.* were paid, and in 1580-1 112*l.* 17*s.* 2*d.*, and a reference is made in the latter entry to Star Chamber proceedings.

12. The accounts included armour, and the expenses of keeping it in repair. The charge was an imperial tax.

13. These would vary with a tendency to increase as the affairs of the Company enlarged and became more important.

14. The difference noticeable in the years 1545-6 and 1555-6 is explained by the abolition of obits under the Chauntries Collegiate Act.

15. These sums are included (so far as they are corporate) in salaries ; and (so far as they were trust) in trust payments ; but they were paid.

16. These exhibitions were paid out of the corporate fund ; in addition to Fish's Battlings. I have thought it best to preserve the names of the exhibitioners as some of them may be traced in their future career in the Church.

		£	s.	d.	£	s.	d.
1570-1.	Sir Huchenson, fellow of St. John's, Oxon	5	0	0			
	John Huchenson, student, Pembroke Hall, Cambridge	5	0	0			
					10	0	0
1580-1.	John Huchenson, student, Pembroke Hall, Cambridge	5	0	0			
	John Fuljambe, student, Peterhouse, Cambridge	5	0	0			
	John Cobb, scholar, in Cambridge, for 3 quarters, 6*l.*, Special Gift, 10*s.*	6	10	0			
					16	10	0
1590-1.	Thos. Harrison, M.A., Trinity, Cambridge	5	0	0			
	¹Ralph Raven, M.A., St. John's, Oxford	3	6	8			
	¹John Perrin, M.A., St. John's, Oxford	3	6	8			
	¹Thos. Cranmer, scholar, St. John's, Oxford	4	0	0			
	Walter Rowse, scholar, Queen's, Cambridge	2	0	0			
	Robt. Wall, scholar, St. John's, Oxford	2	0	0			
					19	13	4
1600-1.	E. Seny, student, Christ's College, Cambridge	5	0	0			
	S. West, student, St. John's, Oxon	3	6	8			
	J. Wicksted, student, St. John's, Oxon	2	0	0			
	J. Sansbury, student, St. John's, Oxon	3	6	8			
	W. House, student, Trinity, Cambridge	2	0	0			
					15	13	4

17. See 6 *ante*. Sometimes the Guild (taking the money of its members) paid it to the Lord Mayor, or purchased corn, and on return, or sale, redistributed it to the subscribers. See Part II, page 234.

18. Was the purchase of the "White Horse," Watling Street, and the "Blue Bear," in Bow Lane from St. John's College.—"Memorials," page 537.

---

¹ As to the future of these scholars, see Vol. 2, Wilson, *passim*.

CHAPTER XI.

THE TRADE MONOPOLY OF THE GUILD DESTROYED.

Persons of various occupations admitted to the Merchant Taylors Company in 1399, p. 197.—The Merchant Taylors became Clothworkers, p. 198.— Charter of Henry VII, p. 198.—Hereditary principle of the London franchise, p. 199.—Impossible for all trades to become hereditary, p. 199. —Complaint of Clothworkers against the Taylors, p. 200.—Controversy of 1550, p. 200.—Claim right of search, p. 200.—Refuse to grind Taylors' shears, p. 200.—Their claims overruled by the Lord Mayor, p. 200.— Order as to apprentices, p. 201.—Claims renewed in 1566, p. 201.— White, Hilles, and other Taylors engaged in clothworking, p. 201.—Vital importance of the question, p. 202.—Lease of the Mora estate by Taylors, p. 202.—Various tenants thereof, p. 202.—Return of the number of Taylors, &c., occupied in clothworking, p. 202.—Appeal to Parliament, p. 202.— Parliamentary Bills prepared by Clothworkers, p. 202.—Rejected by Parliamentary Committee, p. 203.—Other two Bills proposed by the Committee, p. 203.—No Bill passed, and the controversy ended, p. 203.—Complaint of the Haberdashers, p. 204.—Order of 1571 to employ guildsmen in clothworking, p. 204.—The principle of Guild monoply raised in 1571 by fourteen other Guilds, p. 204.—Their case as stated to the Lord Mayor and Council, p. 205.—Remedy sought, p. 205.—Richard Hilles and others as a Committee answer the case, p. 205.—Decision in the Clothworkers' case adhered to, p. 206.—No order made by the Lord Mayor and Council, p. 206.—Attempt at Legislation in 1575, p. 206.—Haberdashers asked by Taylors to join in search, p. 206.—Taylors in the Company, p. 207.— Though Guild monopoly destroyed, Guildsman could not quit his Company without license, p. 208.—Wilkes' case with the Widow Hodgson, p. 208.— Nor sue a brother guildsman without license, p. 208.—Arbitrament, p. 208. —I. Jurisdiction of Master and Wardens: (a) in partnership quarrels, p. 209.—(b.) Apprentices, p. 209.—(c.) Dress, p. 209.—(d.) Bad work, p. 210.—(e.) Recovery of debts, &c., p. 210.—(f.) Slander, p. 210.—II. Manners and Amenities of the Guildsmen: Assault, p. 211.—Hitting in the face, p. 211.—Provoking words, p. 212.—Insult to a Warden, p. 212. —Evil words in anger, p. 213.—Bastardy, p. 213.—Insult to the Master and Wardens, p. 214.—Eminent Guildsmen during the controversy, p. 215.

IT would appear from the earliest existing record of admissions to the Merchant Taylors Company (1399-1400) that persons with occupations other than those of Taylors or Linen Armourers were admitted into the Guild. Thus of the thirty-five persons whose names are entered as "confrers" paying 20s. (then a large sum) we find a chevalier, a brewer, a tallow chandler, a vintner, a barbour, esquires, a parson, a sherman, a tavener, a grocer, a dyer, and a chaundler, the followers of which occupations should have been associated with the several Guilds of the same name.

Whether at that time *any* trade could be followed under the franchise of the Merchant Taylors Company is not known, but, be that as it may, the object of the present chapter is to show how in the latter half of the sixteenth century, if not before, the guildsmen of the Merchant Taylors Company became Clothworkers, and when challenged by, justified their absolute independence of, the Master and Wardens of the Clothworkers Company in respect to search or control, basing their case on the Charter of Henry VII, and the earlier ones.

At the opening of the 16th century a new charter, or as it was then termed, a "New Corporation," was granted to the Guild by Henry VII. The part which FitzWilliam took in procuring this Charter (of 1502) will be explained in his life, but the reasons for obtaining it are not apparent, unless we accept those which are thus set forth in the recitals:

"The men of the Misteries aforesaid, in the city aforesaid, or at least the sounder part of them, have from time whereof the memory of man is not to the contrary, and daily do use, occupy and exercise in all quarters and kingdoms of the world, *all and every kinds of merchandizes*, to the renown, honour, and benefit of our kingdom and subjects, and the great advantage of us and our progenitors formerly kings of England: and that the same men of the said Misteries having during the wholetime aforesaid used, occupied, and exercised the buying and selling of all and every wares and merchandises whatsoever, and especially woollen cloths as well wholesale as retail, throughout our whole realm of England, and particularly with our city aforesaid and the suburbs thereof."

It is more than probable that the alteration about this time made in soldiers' accoutrements had prejudicially affected the trade of a "Linen Armourer," and that more profit was to be gathered up from a trade in clothworking than in making up cloth into garments. If this were so then it was well for the Company that the Masters and Wardens were authorised by their new Charter "to augment and increase the aforesaid Fraternity, and to hold the said Fraternity of whatsoever persons, niatves, whom they may be willing to receive into the same Fraternity, and to retain, have and enjoy, all and singular, persons of the said Fraternity, or received into the same Fraternity, or from henceforth to be received into the same, lawfully and freely, without the hindrance or disturbance of any person or persons, of any other Art or Mystery of the city aforesaid."

What however gave rise to the greatest animosity in the minds of their fellow citizens towards the Company was the right of search which was also given to the Master and Wardens in these terms : " So also within the city, liberties and suburbs thereof they were to make full and entire survey, search, governance, and correction of all and singular the men of the said Fraternity or Mistery, and also of natives, strangers and foreigners[1] using the said Misteries, or anything appertaining to the same Misteries in the city aforesaid, and the liberties and suburbs thereof, as well in the making cutting, and working of men's apparel, as howsoever otherwise using or exercising the same Misteries," and to have " the correction and punishment of all natives, strangers and foreigners, in and concerning all matters appertaining or heretofore belonging to the said Misteries of the Merchant Taylors, or Taylors and Linen Armourers, for their offences therein, so often and when it shall be needful for the advantage and benefit of our liege people or others whomsoever, so that the correction and punishment of such natives, strangers and foreigners, and every of them so offending in the premises be exercised by the Master and Wardens of the said Fraternity for the time being, according to the laws of England, and the ordinances and statutes therefore made, and the customs of our city of London."

The freedom of a Company obtained through the Corporation of London gave trading as well as political privileges, and these were held to be hereditary. Of course trade for one or two successive generations may be so, but even then all a freeman's children could scarcely be Taylors, but must find employment in occupation other than that of their Guild. When, therefore, a guildsman of the Taylors Company was found doing the work of a Clothworker, the question arose whether he should be reckoned as to his trade, craft, or work to be a Taylor or a Clothworker? This

---

[1] The oath points to a prohibition against keeping foreigners, and in 1581 (April 18th) a Proclamation, or Precept, was put out by the Lord Mayor, begging the Guilds to give quiet usage to the French then visiting England, and to appoint two of their members to see the order obeyed. The French and Dutch tailors who had come over for liberty of conscience appear to have been tolerated by agreement in October (14th) 1608.

was the subject of controversy between the two Companies, which was first raised in 1566, and was finally set at rest in 1575 during the mastership of Edward Joans, though no remedy was found. Obviously the Taylors could be no sufficient judges of the competency of the work or workmen of other trades or crafts, and yet they insisted that they only (without breaking up the unity of the Guild or apprenticeship in it) should exercise authority over such freemen of their Company; the Clothworkers contended that the Taylor who desired to work as a Clothworker should previously be affiliated by apprenticeship or service to their Company, thereby becoming amenable to their search and inspection as to his competency as a Clothworker.[1]

The earliest record which the Merchant Taylors have of this contention dates from 1550–1, when their account books[2] show that 26*l*. 4*s*. 9*d*., a vast sum in those days, was spent for the defence of the suit made against them by the Clothworkers. First, the Taylors "occupying the brode shere and rowyng at the perche" would not submit "to the right of searche in their howses from the Clothworkers," and were imprisoned at their instance. Then the Clothworkers would not grind the Taylors' shears, and so 4*l*. 13*s*. 0*d*. had to be spent "in getting up shere grinders to London," when after all this trouble and expense the Lord Mayor "finally made order that the Clothworkers should grind shears for the Taylors."

When the ordinances of 1507 were framed a fine of 20*s*. was thereby imposed on each apprentice after the first, the intention being thus to limit the number of apprentices, but as such an ordinance was held to be an infringement of the statute of 19 Henry VII, cap. 7, any limitation being held to be "against the common profit of the people," and also obnoxious to the 22 Henry VIII, cap. 4, in imposing a higher fee than 3*s*. 4*d*. which the Act authorised,[3] the ordinance (probably about this time) was withdrawn.

It was therefore a grievance that the Taylors should deluge the cloth trade with an unlimited number of apprentices, whereas the Clothworkers had endeavoured to keep up the monopoly by limiting their apprentices to two for each master. Upon this issue it would seem that the Clothworkers appealed to the Common

---

[1] Rep. 16, page 135, under date of 14th November, 1566.

[2] Appendix 24, pages 390–3.

[3] 11 Coke Rep., 55; London case, page 44.; Sayers, 251; Hobart, 210; and 7, Ter. Rep., 543, and page 216, *post*.

Council and were, for a time at least successful—that is so long as the following order of Lord Mayor[1] was obeyed :—

"Adhuc Jovis 33 Marcij a° vij E. VI (1552).

"M^{s}ch*unttayllo^{r}s and Clothwo^{r}kers,

"Itm̄ for certyn good & necessarye consideraĉōns movynge the co^{r}te it was this day orderyd & decreyd by the same that none of the m^{s}ch*unttayllo^{r}s usynge or that herafter shall use the occupaĉōn of the clothwo^{r}kers shall have kepe or Retayne in his s^{a}vice after the Feste of St Mychaell tharch*ungell nowe nexte comynge enye mo apprentycs att once then twoo, as the seid clothwo^{r}kers do kepe any lawe custome or ordyn*unce hertofore made usyd or devysed to the contrary notwthstondynge."[2]

Some other controversy had been carried on for in the following year, 1551-2, probably to clear up all outstanding costs, a further sum of 21*l*. 2*s*. 6*d*. was paid "for the wrongful suit made by the Clothworkers."

In May, 1559, the two Companies came again into conflict and a special Court of Aldermen was appointed to examine into the cause of variance, but in October some members of each Company were committed to prison for riot and released upon recognizances.[3] There the matter rested until in the year 1566, when in the mastership of Thomas Browne, Richard Hilles being absent on the continent, and Sir Thomas White probably in his last illness (as he had made his final appearance at the Court), the subject was revived by the Clothworkers. The question raised was vital to the principle of Guild monopoly on the one hand, and to the commercial interests of those Taylors who were Clothworkers on the other. Of such there were many, and we shall see not the least important members of the Merchant Taylors Company. This is evidenced by what happened upon the application of the Bridewell Governors to the Company in May, 1566, that purchase "might be made from them of woollen cards made by the inmates and not yet uttered or sold." Fifty dozen were purchased by the members present, the following names appearing with others :—

Sir Thomas White 10 dozen, Mr. Richard Hilles 4 dozen, W. Meryche 2 dozen, Gerard Gore 2 dozen, R. Dawbney 3 dozen, J. Mansbridge, 4 dozen.

But the controversy was probably forced upon the Clothworkers by another incident, which was this: In November, 1566,

---

[1] Page 55, *ante*. [2] Extract from City Records, Rep. 13 (1), fol. 36, *b*.
[3] *Ibid.* 14, pages 167 and 225.

the Merchant Taylors Company acquired for a period of eighty years from the Prebend of St. Paul's a lease of the Mora estate (then an open field) for the purpose of using it for racks or tenters in clothworking. The estate was sub-divided by the Merchant Taylors Company into very many tenancies or holdings, and at a somewhat later period (between 1570–1600) was tenanted thus:—

    Of those who had been been Master and Warden of
        the Merchant Taylors Company[1] 15
        Freemen of the same..   21
        The Clerk and Beadle   2
        One Alderman and others, not members   18

Again, from a return extant on the Merchant Taylors' records (as of 21st October), it is shown with names and addresses that the members of the Company did then use and occupy the art or mystery of clothworking in considerable numbers, thus there were:—

    Of householders   38
    Apprentices 66
    Journeymen 11

And the return also shows which of these "do rowe and sheare broad clothes, and also which of them do shere only kersies and cottoning."

There can, therefore, be no doubt regarding the importance of the controversy, both to the two Guilds, parties to it, and to all others whose interests were involved in the principle of keeping up or breaking down the Guild monopoly. Two or more Bills which had been prepared and submitted to Parliament by the Clothworkers to regulate the clothworking, and to settle the controversy in their favour were not accepted by the Taylors, whose opposition before the Parliamentary Committee prevailed, and the Bills were lost.[2]

On the 10th October the Clothworkers submitted to the Taylors another Bill which they proposed to get passed during the session, but the Taylors at once appointed a Committee of John God and fourteen other guildsmen to make influence with the members of the House of Commons and to get the Bill rejected. After an intervening meeting on the 21st October

---

[1] Lady Joan, widow of Sir Thomas White, and Daniel, son of Richard Hilles, were amongst the tenants.

[2] The subject is to be found in the Corporation Records, Rep. (16) pages 135 to 145.

(when a return of all the guildsmen who were Clothworkers was made to the Court) a Committee of Sir Thomas Offley, Lucar, and others were appointed on the 7th November to defend the interests of the Company before Parliament, and after meeting on the 9th, 11th and the 15th presented their answer to the Clothworkers' case to the Lord Mayor, and after other meetings on the 22nd and 23rd in the same month Recorder Fleetwood read out, for approval, the answer to be made to Parliament by the Corporation.[1]

Thus prepared, the Merchant Taylors on the 13th December, 1566, attended the Parliamentary Committee of the Commons, at the lodgings of Sir Ambrose Cave, and after the proposals of the Clothworkers had been fully discussed, the same were declared to be "dasshed and voided;" but in place thereof it was proposed that two Bills should be made by the Committee, the one to be only for certain clothes to be dressed within the realm of England before they should be transported, and the other Bill to be only for the true dressing of woollen clothes.

The Bills are set out verbatim, on the Merchant Taylors' records, the first provides that one in every ten clothes exported shall be dressed within the realm of England under a penalty of 10*l.*, and another provision is added relating to Kentish clothes.

The second Bill provides that no one shall rowe or full any broad cloth or kersey with any iron card but with tassells only, and that every shearman of the broad cloth shall shear the same from end to end with the broad shears only, without the use of any instrument of sleight, under a penalty of 20*s.* and the forfeiture of the instruments. Under this proposed enactment the Merchant Taylors and Clothworkers were to have equal right of search, but the session of 1566 closed without legislation. The rights of the Taylors were never afterwards successfully questioned, so that clothworking became their recognised trade to be carried on without the search or interference of the Clothworkers Company.[2]

But the account books of the Merchant Taylors show another controversy to have been raging at the same time with the

---

[1] Part II, page 271.

[2] In September and November, 1595, the Taylors trading as plasterers, and on 31st March, 1604, Taylors trading as bakers, chandlers, cooks, shoemakers, and other ways, were called on by these several Companies to pay, and were distrained on for quarterages to support their Halls, &c.; but as "these exaction are unlawful (as by trial of the common law in like cases hath been approved), the Court of Assistants stood forward to protect them as learned counsel shall advise and direct."—See Rowe's Charity (1565-9), Memorials, page 287.

"Haberdashers," who, taking exception to the Taylors making hats and caps, appear to have retaliated in the manner thus described in the only entry which the Taylors possess relating to the dispute:

"1566-7.—Master's Account.

"Paid to Mr. Southcote,[1] for drawing of a Bill exhibited to the Mayor and Aldermen in declaration of the unlawful doings and proceedings of the Haberdashers in the making of an Act or Order among themselves that they nor none of them should buy any hats or caps out of their own Company, neither set any awork in the same faculty but of their own Company, upon a certain pain to their own private gain, contrary to the laws of the realm and godly orders and customs of this city, 13s. 4d."

Having possession of the clothworking trade the Merchant Taylors endeavoured to turn it to the profit of their freemen, by publishing an ordinance in December, 1571,[2] on the authority of the Court alone, to oblige their members to put out for dressing half the cloth they made to the men of the Guild, under a penalty of 10s. for each piece of cloth not so put out; which was for a time observed, although the legality of the ordinance was ultimately disputed.

The question of Guild supervision and monopoly was again raised in 1571, when fourteen of the smaller Companies[3] presented a petition on the 15th May to the Court of Common Council praying for relief, but gained nothing. They were in "extreme poverty, decay, and ruin," which they attributed to the then present laxity of the Guild system. "In ancient times (their petition set forth) the Company of artificers or handicraftsmen of the city had reserved the *only* use, trade, or exercise of their several arts and handicrafts, and then the things thereto pertaining were truly, workmanly, and substantially made," because the Wardens and Governors of every handicraft had the "search and punishment of all persons occupying the art, those deserving it were punished,

---

[1] Mr. Southcote was for many years Counsel to the Company, and became in February, 1563, one of the Judges of the Queen's Bench, which office he held until the 29th May, 1584. He was succeeded as Counsel to the Company in March, 1562, by Mr. Jeffrey, of Gray's Inn (at the usual retaining fee of 1l. 6s. 8d.), who, in May, 1576, also became a Judge of the same Court, and afterwards Chief Baron of the Exchequer, which latter office he held till his death in May, 1578.

[2] This was disobeyed by Davenant, and a suit was instituted in the Queen's Bench, when the ordinance was held to be void.—Davenant v. Hurdes, Moore's Reports, 576.—Appendix 25, page 393.

[3] The Dyers, Coopers, Carpenters, Tallow Chandlers, Harness, Upholders, Cutlers, Bakers, Girdlers, Glaziers, Painters, Blacksmiths, Cordwainers, and Stationers.—Rep. 17, pages 14 and 20.

love nourished in the said Corporation, and they (the handicraftsmen) able to live and bear such charges as were cessed upon them for the Queen's affairs, the honour and worship of the city, and the maintenance of their Companies."

The remedy which these petitioners asked the Corporation to apply was to order "that such persons occupying and exercising such handicrafts being free of another Company should thenceforth observe and keep the ordinances of the Company of handicraftsmen as touching their wares and works made, and to pay their fines and duties to the said Company of handicraftsmen accordingly, and that the apprentices already bound to those men who occupy handicrafts free of other occupations may at the expiration of their apprenticeship be made of those Companies of handicraftsmen that they use."

This involved, as it would seem, a double apprenticeship and allegiance, but if skill is to be a qualification for an art, it was not unreasonable that the masters of that art should be the governors of it. "Give this relief," the petitioners went on to say to the Council, and "you shall not only profit the commonwealth and bind your petitioners ever to pray for the preservation of your honourable and worshipful estates, but also purchase yourselves everlasting renown and immortal fame here on earth, with the fruition of the immortal God in the world to come."

The petition was sent by the Mayor to the Merchant Taylors, and probably to all other Companies, for consideration. In May during the mastership of William Kympton (a man of reputation, who was Sheriff in 1570, but was brought before the Star Chamber in 1576), the Court of Assistants appreciating the importance of the questions raised, appointed a special Committee of five of its members, of which Mr. Richard Hilles was the senior member, to investigate the subject, take advice as to their position in law, and put in their answer, Mr. Dalton and Mr. Mattas, both members of the bar, being appointed as Counsel to the Company. On the 21st May the Court met, and a great number of the Livery (not Assistants) were summoned to consider and approve the answer which had been prepared by Counsel on the Company's behalf.

Their case was rested upon "chartered rights" and upon the decision at which Parliament had arrived, when the same question was raised by the Clothworkers in 1556. The meeting adopted the answer prepared for the Company, and entrusted its presentation to Mr. Richard Hilles (as a member of the Common Council) in case any debate should arise in the Council upon the petition.

How this was we have no record, but we know that no order was granted to the petitioners against the Merchant Taylors Company. The Guild monopoly was broken down, but the monopoly of the London freeman lingered on for many years.

The decision also broke up the trade guarantee which a craftsman might gain as being a member of his Guild, nor could the Guild with advantage limit the number of apprentices taken by the members so as to keep up the monopoly when any number of apprentices of other Guilds might practice any trade or handicraft.[1]

The record of this controversy for monopoly would not be complete without mentioning the unsuccessful attempt at legislation which was again made in 1575. A Bill (according to Strype)[2] was drawn up reciting the statutes of 37 Edward III, and 5 Elizabeth cap. 4, prohibiting the exercise of any art or mystery save by such as had been apprenticed to the same. The Bill, which was supported by the Corporation of London, was passed by the Commons but challenged in the other House,[3] and never received the Royal Assent.[4]

The advantage of search by competent judges of the artificers' work and material seems to be obvious, and in August, 1597, the Taylors invited the Haberdashers to a general search of "felt" in the hands of a Taylor, but they took it amiss and summoned the owner of the felt before the Lord Mayor, Billingsley (a Haberdasher), "who was very round" on the Taylors, and committed the

---

[1] Rogers on Prices, vol. 4, page 97. [2] Stowe, Bk. 5, page 252.
[3] Commons Journal, 105.

Monday, 13th February, 1575.
The Bill for the Freemen of the City of London, first reading.
1. Commons' Journals, 106.

Mercurii (Wednesday), 15th February, 1575.
The Bill for the Freemen of the City of London.
The second reading, and ordered to be engrossed.
1. Commons' Journal, 107.

Martis (Tuesday), 21st February, 1575.
The Bill for the Freemen of the City of London. The third reading. Jud'in.
N.B.—The above Bill is sent to the Lords by Mr. Treasurer and others.
1. Lords Journal, 734.

Die Martis, 21st February, 1575.
Hodie Introducte sunt a Domo Communi quattuor Bille.
Tertia. That all the Freemen of the city of London may use the Mysteries and Trades within the same city lawfully quæ 1ª vice lecta est.
1. Lords Journals, 745.

Die Veneris, 9th March, 1575.
Same Bill read a second time.

defendant to prison, but as on the next day he was discharged, no further proceedings were taken.[1]

But although other occupations were opened to the Merchant Taylors under these decisions, it must not be supposed that the art or craft of Taylory was altogether abandoned, though what proportion of the Livery followed the occupation of tailoring is not recorded. In July, 1555, Machyn attended the Company's feast and records the fact that the Master and Wardens "all five" were born in London, and "Taylors' sons all."[2] Later in the same century we find the Master and Wardens certifying to the Lord Mayor "that a goode and experte journeyman or servant in the art or occupation of Tayllory is to have ffower markes wages by yire;" but before they gave that certificate the record states that they did so "by the advice of divers and sundry members of this mysterie using the handicraft of Tayllory, viz., Walter Fish (who in 1580 Stowe describes as Tailor to Queen Elizabeth), Richard Williams, Will Gaye, John Pount, Thomas Widnell, Will Phillips, John Layton, and divers others;" and as pertinent to the same question, it may be noticed that in the warrant of James I, dated May 4th, 1613, on the occasion of his daughter's marriage—the Princess Elizabeth with the Elector Palatine—for the outfit or trousseau, directions are given to the different tradesmen to execute the commissions which are there specified.

Clothes for women as well as for men were made by the Taylors, and orders were given to four persons, as Thomas Spens, Edward Thomasen, Thomas Watson, and Robert Baker, all of whom, save Spens (whose name has not yet been traced), were freemen of the Merchant Taylors Company; Thomasen by redemption on November 14th, 1602; Watson and Baker by apprenticeship on February 27th, 1587, and January 16th, 1584.

The nature of their business may be judged from the warrant. To Spens was assigned the making of gowns—or dresses with

---

[1] " 23rd January, 1622.

[2] " A Petition of the Drapers Merchauntailors Haberdashers and Clothworkers was presented to the Maior and Aldermen praying that an equal number out of the said several Companies may be joined in search with the Company of Weavers, and the one part not to goe without the other whereby the said search may be indifferent and the Weavers as well searched & punished for their abuses as those not free of the Weavers are to be & that in an equal manner and that the number of apprentices & Loomes to be kept by the Silk Weavers of the several Companies may be limited to certain times and yeares of freedom for y' ye Weavers free of other Companies are never to be Bailiffe Wardens or Assistants of the Company of Weavers and soo thereby shall receive much preiudice."

[2] Diary, page 91.

petticoats—the material being mostly cloth, or such like material; to Thomasen, the making the servants' coats or liveries; to Thomas Watson, the suites for the maske; and to Robert Baker, collars of white satin and other material.

But the authority of the Company, though weakened, could not be thrown off nor its membership relinquished without the licence of the governing body. There was then no serving two masters nor membership, save of one Company; whenever, therefore, a conflict of interests or advantages arose, the freeman must make his election for one Company or the other. This dilemma presented itself in the mastership of William Dodworth (1592) to William Wilkes who had engaged the Widow Hodgson, of the Vintners Company to marry him if he could get his release from the Merchant Taylors Company, that he might become a Vintner. His petition[1] was presented and referred to a Committee, who on a conference, found "that the widow will by no means assent to leave her trade." Wilkes, therefore, was released on terms set forth, and gave the Merchant Taylors Company a present of plate, which is duly recorded in the inventory of 1609.

Another consequence of membership, or rather of citzenship,[2] was the inability to sue or take the law of another member of the Company without the previous assent of the Master and Wardens, which in effect obliged a reference of the controversy to their arbitrament and award. Two instances of this licence to sue are here given. On the 5th March to Henry Elston "to take the Lawe of Thomas Brackshawe, Provyded that if Brackshawe complayne there the said Elston to abide the order of the Master and Wardens;" and again on the 7th November, 1585, "licence is given unto Richard Baker to take the Lawe of John Garrett," the Master and Wardens having probably satisfied themselves that the law was Baker's best remedy.

We will therefore take from the Company's records some of the awards made during this period, to show the jurisdiction which was exercised by the Master and Wardens, and what were the manners or amenities of the guildsmen towards each other.

I. *Jurisdiction.*—(a) As to partnership quarrels.—Those who read Sir William Craven's life[3] will notice how he had a con-

---

[1] Appendix 26, pages 394–6.
[2] It rested on the freeman's oath, which was amended 11 George II, so as to enable citizens to sue in the King's Courts.   [3] Part II, Chapter XXI.

troversy with his late master, and afterwards his partner (Hulson), which was referred to the Master and Wardens, who gave an award on November 16th, 1582, in favour of Craven, with an apology from Hulson to him.

(*b*) Apprentices were under the care of the Company, and masters were fined for illtreatment, thus in 1457-8 for assigning him without license 21*d*., and 5*s*. for unlawfully beating him. Further in 1466-7 10*d*. for clothing "him ill to the grete disgrace of the mysterie." In a case of misusing an apprentice, an entry of April 2nd, 1563, shows that very summary measures were taken against his master, thus: "The Wardens have comytted Thomas Palmer to pryson for that he hath broken Henry Bourefelde his apprentice's hedd without any just cause. Henry Bourefelde by composition had comytted his two apprentices to serve with Thomas Palmer during and for so long time, and for such consideration as they were agreed. And for that the said Thomas Palmer hath not onely evill used hymself towards the said apprentices, but also for that they have not had of hym sufficient meate and drynke as they ouygt to have had. Therefore it is decreed by tassente of both the said apprentices, that the said Henry Bourefelde shall immediately take his said apprentices from the said Palmer, and use them as becometh apprentices to be used." But a head was not to be broken for nothing, and, therefore, the Master and Wardens in the year following ordered Thomas Palmer to pay Henry Bourefelde 3*l*. 6*s*. 8*d*. heretofore owing by Thomas to Henry, and pay the surgeon for healing Henry's head broken by the said Thomas."

(*c*) Dress came under their cognizance. Thus as early as 1463-4, we find "fines of 12*d*." entered "for wearing cloaks too short after the manner of gallants contrary to the ordinance," and in later years these entries appear: Item: "Robert Mally is comytted to pryson for that he came to this house in a cloak of fresadowne,[1] a paire of hosen lyned with taffatory, and a shirte edged with sylvr contrary to the ordinance of this house." Item: "Thomas Elliatt is also enjoyned to pay to this house upon Fryday next for a fyne

---

[1] Frizido was a fine cloth of this period of which little appears to be known (Draper's Dictionary, page 134). It appears to have been made by the members of the Merchant Taylors Company, from this Court entry :—

"21st June, 1578, Vol. III, Court Minutes, page 32.

"Certain loving brothers of the Mysterie appointed scassors of the members occupyinge ofryzzadoes for and towards the charges laide owte in the defens of a sute prured by Mr. Hastings againste such as are occupyers of ffryzadoes."

for wearinge a cloke in this house contrary to the ordinance of this house, 5s." Item: "Whereas Richarde Symsone, a brother of this mystry having on apparrell not thoughlie meite for his habilitie to weare, and that admonysion is givene unto hime to reforme himself therein. It is ordered and agreed that yf he be founde faultie therein hereafter, then he is to pay such fyne as is provided for them that mysorder them selves in apparell, according to the ordinances of this house."

(d) In case of bad work, injuring the garment, the appeal was to the same tribunal. Thus on January 12th, 1571: "In the cause of varience betweene Margery Story, plaintiff, and Thomas Taylor, defendant, concerning a Cassock made to litle, it is ordered by the Master and Wardens, with the consent of sayde parties, that the said defendant shall paye to thands of the Clerke of this Mystery, for the use of the plaintiff, before the next Courte the some of fforte shillings, and shall take to hym self the said garment to make his best pffitt thereof accordingly."[1]

(e) Ordinary debts due between members were recovered by the intervention of the Master and Wardens, as the next entry shows: Inter Henrien Bartlett, plaintiff, John Swetser, defendant, yt is ordered by the Master and Wardens, with consent of bothe the saide parties ffor all matters in controversie betweene them. That the said John Swetser shall paye unto the said Henry Bartlett the some of iijli. xs. modo et fforma, viz., at thannunciation of our Lady next ensuinge, iijs. xd., and then iijs. xd. quarterly, untill the said some of iijli. xs. be fully contented, and paide, and so all things to be cleare betweene them from the beginning of the worlde untill the days of the date hereof," &c. Many similar entries are found, and on Sir Thomas White's death his widow came to the Court to assist her in the recovery of his debts from members.

(f) Slander. This case has an especial interest to antiquaries, as Thomas, the apprentice of John Stowe, was the plaintiff. "For the pacyfienge of a controversy depending here betweene Thomas Stowe, plaintiff, of the one ptie, and Thomas Holmes, defendant, of

---

[1] In a case where the plaintiff was not apparently a member of the Company the Master and Wardens avenged her wrong by imprisoning the defendant, a member:—Order of the Master and Wardens, 18th May, 1571, that U. Reynolds is committed to ward for that he will not pay such money as by him is owing unto a poor woman who kept him in the time of the Plague, he lying sick thereof for a quarter of a year, or thereabouts.

the other ptie, both brethenne of this mistery, as well for and concerning undesent and unseemly words spoken, uttered, and reported by the wyfe of the said Holmes againste the wyfe of the said Stowe, as hath beene here witnessed by certen credible persons. It is agreed here by the said Mr and Wardens, by and wth thassente and consente of bothe the said pties as followeth, viz. : That the wyfe of the said Holmes shall forthwth in this place, before the wyfe of the said Stowe, utter, declare, and speak these words as followeth, viz. : 'I am sorry for those undesent woords wch I have heretofore spoken of you, and therefore I praye you to forgive me,' wch, beinge done accordinglie, the wyfe of the said Stowe shall forgive her accordinglie. Further, it is agreed that the said Holmes shall paye to the said Stowe 20s. of lawfull money of England, in satisfaction of all lawe and other charges incurred by him, and that being done, either of the said pties shall release the one other of all manners of actions, &c., &c., as well spiritual as temporal, whatever heretofore rysen between the said pties at any tyme synce the beginninge of the world untill this pnte daye. Whereupon the Wyfe of the said Holmes, in the p'sens of the said Mr and Wardens and dyvrse others of honest neighbors of bothe the said pties did accomplish the said order in asking the wife of the said Stowe forgiveness accordinglie ; and Holmes paid 20s., and so bothe the said pties were made friends by taken of hands the one of the other." (October 20th, 1570.)

II. *As to the Manners and Amenities of the Guildsmen.*—First. Take an ordinary case of assault :—

"On the 15th January, 1568.—Itm, Miles Gilbee is commytted to warde for that he, in the presence of the Master and Wardens openlie in the streete did strike and drewe blud upon Luys Lloyde, a brother of this mystery, contrary to the ordinance of this House, and also to the infringing of the Queen's peace."

In the next case the persons ought to have known more of good behaviour, as both had borne office in the Fraternity. The offender was William Offley,[1] a member of the well-known family, and who had been Warden in 1580. The person towards whom he was guilty of assault and personal abuse had held the office in 1579, and in December, 1581, when Richard Bourne was Master, and another Offley (Richard) Warden, we have this entry :—

"The late Master Phillips[2] complained of (brother) William Offley for his unseemly speeches, and for striking him on the face.

---

[1] He never held office again.

[2] He was father-in law to Daniel, the youngest of Richard Hilles' sons.

Both submitted to the jurisdiction of the Master, and Offley was imprisoned and then fined 10*l*."

Another case is where some freeman complains of William Kympton's conduct towards him. The offender ought to have known better manners, for he was Warden two years later, and became (as we read in these pages) a well-known citizen. This is his case, and another happening to another member of a well-known family :—

"29th August, 1562.—William Kympton fyned 40s. for calling Stephen Myliney, a 'craftie boye,' whereupon the said William lefte in pawne with the Master a ring of gold for the payment of the said 40s. Nevertheless the Master and Wardens upon gentle submysion of the said Kimpton have remytted the moytee of the said fyne."

So again in February, 1563, William Hector is fined 40s. for calling Thomas Wylford a "pratynge boy," and makes a similar deposit.

Unfortunately a Warden was not then free from the malice of a brother guildsman, and had to protect his credit by summoning him before his colleagues, the Master and Wardens (Kympton being a Warden) :—

"22nd March, 1564. Item, At this day Mr. Thomas Browne Warden complavned agaynst Edward Aley a Brother of this Misterie for that the said Edward shulde reporte by the saide Mr. Browne that he was but a shyfter and in thende it shulde appeare that he is not worth a grote with other lyke words of infamy. Whereupon the said Edward was called to make answer thereunto and utterley denyed to speake any suche words by the said Mr. Browne as aforesaid and thereupon the said Mr. Browne for pfe. of the said wordes spoken by the said Aley dyd p'duce one Mrs. Anne Smythe wydowe to wytnesse the same who did take her othe in the p'sens of the said Aley that the said Aley had reported unto her and said that Mr. Browne was but a shyfter and lyved only by making of shifts and in thende his word would prove true that the said Browne is not worthe a grote and thereupon for that the said Aley hath mysbehaved himself in words and deeds towards the said Mr. Browne as aforesaid, contrary to the ordinances of this house, they the said Master and Wardens have comytted the saide Edward to p'son, there to remayne untill he shall make his submyssun for his offence comytted accordingly."

In August, 1583, a similar entry is found of Dawke *v.* Mansbridge. The defendent (who lived in Chiswell Street, Finsbury) became a Warden in 1592, and a donor of a standing cup and cover (gilt), having to pay a fine and, after Dawke's forgiveness, to make this apology in the presence of the Court. "I know I have offended you and not used myself well towards you in speaking such evil words against you. I am sorry for them from the bottom of my heart, and do ask your hearty forgiveness, for they were uttered by me in coller, but rudely, rashly, and immoderately. I pray you that we may be friends and so continue."

The two following entries possibly involved more delicate inquiries: 16th March, 1586, fol. 50: Inter. Alice Wrighte, plt., David Powell, deff., it is ordered by the Master and Wardens, in consideration of 20s. paide unto the saide plt. by the same deff. before the saide Master and Wardens in full satisfaction and paymente, as well of her charges for the carryinge of a childe gotten by the saide deff. uppon the saide plt. into Wales, to be nursed; as also for all mannr of claymes, tythes, and Demandes, and all other controvrsyes between them whatsoever, from the begynige of the world untill the daye of the date of these pntes. that the deff. shalbe acquitted and discharged against the saide plt. for ever. November 29th, 1577, fo. 72: Inter. Andrew Greene, compt., and Francis Coltman, deft. yt is ordered by the Master and Wardens, with the assente and consente of both the saide pties., for a fetherbed, a bolster, and a blankett and coverlett that the sayde Green, his executors or assigns shall paye or cause to be payed unto the sayde Ffrancis Coltiman, the some of xvjs. viijd., and so the sayde Ffrancis to delyor unto the saide Green the sayde ffetherbed, bolster, blanket, and coverlett, and to see the saide Greene discharged againste Isabelle, the mayde wch should have marryed with one Robert Coltman."

The offender in the following entry was a rising man, who was to become Master, and as such entertained King James I. He came of an ancient Worcestershire stock, then and now thriving in that county, but apparently he could not restrain his temper or his speech, when things did not go as he could wish them, and this was the consequence, five days' imprisonment during the mastership of Thomas Wilford.[1]

"John Swynerton, as brother of this Mysterie, being a sewtor to the said Mr. Warden, and Assistants, in which sewte they dealte with him very favorably, and their favorable dealing being opened

---

[1] At and for his funeral dinner at the Hall on the 3rd November, 1608, "the commendable grace at a funeral dinner" was composed.

to him, he said, 'it was not worthe thankes,' saying further 'yt they had neither wysdom, reson, nor conscience in their doinge,' wth other hawghtie and unseemly speeches; and being willed to attend and not to departe or goe away, he very contemptuously went his waye. It is therefore ordered and agreed that he shalbe comitted to pryson, according to the discretion of the said Mr and Wardens." (November 11th, 1585.) "Ordered that the said John Swynerton shalbe released of his imprysonmt uppon his submission wch he hathe made before the Master and Wardens, craving pardon for his rashe mysdemeanor and speeches then uttered." (November 16th, 1585.)

Such then, as we have attempted to describe it, was the position of the Guild in the middle of the latter half of the 16th century. The eminent guildsmen who were influencing its course in the conflict against monopoly were Sir Thomas White, Sir Thomas Offley, Richard Hilles, and Recorder Fleetwood, and the men of lesser note were Sir W. Harper, Gerard Gore, Robert Hulson, Walter Fish, and Robert Dowe. Their names are to be traced in the Court minutes, and the individual acts of some are to be found in the notices of their lives given in the second part of this volume.[1]

---

[1] See Part II, page 212.

CHAPTER XII.

THE GUILD WITHOUT MONOPOLY IN TRADE.
DISINTEGRATION.

Primary use of Guild destroyed, p. 215.—Opening up of foreign trade, p. 215. —Increase of London, p. 215.—Apprenticeship needful for London citizenship, p. 216.—Franchises of Guild and Corporation not sought after, p. 216.—Burthens to be avoided, p. 216.—Apprentices the cheapest labourers, p. 216.—Scot and lot, p. 216.—Return of apprentices and freemen, p. 217. —Freedom not taken up, p. 217.—No presentment, p. 217.—Fleetwood fined, p. 217.—Membership of Company not sought for, p. 217.—Guild offices neglected, p. 217.—Master absent on election, 1565, p. 217.—Refusal of Shottesham, 1572, p. 217.—Assistants absent, p. 218.—Master and four Wardens absent on election, 1589, p. 218.—Auditors absent, p. 218.—Great neglect in 1595, p. 219.—Committee appointed, p. 219.—Report, p. 219. —Ordinances to be amended, p. 220.—Increasing punishment, p. 220.— Neglect in 1602-3, p. 220.— Wardens to be removed from office, p. 220.— Warden a defaulter in account, p. 220.—Dowe's opinion of the evil, p. 221. —Court renewed by thirteen members, p. 221.—Master and Wardens are absent on election in 1611, p. 221.—Result of changes in the Guild, p. 222. —New basis of Guild, without religion or monopoly, p. 222.—Table of apprentices and freemen, p. 224.

ALTHOUGH the primary use of the Guild was injured, if not destroyed, there were other commercial enterprises in which the members became the distinguished pioneers. Trade had burst through the restraints of home monopoly to enter upon a wider sphere elsewhere. The Guilds enlarged their usefulness by becoming the centres of these new projects which, often modelled on their outline, were largely recruited by the resources of the Guild, and of individual guildsmen. Therefore, the Guild as affording facilities for evoking public opinion or substantial help, continued to be an important factor in the trade of London.

However, before entering upon these topics, we must endeavour to show what were the *immediate* effects of the changes upon the Guild in regard to its numbers and government.

London throughout the reign of Elizabeth largely increased in population[1] and size, the flux of people from the country and the

---

[1] See Fleetwood's Life, Part II, Chap. 19, page 269.

new buildings being the frequent subject of interdict. The city was the centre of trade,[1] and no one could enter upon that or any other occupation *there* without protecting himself with the rights of citizenship.

To secure these, apprenticeship to a guildsman was still a necessity, for though the Guild monopoly was destroyed as to its own particular trade, it was in full force as to the larger monopoly of London, to which the Guild remained the sole channel or access. It must not, however, be assumed that Guild membership or that citizenship was otherwise the attraction to or cause of the increase of London. On the contrary, both must be looked at in many instances as conditions imposed upon, rather than as aids to, an industrious man seeking employment. The laws and customs of London were too strong to be broken down by the raw recruits of commercial enterprise, who had therefore to submit to unless they could in some way evade them. Besides which it was the common interest of all guildsmen to maintain this wider monopoly, giving to them the exclusive command of the cheapest labour —that of educated youths as their apprentices.

Hence, the master did not then (any more than he does now) limit his number to two apprentices, for the 5 Elizabeth, cap. 4, sec. 24, allowed three to be employed to every journeyman, a license[2] which the Bachelors in January, 1562, petitioned the Merchant Company for permission to get repealed. Nor was the freeman then influenced (as he is now) by any consideration of letting in another claimant upon the alms[3] and emoluments of membership, or not at least, as a restraining (as now it is an inducing) motive to apprenticeship, for the freeman's advantage was in this manner to get cheap labour.

The constraining motive with the *apprentice* for entering into his contract was not at all times the attainment of citizenship, as the burthen of scot and lot prevented many from taking up their freedom. The London artificer was permitted under the 7 Henry VIII, cap. 5, to earn higher wages than the assize, because of these charges, but these would remain payable though no wages were earned, and the difficulty of obtaining wages in times

---

[1] Rogers on Prices, Vol. 4, page 76.
[2] *Ibid.*, page 97.
[3] Two was the limit by 12 Henry VII, cap. 1, as applicable to Norfolk, which possibly (by custom) extended to London when the 8 Elizabeth became law, and see 200, *ante*.

of keen competition would not be diminished. Hence a practice sprung up until checked by the Charter of Charles II (18th October, 1638) for apprentices to trade without taking up their freedom.[1] The primary irregularity was in the freeman omitting to present the apprentice before entering into contract with him to the Master and Wardens, an offence against which the ordinances provided a penalty, but that this omission was not then deemed to be a grave offence may be inferred when we find Sergeant Fleetwood, the Recorder, one of our guildsmen, from whom a penalty was enforced.

It will be seen by the Table at the end of this chapter how frequent were the omissions to take up the citizenship of London. The number of apprentices and of freemen in the year 1545-6 were all but equal (58 and 56), yet in the four quinquennial periods from 1574 to 1599, it will be seen that 1,825 persons were apprenticed, but only 678 admitted to the freedom, and that in the years 1612-3, 695 were apprenticed, but only 289 admitted,[2] to the freedom. It would seem, therefore, that citizenship was not eagerly sought for during the latter part of the sixteenth century.

In the absence of Court records prior to 1561-2, it is not possible to show whether in earlier years there was the same reluctance to hold office, as there was in these later years to become a freeman in the Guild. All we can do is to point to the fact that, in the ordinances of 1507, such an offence as absence by a Master or Warden on election is not mentioned, and therefore no penalty or punishment provided. It was the experience gained in the latter half of the century which obliged the rulers of the Company to introduce provisions in the ordinances of 1613, making a new offence and increasing the penalties against *official* defaulters. Of this experience we will now give some instances:—

The earliest entry of any seeming neglect is that of "John God," the newly elected Master of 1565, who was absent from the election dinner, and was sworn into office on a later day by Mr. Emanuel Lucar and Richard Hilles.

In 1572 we have a case of absolute refusal to serve as Master, and a fine imposed. The defaulter was Thomas Shottesham, who had served as Warden in 1570. To the Court of the 7th July, he sent his wife to plead his excuse, but this failing to be satisfactory to the Assistants, he was summoned to the Court on the 11th,

---

[1] Norton, page 402.

[2] The admissions would in all the years mentioned have reference to persons who had been apprenticed at least seven years prior to such admission.

when instead of attending he wrote begging their worships would excuse him "in taking an office unworthy of me to hold for divers causes, one is for the ability in substance lacked thereunto; also for that I am aged, remembrance faileth me, utterance in speech I lack, also divers other inconveniences remains in me for that I have not been acquainted with such like dealing as others of our Company have been and who be much worthier for the same office than I." However the Court held these excuses very lightly and fined him 40l., to be levied of his goods without abatement.

Then the Assistants made default, and had to be fined for default as is evidenced by this entry: "18th November, 1585. It is ordered by ye said M^r, Wardens, and Assistants that these psons, Assistants and Councelo^{rs} of this house vidolt Mr Robt. Dowe, Mr Charles Hoskins, Mr. Spencer, Olyver Roe, Wm Offeley, Ric Prockter, and Roger Abdey, beinge warned by the Bedell and have made defaulte, shall pay ther fyne for the same provided wthout a reasonable excuse to be showen to the contrary."

The elections appear to have gone on without improvement in this respect, as at the Quarterly Court of July, 1589, all the Wardens (Richard Gore being one) were absent, as well as many of the Assistants, besides many of the Livery, both "young and old," of which this is the record:—

"And forasmuche as a great number, as well of the younger sorte of the Livery of this Company, as also of the Assistants and older sorte of the Livery of the same were absente this day to the greate discredite of the good governmente of this Company, whileste so many worshipful persons of other Companies heere presente mighte justly note a contempte and disobedience of good orders. Whereas they should see foure Wardens chosen, and none of them presente. It is therefore ordered that the former lawes heretofore made for such as absente themselves from the assemblies appointed for the service and worship of the Company, be severely executed without parciality against all such as have beene absente this day, and cannot lawfully excuse themselves of their absences."

The ordinary work of the Court was delayed on the 26th July, 1595, from the absence of a quorum of four Assistants to constitute a Court, and in August succeeding, as two of the Auditors, Procter and Craven, did not attend, their places had to be specially filled by Mr. George Sotherton and Mr. J. Elwes.

Judging from the next entry matters went from bad to worse, as every year all or most part of the newly elected officers were absent at their election, and not unfrequently at the feast also.

In July, 1595, at the election of Reynold Barker (one who afterwards became a benefactor to the Company), he and three of his Wardens were absent, Richard Gore, the other Warden (having learnt better manners since his last default) being the only elected officer present. The garlands of the absentees had to be delivered to the principal guest, viz., "the Lord Mayor according to antient order," and Gore only was sworn in.

Such an affront could not be passed over, and therefore the Court assembled so soon as they had dismissed their guests, and passed "a resolution adverting to the great disgrace and contempt to the Company that the Master and Wardens yearly elected, or some of them, are for the most part absent, wanting due regard and consideration to the Mystery and of their oaths taken, which the Masters and forefathers in times past held of more account than to offer thereunto any neglect or want of duty," and appointed a Committee[1] of eight Assistants to consider the means for the redress of these disorders."

There the matter was left to sleep, for no meeting of the Committee was held until after one of its members (Roger Abdy) had died, and Robert Hampson been appointed in his room. Then Robert Dowe, "the antientest of the said Committee," warned them to meet at the common hall on the 9th June, 1596, but only three came, while waiting for the others they "did peruse and examine the books and ordinances of the house to learn what pains and penalties be inflicted upon such as shall be absent at the election day, and finding the penalties very small, viz., 3s. 4d., for so great a contempt, and perceiving that by the laws and statutes of this land the Company cannot make any laws or ordinances to inflict any greater punishment, unless with the assent of the Lord Chancellor and others; therefore to the end the same contempt and offence may be reformed, and for that they hold it not fit to move so honorable a personage for one only cause, yet forasmuch as divers others of the ordinances are worn out of use and alteration of this time requireth reformation thereof," the Committee thought "it very convenient that all the said ordinances, or such of them as require amendment, may by such authority be corrected and reformed, and in their opinion they think these penalties very convenient, viz., if the Master, which shall be now chosen, shall be absent at the election to forfeit 5l., and any Wardens 3l. 6s. 8d."

---

[1] Mr. Robert Dowe, Mr. Robert Hawes, Mr. Nicholas Spencer, Mr. George Sotherton, Roger Abdy, Nowell Sotherton, Richard Venables, and Henry Webbe.

But nevertheless they reserved the consideration of the whole premises to a full Court of Assistants.

To reform the ordinances, and to procure their approval by the Lord Chancellor and others, were matters too serious to be taken up to redress an affront, and so the Court were contented to submit to it if it should happen again, and so, surely enough, it did happen when Richard Gore (just mentioned as an absent Warden) was elected the Master for 1602-3. The statement in the Company's records of the 12th July is as follows:—

"And forasmuch as it is generally held and reputed to be a great blemish and disgrace to the government of the Company, that every year either all or the most part of the new elect Master and Wardens are absent on the election day, when they ought above all things to be here present to give countenance and grace to the Company, and minister occasion to strangers, to speak all good of the civil government of the same, the reputation whereof, together with the credit of the same, every brother of the Company ought by oath and conscience to preserve."

Therefore for the reformation of this evil, the Court initiated a remedy by ordering :—

"That every brother which at any time hereafter shall not be present in person in the Common Hall of this Society on election day, when they are chosen either Master or Warden of this Company, and cannot upon their oath show a lawful or compulsory excuse, either by visitation of God, or command of the Prince, or some urgent occupation, having express license granted by the Master and Wardens, at a convenient time before the day of election, shall at the end of his year's service be absolulely removed from his place as an Assistant of this Company, and such as have not been Assistants and shall offend shall not at any time be admitted to the said place, nor receive so much grace and reputation from the Company, who so little regard the honour and credit of the same."

The entry consequent upon this election would lead to the conclusion that the men chosen as office bearers had also deteriorated, for the Renter-Warden, Will Chambre, was a defaulter in his rent accounts,[1] and in 1604 the Company had to take from him a carpet for the King's Chamber, and credit him with 50*l.* on his account, leaving a balance still due.

That this description of laxity was reckoned to be a serious

---

[1] See page 49, note 2. Court Records, Vol. v, page 156.

evil by the antient members of the Fraternity may be clearly seen from the language which Robert Dowe used in his deed of 1605, whereby he gave sums of money " to the officers and principally to the two Beadles that they should put the Master and Wardens in remembrance of the names of such brethren as shall be absent from the quarter days, Court of Assistants, and common assemblies, and for not paying the duties belonging to the hall, wherein they shall take reformation and help of both the said Clerks[1] as need requireth of such absentees and not payers of their duties, and shall procure the Master and Wardens to send for them, to the end that either they do reconcile themselves in seemly order for the first default or else do pay their fines according to the ordinances."

Robert Dowe then goes on to state that he " doth find and take it to be a matter very needful to be effected in these evil days because men were daily more insolent and high minded towards their superiors or governors, and have small remorse or conscience of their solemn oath, taken at their first entry for good government of themselves and the whole Company."[2]

The Court also would appear to have got below the established number of 24 members, so that in 1611 there were added nine Assistants on the 27th January, and four on the 2nd March,[3] which may in part account for the ignorance of the Company's affairs in this respect, which is so painfully noticeable in the Court Minute of the 11th July, 1611, although John Langley, the Clerk, who had made the earlier entries, had become an Assistant on retiring from office. The Minute is:

"Mr. Richard Wright was elected for M^r or Governor, Geo. Lyddiatt, Francis Evington, Thomas Boothby, and John Gore for Wardens, and the said M^r and Wardens being all absent (wch never heretofore hath beyn seene), to the greate greefe and discontent of the grave fathers and governors of this Mystery, there garlands was therefore delivered to the Lord Mayor, being the principall guest

---

[1] History of the Merchant and Bachelors Companies.

[2] "Therefore the said Robert Dowe bestoweth this remembrance chiefly for a mean to help to reform this disorder so much as may be, for it is seen by daily experience that the suffering, neglecting, or not punishing of evil passions in due time emboldeneth them and others to do the like, even so long till the attempt of reformation may breede dangerous, which the said Mr. Dowe prayeth the Governors to consider, and by their daily care and diligence to reform the same in due time."

[3] Court Records, Vol. vii, pages 24 and 25.

according to antient order. The Assistants assembled in their Counsell Chamber, and there considering how greate a blemish it was to this Society to have both M^r and Wardens absent on the Election-day, caused the books to be searched for orders for punishing of such defaults, sett fynes upon the heads of such as have either this yeare or the last byn absent at the Election-day, it was ordered that John Wooller, Upper Warden, who was absent the last yeare, should pay a fyne of 40s. Mr. Richd Wright, now chosen M^r and being absent on the Election-day, shall paye 4l., the 2 Upper Wardens 3l. a-peece, and the 2 Renter Wardens 40s. a-peece, unless they can upon their oathes shew some lawfull cause for their absence."

Without following this disintegration further the thought probably suggests itself to the reader whether this indifference in the apprentice and freeman to become first a guildsman and then a ruler or governor of the Guild was not the natural consequence of the changes which had been made in the functions of the Guild: —First, in disendowing religion; and then in breaking down the trade monopoly, acts by which the Guild was removed from its original basis.

Such, therefore, as we have described, was the *immediate* effect of the changes theretofore made during the century, but it must be borne in mind that the Guild was left in possession of several antient real estates solely applicable to secular uses, and so long as any real government by the Guild lasted its rulers had the power of replenishing their coffers by taxation of the Guildsmen. The real estates, no doubt, were charged with definite payments for charitable or eleemosynary uses, but as these were *fixed* in amount and the rents were rapidly rising in value it needed no special prescience to decide for whose ultimate advantage these arrangements would accrue. Therefore the Guild still offered attractions and inducements to membership, though of a different kind to those of the 14th and 15th centuries, but different as they were, more suitable to the citizens of a later period who, having possession, would use the Guild funds for any which they were pleased to think were Guild purposes. Hence the expenditure and membership of this later period must not be criticised with the hope that they will accord with the rules prevailing at the early existence of the Guild, for in these later years the sumptuary expenses had largely increased and the member had little or nothing to do with the Guild trade, either Tayloring or Clothworking. The Guild when recruited from the young cadets of new families was used as a stepping stone to higher commercial enterprises and to the social pre-eminence which was then accorded to such pursuits.

TABLE OF APPRENTICES AND FREEMEN ADMITTED TO THE MERCHANT TAYLORS COMPANY DURING THE YEARS GIVEN AS UNDER:

	1399–1400.	1453–4.	1469–70.	1545–6.	1574–5.	1592–3.	1597–8.	1599–1600.	1612–3.	1886–7.[19]
Apprentices (no books from 1470 to 1545)	—[1]	—[1]	—[1]	58[8]	270[12]	551[12]	473[12]	531[12]	695[16]	25[12] [18]
Freemen	31[2]	116[3]	91	56[9]	165[13]	165[13]	187[13]	161[13]	289[17]	36[13] [18]
Redemptions	—	1[4]	—[7]	7[10]	—	—	—	—	—	—
Livery	—	17[5]	8[6]	4[11]	12[14]	—	12[14]	—	—	—
Fines for non-enrolment or presentment	—	—	—	—	—	36[15]	38	37[14]	—	—
	£30 6 8	£38 17 4	£33 2 4							

[1] No entry in books.

[2] Confrers I have placed as freemen, two paid only 13*s.* 4*d.* for admission.

[3] One paid 1*s.* 8*d.* and the others 3*s.* 4*d.*

[4] R. Boreman paid 3*l.* 6*s.* 8*d.* for admission to the Liberty of the City and Fraternity.

[5] One paid 6*s.* 8*d.*

[6] 1*l.* each.

[7] Various sums amounting to 9*l.* 19*s.*

[8] At 2*s.* 6*d.* each.

[9] 54 at 3*s.* 4*d.*; one at 5*s.* 10*d.*; Sir John York *nil.*

[10] Seven, varying from 20*s.* to 8*s.*

[11] Three at 20*s.*; York *nil.*

[12] At 2*s.* 6*d.* each.

[13] At 3*s.* 4*d.* each.

[14] At 1*l.* each.

[15] 3*s.* 4*d.* was paid by Recorder Fleetwood.

[16] Of these, four paid no fees as apprentices to Master, Wardens, and Clerk.

[17] Master's son and Warden's man paid no fees.

[18] The Corporation of London in 1835 reduced the fee for purchasing the freedom to trade from 25*l.* to 5*l.*, and again in 1856, by order of Common Council, enabled non-freemen to open retail shops. These measures had this effect upon the Merchant Taylors Company.

Average for	Apprentices.	Freemen.
1831–5	$37\frac{2}{5}$	$27\frac{3}{5}$
1836–40	$35\frac{3}{5}$	$31\frac{3}{5}$
1850–6	$27\frac{5}{6}$	$19\frac{2}{6}$
1856–62	21	$18\frac{3}{6}$

These numbers present a strong contrast to those of 1612.

CHAPTER XIII.

MATTERS MISCELLANEOUS IN THE LATER HALF OF THE 16TH CENTURY.

Matters found on records of the Merchant Taylors Company, p. 225.—School and St. John's College, p. 225.—Claim of the Crown on School site, 1565, p. 226.—Grant from James I, 1620, p. 226.—The Royal Exchange, p. 227.—Corporation desire Percyvale's House, p. 227.—Lombard Street, oldest Burse in Europe, p. 227.—Deputation from Guildhall, p. 228.— Company object to sell, p. 228.—Conference with the Recorder, p. 228. —Offer to exchange land declined, p. 228.—Subscriptions raised, p. 228.—First lottery established (1568), p. 229.—The second, 1585, p. 230. —Lotteries in the city sanctioned by Lord Mayor, p. 231.—Abolished in 1826, p. 231.—Norfolk's treason, 1572, p. 231.—Guard at the city gates, p. 231.—Conduct of citizens towards foreigners, p. 232.—Lord Mayor's precept in 1573, p. 232.—The two terrors of London, p. 233.—Plague in 1563, p. 233.—In 1575, p. 233.—Fire and precautions against, p. 233.—Plays and playhouses, p. 234.—Plays not favoured by citizens, p. 234.—Plays by scholars of the Company's school, p. 234.—Prohibited in the Hall, 1573, p. 235.—Act of Common Council, 1574, p. 235.—Measures of the Crown, p. 235. —Players licensed, p. 235.—Master of the Revels, p. 236.—Lord Mayor's proposal, 1591, declined by the Company, p. 236.—The Bible set up in the Hall, 1578, p. 237.—The Exchequer suit against the Company in 1578, p. 238.—Fish's and Fitz William's scholarship at St. John's, pp. 238-240.— Alleged concealment by the Guilds, 1582, p. 240.—Patent of concealed lands to Adams and others, p. 240.—Negotiations with Sir C. Hatton, p. 241.— And the patentees, p. 241.—Company's tenants proceeded against, p. 242.— Suit dismissed, p. 242.—Offer to pay 200l., p. 242.—Statement laid before Elizabeth, 1587, p. 243.—Sir Philip Sydney's funeral, p. 243.—Thanksgiving at St. Paul's for taking of Cadiz, p. 244.

HAVING dealt hitherto with those subjects of vital importance which affected the religion and monopoly of the Guild, it is proposed in this chapter to bring before the notice of the reader in something of chronological order other matters of general interest, (excluding assessments for pageants, subsidies, or soldiers), which are to be found on the records of the Company in the later half of the 16th century.

The first great undertaking connected with the Company was establishing the school in St. Lawrence Poultney Lane in 1561-2, and the second was connecting the school with St. John's College, Oxford; but as these good works were carried out by the benevolence, not of the Guild, but of Richard Hilles and Sir Thomas White, the history of the events is given in their lives.

However, the school comes before our notice in the 7th Elizabeth from the claim set up by the Crown to military service and homage from the Company in regard to the site of it, which was brought before the Court on the 27th September at the instance of William Beswick, citizen and draper, the owner of the other half of the manor by purchase from Hettie. The entry is as follows :—

"First, whereas a writ is directed from the Court of Exchequer to the Sheriffs of the city of London enjoining them thereby, the said Sheriffs, not only to the tenants of the manor and place with the appurtenances to the same belonging, situate, lying, and being in the parish of St. Laurens Pountney, in London, called the Rose (a great part whereof belongeth to this house, and whereupon and wherein this Company have founded their grammar school), to appear in the said Exchequer at the octave of St. Michael the Archangel now next ensuing, to answer by what title they hold the same, as also to do homage to the Queen's Majesty for the same, for that it is supposed by the said writ that the same manor and place and appurtenances holden of the Queen's Majesty in capite, and forasmuch as the said writ is served upon Mr. Beswick, draper, and that he hath been here to know whether this house will join with him to answer the said writ by order of law or no; and forasmuch as that it is to be proved that the said lands are not holden in capite, but only in free socage. Therefore it is agreed and decreed that this house shall and will be contented to join with the said Mr. Besweke to answer and to bear the said charge in the law as much as our part shall extend unto value for value accordingly if the law will so permit."

The claim then only entailed upon the Company the cost of paying the lawyer's fee (in 1569-70), as under :—

"Item paid to Mr. Cresswell, Attorney of the Court of Exchequer, for the copy of a record concerning a writ of intrusion brought against this Company for their land in St. Lawrence Pountney, whereon their school is erected, in discharge thereof and for the entry thereof, 2*l*." And they were left undisturbed in title until James I obtained 600*l*. for a confirmation of it by a patent of 23rd July, 1620.[1]

In the early part of Elizabeth's reign the great undertaking of the citizens, or rather of one aided by others, was the establishment of "the Royal Exchange." Clough, writing from Antwerp to his

---

[1] Appendix 27, page 396.

master, Sir Thomas Gresham,[1] as to the wants of London in 1561, says "it is a reproach to the citizens, that considering what a city London is, and that in so many years they have not found means to make a Burse, but must walk in the rain when it rained, more like pedlars than merchants." And the description was true, for Stowe writes, "the merchants and tradesmen, as well English as strangers, for their great making of bargains, contracts, and commerce did usually meet twice a day (at morn and evening) but in an open market."

The place of their meeting was Lombard Street, then a narrow street, where Gresham had his shop as a goldsmith, under the sign of "The Grasshopper," upon the site of No. 68, now and for years occupied by Stone and Martin, the bankers of the present generation. The street had been known in commerce since Edward II's reign, when a house was purchased for the Florentines by one Clerke living there. It was a frequent place for the presentment and protest of Venetian bills. Thus on 11th January, 1460, a presentment was made in front of the "dwelling of Humphry Hayford, Goldsmith, in Lombard Street, where merchants of divers nations were wont to meet."[2] Therefore when the Corporation had to acquire a site for Gresham they selected Sir John Percyvale's house, now 71, which has become quasi historic as the intended site of the new Exchange, and from the refusal of a Guild to part with an estate because charged with charitable bequests "by a dead man's will."

On the 10th January, 1564, Rowe warned his colleagues that the Corporation intended to make application for Percyvale's estate. Thus forewarned they looked over the testator's will with the assistance of Mr. Jeffery (their learned Counsel), and decided (four members dissentient) *not* to part with the estate. A committee consisting of Emanuel Lucar, Richard Hilles, and two others was appointed to draft a letter of refusal.

On Friday, the 12th January, a deputation from the Corporation was received at the hall to urge the Court to grant the estate, so that the new Burse might "retain this antient *name*, for that policies made tyme out of mynde there had gained high credit as being made in *Lombard Street*," that Burse being of "longer antiquity than any other in Europe," but the arguments were of no avail, and the letter of refusal was sent. As the matter was urgent, the

---

[1] Burgon's Life, vol. 1, page 409.
[2] No. 354 of 1460, Venetian Papers (Rolls Series).

Master and Wardens were required to attend at the Guildhall for a discussion of the reasons assigned for their refusal, of which a graphic description is given in the Court Minute of the 15th January set out in the Appendix.[1]

To remove their conscientious scruples they were advised by the Recorder to consult their Diocesan or the Dean of St. Paul's. Whether that course was actually taken does not appear, yet they so far conceded to the wishes of the Mayor as to be willing to accept an exchange of the properties set out in their reply (one such being then or lately in the tenure of Sir Thomas White and another). Nothing, however, came of the negotiation, but a century later the necessities of the Company, arising from forced loans, obliged them in 1674 to sell the property (subject to a trifling rent-charge equivalent to the testator's charitable bequests), and thus Sir John Percyvale has ceased to be remembered by the members of many generations as a great benefactor to their Guild.

Another site was therefore obtained, but although the Merchant Taylors Company could not assist the undertaking by selling their estate, the individual guildsmen in answer to the Lord Mayor's precept of December, 1565, readily contributed to it. They were commanded "as ye tender the honor of this city of London," not to "fail at your peril to collect, gather, and receive with all convenient diligence all and every such sum or sums of money, of all Livery persons of the Company (and retain the same with their names) as they have lovingly granted and agreed to give towards the building." In the succeeding month (14th January) a list of seventy-five subscribers was sent up, including many well-known names, with a total sum of 185l. 16s. 8d. towards the Burse.[2]

In 1567-8 lotteries were introduced to the notice of the citizens by the Privy Council, although both Hume in his History of England and Sir John Sinclair in his annals of the "Public Revenue," mention them as originating in the Virginian[3] Lottery, but the Merchant Taylors' records show this statement to be erroneous.

The first lottery ever put forth in England was in the 10th Elizabeth (1567-8) a notice of which is thus given in the Court Minutes, of 4th August, 1568.

---

[1] Appendix 28, page 396.

[2] Sir Thomas White gave nothing, Sir Thomas Offley and Sir W. Harper 10l. each, Sir John Yorke 6l. 13s. 4d., Rowe 10l., Hilles 5l., &c.

[3] Chapter XVII, page 322.

First lottery established.

"First at this day it is agreed by the foresaid Master, Wardens, and Assistants, that for divers considerations them specially moving that all the members of this mystery being of the Livery shall be forthwith called into this place. And to know of every of them what sum and sums of money they will willingly be contented to put into the Lottery all under our posy in the name of this Common Hall, and what gain soever shall grow, arise, or come by the same money so to be put into the said lottery shall be equally divided to and among all the said members of this mystery that shall so put in money under the said our posy into the said lottery as aforesaid. And the said posy to be devised by the said Master, Wardens, and Assistants before the last of this present month of August, accordingly whereupon the whole livery of this mystery being called hither to answer to the premises as aforesaid, granted and condescended to put all such sum and sums of money into the said lottery under our posy to be devised as aforesaid, according as is noted severally upon every of their heds or names hereafter written viz.:—

	£	s.	d.
Mr. William Albany, Master	3	0	0
„ Richard Hilles	1	0	0
„ Robert Rose..	1	0	0
„ John God	1	0	0
„ Thomas Browne	5	0	0
„ Gerard Gore	0	10	0
„ John Travis..	2	10	0
„ N. Lowe	1	0	0
„ E. Jones	0	10	0
„ E. Ley	1	10	0
„ F. Pope	0	10	0

With 29 others at 10s. each.
„ 11 others at 20s. each.
„ 1 at 5l.
„ 1 at 2l. 10s."

On the 28th August, 1568, the Court again met, and "they, the said Master, Wardens, and Assistants have likewise agreed that this posy underwritten shall be put into the lottery in the behalf and names of all such members of this mystery as hath granted to put money into the said lottery as is noted upon every of their heads entered here of record at the last Court of Assistants holden as by the said Court of Assistants among other things therein mentioned doth and may more plainly appear, viz.:—

"One Byrde in hande is worthe two in the Woode,
Yff wee have the greate lott it will do us good."

The object of the lottery was to raise a sum of money for the reparation of harbours and places of strength. It was drawn at the west door of St. Paul's, commencing on the 11th January, 1569, and continuing day and night until the 6th May following.

The second lottery of which these records give us any trace was held under Letters Patent granted to John Calthorp, the originator of lotteries, and was brought to the notice of the Merchant Taylors Company by a Council letter of 12th July, 1585, signed by "Thos. Bromley, L.C.," and other Lords of the Council. Few subscribers came "by reason of the hard opinion and distruste conceived of the last lotterie, and the length of tyme set downe for the execuc͠on of this nowe in hande," and for the "satisfac͠on of such as are disposed to adventure in the said lotterie, the Council redeemed the tyme of the execuc͠on and performance thereof, unto the Eighth daie of November nexte at the furtheste, for the execuc͠on whereof and trewe delivery of the pryces to the wynners," and to secure fair play "we meane to appoynt certaine p̃sonnes of credite and trust to whom the care thereof shalbe committed, that noe man shalbe defrauded of such part or p̃rtes of the armor as shall befall unto him by the event of the said lottery." The Master and Wardens of the Company were to be appealed to and this bait was offered; "There shalbe bestowed upon you the Lord Maior, as of Her Maj^{ties} gift and liberalitie in respecte of the foresaid service of the said Lotterie, one bason and ewre of 100*l.*, and to other of you the Sheriffs, one bason and ewre of 100 markes, to remayne to you the Maior and Sheriffs, and to yo^9 successors Mayor and Sheriffs within the Cittie for ever."

All the guildsmen were called together and a venture was made. The drawing was not as soon as was anticipated, but on the 28th June, 1586, three members were appointed to attend the drawing of the lottery.

"It is agreed by the Master, Wardens, and Assistants that Oliver Thomas Pearson, Richd Prockter and Roger Abdye, Lovinge Brethren of this Misterie, shall give theire attendance in the Lotterie Howse, sett up at the west dore in Pawle's Churche Yarde, where the Lotterie shall be cawled out on Thursday, in the morninge next ensuinge the date hereof, and their to remayne from eight of the clocke of the said morninge until xii of the clocke at noone, and soe uppon everye warninge to p^{9}cede dowards in the Companie untill the same Lottery be called out." It commenced on St. Peter's Day and continued only for two days longer.

Originally the Lord Mayor could veto lotteries being held in the City[1] but so long as they were permitted they were held for various local or charitable objects, as conveying water to London (1630); for Loyalist officers (1674); for the Charitable Corporation (1733); ye Westminster Bridge (1736); and other instances set out in Hone's Every Day Book, pages 703-768.

The Treasury resorted to this means of raising money from 1693 by the 5th William and Mary, cap. 7, and used the same means (more or less) until the year 1826, when the last lottery was held and all future ones prohibited by the 4th George IV, cap. 60. This lottery was drawn on the 18th October, 1826, at Cooper's Hall, from 5 P.M. until 6 P.M.

In 1571 we are brought in contact with the treason of the Duke of Norfolk by a precept in October for actual service, which was rendered necessary as a precautionary measure by his conspiracy, then discovered by Elizabeth. The Duke, resident in what is now used as "the Master's House," at the Charterhouse, had entered into a traitorous correspondence with Mary Queen of Scots, the Duke of Alva, and the French Ambassador, for the purpose of surprising and seizing Elizabeth's person and the Tower of London, and to liberate Mary from imprisonment, with the intention of ultimately marrying her.

On the 5th, Sir R. Sadler was ordered to keep a strong guard upon the Duke's house in the Charterhouse, and on the 8th Elizabeth's government had sufficient evidence against him to order his arrest and detention in the Tower. He was examined before the Council on the 10th and 11th, and the facts as elicited were stated first to the Star Chamber, in a full assembly of nobles with the Lord Mayor and Aldermen, and then to the citizens at Guildhall, by our guildsman, the Recorder, Fleetwood.

As part of the scheme was that the Duke of Alva should transport 10,000 men from the Low Countries to Harwich; it was deemed prudent that the city gates should be guarded, and hence the precept to the Merchant Taylors Company[2] to provide ten able men each tenth day to watch (with ten Vintners) every gate of the city, viz., two at Newgate, at Ludgate, at the Bridge, at Billingsgate,

---

[1] *See* Dribbet's appeal to James I in 1612 against the Lord Mayor's decision.—Col. State Papers, Domestic, page 130.

[2] Appendix 20, page 400.

at Moorgate, at Cripplegate, at the Postern beside the Tower, at Bishopsgate, and at Aldersgate, commencing on the 21st October at 6 A.M., and continuing to remain there till 5 P.M., watching and having "continually a vigilant eye to all and every suspect and idle person as shall pass and return in and at the same gates, and upon suspicion to stay and examine them, and such as they should find faulty to commit to ward," and to apprize the Lord Mayor thereof.

It remains only to add that the Duke was tried for high treason in January and condemned, but his execution was delayed from the irresolution of Elizabeth until the 2nd June, when he was beheaded on Tower Hill by the Sheriffs of London.[1]

The manners of the Londoners towards foreigners were notoriously bad,[2] they looked upon them with extreme jealousy which on the evil May day of 1517[3] culminated in actual riot, for which the ringleader was hanged. Whenever, therefore, an embassy or any great number of foreigners were to be received in London, it was necessary for the Privy Council to put the Lord Mayor, as answerable for the good behaviour of the citizens, upon his guard.[4]

Such a necessity arose at the close of the year 1573, and, therefore, the Lord Mayor, Sir Lionel Duckett, the Mercer, addressed his precept to the Masters and Wardens of the Guilds on the 9th March, setting forth "as some complaynte hathe ben made that the strangers abydinge wthin this citie and the liberties thereof have ben of late molested and evyll entreated goynge in the streates abowte their busynes by servants and apprentices undescretly and wthoute order," the precept "shalbe to require you, and in her Maj^{ties} name to commande you that forthwith you cause all your Companye to be called together at your Cōēn Hall, and to exorte and also strongly to charge all yor saide Companye that, neither they nor any of their servantes or app^{9}ntices do hereafter in anywise misuse, moleste, or evyll entreate any strangers goynge or beinge

---

[1] Camden, Elizabeth, on date and vol. 2, page 177, Bur. Papers.

[2] Rye's England, page 186.

[3] Strype's Stowe, Book 1, page 253.

[4] Resident foreigners increased in numbers during Elizabeth's reign. In 1580 there were 6,462, thus:—2,302 Dutch; 1,838 French; 1,106 Italians, and 1,542 English born of foreign parents, and 664 of countries not specified, an increase of 3,762 over the number in a prior census, thirteen years antecedent. Another authority gives 7,143 as from country districts and strangers in 1571. Vol. 8, Notes and Queries (2nd), page 447.

aboute their busynes, but shall quietly suffer them to pursue without lett or vexation upon payne of disfranchisement," adding[1] "fail ye not hereof as ye will answere for the contrary at your peril." The subject was brought before the Court on the 16th Sir Thomas Offley and Richard Hilles being present, and orders given accordingly.

The two terrors of London in those days—plague and fire—are brought to our notice by the suspension of business and the precautions taken.

As to the plague, on the 17th September, 1563, the calling of "the Livery by name was this day omitted, by reason that the most part of them were departed out of the cytie into the countrye for avoidance of the infectyon of the syckness of the plague that so sore contynueth amongeste us, which God for his Christe sake cease yt and withdrawe his heavye hand from us. Amen."

And again on 1st September, 1575,[2] the business of the Company is stopped by this visitation, thus :—

"It is agreed and decreed by the Maister, Wardens, and Assistants, that fforasmuch as yt hath pleased God to vysite the Howse by takeing awaye of our late Cōēn Clerke, Nicholas Ffuliambe, with the Plague, and his wife also vysited with the same sicknesse, And for that the Worshipfull Mr Edwd Joans, our newe Maister Electe is oute of this Citie, wee have thoughte good that the Quarter daye which usually hath beene kepte the Teusdaye before Mychaelmas, shall be put off and not kepte for this tyme, for the considerac̃ons aforesaid."

Fortunately, considering that gunpowder was placed in storage in the hall premises, fire does not seem to have happened until the great fire of 1666, but precaution was taken against it by this order of March, 1598 :

"It is considered and agreed that our Master and Wardens shall make provision of such quantity of Bucketts for the store of the Hall, to be ready for service to prevent the danger of fire, as the said Master and Wardens, in their wisdome and discrec̃on, shall think convenient. "Notwithstanding this provision, wee humbly

---

[1] Other similar precepts are to be found in the Court Minutes.

[2] As to the precautions to be observed during this plague, Strype's Stowe, Book 5, page 433. From 1st January, 1562, to 31st December, 1563, in London and the suburbs, 23,372 died, and of these 17,404 from plague. No dinner was given at Guildhall, and Sir John White (the Grocer) took his oath "at the uttermost gate of the Tower."— 4 Hol. Chron., 224, and Lodge (*passim*).

pray Almighty God to p̃serve and defend us from the danger of fire, & grant that wee may not have any occasion to use the same."

The order of the Court to be now noticed has a reference to plays, the first of these containing a prohibition against permitting the common hall to be used for their performance, and as Sir Thomas Offley and Mr. Richard Hilles, senior members of the Court, were both present on the 16th March, 1573, when the ordinance was made, we may presume it had their sanction.

The drama would appear to have received scant favour from the citizens in Elizabeth's reign.[1] Until theatres were established the Halls were used, notably that of the Company, for masks and plays, and the earliest theatres or stages in the city[2] were but temporary erections, constructed in the yards of inns, such as the "Boar's Head, Eastcheap," the "Cross Keys," Gracechurch Street; "the Bull," in Bishopsgate Street; and the "Belle Savage" in Ludgate.

The plays written and represented by the University scholars or the Law students raised the drama to a higher level. The boys at the Company's school were instructed in music and singing, and Mulcaster in 1573-6, represented plays before the Court (of Elizabeth) in which his scholars were the only actors.[3] It is probable from the tenour of the order, that they had previously been permitted to make or act some play at the Hall to which the public had been admitted, paying an entrance fee to cover the expenses of the entertainment.[4] However, it is certain that the experiment was not to be repeated, as this order of 16th March, 1573, proves:—

"Whereas at our comon playes and suche lyke exercises whiche be comonly exposed to be seene for money, everye lew'd persone thinketh himselfe (for his penny[5]) worthye of the chiefe and moste comodious place withoute respecte of any other either for age or estimacion in the comon weale, whiche bringeth the youthe to suche an impudente famyliaritie with theire betters that often tymes greite contempte of maisters, parents, and magistrats followeth thereof, as experience of late in this our comon hall hathe sufficyently declared, whereby reasone of the tumultuous

---

[1] See Proclamation against Players, April, 1559, 4 Hol. Chr., page 283, and Plays and Players in Remembrancia, and Part II, page 289.

[2] Applications for leave to play were made to the Lord Mayor by these players, viz., in July, 1582, from the Earl of Warwick's, at "the Bull"; in October, 1594, from Lord Hunsdon's, at "the Cross Keys"; and in March, 1602, from Lord Oxford's, at "the Boar's Head."

[3] Liber Famelicus, Camden Society (1858), page 12.

[4] Part II, page 215.

[5] This was the lowest price, see Collier's Stage, vol. 3, page 341.

disordered persones repayringe hither to see suche playes as by our schollers were here lately played, the Maisters of this Worshipful Companie and theire deare ffrends could not have entertaynmente and convenyente place as they oughte to have had, by no provision beinge made, notwithstandinge the spoyle of this howse, the charges of this Mystery[1] and theire juste authoritie which did reasonably require the contrary. Therefore, and ffor the causes ffirst above saide, yt is ordeyned and decreed by the authoritie of this presente Courte, with the assente and consente of all the worshipfull persones afforesaide, that henceforthe theire shall be no more any playes suffered to be played in this our Comon Hall, any use or custome heretofore to the contrary in anywise notwithstandinge."

In 1574 the Common Council passed an Act to regulate the stage within the city. The preamble sets forth the evils resulting from it, as assignations from the inns being used, the people being withdrawn from Divine Service,[2] waste of money, robberies, seditions, besides the breaking down of scaffolds and stages; again, the plague which was then upon the city spread by such assemblies, and therefore the Common Council, "lest upon God's merciful withdrawing of his hand of sickness from us (which God grant) the people, especially the meaner and most unruly sort, should with sudden forgetting of his visitation without fear of God's wrath .... return unto the undue use of such enormities, to the great offence of God, the Queen's commandment and good goverance," put the stage under regulation, requiring amongst other things that all the plays performed in the city should be licensed by the Lord Mayor.[3]

The measures taken by the Crown were in the same direction. Elizabeth by patent of the 6th May, 1574, gave a licence to James Burbage and others, servants of the Earl of Lycester, to exercise and occupy the art of "stage players," provided the plays were licensed by the Master of the Revels for the time being.

In 1583, twelve of the principal comedians were selected from the companies then subsisting under the licence and protection of certain noblemen, and were sworn as Her Majesty's servants, and

---

[1] "Master's Account, 1572-3 and 1573-4.
"Item, for charges impended at the Cōen Hall when as Mr. Moncaster's scholers did playe before this worshipful Companye as appereth p' bill, summa, 36s. 6d.
"Item, paid for charges impended at the Cōen Hall when as Mr. Moncaster's scholars did playe there as p' bill of the p'ticulers appereth, summa, 49s. 3d."

[2] The plays were often on Sundays, and in 1618 daily from 2 to 5 p.m.—the usual time for christenings, burials, and afternoon service."—Remembrancia (London, 1878), pages 350-7.   [3] Strype's Stowe, Book 5, page 245.

eight of these had an annual stipend of 3*l*. 6*s*. 8*d*. each. Thus the London theatres came under the control of the Crown.

The "Master of the Revels" became an important officer, and the second order of the Court (which we shall print) had reference to him. The first Master patented in Elizabeth's reign was Thomas Benger, on the 18th June, 1560-1; he was succeeded on the 24th July, 1579, by Edmund Tilney, who continued throughout the reign. The salary was 10*l*. a year, but by fees and perquisites squeezed out of others made up to 100*l*. a year, and this or other considerations made the office much sought after.[1]

The Common Council had, as we have seen, ordered that the plays to be acted in the city should be first licensed by the Lord Mayor. Probably the Master of the Revels had given his authority to plays, which sooner or later were brought into the city and there acted; at any rate the Lord Mayor thought it expedient to engage Mr. Tylney's services to redress the grievance that had arisen, as we find on the Court records this entry :—

" A precepte directed frome the L. Mayor to this Companie shewinge to the Companie the great enormytie that this Citie susteyneth by the practice and prophane exercise of players and playinge howses in this Citie, and the corrupc͠on of youth that groweth thereupon invitinge the Companie by the consideration of this myscheyfe to yeilde to the paym^{te} of one Anuytie to one Mr Tylney, mayster of the Revelles of the Queene's house, in whose hands the redresse of this inconveniency doeth rest, and y^t those playes might be abandoned out of this citie."

"An Assembly hereon the xxijth of March (1591), beinge our M^{rs} view daye after they came downe frome dynner out of the Gallarie," took the precept into consideration and determined, " albeit the Comp: think y^t a very good service to be p͡formed yet wayinge the damage of the president and enovac͠on of raysinge of Anuyties upon the Companies of London what further occasions y^t may be drawne unto together wth their great chardge otherwyse which this troublesome tyme hath brought, and is likely to bringe, they thinke this no fitt course to remedie this myscheife, but wish some other waye were taken in hand to expell out of our Citye so generall a c͠otagion of manners and other inconveniency, wherein yf any ende^v or travile of this Companie might further the

---

[1] See Historical Account of the English Stage, Vol. 3, page 40, *et seq.*, of Malone's Shakspeare (London), 1821.

matter they woulde be readye to use their service therein. And this to be certified as the Comp: answere yf y^t shall apeare by conference wth other Companies that the precepte requireth necessarilie a returne of the Comp: certificate, and answere in this behalf." By no means an unwise resolution, or the Crown would have appointed, and the Companies paid the officers; a division of duty little to the advantage of those who provided the salary.

The entry which follows relates to a very different subject. A great number,—indeed a Court minute of 3rd March, 1598,[1] calls them a "great multitude"—of people had occasion to resort to the hall at Court and quarter days, and there to wait for the hearing of their causes. Were they to be left to waste or lose their time, or was some other alternative to be offered?

The Reformation was safe, but the great instrument of the conversion of England to the "new learning" was the Bible, then translated into the mother tongue. Miles Coverdale, one of the original translators, was, as we shall read, an old friend of their most worshipful member Richard Hilles, and had long been the Company's tenant in Fink Lane. On the 30th October, 1578, ten years after the Bishop's or Parker's Bible was put forth, this order of Court, (Richard Hilles being present), was issued:—

"The Master and Wardens decree that a Bible of the new form lately printed by Christopher Barker, the Queen Majesty's Printer, shall be brought and set up in their Common Hall, in some convenient place for such as resort unto the said Hall may occupy themselves at Court days while they attend for the hearing of their cause."

In consequence of objections raised to the Bishop's Bible at a conference of Divines at Hampton Court, a new translation was agreed upon, in which Bishop Andrews and other divines, some of whom had been educated in the Company's School, were engaged. This was printed in 1611, and in process of time supplanted the older edition; for in the Mastership of Mr. Edward Cotton in 1627,[2] a bible was purchased for the Company, as this entry proves:—

"Item paid Mr. Churchman, wch hee laid out for a Bible to stand in the Hall, the summe of 39s."

---

[1] Memorials, page 33 (note).

[2] The Bible was not destroyed by the fire in 1666, but is still in the possession of the Company. It was rebound in the Mastership of Mr. Foster White, and bears the mark of the chain which attached it to the lectern.

This bible escaped the fire of 1666, and is in the present library of the Company, having still the mark of the chain by which it was attached to the lectern.

The troubles of concealment which threatened the Company at a later period were foreshadowed in 1578.

Probably the only obit payable by the Merchant Taylors Company that was ever applied for pious or educational purposes is that of Sir W. FitzWilliam. It would appear that the Royal Commissioners made no return to the Crown under the Chauntry Act of Edward VI, nor did the Company make any payment to the *cestuique* trusts under Sir W. FitzWilliam's deed of May, 1533. As a consequence an information was filed in the Court of Exchequer by one Lytchfielde against the Company, in Robert Dowe's mastership, the result of which will be best explained by these original entries :—

"1578, October 30th.[1]—The Master and Wardens have decreed that the matter of Lytchfielde, by him informed in the Exchequer against this Mystery, for the concealment of 7*l.* a year, for the finding of a prieste to sing masse for Sir W. Fitz-William as he supposeth, to be committed unto ye dealing of the s^d Master and his Wardens, Mr. Anthony Ratcliffe, Thomas Offley, and George Sotherton, loving brothers of this Mystery, according to ther wise discretions."

"April 29th, 1579.[1]—Whereas this Mystery is found to be in arreayre to the Queen's Majesty in her Court of Exchequer for the sum of 103*l.* 5*s.*, for her moiety of 206*l.* 10*s.*, found to be concealed for the stipend of a prieste, to have yearly 7*l.* for to sing in the church of Masham, for the soul of Sir W. FitzWilliam, which sum of 103*l.* 5*s.* is to be paid by 10*l.* a year until the same be fully paid, as appeareth by a decree made in the same Court, the Master Wardens, and Assistants have agreed that the Common Seal shall be affixed unto a safe bond for the payment thereof, if the same may be allowed, by Sir Walter Mildmay."

The bond was sealed by the Court, 10th June, 1579, and while matters were so situate, Walter Fish (Master in 1576), the Tailor to the Queen—if Stowe's authority be accepted—obtained a grant by Patent,[2] dated 3rd October, of the Company's bond, and of the rent of 7*l.* 6*s.* 8*d.* "in consideration of his faithful service, and that he will grant the rents to the Merchant Taylors Company for

---

[1] Mr. Richard Hilles was present at these Courts.
[2] 21 Elizabeth (part 7, M. 3).

pious uses to be specified by him." He came before the Court with his grant from the Crown to arrange for the payment of their debt, and to establish some "pious use." The next extracts, like the last ones, show that the Company was not overburdened with ready money; thus at a Court, 14th November, 1579.[1]

"Item, the said Master, Wardens, and Assistants, do accept and allow of the motion of Mr. W. Fish, a loving brother of this mystery, for the assuring unto them of 7*l*. 6*s*. 8*d*. of lawful money of England, yearly to be bestowed in charitable deeds according to the devise of the said W. Fish.

"And whereas the Master and Wardens of this mystery and their successors stand bound under the Common Seal of this house unto the Queen's Majesty for the payment of 103*l*. 5*s*. of lawful money of England to be paid in her Majesty's Exchequer for certain arrerages of the devise of Sir William FitzWilliam, Knight, deceased; whereof there is paid 3*l*. 5*s*., the rest is 100*l*. to be paid by 10*l*. a year. As also for the payment of 7*l*. yearly for ever; whereof there is due to her Majesty for two years past at Michaelmas last 14*l*. of lawful money of England, the whole sum of 103*l*. 5*s*., and 7*l*. yearly for ever is parcell of the devise of the said Sir William FitzWilliam as by the said obligation it doth and may appear.

"And whereas also there is conceled 6*s*. 8*d*. a year for 31 years past at Michaelmas last which amounts to 10*l*. 6*s*. 8*d*., being also one other parcel of the devise of the said Sir W. FitzWilliam. All which sums of 100*l*. and 7*l*. 6*s*. 8*d*. yearly with the arrerages thereof, &c., the Queen's Majesty hath given unto the said Walter Fish, the said 100*l*. of arrerages unto himself, and 7*l*. 6*s*. 8*d*. in perpetuity for ever to be employed and bestowed in charitable deeds. The whole sum of 7*l*. 6*s*. 8*d*. of the devise of the said Sir William FitzWilliam as also other 10*l*. of yearly rent according to his motion aforesaid. The said W. Fish is contented to assure unto this house to be bestowed and employed according to his devise in consideration whereof, as also to be discharged against the Queen's Majesty, her heirs and successors, as well of the said bond of 103*l*. 5*s*., as also of the said 7*l*. 6*s*. 8*d*. for and with all the arrerages thereof, the said Master, Wardens, and Assistants have agreed and decreed that there shall be paid unto the said W. Fish, by the said Master and Wardens in hand the sum of 74*l*. 6*s*. 8*d*., and 50*l*. more at the feast of St. John the Baptist next ensuing the

---

[1] Mr. Richard Hilles was present at this Court.

date hereof, upon the coming in of 50*l.* due there by Richard Offley, a loving brother of this mistery, being parcell of the fine of his house."

With this money, when paid to him, Walter Fish purchased a freehold house in Cannon Street, from John Marshall (then paying a rent of 10*l.*), and by deed of 22nd May, 1580, between Fish of the first part, John Stanton of the second part, the Merchant Taylors Company of the third part, and the President and Fellows of St. John's College of the fourth part, conveyed the house to Stanton that he might devise the same to the Merchant Taylors Company with trusts declared in favour of "five poor scholars of St. John's, Oxford, which should be most like to bend their studies to divinity, to be divided yearly between them towards the amendment of their victuals and battlings;" such scholars to be nominated by Fish during his life, and after his decease by the Merchant Taylors Company.[1]

This trust has been performed by the Company to the present day, and *by their retention of this real estate*, the income for the benefit of these poor students has grown in these sums :

		£
In 1580 the rent was		10
„ 1829 „ „ „		20
„ 1830 „ „ „		102
„ 1840 „ „ „		120
„ 1868 „ „ „		240

From this concealment these incidental advantages have resulted :—

1. The endowment of 7*l.* has been saved from the Crown and applied to charitable uses by the Merchant Taylors Company.

2. The Company has only been required to pay annually and not to purchase 7*l.* from the Crown by the sacrifice of an estate then bearing an equivalent, but now (like Fish's house) a vastly increased rental.

3. By investing the 100*l.* in real instead of personal estate at interest, the Exhibitions instead of falling below 10*l.* have been raised to 240*l.* per annum.

The troubles of concealment arose in 1582, under the grant of Letters Patent made to Adams and Woodshaw, of lands alleged to be concealed by the Guilds from the operation of "The Act for Chauntries Collegiate." So far as the Merchant Taylors Company's

---

[1] The present scheme of March, 1887, is set out in Appendix 30, page 402, and see in Sir W. Craven's life as to purchase of Creeke advowson, Part II, chapter XXI.

interests were to be imperilled the attempt to obtain money failed absolutely, but as one of the burning questions of that period, which may be revived by modern controversy, it will be well as briefly as possible to state the facts, and set out the records of the Merchant Taylors Company in relation thereto.

The contention of the Patentees appears to have been presented in two aspects:[1]

1. That the *lands* out of which the rent-charges arose, and not *only* the latter, passed to the Crown, for superstitious uses.

2. That both lands and uses had in many instances been concealed from the Crown, notably by eight of the Guilds, as the Grocers, Skynners, Salters, Vinters, Drapers, Clothworkers, Fishmongers, and Haberdashers.

On the 9th May, 1582, these Guilds made application to the Merchant Taylors to join them in a general suit for redress to the Lord Mayor and Aldermen, who had acted for the Guilds in 1549–50, which, thinking reasonable, they consented to do. However, communications were opened with the Privy Council, and at the Court of the 24th the articles of Sir Christopher Hatton were submitted for acceptance, namely, that two judges should be named (one by the City, the other by the Patentees) to hear counsel and decide. If against the Patentees that the contention should cease, but if in their favour, that a favourable composition should be offered to the Companies by the Lord Treasurer; Sir Christopher Hatton's offer was to be considered final, and an early answer to be sent through the Lord Mayor.

At the Court of the 28th May, proposals of a somewhat similar character were received from the Patentees, accompanied by a letter from the Lord Mayor asking for a speedy and definite reply.

Investigations appear to have proceeded at the instance of the Patentees, when other Companies (including six of the smaller ones) were charged with concealment, and an informal suit appears to have been instituted, as under the title of "The Suit of the city of London against the Patentees for concealed Lands,"[2] the reasons of the city of London are found, which Strype has printed. The Patentees were willing to accept 5,000*l*., and a suggestion was made that 580*l*. would be the share to be paid by the Merchant Taylors Company; but when the Court had time to

---

[1] 'Lansdowne MS.,' Vol. 35, page 29.
[2] *Ibid.*, Vol. 38, pages 22–5. *Ibid.*, Vol. 26, page 72.

look into the matter, their resolution was for *no* compromise, and when summoned on the 10th June, 1583, to decide, they came to these conclusions:—

"Item, to the question whether they think good to make composition severally with the Patentees, Adams and Woodshawe, the said Master, Wardens, and Assistants have agreed and decreed that they will make no composition with them."

And again, "to the question if the Right Honorable Sir Christopher Hatton will take upon him to deal generally for all causes of the said Companies, and to compound with them, it is by the said Master, Wardens, and Assistants agreed and decreed to make no composition with him."

The result of this firmness was that the tenants of the Company had proceedings taken against them in the Court of Exchequer, which failed according to the confession of the Attorney-General, and entailed upon the Merchant Taylors Company the costs of their defence. The Master for 1583–4 claims allowance for his expenses in these words:—

"Item, this Accomptant Mr. Richard May asketh allowance for divers particular charges laid out by him in and about our lands in Cornhill and Lombard Street, some time the lands of Sir John Percival, for our lands in the Vintry, some time Cornwallis, lands, and for our house in Tower Street, with a house at Dowgate, which was sold by the Company, called the Talbot, divers of our tenants being served with process out of the Exchequer at the suit of Sir James A. Crofts, as lands said to be concealed from Her Majesty, which was cleared by the confession of Her Majesty's Attorney-General upon the sight of our wills concerning the same as may appear in the Records substitute by the hands of Her said Majesty's Attorney. Total, as appeareth by the particulars, 113*l*. 6*s*. 6*d*."

Notwithstanding the Merchant Taylors Company were not implicated in concealment, they were willing, so as to get their title absolutely cleared from all doubt, to pay 200*l*. "if they could be well assured by learned counsel;" but no payment can be traced in the account books, nor any deed or assurance found amongst their muniments, so that nothing came of this resolution.[1]

---

[1] In the Lansdowne MS., under date of 1585, the Patentees' case is set out with a note upon the statute of Edward VI and on the equity of the case. Then follows their proposals for compromise,[a] but no acceptance having been given the Patentees presented a petition for hearing[b] with a statement of their case against the Grocers, Drapers, Haberdashers, Goldsmiths, and Skynners.

[a] Vol. 38, pages 17 and 19; *ibid.*, pages 20 and 23.   [b]*Ibid.*, Vol. 114, page 21.

Sir Philip Sydney's Funeral.

During the remainder of Elizabeth's reign nothing more was done, for it is said "that to satisfy Elizabeth on this subject, the rental of each Company in 1587 was¹ set out and the particulars of such charitable good gifts as are performed by divers of the Companies of London out of the annuities purchased of King Edward were laid before her², and in this document (which cannot be found in the records) the case of the Merchant Taylors Company is thus stated :—

They purchased of the King in rent per annum, 98*l*. 11*s*. 5*d*.
They sold tenements to buy the same, 124*l*. 1*s*. 8*d*.
Payments yearly out of their rents purchased—

		1586-7.			1587-8.		
	£ s. d.	£	s.	d.	£	s.	d.
In pensions to decayed brethren	58 0 0	*36*	*13*	*4*	*33*	*8*	*4*
In exhibitions to scholars	18 0 0	*17*	*6*	*8*	*20*	*3*	*4*
One grammar school	10 0 0	*62*	*0*	*0*	*16*	*3*	*4*
To their almsmen	42 0 0	*39*	*2*	*0*	*40*	*8*	*0*
	128 0 0	*155*	*2*	*0*	*170*	*3*	*0*

What the Company spent on "charitable good gifts" is given in italics from the extant account books in parallel columns, but in all honesty it was rather for Elizabeth and her ministers to account to her subjects for all the chantry monies received by the Crown for pious uses, than for her subjects to explain how they had spent the rents of estates purchased by them and purged of such uses.

One of the last incidents to be mentioned is the precept here given neither for festival nor service, but for respect "to the noble and virtuous gentleman, most worthy of all titles both of learning and chivalry," Sir Philip Sydney. As indeed he was, and styled by Edmund Spenser, in his Shepherd's Calendar, "as the precedent of noblemen and chivalrie." Sydney, as the reader will remember, was mortally wounded on the 22nd September, 1586, at the siege of Zutphen, on the Yssel, and died at Arnheim on the 17th October following.

The answers[a] of certain Companies and the offers of the Patentees appear to have been submitted[b] to the same tribunal, and the opinions[c] of the Judges are given in certain cases enumerated for the Patentees and in others against them.

[1] 22nd January, 1587, Vol. 55, Lansdowne MS., page 28.
[2] Lansdowne MS., Vol. 16, page 30; and Strype's Stowe, page 337. 3rd February, 1587.
[a] Vol. 49, page 9.   [b] Vol. 44, page 35.   [c] Vol. 14, page 13.

The States, a young nation then fighting for their liberties and their faith, petitioned Elizabeth to allow them to inter their champion at their own cost, pledging themselves to erect "as fair a monument as has ever been set up for any King or Emperor in Christendom, yea, though the same should cost half a ton of gold in the building," but the offer, of course, was declined. His body was conveyed *viâ* Flushing to London, and lay at the chapel[1] of the dissolved convent in the Minories, until the 16th February, 1587, when it was interred in St. Paul's. Such was the national sorrow, that the first general mourning was after his decease. A deputation from the Company, chosen on the precept of the Lord Mayor, attended his funeral to act as pikemen.

The entry from the Company's records is this:—

"10th February, 1586.—A precept from my Lorde Mayor was receaved and redd whereby iiij pikemen in fayre white graven harnesse and gilte rapieres and daggers and fayre apparell gentleman like and ij holberdiers gilte weare apoynted to be by this hall furnished Whereof the M^r and Wardens at this Court took good order in chusinge and sendinge for suche sixe fitt man Bretherren of the Societye, who are all warned to be on Tewsday next at the Artillery Yard to be trayned or sett in the order they shall go yn to the enterring of Sir Phillipp Sydney, Knight, at St. Powles Church, London. Theire harness together wth theire pikes they are apoynted to receive heare on Tewsday and Thusday both at this Hall."

The last precept to be given was for the several Companies to be present in St. Paul's at a general Thanksgiving for the capture of Cadiz in June, 1596. Thus in a meeting of the Court of the 9th August, a precept was read from the Lord Mayor as under: "The Livery of the Company apparelled in their best clothing are upon Sunday next by the hour of 7 in the morning to be at Paulles Church according to her Majesty's pleasure to yield thanks and praise to Almighty God for the great victory given to the Army and Navy in Spain."

In the succeeding chapter we will notice the assessments made against the Company during the period embraced in this chapter, and shew as best we can what was the position of the Company at the close of the reign of Elizabeth.

---

[1] Since pulled down on the union with Aldgate parish.

CHAPTER XIV.

THE COMPANY AT THE CLOSE OF THE REIGN OF ELIZABETH.

Object of the Chapter, p. 245.—Guild consisted of Taylors, Clothworkers, and Merchants, p. 245.—Wealth of the Company, p. 246.—Assessments on Precepts, p. 246.—The Principle of, p. 246.—Assent of Common Council essential, p. 247.—Freemen represented on Assessment Authority, p. 247. —Assessment of Common Council, 1562, p. 247.—Corn assessments of two kinds, pp. 247, 248.—Of 1564, p. 249.—Of 1565, p. 249.—Of 1596, p. 249. —Merchant Taylors assessed in highest amount, p. 249.—Precepts for military service, p. 250.—In 1572, p. 250.—In 1577 and 1579, p. 250.—In 1585, p. 251.—Wealth of the guildsmen, p. 251.—In 1565, p. 251.— Precept to meet the Lord Mayor in gold chains in 1578, p. 251.—Demands for Crown loan of 5,000l. on Privy Seal in 1588, p.—252.—Loan notes issued, p. 253.—Imprisonment of defaulters, p. 254.—Offley and others command trained bands, p. 254.—As to the Merchants, p. 254.—Wealth of citizens in 1557 and 1590, p. 254.—Russia Company, p. 255.—Establishment of East India Company, 1599, p. 255.—Part taken by Guildsmen, p. 256.—Mayors and Sheriffs, p. 256.—Common Councilmen, p. 257.— Political influence, p. 257.—M.P. for London, p. 257.—List of the wisest and best Merchants, p. 257.—High position of the Guild, p. 257.—What were their household expenses, p. 258.—Their house rent, p. 258.—Cost of living, p. 258.—Rise of prices, p. 258.—Wild Durrell's expenses in 1589, p. 259.—Attendant servants, p. 259.—Locomotion, p. 259.—Educational attainments of Guildsmen, p. 260.—The admirable discharge of duty in the 16th century, p. 260.

IN a former chapter we traced the progress of the Guild during the 15th, and endeavoured to show the position which it held at the close of that century. Taking up the same subject, we propose to carry it down in this chapter to the date when England passed from the Tudor to the Stuart dynasty. During this period the members of the Guild had entered upon the employment of clothworking, and when James I came to the throne they were probably divided into three classes, Taylors, Clothworkers, and Merchants, though in what proportion or what wealth and importance was possessed by or attached to each class are facts not easily traceable.

We shall begin, therefore, by examining the assessments made on the Company under precepts issued by the Lord Mayor, as perhaps the best test of the wealth, if not of individuals, yet of the aggregation of such men in the Company. These precepts, though addressed to the Master and Wardens, were not as a rule satisfied out of the "common box," or "treasury," but often by the subscriptions of individual members.

The principle underlying civic assessments we have already shown in dealing with corn assessments, originating in 1521,[1] viz.:—First that the Common Council determined which of and in what amount the several Companies should be assessed, and secondly, that the Master and Wardens distributed this assessment amongst the members; therefore, upon the receipt of the precept by the Merchant Taylors Company, the Court had to determine in what proportion the assessment should be borne between the Merchant and Bachelor Companies; and then distribute the assessment amongst the several members of the Merchant Company.

But it must be emphasised that the assent of the Common Council was essential to the validity of the Lord Mayor's precept for enforcing an assessment upon the citizens. Thus, in the mastership of Anthony Radclyf, in 1577 (Sheriff 1586), the Mayor's precept to the Master and Wardens was obeyed but only under protest from the Company, which stands recorded in the Mayor's Court. Yarmouth Harbour needed completion; money was difficult to raise, and the Lords of the Council pressed the Mayor and Aldermen to procure 1,000*l*. from the City as a loan, to be repaid by yearly instalments of 200*l*. The Lord Mayor, Sir Thomas Ramsay, the Grocer (whose wife, Lady Mary, was a benefactress to the Merchant Taylors Company) yielded to this request, because, as he stated in the precept, the Privy Council had with "sharpness urged the cause," and he thought it expedient to comply "in consideration of the divers affairs of the city depending before the Lords, and for divers other causes that might thereafter happen." Whereupon a precept, on the 11th June, was sent to the Company for 100*l*. to be paid to the Chamberlain before the 24th instant.

The Court of Assistants objected, and replied to the Lord Mayor (1) The amount was excessive, for as one of twenty Companies 100*l*. was more than their fair share; (2) That it was not meet or right to ask for any grant *unless the same had been before the Common Council and agreed to by them.*

---

[1] See Chapter II, page 58, and page 329, note 1.

On the 2nd July a second precept came, that the Company should pay 100*l.* at once, " fail ye not hereof as you will answer to the contrary at your peril," and a deputation waited on the Lord Mayor and gave the former answer. The Court of Assistants was summoned on the 6th, and resolved to stand out and deny as the fourth, if three others would do so. Hampden[1] had not yet lived to show these guildsmen what an English country gentleman dared to do alone. They, remembering the fate of a recalcitrant Alderman who refused to join in an arbitrary loan to Henry VIII, paid their money, but with this protest of the 11th July recorded in the City archives:

"The Merchant Taylors Company deliver the sum of 100*l.* which is prayed of them to be lent for the Haven of Yarmouth with this protestation, that they do not yield to this precedent that such payment be made a precept or command of the Lord Mayor, where no assent of the body of the city by Common Council proceed to find, but understanding Her Majesty's good liking, the earnest request of the Privy Council, and the benefit of the Commonwealth, they are for the same respect content to lend the same sum with this protestation, and that it be not hereafter by this precedent, and they pray that this their protestation be recorded in the registry of this Court."—*Seabright.*

What were the considerations which led the Common Council to fix the amount in which each Guild should be from time to time assessed, or the Master and Wardens the amount which each member should contribute, are not explained, but as the Guildsmen were amply represented both in the Common Council and in their Court; the remedy for any grievance inflicted was to be found in this representation. Taking these assessments as evidence of wealth and numbers, we shall, by following them out, trace the development of the Merchant Taylors Company in these respects during the period under our consideration.

The assessment made in 1548–9 for Bridewell Hospital we have already noticed.[2]

In October, 1562,[3] an assessment was made by the Common Council on 36 of the Companies to provide a loan of 3,928*l.* 6*s.* 8*d.* to enable the Corporation to purchase corn. These corn assessments were originally made by way of "present or loan" to the Corporation of London, and the money was advanced out of the

---

[1] 3 State Trials, page 825. [2] Page 58, *ante.*
[3] This scale of rating probably continued in force for some time. Appendix 32, page 405.

"common box" or by individual members; but in one way or the other the money must be provided, or the Master and Wardens would be in contempt and liable to imprisonment. For the money paid to the Corporation the Chamberlain or Bridgmaster gave bond to the Guild for repayment with interest.

While the loan system lasted the profit and loss of purchase and resale rested with the Corporation, but at a later period, say, 1599, the Corporation required the Guilds themselves to make the purchase and resale, and then the precept was not for money to be lent to the Corporation but for a stated number of quarters of corn to be purchased and resold by the said Guilds at given dates. Thus the precept to the Taylors of January, 1599, was in these words:—

"And that you have the same here at London by the 20th day of March next, to be by you put forth to be ground and sold in meals by yourselves in your halls or in the markets, in such sort as then and from time to time afterwards shall be thought meet by me and my brethren the Aldermen."[1]

To revert, however, to the *loan* assessment of 1562.

The Mercers and Grocers were assessed at 400*l*.; the Merchant Taylors at 350*l*., the Drapers, Fishmongers, Goldsmiths, and Cloth-workers at 300*l*.; and the other Companies at various smaller sums. This assessment was distributed (by order of the 2nd October) on the members of the Company, thus:—

	£	s.	d.
Of every Alderman that hath been Sheriff	10	6	8
Of the same that hath been Mayor	11	16	8
Of every Assistant	4	6	8
Of the rest of the Livery which had not been Warden	3	6	8
Of the common box of the Wardens Substitute	50	0	0

And the Collectors to be Kympton and Johnson.

In the same month another assessment was made for armour, seventy members being assessed. White, Thomas Offley, and Harper, Knights and Aldermen, 3*l*. 13*s*. 4*d*. each; Thomas Rowe, Alderman, and H. Suckley, 3*l*. 6*s*. 8*d*. each; twenty-five others at 26*s*. 8*d*. (including Lucar, R. Hilles, J. God, Albany, Duckington,

---

[1] Extract from prec. pt of 9th January, 1599.

and Hulson); and thirty-eight at 20s.; and on Geoffrey Vaughan[1] and John Godwyn no assessment was made. The Wardens Substitute brought in 33*l*. 6*s*. 8*d*., making a total of 122*l*. 6*s*. 8*d*. collected by William Albany and R. Hulson.

In February, 1564, this assessment was made:—

	£	s.	d.
Each Alderman who had passed the chair paid	5	18	4
Each new Alderman	5	3	4
Each Past Master	2	3	4
Each other of the Court	2	3	4
Each Liveryman	1	13	4

And the residue of this assessment, if any such, was to be made up by the Bachelors Company.

Another assessment was made on 6th May, 1565, White, Offley, and Harper paying 5*l*. 18*s*. 4*d*., Rowe 5*l*. 3*s*. 4*d*., twenty-four others 2*l*. 3*s*. 4*d*., ending with Love and Shotesham, and thirty-seven others 1*l*. 13*s*. 4*d*. each. The Wardens Substitute brought in 38*l*. 8*s*. 4*d*., making a total of 175*l*.

During the latter part of the century the Merchant Taylors were no doubt increasing in wealth and importance, for in the assessment made in December, 1596, we find them standing for the first time at the highest amount, having to provide 280 out of 3,000 quarters of corn. In the previous assessment of 1575, the Mercers and Grocers were rated at higher amounts than the Taylors, "as in right and equity they ought to be be," and the latter found "themselves" as the Court minute recorded, "very hardly and unequally dealt with." However, they complied with the assessment and agreed "to be humble suitors to the Lord Mayor and Aldermen that the Company might be reasonably and indifferently assessed as other Companies were," but as when 55 Companies were assessed for raising 10,000 quarters of corn by order of 22nd December, 1599,[2] the Merchant Taylors Company stood at the highest amount, viz., 936 quarters, it is clear that no relief had been granted to them by the Corporation.

The illustrations given hitherto may be thought to prove the wealth, those hereafter the numbers, of the Company; thus the Lord

---

[1] One of the same name Master in 1522. I presume these Liverymen were in too poor circumstances to meet any assessment.

[2] See Appendix 32, page 405. This scale probably continued in force until raised in 1603-4.

Mayor, by precept or command, called on his fellow citizens to discharge personal service either for military array or duty. Take for instance their array before Elizabeth in 1572, which is mentioned in the pages of Holinshed,[1] thus :—

"On the 24th March,[2] the Lord Mayor sent his precept on Her Majesty's behalf to appoint 188 good, tall, cleanly, and best picked persons of the Company to appear in their proper persons or by other mete and apt persons at their cost to use and beare armes only for the shewe to be made by Her Majesty. They were to parade in the Artillery Yarde in Bishopsgate Without, on the 27th at 8 A.M., and as a preliminary the Wardens Substitute were to warn all the horse soldiers of the Yeomanry of the Company to appear at the hall at 6 A.M., on the 26th, to take order for furnishing the men and armour according to the precept."

The records of the Company show the apportionment of this burden, 107 members (whose names are given) each supplied one soldier; 16 acted in person; 7 were supplied by the house = 130. The names of 58 men with calyvers and shot are given, and probably the cost of these was defrayed by an assessment of 29*l*. 10*s*. 8*d*., made on the Bachelors Company, of which Sir Leonard Halliday was then a member. Though Richard Hilles was present he did not act in person or supply a soldier.

In 1577, a levy of 2,000 men was to be raised by the citizens of London, and of these 200 were assigned to the Company to be trained as soldiers, all being within the age of 19 and 40 years, either apprentices, workmen, or freemen of the city, whereof 50 were to be free of the Guild, whose names and addresses in the city and their commanders were to be certified to the Lord Mayor. This levy was increased in February 1579, to 3,000, of which number the Merchant Taylors had to supply 296, *i.e.*, 100 with calyvers (to be of those that were by the former order trained, and for want of those by death or absence of others to be supplied) and 96 pikemen.

The Wardens Substitute were then directed to go through their quarters to take the names of all the masters and their servants that were serviceable and warn them to attend at the Hall. The corselets were to be furnished by members of the Livery as far as possible, and the rest by members of the Bachelors.

In each instance a burthen of 10 per cent. was borne by the

---

[1] Vol. III, page 128, and Vol. III, page 206 of Nichol's Elizabeth.
[2] Memorials, page 140.

Taylors, and in the assessment of 1585,[1] for men (with armour) and for the cost of maintenance, these figures appear :—[2]

Companies.	Men.	Money.
		£ s. d.
Mercers	294	392 10 0
Drapers	347	567 16 7
Grocers	395	467 10 0
Skynners	174	163 5 3
Taylors	395	273 5 4

The highest number of men being 395, and largest amount of money 567*l*. 16*s*. 7*d*.

The wealth of individual or the proportion of such to poorer members of the Merchant Company, for of absolutely poor there were scarcely any, are facts not easy to ascertain; probably the best guides, when recorded, are the voluntary gifts or loans paid for public purposes. We have already seen that to the Burse in 1565 the members speedily contributed the sum of 185*l*. 16*s*. 8*d*., which was given in various amounts; as the Aldermen (Offley, Harper, and Rowe) 10*l*. each, Sir John Yorke 6*l*. 13*s*. 4*d*., Hilles, Dowe, and Gerard Gore 5*l*. each, Anthony Radcliffe 3*l*. 6*s*. 8*d*., Neu, Tope, and Eden, then partners, 2*l*., Richard Harrison 1*l*., and Reynold Barker 1*l*. 10*s*., and we shall see in a later reign how willing the members were to make contributions to the proposals for planting new colonies. Other criteria suggest themselves,— take for instance the ready answer made to such precepts as that to be now mentioned.

In May, 1578, Casimer (brother to the Elector Palatine), who had commanded troops levied and paid with English gold, on the Rhine, came to visit England to vindicate his want of success to Elizabeth. His host was to be Sir Thomas Gresham, who, on becoming a knight, had left his shop in Lombard Street (such being the usual etiquette of those times),[3] and taken up his residence in his new-built house in Bishopsgate Street. The Londoners desired to give the Prince a becoming reception, and therefore,

---

[1] On 26th July, 1585, when 37 out of 500 were to be raised in Aldersgate Ward the proportion was only 24 per 1,000.

[2] Vol. I, page 253, Ant. Rep.

[3] Sir Baptist Hicks (Lord Campden's ancestor) is said to have been the first knight who continued his shop.—Stowe (1720), Book I, page 287, vol. I, Mait., page 288.

the Lord Mayor (Sir Richard Pipe, the Draper) called on the Guilds to aid him. The Prince was to land at the Tower Stairs, and to be brought from thence in procession to Gresham House. The Mayor's precept was, therefore, issued to the Guilds, and he commanded the Merchant Taylors to appoint thirty-two persons to attend him at eight A.M. "in cotes of velvet with chaynes of gold[1] on horseback and every one of them having a man on horseback to attend upon him." The precept concluded thus: "And as many more as the Master and Wardens thought meet for the purpose."

The Court numbered only twenty-four, and therefore the Livery were summoned and those whose names are recorded in the books "assented to ride accordingly." Though the notice was short, for the Prince arrived the next night, forty-four names are entered as riders. Master Dowe, then Master, and these past Masters, Masters Hilles, Albany, Fish, Radcliffe (then the four Wardens) and others of the Assistants and Livery.[2]

Another instance may be given, though of a totally opposite character, yet as illustrating the ability of the Guildsmen to meet at call the pecuniary demands of the Crown for aid, the occasion being the Spanish Armada, thus:—

"At the Court of Assistants of 27th August, 1588, Mr. Nicholas Spencer, the Master, reported to the Court that he and his Wardens had been sent for with others of the twelve Companies to await on the Lord Chancellor (Hatton), and Lord Treasurer (Lord Burleigh), by whom it was declared unto them that Her Majesty had cause for the better maintenance of her arms and forces prepared against the invasion of this realm to use the help of her loving subjects the citizens of London in the loan of a certain sum

---

[1] The biographer of Sir Thomas Gresham states that at his death a considerable portion of his wealth consisted of gold chains.—Burgon, vol. 1, page 281. Nichols (vol. II, page 411, Elizabeth's Progress) gives an account, under date 17th September, 1583, of an assembly of 3,000 archers "Prince Arthur's knights" (of which corps Hugh Offley and Mulcaster were members), "sumptuously apparelled—942 having chains of gold around their necks"—who assembled at Merchant Taylors' Hall, and marched down Broad Street, where their Captain, "the Duke of Shoreditch" (a sobriquet gained by a great shot, Barlow), lived, to Finsbury and Smithfield, to carry out their military exercises.

[2] There were two other precepts to appear in rich costume with attendants—in November, 1600, when thirty persons of the most grave, tall, and comlie personages were to attend the Queen from Chelsea to Westminster, and the Master and Wardens ordered "the principal members whose bodyes were able to endure the extremity of the weather," to attend the Queen; and the other in January 1603, when James I entered London to take possession of the throne.

of money which the Lords assured the Master would be repaid to the Companies, and the Lords having apportioned the sum purposed by Her Majesty to be borrowed upon the Companies of London, the proportion required in loan of this Company was 5,000*l*. as appeared in a ticket thereof delivered to the Master, who was required to call the Company together; whereupon they resolved as the sum required was very great and hard to be levied, to appoint a Committee of the Master and Wardens, with Robert Dowe, Thomas Wilford, and Roger Abdy to consider upon some platform or proportionall ground how a less sum of 4,000*l*. shall be accepted and performed."

The first action of the Court had relation to the Bachelors' dinner on the Decollation day which was "postponed indefinitely, in consideration of the busy and troublous times of the provision of munitions and other things for the defence of the realm," and the Committee then interviewed the Lords of the Council.

At the Court of the 9th, the Master reported that the Lord Chancellor and Lord Treasurer refused to abate the loan, but that the same might be levied by assessment of the Master and Wardens and all the brethren free of the Company wherever resident, and that the Master and Wardens should return to their honours the names of all refusing to pay, with the sums allotted for payment. It was thereupon decided that the Master and Wardens with the other members of the Court should go through the list of the Bachelor Company and set down the names of all those who were of known ability to pay their proportion, and that the remainder should be assessed upon the Court and Livery.

This was accordingly done, and at a Court of 17th August it was decided that a ticket should be sent to every person assessed, on which should be entered the amount due and the date of payment in this form, viz. :—

"You are to bring in and pay at the Merchantailors Hall, at or before the 28th of this month 50*l*.,[1] to be lent to the Queen's Majesty for six months, parcel to the sum assessed by the Lords of the Council upon this Company, whereof fail you not as you will answer at your peril."

With this entry the Company's records of the transaction end, but not so other records, for the loan was raised when Sir George Bond (the Haberdasher) was Lord Mayor, at the peril of imprisonment. The proceedings taken against defaulters are thus

---

[1] Or such other sum as may have been assessed.

explained to the Lord Treasurer by Martin Calthorp, his successor, in a letter of the 9th November, 1588,[1] "that he had called before him those refusing to pay and living in the city, and entreated them to contribute, and those refusing to pay he had committed to prison, where they do remain."

It is perhaps a remarkable fact regarding this great national deliverance that the Merchant Taylors' records should be absolutely silent, and but for the Queen's necessity for money, no mention whatever would have been made of it. However, from other sources of information we find what array of men were furnished by London, and that the command of three, if not four, brigades was held by Merchant Taylors. Thus Robert Offley was Captain of Basinghall; Gerard Gore of Cripplegate; John Swinnerton of Farringdon; and Medlicote of Queenhithe.[2]

What was the wealth of London or the distribution of employment therein at any early date must be a matter of speculation rather than of fact, but in the mayoralty of Sir Thomas Lodge (1562) there were (it is said) in all 327 merchants in London, and of these Strype assigns only 25 to the Merchant Taylors Company.[3]

How far either estimate may be true we have no definite knowledge, but according to another authority, writing in 1557,[4] "there were many merchants in London who possessed of from 50,000*l*. to 60,000*l*. sterling, all, or the greater part in ready money," which is scarcely consistent with Hume's[5] statement that at a later period, 1590, when wealth and prices had greatly risen, there were only four persons in London rated in the subsidy books so high as 400*l*. That wealth had been accumulated in this reign by the citizens who were also guildsmen is no longer a matter of controversy, and from this class the promoters of the new trading companies which then came into existence were drawn.

---

[1] 2 Burleigh Papers, page 632.

[2] 2 Burleigh Papers, page 606, "Arthur" was the Christian name of our guildsman, and "Anthony" appears in the list.

[3] Vol. 2, Bk. 5, page 291.

[4] Col. State Papers (Venetian), 1884.

[5] Vol. 5, Appendix 3. In the subsidy of 5 Elizabeth Sir B. Hicks stands at the head of the list of Aldermen at 100*l*., four aliens are in the higher assessment of 100*l*., and there are 7,123 on the Roll besides strangers assessed "by poll." In the Roll of 20th September, 1607, Halliday stands at 60*l*., Craven and Swynnerton in 70*l*. "in goods."—Col. S. P. Dom., James I, vol. xxvii i.

CHAP. XIV.] *Establishment of East India Company.* 255

In the reigns of Edward VI, guildsmen, such as Sir Thomas White, Sir Andrew Judde, and others, were the promoters of one of the earliest commercial trading companies, the Russian Company, which is still prosperous, and at the close of Elizabeth's reign a larger commercial enterprise was initiated which opened up India to her subjects.

On the 22nd September, 1599, a day that ought to be had in remembrance, a meeting of citizens was held at Founders' Hall under the presidency of the Lord Mayor (Sir Stephen Some, the Grocer), for the purpose of establishing a company to trade with the East Indies. Amongst the supporters of the project were to be found (Sir) R. Lee, (Sir) L. Halliday, and (Sir) Robert Hampson as Aldermen, with William Offley, John Swynnerton, Thomas Juxon, the Gores (Robert and Ralph) with other Taylors. A subscription was opened, the Lord Mayor heading the list with a sum of 200*l*., and these are some of the other subscriptions:— Sir L. Halliday, 1,000*l*.; Robert Hampson (Warden, 1594), 300*l*.; Ralph Hamer, 200*l*.; Will Harrison and Bond, 200*l*.; Sir Robert Lee, 300*l*.; Will Offley, 200*l*.; W. and S. Gore, 300*l*.; and Sir John Swynnerton, 300*l*.[1]

A petition[2] to the Crown for a grant of incorporation was determined upon, and as the result on the 31st December, 1601, letters patent were issued, setting forth "that for the honour of the realm of England" and "as greatly tending to the honour of our nation, the wealth of our people, and the encouragement of them in their good enterprise," the petitioners were incorporated as "The Governors and Company of Merchants trading unto the East Indies," with a monopoly of the trade for 15 years of those districts which were included in the patent.

The government of the new Company was framed on the analogy of a Guild, that is to say a Master or Governor was appointed with 24 members as a Court or Committee to aid him, all to be sworn in for one year and then a new and annual election was to be had. Apprentices and freemen were to be admitted, the oath of the freeman being in outline the same as the freeman's oath to the Master of his Guild.[3]

---

[1] Cal. S. P. (E .I.), pages 99-101, 105, and the List of Incorporated Members in 1600, page 115, and of Adventurers in 1601-2, page 123.

[2] Besides the other contributors there are included in the letters patent Thomas Juxon, William Chambers, Robert Offley, Robert Brooke, Henry Polstead, William Greenwell, Robert Johnson, Robert Buck, Edmund Spencer, and Richard Wright.

[3] Bruce's Annals of the East India Company, page 159.

Under this charter no joint stock capital was to be subscribed, but each voyage or venture was fitted out by members with such sums as they each pleased to underwrite. The cost of the first voyage is said to have been 68,373*l*., and when the second voyage was completed and the accounts made up the profit of both is said to have been 95*l*. per cent.

Members of the Guild were on the Committee, and of some of the ventures Sir L. Halliday was the treasurer, and William Harrison the auditor. After James I had granted another charter (31st May, 1609), it was deemed expedient by the proprietors or members to subscribe a "joint stock capital" of 429,000*l*., and to conduct the affairs of the Company, with a duly organised staff, which was ultimately established in the House of Sir Will Craven in Leadenhall Street.

The civic or parliamentary offices filled by members of the Guild may be taken as another criterion of wealth, and during the period under our notice the Merchant Company furnished several Sheriffs and Lord Mayors, thus :—

> Thomas Offley, Master in 1547, Sheriff in 1553, Lord Mayor in 1556.
> William Harper, Master in 1553, Sheriff in 1556, Lord Mayor in 1561.
> Thomas Rowe, Master in 1557, Lord Mayor in 1568.
> John Olyff,[1] Master in 1564, Sheriff in 1568.
> William Kympton, Master in 1570, Sheriff in 1576.
> Anthony Radcliffe, Master in 1577, Sheriff in 1585.
> Hugh Offley, Sheriff in 1588.
> Robert Hampton, Warden in 1588–94, Sheriff in 1599.
> Robert Lee, Warden in 1590, Lord Mayor in 1602

While in the early years of James's reign men who had risen to eminence in their Guild, came to hold higher civic offices, as :—

> Leonard Halliday, Warden in 1588–93, Lord Mayor in 1605.
> William Craven, Warden in 1593, Lord Mayor in 1610.
> John Swynnerton, Lord Mayor in 1612.

How many Merchant Taylors other than Richard Hilles were members of the Common Council is not recorded, but it is

---

[1] Son of Sir John, the surgeon to Henry VIII, who died October, 1550; the son died January, 1577, and was buried at St. Lawrence Pountney Hill.

CHAP. XIV.] *Guildsmen who were M.P. for London.* 257

not unreasonable to suppose that many others were so, as the Guilds and the Corporation were in Tudor times far more closely allied than they are at the present day.

Turning to politics the Guild was not without considerable influence throughout the century. This is evidenced by the part which some of its members played (as we read in Hilles' life) when the throne became vacant by the death of Edward VI, and Sir Thomas White was elected as Mayor. His decided action in Wyatt's rebellion threw the weight of the political influence of the Guild in favour of Queen Mary. Neither at the latter part of the century was the Company wanting in men to discharge the higher duty of representing their fellow citizens in Parliament. In that of 1558-9 Richard Hyde and in 1572 William Fleetwood were returned as members, and the latter sat for many years.[1] Of the Parliament in 1592 and 1597, George Sotherton (Master in 1589) was a member; and lastly in the Parliament of 1602, Richard Gore (also Master in 1602) sat for London.

There is another document in Elizabeth's reign which may be taken for what it is worth, namely, a list[2] of "the names of sondry the wisest, and best merchants in London to deale in the weightiest cares of the citie as occasion is offered," found in a handwriting which is unknown, but apparently correct, with the period to which the list refers, and preserved (1683) amongst the Lansdowne MSS. in the British Museum.

The date was probably after Sir Thomas Offley's death in 1582, as his name is not on the list. Many of the names are familiar to any one conversant with the affairs of the Merchant Taylors Company, and of the 99 names, the Merchant Taylors' records show that 27 of the persons so named are on their roll of freemen.[3]

From the materials which have offered themselves to our notice, it is evident that the guildsmen of the Merchant Taylors Company held a very creditable position at the close of the period under notice, and it would be interesting could we find any authentic record of the ordinary expenditure in the households of these men; such, for instance, as held office or formed the Court of

---

[1] William Fishe is given by Stowe as a member of Parliament and of the Merchant Taylors, but he is not found on the books.

[2] Notes and Queries, January, 1877. It also contains the names of lawyers, and Fleetwood is entered as of the Middle Temple, "very learned and riche."

[3] Appendix 31, page 404.

Assistants. The only definite figures that are available to us are the sums paid for house-rent by some two or three,[1] who were tenants of the Company, thus Donkyn's house in St. Michael's, Cornhill, was held at a rent of 2*l*. 13*s*. 4*d*.; Sir Thomas Rowe paid for the house in Bishopsgate Street from 1554 to 1571, 15*l*.; Sir William Harper for Percyvale's house in Lombard Street, from 1553–4 to 1574–5, 10*l*.; and Richard Offley for the same to 1583, 13*l*. 6*s*. 8*d*., subject to fine of 410*l*.; Richard Hilles for a house in the Quadrant, Vintry, paid 200*l*. fine and 3*l*. per annum from 1574 to 1602, or the equivalent at 12*l*. per cent. of a rental of 27*l*. 19*s*. 1*d*.[2]

If the rent formed one-tenth part of the total cost of domestic life in those days, we have an approximate estimate. But the cost of living rose considerably during Elizabeth's reign. "I know" (writes a resident of 1598) "that a gentleman cannot maintain his port or hospitality as his ancestors in former days, for his father and grandfather paid but 20*s*. an ox, 3*s*. a mutton, 2*s*. a calf, 6*d*. a goose, 4*d*. a capon, 2*d*. a hen, and 2*d*. a pig, and for all other household provision the like rate. Now there is not anything that belongs to housekeeping, but it is a triple charge over it, and whereas 100*l*. per annum was a competent living to maintain good hospitality, now 300*l*. a year will not defray the cost of such a house, rateably proportioning all necessaries thereunto belonging, without exceeding his accustomed plenty,"[3] and in the same year Bancroft (Bishop of London) returned "his needful household expenses" at 760*l*. per annum.[4]

The cost of particular items are easily ascertained from works of authority, but these items differ in proportion in each household, and from those of the present day expenditure. When Wild Darrell[5] came up to London with six or seven servants in 1589 he was lodged in Warwick Lane, and the items of his expenditure from the 16th April to the 14th July are preserved. His washing, the first item that presents itself to notice, which was a small

---

[1] See an agreement for ecclesiastical dues on London rents in 1457, printed in Vol. I, Hugh's London, page 102.

[2] The Company extended the lease in February, 1574, for fifty years, from Ladyday, 1575, reducing the rent thereby (at the same rate of interest) to 27*l*. 1*s*. 5*d*. per annum.   [3] Rye, page 197.

[4] Cal. S.P., (Elizabeth) page 44. Whitelock in 1604, living in Fleet Street, spent in the first year of his marriage 172*l*. 1*s*. 11*d*., and in 1612, 389*l*. per annum, his earnings being 188*l*. 6*s*. 8*d*., and 500*l*. and upwards (Camden Society, 1858, page xiv).

[5] Hall's Elizabethan Age, 1886, pages 99, 205–233.

one in many households,[1] shows a greater care for personal cleanliness, and amounted to 17s. 5d. His diet, which was largely supplemented by game, fish, and garden stuff from Littlecote, cost 42l. 6s. 10d., and "his charges of coming down," or in other words, returning home, starting and sleeping at Hounslow on the 14th, at Reading on the 15th, and reaching home on the 16th July, 3l. 7s. 4d. His usual method of getting about London was by boat on the Thames—for the roadways were execrable, and the total cost was 1l. 4s. 3d., the fares ranging from 2d. to 10d. extending on occasions up to Fulham, down the river to Ratcliff. "Horsemeat and shoeing" was a larger item, amounting to some 15l. or more.

Even in and about London there was little locomotion save on horseback, and the servants who were attendants on the master or mistress abroad exceeded the necessity for domestic service. The retired Taylor, Stephen Piers, required in 1467 for himself and wife "an honest man chyld," and "an honest mayde" to wait on them when going abroad, and according to Chaucer, the Alderman's wife:

> "yclelpt Madame,
> And gon to vigilies at byfore
> And have a mantel riallyche i-bore."[2]

These attendants became more numerous in the sixteenth century. "Gentlemen[3] are accompanied by their servants more or less, according to their grades and revenues, all of them in doublets without kirtle or cloak. One servant usually follows with a valise on his shoulder, or a clothe bag containing his master's cloak, hat, a book, and other things, the rest of his servants all carry a little round buckler, with a sword, many of them having two, one out of the girdle, and the other within it. Those who wear a long gown instead of a Spanish cape, have their sword and buckler carried by one of the servants. The 'miladies' use neither carts nor coaches but go on horseback preceded by footmen and followed by maids of honour on foot, or they have one or two of them on horseback." Coaches did not appear in use till 1564, when the Queen had one, and they did not come into common use until 1605, and in April, 1609, the coach hire in London for a day was 2s. 6d.[4]

---

[1] Our English Home, pages 90-2.
[2] Prologue, lines 376-8.
[3] Report of Venetian Ambassador, 1557, App., 1670 [171], Col. State Papers.
[4] Shuttleworth Accounts, Cheetham Society (1857), page 517.

It was, therefore, of necessity that each man whose business took him to the country or even to the suburbs of London, should keep a horse, and hence the guildsmen were sworn to "ridings," and were able to appear on horseback when summoned to any pageant.

The educational attainments of the Taylors was probably on an average with other guildsmen. Sir Thomas White left school at fourteen, but his colleague, Richard Hilles, was more highly educated, and was probably far above the intelligence of those with whom his guild life was passed. The records bear the signatures of Auditors, Renter Wardens, and (after 1572) the Court of Assistants, and looking over these only four guildsman used marks, thus:—

R. Tonge, Warden 1545, Auditor 1549, made mark 66.
T. Pierson, Warden 1584, Auditor 1586-7, made mark P T P.
R. Cox, Warden 1600, made mark R. C.
G. Prescott, Warden 1622, made mark T.[1]

But whatever may have been the social and intellectual status of the guildsmen of the century, we may fairly claim for them an honest desire manifested to do their duty as guildsmen to their fellow citizens. Taking the wants of London to be *grammar schools*, they established a noble one; or the *Universities* to need help, and they, or rather one member planted a College, and others Scholarships. If the *poor* needed succour Donkyn, Dowe, and many others supplied it, and if as it seems to be the case that hospitality or feasting increased, still it conduced to charity, as is evidenced by their gifts which still continue to enrich the Guild, for usefulness in that and succeeding centuries.

---

[1] I am indebted to the search of Mr. Chambers for this note.

CHAPTER XV.

THE COMPANY IN THE EARLIER YEARS OF JAMES I.

James I's reign opens a new era in Guild history, p. 261.—Fortunes of Merchant Taylors at his accession in the ascendant, p. 261.—Lord Mayor, Sir Robert Lee, p. 262.—Sir John Swynnerton, Sheriff, p. 262.—Richard Gore, M.P., Master, p. 263.—Nowel Sotherton, p. 263.—Assessments by precepts, p. 264.—Number of members in the Company, p. 264.—Merchant Taylors premier Company for Lee's year, p. 264.—Payments to John Stowe and for school boys' pageant, p. 264.—Order for Speech by school boy to the King, p. 265.—Plague, p. 265.—Lee knighted, p. 265.—Coronation, p. 266.—Three other members knighted, p. 266.—Fine for renewal of Charter, p. 266.—Reduction thereof by the Lord Chancellor's man, p. 266.—Claim for concealed lands, p. 267.—Reference to Mr. Baron Saville, p. 267.—Letter of January, 1604, from Crown officers, p. 268.—Master and Wardens of that period, p. 269.—Court of 9th February, p. 269.—Recorder retained, p. 270.—Mayoralty of Sir L. Halliday, p. 270.—Session of 1606, p. 270.—Recorder's advice as to claim of Crown, p. 271.—Clothworkers agree to support Bill, p. 271.—Merchant Taylors contribute 100l., p. 272.—Act of 4 James I (local and personal), p. 272.—The case against the Guilds under the Chauntries Collegiate Act, p. 273.

THE reign of James I opened a new era to the London Guilds—one of advancing commercial prosperity, as resulting from new enterprises lying beyond the purposes of their incorporation, which at the instance of the King, were undertaken by them. Upon his accession, James found the fortunes of the Merchant Taylors Company in the ascendant, and one of their members, Sir Robert Lee, in possession of the civic throne.

Elizabeth died at Richmond early in the morning of the 24th March, 1602, and Lee was summoned to Whitehall with the members of the Privy Council to determine the right of succession, and, as the result of that meeting, to subscribe a declaration (to which the names of others were added[1]) " that James of Scotland was the lawful and undoubted heir to the English Crown."[2]

---

[1] Chamberlayne (Present State of Great Britain), states that he subscribed first before all the great officers of State and Nobility, being said to be, on the death of the Queen, the prime person of England.

[2] Lingard, vol. 7, page 3, and page 27, *ante.*

This done, the whole multitude, who were assembled in front of the Palace, proceeded to the Cross at Cheapside, where Sir Robert Cecil with his own voice proclaimed James as King.

In a short interval of only four days, on the 28th, a letter[1] was addressed from Holyrood House by the King to Sir Robert Lee and his brethren, the Aldermen, thanking them for their "great forwardness" in proclaiming him King, and "wherein" (his letter continued) "you have given a singular good proof of your ancient fidelity, a reputation hereditary to that our city of London, being the chamber of our Imperial Crown."

Not only the Lord Mayor—but one of the Sheriffs (Sir) John Swynnerton, was also a Merchant Taylor—who, from the illness of his colleague (Pemberton) had to lead out his fellow citizens on horseback with their cloaks of velvet and chains of gold to Stamford Hill, there to receive the King on the 7th May on his entry into Middlesex from Scotland, and conduct him to the Master's House at the Charter House,[2] the first place in which he was lodged as King in London. Both these members, each from the country, like many others of the successful men whose lives present themselves to our notice in these pages, worthily represented the Company.

Lee came from Bridgenorth, was apprenticed to Anthony Radclyff, a highly respected member of the Guild, and became free of the city in October, 1572. He served only the office of Warden (in 1590), for he escaped service in the Company by becoming an Alderman (of Walbrook) in 1593, Sheriff in 1594, and Lord Mayor in 1602-3. He lived but a short time in James's reign—dying on the 28th January, 1605, and leaving an apprentice loan fund to be administered in favour of the Clothworker members of the Guild. His widow and sons did some injustice to his memory by refusing to provide, as he had promised that his estate should do, for a poor widow in the new almshouses, who, as a consequence, had to be removed, and another widow (readily supplied by another benefactor) installed in her room.[3]

Swynnerton (described on the records as an officer to Her Majesty[4] and by Bishop Hall as a vehement advocate for the press and a lover of learning),[5] was of the well-known family, then, as now, flourishing with honour in the county of Stafford. John, the father,

---

[1] Maitland, vol. i, page 282.   [2] Nichols, James' Progress, vol. 7, page 113.
[3] Court entry, 2nd August, 1606.   [4] Court, 24th October, 1602.
[5] Vol. 5, page 78, of his works (Oxford, 1837).

came into connection with the Company as apprentice to Galfridie Vaughan, and became free on the 12th March, 1562. He was Warden in 1596 and 1600, and Master in 1606–7, dying in 1608, at whose funeral dinner, on the 3rd November, Mr. Robert Dowe's "commendable grace" was first used. The son was free by patrimony in October, 1589. When he was in course of election to the Livery he was elected as Sheriff, and never served in any of the Guild offices, save that of attending the Court of Assistants.[1] He was a man of wealth, farming the Customs[2] duties, and, notwithstanding Fulke Greville's sneer, a man of ancient pedigree, able to purchase from the Marquis of Winchester his mansion house in Austin Friars, in 1602.[3] He died in December, 1616,[4] and both father and son are said to be buried in St. Mary's Aldermanbury.

Besides in these higher offices, in the Mastership the Company was well represented, as the chair was held by Richard, the descendant of John Gore, of 1399, a family distinguished for integrity in their dealings with the Guild, and in later years ennobled. He was also returned as member for the city to the first Parliament of James.

For due reception of the Sovereign, a Select Committee was appointed[5] by the Common Council consisting of sixteen members, four being Aldermen, and one from each of the twelve great Companies. As the Merchant Taylors was the premier Company, so was their member such for the year. The guildsman sent to act for the Company was Nowel Sotherton, of a family which had been honourably connected with the Company, through George Sotherton (the apprentice of Roger Baynton and free on 24th October, 1561); though some of them had fallen into decay. John, his father, was appointed as a Clerk in the Exchequer in 1579, and became a coursetour therein—Nowel, admitted

---

[1] At the Court on 10th July, 1602 (Mr. John Swynnerton, Alderman, being present), "The said Mr. Ald. Swynnerton who was lately elect to the said worshipful degree and calling of an Alderman, and yet never of the Livery of this Company, nor ever bore any office in this house, was with a general consent admitted, and sworn one of the Assistants and Counsellors of this Society, who very lovingly did accept thereof and faithfully promised to do his best endeavour for the credit and good of this Company."

[2] In September, 1613, he wrote to Rochester for a renewal of his farm of the sweet wine duties, urging that he had raised the revenue 60,000*l.* per annum.—Cal. State Papers, page 199, see also page 150.

[3] Nichols Progresses, Elizabeth, vol. 3, page 598. Greville lived in Broad Street Ward, and was assessed in the subsidy of September, 1607, at 9*l.*—Cal. Dom. Ser.

[4] Cal. State Papers, James, I, page 414.

[5] Nichols Progresses, James I, vol. 1, page 376.

to the Company by redemption in September, 1570, was of Gray's Inn —but no lawyer. As connected with the Exchequer, and familiar with its practice, he was made the first Cursitor Baron, an office for taking the Sheriff's accounts, or other[1] formal matters of the department but not then judicial. He had served the Company as Master in 1597, and was a man of reputation.

Of course, the citizens had to be assessed, to meet the expenses of the King's progress, and in these assessments the Merchant Taylors Company stood for and paid, as at the close of Elizabeth's reign, larger sums than any one of the other twelve Companies. For James's entry "into his highest city chamber of his supreme crown as towards his honourable coronation" the members paid 234*l.* out of 2,500*l.*, and 37*l.* 8*s.* 9*d.* for the assessment of 400*l.*[2]

Fortunately for the information of their successors a complete list of the members and of their contributions has been preserved,[3] and it appears from the assessment to James I's coronation that the Master and Wardens, Assistants, and Livery consisted of 80, and the Wardens Substitute, Sixteen Men, and the Bachelors Company (the latter divided into four quarters), stood thus: Watling Street Quarter, 90; Candlewick Quarter, 48; Fleet Street Quarter, 14; Merchant Taylors' Quarter, 47; add the Wardens Substitute and Sixteen Men, 20; making a total of 299 persons.[4]

As "having the Lord Mayor of their Company" at the accession of a sovereign to the throne was an advantage which the Taylors were anxious to enjoy, the precedents of earlier reigns were looked to. When Lee came to the mayoralty they had been, as we have already seen, very anxious to do honour to that pageant. We find from the accounts of special payments for the pageant two entries which throw some light upon their proceedings. The first, "Item, paid John Stow, for great pains by him taken in searching for such as have been Mayors, Sheriffs, and Aldermen of the said Company, 10*s.*"

The second is in these words:—

"Item, p^d to Mr. Haines the Coy's Schoolmaster at their School at St L'cee P'tney hill for his charge for preparing a wagon

---

[1] Vol. 36, Arch., page 27. [2] See Appendix 32, page 405.
[3] Memorials, page 590.
[4] In March, 1624, when for Sir John Gore's mayoralty no brother was to be charged "but such as shall be of ability to beare the same," the numbers were: Bachelors in Foyne 72, in Budge 48, and, say, Freemen of the Bachelors Company 231, or a total of 351 contributors.

& appareling 10 Scholars w^h did represent the 9 Muses and the god Apollo before the Lord Mayor in Cheapside, 7*l*. 13*s*. 4*d*."

The incidents of Elizabeth's progress[1] through the city upon her accession might have been remembered by other guildsmen besides John Stowe, but however that might have been, the Court had the fact within its cognisance on the 3rd April, and made this order :—

"Upon relation given at this Court that at the Coronation of or late most gracious Queen Elizabeth,[2] the Company of Mercers holding then the chief place, before all other companies in regard that Sir Thomas Leigh being one of their Company was then Lord Mayor of this City, the said Company of Mercers did cause a Scholar of their School to pronounce a short Speech unto Her Majesty. It is therefore thought fit in regard that this year our Company have the like precedency and also that our Company maintain a free Grammar School, that the Schoolmaster prepare one of our Scholars to pronounce some such short and pithie Speech as the Schoolmaster (upon good consideration) shall devise, which no doubt shall tend much to his own commendation and the credit of the Company. And it is agreed that as well all such charge as he disbursed in preparing his Scholars to make a show and speech in Cheapside on the day my Lord Mayor went to Westminster as also all other charge which he shall now disburse in preparing one of his Scholars to speak to the King shall be defrayed and borne by the Company."

The plague which was raging in London at this period obliged the authorities to delay the King's *state* progress through the city until March of the following year (after Lee had ceased to be Lord Mayor), but in James's passage from the Tower to his coronation on St. James's Day, 1603, although mention is made in the progress that one of Mulcaster's scholars at the door of the Free School of St. Paul's, founded by the Mercers, delivered a speech to the King, no reference whatsoever is made of the Merchant Taylors School or its scholars.[3]

Sir Robert Lee (who had been knighted on the 22nd May), was present by right at the coronation and the banquet, taking his barge from Three Cranes Wharf, together with such selected citizens[4] (probably the Committee) as he thought fit should accompany him. Upon the day following the coronation, the 26th

---

[1] Hayward's Elizabeth, page 10. [2] Part II, page 152.
[3] Nichol, page 307. [4] Nichol, vol. 1, page 223.

July, three other members of the Court (who were Aldermen) were knighted—Leonard Halliday, William Craven, and John Swynnerton.[1]

The "state" progress from the Tower to Westminster, which had been postponed, took place on the 15th March, 1603. As the Taylors were no longer the premier Company no special mention is made of them; but the various pageants given or performed at the several stations in the city, with the account of the proceedings of the citizens are very fully set out in the contemporary chronicles.[2]

At the commencement of every reign prior to that of William and Mary it was necessary for the Guilds to adjust with the Crown or its officers the fee to be paid by them for the Royal confirmation or re-grant of existing charters, and within a few months after the last incident the Taylors had approached the Lord Chancellor (Egerton) on the subject.

To Elizabeth on her accession the Taylors paid 15l., but the Goldsmiths only 6l., although the latter Company enjoyed precedence over the Taylors, and paid in the assessment of 1562 300l. to the Taylors 350l. On the present accession the Lord Chancellor had assessed the Goldsmiths in 8l., and the Taylors in 30l., or more than treble the fine imposed on the Goldsmiths. Now this was an injustice which the Taylors were loth to put up with, and therefore on the 12th May the Court resolved " (having regard to the great number of poor tailors), that the Goldsmiths were better able to pay than the Taylors, and therefore the Master and Wardens 'were entreated with Mr. Noel Sotherton to attend upon the Lord Chancellor desiring his Lordship that the Company might have reasonable favour, and be rated with other Companies of the city unless the Common Clerk (in the meantime) procure defalcations and abatement thereof.'"

We have no record of any interview with the Chancellor, and possibly Mr. Noel Sotherton, having a better knowledge of the method of adjusting such differences, put the Company into direct communication with "Mr. E. Thomason, the Chancellor's man," who, for the 3l. paid to him, got one-third of the fine reduced, as these entries show: "On the 13th August, 1604, the Court agreed that the sum of 3l. shall be bestowed upon Mr. E. Thomason, my Lord

---

[1] The cost of knighthood was 48l. 2s. 8d., and James, on the 17th July, 1603–4, had ordered that all persons having 40l. or upwards in land should accept knighthood or pay a fine (1 Nichol, page 203, and Vol. 4, page 1001.

[2] 1 Nichol, page 337, and Howes' continuation of Stowe.

Chancellor's man for procuring the fine of 30l., which my Lord Chancellor had taxed upon the Company for the confirmation of the Company's Charter from the King's most excellent Majesty to be reduced to 21l.;" and in the Master's account, 1605-6, the payment is entered thus : " Paid to my Lord Chancellor's man his gratuity for a suit made to my Lord for mitigating the fine of our charter, as by order of Court 13th August, 1604, may appear, 3l."

Scarcely had this claim been adjusted than an old—and to some Guilds a more formidable—one arose in the claim put forward against the Guilds for *concealed lands* under the Chauntries Collegiate Act of Edward VI.

The claim as against the Merchant Taylors Company is set out in a Court Minute of 19th July, 1604, in these words:—

"Whereas there is demanded of the Company divers arrearages (viz.), for a rent going out of a tenement in St. Mary, Wolchurch, at 4s. per annnm for 30 years ended at Michaelmas, Anno Primo James 6th ; and for a pension of 7l. for 55 years and a half, amounting to 488l. 10s. ; and for an other pension of 10l. 13s. 4d. by year for 55 years as aforesaid, amounting to 591l. 6s. 8d. : this day upon perusal of certain evidences taken out of the Treasury, it appeareth that the Company can show sufficient discharges for the same. And forasmuch as diverse other Companies and particular men are called in question upon the like occasions, and the examination thereof referred to Mr. Baron Savile, to whom ye Company are to show their discharge ; therefore two writings were taken out, one marked No. 1, and the other No. 29, and delivered to the Common Clerk ; and Mr. Nowell Sotherton, Mr. Wright, and the Common Clerk are entreated and appointed to attend Mr. Baron Saville, and to take care for the discharge thereof. And allowance given to them to bestow five or six pounds where they think fit for the better dispatch in the business; and it is ordered that a Book of Collections made by Mr. Wright of the Company's evidences when he was Clerk shall be fair engrossed in vellum by the Common Clerk of the Company, with such further additions as shall be requisite, which the Company require to be exactly done, and they will have consideration thereof."

The Company were quite prepared to meet the claim, and they had to do so before Saville, a lawyer of reputation, who, at the instance of Lord Burleigh, had been raised to the Exchequer Bench in July, 1598, and whose commission James had renewed, and to whom, in 1604, he had given the Chief Justiceship of the Palatine of Lancaster. Saville was therefore under obligation to James, which he might have considered himself to have repaid when he gave judgment in Bates' case in the King's favour, and sanctioned the imposition of customs duties by the Crown without the consent of Parliament.[1]

After an interval of six months this letter came from the Crown officers:—

"To our very Loving friends the Master and Wardens of the Company of Merchant Taylors.

"After our hearty commendations Whereas His Majesty finding his loving subjects much troubled and grieved with books of concealments whereby many have been put out of possession and lost their lands to the great disquiet of His Majesty's subjects, wherewith we have acquainted His Highness who hath granted his most gracious Commission under the Great Seal of England commanding us thereby to show all convenient favour we may and with speed to dispatch any his Majesty's subjects that shall seek a composition at our hands, wherein is any mispresion or other defect in their title or letters patent. And for that we understand that daily divers and sundry persons are and have been suitors to His Majesty to have had grants and leases of divers of your lands whereof we have made stay until we might advertize you of the same, who by his Majesty's gracious meaning are to have the preferment of the establishing of your possessions if you do not wilfully decrease your time, for which purpose we have appointed the third day of February next ensuing, at Dorset House, in Fleet Street, London, to sit by force of that Commission, desiring you to come to us yourselves or send some authorized from you, who may as there shall be cause come and compound with us for the same to His Majesty's use. And for readier dispatch with us, whom his Majesty hath appointed Commissioners for such services, we have appointed William Tipper, Gent[n], to attend us daily for such causes, who being always resident in London shall at all times be ready to follow this business and acquaint us with your cause as occasion shall serve. According to the equity whereof you may be sure to have a speedy composition and so be freed from all further troubles. And the arrearages and mesne profits to be likewise pardoned, which is one of the chiefest ends of this His Majesty's most gracious Commission. But if you shall not attend the day above said, then we let you know, that you do still remain subject to informations which by

---

[1] 2 State Trials, page 371. Baron Clarke, who married Barnabas Hilles' widow, concurred in the judgment. Part II, page 226.

any person on behalf of the King shall at any time hereafter be exhibited against you from the which neither we nor any other can free you, but by the benefit of this Commission only. And so we bid you heartily farewell. From the Court at Whitehall this 20th January 1604.

"Your loving friends,

"THO. DORSET.
"SUFFOLK.
"CRANBORNE.
"JO. POPHAM.

"THO. FLEMING.
"JO. SAVILE.
"EDW. COKE."

The Master of the Company at this time was Mr. Geoffrey Elwes,[1] a rising man, and therefore we may presume competent for his office. He was elected Alderman for Farringdon in December, 1605, and Sheriff in 1607. The Wardens were all men of accepted position and benefactors; they were Vernon, Hyde, Gerard Gore, and Medlycott, and these were the men who had to deal with the subject and advise the Court of Assistants as to the best course to adopt. Accordingly, on the 9th February, the Master brought this letter before the Court, apprising the Assistants "that the like letters were written to all or most of the Companies, and that Mr. Recorder hath promised to move the Lords and Commissioners concerning the same; since which my Lord Mayor had sent for the Wardens of the several Companies and demanded whether all the Companies would join together in such a course, as should be advised by learned Counsel, whereunto Master and Wardens prayed his Lordship to give them leave to advise and forbear answering until they had recommended his Lordship's motion to a Court of Assistants, for which purpose our Master specially called this Court. And upon relation now made by Mr. Wright, late Clerk of this Company, and now one of the Assistants of this house, who was the general Solicitor for the City and Companies about twenty years past, when Christopher Hatton procured from the late Queen a Grant of the city's concealed lands, that upon good and sound advice taken by our Company we were found to be clear and out of danger (notwithstanding other Companies found imperfections in their estates). It is now therefore resolved that it is not fit for this Company to join with other Companies, lest as great a burden should be imposed upon us as upon others whose titles are doubtful. And our Master and Wardens

---

[1] Page 183, note 1.

are entreated to make such answer to my Lord Mayor when his Lordship shall send for them. And it is ordered and agreed that Sir Henry Montague, the Recorder of London, shall be retained to be a Standing Counseller to this Company. And a fee of four pounds per ann. which was granted to Mr. Serjeant Crooke, the last Recorder, shall be now satisfied unto the said Sir Henry Montague, to be paid quarterly by 20s. a quarter, and to have continuance only during the Company's pleasure. And our Master is entreated to acquaint Mr. Recorder therewith, and to present him with 20s. presently, which 20s. shall be accounted as paid for our Ladyday's quarter, 1605, next ensuing."

The Recorder had come to his office in Sir Robert Lee's mayoralty, after the accession of James, and at his solicitation.[1] He was fortunately a man of character, and ultimately became the first Earl of Manchester, but so far as the Merchant Taylors were concerned no further notice was taken of this overture, and before any measures were adopted the Chair of the Chief Magistrate was occupied by another Merchant Taylor (Sir L. Halliday), who in September, 1605, was elected to be Lord Mayor.

However, it is certain that some attempt was made at legislation in the session of 1606, as on the 28th August, 1606, the Court came to this resolution :—

"Whereas Mr. Dyas, the Solicitor of the city, did prosecute two Bills in the Parliament House for the good of the several Companies, viz., one Bill for confirmation of land given to charitable uses, and another Bill for giving authority to Masters and Wardens to put their Ordinances in execution without suite or molestation in law. And albeit the said Bills were (engrossed) yet it hath been thought good that the money by him disbursed should be allowed by the several Companies. And whereas he allegeth that other Companies have satisfied and paid unto him five pounds apiece. It is agreed that our Master shall pay unto him the like sum, and the same to be allowed him again in his account."

But other Guilds might have been imperilled in their estates; and the Recorder attended the Court of the Clothworkers on the 13th April, 1607, and advised them to this effect.[2] He said "that there is a Bill pferred to the Parlyament howse touchinge th' assurance of the landes & tenementes belonginge to the severall Companyes of this Cittie, certen rents yssuinge out of wch said

---

[1] James's letters to Sir Robert Lee, 25th May, 1603.
[2] See vol. 1, page 335, London Livery Company Reports.

landes and tenements lymited to supersticious uses were purchased by the said sev'all Companyes of Kynge Edward the sixte in the fourthe yeare of his raigne." Of the legal merits of the claim put forward by the Crown, he spoke thus:—"The iudges & greatest Lawyers of this land then beinge of opinion that onely the rents ymployed or lymitted to supsticious uses were the Kynges,[1] but not the lands whereout those rents were yssuinge yet in these tymes the very landes have bynne & yet are in question."

Then he described the extortion to which the Guilds had been subjected: "And certen patentees in the tyme of the late Queene have gonne about, and yet doe, to entitle the said late Queene and the Kynges Matie that now is to the said lands and tenements (onely for theyr private gayne) as lands concealed from the Crowne, not caringe to bereave a nomber of poor people in this Citty & elsewhere in the Kyngdome of theyr beste and cheifest reliefe & mayntenance & by means of those patentees have drawen from the said sev'all Companyes many greate somes of money for composicon wth the said patentees for the landes, the rents whereof the Companyes had formerly purchased of the said late Kynge Edward the sixte. And so the saide Companyes havinge payd fyrst to the Kynge & after compounded wth the said Patentees for the saide rents and landes sev'ally for all the money they have departed with have at this pnte (of assurance) neither rents nor landes."

Such being the position of affairs, "the said Sr Henry Monntague shewed vnto the Company how beneficiall the passing of that byll in Parliament might be in generall to the whole Cittie & in p̃ticular to every private Company, and did advise that soe good meanes of peace and quiet for the establishinge of theyr landes to them and theyr successors in succeedinge tymes was not to be reiected but to be embraced, and wth all desired to know the purpose & determinacon of this Company whether they wolde ioyne wth the reste of the Companyes & contribute to the chardge of passinge the said byll or desiste and stand vppon theyr own defence."

The decision which the Clothworkers came to was to give (that which an unscrupulous adversary often gets) a sum of money for peace and security. "It was answered that this Company althoughe they knew theyr landes to be as cleare and free from

---

[1] See the statutes and cases collected to this effect in Vol. 1, Stephen's Ecclesiastical Statutes, page 294, and notes.

question as any other Company in London yet in respecte of the generall good w^ch (as is declared) by possibilitie may come to the whole Cittie and to the Companyes in pticuler they will not leave theyr bretheren but ioyne wth them in psequucon of the said Byll & in contribucon to the chardges thereof after a reasonable rate accordinge to the proporcon of the dannger they stand in case of concealement or purchase of rents lymited to supsticious vses."

The Merchant Taylors appear to have been equally patriotic to their fellow citizens, as their records contain the following entry relating to a Court of 6th July, 1607.

"Whereas the Right Worshipful Sir Henry Montague, Knight, Recorder of London hath taken great pains and care in procuring an Act of Parliament for assuring of land, granted and devised to the several Companies of this Citty, and is to bestow many gratifications to such as wellwishers and furthers of the same It is agreed that our Company shall contribute the sum of One hundred pounds towards the same charge. And that our Master shall pay the same to Mr. Recorder, and shall have it allowed in his account."

The Act local and personal of 4 James I, cap. 10, is another parliamentary sanction to the title of the Guilds to the obit lands which they purchased from the Crown. It recites "that the antient devises or grants made of lands, &c., to the several Companies they have used to the comfort of many good subjects and great relief of the poor, and other good and charitable uses." That these grants, &c., have been sought "to be avoided and His Majesty to be entitled thereto as concealed or unjustly detained from him;" but that His Majesty taking "knowledge of the several sums paid for the lands" both in the times of "Edward VI and Elizabeth," and of "the good and charitable employment of the said lands heretofore made, and at this time," and especially His Majesty taking knowledge of the letters patent of 14th July, 1550, since which time "divers doubts and questions have been moved whether the several rents mentioned in their letters or the messuages whereout those rents are mentioned in the same letters to be issuing or employed were concealed or wrongfully detained, and both for the one and the other divers compositions heretofore made."

Therefor as an enactment for taking away of all questions moved or stirred either concerning the said rents or messuages and respectively belonging to the said Companies the King (in

CHAP. XV.]   *Case under Chauntries Collegiate Act.*   273

substance) confirmed the title of the Merchant Taylors and other Companies, under the Letters Patent of the 14th July, 1550.

Thus closed for ever, as it was thought, until the Report of the Royal Commissioners[1] was presented to Parliament in 1884, all controversy between the Crown and the citizens in relation to the conduct of either in the time of Edward VI under "the Chauntries Collegiate Act:" for there is scarcely any transaction at this period less creditable to the Crown than that case presents upon the accepted *facts*, which are these: Parliament—to further the good, or as the statute styled them "pious" purposes, of establishing education and sustaining the poor, placed the Crown in trust of the obit rent-charges, which trust was accepted, but the rents were misapplied to secular uses. The trusteeship was then used to compel the Guilds to buy up the rent-charges from the Crown, on terms of great disadvantage to the purchasers; thus we have seen that, though the Merchant Taylors purchased for Fish's scholars a freehold estate at 10l.[2] per cent., they had to purchase the rent-charges from the Crown at double[3] the value, viz., 5l. per cent., the purchase-money being misapplied as the rents had been, to secular uses.

That the citizens of London, and notably those of the Merchant Taylors' Company, did—from pure motives previously unimpeached by the Crown,—establish schools, promote university teaching, and provide for the poor are matters of history; nor is it less notorious that while so doing they were harassed by false charges of concealment promoted by the Crown for speculative gain.[4] But Parliament, without absolving the Crown from its original trust for pious uses, and certainly not transferring such responsibility to others, has seen fit to confirm the title[5] of the Guilds to the rent-charges and the hereditaments from which they accrue. If, therefore, such a title as the Guilds hold is to be questioned at the instance of the Crown, no dealings with the Crown, even after a Parliamentary confirmation has been given, can ever avail, and the highest title that the law knows will have been destroyed.

The right of the Crown to inquire "into the original objects of the Guilds, and to ascertain how far such objects are now being carried into effect" is now what it was when Sir James Scarlett[6]

---

[1] Page 146, *ante*.   [2] Page 240.
[3] Page 147.   [4] Page 240, *et seq.*
[5] As to Statutes of Edward and Philip and Mary, see page 149.
[6] Parliamentary Papers (1852), Vol. XXII, App. B, page 25.

advised the Merchant Taylors Company on the issue of the former Royal Commission in 1833, that such right did not exist, but the Guilds readily answered the inquiries addressed to them by Her Majesty's Commissioners of 1884. Looking at the valuable reports which other Royal Commissioners have made on some of the more burning questions of the day, and at the reputation, honourable beyond impeachment, which some of Her Majesty's Commissioners of 1884 enjoyed, the Guilds might reasonably have expected after full inquiry made by the Commissioners that none of them would, as they have done, give currency by their Report to any misstatement of fact[1] calculated seriously to mislead Parliament in estimating the moral right of the citizens to their Guild property, which, we venture to submit, either antecedent knowledge or any subsequent inquiry would have prevented them from doing.

---

[1] Extract, page 146, *ante.*

CHAPTER XVI.

THE BANQUET TO JAMES I AND HIS SON HENRY, PRINCE OF WALES, 1607.

*Royal guests in earlier years, p. 275.—The feast of St. John, p. 276.—Celebrated in song, p. 276.—Clothworkers' dinner, p. 276.—James I expresses his intention to dine with the Taylors, p. 277.—Merchant Taylors' record of the feast, p. 277.—Number of guests, p. 277.—Preparations made on 27th June, p. 278.—Money from the Treasury, p. 278.—Standing Committee, p. 278.—Stewards, p. 278.—Two Caterers, p. 279.—Butler and wine, p. 279.—Ben Jonson's engagement, p. 280.—Hangings, &c., for the Hall, p. 280.—Plate hired, p. 281.—Waiters appointed, p. 281.—Watch on the Hall premises, p. 282.—Committee to meet daily, p. 282.—Court of 7th July, p. 283.—King, Prince, and Queen invited, p. 283.—Lord Mayor and Aldermen not to be invited, p. 284.—Recorder attends to remonstrate, p. 284.—Purses of gold to be provided, p. 285.—Provision laid in for the feast, and the cost of it, p. 286.—Butlers, Cooks, and Waiters, p. 286.—Utensils for the table, p. 287.—Messes for the King and others, p. 287.—Preparation of the Hall for guests, p. 287.—Reception of the King, p. 288.—Plague, p. 288.—Lord Mayor and Aldermen at the Hall, p. 288.—Retinue of the King, p. 289.—The physician, p. 289.—Cooks, p. 289.—Lords, p. 290.—Enters the Hall, p. 291.—Performances, p. 291.—Pageant of performers, p. 291.—King's dinner, p. 291.—Dr. Bull's and Mr. Gyle's performance, p. 291.—The Prince's dinner, p. 291.—The Recorder's address, p. 292.—Master presents the purse of gold, p. 292.—The Clerk the roll of Honorary Members, p. 292. —List of these from 1351 to 1562, p. 293.—Notes of these Members, p. 293. —Purse presented to the Prince, p. 304.—Made an Honorary Member, p. 305.—Lords also, p. 305.—Master and Wardens installed into office with garlands, p. 305.—Farewell, p. 305.—Settlement of accounts, p. 305.—Dr. Bull and Mr. Gyles made Liverymen, p. 305.—Ambassadors apply for certificate of freedom, p. 306.—Master's contribution to the feast, p. 306.—Final items, accounts, and total cost, p. 306.—*NOTE. *Items of expenditure for feast, pp. 307-17.*

WE have now to relate a very different incident in relation to James I and the Company, namely, the feast given to him at his own invitation, and at a cost hitherto unprecedented in the history of the Guild. That Sovereigns had been entertained by the Company, is a tradition which gathers round the names of Edward III, and Henry VII; but that such an entertainment was given to James I, is a fact recorded on the books of the Company, with many details of arrangements and expense.

We have already noticed that the Company's great feast of the year, was that on St. John's Day, when the statutes ordained that the Master's election should be proclaimed openly in the hall "afore such estates, honourable and worshipful guests" as were present. That distinguished guests were invited the early accounts show: as entries[1] for "boat hire" paid are found when the Master and Wardens went to invite the Archbishop or the Chancellor, or (as in 1464-5) Edward IV and his Queen, with other noble guests, or (in 1468-9) "Ambassadors" to the feast.

According to the old song said to have been written and sung on this occasion, there were but "four great *Feasts* of England," and that "all others be but dinners called." These were "St. George's Feast the first of all," "the Honoured Mayor of London the second feast" ordains, "The Serjeants of the Law another feast affords," and the fourth which deserved "a gallant grace," was that of "the Taylors Company."[2]

If, therefore, any Company was to be honoured by the King, the Merchant Taylors might not unreasonably expect to be selected to give him an entertainment. Accordingly in July, 1607, after the mayoralty of Halliday had expired, and he had been succeeded in office by Sir John Wait (a Clothworker), the banquet took place.

On the 12th June, James had dined with the Lord Mayor at his house adjacent to Clothworkers' Hall, and after dinner when at the point of departure, the King was interviewed by the Master and Wardens of that Company, and solicited to enter their hall to accept the freedom. This he accordingly did, and drank to them as his brethren of the Clothworkers.[3]

Under what circumstances, therefore, the King so soon after this dinner resolved upon another, is not explained. All that the record states, is that the Company were informed of his intention "to dyne at our hall." Although the event is noticed in the chronicles of the time, the entries in the Merchant Taylors' books relating to it, though printed,[4] have never been published, nor the details, or cost of the "menu" given. These books, therefore, contain a valuable record of a civic feast in the early years of

---

[1] 1454-5, 1455-6.

[2] The Crown Garland of Golden Roses, London, 1692, Vol. 1. Wilson's Merchant Taylors' School, page xxii.

[3] Nichol's Progresses, James I, page 132.

[4] Memorials, pages 153-180.

CHAP. XVI.]   *Record of the Feast.*   277

James I's reign, and extracts from these will be made the basis of the present text.

The reader by looking through the chapter[1] relating to "The Hall and its Contents," will be able to appreciate the resources of the Company in furniture and utensils for such an entertainment. They had no establishment of servants, nor was there any contractor as there is now, able, with equal facility, to feed either 100 or 1,000 guests: but all the arrangements for feasting the King had to be improvised by the Company, and taken in hand by its various members.

The number of principal guests for the hall would approximately appear to have been, say—

Court and Livery	80
President and Fellows of St. John (say)	4
King and Prince	2
Ambassadors and Lords	22
King's attendants named	64
	172

Besides divers esquires and servants to the King, Prince, and noblemen (who would have to be fed after the chief guests had been provided for), and the swarm of servants hired by the Company.

The entries begin on the 27th June, thus:—

"The Company are informed that the King's most excellent Maj^tie. with our gracious Queene and the noble Prince and diverse Honble. Lordes and others determyne to dyne at our Hall on the day of the Elecõn of the Master and Wardens: therefore this Meeting was appoynted to advyse and consult howe everye thinge may be performed for the reputacõn and creditt of the Company and to give his Majestie best lyking and contentment."

The Master in Office was John Swynnerton, the elder, and his Wardens were Richard Wright, Andrew Osborne, Edward Atkinson, and William Albany, all men of experience; and those to be declared as their successors on the occasion of the King's visit, were John Johnson, as Master, and Thomas Owen, Richard Scales, John Wooller, and Randolph Woolley, the two Renters being ultimately benefactors to the Company.[2]

---

[1] Chapter V, page 82.
[2] Memorials, pages 303 and 312.

The election day was usually held early in July, and, therefore little time was available to gather in funds to meet the immediate cost of preparation, therefore, it was "agreed for the present that the whole money shalbe laide oute and disbursed out of the comon Stock of the Company, and when it is knowne what the whole charges will amount to, the Master and Wardens will referr themselves to the consideraĉon of the Assistants what is fytt for them to allowe out of their private purses towards the same chardges."

But responsibility must be delegated, and therefore a Committee was formed. "The Company have entreated and authorized the Master and four Wardens, Mr. Baron Sotherton, four Aldermen and all the old Masters, and Mr. Vernon, or any six of them, to be Committees to determyne, direct and appoynte all matters concerninge the said greate and noble entertaynement and what they or any six of them shall appoynte the Company will approve and allowe." Sotherton had been previously useful, and John Vernon (the noble benefactor of 1615[1]) had served twice as Warden,[2] and was the Company's Master of 1609. He is described "as the blind Merchant Stapler who died without issue," and he lies buried in St. Michael's, Cornhill, where to his memory the Company in 1696[3] erected a bust, which is still standing, to remind the Company at their yearly visitation at Christmas of the charity which he would have them carefully distribute amongst their brethren.

It was usual for the Company to make a fixed allowance for dinner, and to appoint Stewards from the Livery for expenditure and to leave these officers, with the Master and Wardens, to bear any extra expenses which they might be pleased to incur. It became part of the Auditors' duty to protect the corporate funds from any extra charge, which the Stewards and not the Company ought to bear. Stewards were therefore appointed on this occasion. "Mr. Thomas Rowe,[4] one of the Assistants, Robert Jenkinson,[5] Thomas Johnson,[6] and William Greenewell,[7] three of the Livery, to be Stewards to receive money and to make all provisions and perform all other matters which belongeth to Stewards to undergoe."

Accordingly the Stewards would need advice as to the provision to be made for such a feast, and the highest authorities for city

---

[1] Memorials, page 306.
[2] In 1599 and 1604.
[3] Court Entries, 3rd July, 1696, and 18th March, 1697.
[4] Warden, 1599-1603, Master, 1610.
[5] Warden, 1609-12, Master, 1615.
[6] Warden, 1610-13, Master, 1615.
[7] Warden, 1614-16, Master, 1618.

hospitality were the officers of the Lord Mayor and Sheriffs. Accordingly we find "Lansdale the Lord Maior's Cater, and Sotherne one of the Sheriffs' Caters are appoynted to be in attendance upon the Stewards to informe them of all things necessary for such an entertainment, and to consider what number of messes are requisite and howe many and what dishes, and howe and where the same shalbe disposed, and to draw out Bills of the Diett to be considered of by the Committees, and to doe all such services as doth apperteyne to Caters to performe."[1]

But that the Court might be kept informed of his Majesty's wishes and purpose, "Mr. Warden Wright is entreated from tyme to tyme to attend at Court to understand from my Lord Chamberlain and my Lord of Salisbury, what complements are fytt to be performed by the Companye and to knowe if his Majestie hould his purpose and resolucõn to come."

Then and for many years after, the wine for a feast was brought in and specially purchased for each occasion. Here the cellar had to be put in order to receive it, which service Bellew, the Under Butler, did at a cost of 1*l*. 10*s*. 11*d*. Then some competent judge of wine must be appointed to make the selection and give directions in these matters, and therefore "Matthewe Springham,[2] one of the Lyvery, is entreated to be chief, and Master Butler to commaund all the Butlers that shalbe used in this service." The varieties of wine[3] were Gascoine (possibly Mountrose, deemed a liquor for a lord), Cunnock, Canara, Claret, Rhennish, and white. Little importance was attached to the quality of the wine, so long as the spice was strong and aromatic. Thus, Ipocras was hotly infused with spice, and drank after every meal as the favourite of all home made wines. The expenditure with Mr. Atkinson amounted to 61*l*. 12*s*. 7*d*., and 16*l*. 7*s*. 6*d*. for the hire of Butlers. Probably ale and beer fell to the care of the same member to purchase. There were three qualities at 6*s*. 8*d*., 8*s*., and 10*s*. per barrel, with a tun[4] of Court Beere at 1*l*. 16*s*., a total expenditure of 12*l*. 9*s*., which with the wine contrasts strongly (as in Falstaff's time) with " 8*l*. paid for 160 dozen and 6 pennyworth of bread," and 9*s*. paid in addition to Mr. Lansdale for bread.

---

[1] "To Richard Lansdale, the lord maio'rs steward, and Willm. Sotherne, one of the sheriff's stewards, being appointed to be the two caters for this service—viz., to either of them 5*l*. a peece in toto, 10*l*.
 "To William Sothern's sonne for his paynes, 10*s*."
[2] Warden, 1613-15, Master, 1617.   [3] English Home, page 83.
[4] A liquid measure of 4 hogsheads or 252 gallons.

Having Royal guests, a special programme of music and song must be arranged for their entertainment. Some disappointment had resulted from the last demand made on the Schoolmaster for a speech by one of his scholars, when James entered the city in 1603, and therefore other assistance was sought. " Sir John Swynnerton is entreated to conferr with Mr. Benjamin Johnson the Poet, aboute a speeche to be made to welcome his Majestie, and for musique and other inventions which maye give likeing and delight to his Majestie by reason that the Company doubt that their Schoolmaster and Schollers be not acquainted with such kinde of Entertainments."

Mr. Ben Jonson was no doubt engaged, but the speech of eighteen verses devised by him, "which pleased his Majesty marvelously well," has not been preserved either on the records of the Company or in his works."[1]

It was usual to have in the fourteenth century hall at the end opposite to the minstrels or over the daïs a gallery or room to enable the occupants to command a view of the guests and of the entertainment taking place beneath. A room was placed where the present corridor stands, but there was no window commanding a sufficient view of the hall. Therefore "it is ordered that the Mason shall presently cut a hole through the mayne wall at the upper end of the Hall and make a windowe out of the little roome for the King to looke into the Hall, and Mr. Warden Osborne and Mr. Warden Albany to take care to see the same performed."

The inventory of the garniture and furniture of the hall have been placed before the reader. There were not sufficient chairs, stools, or bankers for each guest to be seated, and the hire of such articles was a necessity. Therefore " William Jones,[2] Thos. Owen[3] and Richd. Scales,[4] three of the Assistants, are entreated at the Companies charge to make provision of Hangings, Carpets,

---

[1] Gifford's Ben Jonson, London (1816). The payments made to him by the Company were these :—

"To Mr Beniamyn Johnson, the poett, for inventing the speech to his Ma'y and for making the songs, and his direccions to others in that business, 20l."

" For setting of the songs that were songe to his Ma'y to Mr Copiarario, 12l.

" To Mr Johnson's man for writing out copies of the speech and songes to be giuen to the king and lords with others, 15s.

"To Mr Johnson for the Musitian's dynner the day before the feast, 2l.

" To Powle's singing men by Mr Ben. Johnson, 1l. 5s."

[2] Warden 1599-1605.   [3] Warden 1603-7.

[4] Warden 1604-7, Master 1613.

Curtains, Stools, Chaynes, Pillowes and such other necessaries at the chardges of the Company."[1]

Possibly the reader may have thought the Company had a sufficient supply of plate for any feast,[2] but not so, when it is remembered that glass and earthenware were not used in the hall, and that all the guests were of necessity to be provided with basyns and ewres for washing before and after dinner, and the principal guests with plate, and the other guests with pewter from which their meals were to be taken, therefore the King's plate must be asked for by Mr. Warden Wright and " George Lydiatt,[3] Otho Mawditt, Richard Osmotherly,[4] George Sotherton,[5] James Graves, Matthew Beadles,[6] John Houghton, and Henry Polstrede,[7] being all of the Livery of this Company, are entreated and appointed to make provision of plate at the Companies charge, wherein it is not doubted but they will deale carefully and frugully for the Company. And Mr. Warden Wright is entreated to move the Lord Chamberlain for the use of the King's silver vessel." The result was satisfactory, as the plate was provided at a cost of 25*l*. 14*s*. 9*d*., and the pewter at 9*l*. 15*s*. 6*d*.

It was usual then that the servants of the King should come to cook for and wait upon him, and (as to waiting) the rule applied to noble guests, but in an ordinary way we have already seen that waiters or servants at the Company's feasts were by preference members of the Company, or the Lord Mayor's and Sheriffs' officers;[8] the same assistance was now to be sought for. " The Master and Wardens are entreated to provide a competent and sufficient number of the Officers attending the Lord Maior and Sheriffs to wait at the Dinner. And also p^{9}sonable young

---

[1] The particulars of this expenditure is to be found in these entries:—
"To 2 carmen y^t brought ye hangings from ye wat^d side, 1*s*. 8*d*.
"For the hyring of 18 covered stooles by Griffyn, 10*s*.
"For carrying re-carrying and helping vp with things, 1*s*. 6*d*.
"To the gentlemen that lent the hangings, chaires, stooles, and other thinges for the furnishing of the kinge's chamber and the withdrawing chambers by Mr Warden Owen, 10*l*.
"There was disbursed about the repayring and bewtifying of the howse, as by the accompt of Mr. Swynnerton, maister, appeareth, the some of one hundreth fyfty fower pounds seaven shillinges and sixpence."
[2] Pages 92–8 *ante*. [3] Warden 1608–11.
[4] Warden Substitute 1603, Benefactor, 1612.
[5] Son of George, and admitted by patrimony 18th June, 1599.
[6] Warden 1620–22, then Alderman.
[7] Warden 1621–3, Master 1625.   [8] Page 182, *ante*.

men of the Company to give their attendance in Gownes and to carry up the meate to the inferior tables."

The names of the young men of the Company who *gave* their attendance has not been preserved, but those who were *hired* cost the Company 7*l*. 4*s*. at 4*s*. a head, a heavy charge, but it seems that they were " serjeants."

The safety of the King was the next subject which received attention, and needful it was that it should do so, for since 1586[1] the Company, at the precept of the Lord Mayor, had been obliged to store gunpowder in their hall premises, and the Guy Fawke's conspiracy of 5th November, 1605, had shewn how such a store might be applied to the destruction of the King; therefore with a view to security, " Our Master and Wardens are entreated to cause discreete men to make special serche in and about all the houses and roomes adjoyning to the Hall to prevent all villiany and danger from all which wee doe most humbly beseech Almighty God to blesse and defend his Majestie."

It was etiquette for the Sovereign to dine at a table alone. " The Company are informed that the King's Majestie will dine in the King's Chamber, and the Princes Highness in the greate Hall." Arrangements must be made accordingly. " It is therefore thought fytt the long table at the upper end of the Hall be taken away and three several tables whereby the Prince's Highness may sitt at a table by himself in state, and the noble men at two tables at either end thereof."

Adjacent to the hall was a popular " tavern," either the " Star " or the " Grasshopper," and the roof was fitted up as a place of recreation for the customers, overlooking the hall garden and premises. This might prove an annoyance, therefore " it is considered and agreed that the brick wall in the Garden which adjoineth to the Taverne shall presently be raised up to take away the prospect of such as use to walke upon the leades of the Taverne and thereby woulde overlooke the Garden." And if workmen were to be employed it would be well that " that King's Chamber and the Garden Walls and the Gate and the houses about the same to be bewtified as much as tyme will admytt."

Here the directions given end and the Clerk, as a comment upon the labour of the Committee, adds: " And be it remembered that divers of the Comyttee's mett every day and appoynted officers to attend and also collected the most personable and

---

[1] Note, page 59, *ante*.

proper men, and appoynted every one his service, as well of such as well of the Assistants, Lyvery, and Sixteene Men, as also other young men of the Company and Ushers, and were careful to see everything performed for the creditt and reputacõn of the Company."

All these preliminary arrangements had been made on the bare suggestion of the King's intention to visit the Company, but at the next meeting on the 7th July, " the Company are informed by Mr. Warden Wright that the Right Honble the Earl of Suffolk, Lord Chamberlain, and the Right Honble the Earle of Salisbury, the Kinge's principall Secretarie, oute of theire honourable love to this Companie have invited the King's moste excellent Maj^{tie} to our Ffeast, so as the Company shall not need to trouble his Majestie any further."

The Company were, therefore, certain that the King would be their guest, yet both earls gave " their honourable advice and also thought convenient that some of the chief of the Company should ride to Nonsuch to the Prince's Court to invite his Highness."

The Prince was at this time thirteen years of age, being born on the 19th February, 1594.[1] Nonsuch[2] (which is in Cheam Parish) was begun to be built as a palace by Henry VIII, and after his death completed as such by the Earl of Arundel, who, in 1591, conveyed it to Queen Elizabeth, where she resided occasionally until 1600.[3]

As such an invitation had to be given "Mr. Baron Sotherton, Sir William Craven, Mr. Alderman Elwes, and Mr. Alderman Albany, have undertaken to perform that service;" then "Sir John Swynnerton and Mr. Alderman Elwes have also promised to invite all the Lords that are resident about London," and that the feast might be graced with the presence of the Queen, " Mr. Warden Wright hath also promised to desire the Lord Chamberlain to the Queene to invite her Majestie and such honourable Ladies as usually attend her Highness."

The royal guests being thus secured, the question arose

---

[1] He died at St. James's Palace 9th November, and was buried at Westminster, 7th December, 1612. See the particulars of his illness and death, 2 Nichols, Progresses (James I), pages 469-93, and the sermon of Dr. Joseph Hall (Bishop of Norwich) to the Household of the late Prince, New Year's Day, 1613, Vol. 5, page 66, of his works.

[2] Rye's England, page 243; and Lysons' Environs, Vol. 6, page 151.

[3] Hunting, it is said, every other day, though 67 years of age.

whether the Lord Mayor and Aldermen with their ladies should be invited, and on the 9th the Court was "specially provided to consider and advyse whether it were fitt and convenient to invite the Lord Mayor and all the Aldermen and their Ladies to the Elecõn dynner this yeare," opinions, though given freely were not unanimous, and upon propounding the question, "severall delyvered their conceite and opynions, some holding opinion that it would be an honõr and grace to the Company to see soe many sitt togeather in their Scarlet Robes: other being of opynion that it would much derogate from the private Companie who should be at the whole charge, and soe make it seeme as an entertainment done at the charge of the whole Cytty."

Then the presence of so great an official as the Lord Mayor appeared to some to create a special difficulty. "Some houlding opynion that if wee preferred my Lord Maior and Aldermen to a principal Table it woulde offend the nobles and honourable gentlemen who would reckon my Lord Maior in the presence of the King, to be but as an ordinary Knight *Quia in præsentia Majoris cessat potestas minoris:* others houlding it the duty of us citizens to have a very special care to give satisfacõn and preferr the Governours of the Cytty."

Unfortunately for the credit of the Court others took a lower ground "houlding opynion, that my Lord Maior for the present yere being a clothworker, and having procured to grace that Company and to cause his Majesties name to be entered as one of that Society, he would doe his endeavor to crosse our Companie of that honour which wee understand the Prince's Highness meaneth to confer upon our Company;" however, after "many other reasons and opynions were delyvred, it was put to scrutiny and by moste voices agreed, that neither my Lord Maior nor any of the Aldermen (saving such as be of our Company) shoulde be invyted at this tyme, hoping that none of them shall have any just cause to except against the Companies resolution herein."

Such an affront to the Corporation could not be passed over without remonstrance, and accordingly on the 15th "to this Court resorted Mr. Recorder of London, and did use many perswasive speeches to move the Company to invite the Right Honble Lord Maior and the Right Wor[ll] the Aldermen his Brethren to dyne at the Hall upon the morrowe nexte ensuinge," but in vain, for "upon whose ernest mocõn it was estsones put to question and scruteny whether they should be invited or no, but the major parte remembering how the same was debated at the last Courte, doe stand constant in theire former resolution. And soe by scruteny yt was agreed that they should not be invyted at this tyme."

Such being the decision they made a poor excuse and "praied Mr. Recorder to conceave well of their resolucõn, and to informe my Lord Maior and Aldermen that they feared that the Company of noblemen and ladies woulde be so great that they could not possibly give his Lordshipp and Worshipps that entertaynement as would be fitt for Citizens to give to theire Magistrates, which was the cause they forebore to invite them at this tyme."

The election of Master and Wardens came on in the ordinary way, but having regard to the lax discipline then prevailing[1] the newly elected members were specially enjoined "not to be absent the next day at the publication of their election."

There was, however, one other matter which the Court had to order before the Royal guests were received, viz., that purses with gold therein should be provided; James I was needy, and money was acceptable and readily received by him. On his way from Scotland he accepted purses from Berwick and Newcastle, at Salisbury a cup of silver and also 20l. and a purse containing another 20l. When he passed from the Tower to the Corporation in July, 1603, the city provided 1,000l., 1,000 marks of which was given to James and 500 to the Queen in separate purses. Later, in the succeeding March when he went in State Progress through the city from the Tower to Westminster, three cups of gold (costing 416l. 10s. 5d.) were given by the Recorder to the King, Queen, and Prince;[2] and again when he dined with the Lord Mayor (Wait) at his private house in the June of 1607, he carried away a purse of gold.[3] Therefore the Merchant Taylors Company could not do otherwise than comply with the established custom; and "also at this Court itt was agreed that the Stewards

---

[1] Chapter XII, page 217.   [2] Nichols, Vol. 1, pages 335, 406.

[3] It may be noticed that during the reigns of Edward VI, Queens Mary and Elizabeth, and for the earlier part of James, the custom of giving and receiving New Year's gifts to and from the Sovereign was seldom omitted. The manner of making these in 1603–4 is thus described by Lord Harrington, who then made one:—"You must buy a new purse of about 5s. price and put thereinto 20 pieces of new gold of 20s. a piece; then go to the Presence Chamber at 8 o'clock A.M., deliver the purse and the gold to the Lord Chamberlain." He then mentions the fees to be paid to the King's servants, and how the donor must get a ticket in return entitling him to receive 18s. 6d. in cash and an order for a piece of plate 30 ozs. weight.—1 Nichol, James I's Progress, page 471. It is said that the last trace of this custom in modern times was that the Chaplains in waiting on New Year's day had each a crown piece laid under his plate at dinner.

shall make provision of Three ritch Purses and of Two hundred poundes in faier gold, whereof one hundred poundes to be presented to the King and Fyfty poundes to the Queen, and Ffyfty poundes to the Prynce, and if the Queene doe not come, then that Fifty poundes to be saved."

So much then for the orders of the Court giving directions for due preparation to be made for the entertainment of the Royal visitors, but before reverting again to the Court minutes describing their reception let us see, so far as the cash accounts furnish information, what provision was made for the feast.[1] (1) In flesh, fish, and fowl; (2) In groceries and various items; (3) In cooking, &c.; (4) In waiting on the guests; and lastly, in the equipment of the table utensils.

William Sotherne, the caterer, purchased the "butchers beefe, &c.," costing as a total 40*l*. 14*s*. (with an item of "1*l*. 4*s*. for one dinner with Mr. Alexander, the Princes gent usher"), but there were fourteen bucks presented by members (as Wardens Albany and Atkinson), and from guests as Lord Salisbury, the Lord Chamberlain, and the Prince.[2]

The fish appears to have been purchased at a cost of 22*l*. 19*s*. 4*d*., principally from Mr. Angell, but at whose selection does not appear except that Mr. Swynnerton, the Master, purchased some sturgeon.

The "poultry" was the most various and most costly food provided, amounting to a total sum of 104*l*. 9*s*. 3*d*.,[3] to which must be added 2*l*. 3*s*. 4*d*. for 1,300 eggs at 3*s*. 4*d*. per 100.

The groceries for ordinary cooking cost 32*l*. 9*s*. 10*d*., and for ipocras 3*l*. 14*s*. 6*d*., which after some abatement was paid for by 36*l*. The greengrocer's bill was paid by 30*l*. 2*s*. 8*d*. including 15*s*. 1*d*. for "herbs and nosegaies."

We have now to come to the cooking. Before the Chef (William Beamond) and his deputies could be set to work the kitchen had to be prepared by being provided with utensils, fuel, and candles, and other essential articles, of which the details are preserved. Thus the Chandler's articles cost 3*l*. 3*s*. 7*d*., fuel 7*l*. 7*s*. 8*d*. Dresser clothes 3*l*. 1*s*. 5*d*. and linen 13*l*. 16*s*. 5*d*., besides certain consumable stores.

---

[1] See note at the end of the chapter for the cost, &c., of supplies, page 307.

[2] "Unto which dinner the Prince sent three brace of Bucks, and Sir Thomas Chaloner did, by tre written by his Highness commaundment, signifie that his Highness with his own hand placed the woodman to kill them."

[3] Page 310.

The cooking appears to have cost in wages 15*l*. 13*s*. 6*d*., the distribution being as follows :—" To Mr. Beamond (who was the Company's Cook) for his own pains 5*l*.,[1] and for his apron 6*s*. The cooks under him were 32 in number, and they all dined together at the close of their labours, " there being no cold meat left for them," although their labours were not equal, as some were only partially engaged, as two for one day, eighteen for two, six for three, three for four, and three for four days and one night, each man being reckoned at 2*s*. 6*d*. per day or night, and the work of the kitchen had this number of men : forty-two labourers for one day at 6*d*. each, and four labourers for five days at 1*s*. a day, besides paying three other assistants as :—

" For heating ye oven to the bakers man y^t baked ye pasties, 2*s*."
" To Tho: Jackson for looking to the custards, 2*s*."
" To Walter Bretton for going of errands, 3*s*."

The waiters engaged have been already referred to, and we have now to ascertain what was the table equipment. We notice that glass was introduced at this feast at a cost of 15*l*. 2*s*., but that one pair of knives only appears at a cost of 2*s*.,[2] and no spoons or forks. We find rose water mentioned in Harper's pageant, and for this feast "12*s*. was paid for a gallon of sweete water and the potes."

We come now to the banqueting. For the King the messes were a desert made up of dried fruits and confectionery, that for the King cost 22*l*. 2*s*., that for the Prince 15*l*. 7*s*. 6*d*., that for the Lords 24*l*. 10*s*.

To these must be added the marchpanes, a favourite delicacy made of flour, sugar, and almonds, which cost 9*l*. 3*s*. 4*d*.

For the kitchen and privy kitchen a similar desert at the cost of 5*l*. 14*s*. 2*d*. and 2*l*. 2*s*. 6*d*., to which was added 4*l*., for thirteen dozen and eight plates of glass lost.

Some preparation was always needed to make the hall fit for the reception of guests. If the old rushes had not been taken off the floor after the last feast they had to be covered with clean

---

[1] For made or hackled dishes these payments are entered :—
" For one turky pye, 6*s*. ; for 2 peacock pyes, 11*s*. ; for one pheasant pye, 6*s*. ; for 2 partrich pyes, 4*s*. ; for one phesant py, 6*s*. ; for 2 mallard pyes, 6*s*. ; for 1 swann pye, 6*s*. ; for 1 owle pye, 2*s*.

[2] Note, page 314. Bellew was retired with 3*l*. on 14th July, 1610, "as well in respect of three table knives, a standing carver's knife, and a chipping knife upon two whereof the Company's arms are engraven, and to be left by him for the use of the Fraternity, as also that he is aged and past labour."

ones.[1] The arras hangings which were used to adorn the walls were (as we know) kept in nine bags, and had to be taken out and hung around the hall. A "ship," a popular emblem, was to be used and fitted up for the King's pleasure. These matters must be looked to, and caused a miscellaneous expenditure of which the particulars may be worth the reader's notice.

We may now refer to the proceedings of the 16th July, when the King was received at the hall. The record begins:—

"The Companie made great haste to Church to the Sermon which this yeare was in the Parish of St. Helen, by reason that a howse over against our Church, and some other howses in the Parish were visited with the Plague, which was used by some that would willingly have kepte the King and Prince from our Hall, as a very speciall motive to diswade his Majestie from coming."

The plague here referred to is one of those periodical scourges which visited London before the fire of 1666. It commenced in 1603 and continued for eight years until 1611, and from March to December in the first year 30,561 are said to have died of plague alone according to the bills of mortality which were then established.[2]

The sermon preached by the President of St. John's (Dr. Buckeridge[3]) was finished "in convenient time so as the Company came to the Hall to see all things in order and give entertainment and to attend his Majesty's company." Then to their surprise they found the Lord Mayor and Aldermen standing in the hall to receive the King. "And it is to be remembered that the Lord Maior and Aldermen (albeit they were not invited and some of them discontented therewith) came all to the Hall in their Scarlett, and there staid untill his Maj^{tie}· comyng, and then the Lord Maior and the Master of our Company and some of the Aldermen went to the Gate nexte the streete and the Lord Maior delivered up his sword to the King, and Master of the Companie did welcome his Maj^{tie}· and attended his Maj^{tie}· up into the Hall."

Before entering with the King into the hall we may ascertain who were the officials or servants that accompanied him for protection or state.

---

[1] From the Master's account for 1606-7:—
"Item, for 4 dozen and a half of Rushes at 6s. the bundle, and 12d. over for the Hall, Gallery, &c., 28s.
"Item to Lynsey and Miller for making clean the hall against the Election Day, and carrying forth Rushes, according to former presidents, 10s."

[2] Stowe, Book 5, page 448.

[3] A kinsman of Sir Thomas White's.—See 2 Wilson, *passim*.

It may have been noticed that in the arrangements for this feast no mention has been made of an "Assayer" or taster, yet a modern writer assures us that "from the first of the Norman kings to the days of James I our forefathers ate their meals in fear, and did not consider their lives safe without an assayer or taster." In the Royal Household the physician filled this office, cut off pieces of the various viands which were tasted. So when the "hanap or standing cup" was filled for the master of the house or guest "a portion of the same liquor was poured into the assay cup to which was attached a material for detecting poison."[1] Accordingly we find one of the King's attendants was "Mr. Doctor Hammond, Physician." It was essential to comfort no less than to security that the King's meals should be dressed to his liking, and therefore he brought his own cooks. Their attendance was given with six of "the Guard,'" who kept the entries to the hall and the King's trumpeters at a cost to the Company of 19*l*. 13*s*. 6*d*.[2]

The officers of State were the Lord Admiral, the Lord Chamberlain, and the Principal Secretary of State, with the nobles accompanying him, and holding subordinate offices about the Court.

The King entered the premises at the east door, and went through the garden to the hall at the door on the west end, and from thence was taken to the daïs of the hall as it now

---

[1] Our English Home, page 60.

[2] "Fees to y*e* King's cookes:—

"For 3 aprons to one groome and two children of the kinge's pryvy kytchin by Mr. Roe 12*s*.

"For 5 aprons for the prince's men, by order of Mr. Wright to Hugh Billy, 12*s*. 6*d*.

"Gratuities to the King's men:—

"To M*r* Heiborne, one of his Ma*ts* gent vshers, by order, 5*l*.

"To him for Anthony Gibson and Henry Lyle, groomes of his Ma*ts* chamber, by order from M*r* Wright, 2*l*.

"To one groome of his Ma*ts* privy kytchin, 2 children, 2 turnebroches, two porters and scowrers, one dorekeeper, one sompter man and 4 servaunts by Hugh Billy by the same order, 2*l*.

"To William Lamplough, clarck of his Ma*ts* kytchin, whoe directed the service of the carrying vpp of the kinge's meate by Robt. Belingham, 1*l*.

"To the clark of the check, 1*l*.

"To six of the guard that kept the entries into the Hall, and to the king's chamber, by the clarck of the guard, 3*l*.

"To M*r* Dyer, one of his Ma*ts* pastery, 13*s*. 6*d*.

"To his Ma*ts* trompetors, 40*s*.; and to his droms, 20*s*., 3*l*.

"To M*r* Batty, s*erj*icant of his Ma*ts* pastry, by Mr. Wright, 1*l*.

"To M*r* Traherne, the king's porter, by order of M*r* Wright, 1*l*.

stands. "And at the upper end of the Hall there was sett a Chayre of State where his Maj^tie· satt and viewed the Hall." Then "a very proper Child, well spoken, being clothed like an angell of gladness with a Taper of Ffrankincense burning in his hand, delivered a short speech[1] contayning (xviii) verses, devised by Mr. Ben Johnson the Poet, which pleased his Maj^tie· marvelously well."

At each end of the daïs seats had been erected for the lute players: "Upon either side of the Hall in the Windowe neere the upper end were Gallories or Seates made for Musique, in either of which were seaven singular choice musicions playing on their Lutes."

The singing was performed in a ship which was hung aloft on the rafters of the hall roof thus "in the shipp which did hang aloft in the Hall three rare men and very skilful sung to his Maj^tie·"; and judging from the next description it may be questioned how far the arrangements had been judicious, as the musicians in the minstrels' gallery appeared to have overpowered the other performers, for "over the skreene, cornets and loud musique wherein it is to be remembered that the multitude and noyse was so greate that the lutes nor songs coulde hardly be heard or understoode."

The names and the expense of these performers "who exacted unreasonable sums" of the Company are preserved. The singers in the ship were John Allen (the chief), 4*l*.; Thomas Lupo (His Majesty's musician) 3*l*.; and John Richards, 3*l*.

Those who played on the lute, who were more than seven in number, cost the Company 24*l*. 10*s*.,[2] and the minstrels in the gallery over the skreen (six in number) 10*l*.[3] This entertainment

---

[1] "To Mr Hemmyngs for his direccion of his boy that made the speech to his Ma^ts 40*s*., and 5*s*. given to John Rise the speaker, 2*l*. 5*s*.

"To John, Mr. Swynnerton's man, for things for the boy that made the speech, 13*s*."

[2] "To them that plaid on the Lute:—

"To Thomas Robinson 30*s*., and to John Done 40*s*., 3*l*. 10*s*.

"To George Roselor 40*s*., and to Tho. Sturgon 40*s*., 4*l*.

"To Willm. Ffregosie, by Mr. Roselor, 40*s*., and by Jo. Robson, 40*s*.

"To Nicholas Sturt for himself and his sonne, 4*l*.

"To William Browne, by Sturt, 40*s*., and to Joseph Sherly 40*s*., 4*l*.

"To Willm. Morley for himself 40*s*., and for Robert Kenn^e sly 40*s*., 4*l*.

"To Robt. Bateman and Stephen Thomas who plaid on the treble violens, by Nicholas Sturt and Richard Morley, 1*l*."

[3] "To Mr Educy, Mr. Lancero, and fower others of his Ma^ts musitious players of wynde instruments being placed over the skreene, 10*l*."

took place before dinner and while the King remained in the hall. "Then his Maj^tie. went up into the King's chamber, where he dined alone at a table which was provided only for his Maj^tie. and the Queene (but the Queene came not), in which chamber was placed a very rich paier of Organs, whereupon Mr. John Bull, Doctor of Musique, and a Brother of this Company, did play during all the dynner tyme. And Mr. Nathanael Gyles, Master of the Children of the Kyng's Chapell, together with divers singing men and children of the said Chappell, did sing melodious songs at the said dynner."

What were the songs selected and sung by Dr. Bull are not recorded. That he composed or sang the present National Anthem[1] on this occasion is a fiction, nor do we find any evidence that the song not of eighteen but of seventeen verses before referred to, was then either written or sung. He gave his services to the Company and his name in the list of payments only occurs in this item:—" To M^r. John Bull, Docto^r of Musique, to pay to him that sett vp the winde instruments in the king's chamber where the king dined, and for tuning it, with the carriage of it from and to Ruccolds, 2l. 18s."

Mr. Nathaniel Gyles, appointed Master of the Chapel Boys in January, 1604, also gave his services, and he was granted admission to the Freedom and Livery. Thomas Gyles (possibly a relative) was a dancing master on the Prince's establishment at a wage of 50l. per annum.[2]

Regarding the Prince we have fewer entries. He came (we presume) with the king bringing Mr. Alexander, his gentleman usher in ordinary, and others who were enrolled as honorary members. His trumpeters and drummers also came and received payment[3] from the Company.

It is recorded "that the Prince did dine in the greate Hall, and that the long table at the upper end of the Hall was taken away and three tables distinct one from another placed in the

---

[1] The National Anthem is said to have been first sung in London in November, 1739, and first published in 1742, Henry Carey being the composer.—Sir George Grove's and Mr. Southgate's letters in the "Times," of 4th February, 1878.

[2] Establishment, page 326.

[3] " Gratuities to ye Prynces men :—
" To Mr Alexander, the prince's gentleman usher in ordynary, 2l.
" To the princes trompeto^rs and droms, 1l."

room thereof (viz.), one table in the middle where the Prince sate alone in state, and the tables on either side were wholly furnished with Ambassadors and Noblemen."

The minutes add later information as to the ceremonial that was observed: "The service to the King and Prince for the first course was carried up by the Knights, Aldermen, Masters, Assistants, and Lyvery, which were of the Companie, the Lyvery having their Hoods upon their shoulders, the service being rich and bountifull, as by the charge will appear."

The Recorder was in attendance as the mouthpiece of the Company to address the Sovereign,[1] "and when the King's most excellent Majesty had dyned and withdrawn himself into his inner chamber, the Master and the fower Wardens, Mr. Baron Sotherton and the Aldermen of the Companie, resorted unto his Majestie, and Mr. Recorder of London being there present did in the name of the whole Company most humbly thank his Maj^{tie} that it had pleased him to grace the Company with his presence that day."

The purse of gold was presented by the Master thus: "**And** the Master of the Company did present his Maj^{tie} with a faier purse[2] wherein was one hundreth pounds in gould," and the Roll by the Clerk: "And Richard Langley the Comon Clerk of the Company did moast humbly deliver unto his Maj^{tie} a Roll in Vellum which he had collected out of the ancient bookes and records of the Companie."

The Roll presented to the King is the most valuable record illustrating by the list of honorary members the past history of the Company. When it was framed books were extant which have since been lost, and the roll gives a complete list (as we may assume) of all the honorary members from the reigns of Edward III to that of James I. That it may be more appreciated by the reader we have placed to each name a note to identify the bearer of the name with the general history of England.

"The copy of the Roll delivered to the King and a similar one to the Prince. The names of Seaven Kings, one Queen, &c.

---

[1] Page 30, *ante*.

[2] James endeavoured to solicit money by letters by Privy Seal issued to the Sheriffs of each county, against which St. John protested, and was prosecuted by Bacon in the Star Chamber (2 State Trials, page 899), but in 1627 the nuisance was put down (2 Parliamentary History, page 230).

Edward III.

(1) Roger, Lord Mortimer, 1351.
(2) Humffrey de Baune, Earle of Herford, 1372.
(3) Dame Johan, his Wief.
(4) Symon, Lord Bishop of London, 1373.
(5) Dame Alice, Countess of Kent.
(6) Edmund, Lord Mortymer, Earle of March, 1377.

Richard II.

(7) William Courtney, Lord Bishop of London, 1378.
(8) Henry Percy, Earle of Northumberland, 1379.
(9) John, Lord Hastings, Earle of Pembrooke.
(10) Isabell, Countesse of Pembrooke, 1381.
(11) Robert Breybrooke, Lord Bishop of London, 1382.
(12) John Fferdon, Lord Bishop of Durham.
(13) The Prior of St. Bartholomews, 1383.
(14) The Sub Prior.
(15) The Prior of Elsing Spittle.
(16) King Richard the Second, 1385.
(17) Queene Anne, his wife.
(18) John, Duke of Lancaster.
(19) Sir Roger Walden, Treasorer of Callis, 1387.

---

[1] Grandson of Roger, who was summoned to Parliament in 1306, and in 1328 created Earl of March. He died in 1360.

[2] Cousin to (1). Hereditary Constable of England. Died in 1372.

[3] Wife of (2) and daughter of Richard FitzAlan, ninth Earl of Arundel.

[4] Pages 112, note 4, and 113, note 4.

[5] Daughter of Edmund FitzAllan the eighth Earl of Arundel, and wife of Thomas Holland, second Earl of Kent, only brother to Richard II.

[6] Son of (1). Died in 1381.

[7] Born in 1341, and died in 1396. Riley's London, page 410.

[8] Fourth Lord Percy, father of "Hotspur," made Earl of Northumberland at Richard II's Coronation, July, 1377.

[9] Married Philippa, daughter of (6). Slain at 16 in a joust with Sir John St. John, 30th December, 1389.

[10] Not identified.

[11] The predecessor of (7) in London until 1404, see page 116 *ante*.

[12] Assumed to be John de Fordham, Bishop of Durham, 1382-88, and Ely, 1388 to 1425.

[13] William Sidney, elected 10th June, 1381, till March, 1390, page 115 *ante*. Wat Tyler destroyed the Priory during his incumbency.

[14] Sub-Prior, 1383.

[15] Robert Draycote, Prior, 1400-5, page 115 *ante*.

[16] Born 1366. Died 1399, and the grantor of the second Charter, page 35 *ante*.

[17] The daughter of Charles IV of Germany.

[18] Born at Ghent, 1340, father of Henry IV. Wat Tyler destroyed his house in the Savoy, 1381, and he died in 1391.

[19] Archbishop of Canterbury. Deposed and made Bishop of London. Died 1406.

(20) Thomas, Earle of Nottingham, 1388.
(21) Hugh, Lord Zouth.
(22) John, Lord Willoughby, 1389.
(23) Edmund, Duke of York, 1390.
(24) Thomas, Duke of Gloucester, 1390.
(25) Henry, Duke of Hereford and Earle of Darby, who afterwards was (1390) King Henry the Fourth.
(26) The Duchess of Gloucester.
(27) Edward, Earle of Rutland.
(28) Thomas, Earle of Warwick.
(29) The Countesse his Wief, and Thomas his son.
(30) Thomas, Earle of Nottingham.
(31) John Holland, Earle of Huntington.
(32) John, Lord Roos.
(33) Ralph, Lord Nevill.
(34) Thomas, Lord Ffurnyvale.
(35) Reginald, Lord Gray of Ryffyn.
(36) Walter Skirlowe, Lord Bishop of Durham, 1391.
(37) Phillipp, Lord Darcy, 1394.
38) Robert, Lord Scales.

---

[20] Thomas de Mowbray, sixth Baron, afterwards Earl Marshall, and Duke of Norfolk. Banished and died at Venice 1399–1400 (or in 1413 according to Sir H. Nicholas).

[21] Probably the second Baron Burnell, and husband of Joyce, the next heir of Hugh de Zouche.

[22] Probably "Robert." Died 1452.

[23] Born 1342, fifth son of Edward III. Died 1402.

[24] Born 1355. Constable of England, seventh son of Edward III. Murdered at Calais, 8th September, 1397. Riley's Memorials, page 507.

[25] Son of (18) crowned as Henry IV (13th October, 1399), and the grantor of the third Charter (see page 36 and 132 *ante*). Died 20th March, 1412.

[26] Probably the widow of (24).

[27] Son of (23), created Earl of Rutland 25th February, 1390; succeeded as Duke of York, and slain at Agincourt, 25th October, 1415.

[28] Beauchamp, fourth Earl, banished to the Isle of Man by Richard II, but restored by Henry IV. Died in 1401.

[29] Wife or widow of (28).

[30] Supposed to be the son of (20), and beheaded at York in 1405 for high treason.

[31] Third son of Thomas de Holland, Earl of Kent, by Joane Plantagenet, "the Fair Maid of Kent," and half brother of Richard II. Married the daughter of John of Gaunt, and was beheaded by the mob in 1400.

[32] The sixth Baron, and died in his Pilgrimage to Jerusalem, 1393–4.

[33] Fourth Baron, and created *circa* 21 Richard II, in full Parliament, Earl of Westmoreland. Probably resided in Leadenhall. Died 1425 (see 115a and 135).

[34] Thomas Nevill (fifth Baron Furnival) brother of (33). Sat in Parliament, August, 1383. Died 1406.

[35] Third Baron. Sat in Parliament 1389 to 1439. Died 1440.

[36] Bath and Wells, 1386-88, and Durham until 1406.

[37] Fourth Baron. Sat in Parliament, August, 1377, to November, 1397. Died 1398.

[38] Fifth Baron. Sat in Parliament, November, 1396, to October, 1400. Died 1402.

(39) William, Earle of March, 1397.
(40) Alice, Countess of Oxford.
(41) Edmund Stafford, Lord Bishop of Exeter, 1397.
(42) Thomas, Duke of Surrey, 1399.

Henry IV.

(43) Edmund, Lord Gray, Godnor, 1401.
(44) Thomas Arundell, Lord Abp. of Canterbury, 1401.
(45) King Henry the Fourth and the Prince had the Clothing of this Mistery.
(46) Nicholas Bubwith, Lord Bishop of London, 1406.
(47) William Colchester, Abbot of Westminster.
(48) Lord John, the Kinges sonne, 1407.
(49) Edmund, Earle of Kent.
(50) Lord Thomas, the Kinges son, 1409.
(51) Richard Beauchamp, Earle of Warwick, 1411.
(52) Henry le Scroope, Tresorer of England.
(53) Henry Chichley, Bishop of St. Davies.
(54) Sir Roger Westwood, Baron of the Exchequer.

Henry V.

(55) John, Earle of Huntington, 1412.

---

[39] As Edmund, the third Earl, died in 1381, and Roger, who succeeded as fourth Earl, was slain in battle in Ireland in 1398; it is difficult to identify this person.

[40] Daughter of John, third Lord FitzWalter.

[41] From 1395 to 1419.

[42] Thomas Holland, third Earl of Kent, made by Richard II in Parliament, with his crown upon his head, "Duke of Sussex."

[43] Probably "Richard," who succeeded in 1392 as fourth Baron, and died in 1418.

[44] Son of Richard FitzAlan, Earl of Arundel (29), born 1352, B.A. of Oxford. At 21 Archdeacon of Taunton, and at 22 Bishop of Ely, Lord Chancellor 1386, 1399, and 1412; Archbishop of York, 1388, and of Canterbury, January, 1397. Died 1444.

[45] See (25).

[46] Chancellor of the Exchequer, Bath and Wells, 1407, Salisbury, 1408-24.

[47] "The Grand Conspirator," Abbot, 1386 to 1420. Buried in St. John Baptist's Chapel, Westminster. See Stanley's Westminster, pages 359-381.

[48] The third son of Henry IV, who was John, Duke of Bedford, Earl of Richmond, and Constable of England. The celebrated Regent of France (temporarily Henry VI). Died at Paris, 14th September, 1435. His widow (on remarriage) had a daughter Elizabeth, wife of Edward IV.

[49] The second son of (31). Slain in Brittany, 15th September, 1407.

[50] The second son of Henry IV (25). Married sister of (49). Slain at the battle of Beaugé in 1421.

[51] Son of (28). Born January, 1381, and died at Roan, 30th April, 1439.

[52] Third Baron of Upsal. Sat in Parliament from August, 1408, to 26th September, 1414. In 11 Henry IV was made Treasurer of the Exchequer, and was found guilty of treason and beheaded August, 1415.

[53] The founder of All Soul's College, Oxford, and died February, 1400.

[54] Made such 1st March, 1403, and reappointed by Henry V and VI.

[55] Succeeded his father the Duke of Exeter. Made General, 1416, of all the men-at-arms and archers in the Fleet, and assisted at the Siege of Caen. Died in 1446.

(56) Earle Marshall.
(57) James, Earl of Ormond.
(58) John, Lord Lovell.
(59) Henry Beauford, Lord Bp. of Winchester.
(60) William, Lord Fferris of Groby, 1413.
(61) William, Lord Zouche.
(62) King Henry the Fifth, 1414.
(63) Humffrey, Duke of Gloucester.
(64) Edmund, Earle of March, 1414.
(65) Lord Willoughby.
(66) Henry, Lord Fitzhugh.
(67) Lord Matravers.
(68) The Earle of Salisbury.
(69) Richard Beauchamp, Lord Burgavenny, 1415.
(70) The Abbott of Bermondsey.
(71) Henry Percy, Earle of Northumberland, 1420.
(72) John, Lord Roos.
(73) John, sonne of the Lord Gray of Rytthyn.
(74) The Abbott of Tourehill.

---

[56] John Mowbray, second son of (20), and brother of (30), assumed the title of Duke of Norfolk, 1424. Died in 1432.

[57] James Butler, "the White Earl," Lord Deputy of Ireland, in Dublin, 1407.

[58] Succeeded his father in 1408, and died 1414.

[59] Third son of John of Gaunt (18), Cardinal and Lord Chancellor in 1413, and again in 1424. Uncle to (56). Died 11th April, 1447.

[60] Sixth Baron, sat in Parliament 1396 to 1441, and died in 1445.

[61] Fifth Baron, born 1374. Sat in Parliament 30th November, 1396, to September, 1414, and died 1415.

[62] (See 25). Crowned 9th April, 1413. Died at Bois Vincennes in France, 31st August, 1422.

[63] Youngest son of Henry IV (25), and brother of (62). Regent during the minority of Henry VI, and died in 1446.

[64] Fifth Earl, and grandson of (6). The rightful heir to the Crown through Lionel, Duke of Clarence, and Edward IV (139) succeeded through his title. He died 1424.

[65] Sixth Baron, born 1385. Sat in Parliament 21st September, 1411, to 5th September, 1450. Died 1452.

[66] Third Baron. Sat in Parliament 17th December, 1387, to 1st September, 1423. Died 1424.

[67] Eleventh Earl of Arundel in 1322. Died 1415.

[68] Thomas de Montacote, seventh Earl of Salisbury (his father, a zealous Lollard, and beheaded at Cirencester January, 1400). He died in 1428.

[69] Succeeded his father William in 1410-11; then in 1420, Earl of Worcester, and died in 1422.

[70] Thomas Thetford. Elected 8th June, 1413, and died 1432.

[71] Only son of "Hotspur," and grandson of (8), see page 88 *ante*. Was at the battle of Agincourt, and slain at St. Albans, 23rd May, 1455.

[72] Eighth Baron in 1414. At the seige of Roan, and rewarded with the grant of Basqueville in Normandy. Slain in the Battle of Beaugé in 1421.

[73] Probably the second son of Edmund, the fourth Lord. (See 35.)

[74] The Monastery of St. Mary Graces. "The East Minster" next the Tower of London.

Henry VI.

(75) Philip Morgan, Bishop of Worcester, 1422.
(76) Mr. John Stafford, Privy Seale.
(77) Humffrey, Earle of Stafford, 1423.
(78) Lewes Robessartes, Lord Bourcers.
(79) [William Owborne] the Abbott of Tower Hill.
(80) Mr. William Anwick, Privy Seale.
(81) Harry Werkworth, the Prior of St. Mary Overy.
(82) Wm. Clerk, the Prior of St. Trinitie in Christchurch.
(83) John, Lord Roos, 1425.
(84) John, Lord Talbott.
(85) William, Lord Zouth.
(86) William, Lord Lovell.
(87) William, Lord Harrington.
(88) Thomas, Baron of Carew, 1425.
(89) Walter, Lord Fitzwater.
(90) John, Lord Scroope.
(91) John Kemp, Bishop of London.

---

[75] Translated to Ely, February, 1425-6. Chancellor of Normandy. Died 25th October, 1435.

[76] Probably Bishop of Bath and Wells, 1425-43. Archbishop of Canterbury, 1443-52.

[77] Sixth Earl. Succeeded his father, slain at Shrewsbury in 1403. In September, 1444, created Duke of Buckingham, Constable of Dover Castle, and killed at the Battle of Northampton, 27th July, 1460.

[78] Third Baron Bourcher, a courtesy title only, as having married (when Sir Lewis Robsart, Standard Bearer of Henry V) the only daughter of the second Baron.

[79] See page 115 *ante*.

[80] Bishop of Norwich, 1426-30, and Lincoln, 1436-49.

[81] Elected 1414. Died 1452.

[82] Situate within Aldgate; Clerk. Was elected on 18th October, 1420.

[83] Probably Thomas, who died in 1431.

[84] The renowned "Sir John," who succeeded as Baron, August, 1431. Sat in Parliament October, 1409, to November, 1421, and created Earl of Shrewsbury in 1442. Died 1453.

[85] Son of (61). Sat in Parliament January, 1426, to February, 1463. Died 1463.

[86] The seventh Baron. Sat in Parliament February, 1425, to June, 1453. Died 1454.

[87] The fifth Baron in 1418. Sat in Parliament February, 1421, to September, 1439. Died in 1457.

[88] Not identified.

[89] Born 1400, and succeeded as seventh Baron in 1419. Sat in Parliament July, 1429, to March, 1430. Much distinguished in the French Wars of Henry V. Died in 1432.

[90] Sir John Scroope. Succeeded as Baron when his brother was beheaded at Southampton in 1415. Sat in Parliament January, 1426, to May, 1455. Treasurer of the Exchequer, and died 15th November, 1455.

[91] Bishop of Rochester, 1419-21; London, 1422-26; York, 1426-52; Canterbury in 1452-4, and then died. He was also a Cardinal, and Lord Chancellor in 1426, and again in 1450.

(92) John, Lord Gray of Codnor, 1426.
(93) Raph Nevill, Earle of Westmoreland, 1427.
(94) William Gray, Bishop of London, 1428.
(95) Henry Boucers, Earle of Yew, 1429.
(96) William Poole, Earle of Suffolke, 1431.
(97) John Sutton, Baron of Dudley.
(98) Gaylard, Lord Doros .... ⎫ Three ⎫
(99) Barard, Lord Mounferant.... ⎬ French ⎬ 1431.
(100) Barard, Lord Delamote .... ⎭ Lords ⎭
(101) Thomas Polton, Bishop of Worcester, 1432.
(102) Marmaduke Lomney, Bp. of Carlisle.
(103) Eleanor, Duchess of Gloucester, 1434.
(104) Richard, Duke of York.
(105) Lord Strange, and Constance his Wief.
(106) Robert, Lord Poyninges.
(107) Nicholas, Baron Carewe.
(108) Sir Reginald West, Lord Delaware.
(109) Earle of Oxenford.
(110) Lord Fferris of Chartley.
(111) William Lynwood, Privy Seale.

---

[92] Fifth Baron. Sat in Parliament February, 1420, to August, 1428. Died 1430.

[93] Fifth Baron, and second Earl of Westmoreland. He married the sister of (71). Died 1485.

[94] London, 1426-31 ; Lincoln, 1431-36. In the latter year he died.

[95] On the death of (78) the Barony descended on the Earl of Ewe in Normandy.

[96] Fourth Earl, on the death of his brother slain at Agincourt, 1415. Served for 17 years with distinction in the wars in France. Then beheaded at the port of Dover in 1450. His son married Elizabeth Plantagenet, sister of Edward IV and Richard III.

[97] Fourth Baron. Carried the standard at the funeral of Henry V. Held several offices and sat in Parliament from 1439 to 1487, when he died.

[101] At Hereford 1420 to 1422, Chichester to 1426, Worcester to 1433, when he died.

[102] Translated to Lincoln 1450, and died 1452.

[103] Daughter of Reginald Lord Cobham, and wife of Humphrey Duke of Gloucester, fourth son of Henry VI (63).

[104] Only son of Richard Plantagenet. Slain at the battle of Wakefield, 30th December, 1460 (64 and 139).

[105] Richard seventh Baron, and Constance his first wife. He died 1449.

[106] Fifth Baron. Sat in Parliament August, 1404, to January, 1445. Was in the wars of France (Henry IV, V, and VI), and fell at the seige of Orleans 1406.

[107] Not identified.

[108] Fifth Baron and sixth Baron De la Warr. Sat in Parliament July, 1427, to September, 1449. Died 1551.

[109] Probably John de Vere, Earl of Oxford, a stout Lancastrian, and at the triumph of the Yorkists in 1461, he was beheaded (with his son Aubrey) on Tower Hill.

[110] Fifth titular Baron. Not summoned to Parliament. Died 1435-6.

[111] Probably the Bishop of St. David's from 1422 to 1446.

(112) King Henry the Sixth had the Clothing of this Mistery.
(113) Edward Nevill, Lord Latymer, 1437.
(114) Robert Nevill, Bishop of Salisbury.
(115) Lewes of Lusingbourne, Chancellor of France.
(116) John, Duke of Norfolke, 1438.
(117) Robert Gylbard, Bishop of London.
(118) The Abbott and Prior of Westminster, 1439.
(119) William, Earle of Arundell, 1440.
(120) Thomas Luceus, Lord Scales.
(121) Robert, Prior of St. John's.
(122) Thomas Boucers, Bishop of Ely, 1444.
(123) John Talbott, Lord of Lile.
(124) Sir Thomas Hoo, Chancellor of Normandy, 1445.
(125) The Lord Molynes.
(126) John, Lord Bishop of Rochester.
(127) Thomas Porney, Prior of St. Trinity, London.
(128) Lord Viscount Beaumont.
(129) Thomas, Lord Roos.

---

[112] Son of (62). Born 1421. Crowned 6th November, 1429. Died in the Tower, 1471.

[113] Sixth son of Ralph, first Earl of Westmoreland. Sat in Parliament September, 1450 to 1472. Died 1476.

[114] Brother of (113). At Salisbury, 1427-37. Durham to 1457, and then died.

[115] Brother of (113). Sat in Parliament July, 1432, to 1469, in which year he died.

[116] Third Duke, son of (56). Died 1461.

[117] Robert Gilbert was Bishop of London from 1436 to 1448, when he died.

[118] See (47). Hawarden was Abbot from 1420 to 1440, and Kyrton, a possible relation of the Merchant Taylor of that name, from 1440 to 1466.

[119] Fifteenth Earl of Arundel in 1438, and died in 1488.

[120] Seventh Baron in 1418. Sat in Parliament January, 1445, to October, 1459. Died 1460. Daughter and heiress married Anthony Widville, Earl Rivers.

[121] Robert Botyll. Prior from 1439 to 1469. Malory's successor, page 112 *ante*.

[122] He was son of (95). Bishop of Winchester 1435-43, Ely 1444-54, Lord Chancellor 1455, and Canterbury 1455-86, dying 30th March. A Cardinal.

[123] Son of (84) and second Earl of Shrewsbury. Died 1460.

[124] In 1447 created a Baron. He suppressed the Rebellion in Normandy, and had 11l. per annum granted to him for life. His daughter Anne was the wife of Sir Geoffrey Boleyn, Lord Mayor 1467, and died 1453.

[125] Robert Hungerford, who, in 1445, by right of his wife Aleanore Molines, sat in Parliament January, 1445, to January, 1453. Attainted as Baron Hungerford in 1461.

[126] Bishop of St. Asaph 1433-44, and to Rochester 1467, when he died.

[127] See (82).

[128] The sixth Baron, who held a conspicuous position in the reign of Henry VI. In 1435-6 he was granted the Earldom of Boloine, and 12th February, 1440, made Viscount Beaumont (being the first grant of such a title). He lost his life while fighting as a Lancastrian at Northampton, 10th July, 1459.

[129] The tenth Baron. Born 9th September, 1427, succeeded in 1431. A staunch Lancastrian, and being with the King at York, on 29th March, 1461. On hearing of the defeat at Towton Field, he fled with him to Berwick, and upon the surrender of the town was attainted in November, 1461.

(130) Raph Botelor, Knt., Lord of Sidley and Tresorer of England.
(131) Lord Wells.
(132) Kemp, Bishop of London, 1449.
(133) John Tiptough, Earle of Worcester, 1451.
(134) William Wainflete, Bishop of Winchester, 1452.
(135) Richard Neville, Earle of Warwick.
(136) Henry Beauford, Earle of Dorset, 1453.
(137) Richard, Lord Lawarre, 1458.
(138) George Neville, Bishop of Winchester and Chancellour of England, 1459.

Edward IV.

(139) King Edward the Fourth, 1460.
(140) Lord Humffrey Stafford, Lord of Southwark.
(141) Lord William Hastings.
(142) Henry, Lord Fitzhugh.
(143) George, Duke of Clarance, 1462.
(144) Richard, Duke of Gloucester, who was after King Richard the Third.
(145) John Neville, Earle of Northumberland, 1465.

---

[130] Created Baron Sudeley in September, 1441. Died 1473.

[131] Sixth Baron. Sat in Parliament February, 1432, to July, 1460. A staunch Lancastrian, and was killed in Towton Field on Palm Sunday, 1461.

[132] The same as 91.

[133] John Tiptoft, born 1428. Created Earl 16th July, 1449. A Yorkist during the temporary restoration of Henry VI. He was arrested, brought to London, and beheaded on Tower Hill in 1470.

[134] (*Alias*) Pattyn, Provost of Eton College. Lord Chancellor 1456. Bishop of Winchester from 1447 to 11th August, 1487, when he died.

[135] The son of (33) and brother of (113). Married Alice Montacote, and created Earl of Salisbury, 4th May, 1442, and Earl of Warwick; also Baron Montacote, *jure uxoris*.

[136] Assumed to be a courtesy title held by the eldest son of Edmund Marquis of Dorset, and fourth Earl of Somerset, who eventually became second Duke of Somerset, and was beheaded by the Yorkists after the battle of Hexham, May, 1464.

[137] Son of (108). Born 1432. Succeeded in 1451. Sat in Parliament, January, 1456, to August, 1472. Died 1476.

[139] Son of Richard Duke of York (164) by Cicely, daughter of (33). Born 1441. Crowned 1461. Died 1482.

[140] Sat in Parliament, July, 1461, till 1463. Created Lord Stafford 1464, and Earl of Devon May, 1469, after Thomas Courtnay, Earl of Devon, had been captured at Towton and executed. He deserted the King's army with 800 archers, and was captured and beheaded at Bridgewater on the 17th August, 1469.

[141] First Baron. Sat in Parliament July, 1461, March, 1482. The Chamberlain of Edward IV. Beheaded by Richard III in 1483.

[142] Fifth Baron. Born 1430. Sat in Parliament May, 1455, till 1470. Brother-in-law of (141).

[143] Third son of Richard Duke of York (104). Condemned for treason, February, 1478, and died in the Tower, as some say in a butt of Malmscy.

[144] Brother of (143) and Richard III.

[145] Third son of Richard Earl of Salisbury. Summoned to Parliament by Henry VI, 1460, as Baron Nevill; and by Edward IV, in May, 1467, made Earl of Northumberland. He defeated the Lancastrians under the Duke of Somerset, at Hexham. He resigned the Peerage of Northumberland, and became Marquis of

CHAP. XVI.]   *Roll of Honorary Members.*   301

(146) Lord John, Earle of Oxenford.
(147) John, Sonne and Heire of the Lord Fitzwater.
(148) Duke of Suffolk, 1466.
(149) Earle of Shrewsbury.
(150) Thomas, Lord Stanley.
(151) Richard Ffynes, Lord Dacre.
(152) William, Lord Harbert.
(153) Lord Fferries.
(154) John May, Abbott of Chertsey.
(155) Wm Abbott of St. Austin's nere the City of Canterbury.
(156) John, Duke of Norfolke, 1469.
(157) George, Duke of Bedford.
(158) William Lovell, Lord Morley.
(159) Lady Fferries.

Montagu. He joined his brother, the Earl of Warwick, in attempting to restore Henry VI, and both brothers fell at Barnet, 14th August, 1471.

[146] Second son of (109). In 1470 restored as thirteenth Earl of Oxford, and sat as High Steward at the trial of John Tiptoft, Earl of Worcester, who was beheaded on Tower Hill (133). After the battle of Barnet he was attainted and pardoned his life, escaping from prison and doing good service at Bosworth Field for Henry VII, he was restored to his title and position. Made High Constable of the Tower and Lord High Admiral. On the accession of Henry VIII he was restored to the office of Great Chamberlain. Died 1513.

[147] Sir John Ratcliffe. Succeeeded as the eighth Baron. Sat in Parliament September, 1485, October, 1495. For treason in connection with Perkyn Warbeck he was attainted, endeavouring to escape in going to Calais. He was there beheaded, 1495.

[148] Son of (96). On the accession of Henry VII made Constable of Wallingford. Married Elizabeth, the sister of Edward IV (139), and died 1491.

[149] George Talbot, the third Earl and grandson of (123). Died 28th June, 1473.

[150] Second Baron Stanley, succeeded in 1458-9. Sat in Parliament July, 1460, to December, 1483. Brought Richard III's crown and placed it on the head of Henry VII at Bosworth. Created Earl of Derby, 27th October, 1485. His second wife was Margaret Countess of Richmond, mother of Henry VII, and foundress of St. John's and Christ College, Cambridge. He died 1504.

[151] Married Joan Dacres, and was declared Lord Dacres by Parliament 7th November, 1458. Sat in Parliament October, 1459, to November, 1482. Died 1484.

[152] First Baron. Created Earl of Pembroke in 1468, and beheaded in 1469.

[153] Walter Devereux. Married Anne, the heiress and only daughter of Will de Ferrars, and was summoned to Parliament in 1461, *jure uxoris*. He was killed at Bosworth Field, 1485.

[154] Chosen 1467. Henry VI was interred at Chertsey during his incumbency, which ended in 1479.

[155] James Sevenoak, elected 1457, or William Selling, who died 1480.

[156] John Mowbray, fourth Duke. Died 1475.

[157] Created 5th January, 1469, by Edward IV, with intention of his marrying his eldest daughter, Elizabeth, but by the attainder of his father (Marquis Montagu) all his estates were forfeited, and he was degraded by Parliament in 1477, and he died in 1483.

[158] The seventh Baron. William Lovell, the husband of Alianore Morley, heiress of the sixth Baron, and who was summoned *jure uxoris* as Lord Morley to Parliament, August, 1469—July, 1476, until he died.

[159] Only daughter of (153).

(160) Laurence, Bishop of Durham.
(161) John, Bishop of Exeter.
(162) Lord of Northumberland, 1471.
(163) Anthony Woodvile, Lord Ryver, 1476.
(164) John Russell, Bishop of Rochester.

Richard III.

(165) Sir John Wood, Kn^t, Tresorer of England, 1483.

Henry VII.

(166) King Henry the Seventh.

Henry VIII.

(167) Edward, Duke of Buckingham, 1510.

Elizabeth.

(168) Thomas, Earle of Sussex, 1562.

James I, 1607.

Ambassadors.

(169) John Berk, Lord in Godshalckoort, &c., Councellor of Dort in Holland.
(170) Sir James Du Maldere, Kn^t, Lord of Hayes, Councellor of Zealand.
(171) Sir Noel de Caron, Kn^t, Lord of Schoonewall, &c., Ambassador from the Stats, &c.

Noblemen.

(172) The Duke of Lenox.

---

[160] Botle or Bootle. Bishop of Durham 1457-76. Lord Keeper 1473. York to 19th May, 1480, when he died.

[161] Half-brother to (160). Baron of Exchequer 1465-1478, dying 5th April. Both were sons of John Bootle, of Barton, Lancashire, in Richard II's reign.

[162] Henry fourth Earl, son of Henry the third Earl, who was slain 1461. Restored in 1470, and died April, 1489. (See 145 and 157.)

[163] Anthony Widville (son of Sir Richard, of Grafton, who was Governor of the Tower in Henry VI's reign, and created Baron Rivers), married Elizabeth, the heiress of Thomas Lord Scales (120) and sat as Lord Scales December, 1462—February, 1463. Succeeded as Earl Rivers, 1469, and was beheaded with his second son, John, at Pontefract, 1483.

[164] Rochester 1476-80, Lincoln to 1494, Lord Chancellor, 1483 for Edward V and Richard III, and died 30th December, 1494.

[165] Sir Richard, not John, was Treasurer in 1484.

[166] See page 37. Died 22nd April, 1509.

[167] Edward Stafford, the third Duke, who succeeded 1483. Lord High Constable. Beheaded in 1521, as his grandfather and father had been in 1483 and 1486.

[168] Thomas Ratcliffe, third Earl of Sussex, and was grandnephew of (167). Lived in Bermondsey, and there died 19th June, 1583.

[171] (See, 80, note and *ante*).

[172] Ludovick, second Duke, born 29th September, 1574. Attended King James to England in 1603, and represented his Majesty in the Parliament of Scotland 1607, and was created the Duke of Richmond, 17th May, 1623. He died on 16th February, 1624, and was buried in Westminster Abbey.

(173) Earle of Nottingham, Lord Admirall.
(174) Earle of Suffolk, Lord Chamberlain
(175) Earle of Arundell.
(176) Earle of Oxenford.
(177) Earle of Worcester.
(178) Earle of Pembroke.
(179) Earle of Essex, absent yet entered by order from the Prince under his Highness own hand.
(180) Earle of Northampton.
(181) Earle of Salisbury, principall Secretary to the King.
(182) Earle of Montgommery.
(183) Earle of Perth.
(184) Lord Viscount Cranborne.
(185) Lord Eure.
(186) Lord Hunsdon.
(187) Lord Knolles.
(188) Lord Hay.
(189) Lord Sanker.
(190) Lord Burghley."

The names following are members of the Prince's household, and their annual remuneration has been added from the Household Establishment of the Prince, published 1790 by the Society of Antiquaries.

---

[173] Charles Howard (second Baron of Effingham). Created Earl 22nd October, 1597. Died 1624.

[174] Thomas Howard, first Baron de Walden. Created Earl 21st July, 1603. Died 1626.

[175] Thomas Howard, twenty-third Earl. Created Earl of Norfolk, 6th June, 1644, and Earl Marshall. Died 1646.

[176] (See 146.) Henry De Vere, Lord Great Chamberlain, died 1625.

[177] Edward Somerset, ninth Earl, succeeded 1589. Died 1628.

[178] William Herbert, the twenty-second Earl, succeeded 1601. Died 1630.

[179] Robert Devereux, twentieth Earl (son of Robert, who was beheaded 1600). Restored in 1603. Died 1646.

[180] Henry Howard (second son of Henry Earl of Surrey). Created Baron Howard of Marnhill, and Earl of Northampton, 13th March, 1604. Died 1614.

[181] Robert Cecil, first Viscount Cranborne. Created Earl of Salisbury, 4th May, 1605. Died 1612.

[182] Philip Herbert, brother of (178). Created Earl 4th May, 1605, and succeeded (178) in 1630. Died 1650.

[183] Lord Drummond. Created Earl, 4th March, 1605.

[184] Eldest son of (181).

[185] Ralph Eure, third Baron, succeeded in 1594, and living in 1623.

[186] John Carey, third Baron, succeeded in 1603. Died 1617.

[187] William Knollys. Created May, 1603. Viscount Wallingford, March, 1616. Earl of Banbury, August, 1626. Died 1632.

[188] John, seventh Lord Hay of Yestr, died 1609.

[190] William (son of Thomas Cecil, second Baron Burleigh, who was created Earl of Exeter, 4th May, 1605). He succeeded as Earl in 1622, and died 1640.

"Mr. Howard, Sir John Harrington, Mr. Sheffield, Sir Thomas Challoner, Governor to the Prince (66l. 13s. 4d. and diet ; he was the son-in-law to Fleetwood the Recorder, and built a residence for himself in Clerkenwell Close) ; Sir Thomas Vavasor, Knight Marshall, Sir David Fowlis (66l. with diet), Cofferer ; Sir David Murray (22l. 6s. 8d. with diet), Groom of the State ; Mr. Dr. Montague, Deane of the Chapell ; Mr. Newton, Dean of Durham and Tutor to ye Prince ; Sir Thomas Savage, Sir Lewes Lewknor, Master of the Ceremonies ;[1] Sir Robert Darcy, Mr. Erwyn, Gentlemen Ushers of the Privy Chamber to the Prince (20l. with diet) ; Sir John Wentworth, Mr. Moore, Gentlemen of the Privy Chamber to the Prince ; Sir Edward Michelborne, Sir Thomas Munson, Sir Robert Maunsell, Sir John Wentworth, Sir Thomas Penruddock, Sir Robert Carew, Sir Henry Mountague, Recorder of London ; Sir Henry Helmes, Sir Gregory Cromwell, Sir John Key, Sir George Hay, Sir Robert Filligray, Sir Robert Osborne, Sir Edward Torbuck, Sir Thomas Mettam, Sir James Ouchterlony, Sir Alex^r Stratton, Lord of Louriston, Sir William Anstrowder, Sir John Digby, Sir Richard Preston, Sir Edward Gorge, Sir Raph Winwood, Sir Roger Dallison, Sir Richard Wigmore ; Mr. Bruce, Mr. Hetley, Mr. Puckering, Pages of Honor to the Prince ; Mr Sandelaus, Mr. Burchmore, Mr. Ramsey, Mr. Gybb, Grooms of the Bed Chamber to the Prince (13l. 6s. 8d. each with diet) ; Mr. Douglass, Equerie ; Mr. Abington, Mr. Alexander, Mr. Lumley, Gentlemen Ushers ; Daily Waiters, (20l. and diet), Mr. Dr. Hammond, Physicion (140l.) ; Mr. Gwynne ; Mr. Tyrrell, Gentleman of the Bowes ; Mr. Cannock, Auditor to the Prince ; Mr. Richard Martyn, Counsellor at Lawe ; Mr. Manley, Clarck Comptroler (32l.) ; Mr. Fflood, Clarck of the Kitchen (32l. and diet) ; Mr. Knolles, Clarck of the Spicery (20l. and diet) ; Mr. Wilson, Yeoman of the Robes (5l. and diet) ; Mr. Knightley, Gentlemen Usher, daily waiter to the King ; Thomas Morgan, Mr. John Hebborne, Gent. Usher, daily waitor to ye King ; Mr. Alexander Serle, Bachelor in Lawes ; John Wydopp the younger, one of the Groomes of the Princes Privy Chamber, William Hay[2] ; and divers Esquiors, Gentlemen and Servaunts to the King, Queen, Prince and Noblemen."

"This Roll his Majestie gratiously accepted and said that he himself was free of another Company, yet he would soe much grace the Company of Merchant Taylors' that the Prince his eldest sonne shoulde be free thereof, and that he would see and be a witness when the Garland should be put on his head." It was in accordance with the custom of the times that the member could not serve two masters, and hence the King's action.

"And then they in like manner resorted to the Prince, and the said Master presented his Highnesse with another rich purse wherein were fiifty pounds in gould, and the Clerke delivered his Highness a like Roll which also were gratiously received, and his Highnesse said that not only himselfe woulde be free of the

---

[1] Rye's England, page 182.
[2] Taylor to the Prince, page 334.

Companie, but commaunded one of his Gentlemen and the Clerk of the Companie to goe to all the Lords present and require all of them that loved him and were not free of other Companies to be free of his Companie, whereupon these Lords whose names ensue 'with humble thanks to his Highnesse,' accepted of the Freedom.[1]

The proper business of the day then proceeded.[2] "The Master and Wardens according to their usuall manner went with their Garlands on their heads to Publish the Eleccōn. It pleased the King's moast Excellent Maj$^{tie.}$ to resort into the little Lobby out of whiche there was a faier windowe made on purpose for his Maj$^{tie.}$ to looke into the Hall, and there his Maj$^{tie.}$ observed the whole manner of the ceremonie: And it did moast gratiously please the Prince to call for the Master's Garland, and to put the same upon his owne head, whereat the King's Maj$^{tie.}$ did very harteley laugh; and soe the Old Master and Wardens proceeded to the publicačōn of the Eleccōn of the Newe Master and Wardens whoe were all here present to the good liking of the Companie."

The farewell at last came. "After all which his Maj$^{tie.}$ came downe into the Greate Hall, and sitting in his Chayre of State did hear a melodious song of farewell, sung by three men in the shipp being apparelled in watchett silke like seamen, which song so pleased his Maj$^{tie.}$ that he caused the same to be sung three times over. And his Maj$^{tie.}$ and the noble Prince, and Honourable Lords gave the Company hearty thanks and so departed."

No delay was to be allowed in clearing out the hall[3] and in settling up the accounts for this entertainment, and on the 17th 300*l.* was taken out of the Treasury and given to the Master on account. Then they conferred the Livery upon Dr. John Bull (who was a freeman), and the freedom and Livery on Nathaniel Gyles.

"At this Court the Company accepted Mr. John Bull, Doctor of Musique and a Brother of this Companie into the Clothing and Liverye of the Companie.[4] Also they have accepted and taken Mr. Nathanael Gyles who hath his grace to be Doctor of Musique, and is Master of the Children of the King's Chappell into the Freedom of this Society, and also into the Clothing and Livery of the same

---

[1] These persons made no payment to the Company as the honorary members usually did according to antient custom.

[2] As to these, see pages 48-50.

[3] "To Elizabeth Edwin for making cleane the howse, having 2 women to help her the space of 14 daies, 1*l.*"

[4] Page 134, *ante*. John Bull D.M., admitted free of the Company, 15th December, 1606, on apprenticeship to the Earl of Sussex in 1577-8. He died in 1628, but one of his name was admitted to Dowe's pension when nearly 100 years of age.

And it is ordered that they shalbe placed in the Lyvery next unto the Assistants. And note that the Lyvery Hoods were put upon their shoulders but neither of them sworn. And the Company are contented to shewe this favor unto them for their paynes when the King and Prince dyned at our Hall, and their love and kindness in bestowing the musique which was performed by them, their associates and children in the King's Chamber gratis, whereas the musicians in the greate Hall exacted unreasonable somes of the Company for the same. The Companie therefore meane that this calling of Mr. Doctor Bull and Mr. Nathanael Gyles into the Livery shall not be any burthen or charge unto them further than shall stand with their own good likinge."

The Ambassadors gratified at the honour of admission into the Company, applied for a formal certificate of membership, which was granted to them, on the following day.

The Treasury was again resorted to, and 208*l*. 15*s*. 1*d*. paid to the Master; but in August, when the time of audit drew nigh, they made an appeal to John Swynnerton to help them pay the great charges of the entertainment.

"The Companie falling into consideracõn and reckoning of theire greate Charges in the Entertaining of the King and Prince, amounting to above 1,000*l*., being all disbursed out of the common Stock of the Companie, doe therefore desire to understand of Mr. Swynnerton, late Master, what he will allowe towards the same charges, whoe of his owne accord doth offer (that he beinge allowed the usual allowance to other Masters for his Quarter dinners and also his Wardens 30*l*., and the Brotherhood money) that then he will bestowe towardes the said charges the sum of one hundred forty pounds, the which sum (albeit they hold it not so much as they expected) the Companie have accepted, upon hope that Mr. Swynnerton will be a good Member and Benefactor to our Company."

The accounts were then framed with accuracy, the last three items being:—

"To a youth that copied the draught of the accompt p^{r}sented by the stewards, 6*s*. 8*d*.

"For dribletts forgotten to be written by the payer that kept the money alone, the some of 8*s*. 1*d*.

"Giuen to Henry Beamount, the companies cooke, for 32 maister cooke's dynner, there being noe could meate left for them, 2*l*."

So that if we may believe the last item, the provision laid in was not sufficient for the meals of all those employed in furnishing this grand entertainment, the total cost of which was 1,061*l*. 5*s*. 1*d*.

NOTE.—ITEMS OF EXPENDITURE FOR THE FEAST.

Wine, ale, and beer, that was laid in, and the expenses of the cellar and butlers.

To Bellew.

	£	*s.*	*d.*
For 8 dozen of ashen cupps at 16*d*.	0	10	8
For 2 payles at 18*d*. the payle	0	3	0
For tilters 2*s*. 6*d*., and trayes 4*s*.	0	6	6
For berebarrells to make tubbs for the celle^{rs}	0	4	0
For carying and cutting	0	0	6
For mending a copper cesterne	0	1	0
For 2 quier of paper	0	0	8
For a padlock and staple for the wine cellar	0	1	0
To Silverwood, Griffin, and Belewe for their dynne^{rs}	0	2	0
For mopps to wash the howse with	0	1	0
For a lock for the beere celler dore	0	0	7

Wine of Mr Atkinson.

For 2 hogesheads of gasconie wine at 6*l*. 5*s*.	12	10	0
For one hogeshead of high countrywine rackt	6	10	0
For one hogeshead of cunnock wine	4	10	0
For a rundlet of canara wine con^t 52 gallons	7	16	0
For a tierce of gasconie wine rackt	4	10	0
For 22 gallons of claret wine for the cookes	2	4	0
For the Rundlet for it	0	2	0
For 2 rundlets of rhennish wine con^t 51 gallons at 2*s*. 6*d*.	6	7	6
For the 2 Runletts	0	5	0
For a runlet of white wine con^t 21 gallons and a potle at 2*s*. 2*d*. the gallon, and for the runlet 2*s*.	2	8	3
For one runlet of canara wine con^t 22 gallons at 3*s*.	3	6	0
For the runlet	0	2	0
For 13 gallons of veniger at 18*d*. the gallon	0	19	6
For the runlett	0	1	4
For 2 empty runletts	0	2	0
For 6 hogesheads of empty caske 15*s*., and portage 6*d*.	0	15	6
For a runlett of veniger, 7 gallons	0	10	6
For 2 runletts of rennysh wine, 25 gallons 1 potle, at 2*s*. 6*d*. the gallon 3*l*. 3*s*. 9*d*., and the rundlet 3*s*.	3	6	9
For a runlett of rennish wine, 25 gallons at 2*s*. 6*d*. the gallon, 3*l*. 2*s*. 6*d*., and the runlet 2*s*.	3	4	6
For cartage and portage of all this wine	0	6	8
For 3 gallons of canara wine from the tavarne	0	10	0
For 3 potles of redd wine to make Ipocras	0	3	3
For cariage of 3 runlets of rennish wine	0	1	6

	£	s.	d.
For a gymlett broken 12d., and a dozen of canns 18d.	0	2	6
For a potle of white wine for the cooke	0	1	2
For cariage of 3 runlets of wine	0	1	4
To Mr Bray for his charge of the wyne celler 10s., and to Pryce 2s.	0	12	0
To Mr Roe for wine, one saterday to dynner	0	3	4

Chief Butlers.—Hyer of Lynnen.

	£	s.	d.
To John Hudson for his paynes beinge chiefe butler	5	0	0
To him for the vse of his lynnen being 6 damaske table clothes, 8 dozen damaske napkins, 6 diaper table clothes, and 3 diaper towells, whereof diaper was mangled and cut in the high gallery, and 19 damaske napkins, and one diaper napkin was lost	2	10	0

Comon butlers.

	£	s.	d.
To Nicholas Bellewe for his fee 40s., and gratificacion 10s.	2	10	0
To John Story 6s., Roger Rany 6s., Tho. Chamberlen 6s.	0	18	0
To Gilbert Yailes 6s., Henry Cocks 6s., and Tho. Leich 6s.	0	18	0
To Thomas Dikes 6s., Richard Morton 6s., to Jo. Fferrer 4s.	0	16	0
To Arthur Godfrey 3s. 6d., Brafford 3s., Wm Bond 2 daies 2s.	0	8	6
To John Ash, Ric. Gardn⁹, Ro. Chapman for 2 daies, &c.	0	6	0
To John Pierce, Ffloid, Tyme, Bretton, Cooly for each 2 daies....	0	10	0
To Briggs 4s., to Browm⁹, 2s., to Thompson 2s., to stanger 3s. ...	0	11	0
To Vaughan 2s., to Heywood 2s., to Murrey 12d., to Tomkins 12d.	0	6	0
To Lownes 12d., Lane 12d., Morris 12d., Bread-stealer 12d.	0	4	0
To John Williams 12d., to Jarvis 12d., Newbut 12d., Munday 12d.	0	4	0
To Parry 12d., to Orton 12d., to Wilson 12d., to Levet 12d.	0	4	0
To Story for his apron	0	1	6
To 8 butlers, to watch the plate one night 4s., for their suppers 6s., paper to pack the King's plate in 6d., washing of it 6d.	0	12	6
To Myles Okeley the butler for his paynes	0	6	0
To Thomas Wiborne for drawing of drinck	0	2	0

	£	s.	d.			
For 6 barrels of beere[1] at 8s.	2	16	0	7	14	0
For 13 barrels of beere at 6s. the barrell	4	18	0			
For a tunn of court beere to Mr. Campion				1	16	0
For carring vp of beere to the high gallory				0	1	0
For 4 barrells of 10s. ale				2	0	0
For 4 barrells of 8s. ale				1	12	0
For 1 barrell of 6s. ale				0	6	0

---

[1] A barrel of beer was 36 gallons, of ale 32 gallons. The tun was 252 gallons, by 2 Henry VI, cap. 11, but the wine gallon was 231 cubic and the ale gallon 282 cubic inches. (See Report of H. of C. 1758, page 48, and 7 Rept. 1873, of Board of Trade on W. and M.)

CHAP. XVI.] *Expenditure for Feast.* 309

Payments by William Sotherne, one of the Caters.
Butchers' Beefe, &c.

	£	s.	d.
For 4 surloynes and ribbs to rost 21 stone at 20d.	1	15	0
For 42 stone of beefe for labourers at 18d.	3	3	0
For 79 stone of mutton at 2s., leggs at 4s., 8l. 2s.	8	2	0
For veale, 5 calves and a halfe, 5l. 19s., and brest and loyne	6	5	0
For lambs 7 at 6s., and mutton 4s.....	2	6	0
For suett lbs. 104, at 4d. the pounde	1	14	8
For mary bones, 10 dozen at 5s. the dozen, 50s.	2	10	0
For sweete breds and land lambs stones	0	2	0
For pricks 12d., and 88 neats tongues at 14d.	5	3	8
For 3 dozen of sheepes tongues	0	3	0
For 8 dryed neats tonges 12s., and 3 dozen at 16d.	3	0	0
For 18 dryed neats tongues at 16d. and 12 at 18d.	2	2	0
For 20 neats tongues at 14d. the peece	1	3	4
For 4 leggs of mutton 7s., and 4 leggs of veale 7s. 8d.	0	14	8
For 3 dozen of deeres tongues 3s., and 2 dozen of sweet breds 4s.	0	7	0
For 6 dozen of lambs dowsetts	0	6	0
For 2 leggs of mutton for the m^{rs} dynner	0	4	0
For half a lamb at that tyme	0	4	4
Paid William Sotherne for a porter to attend him 4 daies, etc.	0	4	4
Paid for our dynner wth m^r Alexander ye princes gent. vsher	1	4	0

Fish.

	£	s.	d.
For fresh salmon, one at 35s. and 2 at 25s. ye peece	4	5	0
For one 22s. and 4 others at 19s. the peece	4	18	0
For 3 of m^r Angell at 23s. 4d. the peece	3	10	0
For a salmon peale 4s. 6d., and a side and chyne 12s.	0	16	6
For 8 playse 6s. 2d., a lynge 3s., att butt 2s.	0	11	2
For a salt fish 10d., for a lobster 16d.	0	2	2
For 2 greate playse, a paier of soles, and a dorie ...	0	8	6
For 3 greate lobsters and 200 praunes	0	7	2
For porters to carry fysh from m^r Angells	0	1	6
For a turbut to m^r Angell at 3s. 4d.	0	3	4

	£	s.	d.		£	s.	d.
Pikes, large cont 24 inches, 16 at 6s. the pike	4	16	0	}			
Carpes, 12 at 2s. 6d. the carpe	1	10	0				
Tenches, 12 at 2s. the peece....	1	4	0				
Pikes, large, cont 24 inches, 6 at 6s. the peece	1	16	0	}	15	0	0
Pikes, midle, cont 22 inches, 14 at 4s. the peece	2	16	0				
Pikes, cont 20 inches, 14 at 3s. 4d.....	2	6	8				
Pikes, cont 18 inches at 2s. 8d.	1	1	4				

These 7 sommes amount to 15l. 10s., but 10s. abated, so paid.

	£	s.	d.		£	s.	d.
Paid for a pike by m^d Lansdale	0	2	2	}	0	3	2
To m^r Osborns man for bringing a fresh salmon	0	1	0				

310   Banquet to James I and his son Henry.   [PART I.

Sturgeon.

	£	s.	d.
To m^r Swynnerton for 2 firkins at 26s.	2	12	0
To mr Angell for 2 firkins at 26s.	2	12	0
To m^r Barnes for 2 firkins at 26s.	2	12	0

The Poultry.

	£	s.	d.
For 11 swanns at 10s. the peece	5	10	0
For 6 swans to Mr Swynnerton at 11s.	3	6	0
For 10 old phesents at 10s.	5	0	0
For 16 phesant pouts at 6s. the peece	4	16	0
For 2 phesant cocks	1	0	0
For 16 geese at 22d., and 16 at 21d. the peece	2	17	8
For 62 capons at 2s. 4d. the capon	7	4	8
For 158 pullets at 18d. the peece	11	17	0
For 36 turky chickins at 18d. the peece	2	14	0
For 40 large chickins at 7d. the peece	1	3	4
For 18 large chickins at 7d. the peece	0	9	0
For 162 chickins at 6½d. the peece	4	7	9
For 114 chickins to bake at 6d. the peece	2	17	0
For 47 chickyn peepers at 6d. the peece	1	3	6
For 172 quailes at 10d., and 6d. over for portage	7	3	10
For 23 hernes at 3s., and 22 at 3s. 4d.	7	2	4
For 2 hernes at 3s. 4d.	0	6	8
For 10 bitters at 3s. 4d.	1	13	4
For 13 shovelers at 5s. the peece	3	5	0
For 17 godwitts at 3s. 4d. the peece	3	6	8
For 81 partriches at 18d. the peece	6	1	6
For 14 rouffs at 3s. 4d. the peece	2	6	8
For 14 brewes at 3s. 4d. the peece	2	6	8
For 52 pewetts at 16d. the peece	3	9	4
For 87 rabbets at 8d. and 6 rabbet suck^rs at 6d.	3	1	0
For 66 ducklings at 6d. the peece	1	13	0
For howse pigions 57 at 8d. and 56 at 9d. the peece	4	0	0
For 10 owles, 7 at 12d. and 3 at 8d.	0	9	0
For 2 cookoes at 12d. the peece	0	2	0
For 2 ringdoves at 9d. the peece	0	1	6
For 2 leverets at 2s. 6d. the peece	0	5	0
For 2 peacocks at 10s. the peece	1	0	0
For a greate turky	0	6	0
For a mallard	0	1	0
For 24 teales at 7d. the peece	0	14	0
For 6 martins	0	0	6
For 9 browsses at 3s. 4d. the peece	1	10	0
For 2 capons on the 17 of July for ye M^r and Wardens	0	4	8
For a mallard to hackle by Lansdale	0	2	6

CHAP. XVI.] *Expenditure for Feast.* 311

Grocery.

	£	s.	d.	£	s.	d.
Suger powder, 250 lbs. at 13*d.* the pound	13	10	10			
Svgar refyned 96 lbs. at 15½*d.* the pound....	6	4	0			
Currance fyne 20 lbs. at 6½*d.* the pound	0	10	10			
Pruons 24 lbs. at 2*d.* the pounde	0	4	0			
Reasons of the sonne 6 lbs. at 5*d.* the pounde	0	2	6			
Jorden Almonds 6 lbs. at 18*d.* the pounde	0	9	0			
Figgs 6 lbs. at 6*d.* the pound	0	3	0			
Dates 12 lbs. at 2*s.* 4*d.* the pound	1	8	0			
Pepper beaten 8 lbs., and vnbeaten 12 lbs. at 2*s.* pound	2	0	0			
Nutmeggs beaten 2 lbs. and vnbeaten 4 lbs. at 4*s.*	1	4	0			
Synamon beaten 1 lb., and vnbeaten 2 lbs. at 3*s.* 4*d.*	0	10	0	32	9	10
Gynger beaten 2 lbs. vnbeaten 2 lbs. at 16*d.*	0	5	4			
Mace, large, 3 lbs. at 8*s.* 6*d.* the pounde	1	5	6			
Mace, midle, 8 ounces ½ beaten ½ vnbeaten	0	3	4			
Cloves one pound	0	5	4			
Saffron 2 ozs. at 2*s.* 4*d.*	0	4	8			
Saunders 1 lb. at 4*s.* 6*d.*	0	4	6			
Rice 12 lbs. at 4*d.* the lb.	0	4	0			
Suger powder, 100 lbs. more, at 13*d.* the pound	5	8	4			
Reasons of the sonne more 8 lbs. at 5*d.*	0	3	4			
Dates, 4 lbs. more, at 2*s.* 4*d.* the pounde	0	9	4			
Almonds Jorden 6 lbs. at 18*d.* the pounde	0	9	0			
Pepper casse 6 lbs. at 2*s.* the pound	0	12	0			
Paid 3 porters for portage of this	0	1	0			

Grocery for Ipocras.[1]

	£	s.	d.
For synamon, large, 4 lbs. at 4*s.*	0	16	0
Suger 3 lbs. at 16*d.* the pound	0	4	0
Nutmeggs 3 q's of a pounde	0	3	0
Suger powder 46 lbs. at 13*d.*	2	9	10
Cloves 4 ounces at 4*d.*	0	1	4
Coryander seedes 4 ozs.	0	0	4

For Fruite.

	£	s.	d.
For 3 syves of cherries, and 20 lbs. more at 3*d.*	1	15	6
For strawberies for the king's cookes	0	2	0
For 3 gallons of gooseberies	0	3	0
For a gallon and half of raspices	0	5	0
For certen seeds for the cookes	0	1	10
For 2 hamper of quodlings	0	12	0
For a hamper of pyppyns	0	6	0
For goosberies, peaches, and cheries, wth portage	0	7	0
For greene fruite, peares, apples, and damsyns	1	4	6

---

[1] See recipe for this in footnote at page 49.

	£	s.	d.
For fower score greate lemans at 8d.	2	13	4
For fower score midle lemans at 4d.	1	6	8
For 150 grete orenges at 4d. the peece	2	8	0
For 250 midle orenges at 1d. the peece	1	0	0
For 60 lbs. of potatoes at 10d. the pounde	2	10	0
For 136 quinces at 4d. the peece	2	3	0
For 40 large quinces to Mr. Wallis at 6d.	1	0	0
For ffyfty large quinces to him at 6d.	1	5	0
For 10 dozen of artechoks at 5d. the dozen	2	10	0
For 6 gallons of gooseberies at 16d. the gallon	0	8	0
For 3 quarts of redd currens	0	3	0
For parsly 6s., lettis 5s., and purslane 2s.	0	13	0
For spynnage 3s. smale sallett 2s. 6d.	0	5	6
[1]For corne sallett 2s., tarragon and rockett 12d.	0	3	0
For flowers of all sorts 6s., rosemary and bayes 5s.	0	11	0
For burredge and burnet 12d., carrets, and turnepps 3s.	0	4	0
For sweetherbes of all sorts 3s., onyons and herbs 12d.	0	4	0
For sorroll and fennell 18d., for reddishes 6d.	0	2	0
For hartechoke suckers	0	1	0
For 5 barrell of pickled oysters at 2s.	0	10	0
For a gallon of large olyves	0	5	4
For a potle of small olyves	0	2	0
For 6 lbs. of capers 7s., and 2 lbs. of capers at 5s.	0	12	0
For 14 pickled lemons	0	2	4
For a gallon and a pinte of candy oyle	0	6	9
For 5 lbs. and a half of bolonia salsadg	0	16	6
For 5 barrells and a bottle 2s. 6d., for portage 4d.	0	2	10
For 3 lbs. of balonia salsage to Mr Angell at 3s. 4d.	0	10	0
For 70 wardens to Mr Swynnerton at 4d. the peece	1	3	4
For a gallon of barbaries	0	6	8
For portage of meates	0	2	6

Herbs and Nosegaies.

	£	s.	d.
For 13 baskets of strowings at 6d. the baskett	0	6	6
For flowers about the hall and church	0	4	0
For 9 dozen of nosegaies at 6d. the dozen	0	4	6
For onyons and parsly	0	1	0

For the Cook.

	£	s.	d.
Inprimis for boyling pipkins, 11 dozen and a half at 18d. the cast	0	16	6
For pans 2s. 6d., for 4 porringers 4d.	0	2	10
For 16 candlesticks 8d., and 2 chafing dishes 2d.	0	0	10
For 8 lbs. of candles 2s. 9d., and half a pound of wax 9d.	0	3	5

---

[1] Still to be obtained in London. It is a native edible plant (*Fedia Olitona*), Latham's English Dictionary. *Corn Salad* is an herb whose top leaves are *sallet* of themselves, Mortimer Husbandry. It should be dressed with an admixture of oil and vinegar in the proportion of three to one. Slices of beetroot may be added —E. N.

CHAP. XVI.] *Expenditure for Feast.* 312

	£	s.	d.
For vergis 5 gallons at 8d.—3s. 4d., for rosen 2d.	0	3	6
For mustard 6d., packthreed 4d., ladles 3d.	0	1	1
For oatemeale 6d., and 3 torches 3s., and a linck 4d.	0	3	10
For vinyger 1d. and 5 lbs. of candles 20d.	0	1	9
For 6 lbs. of candles 2s., 4 candlesticks 2d., packthred 6d.	0	2	8
For cords 4d., wooden cans 6d., butter 2d., oyle 4d.	0	1	4
For bay salt for the beere 2d., white salt a bushell 2s.	0	2	2
For 8 dozen of pottle potts at 18d. the dozen	0	12	0
For 8 dozen of temple potts at 12d.	0	8	0
For tapps 12d., candles 7 lbs. 2s. 4d., a firkin 4d.	0	3	8

Other Expenses.

Payd for paynting the signe of the lambe on ye dresser clothes	0	1	0
For making and marking the said dresser clothes	0	5	0
For a dynner on Munday befor the feast	0	10	6

Gammons of Bacon.

For 18 gammons of bacon waying 22 stone at 2s. 2d.	2	7	8
For 8 Westphalia gammons of Mr Angell at 5s. 6d.	2	4	0
For 44 lbs. of lard at 10d. the pound	1	6	8
Butter 160 lbs. of Watson and 200 lbs. of Lansdale	6	0	0
For 14 gallons and a q^{rt} of creame	0	19	0
For forty bushells of fflower by waight at 34 lbs. to a bushell at 4s. 6d. the bushell	9	0	0
For 160 dozen and 6 penny worth of breade	8	0	0
For breade by Mr Lansdale	0	9	0

Fewell.

For 3 loades of old greate cole at 26s. the loade	3	18	0
For 4 sackes of smale coles at 6d. the sack	0	12	0
For 2 thowsand of billets at 15s.	1	10	0
For 400 of ffaggots at 6s. 8d.	1	6	8
For a porter to help Sotherne	0	1	0

7*l.* 7*s.* 8*d.*

Necessaries for the Cooke.

For a reame of capp paper 5s., and a reame of white 4d.	0	5	4
For a hand basket, an herb basket, and treene dishes	0	1	4
For a hoggshead made into 2 tubbs	0	3	0
For 5 lbs. of packthridd	0	3	0
For 3 lbs. of isinglasse at 12d. the pounde	0	3	0
For 3 shovels 3s., for 2 payles 18d., for 3 poles for ovens 9d., for buttons and allowes 6d., and for 2 dozen of broomes 2s.	0	7	9
For bread for the kytchin 18d., and carring stuff 5s.	0	6	6
For a realme of capp paper for the cookes	0	5	0
To Jennyns for scowring of vessell	0	2	0
Ffor our dynner at the Mermaide for Mr Wright and others	0	16	0
For an other dynner for Mr Webb ye butler and others	0	8	6

3*l.* 1*s.* 5*d.*

Lynnen.

	£	s.	d.
For 29 ells of holland for butler's aprons	2	8	0
For 28 ells of canvis for dresser clothes at 12d.	1	8	0
For 33 ells ½ of vemounter canvas at 18d.	2	10	3
For 20 ells ¼ of holland at 2s. 8d. for cooks' aprons	2	13	4
For 5 ells of course canvas at 10d. the ell	0	4	2
For 2 ells of browne ministers to wrapp yᵉ towells	0	1	10
For 5 ells of cambrick at 7l. 2d. the ell	1	15	10
For 6 ells ½ of Ozenbriggs to wipe hands	0	6	6
For 9 ells of 3 qʳˢ of lockerome at 16d. the ell	0	13	0
For one ell ¼ of cambrick for Mʳ Cordall	0	11	0
For 9 ells 3 qrs. of heasings for yᵉ cooks to wipe one	0	9	6
For 14 yards for straynors at 12d., and 2 yard corse 12d. ...	0	15	0

13l. 16s. 5d.

Table Equipment.

	£	s.	d.
For yᵉ loane of plate to Mʳ Terriey yᵉ gouldsmith, wᶜʰ was hired by Mʳ Georg Lydiat and other Comytties appointed	12	0	0
Paid him for 28 oz. ¾ of plate guilt and vngult, by agreement made by George Sotherton—7l. 18s. wᵗʰ proviso that if the same plate be found againe, and not spoyled, to allowe like pryce againe for it	7	18	0
For cartage of silver vessell from the Tower 14d., and to the Tower back againe 16d.	0	2	6
For a padlock for the truncke for the plate	0	1	0
For a doble lock for the plate chamber dore	0	5	0
For bringing and carrying plate from and to Mʳ Hudson's ...	0	8	3
For loane of the King's plate to Mʳ Warden Atkinson	5	0	0

Trenchers.

	£	s.	d.
For 20 grosse of round trenchers at 4s. 6d. yᵉ grosse	4	10	0
For 24 gallon pots at 20d. the peece	2	0	0
For 3 dozen of playne potts at 8s. the dozen	1	4	0
For 4 dozen of playne pots at 4s. the dozen	0	16	0
For 1 paier of table knyves....	0	2	0

23 10 0

Glasses.

	£	s.	d.			
For 2 dozen of water glasses at 8s.	0	16	0			
For 12 dozen of venis glasses at 18s.	10	16	0	14	12	0
For 2 dozen of fyne venis glasses, covered, at 2s. 2d. the peece	3	0	0			
For one venis table baskett 4s., and one square 3s.	0	7	0			
For 2 dozen of ashen cupps at 18d.	0	3	0			

23l. 14s. whereof 4s. abated, and so pd. .... } 23l. 10s.

CHAP. XVI.] *Expenditure for Feast.* 315

For the loane of black Jacks.

	£	s.	d.
To Robert Appleby for the loane of 18 black jacks	1	0	0
For him for 2 of them lost	0	13	0

33s.

For the hyer of Pewter.

	£	s.	d.
To Robert Hurdys for the loane of 63 ——— garnish of pewter vessell being rough, at 18d. the garnish	4	16	0
For the loane of 42 pewter potle potts at 6d. the pott	1	1	0
For the loane of 20 long pasty plates at 8d.	0	13	4
For the cariage in and out of the vessell	0	3	0
For the loane of 2 dozen of chamber potts	0	4	0

	£	s.	d.		£	s.	d.
To Robert Herdis for pewter lost—one 7 lbs. platter, 5 fower pound plates, 4 three pounde plates, 2 midle platters, and eleaven pye plates poiz.—all 74 lbs. at 9d. the pound		1	17	4			
For one longe plate 8½ pounde at 10d. the pounde		0	7	1	2	17	8
For 3 pottle pots poiz., 18 lbs. at 8d. the pownd		0	12	0			
For 1 chamber pott 18d., and 14 sawcers 3d.		0	5	0			

3l. 1s. 5d.

	£	s.	d.
Whereof defalked for one dish and one pye plate poiz. 4½ lbs. at 9d. the pound	0	3	9

For the King's Messe.—Banquetting.

	£	s.	d.
Inprimis plums of Janua 1 lb. 8s., and plums of Damasco 1 lb. 6s. 8d.	0	14	8
Pruons de roy 1 lb. 6s. 8d., and Venis apricocks 1 lb. 8s.	0	14	8
Venis azer plums 1 lb. 6s. 8d., and plums of Arabia 1 lb. 6s. 8d.	0	13	4
Plums Valencia 1 lb. 6s. 8d., and Venis dat plums 1 lb. 6s. 8d.	0	13	4
Pruons of Genoa 1 lb. 8s., Venis peach stond 1 lb. 7s.	0	15	0
Dryed aprecocks 1 lb. 8s., peach of Genoa 1 lb. 8s.	0	16	0
Venis verduse plums 1 lb. 6s., French aprecocks 1 lb. 6s.	0	12	0
Venis amber plums 1 lb. 5s. 4d., dryed peach 1 lb. 6s.	0	11	4
Canded plums of Genoa 1 lb. 6s. 8d., dried pedrogots 1 lb. 6s.	0	12	8
Gooseberies dryed 1 lb. 5s., and plums of Marcelis 1 lb. 6s. 8d.	0	11	8
Peares of Roan 1 lb. 4s., and past of medlers 1 lb. 4s.	0	8	0
Past of verduces 1 lb. 4s., and past of redd dates 1 lb. 4s.	0	8	0
Past of gooseberies 1 lb. 4s., and past of damsons 1 lb. 4s.	0	8	0
Past of Genoa 1 lb. 5s. 6d., and past of green dates 1 lb. 4s.	0	9	6
Past of aprecocks 1 lb. 5s. 6d., and past of amber plums 1 lb. 4s.	0	9	6
Past of red peach 1 lb. 4s., and past of green verduses 1 lb. 4s.	0	8	0
Past of rubies 1 lb. 4s., and cakes of Janua 1½ lbs. 9s.	0	13	0
Past of muske millions 1 lb. 4s., and past of grapes 1 lb. 4s.	0	8	0
Past of greene peach 1 lb. 4s., and past of orenge 1 lb. 4s.	0	8	0
Past of musk peach 1 lb. 4s., and dryed plums 1 lb. 4s.	0	8	0

316   *Banquet to James I and his son Henry.*   [PART I.

	£	s.	d.
Pruons brembe 1 lb. 4s., and apples of Damasco 1 lb. 4s.	0	8	0
Buccones of Genoa 1 lb. 5s. 4d., and past of greene petrogots 1 lb. 4s.	0	9	4
Past of greene reddish 1 lb. 4s., and white peach 1 lb. 4s.	0	8	0
Past of rasberies 1 lb. 4s., and frayses of Genoa 1 lb. 5s. 4d.	0	9	4
Plums, Damesine 1 lb. 6s., pruons of Mercelis 1 lb. 6s. 8d.	0	12	8
Peach of Roane 1 lb. 6s., and quartered pruons 1 lb. 5s.	0	11	0
Past of quinces 1 lb. 4s., Madere citrons 1 lb. 4s.	0	8	0
Candied nutmeggs 1 lb. 5s., candied Damasco plums 1 lb. 6s. 8d.	0	11	8
Canded aprecocks 1 lb. 6s., oranges canded 1 lb. 5s.	0	11	0
Canded date plums 1 lb. 5s., and canded peches 1 lb. 5s. 4d.	0	10	4
Canded cloues 1 lb., 5s. 4d., canded goosberies 1 lb. 5s. 4d.	0	10	8
Canded eringas 1 lb. 5s. 4d., and canded gilliflowe^{r}s 1 lb. 5s. 4d.	0	10	8
Canded musk peares 1 lb. 5s., and candied cheries 1 lb. 6s.	0	11	0
Canded white date plums 1 lb. 5s., and candied plums of Roan 1 lb. 5s. 4d.	0	10	4
Amber greete comfitts 1 lb. 4s. 4d., and Mucakine conf. 1 lb. 3s.	0	7	4
Fyne syneamond 1 lb. 3s., annis seed conf. 1 lb. 14d. cheries p^{9}served 3s.	0	7	2
Damsins 1 lb., French apricocks 1 lb., greene verduss quinces 1 lb. all p^{9}served 13s. 4d.	0	13	4
Rasberies 1 lb., date plums 1 lb., goosberies 1 lb., apricocks 1 lb., peches 1 lb. p^{9}served 13s. 4d.	0	16	8
Damsins white p^{9}served 5s., and pippins p^{9}served 3s.	0	8	0
For the vse of 70 dozen of plate glasses	1	3	4

22*l.* 2*d.*

MISCELLANEOUS ITEMS OF EXPENDITURE.

Joyners.

	£	s.	d.
To Thomas Collins for joyner's worke done by him, for nailes, stuff, and workmanshipp vt. p. bill	2	6	0
To William Gossen for carving worke donne for the Company as by his bill	0	11	0

For hanging the Hall.

	£	s.	d.
For hanging the hall to Silverwood and Griffeth	0	2	6
To Griffyn for serving a sewer at o^r M^{rs} election	0	2	6
To Silverwood for a gratification	0	2	6
To Griffyn for a gratification	0	2	6
To Myller for a gratification	0	3	0

Porters.

	£	s.	d.
To Olyver Prichard and ———— Osborne for keeping the back dore	0	6	0

CHAP. XVI.] *Expenditure for Feast.* 317

	£	s.	d.
To Thomas Lynsey for keeping the gate 4 days....	0	10	0
To Evan Griffyn for 3 daies 4s., to Jo. Wotton for 4 daies	0	6	0
To Andrewe Richardson for one day 18d., to Edward Roper 18d.	0	3	0
To Robert Lendsey and to William Midgley for one day 18d.....	0	3	0
To William Bond for going of errands	0	2	6
To Robert Cryñ for clensing the water gutters....	0	1	0
To the marshall's men for their paynes	1	0	0

30s. 6d.

For the Shipp.

	£	s.	d.
For 19 lbs. of rope at 3d. the pound, and 31 lbs. of rope at 3d.	0	12	0
More for three pullies for to hoise vp the shipp 6d. the peece....	0	1	6

13s. 6d.

For taffita for ye garm^{ts} of the singers in the shipp and robes for the speaker.

	£	s.	d.
To Mr Springham for 19 ells ½ of taffite to make clothes for the three singers in the shipp, and for him that made the speech to his Ma^{ty.} at 13s. 4d. the ell, the some of	13	0	0

To ye Tayler.

Viz. :—For garters, stockings, shoes, ribons, and gloves.

	£	s.	d.
For making of the two robes 6s. 8d., for the ribons and tapes 2s. 6d., and for the fring 8s. 8d.	0	17	10
For buckroms for the babes 18d., for flowers for the garlands 3s. 6d.	0	5	0
For sowing silke 2s. 4d., for making of ye garments 25s.	1	7	4

Sweete Water.

	£	s.	d.
For a gallon of sweete water and the potts	0	12	0
For 24 dozen of rushes, at 3s. the dozen, by Guy Robinson	3	12	0
For 7 dozen ½ of whitestanes at 3s. 6d. the dozen	1	6	3
For making cleane of St. Martin Outw^{ch} church to the clarck	0	5	0
For making cleane of St. Hellen's church to the clarck	0	5	0
To the constables of two wards for the paines of howshoulders which warded in the streetes to keepe quiet order....	1	10	0
For butter 4d., blue tape 4d., smale cord 4d., and sugar 4d.	0	1	4
To Pigion for water 10s., and to ye kep of the conduit 2s.	0	12	0
To Mr. Salter for 30 boxes of wayfers at 20d. ye box	2	10	0
To John Miller for receaving the pewter and deliuering of it, and to 4 men y^t did help to scower and wash it	0	10	0
For 8 horsload of birch for to make the windowes for them that plaid on the lute	1	5	0

12l. 8s. 7d.

Guifts to the King and Prince.

	£	s.	d.
Gyven his Ma^{ty} in a purse 100*l.* in 20*s.* peeces	100	0	0
Memorandum that it was agreed that 50*l.* should haue been giuen to the queene, but by reason that she came not 50*l.* was saved.			
Item, gyven to the prince 50*l.* in 20*s.* peeces	50	0	0
For three purses, one for the king, 40*s.*, one for the queene 30*s.*, and 'one for the prince, 30*s.*	5	0	0
For the change of the 200*l.* in gould	2	0	0

CHAPTER XVII.

THE COMPANY TO THE DATE OF THE NEW ORDINANCES (1613).

New enterprises in Elizabeth's reign, p. 319.—*Contract with Rochelle merchants*, p. 320.—*In James's reign London population excessive*, p. 321.—*American (Virginia) Plantation*, p. 322, *et seq.—Lottery*, p. 325.—*Disastrous result*, p. 326.—*Ulster plantation*, p. 326.—*Precept for voluntary offers*, p. 327.—*Result*, p. 327.—*Compulsory assessment of the Guilds*, p. 328.—*Merchant Taylors' payments of first and second instalments*, p. 328.—*New Assessment*, p. 329.—(*Note on same*, p. 329.)—*Payment of third and fourth instalments*, p. 329.—*Irish Society*, p. 330.—*Allotment of lands to the Guilds*, p. 330.—*Manor of St. John Baptist*, p. 330.—*Plantation of Church and people*, p. 330.—*Taylors' Irish estates sold*, p. 330.—*Ill behaviour of members*, p. 331.—*Difficulty in filling Guild offices*, p. 331.—*Power of fine and imprisonment*, p. 333.—*Guilds upheld by the Crown*, p. 333.—*Lady Elizabeth's marriage portion*, p. 333.—*Favours solicited from them*, p. 333.—*Prince Henry's request*, p. 333.—*Lady Elizabeth's for Cook's place*, p. 334.—*Sir John Swynnerton's mayoralty*, p. 334.—*Dekker's Pageant*, p. 335.—*Opening of New River*, p. 339.—*Masque at Merchant Taylors' Hall*, p. 340.—*Ordinances of 1613 confirmed*, p. 341.—*Eminent members of the Company*, p. 342.—*Conclusion*, p. 342.—*Expenditure for 1612–13*, p. 343.

WE have already observed that the reign of James I opened a new era to the City Guilds, and they entered into commercial enterprises lying beyond the purposes of their incorporation. These commenced in the previous reign, and were initiated by the Lord Mayor's precepts requiring the Guilds to subscribe funds (either corporate or individual) to supply London with corn, and after 1599, to bear the risk of profit or loss on each purchase and sale.

The Guild organisation being found available for such enterprises, the members were invited by the Crown to adventure their money in lotteries,[1] and in 1572 the Lord Mayor and Lord Bishop[2] of London invited their co-operation in a quasi-charitable scheme to trade with their fellow protestants needing support at Rochelle.

It may be remembered by the reader that the salt tax imposed

---

[1] Page 229, *ante*.
[2] He had three sons in the Company's School in March, 1571, who became eminent men in after life, Edwin, Samuel, and Myles.

upon its inhabitants had provoked them to rise in rebellion against Francis I, and that the people purchased exemption from the tax in 1568.

The subject appears to have interested the Bishop of London (Sandys), and came before the Company on the 7th February, 1572, when this decision was arrived at :—

"Item, concerning the motion and request made by the right honourable Sir Lionel Ducket, Knt., Lord Mayor of London, and the bishop of the same, to know what this worshipful Company (as well as others) will defray towards the furnishing of a more sum of money, intended to be employed in a contract to be made with divers merchants of Rochelle for wine and salt to be delivered at such prices (?), days, and place, as may be most profitably concluded and determined by such persons as shall be Committees specially appointed by them to deal with the s^d merchants of Rochell, and it was finally (after due consideration and consultation had thereof) accorded and decreed that this r^t w^oful Society shall furnish and defray the sum of 300l. or under, of such money as is appertaining to the body of this mystery, to be employed in the said contract with such expedition as shall be conveniently required. And Mr Wm Kympton and Mr Walter Fish, now one of the Wardens, are appointed and requested to accept the pains to deal in this matter by their good providence in such sort as may to their wisdoms be thought best for the worship and profit of this house accordingly."

The matter needed some little care, and the Bachelors were consulted as to the part they should be willing to take in this enterprise, and accordingly we find on the 16th February, 1572, it was "agreed that Mr. A. Dawbney, Robert Dowe, Anthony Ratclif, and William Salkyns shall confer together for the better understanding of the 'Asshewerance' which the merchants of Rochelle are able to make for the delivery of wine and salt for such moneys as this Company shall deliver to them, therefore, according to their grant heretofore made that their report being made, the bargain may be concluded, and the money delivered accordingly.

"Item, the Warden Substitutes and Sixteen Men of the Bachelors Company have granted to disburse presently the sum of threescore pounds of lawful money of England, and also forty pounds moveover at Whitsuntyde next ensuing, for the better furnishing of the s^d 300l., w^h this wor^{s}pful Coy have promised to employ in a contract to be made with the merchants of Rochell as aforesaid, requesting humbly that this w^spful Comp^y w^{ld} see them answered, therefore, again either by the said commodities or otherwise, w^h was granted by them accordingly."

The next entry is on the 20th, when "200*l*. was taken out of the Treasury.

"Item, the said 200*l*. with 60*l*. received of the Bachelors Comp^y, and 20*l*. of Mr. Warden Borne, and also 20*l*. of Mr. Warden Jacob, that is in all 300*l*., was this day delivered by the said M^r, Mr Warden Fish, and others, unto the hands of the Reverent ffather in God, Edwyn, Bishoppe of London, for to be employed in the contract to be made with Merchants of Rochell, if it shall go forward and take effect as it was pretended or otherwise, to be rendered again to this Company, w^h the s^d Bishop hath faithfully promised to be observed accordingly."

The massacre of St. Bartholomew happened in the following August, and Rochelle, the refuge of the Huguenots, was besieged by the Duke of Anjou, and all but destroyed, the siege being raised on the 25th June, 1573, after a loss of many thousands of its citizens. Time was, therefore, asked by the merchants of Rochelle to fulfil the contract and given, as the Court minute of the 11th September, 1573, shews :—

"The contract made with divers merchants of Rochelle by the several wpfull Cos. of this hon. City, was read by the Common Clerk, and after full consideration had thereof, and consideration of the request of the said merchants, viz., to have leave to depart home and to have year, year, and year granted unto them for the performance of the said contract, it was finally agreed that the r^t w^spfull Comp^y should agree in the course taken by the other Companies."

For many years the 300*l*. was entered as a debt; but on the 12th February, 1579, from "his house in St. Paul's Churchyard," the Bishop of London (Bancroft) wrote to the Corporation with letters from Rochelle, praying that the loan might be remitted, "as they had to stand upon their defence for the maintenance of the common cause, 'true religion.' "[1]

After the banquet given to James, it was not unreasonable for him to suppose that the resources of the Guild were very great, and that they would readily be applied by the citizens to the relief of the distress then surrounding them. London was supposed to be suffering from a plethora of population, though Elizabeth had

---

[1] Remembrancia, page 185.

endeavoured, vainly, as it seems, to stay its increase, and to prevent additional houses being erected for the people. A wiser policy was to find an outlet for them. "If," wrote the Council, " multitudes of men were employed proportionally to the comodities which might be there by theire industry attained many thousands would be set on worke to the greate service of the King, strength of his Realmes, advancement of several trades, and benefitt of the peculiar persons whome the encreasing greatness (that often doth mynister occasion of payne to itself) of this Citty, might not only conveniently spare but also reape a singular comodity, thereby easing themselves of an insupportable burthen which soe surchargeth all the partes of the cittie, that one Tradesman can scarce lyve by another, which in all probability would be a meanes also to free and preserve the City from infection, and by consequence the whole kingdome, which of necessity must have recourse hither, which persons pestered or closed up together can neither otherwise or very hardly avoid."

This policy of colonisation had been originated, when in 1574 a Commission was appointed by the Crown, having (*inter alia*) the names of Spencer, Slanye, Staper, Maye, and Leake, for the discovery and plantation of new settlements in America. As the result of this measure, in 1585 Lane sent to Sir P. Sydney a report upon the country of Virginia, and in October Sir Richard Grenville took possession of it in the Queen's name.

The attention of the leading men in James' reign was therefore directed to the formation of new plantations or settlements, to which the surplus population of London could be sent, and in the year 1609 proposals, which we are about to mention, were made to the citizens to aid in two new enterprizes, viz., to colonise Virginia and Ireland with Londoners.

With regard to Virginia, the early history of its colonisation is not a narrative of success. But little was done prior to April, 1606, when a grant of the land was made to Gates, Somers, and others for the purposes of colonisation, and in 1609 a Company was formed as "The Treasurers and Company of Adventurers and Planters for Virginia," of which Sir Thomas Smyth was the Treasurer, and the Earl of Salisbury and others the members, to whom a patent was afterwards granted on the 23rd May, 1609.

In anticipation of this grant the Council of this new Company addressed a circular to the Lord Mayor, which he sent to the Guilds, and came under the consideration of an Assembly of the Merchant Taylors on the 28th March.

CHAP. XVII.]   *Virginian Plantation.*   323

The Council professed themselves as "desirous to ease the City and Suburbs of a swarme of unnecessary inmates, as a contynual cause of dearth and famyne, and the very originall cause of all the plagues that happen in this Kingdome," and invited subscriptions for the removal of these people to Virginia. They would issue no Bill of Adventure under 12*l*. 10*s*. 0*d*., but if "any voluntary contribution from the best disposed and most able of the Companies were raised, wee are willing to give our Bills of Adventure to the Master and Wardens to the generall use and behoofe of that Companie." Should the emigrants "demaund what may be theire present mayntenance, what maye be theire future hopes, it maye please you to let them knowe that for the present they shall have meate, drink, and clothing, with an howse, orchard, and garden, for the meanest family, and a possession of lands to them and their posterity, one hundred acres for every man's person that hath a trade, or a body able to endure day labour as much for his wief, as much for his child, that are of yeres to doe service to the Colony, with further particular reward according to theire particular meritts and industry."

The appeal was not for men but for money, and the plenty described was put forward as an inducement or to stimulate the wealthy to provide a fund to transplant the poorer citizens to this promised land.

The Lord Mayor called for a reply early in April, and therefore an immediate communication was made by the Merchant Company to the Wardens Substitute requiring them to consult the members of the Bachelors and obtain such subscriptions from them as they were disposed to offer.

From the Taylors nearly 800*l*. was obtained, a small part as a gift, and the residue by way of gain. Then, on the 31st March, divers of the Livery[1] (on summons) attended the Court, and it was agreed that 100*l*. should be taken from the stock of the house, and those assembled agreed that the profit of the venture (if any) should go to the poor of the Company.

Then another Court was held on the 29th April, and the result of the appeal is shown in these figures:

---

[1] Memorials, page 143.

	li. s. d.	£
[1] Out of the Stock of the Company....	c.	} 124
[1] Of the free guift of 23 of the Lyvery whose names ensue	xxiiij.	
[2] Of the free guift of 121 of the Bachelors Company whose names also ensue	liiij. iij. iiij.	} 76
Adventurers (5) of the Bachelors Company, whose names also ensue, expecting gaine	xv. xij. vj.	
[2] Supplied by the Bachelors' Company out of theire Th'rory	vj. iiij. ij.	
	cc.	200

The gifts of the Livery were (save in two instances of 2*l*.) only of 1*l*. each, and those of the Bachelors varied from 1*l*. to 4*s*. each.

But in addition to this 200*l*., nineteen Merchant Taylors adventured "for themselves, their children, and friends," 581*l*. 13*s*. 4*d*., in sums varying from 75*l*. to 6*l*. 13*s*. 4*d*. each, and the return of these subscriptions was made to the Lord Mayor on the 29th April.

The appeal, it will be noticed, was from a private Company of Adventurers to the several Guilds at the instance of the Lord Mayor, for subscriptions which were made by the Guildsmen as purely voluntary offerings. The Merchant Company granted, with the assent of the Livery, 100*l*., and the Bachelors, with the assent of the Freemen, 6*l*. 4*s*. 2*d*., out of their separate treasuries.

A Bill of Adventure for 200*l*., with the Great Seal of England, was given to the Company on the 4th May, entitling them rateably to the same benefits as other holders, viz., "theire full parte of all such lands, tenements, and hereditaments, as shall from tyme to tyme be there recovered, planted, and inhabited. And of all such mines and minerals, of gould, silver, and other metals or treasure, pearles, precious stones, or any kind of wares or merchaundizes, comodities, or profitts whatsoever, which shalbe obteyned or gotten in the said voyage according to the porcōn of money by them employed to that use, in as ample manner as any other adventurer therein shall receave for the like some."

In May about 150 persons were sent off with three vessels, two of which were beaten by stress of weather upon Bermuda (which for the time was taken as part of the Virginia scheme)

---

[1] and [2] The profits (if any) to the poor (1) of the Company, (2) of the Bachelors.

and the cargo was re-shipped to Virginia, arriving at James Town; the people who were already there being in a state of starvation.

These early settlers were described by Sir Thomas Dale in August, 1611, as being so diseased in body that only few could work, and that the wants of the Colony were for 2,000 men, with six months' provisions. A profitable return for capital was so hopeless that the original subscribers refused to pay their instalments, and the Court of Chancery was invoked against them in 1613. Gates, therefore, returned to England in May, 1614, to urge upon the Council that a collapse was imminent unless Parliament would, which we do not find that it did, assist the colony.

Resort was then had to a lottery—the third[1] (so far as we believe) that was ever held in this kingdom. This was initiated by the Privy Council, who wrote to the Lord Mayor, sending to him—and he forwarding to the Guilds—1. Paper book, by Sir Thomas Smyth, the Treasurer; 2. A true declaration of the state of the Colony, &c., printed by the advice and direction of the Council of Virginia, by William Barnett (4to.), London, 1606; and 3. The Virginia Company's scale for such as should venture in the lottery. The enterprise was urged upon the citizens as "worthy and Christian"—"full of honour and profit to his Majesty and the whole realm"—but it received little support from the Taylors, for on the 8th May all that the Court of Assistants did was to vote only 50l. out of the common stock at the risk and for the profit of the house, and to order the whole Livery and all the Bachelors Company to be summoned into the hall that they might know the pleasure of his Majesty's Council, and venture for themselves such sums as they saw fit; but no later minute is found relating to the Virginia Company.

Probably the venture of 50l. out of the stock of the house brought no beneficial result to the Company, for the great prizes were purloined by some merchants, who were prosecuted in the Star Chamber.[2]

We will add only a few lines to complete the narrative. In 1618 the city shipped to the colony "one hundred boys and girls laying

---

[1] See page 228, *ante.*   [2] Hudson, page 136.

starving in the streets," at the cost of 500l.,[1] but as the legality of this appears to have been questioned, leave was asked of the Council before making another shipment in 1620. Something of terror must have been felt by the victims of this transportation, for in October, 1618, the Council was informed by Sir E. Hext, J.P. for Somersethire, that forty girls had ran away from one parish to obscure places, and could not be recovered by their parents, only on the appearance of a man representing himself to be the Council messenger having authority to press them for shipment.[2]

Out of the Virginia Company sprang that for Bermuda, and amongst the early promoters of this are to be found the names of these Merchant Taylors: Robert Gore, Will Greenwell (Master 1618), Ralph Hamer (Warden, 1610), Robert Offley, and Elias Roberts.

The settlement of the Londoners in Ulster arose about the same period and out of the same necessity of disposing of the surplus population. It was made direct from the Crown, and put forward by the Lord Mayor to the London Livery Companies in the spring of 1609, in this manner. Printed papers were sent in May (25th) of the motives and reasons to induce the city of London to undertake the work, and all the advantages in quality of soil, sea, and river commodities, and the profit to be reaped were formulated for the consideration of the citizens.

The Lord Mayor sent on the proposal to the Guilds on the 1st July, with an intimation of the "King's most gracoeus favour and love to the city—to grant to us the first offer of so worthy an action which is likely to prove pleasing to Almighty God— honourable to the city, and profitable to the undertakers." He requested that each Company should appoint four of their members as a Committee to meet at Guildhall on the 7th instant. A Court

---

[1] This was possibly "assisted emigration" by the parishes of London, acting (as to repayment of expenses) on the precepts of the Lord Mayor. Thus in the Master's Account of 1618-19 these items appear :—

"Paid by virtue of precept from Lord Mayor for setting forth children to Virginia, after the rate of 3d. a week, which the Company pay to the poor of St. Benetfink, 1s. 6d.

"The like after the rate of 2s. 6d. a week, which the Company pay to the poor of St. Martin Outwich, 15s."

[2] James I, Domestic Series, pages 586 and 591.

was therefore summoned on the 5th, at which Sir W. Craven, Robert Dowe, and nine other members were present, and such a Committee appointed consisting of Richard Gore, Thomas Juxon, Thomas Owen, and Randolph Woolley.

The matter does not appear to have been taken up very cordially, for a third precept was issued on the 24th July in terms somewhat peremptory, "These are therefore to require you in His Majesty's name on Wednesday next to assemble in your common hall all the Aldermen of your Company, and the four Committees by you formerly named and all other the Assistants, Livery, and men of note of your Bachelors Company or Yeomanry by special summons, then and there to understand and be informed by your Aldermen and Committee of the whole proceedings that have been taken concerning the said honourable intention of plantation, and to make a book of all their names, and to understand every man's answer what he will willingly contribute to the furtherance of so famous project, to the intent His Majesty may be informed of the readiness of this city in a matter of such great consequence, and to the end, if any, of your Company shall be then absent (being specially summoned) he may be fined for his contempt, that all such as shall be then absent, may be afterwards dealt withal concerning the same, and a note also to be taken of those that shall refuse, wherein you are not to fail as you tender His Majesty's service, for that the Committees are to return an answer to the Lords of His Majesty's Privy Council and if occasion be to confer with the Council of Ireland on Friday next. From Guildhall, 24th July, 1609."

The Company consisted of 338 members, divided thus :—86 of the Merchants and 252 of the Bachelors, and the formal return was sent to the precept in the 14th August, showing this result :—

Of the Merchants as willing to adventure, (omitting Sir W. Craven and Alderman Elwes, who signified their resolution direct to the Court of Aldermen) there were only five, Sir L. Halliday giving 100*l*., and the other four 87*l*. 10*s*. = 187*l*. 10*s*. As willing (in sums varying from 20*l*. given by Richard Gore, to 2*l*. generally given) freely to contribute without expectation of gain only 23 members, 88*l*. 13*s*. 4*d*.; while seven of the Assistants, including G. and R. Gore and George Sotherton, refused either to adventure or to contribute. As being in the country there were returned Sir John Swynnerton and 68 others of the Court and Livery, whose names were given.

The Bachelors were thus returned:—six as willing to adventure (in sums varying from 85*l.* to 12*l.* 10*s.*) 147*l.* 10*s.*; four as willing to contribute 2*l.* each, without expectation of gain, 8*l.*; seventeen, including three Wardens Substitute of the Bachelors, who refused either to contribute or adventure, while some of the Bachelors, whose names are not given, were returned as out of town, to be summoned to appear before the Court upon their return.

It is clear, therefore, from these figures, that the undertaking was received with little favour, for of the Merchants only five, and of the Bachelors only six, were willing to adventure a total sum of 335*l.*, and twenty-five of the former, and four of the latter would only bestow 96*l.* 13*s.* 4*d.* as a free gift without expectation of gain.

The course taken by the Corporation was the converse of that now adopted in compulsory dealing with lands, for they used powers of acquisition—not against the landowner to take his land, but against the capitalist to take his money and to compel him to pay for that which he did not desire to purchase. However, what else could be done, for James had the Irish Committee down to Greenwich and upbraided them for neglect.[1]

A deputation of four was sent over to Ireland to survey and report on the proposed purchase by the Corporation, and their reply being in favour of the undertaking the Common Council adopted their report, ordered that 20,000*l.* should be forthwith raised from the London Livery Companies, and that 1,872*l.* was the share to be paid by the Taylors in four equal instalments as called for by the precepts of the Lord Mayor.

Accordingly in June, the Lord Mayor in His Majesty's name charged the Master and Wardens to call a Court of Assistants and to make this "assessment of 1,872*l.* by the poll within the Company," and on the 15th January such a Court was held, and a Committee consisting of Sir W. Craven, Robert Dowe, and others was appointed to meet on the 20th to levy and raise this assessment, which was raised as to the first and second instalments on the 23rd March and 16th June, 1610, thus:—

Thomas Vernon, though the Master, paid only 1*l.* 6*s.* 8*d.*, possibly at that time a poor man. The four Wardens paid only 1*l.* 5*s.* each. The four Aldermen 10*l.* each, nine other Assistants 3*l.* 6*s.* 8*d.*, and twelve others only 2*l.* 13*s.* 4*d.*; but

---

[1] 2 Maitl., Vol. 1, 294.

Gerard Gore paid nothing. Of the Livery, four paid nothing, and fifty-one paid 45s. each. Of the Bachelors 104 paid 25s., and 148 only 16s. 8d. each, the distinction probably being in Foyne and in Budge. There were no defaulters in those assessed, and therefore the two Gores and other dissentients had to contribute to, though they did not like the Ulster plantation.

The third and fourth instalments were soon called for, but the Common Council enacted before the precept was issued that the former assessment should be readjusted[1] and the precept of the 3rd August, 1610, issued to the Merchant Taylors stated that the Company had been re-assessed by this later Act (for rating Companies at 1,050 quarters of corn), and therefore that the Master and Wardens were to gather up their third assessment of money for Ireland at this higher rate "under pain of imprisonment." The assessment was accepted, though the Company was raised by 57l. The Master and Wardens had to confer with the Wardens Substitute, and propose that they should bring in Bachelors from the outstanding freemen and gather up this extra sum from them. Accordingly in the third and fourth assessments new members are found added to the Bachelors Company, but though 1,050l. had to be and was paid to the Corporation, only 1,021l. 13s. 4d. was collected.

The instalments were paid originally for the individual benefit of each member, who we presume expected to obtain an estate or some part of one from the city, but at a Court of 17th June, 1613, all the assistants present surrendered their rights to the Company in regard to the past payments, and many other members did the

---

[1] The method of assessing by the Common Council of London appears to have been as follows :—A Committee was constituted by one member from each of eighteen of the different Companies (ten being a quorum), and the Merchant Taylors were represented by William Greenwall (Master in 1618). This Committee brought up the scheme of assessment for raising 10,000 quarters of wheat and 10,000l. still required for Ireland. By it fourteen Companies were increased[a] and nine were decreased as to their former assessments, but 192 quarters were raised over the 10,000 quarters required. The Common Council, by act of 18th July, accepted the scheme, and remitted it to the Lord Mayor and Aldermen to abate the 192 quarters from such Companies and in such proportions as they deemed fit. And that done, it was enacted that the final assessment should be entered into the Journals of the City, and adopted till amended and reformed. This abatement was made on the 11th September, in favour of five Companies: the Ironmongers 42, Mercers 80, Skinners 30, Goldsmiths 20, and Sadlers 20. The Merchant Taylors had the highest assessment 1,050, and then came the Grocers at 1,000 quarters.

[a] As to these see note to Appendix 32, page 405.

same upon the understanding that the common stock of the house should answer all future assessments made upon them. The Lord Mayor (Swynnerton) being absent was waited upon by a Committee to obtain his approval to the order or arrangement, and to entreat him that such brethren as should refuse to obey the order (or in other words to surrender their rights) might be committed on his Lordship's command.

Thus was originated and set on foot the plantation of Ulster by the Corporation of London, but as the Taylors have long since ceased to hold their share, which was one-sixth part[1] of the land granted by the Crown, we shall only add a few more sentences regarding the completion of the plan.

A Company called the "Irish Society" was formed consisting of a Governor, Deputy, and twenty-four Assistants, the Governor and five others being Aldermen, and the remainder being the Recorder and Commoners. To this Society the lands were granted by the King, subject to certain conditions for building upon and for peopling the district.

Of these lands after retaining certain estates to cover their corporate expenses, a distribution was ultimately made by the "Irish Society" to the various guilds, and the Taylors had an estate granted to them by indenture of 30th October, 1618, which they designated "as the Manor of St. John Baptist," and a share of another estate held by the Clothworkers. Upon the Manor of St. John they built a church (which they furnished and also equipped with communion vessels) holding the patronage of the advowson. This expenditure was necessitated by the terms of the grant as the land would have been forfeited had not the expenditure been made.[2]

The Taylors sold the "Manor" and these estates in 1727 for 20$l.$ 6$s.$, and a rent-charge of 150$l.$ per annum, and the land held with the Clothworkers, before any Irish Land Act was passed. The proceeds of the last sale they invested in purchasing the Charter House, and re-establishing their school for the benefit of London residents.

It may be thought that these new enterprises induced a higher class of citizens to come into the Guild, both better behaved and more ready to fill its offices; but the contemporary records do not show this to have been the case.[3]

---

[1] Court Minutes, 1st February, 1614.
[2] Return by Court to Irish Committee, 22nd March, 1620.
[3] See the List of Masters and Wardens in Part II, Appendix 1, and notes thereon.

Let us take the matter of behaviour which ends in the committal of the offender to prison. It is entered thus on the 20th August, 1613 :—

" At this Courte came William Wright, a Brother of this Society, who had been three several times before summoned to appear for many peremptory speeches which he had used to our Master and Wardens in their presence as taxing Mr. Wm. Jenkinson with partiality, and telling him he would talk with him in another place, and likewise for using many unseemly words and bad speeches to Edward Katcher, one of the Livery of this Company, before he went out of the Hall; against the Comon Clerke of this Society, as terming him saucie knave and scurvey fellow, with divers other opprobrious speeches heard as well by the said Katcher as by others in the howse, some parte whereof he confessed before this Courte. And being spoken unto by Sir Wm. Craven, a worthie member of this Societie, did not spare, in the presence of this Courte, to tell him also of partialitie : All which offence deservinge greater punishment than could be inflicted upon him, it was ordered at this Courte that Mr. William Gore and Mr. Greenwell should goe to my Lord Maior to informe his Lordshipp what had passed at this Courte concerning the said Wright, and that it was the Companies' desier that he should be committed as well for his owne due deserts as for example for others. Whereupon my Lord Maior,[1] giving good allowance to that which the Company had done, caused him presently to be committed to Prison."

The refusal to serve in office was the occasion of greater trouble, as the defaulters, the Master elect and two Wardens (Robinson being one), had retired to the country, and while there were beyond the jurisdiction of the city authorities. The Court of July, 1613, "therefore ordered that sev'all lres should be sent unto them, which lres were readie written and signed at this Court by the M^r and Wardens and divers of the Assistants then present, for their present appearance to take their oathes and charges, and that the Beadle of the Livery should be sent unto Mr. Symon Clynt, M^r, and Martin Leather, one of the Wardens, with all convenyant speede, and the Beadle of the Batchelors' Company should be sent to John Robinson, one other of the Wardens, and that they should take with them sev'all bonds, viz. :—one for Mr. Symon Clynt to be bound in two hundreth

---

[1] Sir John Swynnerton.

pounds for the payment of one hundred pounds at five months for his fyne if he should refuse the service, and other two for Martyn Leather and John Robinson, with either of them a good suritie in one hundreth pounds for the payment of fifty pounds a peece at the like tyme."[1]

We had lately had dealings with Mr. Cartwright, the Lord Chancellor's officer in the approval of the ordinances, and therefore, as the Beadles could not arrest out of the City, it was "further ordered that the Comon Clarke should give Mr. Cartwright two double sovainges, and to entreate him to move the right honourable the Lorde Chauncellor that it would please his Lo. to grant severall pursevants for the said pties that if they should refuse to submit themselves to their several service or paye their ffynes, the said pursevants migh by authoritie compell them to make their appearance in London."

Two of the offenders readily came to terms, but not so Robinson, and as a consequence he was fined for not serving Renter Warden :—

" Mr. John Robinson appeared at this Courte and refused either to serve the office or to pay his fine for not serving Renter Warden.

" The Lord Mayor, before whom he was summoned, made a mild speech to him concerninge his Oath, which he still refusing to take, his Lordshipp informed him that when mildness of persuasion would not do, Justice must follow. He then required him to enter into a recognizance of 100*l.* to appear the next day by 8 of the clock at the Guildhall, which he also refused, and was accordingly committed on the morrow to Newgate.

" A copy of Recognizance was made out and he appeared on Nov^9 3, 1613, at a Court of Assistants, and after again refusing to serve or fine he at last being better advised he entered into an agreement (Mr. Isaac Kilborne) for his suretie to pay the sum of 25*l.* on the 3^d of Nov^9, 1614, and 25*l.* on the 3^d of Nov^9, 1615."

However, it was cheaper for him to pay than to serve, and on the 3rd November Robinson "made his personal appearance at this Court and agreed to submit himself unto the Company for his fyne, 'hopinge they would deal lovingly and kindly with him,' when after a lengthened negociation he agreed to pay 50*l.*

---

[1] W. Jenkinson, Warden in 1609-12, and he paid 100*l.* as a fine for not serving as Master in 1615.

to be excused from all offices and liabilities (for the payment of this amount, he ultimately obtained two years' time)."

This power of fine and imprisonment was at this period, and for many years afterwards of the very essence of civic and Guild rule. If the apprentice did not come in as a freeman he could be stayed from trading, if as a freeman he did not take up first his livery and then office on call from his Guild, he could be fined and imprisoned. So again with civic assessments to be distributed by the Court on the several members of the Guild. If no such distribution were made the Master and Livery were fined, and if such was not paid the defaulter was imprisoned.

So long as the government of the London Livery Companies was in practical operation, there was no escape from it, for there was no public pressure either in or out of Parliament to alter or destroy this authority. To the Crown the Livery Companies were not only innocuous, but contributory by way of largess to the Royal Family. Thus on the 2nd December, 1612 (there being no legal claim on the Company), this entry is found :—

"It was ordered that 20l. should be paid to Sir Thomas Lowe, Knight, one of the Commissioners for the receiving of the aid money for the Lady Elizabeth, the King's Majesty's eldest daughter, in full payment of all such lands and tenements as belong to this Company in the City of London and the suburbs thereof."

The Livery Companies were also available even to the King's children for the soliciting of favours. Of these two instances from the Merchant Taylors' records are given. In the first Prince Henry writes from St. James's on the 1st May, 1612, thus :—
"On some occasions of our service having emploied (sic) our beloved Arthur Ingram, Gn., Comptroller of our Father's Custom House, and fynding his faithful and industrious carriage in these our employments to deserve from us some kynd of respect," therefore the Prince asked the Master and Wardens that he might have his lease of the Company's house in Fenchurch Street renewed to him, which was granted, to the prejudice of the loving brother of the mystery John Speed.[1]

---

[1] Part II, Chapter XXII. It is only fair to give the other side of the case. In this entry of the 12th August, 1611 :—
"Two brace of fatt bucks being brought to the Hall in a coach and presented from his highness (Henry Prince of Wales) by Mr. Alexander, one of his highness gentlemen ushers, whereupon Mr. Thomas Row did deliver to the said Mr.

The other when the Lady Elizabeth, shortly before her departure wrote to Sir John Swynnerton and to the Master and Wardens stating that as their Cook[1] was an old man they would perhaps bestow his place on the bearer of that letter, John Warde), and if she should hear of his appointment before her departure " it shall settle an affection in me to contynue your friend, Elizabeth." But as the letter reached the Court on the 4th May after her departure from England it was not deemed necessary to make any reply.

Possibly she might have thought it a request which Sir John Swynnerton would readily procure for her, as, though no longer in office, he had been such when the Elector Palatine arrived in London to marry her, and she, Lady Elizabeth, had often been brought into social contact with him.

Swynnerton's mayoralty was marked by the event of her marriage and by one other notable event. He entered upon office " with showes, pageants, chariots of triumph, with other devices (both by land and water) fully expressed by Thomas Dekker," at the expense of the Bachelors Company.[2]

Alexander, to bestow upon the keeper or where he should think fitt the some of fowre pounds, and to the keeper's men that came with him 20s., and to the coachman 5s., amounting in the whole to 5l. 5s., the which the auditors did forbeare to allow. Now upon consideration it is ordered, that for as much as it is fitt that the messenger from so greato a Prince should receive a good reward, to demonstrate the Companies thankfulness and to encourage other Maisters hereafter to be bountiful, 4l. shalbe allowed to Mr. Rowe, and whensoever the Prince shall send any more bucks or does, the house (over and above such gratuity as the M^r shall allowe out of his owne purse) shall allow 20s. for every buck or doae to be sent from his highness, and Mr. Thomas Rowe did willingly give the 25s. out of his owne purse for a good example of them that shall succeede." Thomas Rowe was the Master, and the audit was against him. 1l. 1s., if I mistake not, is still the fee for killing a buck sent by custom to the Secretary of State.

[1] Page 184 (note) *ante*.

[2] Sir J. Swynnerton's Triumph, and page 74 as to other Triumphs.

Receipts :—

	£	s.	d.
Bachelors in foyne, 81 at 3l. 6s. 8d.	270	0	0
Bachelors in budge, 46 at 2l. 10s.	115	0	0
Watling Street Quarter	154	1	0
Candlemas ,, ...	86	17	4
Fleet Street ,, ...	98	0	0
Merchant Taylors ,, ...	83	3	4
Received from Lord Mayor	20	0	0
From Treasury of Bachelors Company	181	11	10
	£1,008	13	6

Of this 978l. 12s. 11d. was spent, leaving a balance of 30l. 0s. 7d. in hand.

The detail of the expenditure in about 70 items has been preserved, but only two of these need be noticed, which are:—

"Item paid to Mr. Hemynge and Mr. Thomas Dekker the poet, for the devise of the Land Showes, being a Sea Charriott drawne by two sea horses, one pageant called Neptune's Throne, with the seven liberall Sciences, one Castle called Envy's Castle, one other pageant called Virtue's Throne, and for the printing of the book of the Speeches, and for the persons and apparel of those that went in them the sum of 197*l*. Also to Nicholas Sotherne and George Jackson the two master painters for the making, painting, gilding and garnishing of all the same several Thrones before mentioned and for new painting the Company's Ship, the sum of 181*l*."

The description and speeches have been printed and published by the Percy Society[1] under the title of "Troia Nova Triumphans." Dekker[2] had prepared for the city the triumph upon James's entry in 1603, and as it was known that the Prince Palatine would be present as a spectator of the triumph, it may be presumed that it was one got up by him with greater care.

The poet begins this work with an epistle dedicatory to Swynnerton "as the Deserver of all these honours which the customary rites of this day, and the general love of this City bestow." He then presents "the labours of his pen" as undeserving of acceptance, as "notwithstanding you will give them a generous and gratefull entertainment in regard to that noble fellowship (of which you yesterday were a brother and this day a father) who most freely have bestowed their loves upon you." He then adds: "The colours of this piece are mine own; the cost theirs: of which nothing was wanting that could be had and everything had that was required. To their lasting memory I set downe this and to your noble disposition this I dedicate."

A description of the triumphs follows. In the first on land Neptune is represented as addressing the Lord Mayor on his landing at Paul's Chain thus:—

> "Every gale
> Will not perhaps befriend thee : but howe blacke
> So ere the sky looke, dread not thou a wracke,
> For when Integrity and Iunocence sit,
> Steering the helme, no ship can split."

---

[1] Vol. 10.
[2] See his life in the Mermaid Series of British Dramatists (London), 1887.

The trytons then sounding, Neptune in his chariot passeth along before the Lord Mayor. The four windes dressed up drive forward the shipe of which Neptune spake into St. Paul's Church Yard, where another Chariot stands which displaces Neptune's, which is sent on to Cheapside.

The second triumph is a Throne of Virtue gloriously adorned and beautified. Upon the height sits Arete, her temple shining with a diadem of starres, her robes rich, her mantle white, with starres of gold. Beneath her sit the seven liberal sciences.

Other details are given too long for us to quote, but the Lord Mayor being approached to this throne, Virtue thus salutes him :—

> " Hail, worthy Prœtor, stay and do me grace,
> (Who still have called thee patron) in this place,
> To take from me heapéd welcomes who combine
> These people's hearts in one, to make them thine.
> Bright Vertue's name thou know'st, and heav'nly birth,
> And therefore, spying thee, downe she leaped to earth,
> Whence vicious men had driven her. On her throne,
> The Liberall Arts waite ; from whose brests do runne
> The milke of knowledge, on which sciences feed,
> Trades and professions ; and by them the seed
> Of civill popular government is sowne,
> Which, springing up, loe ! to what height is growne
> In thee and these[1] is scene. And to maintaine
> This greatnesse, twelve strong pillars it sustaine,
> Upon whose capital twelve societies[2] stand,
> Grave and well ord'red, bearing chiefe command
> Within this city, and with love, thus reare
> Thy fame, in free election, for this yeare.
> All arm'd to knit their nerves in one with thine,
> To guard this new Troy.
>
>   *   *   *   *   *   *
>
> Thou must be now stirring and resolute,
> To be what thou art sworne a waking eye,
> Afar off, like a beacon, to descry
> What stormes are comming, and being come, must then
> Shelter with spread armes the poor'st citizen.
> Sit Plenty at thy table, at thy gate
> Bounty and Hospitality ; hee's most ingrate
> Into whose lap the publick-wheale having pour'd
> Her golden showers, from her his wealth should hoord ;
> Be like those antient spirits, that long agon,
> Could think no good deed sooner than 'twas don
> Others to pleasure. Hold it then more glory,
> Than to be pleas'd thy selfe, and be not sorry
> If any strive in best things to exceed thee,
> But glad to helpe thy wrongers, if thy need be."

---

[1] The Aldermen.   [2] The twelve Companies.

This chariot then sets forward taking the place of Neptune's before the Lord Mayor.

The third triumph is a forlorn castle built by the Little Conduit in the Cheape, in which, as Virtue approaches, appears Envy with Ignorance, Sloth, Oppression, Disdain, &c., as her followers. At the Castle Gates stand Ryot and Calumny to stop the passage of Virtue, "but she onely holding up her bright shield dazzles and confounds them."

The procession then passes; Virtue having brought the Lord Mayor safely through the jaws of Envy on "to the Crosse in Cheape" and to the house of "Fame," where in an upper seat she sits crowned in rich attire with a trumpet in her hand, and in several places sit kings, princes, and nobles, who are free of the Merchant Taylors Company, a particular room being reserved for one that represented Henry Prince of Wales.

In this fourth Triumph, Fame addresses the Lord Mayor:

> "Welcome to Fame's high temple: here fix first
> Thy footing; for the wayes which thou hast past
> Will be forgot and worn out; and no tract
> Of steps observ'd, but what thou now shalt act.
> * * * * * *
> Erecte thou then a serious eye, and looke
> What worthies fill up Fame's voluminous booke,
> That now (thine owne name read there) none may blot
> Thy leafe with foule inke, nor thy margent quoate
> With any act of thine, which may disgrace
> This cittie's choice, thy selfe, or this thy place;
> Or that which may dishonour the high merits
> Of thy renown'd society."

Then follows a description of some of the members of whom a list was given in the last chapter, and "Fame" concludes thus:—

> "Fame hath them all en-rold,
> On a large file (with others), and their story
> The world shall reade, to add unto thy glory,
> Which I am loath to darken; thousand eyes
> Yet aking till they enjoy thee; win then that prize,
> Which Virtue holds up for thee, and (that done)
> Fame shall the end crowne as she hath begun."

The speech is ended. Fame's temple takes its place before the Lord Mayor, and a song is heard (the music being conveyed in a private room and not a person discovered) of which the last verse is this:—

> "Goe on nobly, may thy name
> Be as old and good as fame,
> Ever be remembered here,
> Whilst a blessing, or a teare
>   Is in store,
>   With the poore.
> So Swynnerton nere dye,
> But his virtues upward flye,
>   And shall spring
>   Whilst we sing
> In a chorus ceasing never,
> He is living, living ever."

After returning back from the Guildhall to perform the ceremonial customs in St. Paul's Church,[1] the pageants move on, and when the Lord Mayor is brought home, "Justice, for a farewell, mounted on some scaffold close to his entrance gate," thus addresses him :—

> "May this dayes sworne protector, welcome home,
> If Justice speake not now, be she ever dumbe;
> The world gives out shee's blinde; but man shall see,
> Her light is cleare, by influence drawne from thee.
> For one yeare, therefore, at these gates shee'l sit,
> To guid thee in and out: thou shalt commit
> (If she stand by thee) not one touch of wrong.
>
>   *   *   *   *   *
> *   *   *   *   *   *
>
> Do good for no man's sake now but thine owne,
> Take leave of friends and foes, both must be knowne
> But by one face; the rich and poore must lye
> In one even scale; all suitors in thine eye,
> Welcome alike, even he that seems most base,
> Looke not upon his clothes, but on his case.
> Let not oppression wash his hands i' th' teares,
> Of widowes, or of orphans; widowes' prayers
> Can pluck downe thunder, and pore orphans' cries,
> Are lawrels held in fire."

Then referring to the insignia of the Lord Mayor's office, Justice continues :—

> "That collar which about thy necke is worne,
> Of golden esses, bids thee so to knit,
> Men's hearts in love, and make a chayne of it,
> That sword is seldome drawne, by which is meant,
> It should strike seldom; never th' innocent,
> 'Tis held before thee by another's hand,

---

[1] Pages 23–4, *ante*.

> But the point upwards (heaven must that command),
> Snatch it not then in wrath, it must be given,
> But to cut none, till warrented by heaven.
> The head, the politicke body must advance,
> For which thou hast the cap of maintenance,
> And since the most just magistrate often erres,
> Thou guarded art about with officers,
> Who knowing the pathes of others that are gone,
> Should teach thee what to do, what leave undone."

It was time for the labours and pleasures of the day to end, so Justice adds this parting advice :—

> "Night's candles lighted are and burn amaine,
> But therefore bere off thy officers traine,
> Which love and custom lend thee ; till delight
> Crowne both this day and city ; a good night
> To thee and these grave senators, to whom
> Thy last farewels in these glad wishes come,
> That thou and they (whose strength the city beares)
> May be as old in goodness as in yeares."

The shows by water are not given, "I suffer them to dye (writes Dekker) by that which fed them, powder and smoke. Their thunder[1] (according to the old gally-foist fashion) was too loud for any of the nine Muses to be bidden to it."

Prince Henry was not well enough to appear, but the Prince Palatine was present at the feast, and received from the Corporation a present of plate. On the 14th February the royal marriage took place.

The other notable event in this mayoralty was the opening of the New River.

> "Flow forth precious spring,
> So long and dearly sought for—and now bring
> Comfort to all that love thee."[2]

Words at which the sluices were opened by Swynnerton on Michaelmas Day, 1613; the completion of a work which was commenced by Sir Hugh Middleton in 1608.[3]

---

[1] See Harper's pageant, Part II, page 260.

[2] 2 Maitl., 1270.

[3] The Taylors brought the water to the Hall in 1615-16, thus :—

"Item, p^d to Mr. Middleton, for suffering the water to come into the Hall, the sum of 40s.

"Item, p^d more to Mr. Middleton for ¼ of a year rent for the said water, after the rate of 40s. per annum, the first payment due at Xmas and the last ending at Mids^r 1616, 30s.

"Item to the plumber upon his bill for taking in of Mr. Middleton's water into the Hall, 7l. 10s." As to the earlier supply, Part II, page 247.

Another event at this period with which Swynnerton's name is associated is the ball and mask given by the Corporation in the Company's hall (but not in any way mentioned in their records) to the Count Palatine and the Lady Elizabeth in January, 1614. It would appear that on the 31st December James (as on other occasions) sent to the Lord Mayor a notice of his intention to visit him.[1] The Court of Aldermen adopted the entertainment, which was to be a supper, as one to be paid for by the city, and ordered that Sir W. Craven, Sir John Swynnerton, and others should meet as a Committee, and make arrangements.

"Lastly," so stands the entry in the Corporation Order Book, "because the Lord Mayor's house is not spacious enough, it is agreed and so ordered that the Merchant Taylors' Hall shall be prepared and made ready against that night for these solemnities."

Accordingly on the 4th January, 1613-14, the bride and bridegroom, with others, came to Merchant Taylors' Hall, where the Lord Mayor and Aldermen entertained them with hearty welcome and great magnificence. The Masque, which was acted, was probably "The Irish Masque at Court," by Ben Jonson.[2]

It was possibly through Swynnerton's influence that the ordinances of the Company, which had been varied and departed from in practice, were submitted to the constitutional authorities for and obtained sanction from them.

It has been remarked that great constitutional changes were made in the Guild in the earlier half of the sixteenth century, only to be traced in their effects, as the Company have no records extant to show when or under what circumstances they were made. On the 20th June, 1581, a "Booke of Orders, devised by Mr Anthony Radcliff, Mr Robert Dow, Richard Maye, and George Sotherton, Lovinge Brethren of this Misterye, was openly redd by the cōen clark and verye well lyked of by the saide Mr, Wardens, and Assistants, who have ordered, agreed, and decreed that the same booke shalbe followed and executed accordingly," but this book is not to be found.

Lord Ellesmere was Lord Chancellor, and on 24th June, 1612, we find this minute:—

"Whereas informacon was given at this Co*te by the Comon Clerke of this Society, that it was Mr. Recorder's[3] advise and

---

[1] 2 Nichols (James), page 731.
[2] Cat. State Papers (James I), pages 215-20.
[3] Henry Montague, Chief Justice of England in 1616.

counsell to have the booke of Ordinance first p'sented to the Right Hon. The Lo. Chancellor of Eng⁴ and that his Lo^(pp) should alsoe be psented with some remembrance from the Comp. for the better furtherance and fynishinge of that busyness. It is therefore ordered and agreed that the Comon Clerke shall attende Mr. Recorder, intreating him to move His Lo^(pp) in their suite.[1] And alsoe to psent His Lo^(pp) with tenne double sufferants in gould; and further ordered that what other monies shalbe disbursed by the consent of the M^r and Wardens to any Judge or Counsellor for the said business shall be paide by our M^r."

The effect of this distribution of money was that the ordinances were confirmed with this preface, "To all trew Christian People to whome this present writing shall come, Sr Thomas Egerton Knight, Lord Ellesmere Lord Chauncellor of England, Sir Thomas Fflemyng Knight, Lord Chief Justice of the King's Bench, Sir Edward Coke Knight, Lord Chief Justice of the Common Pleas, senden Greeting in our Lord Everlasting." Then follows a recital of the 19 Henry VII, cap. 7, and that "the Maister and Wardens of the Marchant Tailers of the Fraternitie of St. John Baptist in the Cittie of London, willing and desiryng the said Act in every behalf to be observed and kept." On the 20th January, 1612, "have exhibited and presented unto us theire Peticōn with a Book conteyning diverse Statutes, Acts and Ordynaunces, by them ordayned divised and made, for the said Ffraternity and their successors, and for the comōn weale and conversation of the good estate of the Mistery of the said Marchauntailors and for the better governing, ruling and ordering of the same Ffraternity to be established, ordayned and used & thereupon have instauntlie desired us, that wee would peruse and examyne all and every the said Statutes, Ordynaunces, Acts and Oaths by the same Maister and

---

[1] The fees paid under this order were these:

"*Master's Account*, 1612-13.

"Item p^d & given to the Recorder by order to peruse the book of ordinances, & to make the same ready for the Lords, five double souveraignes, 5*l*. 10*s*.

"Item p^d to my Lord Coake, lord Chief Justice of the Common pleas, for his fee for his hand to the book, 6*l*. 12*s*.

"Item to his doorkeeper & porter, 7*s*.

"Item p^d to my lord Fleminge, Ld Chief Justice of England, 6*l*. 12*s*.

"Item p^d to the Ld Chancellor, 11*l*.; and to his man, 2*s*. 6*d*.

"Item p^d to the 3 Lords men for examining & procuring the scales of their Lords to the book at 40*s*. a prece, 6*l*.

"Item p^d to Mr. Cartwright for engrossing the book & for passage with the Ld Chancellor for to have the fines stand as the Lord Chief Justice had agreed, 21*l*. 17*s*.

"Item to his clerk, 1*l*."

Wardens of the Merchauntailors of the said Fraternitie and by theire predecessors, to the foresaid intent made ordeyned and established and the same and every of them correct and amend in due forme, and as the foresaid Act made in the said Parliament requireth, Wee having perused the said Petition and fynding the same fitt to be graunted according to their desires, have also by the authority of the said Act of Parliament perused and redd, all and every their Ordynaunces, Statutes, Acts and Oathes in the said Booke specified and the same have corrected, reformed and amended as Wee sawe fitt, The Tenor whereof hereafter ensue and followe in these words."

These ordinances have been supplemented by others of a later date—but they are (with the oaths) the rules of government by which the Merchant Taylors are ordered at the present day in relation to their Guild.

Little further remains to be written but to point out that the men by whose counsels the Guild was governed during the earlier years of James's reign were Robert Dowe (whose noble benefactions we have previously described) Richard Gore, the M.P. for London, the Swynnertons (father and son) John Vernon (the benefactor), Sir Leonard Halliday and Sir W. Craven—and the expenditure of the Master and Wardens for the year 1612-13 which they sanctioned is shown on the opposite page. It will be noticed that London rents were gradually rising in value, and that the expenditure in entertainments and education and charity had increased. No reference is made to Virginia, but the plantation in Ireland adds items to each side of the account.

CHAP. XVII.] *Expenditure for 1612–13.* 343

MERCHANT TAYLORS COMPANY 1612–13.[1]

RECEIPTS.	£ s. d.	PAYMENTS.	£ s. d.
Apprentices' fees.. ..	86 7 6	Salaries, pensions &c. ..	131 18 8
Freemen's admission fees	48 3 4	Entertainments	192 1 5
Sundry fines	10 12 0	Repairs and work ..	59 18 4
Other receipts—fines on leases, &c.	411 0 0	Legal expenses (new ordinances 65*l*. 15*s*. 6*d*.) ..	97 11 8
Interest on loans.. ..	236 7 4	Soldiers	31 1 7
Rents	1,118 11 8	Sundries	62 13 3
	£1,911 1 10	Trust payments and quit-rents	705 12 5
Repayment of loans ..	1,200 0 0	Lord Mayor (Swynnerton)	77 0 0
Corn money	51 0 11	Exhibitions	20 10 0
Bequests	366 13 4	School	84 6 8
On account of Irish plantation	255 16 8	Charitable expenditure ..	143 7 6
	£3,784 12 9		£1,606 1 6
Balance brought from last account	702 2 0	Purchase of corn ..	440 16 3
		Loans	310 0 0
		Purchase of property[2] ..	900 0 0
		Plantation in Ireland ..	1,175 0 0
			£4,431 17 9
		Balance	54 17 0
	£4,486 14 9		£4,486 14 9

[1] The Master was Andrew Osborne, and the Wardens were Robert Jenkinson, Ralph Hamer, William Gore, and Charles Hoskyns.

[2] 24 and 26, Basinghall Street, and 1 and 2, Sambrook Court, purchased of Sir Wolston Dixie, and now let at (say) 2,000*l.* a year. This was the final payment to complete the purchase at 1,840*l.*

APPENDIX 1.

Indenture of Apprenticeship of 20th December, 1451 (30 Henry VI).[1]

John Harrietsham contracts with Robert Lacy to serve the said Robert as well in the craft and in all his other works and doings such as he does and should doe, from Christmas day next ensuing for the term of seven years. *He is to receive 9s. 4d. at the end of the term, and he shall work one year after the seven at the wages of 20s.*[2] Robert is to find his apprentice in all necessaries, food, clothing, shoes, and bed, and to teach him his craft in all its particulars without concealment. During the term the apprentice is to keep his master's secrets, to do him no injury, and commit no excessive waste on his goods. He is not to frequent taverns, not to commit fornication, in or out of his master's house, nor make any contract of matrimony nor affiance himself without his master's leave. He is not to play at dice-tables or chequers, or any other unlawful games, but is to conduct himself soberly, justly, piously, well, and honourably, and to be a faithful and good servant, according to the use and custom of London. For all his obligations Robert binds himself, his heir and executors, his goods and chattels, present and future, wherever found. Signed, sealed and delivered by the two parties."

APPENDIX 2.

Petition of the Tailors and Armourers of London to Edward III for a Charter granted 10th March, 1327.[3]

"To our Lord the King and to his Council, pray humbly the Tailors and Armourers of London, that whereas they have hitherto held their guilds every year from a time beyond which memory

---

[1] Rogers on Prices, Vol. 4, page 59.

[2] The words in *italics* are not in the form in use by the Merchant Taylors Company.

[3] This document, as will be noticed, bears no date, but when sent to me the words of it were identified as being the same as those recited in the Charter. This identity proves it to be (what I have described it to be), viz., the petition for the Charter. Mr. Trice Martin has rendered it into English.

runneth not. In which guild they are wont to rule their mystery and order the state of their workmen and servants and redress all faults by them committed, for the honour of their mystery and the common profit of the said city of London, and of all the people, citizens and foreigners. And of late every one who has become a Tailor and Armourer has taken and kept a shop of his mystery in the said City, as well foreigners as those free of the City. And by such foreigners who were not ruled by the good folk of the said guild, many folk have received great damage, whereof the good folk of the mystery have been defamed and slandered evilly and wrongfully, to the great damage and dishonour of the said City. May it please you, dear Lord, for God's sake, for the profit of your said City and for the common profit of all the people, to order that the Tailors and Armourers of London and their successors, may hold their guild once every year, and in their guild order and rule their mystery and redress their wrongs by the Mayor of London for the time being, and the best and most sufficient folk of the mystery. And that no man may keep table or shop of the mystery, unless he be free of the City. And that none may be enfranchised, unless he be vouched for by the best of the mystery, as good and loyal and useful to the mystery.

"Endorsed.—Let what is asked by the petition be done with the advice of the Mayor, etc.   Enrolled."

From the original in the Public Record Office.

APPENDIX 3.

Nota Bene, &c., of the Great Costs, Tempore Lokok, Master, 1439–40.

These are divers payments and costs made by the Master and Wardens upon divers men for the new great Charter:—

	£	s.	d.
First, pd. to Radeford Vampage Lymyngton Brown, of the Common Pleas, and Wolston, men of law, for their counsel at divers times, 4 marks	2	13	4
It. expended on them in dinners and suppers divers times, and on divers matters of the Mistery, as appeareth by bills	1	10	5
It. pd. to John Panycook, yeoman of the robes of our Lord the King, for the pursuit and getting of our great Charter	20	0	0
It. given to him a gilt cup, 4 marks	2	13	4
It. given to him a box of silver and gilt	1	0	0
It. given to his servants in money	1	13	4
It. boat hire to the Privy Seal at Barnes	0	3	4
It. pd. to the Privy Seal for writing and sealing	1	13	4

		£	s.	d.
It. pd. for writing of the great Charter in the Council		2	6	8
It. pd. the seal of the great Charter to the Clerk of the "hampio"		8	9	0
It. pd. a ring of gold to the Chancellor		4	0	0
It. pd. damaske to John Norys		4	0	0
It. pd. divers costs for Penycook at Dogmansfeld		0	6	8
It. pd. to Geoffrey Goodlok for his labour		2	0	0
It. pd. to Appelton, an Esquire of the Chancellor		0	6	8
It. pd. to Clerk of the Council		7	6	8
It. pd. Master Thomas Kirkeby, of the Chancery, for the examination of our Charter		1	0	0
It. to a yeomen of the Crown, Waplode		1	0	0
It. expended at divers times to John Penycook, and other men of the Mystery, ―――― on dinners and suppers, as appeareth by divers bills		3	1	7
It. pd. for a copy of a bill wh the Mayor of London brought to our Lord the King and to the Council for the Charters of all the different Mysteries of the City		0	1	8
It. pd. to fformory, Scrivener, for writing diverse copies of our Charter, and divers bills and indentures, as appeareth by a bill		0	15	0
It. expended in hire of horse, meat, and drink to Dogmansfeld, and home 4 days, 3 men, for the suit of the new Charter		1	2	9
It. given to Lowthe, for his great labour and business about our Charter in many wise, 4 yards of scarlet		2	4	0
It. to his two clerks at Dogmansfeld		0	3	4
It. to the Chafferer of wax, for his fee		0	1	8
It. to a man that rode with us for his labour		0	1	4
It. given to a man to be our guide		0	0	8
It. spent on a dinner and supper on Lowthe, when he came to London, and on our men of the Craft		0	18	10
It. for pears and plums that were sent to my lord		0	1	6
It. pd. to Grenchode, limner, for limning of the head of the great Charter		0	5	0
It. pd. to John More, for a copy of the Charter of the Rolls		0	3	4
It. pd. for a pair of Boges that Penycok had of Wilcocks' wife of the late		0	2	0
Sum of the payments of the Charter	£71	5	5

APPENDIX 4.

22 HENRY VI (1443), WILLIAM AUNTRUS, MASTER.[1]

THISE BEEN THE PAIEMENTZ AND COSTZ MADE BY THE MEISTRE AND WARDEINS UPON DYVERS MEN FOR THE SERCHE OF BARTHILMEW FAIRE.

First spended in mete and drinke and horsemete to Dogmansfeld and home, and fro London to the kynge's hous for a letter fro the kyng, and a nother tyme to Penycoke's place, xxiiijs.

---

[1] He was the Esquire for the King's person. See surrender and quit claim by his heir-at-law in favour of the Carthusians at Boston, 20th March, 1486.—Materials for History of Henry VII, page 58.

Item, paid to Lowthe's clerk for writyng of the charter and certein writtes, xjs. viijd.

Item, paid to Gedeney, under secretarye for devysyng and writyng of a letter fro the kyng to the Meir of London, vjs. viijd.

Item, paid to Lowthe, of the Chauncerie for his labour, dyvers tymes rydyng fro Dogmansfeeld[1] to London and to the kynge's hous and other places for our mater, xls.

Item, paid to men of our crafte and other that wer in Newgate, vjs. viijd.

Item, spended in horshire, horsmete to Eltham, and bothire dyvers tymes to Westminster for that matter, ijs. vjd.

Item, espended in dyvers tymes at dyners and sopers upon Lowthe, Gedeney, and other men of lawe for the serche forseid, xxxvijs.

Item, paid to Lakyn and Wolston, men of lawe, for seyng of our charter, vjs. viijd.

Item, spended in horshire and horsmete whan Jeorge rode to Shene and fet Thomas Davy and the clerk another tyme, ijs. iiijd. = vjli. xijs. jd.

APPENDIX 5.

AGREEMENT WITH HENRY VII, THAT IN CONSIDERATION OF THE NEW CHARTER CERTAIN RELIGIOUS CEREMONIES SHALL BE OBSERVED AND MASSES SAID FOR HIM.[2]

To the most Christian and most excellent Prince and Lord, our Sovereign Lord Henry seventh of that name, most unconquered King of England and France, and most illustrious Lord of Ireland, your humble, devoted and faithful servants and subjects, Edmund Flowre, Master, also Richard Conhyll, Thomas Speight, Robert Colson, and John Wright, Wardens of the Brotherhood or Company of Merchant Taylors called of St. John the Baptist, of your city of London, and all the Company of the same Brotherhood [wish] prosperous and happy state in Him by whom kings reign and princes govern, and perpetual increase of your most happy succession, and happily to earn eternal joys in the Lord.

Whereas your most serene Majesty has not only deigned always graciously with the eyes of your Highness to look upon

---

[1] In Hants, now the seat of the Mildmays, but then of the Archbishop of Canterbury, who was Lord Chancellor. Henry VIII gave it to Wriotesley, Earl of Southampton.

[2] Rendered into English by C. Trice Martin, B.A.

and increase us and our foresaid Brotherhood with special privileges and favours, but also, as the original and most pious founder and erector, you have graciously caused to be favourably brought to light, raised up and made known, and have changed the name of the same Brotherhood, which has long lain hid in concealment and shade; and because we are not able in the earthly and transitory gifts of this world in a worthy and equal manner to reply, repay, or recompense your Highness's great and ample kindness and benevolence, shown to us only by your graciousness, not in consequence of our merits, and because revolving in our inner mind how purely, how piously, by reason of its devotion your soul as the noblest of all creatures is worthy by the Divine mercy to be crowned with a crown of glory in the heavens among the hosts of Holy Angels; and because the singular fervour of devotion which we see that your foresaid Highness ever has in the petitions of prayers, strongly urges us, Most Christian Prince, and compels us in the love of Christ to devise the making and pouring out of prayers and petitions for the safety of your soul.

Therefore we, the said Edmund Flowre, Master, and Richard Conhyll, Thomas Speyght, Robert Colson, and John Wryght, Wardens, *and the whole of the aforesaid Brotherhood* treating carefully in this behalf of and concerning the premises in common *amongst ourselves*, by our *unanimous express consent*, knowingly and deliberately have granted and grant for us and our future successors of the said fraternity for ever, and to this charge and bind us and them for ever by these presents, that is to say, that we and our said successors at our and their own charge and expense yearly, during the natural life of your aforesaid most serene Majesty, on the day when it happens that the exequies of the deceased are celebrated in the Conventual Church of your Monastery of St. Peter's, Westminster, for your good and happy estate, we and our successors will cause the office of exequies with nine lessons and lauds and with a mass of requiem on the next day then immediately following, with all and single prayers, suffrages, lights, tolling of bells, and other ceremonies requisite and fit in that behalf, with music to be celebrated solemnly and devoutly[1] in the parish church of St. Martin's Outwich, of the city of London, on the same days, for your aforesaid prosperous and happy estate, as for our original and most devout founder; as also by these presents we grant to hold and celebrate for ever another office of exequies or exequies of the dead, whatever they may be,

---

[1] *Solemni tam* is probably an error for *solemniter*.

every year on the day of the Nativity of St. John the Baptist for the souls of the brethren and sisters of the said Brotherhood in all the most solemn manner, form, and effect, as is most solemnly and devoutly fitting. And thus every year in future during your foresaid natural life shall be done; and we and they will cause to be held a service of the dead, *i.e.*, *Placebo* and *Dirige*, with nine lessons and with mass of requiem on every next day then following, for your happy estate in manner, form and effect aforesaid.

And we the aforesaid Master and Wardens *and the whole Brotherhood* aforesaid and our and their aforesaid future successors are bound to be present at the same exequies with the whole Company of the aforesaid Brotherhood, or at least with the greater and better part of the same Brotherhood, viz., each in his decent and better clothing, as seems most decent and best to us and them, publicly and in common every year for ever.

And on the day next following we and they will be bodily present at the mass of requiem in the like manner, form, and effect, and each one of us and them and each of us and them will be bound to offer to God and devoutly display offerings for each of us and them in the same mass for your said good and prosperous estate, and we and they will offer them effectually to the praise of God.

We will also and by these presents grant for ourselves and our said successors, and to this by the tenor of these presents we charge and bind ourselves and them by strict law, that when the day of your obit is announced to us, or we are certainly informed thereof in any way, that then on the very day on which as is aforesaid the office of exequies is celebrated and sung in the Conventual Church of your Monastery of St. Peter's, Westminster aforesaid for your soul, we in like manner and form aforesaid will cause to be said for ever devoutly and celebrated solemnly and with music, in the said parochial church, the office of exequies with nine lessons and lauds, and with the mass of requiem on the morrow then following with all and single prayers, suffrages, lights, tolling of bells, ceremonies, offerings, and other things aforesaid, on every day of your obit and on every next day then following annually every year for ever, for your soul.

In witness of which thing we Edmund Flowre, Master, also Richard Conhyll, Thomas Speyght, Robert Colson, and John Wright, Wardens aforesaid, *and the whole Brotherhood*[1] aforesaid

---

[1] The words in *italics* show this to be a contract made with the full assent of the whole Brotherhood assembled in the Common Hall.

ave unanimously, knowingly, and deliberately affixed to these presents our common seal which we use instead of our signatures in this behalf. Dated at London in the Common Hall of us and the aforesaid Brotherhood, on the third day of the month of December, in the year of Our Lord, 1503, and the nineteenth year of your most excellent reign.

APPENDIX 6.

"TH'ORDYNNAUNCE FOR THE KEPYNG OF THE QUENE'S OBITE and OF THE KYNGES WHEN IT SHALL HAPPEN.

"Also it is ordeigned & enacted that every broder of the said fraternitee beyng duly sommoned by the bedell every yere herafter and for evermore shalbe personally present in his hole lyvery atte obite of the moste excellente Prynce of famous memory our late Soveraigne Lorde Kyng Henry the vijth in the parisshe Chirche of Saynte Martyn Oteswyche of London, and afterward continuelly & for ever atte obite of the same our soveraigne Lord whan it shall please Almighty God that his moste graceyous persone shall departe from this present lyfe as the said fraternitee have bound theymself to do according unto the effecte of a draunte by theym late made in writyng under their common Seale, and delivered unto the Kynges Highnesse more plainely doth appere. And what persone of the said fraternitee beyng duely sommoned as is afforsaid and cometh not to the said obite and wole not tary there tyll Dirige and Masse be don, nor offer atte said mass ej^d, shall paye to th'use of the said fraternitee as often and whan as any is founde fauly iij^s. iiij^d. reasonable lette & lawfull excuse alwey excepte."

[There is no mention made of the Queen in the body of this Ordinance, but there is an evident erasure where her name should stand and an insertion of the King's instead, who thus becomes mentioned twice over and is spoken of as "our late Sovereign" before his death. The words underlined are later than the others and those marked through are crossed out to agree with the former alteration, which was made after the 11th February, 1503, on which day the Queen died at the Tower of London in childbirth.]

APPENDIX 7.

EPITOME OF THE ORDINANCES OF THE MERCHANT TAYLORS COMPANY RELATING TO THE PERSONS UNDERMENTIONED: (A) FREEMEN; (B) APPRENTICES; (C) WARDENS; (D) ASSISTANTS; (E) MASTER; (F) MASTER; (G) BEADLE AND WARDENS, AS APPROVED IN 1507, UNDER 19 HENRY VII, CHAP. 7.

(A) Ordinances relating to the Freeman.

Every brother or freeman shall—

(1.) On summons be present with the Master and Wardens in his whole livery or otherwise at any place and hour assigned for any noble triumph for the Kinge's Highnesse, his noble issue, or other grater estates, concerning the honour of the King and of his realme, or elles for any quarter-day obit, dirge, offering, pression riding, or other assembly (except he be Mayor or Alderman or Sheriff) or pay 8*d.* for the first; 16*d.* for the second, and 6*s.* 8*d.* for the third offence.

(2.) Shall not wear costly array other than is fitting for his calling as a citizen or merchant under a penalty of 100*s.*

(3.) Every freeman or of the Livery to pay for each apprentice, 3*s.* 4*d.*, and for every such over two apprentices, 20*s.*, but if the Freeman be of the Bachelors Company, half moiety of the 20*s.* to go to the Common Box of the Bachelors Company,[1] and every freeman before taking his apprentice shall present him to the Master and Wardens for their examination as to his birth, &c., under a penalty of 40*s.*, and after taking him, enroll his apprenticeship with the Chamberlain, under a penalty of 6*s.* 8*d.*

(4.)[2] Not set up a shop without a licence from the Master and Wardens if he has stock to the value of 10 marks paying to the Fraternity 3*s.* 4*d.*, and for his "incomyng to the Batchelors Company and to be broder" with them 3*s.* 4*d.*, and shall produce his freedom and enter it of record under a penalty of 40*s.*[3]

(5.)[2] The preface to this section is as follows :—

"Also where" dyvers persones aswele of the same misteere as also estraungers born in the parties of beyond the see and also

---

[1] The preceding paragraph is omitted from the ordinances of 1613, so that the fees were regulated by 22 Henry VIII, c. 4.

[2] These sections are not in the ordinances of 1613, as the Freeman's oath to the same effect was prohibited by 28 Henry VIII, c. 5.

[3] A proviso is added that this ordinance is to stand only till complained against, and then to be reformed "as the King's noble grace and his Council shall be advised."

foreyns use dayly to kepe Chambers secretly in aleys and upon steyers & houses in corners, and cutte & make almaner of garmentes, and the same persones be nother free of the Citee nor of the said feliship of Merchaunt Taillours, nother obedient to the good & lawfull ordynaunces made & provyded for the said feliship, nother contributory to any imposicions or other charges paid to the Kyng's grace for the common weale of the Citee, nor chargeable with the payment of any money toward the supportation and mayntennaunce of the said misteere and the fynding and releef of the pore almesbredern of the same which abusyon is lykely to be the grete hynderaunce & impoverysshyng of the freemen, householders and kepars of shoppes of the same misteere and to the decay and hurt of the libertees of the said Citee yf due remedy therein be not the sooner provyded and had, the premisses considered."

Not to keep any secret chamber or house in alleys or upon stairs, or cut or make any manner of garment therein unless it be for his wife and children under a penalty of 6s. 8d.

"Also whereas there is a grete noumbre and multitude of aliauntes, foreyns, denizens and straungers dayly repayring to this Citee and use th'andicrafte of Tailloury in dyvers Citezeins houses of other mysteeres which is to the grete hurt & hynderaunce of th'artificers of this ffraternitee."

(6.)[1] Not to employ any foreign stranger or denizen in his house in the handicraft of tailory unless for some work which must be done for some noble triumph, &c., under a penalty of 20s.

(7.)[1] Not to attend or make any unlawful assembly for making of ordinances to the subversion of the Fraternity, under penalty, if of the Livery, to be put out of the same, and be excluded from all alms and other benefits; and if a Batchelor (or Yeoman) of 10l., and to be imprisoned by the Mayor.

(8.)[1] Not to take by cosen or fraud any tenement in the city of the lord of the soil, whereby any occupying tenant should be expelled, under a penalty of treble the value of the rent, one-half going to the tenant so expelled, and the other part to the Fraternity.

(9.) Not to use rude words or revile another, or otherwise misbehave himself to any person in any cause or matter proposed before the Master and Wardens in open audience, under a penalty of 40s.

(10.)[1] To attend on summons in livery the Master and Wardens at the burying of a brother and sister, and to carry such to burial

---

[1] These sections are not in the ordinances of 1613.

(unless himself ill or the deceased died of the great pestilence), under a penalty, if the deceased had not been Master or Warden, of 6s. 8d., provided that a past Warden was summoned for the burying of a Master, who made default should pay 10s.

(11.) To pay immediately ensuing the feast of Midsummer his duty for the same feast to the Warden under penalty of being put out of the Livery, and if not of the Livery shall forfeit to the Fraternity double the value of the debt he oweth to the said craft.

In the ordinances of 1613 the fees for the feast were inserted as "3s. 4d. for the Livery, and such person as be not of the clothing and able to pay their duty shall pay at the general feast 12d., whether he be present or not, and shall also pay his quarteridge of 2s. 2d. yerely to the use of the poore of the said fraternite upon payne of forfeiture of double the value of the several duties that he oweth to the said craft without any remission or pardon."

(12.)[1] To obey the Master and Wardens for peace, or "such rebels being obstinate," to be punished at the discretion of the Master and Wardens.

(13.) Not disclose secrets of trade or the counsels of the Fraternity, under a penalty of 10l.

(14.) To bear charge of all cessings, prest-costs, contributions, and all other charges pertaining to the worship, benefit, and credit of the Mysterie as thought fit by the Court, under of penalty of 40s.

(15.) Not to entice any man's apprentice or covenant servant away under a penalty of 20s. to the craft, and to the master of the apprentice or servant, 10l.

(16.)[1] Not to keep open shop on any holy day appointed by the Church, except St. Bartholomew's Day, or on this if it fall on a Sunday, under a penalty of 40s.

(17.) Not to deliver vendible goods, cloth, wares, merchandise, plate or jewels to any man's apprentice or servant (save on special token from the master) save at his own adventure.

(18.) Not to take an alien as apprentice, under a penalty of 20l.

(19.)[1] Not to associate with a breaker of the ordinances (after warning) under a penalty of 100s.

(20.) No person to leave the Fraternity without licence from the Master and Wardens on payment of such fine as they, or on appeal, the Chancellor and Treasurer of England and the two Chief Justices of either bench for the time being, or three of them, shall assess according to his condition and quality.

---

[1] These sections are not in the ordinances of 1613.

(21.) Upon a Mayor's election from the Fraternity the Bachelor's Company was appointed to certain services, thus if any of those persons appointed by the Master and Wardens[1] to be Master's Bachelor of the Barge (in Foynes)[2] refuse attendance in such sort as is for the worship of the Fraternity, and do not supply and bear such usual rates as are usually borne by such as are elected, each shall pay 100s. to the mysterie; and if any other Bachelor (in Budge) for the same cause named do not obey the same attendance and contributions as are usually borne, he shall pay 20s. to the Mysterie. Further each of the said Bachelors to give his best attendance at the Mayor's and Sheriffs' feast of the said Fraternity as by the said Master and Wardens appointed, under a penalty of 6s. 8d.

(22.) To bear the room and office of Master, if elected, or pay a fine of 40l. (increased to 100l. by the ordinance of 1613).

(23.) Not to be a servant of a man of another mysterie, save for higher wages under a penalty of 40s.

(24.) Not to instruct children in the art of the mysterie save as apprentices enrolled, under a penalty of 100s.

(25.)[3] To keep the Queen's obit and the King's (Henry VII) when it shall happen, and offer at the said masse a 1d., under a penalty of 3s. 4d.

(26.) Not to permit their servants or apprentices to buy or sell for their own or another's use, save for their master's, under a penalty of 20l.

(B) *Apprentices.*

Not to wear any weapon within the city unless going into the country with his master or other honest company.

(C) *Ordinances relating to the Wardens.*

(1.) The search at St. Bartholomew's Fair under the charter of Edward IV (1465), which is recited as a preface to the ordinance.

(2.) To appear on summons at the Common Hall (Mayor, Alderman, or Sheriff being excepted), under a penalty of 4s.

---

[1] In 1507 the appointment might be made by the "Livery," but in 1613 it was changed to Assistants.

[2] It is perhaps needless to say that this designation is by the skin which each Bachelor wore as part of his Livery. Foyne, being the skin of the marten, and Budge the skin of the lamb, these terms first appeared in the ordinance of 1613, but whether the first was a master and the other a workman has not come under my notice. The contributions made for Sir John Gore's Mayoralty in 1624 was by each 3l. 6s. 8d. as Foyne" and 2l. 6s. 8d. as "Budge" Bachelors.

[3] This section is not in the ordinances of 1613.

(3.) No Warden to misuse himself against the Master by hasty speech or violent misdemeanor, under a penalty of obeying the order thereon of four or six of the Assistants, or paying 40s. to the use of the Company.

(4.) To act without partiality or fear to all alike in carrying out the acts and ordinances, under a penalty of 5l.

(5.)[1] The old Wardens shall assist the new Renter Warden in getting in the rents, under a penalty of 10s.

(6.)[1] The fourth Warden to gather in rents, buy stuff for reparation of houses, and account to the Master four times a year before the August next after the feast of Midsummer under a penalty of 10s.

(7.)[1] Two Liverymen to be arbitrators and counsellors with the Fourth Warden in all measures belonging to the common profit, to true attendance, and advice at all time, under a penalty of 100s.

(8.)[1] The Fourth Warden shall buy at Kingston Pentecost Fair, or other place, preceding Midsummer, timber, &c., at easy prices to the sum of 12l. or thereabouts, and stow the same in the Common Hall, and make to the Master a true account of such costs paid before the engrossing of the Master's account under a penalty of 20l.

(D) *Ordinances relating to Assistants.*

To appear at the Common Hall or (elsewhere on summons) for any matter or cause concerning common worship and profit of the Mysterie, under a penalty of 3s. 4d.

(E) *Ordinances relating to the Master.*

(1.) To order search throughout the city at St. Bartholomew's by ye Wardens.

(2.) To appear at the Common Hall or elsewhere on summons for any matter or cause concerning the common worship and profit of the mysterie, under a penalty of 5s.

(3.) Every year before the 14th August after the Midsummer Feast to yield up his accounts openly in the Common Hall before the whole body of the Fraternity of all money received and paid by him, and there to be allowed or disallowed of all his reckonings. If any sum be due to the said Fraternity then to pay the same (under penalty of double the amount), or if any sum be due to the old Master then the new Master shall pay such out of growing receipts.

(4.) Every year to view the lands of the Fraternity, not paying for ye expenses of such view more than 20s.

---

[1] These sections are not in the ordinances of 1613.

(F) Same as to the Master and Wardens.

(1.) To nominate eight of the Livery on the eve of St. John Baptist's Day for the Court of Assistants to elect four thereof as Wardens.

Same as to the Master and Wardens with the Court of Assistants.

(1.) To elect a Master and four Wardens on the vigil of the Nativity of St. John Baptist.

(2.) To present to the benefice of St. Martin Outwich.

(3.) To [appoint and] remove almsmen.

(4.) To use the common seal if the Master and Wardens and ten Assistants be present and consent.

(5.) To assist the Master and Wardens generally in matters submitted to them when summoned.

Same to the Bedel.

The Bedel, on notice of the decease of an Assistant or Liveryman, or his wife, to summon the whole Company to be present with the Master and Wardens in livery, at the place and hour for burial, and his fee for such summons from the executors to be 2s. 4d., and for a Master 3s. 4d.

Same to the Clerk.

To make all the indentures of apprenticeship and obligations (under a fine of 5s.) and receive 12d. for each indenture and obligation.

ADDITIONAL ORDINANCES IN 1613.

25. If any person of the Fraternity named and elected Warden will not serve he shall forfeit 50l., and if any person of the Bachelors Company, not of the Livery, being chosen shall not serve he shall forfeit 40l.

26. That an Assistant withdraw from Court or assembly during such time as any cause or matter be considered in which he or any brother or servant is concerned under a penalty of 40l.; and the Clerk to put the Master, Wardens, and Assistants in mind of this ordinance under a penalty of 10s.

34. (*a.*) That in all controversies between any brother and his apprentice leading to separation, the master to bring the indenture to the hall for differences to be examined, and apprentice to be delivered to the Master of the Company (*ad interim*) till another master can be found for him.

(*b*). If any brother fall into decay or depart the city leaving the apprentice destitute, the Master of the Company may put such apprentice to another master for the residue of the term.

The Oath of the Four Wardens Substitute of the Bachelors Company.

The Oath of the Sixteen Men or Assistants to the Wardens Substitute of the Bachelors Company.

APPENDIX 8.

The Ordinance (1507) for the Election of the Master and Four Wardens.

Also it is enacted and ordained that the M & 4 W^s being in office and authority from henceforth shall do, call, and cause to assemble togeder the 24 Assistants and Counsellors of the s^d Fraternity, or the more part of them in the vigil of the Nativity of St. J^n Bptist to be present with the s^d M & 4 W^s in their Common Hall at a certain hour limited, and incontinently upon the said Assembly the said M & 4 W^s being in office of one mind after their wise discretion shall name and appoint unto the said Assistants 8 sad, wise, and able persons of the clothing and livery every of them to bear the room of a Warden, out of w^h 8 persons so as is aforesaid named the same Master & 4 Wardens with the consent of the s^d Assts. then being present shall take, admit, and elect 4 of them w^h have most of the common voice of the same fellowship to be Wardens for the year ensuing,[1] and the Master

---

[1] From these words the ordinances of 1613 concludes thus :

"Which being done, then the said Maister and Wardens shall name and appoint two of the Assistaunts of the said Fraternitie which have formerly served in the place of Upper or Second Warden, out of which two the said Maister and Wardens together with the assent of so many of the Assistaunts as have formerly borne the office of a Maister of the said Fraternitie shall proceede to the electon of a newe Muister to governe the Company for the yeare ensuing. And thus the electon of the Maister and fower Wardens is in manner aforesaid to be performed. Which Electon so made, is to be kept secrett until their ffeast or dynner, called the Dynner of the publishing of the Electon of the Maister and Wardens, and then, nigh about the end of the same ffeast the Maister and Ffower Wardens, with their garlands* upon their heads, and two others that have bene Maisters, that shalbe for the same appointed, and their Officers attending upon them shall come forth openly into the Hall afore such Estates, Honourable & Worshipful Guests as shalbe then and there present, and shall there publish theire late election and choice of the newe Maister that was aforenamed in the said day of elecŏn. And after that done, then the ffower Wardens and every and each of them in his order, shall publish

* When this custom was discontinued has not come under my notice, but on the 20th June, 1674, the Court ordered, and Warden Sewell was requested to provide, five garlands for our Master and Wardens, against the Election day, as was formerly before the late dreadful fire.

that shall be chosen for the same year ensuing shall be elect and put into room by him that is their Governor, the 4 Wardens there being & the Assistants such as have been Masters aforetime and when the same election of the M & 4 W^s is in manner aforesaid finished then the same election to be kept secret unto the morrow then next ensuing w^h is the day of the Nativity of *St. John the Baptist in whose honor they keep their feast* according to sundry grants given & granted unto them by the King's noble progenitors as by their letters patent under their great seal made & by the king's grace that now is ratified & confirmed more plainly appeareth & then nigh about the end of the same feast the Master & 4 Wardens with garlands upon their heads & 2 other that have been Masters that shalbe for the same appointed & their officers attending upon them shall come forth openly into the Hall afore such noble Estates, Men of Honour, & Worshipful Guests as shalbe then & there present and do admit & choose the new Master that was afore named in the s^d Vigil & none other & after that done then the four Wardens & every of them in his order shall elect & admit openly the same 4 persons that were afore appointed to be Wardens in the s^d Vigil & none other.

Provided always that as soon after as the Dinner of the s^d feast is finished then every brother of the s^d Frat^{ty} or the more part of them shall repair & go in his whole livery unto the Church of St. Martin Outwich, whereof the said M W^s & fell'ship be patrons where for ever shall be kept a solemn dirge by note for all the brethren & sisters of the said fraternity deceased and on the morrow next following every brother of the same fraternity to be

their late election of the said severall fower Wardens formerly elected in the said day of election, according to the usual course, lawdable & ancient custome heretofore used in the publishing of the election of the Maister and Wardens of the Merchauntailors. And for the election of the Wardens substitute of the Bachelors company of this Mistery, and their Assistants, the same to be holden, done & performed yearely upon the Even of the Decollation of St. John Baptist according as heretofore hath bene accustomed.

" And it is further ordayned that yff the newe Maister & Wardens or any of them shalbe absent at the said feast or dinner of the publishing of the same Electon of Maister and Wardens unlesse they be letten by sickness or some such other necessary and ymportant occasion as they cannot be present, then they which are absent shall forfeit to the said Maister and Wardens to the use of the Poore of the said Fellowshipp, the severall penalties and forfeitures following—viz.,

" The Maister for his absence, Fforty shillings. The Upper Warden for his absence, Thirty shillings. The Second Warden for his absence, Thirty shillings; and the two Rentor Wardens for their absence, Thirteen shillings fower pence apiece.

" The same penalties and forfeitures to be paid before they take their Oathes for the execution of their severall offices respectively."

at s[d] Church at Masse at 9 (IX) of the clock or soon after, & every of them to offer there a penny or else to send thither by one of his brethren or by the Clerk or Beadle for his offering a penny & he that is not at dirge & Masse there nor do his dirge as is aforesaid shall forfeit & pay to the use of the said fraternity a fine of 12d. as often & when any is found defective, reasonable and lawful excuse alway except & reseived.

APPENDIX 9.

(*The Prayer of the Guild.*)
THE FIRST ENTRY IN THE MERCHANT TAYLORS' ORDINANCE BOOK OF HENRY VII's REIGN.

Most mighty and most glorious God which are great and fearful yet loving and mercifull to all such as call upon thee in sincerity and truth, and our most gracious and mercifull and loving Father in Christ Jesus. We most wretched and sinful creatures here prostrate ourselves before thy throne of mercy in the name and mediation of thy beloved sonne our most gratious saviour and Redeemer, humbly beseeching thee (for his sake) to cast all our offences behind thee and to bury them in his grave, who died for our synnes and rose agayne to bring us both in body and soul unto thee, and we beseech thee (good Lord), to preserve our king's most excellent Majesty, our gratious Queen's majesty, the noble Prince, and all the rest of the King's royal offspring and progeny. Good Lord keep this noble city of London and defend it from grevious plagues and contagious sicknes that we may often in Brotherly and true love assemble and meete together to thy glory and our mutuall comforte in Christ Jesus. And merciful father bless this Society and brotherhood and be present with us in all our assemblies and counsells that we may use them to thy glory and discharge of our duties; make us thankful for all the benefits which we have received and daily in thy mercy are continued towards us through our Lord and Saviour Christ Jesus. Bless thy good covenant amongst us (O Lord) and multiply thy mercies towards us with increase of well wishers, benefactors, and sound members of the same, settle and confirm faithfull and harty love amongst us all. Bless and direct (by the Holy Spirit) all our actions and endeavours, and give us grace faithfully and honestly to discharge the trusts reposed in us as well by our good friends and bretheren deceased, as any other way belonging to us to the glory of thy holy name and peace and comforte of our owne soules and good example and incitement to others. For these thy mercies and whatsoever ells thou in thy wisdome knowest most needeful for us and for thy whole church we shutt up these prayers in yt effectuall prayer which Christ himself hath taught us saying :—

APPENDIX 10.

June 13th, 1567.
Muster and Shew of the Standing Watch.

To the Wardens of the Company of Merchauntailors for the ffurniture of xij cressetts & v Bagge Bearers wth convenient Lyghtes for the same.

By the Mayo^r.

On the Quene o^r Sovreigne Ladyes behalf we straightly charge and comande you, that ye with all convenyent spede do p̃vide & p̃pare in p̃fecte redines xij fayre & comely cressitts wth good & sufficient lights for the same for the necessary muster & showe of the standing watche wch we have appoynted and are fully determyned and mynded, God willinge, to kepe and make within this o^r Sovreigne Lady the Quenes Maties Cittie of London upon the Vigill or Even of the Ffeaste of the Natyvitie of St. John Baptyste nowe nexte cominge, that ye p̃pare for only ij Cressett Bearers one Bagge Bearer to beare cressett lyghts with streamer hatt upon theire hedds havinge your armes thereupon. And that ye do cause all the same men and Cressetts wth so many good lyghts as shalbe suffycient to shyne durynge the tyme of the same Watche to be brought and conveyed to the Leadenhall within the said citie before vij of the clocke in th'afternoon of the sayd Vigill or Even of St. John Baptiste next cominge.

Fayle ye not thereof as ye will tender ye honor of the sayde cittie and the good pleasure of our sayde Sovreigne Ladye the Quene; and as you will answer for the contrarye at yor p̃rlls. Geven at the Guildehall of the sayde Cittye, the xth daye of June, anno 1567.

APPENDIX 11.

Assessments made upon the Company to Provide for the Purchase of Corn.

By the Mayor.

A Precepte directed to this Howse concerninge the levyinge of clxxv*l*. of the Members of this Mystery to be disbursed to the

APP. 11.]   *Corn Assessment.*   361

Chamber of London towards the makinge of pᵼvision of Grayne for the Servinge of the Citye was openly redd: The tenor whereof followeth in these words, viz. :—

"Forasmoche as we at this pᵼsent beinge very careful & mindefull accordinge to oᵼ duties to pᵼvide in tyme convenyent for the common Weale, comoditie & profitt in all things of this oᵼ Sovereign Lady the Queene's Highness Citie and Chamber of London, & of all the Citizens and Inhabitants of the same as moche as in us lieth, and consideryngc also the greate and excessive price of Wheate, and of all other kinds & sorts of grayne, mete & necessary for Man's sustenance which of late hath bene sore & felte, and willinge therefore to guard agaynst the danger & pᵼll throughe the gredy avourise and covetous mindes of the people, owners and possessors of the same grayne, that unhappely with a shorte tyme might ensue for th' avoiding & eschewing of such pᵼills & inconvenience as might ensue by th' occasions above recyted, to take uppe & make withall convenient spede of the Company's and Fellowshipps of the said Citie a very good & substantiall Masse and Some of Money to pᵼvide & buy Corne withall as well beyond Seas as on this side (and if need shalbe for th' use & common pᵼvision of the sayde Citie), towards the payment & makynge uppe of which Masse & Some of Money We have assessed yoᵼ said Company at the Some of Money of One hundrith, threscore & fyvteene pounds, which Some of clxxv*l*. We straightlie charge & command you that ye immediately upon the receipt hereof callinge your said Company together at the Hall do forthwith assese, taxe, levye & gather of the welthie and able pᵼsons of the same Company in suche sorte that ye fayle not to paye the same to Mr. Lyonell Duckett, Aldermⁿ within v day's next ensewing the date hereof, upon the delivery of whose bill witnessing the rescript of the said Some to the Chamberlyn, ye shall receyve the same Chamberlyn's bill for the futer payment of the same unto you ageyne. Ffayle ye not hereof as ye tender the Common Weale of the same Citie, and also your owne private welthe, and as ye will answer for the contrary at yoᵼ pᵼill.

"Given at the Guildehall of the saide Citie the xiiijth day of February 1565."

Whereupon the Company agreed and decreed that the foresaide clxxv*l*. shalbe assessed, taxed & levyed of the Members of this Mystery after suche & like order as was the clxxv*l*. that this Howse disbursed to the Chamberlayne for like pᵼvision of Wheate for this Citie accordinge to the tenor of like Precepte bearing date the viijth of February A⁰ 1564, which is as yet Owinge to this Howse, in & by all things.

APPENDIX 12.

Account of the Repayment of Corn Money which the Corporation had made to the Master and his distribution of it.—List of the Merchant Company.

1546-7. Master's Account.—Richard Holte.

This Accountant prayeth to be allowed of and for the payment of 51*l*. 3*s*. 4*d*., which he paid unto the Company for that they had lent the same for the provision for wheat, and hereafter is particularly declared to whom the same is repaid.

First, to Sir Henry Hobthorne (Lord Mayor). Item, Mr. John Wilford, Alderman, Mr. Thomas White, Alderman, each, 30*s*. Mr. John Suckley, Mr. William Wilford the elder, Mr. Wethypoll, Mr. Benett, Mr. Holte, Mr. Scult, Mr. Malte, Mr. Ryrton, each, 20*s*. Mr. Brooke, 3*l*. Mr. Dawbney, 20*s*. Thomas Offley,[1] 13*s*. 4*d*. Nicholas Cosyn, 20*s*. Richard Waddington, 13*s*. 4*d*. Henry Brayne, 20*s*. Richard Botyll, John Fording, Robert Mellish, Nicholas Wilford, Ralph Foxley, William Harper, Robert Herde, George Briggs, John Canon, John Jaks, John Mylner, Ralph Davenett, Richard Pawlyn, William Barlow, each, 10*s*. Walter Young, Richard Tongue, each, 20*s*. John Fisher, John Smith, Christopher Lording, Christopher Nicholson, William Wyld, Thomas Ridley, Henry Cook, William Rigeley, William Wolberd, Nicholas Wolberd, Emanuel Lucar, Thomas Emerey, George Heton, William Grene, Richard Newport, Richard Holt, jun., William Body, John Wethers, William James, Thomas Rowe, Edward Lee, William Sadok, Robert Dawson, Thomas Richards, Thomas Ackworth, John Bidge, John Apsley, Gye Wade, Thomas Walker, Thomas Middleton, Reynold Conygrave, Symon Low, Robert Brook, Robert Roos, Thomas Haile, John Whytpayne, William Clyfton, each, 6*s*. 8*d*., and the Bachelors Company, 10*l*. Total, 51*l*. 3*s*. 4*d*.

---

[1] The title "Mr." denotes a Master or Past Masters. Mr. Holte was Master in 1546-7, and Offley in 1547-8. This is the earliest list of the Company which I have met with in the Company's records.

APPENDIX 13.

Octo[r] 8th, 1586.
A THREAT OF IMPRISONING THE MASTER AND WARDENS FOR NOT MAKING A PROVISION OF GUNPOWDER.

By the Mayor.

Whereas by my late Precepte you were appoynted to receive of Henry Dale, Haberdasher, 1776 poundes of gunpowder & to paye him after the rate of x^d for everie pownde, the which my Lordes of the Privye Counsell are informed you have not done, Whereupon theire Lordshipps have written to me verie ernestlie to Commit you the Maister and Wardens to Warde for youre contempte and disobedience therein if you doe not spedilie accomplishe the same. Theise therefore shalbe Eftsones to require and commande you presentlie upon the sighte hereof to fetch all the saide complimente of powder and to make present paymente accordinge to my fformer Precepte, Otherwise I must comitt you to Warde according to theire Lordshipps commandement, and advertyse theire house thereof.

Whereuppon the Maister & Wardens have ordered that Mr. Rob[t] Dowe and Mr. Rich[d] Maye shalle conferre with the saide M[r] Henry Dale for 1,000 Weight of powder and not above, but as muche under as theyre discrecons shall seme mete, soe as the said powder shalbe judged & decreed good serviceable powder for Caleaver Shotte.

The same Rob[t] Dowe & Rich[d] Maye to conferre wth Mr. Bracie & such others as they know for the provydinge of 50 Corsletts and 16 or 20 Halberds to be boughte & provided by them to the moste proffite of this howse.

Also to provide 50 Arminge Swordes & Hangers to the moste proffite of this howse.

APPENDIX 14.

EDEN'S CASE IN THE STAR CHAMBER.

These documents illustrate the case: In the Star Chamber before the Council, June 7th, Elizabeth 23 (1581).—This day were heard the matters of account which have of long, long time depended in the honourable Court betwixt John Eden, plaintiff, and Walter Fish, Mrs. Hodgson, and others, defendants, touching an award made by them, bearing date November 28th, 15 Elizabeth (1573), premised by the plaintiff to be unduly and corruptly made by some of them, the said defendants, then being Master and Wardens of the Company of Merchant Taylors in London, touching certain matters then in controversy between the said plaintiff and one John Toppe, both brethren of the same, for the partnership of a certain stock then in question between them, and also touching perjury supposed to be committed by them in affirming the same in her Bench to be a true award, or writing and other several perjuries likewise supposed to be committed by the said defendants before the Lord Mayor in London, and in their examination to interrogations ministered by the plaintiff upon his first bill exhibited against them by the said plaintiff here in this Court, and for diverse other supposed misdemeanours as by the said several bills of complaint more at large appeareth. In the hearing and debating thereof, and specially of the proof of the plaintiff, the Court spent very long time, but forasmuch as in the end there appeared to the Court no cause or proof at all whereby they might be led or moved to give judgment against the defendants or any of them for any of the said supposed offences wherewith they were charged, but that they dealt simply and plainly, and that the same was by the said parties' full consent without any manner of corruption or suspicion of corruption very indifferently for the appeasing of all matters of controversy then depending between the said parties according to a covenant comprised in a pair of indentures made between the said parties which was this day openly read in Court touching the ordering of all striffe concerning the said partnership between them. Therefore they are this day clearly acquitted of all matters in the said bills contained and dismissed from this place with their costs sustained in the defence of the same cause with the good favour, opinion, and liking of this Court, of their dealing in all points. Nevertheless, the Court graciously respecting the poverty of the plaintiff, although produced by his own troublesome suit as it was informed, and also the good liability and estate of the defendants, have ordered that if the same plaintiff shall openly and personally by his submission before the Master, Wardens, and Assistants of the said Company of Merchant Taylors in their common hall on some day of their assembly there between this and the next term acknowledge and confess that he hath rashly, unadvisedly, and untruly charged the said defendants with the matters contained in his several bills of complaint, and then and there ask the defendants' forgiveness for the same, then they shall be allowed no costs at all in that behalf aforesaid. Otherwise to have allowance of their costs.

Eden's Star Chamber Case.

Court of June 14th, 1581.—Item, It is by the said Master, Wardens, and Assistants agreed and decreed that John Eden shall be warned at every Court of Assistants between this and the next term to come in and make his submission according to the order taken in the Star Chamber. Eden submitted himself to the Court, November 11th, 1581. Eden further claimed from John Toppe a sum of 30*l*., which, on coming before the Court for hearing, was settled by mutual agreement, and the matter was considered to be finally ended.

Such might have been the intention of the Merchant Taylors Company, but it was not so with Eden, for on February 14th, 1581, he renewed his application to the Court, through Lord Chancellor Bromley, thus:—

Item, A letter directed unto the said Master, Wardens, and Assistants, was openly read, containing as followeth: "After my hearty commendations, whereas upon occasion of my letters directed unto you the last term (as the poor man, John Eden, informed me) you did offer to admit him one of your almsmen, which manner of relief, though he do not despise, yet, as he sayeth, he may not take it, because the taking thereof may hinder and make him seem unfit for a much better preferment, whereof he is in possibility, and therefore requireth your benevolence to be extended towards him in such sort as the same hinder him not in a greater matter, and to that end hath humbly beseeched me to write again unto you in his behalf. Wherefore, considering the poor man's extremity, I pray you to have consideration of the premises; and, notwithstanding the late suit and trouble, which is past, yet, considering he hath humbled himself and made his confession before you according to order, I would wish you should bend your good wills towards him and relieve his necessity as much as you may. And touching the 30*l*. in question between him and Mr. Topp, which I have referred unto you, if it be true that Eden saith that they both have referred themselves (touching that matter) to be judged by the account which you made between them, then in reason the accounts ought to be seen and viewed, that the truth may be tryed. And so fare you well.—From my house near Charing-cross, the 9th day of February, A.D. 1581.—Your loving friend, THOMAS BROMLEY, Chancellor."

Whereupon and the rather at the contemplation of the said letter, the said Master, Wardens, and Assistants have granted unto the said John Eden one yearly pension of 5*l*. during his natural life at the will and pleasure of the said Master, Wardens, and Assistants, to be paid unto him quarterly, the first payment to begin at the feast of the Annunciation of the Blessed Virgin Mary now next ensuing. And yet for his better relief the said Master, Wardens, and Assistants have ordered and agreed that this first year's pension shall be paid unto him in hand, and after, quarterly, provided always that from henceforth the said John Eden be of good and honest behaviour.

Court of 2nd May, 1582.—Mr. Richard Burne, Master.—Item, as touching the request and petition of John Eden to the said Master, Wardens, and Assistants for their charitable relief to be bestowed upon him. The said Master, Wardens, and Assistants willed him to set down his request and petition in writing, and to bring the same unto the same Master and Wardens, and they should see him answered.

Court of 9th May, 1582.—Mr. Richard Burne, Master.—The 4th of May, 1582.—Whereas heretofore I, John Eden, was enjoined by decree in the Star Chamber to make my submission before the Master, Wardens, and Assistants of the Merchant Taylors, in these words following, viz. :—" That I have rashly, unadvisedly, and untruly charged sundry persons of you—which I, the said John Eden, have performed accordingly. And, forasmuch as now my private necessity is so great as I am driven to crave of you, the said Master, Wardens, and Assistants, your alms and charitable relief; and that it may please you to forget my former evil doings towards you upon this my aforesaid submission, and acknowledging mine necessity for God's cause to relieve the same, the rather for that the Right Honourable the Lord Chancellor hath, by divers his letters, recommended my necessity unto you. And that this my relief may be no longer chargeable unto you than I shall be found of good and honest behaviour towards you.—Subscribed by me the day and year abovesaid, your Worships' poor orator, JOHN EDEN.

APPENDIX 15.

"THE OTHE OF EV^{9}Y FOREYN BRODER ADMITTED INTO THEIR SAID FRATERNITEE.

" Ye shall swore that ye shalbe true to the kyng oure soveraigne lorde and to his heires kynges of England, ye shalbe goode and lovynge broder unto the Merchaunte Taillours of the fraternitee of Saint John Baptist, of the Citie of London, into the whiche ye be now received and admitted. And if ye at any tyme hereafter here or knowe any ill spoken of the said fraternitee which shulde growe sounde or redown to the reproche, infamye, or sclaunder of the same fraternitee, ye shall do as moche as in you is to reforme and amende the same in conservation of the honoure and worship of the same fraternitee. Also ye shall gyf in your lyf tyme or elles bequethe in youre testament to th'use and behofe of the said fraternitee more or lesse after youre estate and devocion that ye bere and have to the same in supportyng and mayntenyng of the prestes and pore almesmen of the said fraternitee. All these articles and poyntes aboverehersed ye shall on youre behalf and to youre power observe and keepe as nyghe as god shall sende unto you grace. So helpe you god and all Saints and by all tholy contentes in that boke."

APPENDIX 16.

1467, February 22nd.—Agreement transfering a Taylor's business from father to son on terms.

Thomas Burgeys, Magister. Memorandum that I Stephen Piers, citezein and Tayllour of London, have graunted and possessed the xxij day of Feverer in the yeer of our Lord mccccxlvij, my trusty and well-beloved sone John Piers in the house there I dwell in in Bokeleresbury, sett in the paryssh of Seint Mary Colchirch in London, to have and to occupie the said house duryng my termes that be to come, as is comprehended in wrytyng betwene my landlord and me, reservyng unto myself and Julyan my wyf always the chaumber that I lye in called the Whyte Chaumber, and another annexed to the same called the Rede Chaumber, and that the said John Piers shall acquite me and my wyf from all maner charges of the said house during the said termes as is aforeseid.

Also I will and graunt that my said sone shall have all my servauntes and apprentises them to teche and enfourme or do theim to be taught and enfourmed in their occupacions in the best wyse that he can, and also them to fynde mete, drynk, clothing, and all thinges as is belongyng unto such prentises, and I will that the said apprentises shall obey all maner rules commaunded or taught by my said sone or his wyf, and to obey their due correccions; and so my said sone to acquite me and my wyf of all maner charges of the said apprentises.

Also I will that my said sone shall fynde and kepe honestly one Anne Parys, a pore·mayden, that is deef and dome, mete, drynk, and clothing as nedeth.

Also I will that at all due tymes whan that I or my wyf walketh oute, that my said sone shall late me have an honest man chyld to wayte upon me, and an honest mayde chyld to wayte upon my wyf at his owne propre cost yef we desire it.

Furthermore to acquite all these charges and other charges hereafter suyng, I the said Stephen Piers have graunted, geven, and delivered the day and yeer abovesaid unto my said sone diverse goodes, wares, and dettours, as it more pleynly specifieth in diverse billes made betwene me and my said sone, the which amounteth to the some of ccxx*li*. sterlinges, to have and enjoye the said goods, wares, and dettours, to by and sell wyth all in the best wyse that he can to moost profite and encrese; of the which the said John Piers shall pay or do to be payed to me and to my said wyf, and to either of us that lengest leven, for our sustentacion in mete, drynk, and clothing, and all other thinges to us and either of us necessary, x*li*. sterlinges yeerly, to be payed at iiij termes in the yeer; that is to say, atte fest of the Nativite of Seint John the Baptist next after the date aforesaid 1*s*. atte fest of Seint Myghell tharchaungell than next suyng, 1*s*.; atte fest of the Nativite of our Lord than next suyng 1*s*.; and atte fest of the Annunciacion of our Lady than next suyng, other 1*s*., and so from quarter to quarter, and from yeer to yeer duryng my lyf, my wyves lyf and either of us longest lyvyng as is aforeseid. And yef so be that my said sone perfourme and kepe these desires aforeseid, and therto will agree in all goodly wise, I woll and graunte at this tyme present in the day and yeer abovesaid, that I duryng my lyf nor none of myn executours in tyme to come nor none other persone in my name, shall never interupt nor encounter my said sone John Piers of the said goodes, wares, and dettours from this day and yeer aforeseid unto the ende of the world.

Also I will thet my said sone shall ones in the yeer, that is to sey, betwene Cristmasse and Candelmasse make a due rekenyng wyth his house that in counfortyng of myself I may knowe that he goth forthward and encrese, the whych shall be to me grete pleasire.

Also I will that in cas be me lyst to have eny money bestowed in merchaundise of myn owne, besyde the goodes, wares, and dettours aforeseid, that my said sone shall ley it in his shop and so to occupie it in merchaundising in the best wyse he can, reservyng to myself that one half of the geyn, and to my sone for his labour that other half, with Goddes blessing and myn.

To the which desires and grauntes as is aforeseid, I the said John Piers sone to my right reverend fader and moder Stephen

Piers and Julyan his wyf afore named, aggree and consent to all and singler that is afore desired or willed by my said fader, that is for to sey:—first, wheras my said fader heth possessed me in his house as is aforeseid, I beryng all the charges of the same and them conveniently discharge, I aggree therto accordyng to my said fader's desire.

Also, where as my said fader woll that I shall have the rule and charge of his servauntes and prentises, theim to teche or do theim to be taught wyth sufficient fyndyng and all other things as is aforeseid, I aggree accordyng to my said fader's desire.

Also in kepyng and fyndyng of the seid Anne Paryse, I aggree therto accordyng to my fader's desire.

Also as towching my children to awayte upon my fader and moder at all deive tymes, I aggree therto accordyng as is aforeseid.

Also as towchyng to the pension of xli., the which shuld be payed at iiij termes yeerly by even porcions as is aforeseid, I aggree to be bound in an obligacion of ccli., that in cas be that I be behynde of payment after eny day of payement as is aforeseid post ij monethes, that than it shall be liefull that the said obligacion to stond in full power and strenketh, and yef it so be that the said dayes of paiement be sufficiently content or within ij monethes after eny of the said dayes be content, that than the said obligacion to stand in no strenketh or effect.

Also where as my said fader desireth to have in knowelech ones in the yeer of the rekenyng of my house, I aggree therto, that in cas be there can be due proof made that at every day of rekenyng my goodes, wares, and dettours be found worth ccli., that so longe my fader to holde him pleased and aggreed, and I to reioyse, and the said goodes, wares, and dettours for evermore withoute eny interupcion, and yef it so be that eny said goodes, wares, and dettours be otherwyse fowade by due proffe made, not worth ccli. as is aforeseid, that than it shall be lefull for my fader to enter into my goodes, wares, and dettours, wher som ever they may be found, and so to keep my said goodes, wares, and dettours in his owne possession till I sett him in veray suerte of his dicete.

Forasmoche as Stephen Piers and his sone John Piers, bothe afore named hath knoweleged, aggreed, and consented ech of them to other the day, moneth, and yeer abovesaid unto all and singler articles aforesaid, and for the more sertente of trouth and record, ech of theim to perfourme and kepe the said articles they of theim self ar come joyntly unto Tayllours Hall before the Right Honurable and Worshipfull Maister[1] and Wardeins in the said day and yeer beyng, proying theim that the seid articles myght be regestred and entred in to their bookes of record beryng the said date.

(Amended Agreement.)

The Monday the iiijth day of Decembre the ixth yeer of the reign of Kyng Edward the iiijth (1469) cam personnelly before William Parker, Maister, John Stone, John Stodard, and John Phelip, somtyme Maisters, John Kyffyn, Richard Wayler, Ric. Warner, and William Crosseby, Wardens of the Fraternite of Seint John Baptist of the Craft of Taylours in London at Tayllourshall, Stephen Piers and John Piers his sone, Citezeins and Tayllours of the said Citee of London, and there by the meanes of the said Maisters and Wardeins appointed and aggreed in forme folowyng, that is to say, that the said Stephen shall kepe all thappointementes on his parte specified and writen in the leef next heer before, and that the same John Piers shall have and reteign to him selff freely and quitely unto his owne propre use withoute eny interupcion, as well all maner goodes, wares, dettours, and stuff conteigned and specified in the said leef, as all other duetees and thinges that hath been due by the said John Piers unto his said fader, and also his moder, or which they or either of hem of hym in eny wyse might cleime att eny tyme sithen the begynnyng of the world unto the day aforeseid. The same Stephen and Julyan his wif from hensforth beryng good fader and moder to their sone and his wyf in all things that goodly belongeth.

For the full contentacion of which premisses the said John duryng the lyves of the said Stephen and Julyan his wyf, fader and moder to the said John, shall pay to the said Stephen xx mark yeerly, and immediately after the decese of one of them to him or hir overlyvyng during the lyf of him or her overlyvyng x marcs yeerly in the said Hall, at iiij principall termes of the yeer or within ij monethes next suyng everych of the said termes by even porcions.

And that these agrementes be kept and perfourmed from hensforth betwene the said partyes, they by good advise shall make sufficient writyng for the confirmacion and record of the same.

---

[1] These were Thomas Burgeys, Master ; John Kyffin, William Marshall, Roger Warren, Richard Naylor, Wardens.

APPENDIX 17.

THE PAYMENTS MADE IN THE YEARS PRECEDING AND SUCCEEDING THE ACT ARE THUS SHOWN IN THE COMPANY'S CASH BOOKS.

In 1545-6, the last year of paying priests, the sum of 99*l.* 13*s.* 4*d.* was paid by the Master, and is shown in his account against the Company; but in 1546-7 only three quarters of the year was due to the priest and one quarter to the Crown. In later years all was paid to the Augmentation Office, as will be seen from these entries:—

1547-8. Item, at the obit of J. Churchman, 5*s.* 10*d.*

Item paid to John Wylkynson, singing at St. Martin Outwich for Mr. Churchman for 3*s.* 4*d.* *salary* due to him at th'annunciat^n of our Lady Anno 1548, after 7*l.* 1*s.* 8*d.* per ann., 5*l.* 7*s.* 6*d.*

Item, pd. to Sir Rothe Palmer, his half salary for 3 *quarters* to same date, 2*l.* 10*d.*

Item, Oyle spent according to the will of J. Churchman, 10 pottles of oil at 8*d.* the pottle, 6*s.* 8*d.*

1548-9. Item, paid 26° October to Mr. E. Mildmay one of the King's collectors for a half year's quit rent, due to his highness at the feast of St. Michael the Archangel, within the time of this account, which said sum heretofore was paid to priests, clerks, &c., for keeping of obits now dissolved, as by a quittance thereof made ready to be showed more plainly may and doth appear, 44*l.* 5*s.* 11*d.*

Item, paid 28° May for 6 mos. to Lady Day, 49, 40*l.* 9*s.* 3*d.*

Item, paid quit rent for one year on account of Beatrice Roes and Bp. FitzJames Chauntries, 22*l.* 6*s.* 8*d.*

APPENDIX 18.

THE FINANCIAL EFFECT OF THE SALES (1549-50) UPON THE YEARLY REVENUE OF THE COMPANY AT THAT AND AT THE PRESENT TIME.

	£	s.	d.
In 1549-50 the rents amounted, as we have stated, to a total sum of	440	13	10
Which these sales (to purchase 98*l.* 11*s.* 5*d.*) reduced by	122	14	2
Leaving a residue of	317	19	8
From this residue the sales after the fire of 1666 caused a further reduction of rent, viz.	86	0	0
Leaving an ultimate residue still held by the Company of..	£231	19	8

The annual loss in 1549–50 (viz., of 122*l*. 14*s*. 2*d*., less 98*l*. 11*s*. 5*d*.) was 24*l*. 2*s*. 9*d*. (equal to 5*l*. 9*s*. 6*d*. per cent. on the total income of the Company), and in 1885–6 is 10,215*l*. 1*s*. 3*d* Thus the ultimate residue, *i.e.*, 231*l*. 19*s*. 8*d*. still held, now produces to the Company a yearly rental of 19,730*l*. 9*s*. 2*d*., or a difference of 19,498*l*. 9*s*. 6*d*., which is equal to 8,405*l*. per cent. increase on the rents of 1549–50. Apply this same rate of increase to the estates sold in 1549–50, *i.e.*, 122*l*. 14*s*. 2*d*. at 8,405*l*. per cent., and the sum of 10,313*l*. 12*s*. 8*d*., less 98*l*. 11*s*. 3*d*., or 10,215*l*. 1*s*. 3*d*. is shown as the loss to the Company in the year 1885–6 from these sales.

APPENDIX 19.

IN CHANCERY (1514). MERCHANT TAYLORS COMPANY *v.* THOMAS HOWDEN'S EXECUTORS.

To the Most Reverent fader in God William[1] Archibusshope of Caunturbury, and Chaunceler of England.

Sheweth unto your gracious lordship your dayly oratours the Maister and Wardens of the occupacioun of Marchaunt Taylours, within the citie of London:

That wher as one Thomas Howdan late Marchaunt Taylour (of) London in his lyfe tyme came to the comen hall belongyng to the hole body of the Marchaunt taylours aboveseid, and at a councell a mongest theym ther holden, of his own mere mocion instaintly desyred your said oratours to understond and perceyve his mynde and purpose; at whiche tyme the seid Thomas Howdan, amongest oder thynges shewed theym, he hadde layde to gyder V.C. marke redy told in angels to theutent that your said oratours should founde therwith a specyall chauntry[2] within the parisshe churche of Abchurche in London and that they should distribute yerely amongst the pore house holders of the said parisshe certeyn quarters of coles, and ther to have an honest preest at ther eleccion and wyll ther to syng for his soule and other, whome he wold more at large name in his last will and testament. Entendyng and openly saying the said summe of V.C. mark should be delyvered

---

[1] William Warham was Chancellor from 1506 to December, 1515, and was succeeded by Cardinal Wolsey. As Howdan's gift was in 1514, the Bill is addressed to Warham.

[2] In 1547 the Company made a return that they held certain vestments and church ornaments in the custody of Sir Robert Waterall, Priest, serving for Mr. Howdan at Abchurch.—Memorials, pages 103 and 528.

in his lyf tyme to your said oratours, to whose mocion and desyre your said oratours were then perfitely agreyd and concluded and theruppon the same Thomas gave to your said oratours over and besyde the said V.C. marces a standyng gylt cuppe and ij saltes. [These articles are in the Company's inventory of 1592.] And according therto declared in his testament and last wyll by expressed wordes saying " Wher as I have gyven and delyvered to the said Master and Wardens of the said Fraternitie now beyng V.C. marc." And so theruppon made executours Isabell his wyf, Henry Heyward clerk, Richard Howdan, and Henry Mayor.[1] And so sodenly preventyd by deth, dyed afore the delyveraunce of the same summe and plate or any part thereof, and left it in the kepying of his said executours enclosed to gyder in a bagge.

Off whom your saide besechers hath many and dyvers tymes requyred the said summe and plate, and desired theym to fulfill and kepe the promyse and gyft gyven by the said Thomas in his lyfe tyme made, but that to do they at all tymes hath denyed and yet denyeth contrary to right and conscience. Purposyng by synystre counsell to employe the said summe of money to the augmentacion of the porcion of his said wyfe accordyng to the custume of the Citie of London, unlesse your gracious favoure be to theym shewed in this behalve.

And forasmoche as your saide oratours hath no wrytyng or specyaltie but as afore is rehersed wherby they may clayme and opteyne the said summe by the comen lawe, nether specyall wordes in his will or testament to calenge it as a legacie by spiritual lawe, they ben remedylesse as well by spirituall as temporall lawe, and can not in any wyse perfourme their graunt or promyse made to the said Thomas in his lyf tyme to the great hynderaunce and utter breking of the will and mynde of the said Thomas agayn right and conscience.

> Plesith therefor your gracious lordship the premisses tenderly considered to graunt severall wryttes of sub pena to be directyd to the said Isabell, Henry, Richard, and Henry, commaundyng them by the same to appere before the king in his High Court of Chauncery at a certeyn day there to make answer to the premysses. And your oratours shall dayly pray to God for the preservacion of your good grace long to endure.
> Pleg.' de Pros':—THOMAS GRENEWAY and
WILLS. BEXLEY.

Endorsed.—Coram Rege in Concellaria sua
    in Octabis sce trinitaris.

---

[1] This was the Clerk of the Company.

APPENDIX 20.

Memorandum of the Merchant Taylors Company.

[The Company were indebted to a Liveryman (Walter Clode) for the preparation of this paper.]

The Royal Commissioners to enquire into the condition of Livery Companies having sent to the Merchant Taylors Company, for their perusal, the evidence taken on the first eight days of their enquiry, the Company deem it to be their duty, no less than their right, to point out *substantial* misstatements of fact, and erroneous conclusions drawn from them, which two of the witnesses have laid before the Commissioners.

The charges against the Company have not been stated with an explicitness such as might reasonably have been expected in so serious an enquiry, but they are to be found rather in a multitude of insinuations spread over some twenty pages, which, however, so far as they are capable of taking any form, seem to take the following:—

1. That the Merchant Taylors Company have appropriated moneys of which they were trustees;
2. That they have also misconducted themselves in their capacities of landlords;
3. And as Governors of their School; and this conduct is rendered all the more heinous, as in so acting they are doing violence to the rights of the London poor.

Each of these charges will be met and answered in turn. It may, however, be convenient here to dispose of the question whether the poor have any, and what, special claim on the funds of the Merchant Taylors Company.

It is obvious that the purpose of some of the witnesses is to represent the Livery Companies as Corporations created by the poor, and for the special benefit of the poor, as being the recipients of wealth accumulated from yearly contributions levied upon the poor freemen in former centuries. This representation, the Merchant Taylors Company have here to submit, has *no* historical foundation. These Guilds in their initiation were promoted, and during their continuance have been fostered, by the middle as distinct from either of the other two classes: individual members may have ascended from a lower to a higher class in society; but the Guilds themselves have continued to be as they now are, middle-class institutions.

The only way in which the poor can now in any sense be said to be connected with this Company is as recipients of their bounty, and as enjoying the funds which have been accumulated heretofore by the middle as distinct from the poorer classes.

Their relations with the Company may be either those of beneficiaries of a trust created for them by men of the middle class, in which capacity they may be honestly said to have received the whole, if not more than the whole, of what is due to them; or they may be considered as the recipients of a bounty which the Company, in recognition of the duties of the rich towards the poor, have voluntarily and spontaneously made to them; but in neither case can these voluntary benefactions be allowed to ripen into a legal claim upon the funds of the Company.

As has been before stated the allegation that the Company must be considered as the heirs of the accumulated contributions of the poor in former times has really no historic foundation. That the Company used, under the name of "quarterage," to levy contributions upon the whole of their members, including the freemen, who were generally of the poorer class, is perfectly true, as will be seen from the 13th Ordinance;[1] but it is also equally certain that so long as any portion of these contributions were so raised from the poor, the whole, and not only the proportionate part which had been derived from the freeman was expended upon the poor: and so far from the Company being in possession of any accumulations derived from such a source, they are annually out of pocket by the transaction, as, while the wholesome custom of contribution has been discontinued, the Company's disbursements under this head continue.

Wealth, in the hands of a man or of a guild, may be coveted under the beneficent plea of using it for the alleviation of poorer men's burthens, but the security for property would be lost if poverty was a justifying plea for confiscation.

I.—To revert, then, to the first of the special charges against the Merchant Taylors Company, viz., that they have appropriated moneys of which they were trustees.

As the answer to this charge involves principally the correction of certain misstatements of Mr. Beal, this may be perhaps the

---

[1] Memorials, page 214.

best place for the Company to explain how it is that they come to attach so much weight to Mr. Beal's utterances as to deem it necessary to devote no small portion of this paper to answering them.

In the first place, Mr. Beal speaks in a certain sense *ex cathedrâ*: he is, in the opinion of one at least of the Royal Commissioners,[1] the leading authority upon municipal matters, and from his unique collection of literature upon the subject, he is not only justly thought to be in possession of the means of acquiring accurate information, but also, when he gives it, it is usually received as such: he lectures also to the working classes upon this subject; and as the audiences are crowded,[2] and are reported to be so unanimous as to "assent universally to the ideas there expressed," it is a satisfaction to feel that in stopping error here, it is stopped at the fountain-head.

In the second place, the Commissioners themselves appear to have accepted, to some extent, his assistance, if not guidance, by giving him peculiar facilities for prosecuting his enquiries into the affairs of the City Companies with a view to framing his indictment against them; and the man entrusted with such a task should be proved, not only to be honest, which in Mr. Beal's case, needs no demonstration, but accurate, which Mr. Beal certainly is not.

Upon what evidence, it is asked, does this first charge rest? Apparently upon the misdoings of the Merchant Taylors Company in regard to Donkyn's Charity.

It is proposed to give, first Mr. Beal's version of this affair, and then the true one, remembering always that even for an erroneous misstatement in such a matter there can be little excuse, as the whole history of this case is public property, and not only public property, but this very case of Donkyn's Charity has been singled out[3] by Mr. Beal himself for especial study, as a leading one upon the whole question of charitable trusts.

---

[1] Mr. Firth thus speaks of him, at page v of his preface to his work, "Municipal London":—"The author has to express his deep obligation to Mr. James Beal, who may be justly regarded as the father of municipal reform. It is to his energy and patriotism that the present advanced condition of the question is mainly due; and if ever from existing chaos there should come forth a London Municipal Government worthy of that name, it is to him that the thanks of the citizens should be given."

[2] "509. I have lectured at all the working-class clubs throughout the metropolis for years past, and in every case they universally assent to the ideas there expressed."

"513. The Eleusis Club is 1,000 strong."

"514. The Hammersmith Club has 460 members; that is the smallest, I think."

[3] "915. I have read Donkyn's and the Wax Chandlers," &c.

So far as any connected account can be garnered from Mr. Beal's somewhat incoherent statements, it would seem that a more than usually vigilant Attorney-General[1] haled the recalcitrant Company to the judgment-seat, and did not relax his grasp until the Company had disgorged the whole of their ill-gotten gains. Since that day Mr. Beal inclines to think that the race of Attorney-Generals has declined, and that it will be a long time before we have another of equal pugnacity.

The true facts are as follows:—

Robert Donkyn, by his will, dated 1570, gave to the Master and Wardens of the Merchant Taylors Company, in fee, certain lands and tenements, with their appurtenances, to the intent as to the rents and profits thereof, to make certain specific payments thereout; and he directed the whole of the residue of the rents to be gathered into the Company's stock, to repair and, if need be, rebuild the said tenements at their discretion.

The year after Donkyn's death, after providing for all the specific payments, there remained a residue of 9l. 13s. in the hands of the Company, which was carried to the Company's corporate account, and, until 1862, this was regularly done; at the same time it should be said that all the expenses of repairings or rebuildings were discharged out of the same fund.[2]

Now, in the first place, it should be noticed, in passing, that at the time when the residue was carried to the corporate account, viz., in the year 1571-2, it is more than probable that the Company were absolutely right in so disposing of it, for the question of what should be done with residues in such cases seems to have been decided for the first time in 1610.[3]

In the second place, it should be noticed that, even supposing that they were wrong, it was in the power of the Crown, under the statute of Elizabeth (43 Eliz., cap. 4), to call them to account, and to have a full inspection of all their deeds for that purpose; and the fact that the Crown, at a time when it kept a vigilant eye

---

[1] "637. Look at the case of Donkyn: the public were represented, and the Attorney-General made a great fight."

"911. Q. Who is to begin all this (*i.e.*, litigation to stop the misappropriation of trust moneys)?—*A*. The Attorney-General began Donkyn's case, and won it."

"741. Q. Surely, if it is public property, the Chancery Division of the High Court of Justice would enforce its being applied to public purposes?—*A*. Take the case of Donkyn's Charity as an example; but where will you get an Attorney-General to fight a battle again like that?"

[2] The annual residue for 1880-1 was 1,831l. 2s. 2d.

[3] Thetford School case, 8th Report, 130[b].

upon the doings of the City Companies,[1] never thought it worth while to interfere with them, is some, if not conclusive evidence that their disposition of it was right.

Coming to later times, we shall find that so far from the Company's keeping back or concealing anything in this matter from Commissioners or others appointed to inquire into their disposition of this income, they have always been ready and willing to make such a disposition of it as the law or its officers should deem right, and (even incredible though it may seem to Mr. Beal) have themselves instituted those proceedings against an unwilling and recalcitrant Attorney-General, which Mr. Beal supposes the vigilant Attorney-General to have instituted against them.

This is literally true. The Merchant Taylors' Company were plaintiffs, not defendants, in the case of Donkyn's charity.

How this came about the following short history of the facts will show.

The Royal Commissioners may be reminded that from 1828, in which year the Commissioners of Inquiry, acting under 58 Geo. III, cap. 91, printed their Report relating to the Merchant Taylors Company's charities, Donkyn's will, and the dealings of the Company with the property devised under it, have been absolutely public property; and that if, after such a full disclosure no action was taken against the Company, it can only be accounted for by the supineness of the Attorney-General, according to Mr. Beal's theory, or what is perhaps more probable, by the fact that the point as to the disposal of the residue was not so clear as to warrant any proceedings against them.

The year 1853 saw the appointment of the present Charity Commissioners; and it is, perhaps, not unreasonable to imagine that if any flagrant act of misappropriation was taking place, they were the persons, armed as they were with the very fullest powers of search and discovery, and having the reports of the Commissioners of Inquiry before them, to correct the error and place matters upon their right footing. It certainly never occurred to the Company, who saw what was going on elsewhere, to account for the Charity Commissioners' inaction by assuming that they, in company with the Attorney-General, were suffering from an inordinate lethargy; they thought, perhaps unreasonably, but still perfectly honestly, that no reform was made in their administration of the charity because none was needed, and they still went on

---

[1] Memorials, page 657.

carrying the residue, whatever it was, to their corporate funds.

At last, in 1862, the present Charity Commissioners issued their order for Mr. Hare, their inspector, to examine into all the charities held by the City Guilds; and, in performance of this duty, Mr. Hare, in or prior to January, 1863, came to the Company's Hall; he saw the will in question, and, in the year 1864, in his report to his Board writes as follows:—"The construction always adopted by the Company, and which seems to have been acquiesced in by the Commissioners of Inquiry, is that the residue, after keeping the estate in repair, is given to the Company for their own use;" and he then adds, that "it may be a question for the consideration of the Board whether the actual construction of this gift should be determined by any legal proceedings, and whether the Company should be required to render the account of the estate as of an endowment wholly charitable."

But the Court of the Merchant Taylors Company, desirous of doing what was right, did not wait for this Report, as, in fact they never knew of its existence until Mr. Hare referred to it in his evidence before the Royal Commissioners. The doubts contained in that Report Mr. Hare mentioned verbally to the Company's officers as early, at least, as 1863; whereupon the Court, on the 28th of January of the same year, ordered the residue to be held intact for the charity as from 25th December, 1862, and empowered their Clerk to consult Sir R. Palmer as to the proper construction to be put upon Donkyn's will.

The opinion of Sir R. Palmer was given in the ensuing March, and was to the following effect:—"That, subject to the provision for the twelve poor men and twelve poor women (the donees of the specific payment mentioned above), the Company are to be considered as trustees of the property, and, as such trustees, bound to render to the Charity Commissioners an account of the rents and profits arising therefrom."

The Merchant Taylors Company lost no time in acting upon the opinion here expressed, and, as early as April of the following year, had submitted to the Charity Commissioners, for their sanction, a scheme disposing of the whole of the residue to charitable purposes. This scheme, however, the Charity Commissioners did not feel able to accept, on the ground that it proposed to devote the residue in question to persons of a higher class than the original recipients of the charity; and in January, 1865, they referred it back to the Company for reconsideration.

It would not be unreasonable to imagine that, upon the refusal of this kind, made at the time when the Company were under no legal obligation to defer to the opinion of the Charity Commissioners, the Company would consider that their duties were at an end, and that it remained for the Commissioners to take the initiative in any further proceedings; but so far from this being the case, the Company cheerfully accepted the decision of the Commissioners, and applied themselves to the task of seeing how best they might meet their wishes.

With that object in view, a conference was held with the Charity Commissioners, in which it was suggested and conditionally agreed that a convalescent home should be established by the Merchant Taylors Company, to be ultimately supported out of two funds—those of Donkyn (which are the subject of the present Memorandum) and of the Prison Fund[1] (the history of which fund is with the Royal Commissioners)—so soon as the equitable rights affecting the same should be decided.

At the close of the year 1869 the Corporation of London notified their intention of obtaining Parliamentary sanction for the use of the Prison Fund to establish a reformatory for boys, which led the Merchant Taylors, with other Companies, into a Parliamentary contest, in the session of 1870, to protect these funds from the Corporation representing the ratepayers of London.

However, not daunted by these difficulties, the Company in January, 1869, appointed a Special Committee to consider and select a site for a convalescent home. This committee consulted Dr. Gull, Mr. John Birkett, and other medical authorities as to its position as inland or seaside; and then, carefully considering nine different sites offered to them, ultimately selected Fitzlett House, Bognor, where the home is now established.

This estate was purchased, and taken possession of by the Company early in the year 1870. The house was immediately converted into a home, with thirty-six beds, now increased to fifty, and opened as such on the 5th July, 1870, for poor patients from any of the London hospitals.

As the Merchant Taylors Company had then pledged themselves to carry on a convalescent home, how, it may be asked, was it that they subsequently appealed to the Court of Chancery for the proper construction of Donkyn's will? The answer almost suggests itself when it is noticed that the Wax Chandlers' case,

---

[1] The history of this fund, Memorials, page 336.

which was decided in August, 1869, wholly altered the law, and gave, as it was thought, all residues devised in similar terms to the trust devisees. Obviously such a question could not be left in doubt, and, under these circumstances, the Company placed the papers again before Sir R. Palmer and Mr. M. Cookson, who in April, 1870, wrote as follows:—

" We are of opinion that this case, though in some respects more favourable to the contention of the Attorney-General, is not substantially distinguishable from the Wax Chandlers' case; and that accordingly the Merchant Taylors Company must, while that case remains law, be treated as entitled to the property devised to them by Mr. Donkyn's will, or its present representatives, for their own benefit, subject only to such deductions as are specifically mentioned in the will.

" In coming to this conclusion, we have taken into account the order of the Charity Commissioners of the 26th February, 1870 (to which our attention was called in consultation), and which treats the accumulations lately invested in the purchase of the house at Bognor as trust property. Having regard to the terms of that order and the facts stated in the case, that since Christmas, 1862, accounts of receipts and payments in respect of the entire property have been rendered to the Charity Commissioners, we think it expedient that the Company should obtain an authoritative declaration on the point raised by the case, through the medium of the Court of Chancery. This may be done by filing a Bill against the Attorney-General, for which, the claim of the Company being adverse to the charity, the leave of the Commissioners need not be first obtained."

A Bill was accordingly filed, and the case was decided by the Court of First Instance on the 3rd November, 1870, and of Appeal in April, 1871, declaring in both instances that the residue was a trust estate. The words in which these judgments were given furnish a justification to the Company, if such be needed, for their having taken the case before the Courts for decision. In the lower Court the judge (Lord Romilly)[1] expressed his opinion that the litigation "raised a question which it was desirable to have settled;" and in the higher Court the Lord Chancellor (Hatherley) described the case "as one of very great nicety," in which he came to this "conclusion with considerable hesitation."

To complete the statement of facts as to the Prison Fund, it

---

[1] Merchant Taylors Company v. Attorney-General, L.R., 11 Equity Cases, page 35. *Ib.*, 6 Ch. App., page 517.

should be mentioned that Parliament, in the session of 1870, threw out the Bill promoted by the Corporation of London; and then came the question of appropriating these funds to charitable purposes, which had to be dealt with by the Court of Chancery. This was done in 1873, by the reported case of Prison Charities, in 16 "Equity Cases," page 145, which resulted ultimately in a transfer of these funds to the credit of the Convalescent Home.

The Company did not, as it will be seen, wait for this decision before establishing that Home, although the scheme for that purpose was not finally approved and sealed by the Charity Commissioners[1] until the 6th March, 1872.

What then could any trustees, individual or corporate, do, more than the Merchant Taylors Company have done, to carry out a beneficient object; and where does Donkyn's case furnish a justification for Mr. Beal's contention that a new municipality should be originated to take the City Companies by the throat and deal with them?

II.—To revert to the charges of their misconduct as landlords.

The other witness to whom reference has been made is Mr. W. Gilbert, who has requested the Commissioners to take his evidence (1500). He assures the Commissioners that "he has given a good deal of attention to the city generally, including the Companies;" (1472) and his mission is to show that "he has formed and expressed a strong opinion as to the action of the City Companies in connection with the poorer population of the city" (1475).

In general terms he accuses the City Companies of "driving the poor out of their districts" (1476). "Whenever a house is destroyed and a new one is erected, in almost every case, especially with regard to those of City Companies, a clause is inserted that no person shall be allowed to sleep upon the premises, thereby totally prohibiting the poor (though why only the poor?) from returning."

In specific terms he formulates his accusation against the Merchant Taylors Company "by an example, to explain better what he means."

He states his facts thus,—that in Coleman Street the Merchant Taylors Company own a property which, some ten years ago, they leased at 2,300*l.* a year "under a condition that the whole building should be pulled down and about 200,000*l.* expended in building chambers, with a strict clause in the lease that no one should be allowed to sleep upon the premises" (1480).

---

[1] See Memorials, page 380.

When cautioned by one of the Royal Commissioners, lest he should be imputing blame to the Company upon imperfect information, he repeats his accusation " from his own personal experience " as a director in a large Assam Tea Company, which, by the by, has, on another occasion enabled him to furnish the Royal Commissioners with other information (1520). It is suggested by the same Royal Commissioner that the leaseholder, and not the freeholder, has inserted this condition (1571–3); but as his accusation against a City Company, and his *raison d'être* for appearing before the Royal Commissioners, would fall to the ground if Mr. Gilbert accepted this (almost obvious) explanation, he answered, "No ; the freeholders would not grant the lease, except upon that condition."

Now, whether the leaseholder has or has not inserted such a condition is not known to the Merchant Taylors Company; but they do know that the terms in which the Inhabited House Duty Act[1] is framed did formerly, until the Act was amended, oblige persons letting premises for offices or warehouses to insert such a stipulation, not against the poor, but to escape this very heavy taxation.

The facts are these.

The premises in question, prior to the re-letting referred to, were used as offices and warehouses, in which it is not probable that any persons resided, more than the occupiers required there for their employments. Be that as it may, the Merchant Taylors Company did not seek or desire to alter in any way the purpose for which the premises should thereafter be used.

In the years 1875 to 1881[2] they granted ordinary building leases of these premises to A. A. Croll, Esq., at a ground rent, and with a covenant for an expenditure, not of 200,000*l*., as Mr. Gilbert asserts, but of 20,000*l*.

Whether Mr. Croll built offices or warehouses with or without residences for the rich or poor, was a matter as to which the Merchant Taylors Company made no stipulation whatever; and it may be added, that neither in this nor in any other case, when granting a building lease, have the Company ever inserted such a covenant as Mr. Gilbert affirms them to have included in the leases in question.

III.—As Governors of their school.

---

[1] 32 and 33 Vic., cap. 14, sec. 11, and 41 Vic., cap. 15, sec. 13.
[2] 1875, July 14 ; 1876, June 7 ; 1879, July 14 ; 1881, February, 20.

Before adverting to the statement of Mr. Gilbert on this head, the Merchant Taylors Company may be excused if they preface these remarks by a short statement of their recent action as Governors of that institution. This statement, it is hoped, will furnish reasonable justification, if such be needed, for their not having contributed as largely as other Guilds have done to the Technical Institute.

Rightly, as they venture to think, the Merchant Taylors Company recognised in 1866 an opportunity of largely increasing the usefulness of their own school as a high-class day school for the benefit of the residents in and about London. These matters are stated plainly in the Master's letter of the 23rd June, 1866, to the Governors of the Charter House, which is printed at length, page 426 of the Company's Memorials; but the paragraph to which attention is invited is as follows :—

" In conclusion, I have only to add, that the Company desire—whatever may be the result of this communication—that I should express to the Governors their thanks for the opportunity offered to them of becoming the purchasers of their estate.

" All that the Merchant Taylors Company have it in desire to do, is to supply the want which obviously must arise—unless the Governors of the Charter House are prepared to make some provision for it, after their relinquishment of that sphere of usefulness which, for upwards of 250 years, within the City of London, and partially towards its citizens, the Governors of the Charter House have occupied—a want arising from no fault in the citizens of London, but necessarily resulting from the removal of an ancient educational establishment far beyond the walls. To aid in the supply of this want (so far as their corporate means will allow) is the only motive that has induced the Merchant Taylors Company to give such anxious consideration to the proposals of the Governors. How far the Company may be enabled to accomplish this object is dependent in some degree upon the result of this negotiation; but whatever the result may be, I shall ever feel conscious that my colleagues and myself have manifested every desire to meet the proposals of the Governors of the Charter House in a candid and unselfish spirit."

At that date, and when the " Royal Commissioners on the Public Schools " reported the annual cost of the school to the Merchant Taylors Company was (say) 2,000*l*. per annum, they were left free and untrammelled by the Parliamentary enactments which were extended to the other schools, the subject of that inquiry. The confidence thus reposed in them by Parliament, the Merchant Taylors Company venture to think has not been abused. Since that date they have sold their Irish estate, and devoted the proceeds thereof, with other moneys, to the purchase of the site and erection of the school in Charter House Square at a cost of 91,600*l*. They have increased the number of scholars from 250 to 500 boys; and their annual expenditure on the school has been increased from 2,000*l*. to 7,724*l*. These figures, it is hoped, will satisfy the Royal Commissioners that the Merchant Taylors Company are not indifferent to the cause of education for the middle-class of London residents.

But to advert to Mr. Gilbert's charge against the Company.

It is not, as against Eton and other public schools, alleged that the Company's School was instituted for paupers (730, 555); but it is insinuated that it was founded for the sons of working tailors, for Mr. Gilbert, on being asked " if a proportion of the Merchant Taylors' fund should be applied for the benefit of the tailors generally ?" he replies (1565), "Yes; and that used to be the case. If you look at Machyn and Stowe's Diaries, you will find *they* give a description of a dinner at Merchant Taylors' Hall, and also describes the Merchant Taylors' School, in which there was not a boy in the School that was not the son of a tailor."[1]

The dinner will not probably be thought worthy of further notice by the Royal Commissioners, though that allegation might be easily answered; but the statement in relation to the School is one of graver moment.

As authorities for this strange assertion, Mr. Gilbert refers the Royal Commissioners to two authors, both of whom were members of the Merchant Taylors Company; but, before dealing with these let it be noted, as dates are material, that the School was opened in the year 1561, under statutes framed by the Company.[2] Though the number was limited to 250 boys, it was laid down in Rule 25 that "children of all nations and countries indifferently" should be taught; and as proof that children of different social grades should be accepted, Rules 5 and 6 should be referred to, as these provided that a hundred should be taught freely, fifty paying 10*s*. a year, and a hundred paying 1*l*. a year. There is not a scintilla

---

[1] Why the witness should have given his preference to Taylors when possibly half the Company were Clothworkers is not apparent, unless he was ignorant of the fact.—C. M. C.

[2] Printed in Memorials, page 417.

of evidence in these statutes or elsewhere that the Company had any intention whatever of founding a class-school for tailors' sons.

But, to refer to the authors quoted, Machyn's Diary closes, as will be seen on referring to it, in the year 1562-3,—that is, within a few months after the School had been opened. Had he made the assertion imputed to him, its veracity might reasonably have been doubted, and the fact questioned whether 250 sons of tailors could have been found *instanter*, at the opening of the School doors, eligible to enter. But, leaving this question for others to decide, it is certain that Machyn made no such assertion as is imputed to him. He does refer to "tailors' sons," so that he had his eye upon the craft; but his reference is not to the "scholars," but to the "Wardens" of the Company, who in the year 1555 he notes to have been all " taylors' " sons.[1]

Stowe, in his "Survey," which work, it is presumed, Mr. Gilbert means by his reference to it as a "Diary," is equally silent on the subject; and well it is for Stowe's reputation as a chronicler that he makes no such ridiculous assertion.

Wilson,[2] in his School History, which an author of Mr. Gilbert's reputation cannot be ignorant of, asserts that in 1566 the scholars[3] came not only from the districts adjacent, but from the counties of "Oxford, Northampton, Dorset, Somerset, and even York;" and this is nearer the truth. However, the parentage of many of the earliest scholars in Merchant Taylors' School is biography within the ken of any tyro in history; and had the witness shown his authorities (if he ever found them) to any such friend, it is to be hoped that he never would have committed himself to the statement he has made to the Royal Commissioners.

For conclusive proof it may be mentioned that the Merchant Taylors Company possess a printed record of all entries in the school register from its opening until 1699, thus covering a period long after Stowe's death in 1605; and every page of this register furnishes a contradiction to Mr. Gilbert's assertion. Taking the first ten years, up to 1571, as a test period, one tailor's son only, "William Hodgson, son of Robert, tailor," is entered, viz., on the 12th July, 1566; and not even the majority of the scholars are "Merchant Taylors," though this term would not, having regard to

---

[1] Page 191, and see note page 345.

[2] Vol. 1, page 34.

[3] Sir James Whitelock entered the school in 1574-5, and George, son of Thomas Wright, Vintner, "that dwelt at the Bore's Hed in Eastcheap," in the same year. Both were elected to St. John's, Oxford, in 1588.—C. M. C.

the terms of Henry VII's charter,[1] necessarily show the father to have been a "Taylor."[2]

Passing from Mr. Gilbert's evidence, the Company confess that they have commented upon it with some degree of severity; but they hope that their criticism will not be taken for detraction; it was necessary to proclaim with no uncertain note the fallibility of one who claimed to be an expert upon the subject of municipal reform, and to bring to the consideration of the subject a judgment ripened by his researches into the usage prevailing in all the capitals of Europe besides our own. If Mr. Gilbert has allowed himself to be betrayed into such misstatements with regard to subjects upon which it is possible for any one to form a correct opinion, is it unreasonable to ask that his statements elsewhere should be tested and weighed before being accepted as facts?

But a word in conclusion. The Company wish it to be distinctly understood that in thus entering the arena of controversy they come not as defendants, since their conduct as a Company needs no defence, and as for their reputation as honest men they are content to leave it in the hands of the Commissioners; but they come rather to dispel the cloud of prejudice and aspersion which seems to envelop the consideration of their case, and which is mainly due to the intemperate and inaccurate statements of their detractors. Mindful of this, they have confined themselves to a bare, and they hope a conclusive, contradiction of material facts, and have never descended, so far as they know, to the language of extenuation. Their war is with error, not with individuals, and they hope that no word in the preceding pages is calculated to give offence to any one who is honestly and earnestly endeavouring to promote the public good, even though it should be at their expense.

It is, however, with some difficulty the Company candidly admit that they have brought themselves to include Mr. Beal in this category, since errors, which in one of less pretensions to knowledge would be venial, from his mouth can be considered little less than reckless; in such a case omission is more apt to be suppression, and misstatement distortion.

Whatever misgivings, however, they may have had upon this

---

[1] Printed at page 195 of Memorials.
[2] This register has been carefully compiled by the Rev. Charles J. Robinson, M.A., one of the former scholars of the Merchant Taylors' School, and is on the eve of publication. [It has since been published, in 1883, by Farncombe and Co., Lewes.]

score they have been able to dispel by considering that perhaps, after all, Mr. Beal is not to be taken at his own valuation, and that though he has assumed the *rôle* of omniscience with an airiness and jauntiness such as are seldom seen in one who is alive to its duties and responsibilities, his claim to the title has yet to be established.

JAMES FENNING,
Master,
On behalf of the Master and Wardens.

Merchant Taylors' Hall,
Threadneedle Street,
10*th August*, 1882.

APPENDIX 21.

ROBERT DOWE'S MIDNIGHT EXHORTATION TO THE CONDEMNED PRISONERS IN NEWGATE.

"Yee Prisoners within who for your wickedness and sinns after many former mercies shewed you are nowe appointed to be executed to death to morrow in the forenoon give care and understand that to morrow morning from six of the clock till tenn the greatest Bell of St. Sepulchres parish shal be touled for You in manner and order of the passing Bell used to be touled for those that lye at the point of death to the end that all godly people hearing that bell and knowing that is for You going to your death maie be stirred up to praie hartelie to God to bestow his mercie and his grace upon You while you yet live and therefore seeing the praiers of other Men can doe you noe good unless you turn to the Lord in true sorrow for your own wickedness and praie with them for yourselves also I beseech you all and everie of you for Christ his Sake to continue this night in watching and hartelie praier for the Salvation of your own sowles while there is yet time and place for mercie considering that to morrow You are to appeere before the Judgment of yor Creator and to give an accompt to him of yor lives past and to suffer eternal torment for your sinns comytted against him unlesse upon your hartie and unfeigned repentance in this world by faithful and earnest praier you obtain pardon and forgiveness at the hand of God through the death and passion of your Redeemer Ihesus Christ who came to save Synners and now sitteth at the right hand of his ffather to make intercession for as manie of you as penitentlie turn to God by him (then end saying two severall tymes) our Lord take Mercie on You all our Lord take Mercie on You all."

APPENDIX 22.

ROBERT DOWE'S MORNING EXHORTATION TO THE PEOPLE TO PRAY FOR THE SAME PRISONERS.

"All good People praie hartelie to God for these poor Synners going to their deaths for whome this greate Bell doth toule and all you that are condemned to die repent yourselves with lamentable tears and ask mercy for the Salvation of your Souls by the merritts passion and death of Ihesus Christ our onely Saviour and Redeemer (and then with a lowde voice say two several times our Lord take mercie upon You all our Lord take mercie upon You all."

APPENDIX 23.

SIR RICHARD LEE'S MAYORALTY.
Master's Account, 1602–3.

	£	s.	d.
Paid to Sir Richard Lee, Lord Mayor, the sum of 100 marks, being a gratuity to him as a member of the Company	66	13	4
Paid to Sir J. Swynnerton, Knt., one of the Sheriffs, and a member of this Company	33	6	8
Dinner at the Hall when the Lord Mayor took his oath at Westminster[1]	3	0	0
To the Lord Mayor of London on the day the Company dined with his Lordship to bear the charge of the Master and Wardens according to ancient precedent	10	0	0
Then for exchange of the same into gold at 4d. the pound	0	3	4
	13	3	4

---

[1] This was an annual charge made to the Stewards of the Livery who entertained him.

PAYMENTS.

1602.

	£	s.	d.
Flags, &c.	159	0	3
The ship	38	0	0
The Pageant	78	17	7
The Lion and Camel	8	16	6
Trumpeters	33	7	6
Greenmen	5	3	4
The poor men's gowns	178	18	0
The barge cloth, barge, and gallifoyst	78	3	4
Chambers discharged double at Lambeth and Bankside	11	6	8
Sword players, banners, and standard bearers	32	10	5
Hire of hangings	2	2	0
Staves	5	4	6
Torches and links	35	13	4
Casual charges	79	19	5
	747	2	10

APPENDIX 24.

EXPENSES CONCERNING THE LAW FOR OUR DEFENCE IN THE SUIT MADE BY THE COMPANY OF THE CLOTHWORKERS.

1550–1.

	£	s.	d.
First paid to Mr. Burnell, the 17th day of March, for his retainer in the same suit	1	0	0
Item paid the same day to Mr. Stapleton, Mr. Cholmeley, and Mr. Dyer, men of law, for their retainers	2	10	0
Item paid the 22nd day of March to Mr. Burnell and Mr. Dyer, 26s. 8d., and to Master Cholmeley, Mr. Stapleton, and Master Suthcott, 30s., at the time that Mr. Recorder and the Council of the City heard all the circumstances of the suit, and what the Counsellors of both parties could say in the same	2	16	8

Item paid the 28th of March to the said Mr. Burnell, Mr. Stapleton, Mr. Cholmeley, Mr. Suthcott, and Mr. Weston, the

	£	s.	d.
said day they pleaded before the Lord Mayor, Aldermen, and Common Council, to every of them 30s. apiece....	7	10	0
Item paid for a Dinner prepared and made for the said Counsellors at the "Gote in Chepe," and for bread and wine divers times had at the Three Tuns, at Yeld Hall Gate, where our men of law met together at sundry times about the said matter	1	13	9
Item given in reward[1]———	5	0	0
Item in reward[1]———	1	0	0
Item paid to sundry Clerks and Beadles of the most part of all the Companies within the city, by the hands of the Warden Substitutes for certifying us to this house the names of such persons as did use and occupy other occupations and arts than they were free of, notwithstanding they made their apprentices free of that art whereof they were free	1	13	0
Item paid as well for writing all the said names fair within one book, which was showed to our men of law, and for writing four sundry bookes of the draught of our men of law, whereof two was delivered to the Mayor, and the other two our Counsellors had. As also for the copy of the Clothworkers' bill, and the copy of the certificate made to the Mayor by Mr. Blondell, Mr Bacon, and other, which was hearers of the said matter afore the Common Council passed the matter	0	15	4
Item paid to the Town Clerk for making our part of the bond that the Company stands bound in to the Chamberlain of London, for the performance of such direction and order as the Lord Mayor and Aldermen shall make at any time before Michaelmas, between the said Clothworkers and us	0	6	0
Item given by this Accountant to my Lord Mayor, according to the old precedents[2]	2	0	0
Summa	£26	4	9

Expenses concerning divers our brethren occupying the broad shear and rowing at the perch which was imprisoned by the procurement of the Clothworkers, for that some of them would not suffer the said Clothworkers to make search within their houses, and for keeping of foreigns, as they alleged.

	£	s.	d.
First paid to Thomas Cowdale, Robert Austen, and Baldwin Walton, towards their charges of imprisonment, and of three of their servants	0	13	4
Item to John Williams, for himself and two of his apprentices, imprisoned in like case....	0	3	4
Item to Nicholas Parker, in like case	0	3	4
Item to Robert Bogas, in like case....	0	10	0
	£1	10	0

---

[1] Names written but carefully scored out.

[2] This payment is made annually and is not, I think, in reference to this suit, though on the same page.

Expenses concerning provision made for to have shear-grinders out of the country hither to London, at such time as the Clothworkers took order that they would not grind shears to this Company.

	£	s.	d.
First paid to Thos. Worlyche for riding into Suffolk, and bringing of a shear-grinder hither who remained here a certain time at the request of the Company—for his charge and reward	2	10	0
Item paid to Thos. Middleton of Reading, shear-grinder, for his costs coming to London, and abiding here a month until order was taken by the Mayor that the Clothworkers should grind shears to this Company....	2	3	0
Summa	£4	13	0

1551-2.

	£	s.	d.
First paid the 16th day of September to Mr. Bornell, our councillor, for opening of our matter afore the Mayor, and being against the said Clothworkers the said day	0	5	0
Item paid more to him for his counsel given the 27th day of September, in the same suit	0	10	4
Item paid more the 28th day of September, for counsel and pleading our cause afore the Mayor, Aldermen, and Common Council, against the said suit of the Clothworkers, viz. : to Mr. Bornell, 13s. 6d. ; Mr. Stapleton, 10s. ; Mr. Williams, 10s. ; and Mr. Southcott, 10s.....	2	3	6
Item paid more the said day to other learned men of the law for their counsel given us in the same suit, as by a bill appeareth	14	14	0
Item paid to our Clerk for making of certain abstracts out of our grants to every one of our men of law	0	6	8
Item paid to the Sword-bearer and Common Crier for their pains taken at sundry times in warning the said Clothworkers to appear before the Mayor, at our request, concerning the same suit	1	0	0
Item more given to the Officers of the Chamber....	0	2	0
Item paid for the copy of a view made by the Common Viewers of our ground in Coleman Street, for making a fence between Baskerfild, mercer, and this house	0	1	0
Item paid for a hogshead of wine given to Mr. Common Sergeant[1]	2	0	0
Summa	£21	2	6

---

[1] On 25th January, 1556-7, 2l. 4s. is charged for wine sent to Lord Chief Justice Brooke.

APP. 25.] *Ordinance* (1571) *as to Poor Taylors.* 393

1552–3.

	£	s.	d.
Item paid to the said Town Clerk for the copy of a decree made by the Court of Aldermen, the 23rd day of March, A° 7th Edward VI, between us and the Clothworkers	0	1	0

1554–5.

	£	s.	d.
Item paid to Mr. Blackwell, Town Clerk, for the copy of the Clothworkers' Bill, by them exhibited to the Mayor and Aldermen against this Company	0	3	0

APPENDIX 25.

An Ordinance for Nourishing and Relieving the Poor Members of the Merchant Taylors Company.

A Quarter day, 3rd December, 1571.

Forasmuch as it is the duty of every Christian society to help and relieve every willing and labouring brother in the Commonwealth, and specially such as are incorporated, grafted, and knit together in brotherly society, remembering the scripture written he which doth not provide for family and household is worse than an infidel, calling more to remembrance many and grievous complaints of a great number of such of the poor brethren of this our Company of the Merchant Taylors, who only live by their labour in and by the art of rowing, shearing, and dressing of woollen clothes within this City of London, whose need is much and poverty great, and more like to be if charitable order be not taken to relieve them. Wherefore it is accorded, ordained, and established for reformation thereof by the right worshipful the Master and the Wardens and all the Assistants and Councillors of this Compannie in a plain and full Court assembled the 3rd day of December, in the 14th year of our Sovereign Lady Elizabeth by the grace of God Queen of England, France, and Ireland, F.D., &c. That from and after the feast of the birth of our Lord God next coming every brother of this our said fellowship and Corporation which shall have after the said feast of the birth of our Lord God (called Christmas), and put forth to be dressed, rowed, or shorn, any manner of woollen cloth, broad or narrow frize, or cotton unto any person or persons which exerciseth, or hereafter shall exercise the art of clothworking, or useth or shall use the art of clothworking, or being free of any other art, mystery, craft, fellowship, or company within the said citie of London than of this our said fellowship and mystery of the Merchant Taylors, shall within eight days next after the said feast of Christmas without delay put forth to be rowed, shorn, and dressed to some brother of our said mysterie or fellowship of Merchant Taylors, as well to such as now use as also to such as hereafter shall use the craft and mysterie of cloth dressing, the one half or moiety at the least of all and singular such clothes as he or they shall put to dressing, rowing, or shearing in nature, kind, and quality as they shall fortune to have occasion hereafter to put forth to dressing in manner and form aforesaid, upon pain that every owner of such clothe or clothes so put forth, contrary to the true meaning of this present ordinance, to forfeit for every clothe to the use of the Master and Wardens of the fellowship of the Merchant Taylors of the Fraternity, of St. John Baptist for the time being, and to their successors, 10s.

APPENDIX 26.

Mr. Wilkes's Petition to Marry and to be Translated from this to the Vintner's Company.

"*April* 11*th*, 1591.

"The Petition signifieth that he hath proceeded in communication and speach of marriage with one Helen Hodgson, widowe, late the wyfe of one Gyles Hodgson of London, Vintener, deceased, and the matter and full agreement of the marriage resteth upon his translation and settinge over frome this Ffraternitie to the Company of Vinteners, without the obteyning whereof she meaneth not to proceed any further in the mache. The state of which cause being considered with the event thereof (viz.) the losse of such a Brother beinge himselfe a good member of the Company, and the losse of other branches and good members of this societie which myghte rise out of him which by privation in this course will be cut off. It is a mocyon that the Companye cannot with anye readiness or forwardness entertayne, yet rather than he should be prejudiced in his advancement by the straightnesse of the companie, some consideration is thought fitt to be had how his sute maye be yielded unto, but ffirst yt is resolved & ordered that those persons hereafter named shall repayre unto the widowe and see how they can prevayl with her by perswasion to proceed in the marriage and to become a sister of this Companie, and as they shall find her addicted to the motion, further order be taken.

"The persons nominated to this conference are—
"Mr. Wilforde, Chamberlain of London.
"Mr. George Sotherton.
"Mr. Nowell Sotherton.
"Mr. Roger Abdy."

"THE WIDOW HODGSON'S REPLY, AND FURTHER DELIBERATION ON MR. WILKES'S CASE.
April 10th, 1591.

"The reporte made at this Courte 'that she, the Widowe Hodgson will by no meanes assente to leave her trade.'

"The subjecte therefore is again considered, and forasmuche as either the saide Wm. Wilkes is to be licensed to change his copie, or else he is lyke to loose the benefit of his marriage, the companye doe so farr tender the benefitte & preferrmente of the saide Wm. Wilkes that they are content for his good to license him to be translated over to the Vinteners hopeinge, that howsoever the necessitye of the cawse dothe drawe him to another societye yet they hope his good affection towards this howse will not be withdrawne nor discontinued, and in hope thereof they are content to yield to his sute, and to leave the fyne of dispensation in such lyke case used, to his owne discretion, but with this, that ffirste he be bounde that his sonne who is bounde apprentize to a Freeman of the Company of Clothworkers maye be kepte from beinge enrolled to th'ende he maye be free of this Company by patrymonie. And further that such apprentizes as he hath already bound unto hym may be presentlie enrowled in the Chamber of London, and that those which he shall hereafter take into his service to employe in Merchandize and Draperie be bounde apprentize to some merchant tailor, and soe to be sett over to him to th'ende they maye become brethren of this Companie. Whereunto he willingly assenteth and doeth voluntarily offer to this Companye a remembrance in Plate suche as he hopeth they will accepte of, and will otherwise hereafter shewe some further arguments of his affection to this Companye as God shall enable him, which is lefte wholly to his discretion with this further injunction, that he promyse at all dayes of Election of the Maister of this Companye to which he and his wyfe shall be invited as guests, that they both shall come to this Howse."

"MR. WILKES'S PRESENT OF PLATE TO THE COMPANY.
June 7th, 1592.

"At this Courte, Mr. Wilkes, a late Brother of this Companie.

and at his earneste sute to this House, licensed to be transferred over to the Companie of Vintenors, hathe in thankfulnesse to this Companie for theire saide assente given him ffor his Preferment, brought and delivered to this Howse a Bason and Ewre of Silver gilt with his name and his wyfe's name graven thereupon as his guifte and remembcrance of his thankfulness to this Societye."

APPENDIX 27.

CONFIRMATION BY JAMES I (1620) OF TITLE TO SCHOOL SITE.[1]

The King &.

Whās the Master &. held &. (inter alia) all these 3 meñes with their appurts situate and existing in the p̄sh of St Lawrence Poultney, in the ward of Dowgate, London, now or lately in the tenure of Ralph Hollande[2] or his assigns;

And also all that meñe with its appūrts, commonly called or known by the name of the Merchant Taylors School, situate and existing in the afs^d p̄sh of St Lawrence Poultney; &

Whas s^d master has petitioned us to confirm & ratify to them the afs^d heres and further for ourselves and heirs and successors deign to give and concede the same;

Know therefore, that we, for ourselves, our heirs and successors, in cōson of 600l., have confirmed, remitted, released, and ratified to the s^d Master &. the afs^d premes.

Habendum.

To s^d master &.

Tendendum.

Of us our heirs and successors *in free burgage of the City of London and not in chief (in capite), nor by military service,* &.

[17 Jac. p. 8 n. 8.]

APPENDIX 28.

1564.—INTERVIEWS BETWEEN THE CORPORATION OF LONDON AND THE COURT OF MERCHANT TAYLORS COMPANY AS TO THE ACQUISITION OF PERCYVALE'S HOUSE FOR THE BURSE.

Friday, Jan. 12th, 1564.

At this day the Right Worshippful Sr William Chester,

---

[1] Quoted in Wilson's "Psh of St. Lawrence Poultney," London, 1531, page 231.

[2] Ralph Holland was the churchwarden of the parish for the years 1621-2 and 1622-3 (page 112), and was buried there 18th September, 1625 (page 12).

S˚ John Whyte, M˚ William Alleyn, and M˚ Rowland Heyward, Aldermen, beying accompanied wth certen Comoners of this Citie that ys to wete, M˚ Geffery Walkeden, M˚ Barneham, Bannester Huggyns, and Robert Dowe, Marchaunttaillors came to this Howse as sente in Message frome the Ryght Honorable Lorde Maire & the Worshipfull Aldermen his Brethren.

And there the said S˚ William Chester declared how that S˚ Thomas Gressham, Knyght, for the greate good will and love he hath to this Citie was contented and had already p̄mysed unto the said Lord Maire and Aldermen to buyld and plant within this Citie a Burse to be more faire and costly buylded in all points than is the Burse of Antwerp, so that the said Lord Maire and Aldermen would p̄vide hym such a Plot of grounde as the said Lord Maire and Aldermen shulde think most mete to plant the said Burse upon. And further declared how that the p̄myses made by the said S˚ Thomas Gressham in that behalf was by the Lord Maire and hys Brethren thankfully accepted and receyved, and howe that they the said Lord Maire and Aldermen hath already vewed dyvers grounds wth in this Citie for the planting of the said Burse upon, and could fynde none so fytt for to buylde the same upon as was the ground belonging to this Company adjoyning upon Lomberd Strete & Cornhill. Whereupon the said Lorde Maire & Aldermen were fully resolved that the said Burse should be there planted yf this Company woulde be contented to dep̄te wth there said Lands there upon such consideracõns as they shulde be contented wth all for dyvers respects and consideracõns them moving amongst wch this was come to the chiefest that moved them to request the said Lands to buyld the said Burse upon, for that it did so joyne upon Lomberd Strete whereby the said Burse myght thereby retayne and kepe the ancient name of Lomberd Strete, for that the Policies that hathe been made tyme out of mynde, between Marchaunte and Marchaunte in other forren regions hathe had relacions, to be of as good effecte to all respects as the Policies usually made in Lomberd Strete was of, whereby it dothe appeare that the Burse of Lomberd Strete is of longer antiquitie than any other Burse is known to be of, that is wth in all Europe. And further he shewed that the planting of the same Burse there woulde be a worthie ornament to this Citie whereby not onely the same Citie shoulde be the more frequented by Marchaunts and thereby wynne the more fame, but also be the better beloved and favoured as well of the Prince as of others. Wherefore the consideracõn by them considered and well weyed, he trusted that this Company as good and loving members of this Citie for the furtherance of the saide goode intended acte wolde willingly be contented to dep̄te wth theire forsaide lands and tenements as aforesaide whereof he in the name of all the reste of his associats there present required theire gentill answere.

And thereupon the foresaid Maister in the name of the whole Company then assembled desyred his Worshipp and th'other his Associats respecte, to answere upon theire saide demand: Whereunto they assented and in the meantyme of theire conference had, dyd wthdrawe themselfs into the Com̄on Hall of this Mystery.

And in the meane tyme of theire being absent, yt was fully agreed that theire answere wch was already devised, made, and put into wryting by the forsaid Marster, Wardens, & others, thereunto appoynted and by theire learned counsell shulde not be delyv̄red before five or vj of the clocke this day in the afternoone, notwithstanding that it should not be otherwyse declared unto the said Sir William Chester & others his associats thereof, but that they coulde not in so short tyme as they wyshed give unto theire Worshipps answere to their demande, considering the greate ymportance thereof.

Where upon the said Sr William Chester and the reste of his Associats were called in after they had been absent owte of this place almost an houre, and there yt was said unto them that they were very sorry they had deteyned them so long as they had done, and yet they nevertheless were not fully resolved of theire answere and requested theire Worshipps not to be discontented with them for that they had made theire Worshipps to tarry so longe, and also prayed them to be contented to dep̄te for that tyme and that the Company shulde this p̄sent daye before v or vj of the clocke delyver theire answere to the said Sir William Chester wth wch answere they the said Sr William Chester and his associats dēpted conténted.

And in the afternoone the Company's answere wch before they had devysed was delyv̄red accordingly wch followeth in hæc verba.

Fyrste, for that one Sr John Percivall, Kynght, late Alderman and Maire of London, and late Citizen and Merchaunttailo^r, then being one of the heade and chief of theire Company, by his great industrie and long travaile, obteigned the said Messuages and Tēñts, and in one of them there planted himself durying all his lyfe tyme, as a great stay to the whole Company, and as a bountifull Benefactor unto them, ordeyned by his last Will and Testament, that the said Messuages and Tēñts shuld remayne and contyneu in the said Company for ever as a declarac̃on of his good will and greate benevolence towards them ffurther putting them in trust wᵗʰ the contynuall extenc̃on of suche godly and charitable deedes as he had ordered and devysed by his said Will for eṽ.

Seconde, yf this request shulde be graunted the said Messuages and Tẽnts shulde be altered and changed and to such other purposes & use ymployed that the memoryall, intent, and purpose of so good and liberall a Benefactor shulde shortly perishe and from whence he was, where he buylded and planted hymself woulde soon be oute of mynde.

The said Company are in good hope, yea in mañ, assured of the lyke or greater benefitts to be done unto them in p̃petuytie for the continuance whereof longe travaill, learned counsell and greate advice hath bene taken, if the said Company shulde assent to any acte whereby so greate and liberall a benefite of the said Sʳ John Pͬcyvall shuld be comytted to oblivion they myght think themselffs unworthie of the like benefite, or to be put in the like trust.

The said Company have placed in the said Messuages dyvers of theire own Company and other good Citizens wᶜʰ yf this grante shulde passe, shulde be in greate p̃ill to be displaced to theire greate greves & disquietness, and therefore they shulde not from thensforthe have so good occasion to wysshe for the prosperous state and long contynuance of the said Companye as they before this tyme have had gratefull memory of our p̃decessors and Benefactors.

And, fynally, the said Company p̃ͬtest that they are as desyrous of the said goode intended p̃ͬpose wᶜʰ is like to be for the c̃oen welthe of this Citie as any other Company or Citizens of the same, and yf any other convenyent place may be therefore had they shalbe as willing and as liberally assysting thereto as any Company of this Citie. And this wee trust may be to the demaunde of youre honor and Worshipps, a reasonable answere.

Tuesday, Janʳ 15, 1564.

At this day the forsaid Maister & Wardens did make relac̃on unto the forsaid Assistants how that upon Saturday last past, they were called into the inner chamber of the Guylde Hall before the Lord Maire and Courte of Aldermen then and there assembled, Whereas the said Lord Maire and certen of his Brethrene th' Aldermen as well by themselfs as by the mouthe of Mʳ Recorder, dyd reply to eṽry of their Articles and reasons by them alledged in theire answere exhibit by us to Sir Wᵐ Chester upon Fryday last past consernyng such causes as dyd p̃swade them not to be contented to dp̃te wᵗʰ these o͛ Lands by them demanded, wherein they said that the greatest matter therein alledged wᶜʰ dyd seme to them that dyd p̃swade them not to dp̃te wᵗʰ the said Lands was onely theire conscience of breaking the dead's Will yf they shulde graunte to departe with them, wherein Mʳ Recorder said, that the Dead's Will myght be as well fulfilled and p̃ᵉformed out with other Lands wᶜʰ they shulde have in lieu thereof as owt of the same Lands wᶜʰ they now holde, and yf the Companye did strive so moche upon the p̃suasion of theire consenting, he doubted not but that the Bishopp of London, or Mʳ Deane of Poulls, yf they would be so contented thereby, to resolve them therein. And also further said that yf this Company would be contented to dp̃te with theire Lands for the furtherance of the said good intended acte he dyd not doubte but that they shulde obtteigne for the Company as moche other Lands and' of lyke yerely value as oures was of, out of the Quenes Maᵗⁱᵉˢ Londs lyeing either within the Citie or in the Countrye. And here withall he and they trusted that the Company woulde be contented, Whereunto yt was answered and replyed by the said Maister & Wardens that they were so p̃csuadyd by theire Conscience that they could not assente & dp̃te with the said Lands in demande, wᵗʰout breach of the Deades Will, howsoev͛ Mʳ Recorder had alledged to the contrary. Thereunto it was answered by Mʳ Recorder that yt should appeare to hym that wee dyd refuse to consente more of a Will than of any Conscience, for said he, a man may not make to hymself a Conscience of that there is no conscience to be made of. After which answere so made by Mʳ Recorder the Lord Maire dyd redelyver and restore to the said Maister and Wardens theire Bill of Answere agayne and said he woulde not accept the same for a full or absolute answere to theire demand, But dyd give them in commandement to assemble the Company together and estsones to p̃suade them to be contented to dp̃te wᵗʰ theire said Lands for the furtherance of the said good intended acte as before they had requested them and to bringe theire answere thereof to that Courte as upon the Tuesday next.

APPENDIX 29.

October 20th, 1571.

A Precept to Watch at ev'ry Gate and Posterne in the City.

Ffirste at this daye, a Precepte directed from the Mayo͛ to the Maister and his Wardens, conserninge the appoyntinge and nominatinge of some sufficient, hable, and discreete men to joyne with the Company of Veynteners, who are likewise appoynted to set forthe other and hable and discreete men to joyn with this Company in watche, on Monday nexte, beinge the 22nd daie of this instante month of Octob⁹, at ev'ry gate and posterne, as in the said Precepte hereafter wrytten mencōned, was openlie redd, the tenor whereof followeth :—

"Wee straightlie charge and commande you that you immediatelye upon the receipt hereof, do call and assemble togeder so many of your Companie as you shall think mete and expediente, and that ye take such order forthwithe among yourselfs that ye appointe tenne sufficient, able, and dyscrete p⁹sones to joyne wth the Companie of Vynten⁹s, who are likewise appoynted to sett forthe tenne able men to joyne with you to watch at every gate and posterne hereafter named, that is to say: at Newgate two, at Ludgate two, at the Bridge two, at Billingsgate two, at Moregate two, at Cripplegate two, at the posterne beside the Tower two, at Bishoppsgate two, at Aldersgate two; and that they be ready uppon Munday nexte, being the 21st daie of this instante monthe, by sixe of the clocke in the morninge, and they theire continuallie to remayne from the said houre of six until five of the clocke at night, watchyng and havinge continuallie duringe the sayde tyme a vigillant eye to all and ev'ry suche suspect and idle p⁹sones as shall passe and returne in, at, and by the same gate, and upon suspicion to staie and examine them, and so manye as they shall fynde suspecte and faultie to commit to warde under safe custodie until o⁹ pleasure shall be knowne therein for their deliv⁹rance, and that ye certifie me, the said Maior, of the names and surnames of such as ye shall comyt, and in what prison they shall remayne, and the cause ye comyt them for, to th'ende I maye take order for theire further examinacōn, and forasmuche as other Companies of this Cittie are by us appoynted to followe you in the like watche, so as your turne cometh agayne to watche the tenthe daie from yo⁹ saide first daie of watchinge.

"These are therefore also to commande you to observe the saide order of watchinge ev⁹ry tenth daie as y⁹ turne comethe untill you shall have otherwise from us in commandement. Ffayle ye not hereof as you will answere for the contrarie to yo⁹ p⁹rilL"

APPENDIX 30.

Sir W. FitzWilliam's Obit and Fish's Exhibitions.[1]

The Exhibitions are at present regulated by a scheme (604) of the Charity Commissioners, dated 20th May, and approved 28th November, 1887, of which these are the principal stipulations:—

"8. The income of the Foundation shall be applied by the Governors in maintaining Exhibitions to be called Junior Fish Exhibitions and Senior Fish Exhibitions respectively. The Exhibitions of each class shall be as nearly as may be equal in number.

"9. The Junior Fish Exhibitions shall be each of the yearly value of 80*l.*, and shall be awarded for proficiency in the study of Hebrew and Divinity, and competed for by boys in Merchant Taylors' School, or, in default of fit candidates so qualified as aforesaid, by members of St. John's College in the University of Oxford who have not completed more than four terms from the date of their matriculation. Each of these Exhibitions shall be tenable at St. John's College aforesaid until the beginning of the University term next after the expiration of two years from the date of the election, and shall then determine, unless the President and Fellows of the said College shall by resolution have declared themselves satisfied with the industry and good conduct of the holder, in which case his Exhibition shall be renewed for a further period of two years reckoned from the expiration of the two years from the date of his election.

"10. The Senior Fish Exhibitions shall be each of the yearly value of 60*l.*, and shall be awarded on the ground of merit as shown by honours or distinctions gained in the public examinations of the University of Oxford to members of St. John's College aforesaid who have completed not more than eighteen terms from the date of their matriculation, and who at the date of the election have passed all the examinations required for obtaining the degree of Bachelor of Arts in the said University. The Senior Fish Exhibitions shall be tenable for not more than two years at any University in the United Kingdom or at any Theological College approved by the Governors and the said President and Fellows. The holder of a Senior Fish Exhibition shall, whenever required by the Governors or the said President and Fellows, furnish satisfactory evidence that he is actively pursuing the study of Divinity.

---

[1] The Company are indebted to their guildsman the Right Hon. Sir Richard Baggallay for the preparation of this scheme.

"11. Subject as herein provided, the Exhibitions under this Scheme shall be awarded and held under such regulations and conditions as the Governors with the concurrence of the said President and Fellows may from time to time prescribe. The election to a vacant Exhibition shall in each case be made by the Governors with the consent of the said President and Fellows regard being had to the circumstances of the candidates. Any Exhibition for which there shall be no duly qualified candidate who shall be adjudged worthy to take it shall for that turn not be awarded.

"12. If the holder of an Exhibition shall, in the judgment of the Governors and the said President and Fellows be guilty of serious misconduct, or, in the case of a Senior Fish Exhibition shall fail, when required as aforesaid, to produce satisfactory evidence that he is actively pursuing the study of Divinity, the Governors with the consent of the said President and Fellows may deprive him of the Exhibition, and for this purpose, in the case of an Exhibition held elsewhere than at the said College, may act on the report of the proper authorities of the place of education at which the Exhibition is held, or on such other evidence as the Governors and the said President and Fellows think sufficient. Under this clause the decision of the Governors made with such consent as aforesaid shall be final in each case.

"13. Subject to the payment of the expenses of management of property and business and of any necessary or proper outgoings, any income of the Foundation not applied under the foregoing provisions and not needed as a balance to meet current expenses shall be invested in the name of the Official Trustees of Charitable Funds in trust for the Foundation in augmentation of its endowment.

"14. No boy shall by reason of any exemption from attending prayer or religious worship, or from any lesson or series of lessons on a religious subject, be deprived of any advantage or emolument out of the endowment of the Foundation to which he would otherwise have been entitled.

"15. Religious opinions, or attendance or non-attendance at any particular form of religious worship, shall not in any way affect the qualification of any person for being one of a Governing Body under this Scheme.

"16. Within the limits prescribed by this Scheme the Governors shall have full power from time to time to make regulations for the conduct of their business and for the management of the Foundation, and such regulations shall be binding on all persons affected thereby."

APPENDIX 31.

List of Freemen in the Lansdowne MS.

Albanye, William, free 11th November, 1586.
Allen, Thomas, free 25th January, 1590.
Bond, George, free 5th December, 1567.
Browne, Thomas, free 26th May, 1564.
Cocking, William, free 3rd April, 1584.
Denham, John, free 15th May, 1556.
Dove, Robert, free 9th August, 1550.
Dawbney, Arthure, free 16th December, 1552.
Gore, Gerard, free 7th September 1582.
Gore, Thomas, free 7th September, 1582.
Howse, Robert, free 13th July, 1543.
Harte, John, free 26th May, 1552.
Hilles, Richard, free 1535.
Hoskins, Charles, free 21st April, 1550.
Harrison, John, free 5th August, 1558.
Lambert, John, free 13th December, 1558.
Maye, Richard, free 22nd April, 1555.
Offley, Robert, free 27th October, 1598.
Phillipps, William, free 24th February, 1547.
Riche, John, free 27th April, 1582.
Reynolds, Richard, free 20th December, 1596.
Ratcliff, Anthony, free 11th October, 1555.
Sotherton, George, free 24th October, 1564.
Spencer, Nicholas (Master 1588).
Starkie, Thomas, free 15th October, 1573.
Spencer, John, free 8th July, 1566.
Smith, Richard, free 5th February, 1564.
Thorogood, William, free 22nd February, 1554.
Webbe, William, free 23rd January, 1572.
Warren, Richard, free 11th June, 1540.
Widnell, William, free 7th June, 1555.

APPENDIX 32.

Table shewing Assessments of the Livery Companies by the Corporation of London at the date under-mentioned.

Names of Companies.	In 1548–9.	In October, 1562.			In 1599.	In 1603–4 (14 Feb.).		
		£	s.	d.	Quarters of corn.	£	s.	d.
Mercers[4]	xxiiij[li]	400	0	0	820	32	16	0
Grocers[3]	xx[li]	400	0	0	874	34	19	2
Drapers..	xx[li]	300	0	0	768	30	14	4
Fishmongers	xvj[li]	300	0	0	565	22	12	0
Goldsmythes[4]	xvj[li]	300	0	0	809	32	7	2
Skynners[4]	xiij[li] vj[s] viij[d]	150	0	0	553	22	2	4
March'unttaylors[3]	xx[li]	350	0	0	936	37	8	9
Salters[4]..	xij[li]	150	0	0	514	20	11	2
Hab'dasshers[3]	xvj[li]	250	0	0	724	28	19	2
Iremongers[4]	ix[li] vj[s] viij[d]	200	0	0	440	17	12	0
Vynteners	ix[li] vj[s] viij[d]	66	13	4	520	20	16	0
Clothw'kers	xvij[li] vj[s] viij[d]	300	0	0	565	22	12	0
Dyers[3]	iiij[li]	40	0	0	100	4	0	0
Brewers[4]	xij[li]	66	13	4	200	8	0	0
[1]Bakers..	v[li] vj[s] viij[d]				120	4	16	0
Lethersellers[3]	x[li] xiij[s] iiij[d]	200	0	0	200	8	0	0
Talowch'undlers[4]	v[li] vj[s] viij[d]	40	0	0	80	3	4	0
Carpenters	2l. 13s. 4d.	15	0	0	50	2	0	0
Pastelers	2l. 13s. 4d.							
Tylers ..	xl[s]	10	0	0	20	0	16	0
Fruterers	2l. 13s. 4d.	10	0	0	16	0	12	9
Butchers	2l. 13s. 4d.	20	0	0	30	1	4	0
Masons..	xxvj[s] viij[d]	10	0	0	25			
Scryveners[3]	xxvj[s] viij[d]	20	0	0	70	2	16	0
Joyno[r]s..	xxvj[s] viij[d]				41	1	12	9
Woodmongers[3]	xxvj[s] viij[d]				20	0	16	0
Playsteres	xxvj[s] viij[d]				10	0	8	0
Blacksmythes and Sporryo[r]s	2l. 13s. 4d.				16	0	12	9

[1] No baker who made "white" could lawfully make or sell "brown" bread. Denton's England (15th century), page 244, note 4.

These ([3]) had increased, and these ([4]) had decayed in worth since the last assessment, and therefore in the assessment of 18th July and 11th September, 1610, ([3]) were raised and ([4]) were diminished accordingly. See note on page 329.

Names of Companies.	In 1548–9.	In October, 1562. £ s. d.	In 1599. Quarters of corn.	In 1603–4 (14 Feb.). £ s. d.
Botyllmakers and Horners	xiij^s iiij^d	..	..	
Ferrors	xiij^s iiij^d			
Pavyers	xiij^s iiij^d			
Founders	xxvj^s viij^d	10 0 0	15	0 12 0
Wevers	xxvj^s viij^d	..	25	1 0 0
Paynters	iiij^{li}	..	11	0 8 9
Cutlers[3]	iiij^{li}	20 0 0	45	1 16 0
Pewterers	vj^{li} xiij^s iiij^d	..	60	2 8 0
Sadlers[3]	v^{li} vj^s viij^d	30 0 0	90	3 12 0
Barbor S'geons[3]	v^{li} vj^s viij^d	20 0 0	50	2 0 0
Gyrdelers[3]	viij^{li}	50 0 0	70	2 16 8
Corryo's	iiij^{li} xiij^s iiij^d	20 0 0	11	0 8 9
Inholders	v^{li} vj^s viij^d	30 0 0	50	2 0 0
Bowyers	iiij^{li}	10 0 0	5	0 4 0
Cowpers	iiij^{li}	50 0 0	70	2 16 0
Broderers[3]	2l. 13s. 4d.	..	33	1 6 6
Plūmers	xxvj^s viij^d	..	20	0 16 0
Wexch'undlers	xxvj^s viij^d	..	20	0 16 0
Cordwayners[4]	2l. 13s. 4d.	20 0 0	70	2 16 0
Armorers	2l. 13s. 4d.	10 0 0	10	0 8 0
Fletchers[3]	2l. 13s. 4d.	10 0 0	5	0 4 0
Wolpackers	xxvj^s viij^d	10 0 0	5	0 4 0
Pulters	2l. 13s. 4d.	..	20	0 16 0
Lorymers	xiij^s iiij^d			
Stacyoners[3]	2l. 13s. 4d.	40 0 0	100	4 0 0
Upholders	xiij^s iiij^d	..	11	0 8 9
[1]Browne Bakers[4]	xiij^s iiij^d	..	30	1 4 0
Graye Tawyers	xiij^s iiij^d			
Longe Bowestryng makers	xiij^s iiij^d			
Turno's	xiij^s iiij^d	..	17	0 15 7
Glasyers	xiij^s iiij^d	..	8	0 5 4
Cooks	..	..	50	2 0 0
Minstrels	..	..	5	0 4 0
Basket makers	..	..	8	0 5 4
				400 0 0[2]

[1] No baker who made "white" could lawfully make or sell "brown" bread. Denton's England (15th century), page 244, note 4.

[2] See Vol. 1, page 400, of Nichol's Progresses (James I.)

[3] These ([3]) had increased, and those ([4]) had decayed in worth since the last assessment, and therefore in the assessment of 18th July and 11th September, 1610, ([3]) were raised and ([4]) were diminished accordingly. See note on page 329.

APP. 33.]   *Antient Acquisitions of Company.*   407

APPENDIX 33.

ANTIENT ACQUISITIONS OF THE MERCHANT TAYLORS COMPANY 1331 TO 1531.

[The Company are greatly indebted to Mr. Chambers for the assistance given by him in the preparation of these rentals.]

NOTE.—The rental of A and B 1 is included in this printed at page 521 Memorials for the year 1468-9. It is also included, though possibly at a higher sum, with B 2, in the rental printed at pages 523-4 for the year 1545-6.

A.—*By Purchase.*

No.	Date.	Vendor.	Purchaser.	Premises.	Situation, Parish, &c.	Rent. Antient.	Rent. Present.	Remarks.
1	1331	Edmund Crepin...	John de Yakesley	A principal mansion house abutting on Broad Street and Cornhill A gatehouse in Cornhill The Great Chamber, let to a "Steynour" The garden and appurtenances *Now houses Nos. 22, 28, and 29, Threadneedle Street*	St. Peter's, Cornhill St. Benedict Fink St. Martin Outwich	1545 £ s. d. ... 3 0 0 4 2 0 28 17 6	£ s. d. } 3,522 0 0 1,190 0 0	The Hall was then as now in occupation. The rent inserted is Poor Rate assessment 1885.
2	1400	Unknown...	Merchant Taylors' Company	All that great messuage called the "Saracen's Head" in Friday Street, *Now Nos. 5, 6, and 7.*	St. Matthew's, Friday Street	2 5 10 18 11 8	*650 0 0	The property was taken probably as a loft and the hostell built by the Company, for in 1404 and onwards it was let for 6l. See Memorials, page 65-68.

By deed of 1st March, 1392, by the Masters and Wardens, to Richard Jykenove, Draper, 8l. was granted from tenements in St. Benet Fink, St. Martin, Outwich, and St. Peter's, Cornhill.
By deed of 5th March, 1468, for a valuable consideration, the Company charged these premises with a rent charge of 8l. for a chantry priest at the north gate of St. Paul's, at the ordinance of Beaurioe de Roos.

(Item. Note to 1 ante.) * This property as now held includes purchases made in 1843-4. Also 1526 charged with a rent of 9l. 13s. 4d. in favour of James Wilford.—(Memorials, page 283)

B. 1.—*By Benefactions.*

No.	Date.	Donor.	Description.	Parish, &c.	Rent. Antient.	Rent. Present.	Limitations in favour of the Merchant Taylors Company.
3	1382 Dec. 20	*Carleton, Thomas *Sold* 1549-50.	Tenements ..	Ad Lane, St. Alban's, Wood Street	1545 £ s. d. 4 4 10 *as in* 1406. 9 8 0	£ s. d. ..	To the Master and Wardens and their successors for ever for chauntry priests at Paules.
4	1392 June 24	Wyncheombe, Simon Memorials, page 65.	Two houses and eleven shops	St. Benet Fink, St. Martin Outwich, and St. Peter, Cornhill	included in	Nos. 1 & 6.	To the Master and Wardens.
5	1404-5 Jan. 21	Sibsey, Thomas (See No. 20, i.)	"Saracen's Head" ..	Bread Street, All Saints	7 6 8 7 13 4	300 0 0	To the Master and Wardens and Brethren and Sisters of the Brotherhood of St. John Baptist, London.
6	1405 July 20	*Churchman, Thomas (1)*Sold* in 1688 for 750l., retaining a rent-charge of 24l. per annum. (2)*Church Site sold in* 1874 *for* 38,179l. *and parsonage in* 1875 *for* 15,000l.	(1) Four messuages (2) Seventeen shops Now 117, Bishopgate St., & 31, 37, & 38, Threadneedle St. (3) The Advowson of 6s. 8d., rent-charge from St. Michael's, Crooked Lane.	St. Martin Outwich.. St. Martin Outwich.. St. Martin Outwich. St. Michael's, Crooked Lane.	} 26 13 0 30 6 8	24 0 0 2,420 0 0	To the Master and Wardens, Brethren and Sistren of the Guild and Fraternity of St. John Baptist, London. (*N.B.*—2s. 5d. paid to St. Martin's yearly.)

* The estate came to the Company charged with quit rents of 7s. to Christchurch (Grey Friars), and 8s. to St. Mary Overy, Southwark, which were redeemed in 1549-60.

APP. 33.]   Antient Acquisitions of Company.   409

7	1412 Sept. 6	*Mason, Peter	..	Tenements and shops near the Old Conduit	St. Mary Colechurch 1, 4, 5, *Poultry*	11 16 8 *13 6 8*	590 0 0	To the Master and Wardens of Tailors and Linen Armourers of the Brotherhood of St. John Baptist, London. "In pure and perpetual alms, for perpetually relieving the poor needy Brethren of the Brotherhood."
8	1418 Nov. 22	* Creek, John, by Wm. Turnell. *Part sold* 1549-50.	A tenement ..	Tower Street, No. 8, St. Dunstan's-in-the-East	2 0 0 *as in* 1468 *7 6 8*	182 0 0	To the Master and Wardens. (i.) Superstitious uses. (ii.) To give thirteen quarters of coal to thirteen poor persons of St. Dunstan's yearly. (iii.) For repairs.

19th March, 1419. All the lands and tenements of the Company were by contract of this date made liable to a perpetual rent-charge of 40s. to provide an obit for Sir Gerard Braybrook.

9	1422 Jan. 26	Buck, John .. *Sold* 1549-50.	..	The Scule on the Hoppe, or Lyon's Alley	Gracious Street, Allhallows	2 4 2 0 4 0	..	To the Master and Wardens for the poor of the fraternity.
10	1432	Sutton, Thomas	..	(¹)Lands, shops with wharf near the Thames (²)Lands (*sold in* 1871 *to Railway Company and invested in Consols, now reinvested in* 10, *St. Swithin's Lane.* 689*l.* 1*s.* 1*d. left in Consols.*)	Greeningham Lane (*Anchor Alley*), St. James' Garlickhithe ⎫⎬⎭ Trinity the Less	10 12 0* *25 8 4* ..	350 0 0 *now unlet* 617 2 6 *Dividend* 20 13 4	To the Master, Wardens, &c. (i.) Towards the relief and sustentation of the poor Brethren and Sisters of the fraternity in their Almshouses near the Hall. (ii.) To pay 2*d.* a week to every poor Brother and Sister in the Almshouse to the end to pray specially for testator's soul. **This rent is so entered in* 1434 *with* 9*s. of arrears.*

ANTIENT ACQUISITIONS—*continued*.

No.	Date.	Donor.	Description.	Parish, &c.	Rent. Antient.	Rent. Present.	Limitations in favour of the Merchant Taylors Company.
11	1451 Oct. 12	Halleyate, Idonia. *All these lands were sold in 1549-50, the rents then being*	Lands	St. Margaret Patyns	*1545* £ s. d. 1 6 8 *as in 1453* 4 16 4	£ s. d. ..	To the Master and Wardens of the Brotherhood of Tailors and Linen Armourers of St. John Baptist, and also the commonalty of Tailors aforesaid, on condition:— (i.) To insert her name and the name of her husband in the list of Brothers and Sisters prayed for. (ii.) 6s. 8d. for superstitious uses.
12	1452 May 2	Holland, Ralph (First Will) 1, 3 (*in part*), *and 4 sold in* 1549-50, *and* 2 *at some time anterior*.	1. Lands and tenements 2. Shops and garden 3. Basset's Inn 4. Perbright Inn	St. Alban's, Wood Street. St. Clement's Lane, Eastcheap St. Mary, Aldermanbury St. Andrew's, Cornhill, Lime Street	1 13 4 *as in 1454* 10 16 8 10 5 0 17 11 4 23 1 0	.. .. 165 0 0 ..	To the Master and Wardens in pure and perpetual alms of the Brotherhood, *i.e.*, for perpetually relieving the poor and needy persons of the Brotherhood, and especially to pray for the souls of the Brethren and Sisters of the said Brotherhood.

APP. 33.] *Antient Acquisitions of Company.* 411

13	May 3	*(Second Will) 5, 6, *and* 7, also sold in 1549-50. *It is said that he also gave land in this parish to this parish, see C. C. Report, viii, page* 265.	5. One tenement 6. One ditto 7. One ditto opposite Houndsditch	St. Dionis Backchurch, Fenchurch Street *St. Margaret, Patyn Lane St. Botolph, Aldgate The "Three Kings"	2 0 0 1 6 8 3 6 8 *4 16 8*	.. .. ..	⎧ To the Master and Wardens, &c. ⎪ (i.) To repair; (ii.) 13s. 4d. for superstitious uses; (iii.) 1d. weekly to every poor Brother and Sister out of the alms of the Brotherhood. Residue in pure and perpetual alms (*as ante*).
14	1460	*Candish, Hugh, by Richard Tolle. 1 and part of 2, *sold* 1549-53.	1. One messuage 2. Alley and messuage, Candish Alley	Walbrook *Memoriale*, 521. Fenchurch Street No. 30, St. Gabriel	2 13 4 *as in* 1463 (?) 3 13 8 *9 0 0*	.. 560 0 0	⎧ To the Master, Warden, Brethren, and Sisters of the Brotherhood. ⎪ (?) *The Fenchurch Street rents were in 1646 increased by this amount for two tenements, the other eight tenements of Holland yielding then 6l. 4s.*

B. 2.

15	1467 Feb. 9	*Langwith, Ellen	Tenements ..	Sherborne Lane, and Candlewick Street, St. Mary Abchurch	12 6 8	1,700 0 0 *up to* 2,000 0 0	To the Master and Wardens (named), and the Brotherhood of Tailors and Linen Armourers of St. John Baptist, London. (i.) For superstitious uses; (ii.) for bread and ale, 6s.; (iii.) 26 quarters of coal to 13 poor men and women of St. Mary; (iv.) 6s. 8d. for Master and Wardens for their presents at obit.

This estate came to the Company charged with quit rents of 2s. 6d. to the Abbot of Bermondsey, and 17s. to the Prioress of Kilburn, which were redeemed in 1549-50.

16	1507 Feb. 21	*Percivel, John *Sold* in 1688 *subject to* 5l. *rent-charge on* 71, *Lombard Street.*	Twelve messuages ..	Lombard Street, St. Mary Woolnoth	45 0 0	5 0 0	To the common box of the fraternity, for the maintenance and supportation of the common charge.

ANTIENT ACQUISITIONS—continued.

No.	Date.	Donor.	Description.	Parish, &c.	Rent. Antient.	Rent. Present.	Limitations in favour of the Merchant Taylors Company.
17	1508	*Percival, Dame T. (*Part sold in 1878*).	Six messuages	Vintry of St. Martin 12, 13, 14, 15, *College Hill.* 179, 180, *Thames Street*	*1545* £ s. d. 21 13 4	£ s. d. 755 0 0 110 0 0	} To the common box, as in the last will.
			One messuage	Fenchurch Street, No. 21, St. Dionis Backchurch		370 0 0	For an obit for John Hadleigh.

By deed of .... the Vintry property was made liable to a rent charge of 20s. for an obit for John Hadleigh.

| 18 | 1508 June 28 | *Pemberton, Dame Katharine (In pursuance of Sir Hugh P.'s will). *Sold with No. 25, and repurchased.* | Tenements, crane and wharf | St. Martin Vintry | 24 14 8 | 600 0 0 | To the Master and Wardens. |

By deed of 4th March, 1514, certain lands owned by the Company were made liable to a rent charge of 8l. 12s. for an obit for Thomas Howden.

| 19 | 1515-6 Mar. 1 | Smith, Richard *? Sold in Nov., 1669, to W. Priestman and J. Gardiner for 800l.* | Two messuages and garden called the Great Messuage | St. Mary, Fenchurch | 10 13 4 | .. | To the Master and Wardens, and to the Brethren and Sisters of the same fraternity for their proper use and behoof for ever. |

APP. 33.] Antient Acquisitions of Company. 413

20	1518	Tresswell, John 3 and 5 only are now in possession of the Company.	1. 6s. 8d. rent-charge on the "Saracen's Head" (via 5 ante) 2. Seven tenements and gardens 3. 13s. 4d. quit rent on the "Three Legs" 4. 13s. 4d. rent-charge on "Unicorn on the Hoop" 5. One tenement	All Hallows, Bread Street Aldgate Basing Lane, All Hallows St. Nicholus Olyf Bread Street, No. 61, All Hallows	.. .. 0 13 4 0 13 4 3 0 0	.. .. 0 13 4 .. 400 0 0	To the Master and Wardens of the fraternity of St. John Baptist, London, "In mere pure and perpetual alms for ever."
21	1520 July 20	Harrys, John	One messuage, "The Bell"	Bowyer Row, St. Martin 40, Ludgate Hill	4 0 0	273 0 0	To the Master and Wardens, Brethren and Sisters of the same fraternity, to do and dispose of their own free will
22	1521 Mar. 1	Slater, Giles Part, "The Helme," sold 1549-50, and part in 1686	Three messuages	In Gindre St. Michael's Cornhill, No. 21	10 0 0	900 0 0	To the Master and Wardens, Brethren and Sisters of the same fraternity, to do and dispose of their own free will
23	1521 Mar. 1	Moncester, William. Sold 1549-50.	"Three Nuns" One tenement and garden	Aldgate Leadenhall Street, No. 140, St. Andrew Undershaft	7 0 0 2 0 0	800 0 0	To the Master and Wardens, Brethren and Sisters, to do and dispose at their own will and pleasure.
24	1522 Mar. 1	Harrys, John Sold 1549-50.	A tenement against the church door	Thames Street, All Hallows	5 0 0	..	To the Master and Wardens of the Merchant Taylors Company.

By deed of 13th June, 1522, for 800 marks paid by Richard Fitzjames, Bishop of London, the Company charged all their tenements in London and the suburbs with an annuity of 20 marks.

ANTIENT ACQUISITIONS—*continued.*

No.	Date.	Donor.	Description.	Parish, &c.	Rent. Antient.	Rent. Present.	Limitations in favour of the Merchant Taylors Company.
25	1527 Dec. 10	Speight, Thomas. *All sold in 1817–18 to the S.B.C., and the surplus land repurchased by the M.T.C. in 1818–19*	Messuages, wharf and crane against the south part of the parish church	In Thames Street, St. Martin's Vintry, *Queen Street Place*	*1545* £ s. d. 45 6 8	£ s. d. 494 0 0	To the Master and Wardens, Brethren and Sisters of the fraternity to do and dispose of at their own free will, liberty, and pleasure.
26	1527 Jan. 24	*Jennings, Sir Stephen, by John Bennett	One tenement / Three messuages / A garden	Thames Street, All Hallows, *No.* 89 / Coleman Street *Nos.* 27, 28, *and* 29 St. Stephen's. / St. Michael's Bassishaw	.. / 7 13 4 / ..	200 0 0 / 1,500 0 0 / ..	To the Master and Wardens and Commonalty of the fraternity of the Merchant Taylors.
27	1530 Jan. 24	*Acton, Hugh by Thomas Speight	Two messuages	St. Martin's Ludgate, *Nos.* 36 *and* 38	11 0 0	{ 602 0 0 / 17 0 0 }	To the Master and Wardens of the Merchant Taylors Company.

[APP. 33.]   *Antient Acquisitions of Company.*   415

					£ s d		
28	1531 Feb. 26	*Buckland, Richard by Thomas Speight	One tenement	Bowyer's Row, St. Martin's Ludgate, No. 34	5 0 0	⎡330 0 0⎤ ⎣ 33 0 0⎦	To the Master and Wardens of the Merchant Taylors Company, and of fellowship of the same.
29	No date	Thomason, Richard. *All sold* 1549-50	Lands and tenements	St. Bartholomew-the-less	6 1 4	..	(i.) For repairs. (ii.) To provide an obit. (iii.) Residue to the Master, Wardens, and Commonalty of the fellowship of Tailors of London.
			Total ..		404 12 10		
		Add—R. Sheather, leasehold, A. Watling Street. B. Laurence Pountney.		St. Mary Axe Donor not known. do.	4 1 0 5 13 4 26 6 8		
		Total—*See* Memorials, folio 523-4		Rental 1545-6 ..	440 13 10	19,680 9 2	

THE END OF PART I.

LONDON:
HARRISON AND SONS, PRINTERS IN ORDINARY TO HER MAJESTY,
ST. MARTIN'S LANE.

www.ingramcontent.com/pod-product-compliance
Lightning Source LLC
Chambersburg PA
CBHW051728300426
44115CB00007B/510